The Changing American Presidency

New Perspectives on Presidential Power

Richard W. Waterman
University of Kentucky

ATOMICdogPUBLISHING

Cincinnati, Ohio
www.atomicdog.com

352.23
W328c
2003

Cover: U.S. Air Force photo

Copyright © 2003 by Atomic Dog Publishing. All rights reserved.

ISBN 1-59260-030-1

Library of Congress Control Number: 2002113374

No part of this publication may be reproduced, stored in a retrieval system, or transmitted,
in any form or by any means, electronic, mechanical, photocopying, recording, or otherwise,
without the prior written permission of the publisher.

Printed in the United States of America by Atomic Dog Publishing,
1203 Main Street, Third Floor, Cincinnati, OH 45202

10 9 8 7 6 5 4 3 2 1

This book is dedicated to
President Samuel Tilden.

METHODIST COLLEGE LIBRARY
FAYETTEVILLE, NC

Brief Contents

Contents

Chapter 3

**Active Presidents: The Path
to Presidential Greatness   49**

Chapter 4

**Domestic Policy, Constitutional Ambiguity,
and the Growth of Presidential Power   77**

Chapter 5

The Constitution and Foreign Policy   105

Chapter 6

Presidential Elections in a Constitutional Framework   125

Chapter 7

The Presidency and the Public: A Double-Edged Sword   157

Chapter 8

A New Intermediary: The Decline of the Political Parties and the Rise of the Media   183

Chapter 12

The President's Cabinet: An Internal or External Political Resource?   281

Chapter 13

The Search for New Political Resources   297

Chapter 14

A New Role for the Vice President   329

Chapter **15**

How Internal and Informational Resources Can Increase Presidential Influence: The Case of Presidential Appointments   339

Chapter **16**

Of the Presidency: Past, Present, and Future   359

Preface

Preface

This book began with my dissertation, though it was not the subject of my dissertation. Let me explain. As I read many books on the presidency for my dissertation, I was struck by one seemingly simple question: How had the presidency developed from a relatively weak office, clearly subservient to the legislative branch, to the most powerful political office in the world? As I read book after book, I noticed that many of them addressed the subject of presidential power. Most, however, focused on how presidents could increase or better use their power or alternatively argued that presidents had too much power. Although they provided some insight into the development and transformation of the presidential office, they did not directly address the question.

While writing my dissertation, I therefore began to take notes for a book that I knew I did not have the time to write, certainly not until I finished the dissertation, and probably not before I got tenure, but someday. For more than a decade, every time I read or wrote a book on the presidency, I would take notes for this someday project. After almost two decades, the someday project is completed, and as Rod Serling, the creator of the "Twilight Zone," used to say, it is "Presented for your consideration."

As for my experience with this book, it has been like a game of connect the dots. Over time, I found a lot of material that seemed to be relevant to the development of the presidential office. I also found some excellent books that had more than just a little bit to say about it, all of them cited herein. When I began writing this book in the spring of 2001, however, I still did not fully see how the dots were connected. This book evolved as I wrote it, as I took long walks and thought about it, and as I got feedback from the reviewers and the people at Atomic Dog. I hope that I have connected many of the dots and even provided a rudimentary theoretical rationale for these various connections. Like any good game, however, I am sure that I have left room for improvement, that I have not connected all of the dots. I hope that as students and scholars read this work, they will find new dots and new connections that I have missed and that, as a result, through different editions of this work, we can develop a more detailed and comprehensive answer to the question that initially drove this research.

Pedagogy

The Changing American Presidency has a number of unique characteristics that I hope will help you get a more realistic feel for the American presidency.

- Each chapter opens with a ***Chapter Outline*** that previews discussion topics.

- ***Key Terms*** in both the print and online versions of the text are highlighted and defined on first appearance. In the print version, key terms are also defined in the text margins and listed in alphabetical order at the beginning of each chapter. A ***Glossary*** at the end of the print book presents all of the definitions alphabetically. In the online version of the text, "pop-up" definitions of key terms provide you with immediate clarification of a term's meaning.

- A ***Chapter Summary*** at the end of each chapter highlights the major topics of discussion.

- ***Review Questions*** at the end of each chapter allow you to check your comprehension of the chapter's major concepts, while ***Discussion Questions*** suggest interesting issues for essays and class interaction.

- A comprehensive list of ***References*** appears in both the print and online versions of the text. These references can be used to study the entire article from which an in-chapter citation came or as the basis for further study on the topic.

Online and in Print

The Changing American Presidency is available online as well as in print. The online version demonstrates how the interactive media components of the text enhance presentation and understanding. For example,

- Animated illustrations help to clarify concepts.

- Interactive activities engage you in the learning process and give you hands-on experience in political science.

- Clickable glossary terms provide immediate definitions of key concepts.

- Highlighting capabilities allow you to emphasize main ideas. You can also add personal notes in the margin.

- The search function allows you to quickly locate discussions of specific topics throughout the text.

You may choose to use just the online version of the text, or both the online and print versions together. This gives you the flexibility to choose which combination of resources works best for you. To assist those who use the online and print versions together, the primary heads and subheads in each chapter are numbered the same. For example, the first primary head in Chapter 1 is labeled 1-1, the second primary head in this chapter is labeled 1-2, and so on. The subheads build from the designation of their corresponding primary head: 1-1a, 1-1b, etc. This numbering system is designed to make moving between the online and print versions as seamless as possible.

Finally, next to many of the figures, tables, and boxes in this print version of the text, you will see one of the interactive icons on the left. The icons indicate that this figure, table, or box in the online version of the text is an interactive animation or simulation that is designed to apply, illustrate, or reinforce the concept.

Acknowledgments

Of course, in writing books, there are many people to thank. Since this one started so many years ago, I have a long list of people to include. I would like to thank my mother and father for encouraging me to be curious and to learn. I would like to thank the best friend anyone ever had, Beverly Elliott, who encouraged me to be the best person and scholar I could be. I would like to thank Michael Spikes and Ernest Guevara, who were with us for far too short a time, but who over the years watched me read numerous books on the presidency, and Sendil Nathan, who eventually watched me write this one. They showed extraordinary patience, and I am forever thankful to them.

I would like to thank the people and institutions that played a role in the actual writing of this book. The University of Kentucky provided me with a light teaching load, which allowed me to dedicate a concentrated amount of time to the writing of this manuscript. Kendra Leonard is simply the best editor that I have ever had, and I have had some good ones. She particularly encouraged me during a detailed final rewriting of the book. Chuck Hutchinson provided a thorough copy editing, which of course makes me look like a much better writer than I actually am. I would also like to thank Ed Laube and the other folks at Atomic Dog, an "instructor's best friend," for their support and encouragement throughout the writing of this book. My thanks also go to my conscientious and helpful reviewers: William D. Baker, Janet M. Clark, James P. Pfiffner, Beth Rosenson, and Ray Tatalovich.

Finally, I would like to thank the New England Patriots, who showed me that if you work hard enough, good things can happen to you. Unfortunately, at least at this date (the summer of 2002), my beloved Boston Red Sox have yet to learn this lesson. Maybe they too will finally learn how to connect the dots and bring a World Series back to Boston.

About the Author

Richard Waterman is Professor and Chair of the Department of Political Science at the University of Kentucky. He received his Ph.D. in political science from the University of Houston. He is the author of seven books on the presidency and bureaucratic politics. He also has published articles in such journals as the *American Political Science Review*, the *American Journal of Political Science*, and the *Journal of Politics*. Most important, he is a long-suffering fan of the Boston Red Sox.

Introduction

Suppose the economy of the United States were to suddenly experience a recession, perhaps even a depression. Businesses fail at an alarming rate. Ordinary citizens flock to their banks only to find that all of their money is already lost. The nation teeters on the brink of disaster. Meanwhile, the president of the United States announces that under the Constitution it is the Congress that has the authority to deal with economic matters, not the president. What do you think would happen to this president in the next election? The answer is that he was re-elected without opposition: James Monroe, 1820!

Let me present another case. Poorly prepared for war, the United States is invaded by a foreign country. The nation loses battle after battle, and its military readiness becomes a topic of increasing concern. Finally, the invading army marches on Washington and burns the White House as the commander-in-chief and his wife escape to safety. Surely, he would be rated as the worst president of all time? Yet, a recent poll ranked this president, James Madison, eighteenth out of forty-two presidents, just behind John Adams and Grover Cleveland, and just ahead of John Quincy Adams, George Herbert Walker Bush, Bill Clinton, Jimmy Carter, and Gerald Ford.

Now let me ask a question: What do you think would happen if a president today was thought to have done nothing about an economic downturn, even a mild one? George Herbert Walker Bush did not have a clear program to deal with the relatively mild recession of 1990–1991. He was defeated when he ran for re-election in 1992.

And what do you think would happen if the United States were invaded? Unfortunately, this is no longer merely a hypothetical question. The September 11, 2001, attacks on the World Trade Center and the Pentagon demonstrated that America is vulnerable to terrorism. This event will likely change the way we live and think about security issues for many years to come. But will it also transform the presidency, and will it translate into long-term support for President George W. Bush? Will the public and history blame him for a failure of U.S. security to identify the terrorist attack in advance, or will they reward him for successfully responding to the terrorist threat?

To better understand the dynamics of this situation, we must remember that his father, George H. W. Bush, lost the 1992 election, despite having won a war in the Persian Gulf the year before. On the other hand, after the Japanese attack on Pearl Harbor, Franklin Delano Roosevelt successfully prosecuted World War II and became one of our greatest presidents. Today, one can only surmise what fate would befall a president if the United States were invaded by a foreign nation (as occurred during the War of 1812), but presidents such as Harry Truman and Lyndon Johnson saw their approval ratings decline precipitously as the result of unpopular wars (Korea and Vietnam), and Jimmy Carter lost the 1980 election with American hostages in captivity in Iran and a weak economy at home. Clearly, then, presidents today are severely punished in public opinion polls and in re-election campaigns when they fail to provide *expected* leadership in economic and foreign affairs. In short, *expectations* of presidential performance have changed considerably since the early days of our nation, and the presidency has changed with them.

This book is called *The Changing American Presidency: New Perspectives on Presidential Power* and, as its title suggests, it is all about *change—both how and why it occurs.* The office that the Founders created in 1787 is not the same one that presidents now occupy. Today we commonly refer to the president as one of the most powerful people in America, even the world. But this is not how the presidency was always described. For instance, in 1835 in his classic work *Democracy in America,* Alexis de Tocqueville wrote, "In America, the President cannot prevent any law from being passed, nor can he evade the obligation of enforcing it. His sincere and zealous co-operation is no doubt useful in carrying on public affairs, but is not indispensable" (1945, 12th edition: 132).

He then continued:

> Hitherto, no citizen has cared to expose his honor to become the President of the United States, because the power of that office is temporary, limited, and subordinate. The prize of fortune must be great to encourage adventures in so desperate a game. No candidate has as yet been able to arouse the dangerous enthusiasm or the passionate sympathies of the people in his favor, for the simple reason that when he is at the head of the government, he has but little power, little wealth, and little glory to share among his friends; and his influence in the state is too small for the success or the ruin of a faction to depend upon his elevation to power.

Yet, within a century, in 1923, before Franklin Roosevelt is credited with creating the *modern presidency,* scholar Frederic Haskin (1923: 51) described the president in quite different terms: "The President of the United States has greater power than any individual in this or any other land. He is the foremost ruler of the world." Some forty years later, Finer (1960: 119) elevated the presidency even further, arguing "the presidential office is no trifle, light as air, no bauble; it belongs rightfully to the offspring of a titan and Minerva husbanded by Mars."

Still a mere decade later, the presidency fell from this god-like incarnation to become an "Imperial Presidency," "out of control" and badly in need of "new definition and restraint" (Schlesinger 1973: x). Hardin (1974: 1) wrote the "president all too often was out of control" and that the "heritage of Washington, Jefferson, and Lincoln . . . was crumbling to dust."

So what is the presidency? Is it an office with little power or the most powerful office in the world? Does it rank among the gods, or is it crumbling to dust? How, in short, can the presidency have both too little and too much power? The answer is that when we speak of the presidency we are not speaking of one monolithic institution over time. Instead, we are talking about an institution that changes continually. Sometimes it is too powerful, and sometimes it is not powerful enough. This is not merely due to the constant change in the Oval Office's occupants. Clearly, some of them have been more active in promoting presidential power than others, while some have been content to let others (e.g., Congress or the states) take the lead in governing the nation. But that is only one aspect of the change that we will talk about in this book, and not even the most important element of it. Rather, the office itself has changed over time. The presidency and our expectations of it have been continually re-invented. In fact, like an organism, the

Box I-1

Personal Expectations for the President

Answer "Yes" or "No" to each of the questions that follow.

Do you expect the president to:

1. Preserve the peace? (Yes or No)

2. Provide for a strong economy? (Yes or No)

3. Work well with Congress? (Yes or No)

4. Be a moral leader? (Yes or No)

5. Put the nation's interests ahead of the president's own political interests? (Yes or No)

6. Always tell the truth? (Yes or No)

7. Avoid swearing, even in private? (Yes or No)

8. Avoid smoking? (Yes or No)

9. Avoid alcoholic beverages? (Yes or No)

10. Avoid telling offensive jokes, even in private? (Yes or No)

11. Be faithful to his spouse? (Yes or No)

12. Work hard every day? (Yes or No)

13. Be an effective public speaker? (Yes or No)

14. Look good on television? (Yes or No)

15. Keep an open mind on most major policy issues? (Yes or No)

16. Improve education? (Yes or No)

17. Balance the budget? (Yes or No)

18. Protect the environment? (Yes or No)

19. Increase defense spending? (Yes or No)

20. Help the poor? (Yes or No)

21. Lower the divorce rate? (Yes or No)

22. Lower the crime rate? (Yes or No)

23. Protect Social Security? (Yes or No)

24. Provide for Homeland Security? (Yes or No)

25. Stay out of issues best run by the state and local governments? (Yes or No)

Evaluating Your Responses

Give yourself one point for each "yes" answer, zero points for each "no" answer. Then group your points into three dimensions: Dimension 1 includes questions 1–5; Dimension 2 includes questions 6–15; Dimension 3 includes questions 16–25. Find your score for each dimension.

Dimension 1: Most people expect the president to provide leadership on the first five questions (peace, prosperity, work with Congress, be moral, put the national interest first). The higher your number of "yes" answers, the more you expect of the president in this dimension.

Dimension 2: These questions involve personal qualities of the presidency, and there is usually greater disagreement as to what people expect. The higher your number of "yes" answers, the more you expect of the president in this dimension.

Dimension 3: These questions involve particular issues. The higher your number of "yes" answers, the more you expect of the president in this dimension.

Now compare your answers on all three dimensions with those of other students in your class. This will tell you how much you expect in comparison to other students.

---

presidency is in a constant state of change. The office that George Washington occupied was nothing like the one that Theodore Roosevelt held. Likewise, the presidency changed considerably by the time the next Roosevelt, Franklin, was in charge. And the office that FDR held was nothing like the one that Ronald Reagan, George H. W. Bush, or Bill Clinton inhabited or that George W. Bush presently occupies. The story of the presidency then is all about change. Our primary objective in this book will be to examine how and why the presidential office changes. The framework that we will use to examine this changing presidency is the focus of Chapter 1.

Answer the questions in Box I-1 to determine what your expectations for the president are.

Public Expectations and the Political Resources of the Presidency

Key Terms

electoral resources
expectations gap
external resources
honeymoon
informational resources
internal resources
legal resources

modern presidency
new political resources
personal resources
political ecosystem
post-modern presidency
rally round the flag effect
traditional political resources

1-1 Public Expectations and the Political Resources of the Presidency

In 1960, noted presidential scholar Richard Neustadt (1980 edition: 7) wrote that the public has come to believe that "the man inside the White House [can] do something about everything." By the end of the same decade, Seligman and Baer (1969: 18–35) wrote, "A major political trend of our time is the growth in public expectations of the presidency and the expanding scope of presidential action." What these scholars identified was nothing less than a fundamental transformation in the structural dynamics of American politics. In the twentieth century, as public attention and demands for governmental action shifted toward the federal level, the presidency became the most powerful office in the American governmental system.

This was quite a change from the eighteenth and nineteenth centuries—the traditional era of American government. During that era, the American public focused its attention primarily on state and local officials, as well as the U.S. Congress, then considered the dominant branch of the federal government. But by the late nineteenth century, the federal legislature's perceived inability to deal with a variety of pressing issues led a young scholar by the name of Woodrow Wilson to argue that Congress lacked the ability, and the presidency the capacity, to lead. Other contemporaries were likewise concerned with the limitations of the presidential office. After visiting the United States from England, Lord Bryce wondered why men of limited stature most often occupied the presidential office. One answer is that in the nineteenth century the public had limited expectations of presidential performance and therefore placed relatively few demands upon it. The public looked to Congress, and it in turn dominated national politics.

1-1a Fundamental Transformation

By the beginning of the twentieth century, however, particularly with the advent of the presidency of Theodore Roosevelt, a radically different view of our constitutional system began to emerge. With ever increasing frequency, the public focused its demands and expectations directly on the presidential office. As he did, most of Teddy Roosevelt's twentieth century successors encouraged this trend to look to the White House for leadership. As a result, as Brownlow (1969: 35, 43) writes, the public came to expect the chief executive to be "a competent manager of the machinery of government; . . . a skilled engineer of the economy of the nation, . . . [and] a faithful representative of the opinion of the people." In addition, in time of war the public also expected the president as commander-in-chief "to lead us to victory." In short, public expectations of the presidency were expanding, and with them the potential power of the presidential office.

What accounts for this radical transformation in public expectations of the presidency? The explanation is multifaceted. Clearly, presidents today are armed with new communication and transportation technologies that allow them to take their message directly to the people. Whereas nineteenth century presidents had only a limited megaphone to communicate their message to the public, today presidents can use national newspapers and magazines, radio, television, the Internet, and other technologies (e.g., faxing messages directly to the media, communicating via satellite, or staging media events in historic locations such as Normandy Beach) to get their message out.

Whereas nineteenth century presidents were constrained in their ability to travel, and no president left the borders of the United States until Theodore Roosevelt visited the Panama Canal, transportation advances allow today's presidents to travel around the country and the world with increasing speed and frequency. Presidents can even employ sophisticated equipment on board Air Force One to conduct their governmental business en route to their destination.

Along with these technological changes, presidents today can rely on a large presidential bureaucracy or White House staff organization to assist them in policy formulation and implementation. This bureaucracy also performs outreach to various communities of political importance to the president, provides expert information on foreign and domestic policy, and helps to create better public relations with the media, interest groups, and the public. Whereas the presidency of the nineteenth century consisted largely of the president and his Cabinet, today presidents can rely on thousands of individuals in the Executive Office of the President (EOP). The influence of the Cabinet has been eclipsed by the White House Staff, and the second most powerful executive branch official is often the chief of staff, a position that did not even exist until the Eisenhower presidency.

1-1b Why Have Expectations Changed?

There are many reasons why the public has higher expectations of presidential performance, while other explanations cannot adequately explain the change in presidential power over time. For instance, we cannot explain the growth of presidential power by examining changes in the wording of the Constitution. The president's constitutional authority is essentially the same as it was in 1787. The words are basically the same, though the way in which they are interpreted is often vastly different. For instance, the president's increased power as commander-in-chief in the twentieth century derives not from an amendment to the Constitution, but rather from different perceptions and expectations regarding what those words mean.

Specifically, with the ascension of the United States to the status of a world power, twentieth century presidents took on greater authority and responsibility. With the rise of a permanent threat to national security (the Soviet Union and the Cold War, the invention and deployment of nuclear weapons, the rise of terrorism abroad), the public came to look to the president for leadership on foreign policy. As technologies allowed presidents to travel overseas, the status of the presidency grew as presidents negotiated directly with world leaders in various foreign capitals. In sum, no alteration in the Constitution was necessary to imbue the presidential office with extraordinary new power.

Instead of changes in the president's constitutional authority, expectations changed. Presidents themselves encouraged a growth in presidential power. Whereas many of the nineteenth century presidents believed that it was Congress that played the primary role in the governing process, presidents today (even our weaker ones) are expected to set the tone for the policy agenda. The public, and even Congress itself, looks to the White House for cues about policy priorities. In this process, presidents are expected to lead. Presidents who do not actively set an agenda generally face the electorate's wrath at the next election.

1-1c Presidents Who Increased Expectations

Theodore Roosevelt and Woodrow Wilson played a critical role in this development, but it was Franklin Roosevelt, using the radio (a newly evolving technology) to speak directly to the American people, and improved transportation technologies (air travel) to travel around the country (and even the world), who took his political message directly to the people, in turn transforming public expectations of the presidential office (see Box 1-1).

Franklin D. Roosevelt

AUDIO

Box 1-1

Franklin D. Roosevelt's Pearl Harbor Speech

To the Congress of the United States:

Yesterday, Dec. 7, 1941—a date which will live in infamy—the United States of America was suddenly and deliberately attacked by naval and air forces of the Empire of Japan.

The United States was at peace with that nation and, at the solicitation of Japan, was still in conversation with the government and its emperor looking toward the maintenance of peace in the Pacific.

Indeed, one hour after Japanese air squadrons had commenced bombing in Oahu, the Japanese ambassador to the United States and his colleagues delivered to the Secretary of State a formal reply to a recent American message. While this reply stated that it seemed useless to continue the existing diplomatic negotiations, it contained no threat or hint of war or armed attack.

It will be recorded that the distance of Hawaii from Japan makes it obvious that the attack was deliberately planned many days or even weeks ago. During the intervening time, the Japanese government has deliberately sought to deceive the United States by false statements and expressions of hope for continued peace.

The attack yesterday on the Hawaiian Islands has caused severe damage to American naval and military forces. Very many American lives have been lost. In addition, American ships have been reported torpedoed on the high seas between San Francisco and Honolulu.

Yesterday, the Japanese government also launched an attack against Malaya.

Last night, Japanese forces attacked Hong Kong.

Last night, Japanese forces attacked Guam.

Last night, Japanese forces attacked the Philippine Islands.

Last night, the Japanese attacked Wake Island.

This morning, the Japanese attacked Midway Island.

Japan has, therefore, undertaken a surprise offensive extending throughout the Pacific area. The facts of yesterday speak for themselves. The people of the United States have already formed their opinions and well understand the implications to the very life and safety of our nation.

As commander in chief of the Army and Navy, I have directed that all measures be taken for our defense.

Always will we remember the character of the onslaught against us.

No matter how long it may take us to overcome this premeditated invasion, the American people in their righteous might will win through to absolute victory.

I believe I interpret the will of the Congress and of the people when I assert that we will not only defend ourselves to the uttermost, but will make very certain that this form of treachery shall never endanger us again.

Hostilities exist. There is no blinking at the fact that that our people, our territory, and our interests are in grave danger.

With confidence in our armed forces—with the unbounding determination of our people—we will gain the inevitable triumph—so help us God.

I ask that the Congress declare that since the unprovoked and dastardly attack by Japan on Sunday, Dec. 7, a state of war has existed between the United States and the Japanese empire.

The available evidence suggests that he was extraordinarily successful in making this personal connection with the American people. Prior to Franklin Roosevelt's presidency, the "daily grist of letters and telegrams frequently" ran "as high as 2,000 or 3,000. . . ." One clerk at the Executive Office classified all of the incoming mail (Haskin 1923: 54–55). But under Roosevelt, a staff of 50 had to be hired to handle his correspondence. His mail averaged 5,000 letters per day, increasing at times to 150,000 letters. The man who was in charge of answering Roosevelt's public correspondence commented that when the president "advised millions of listeners in one of his fireside chats to 'tell me your troubles,' most of them believed implicitly that he was speaking to them personally and immediately wrote him a letter" (Leuchtenburg 1988: 7–40). Thus, a relatively new communication technology, radio, and an innate ability to communicate allowed Roosevelt to build a personal relationship with the American public. By so doing, he was able to focus public expectations directly upon his own presidential office.

The crisis of the Great Depression also provided opportunities for the expansion of presidential power. Roosevelt's New Deal called for a greater level of federal governmental participation in the daily lives of average Americans than at any prior time in American history. In successive initiatives, Roosevelt promised the American people that he would provide jobs for the unemployed, stabilize the banking system, establish price supports for farmers, provide electricity for the Tennessee Valley, grant social security for the elderly, and grant protection for union employees. Each of these actions expanded the scope of federal activity. In keeping each of these presidential promises, Roosevelt demonstrated that politicians who espoused an expanded governmental role would be rewarded with continued electoral success, a lesson that was not lost on other contemporary politicians.

Enthusiastically, politicians in the Democratic, and later the Republican, party promised their constituents that the federal government could provide solutions to the nation's most vexing problems. The public, in turn, with its expectations for governmental action heightened, increasingly focused its attention on Washington and the presidency, generally returning to office incumbents who made even grander promises, which in turn further increased public expectations for governmental action. In this process, a cycle of escalating public expectations was firmly established.

One important short-term effect of this cycle was that presidential power was substantially increased. As people turned to the presidency for action on a wide range of issues, presidents gained greater prestige and often with it new statutory authority. A long-term effect of the cycle, however, threatened to undercut this newly gained presidential power. If presidents could not deliver on their myriad promises (if the economy went sour or the international situation destabilized), their future electoral prospects (and job approval ratings) could be imperiled.

1-1d The Dangers of Excessive Public Expectations

But as time progressed, the scope of presidential promises continued to escalate. Predominant among them was Franklin Roosevelt's 1944 promise of a "second Bill of Rights." While it was largely a campaign promise, Roosevelt asserted that the U.S. government should be responsible for the "economic security and prosperity" of all Americans (Sundquist 1981: 62). In 1946 Congress enacted the Employment Act "which committed the government to a continuous policy of economic activism" (ibid., 62), thus assigning the presidency the responsibility for maintaining a healthy economy. The Employment Act of 1946 increased presidential power by expanding the president's legislative responsibilities and most importantly by increasing public expectations of presidential performance. Presidents would now have to deliver a healthy economy, as they had promised, or face the voter's wrath on Election Day.

Through a similar process, over time, a pattern of presidential promises and acquired presidential responsibility was established. Unfortunately, during this same period, there was another development that made it more difficult for presidents to follow through on their promises. The utility of many of the presidency's **traditional political resources** was declining. For example, the influence of the political parties was waning. New and powerful single-issue interest groups were

Traditional political resources: Resources that consist of the president's personal, legal, electoral, and external political resources.

becoming more demanding. In Congress, such developments as the election of a new cohort of independent-minded legislators, the decline of seniority, the reduced influence of the Senate and House leadership, and greater decentralization as exhibited by the increased prominence of subcommittee government, all made it more difficult for presidents to effectively negotiate with the legislative branch.

1-2 The Expectations Gap

Given these concomitant developments, rising public expectations, and a steady decline in the utility of many of the presidency's traditional political resources, it is not surprising that political pundits began to argue that public demands for action were simply out of touch with political reality. For example, the former head of Franklin Roosevelt's Committee on Administrative Management, Louis Brownlow (1969: 35) writes,

> The nation expects more of the President than he can possibly do; more than we give him either the authority or the means to do. Thus, expecting from him the impossible, inevitably we shall be disappointed in his performance.

Other scholars echoed this theme.

Cronin (1974) writes that the public has "inflated and unrealistic" expectations regarding the presidency. Moe (1985: 269) states, "the expectations surrounding presidential performance far outstrip the institutional capacity of presidents to perform." Mezey (1989) adds that public expectations must be reduced before the president and Congress can begin to responsibly deal with many of the nation's problems.

1-2a What Is the Gap?

Expectations gap: The difference between what the public expects presidents to do and what presidents are actually capable of doing.

This problem of excessive and unrealistic expectations became identified in the presidential literature as the **expectations gap**, which is generally described as the difference between what the public expects presidents to do and what presidents are actually capable of doing (see Waterman 1993). Because of the gap's impact, presidents are hypothesized to

1. Have lower approval ratings over time (Stimson 1976; 1976/77; Raichur and Waterman 1993)
2. Be more vulnerable to electoral challenges, both from within their own party and in general election contests at re-election time
3. Have a higher likelihood of experiencing a "failed" presidency overall (Lowi 1985)

In fact, since the 1960s, the expectations gap is one of the primary explanations presidential scholars provide for the failure of the presidency.[1] Scholars provide specific evidence for this failure:

1. Lower job approval ratings for most incumbent presidents
2. Three incumbents defeated for re-election (Ford in 1976, Carter in 1980, and Bush in 1992)
3. A series of major political scandals (Vietnam and Johnson; Watergate and Nixon; Iran-contra and Reagan; Whitewater, the Monica Lewinsky scandal, and Clinton's subsequent impeachment)

The gap is conceptualized in two primary ways. The first is the idea that the longer an incumbent president serves in office, the wider the expectations gap will

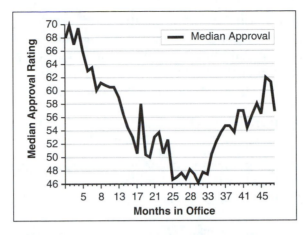

Figure 1-1
Median Approval Ratings

be. Accordingly, it should be relatively easy for most newly elected presidents to satisfy expectations. There is a period of good will, the "**honeymoon**," in which the public, the media, and even the president's political opposition are generally restrained in their criticism and often effusive in their praise.[2] During this period, presidents generally exhibit high levels of public approval. This is the period in which Pfiffner (1996) recommends presidents should "hit the ground running" to take advantage of this time-limited favorable political mood. Likewise, Light (1983) believes this is the time in which presidents have the greatest political resources, if not yet the greatest political skill.

As the honeymoon period ends (within about five months of the inauguration), as the president is forced to address unpopular issues or make difficult decisions, as the economy, events, or scandal raises questions about the president's leadership capabilities, it is postulated that the president's approval ratings will decline and the expectations gap will widen. According to Stimson (1976; 1976/77) and Raichur and Waterman (1993), after the honeymoon, a president's job approval ratings decline steadily, reaching their lowest ebb at midterm. They then remain low throughout much of the president's third year in office and only begin to climb again during the re-election year as the excitement of the election contest brings partisans back to the president's side.[3]

This pattern can be seen in Figure 1-1, from the work of Raichur and Waterman (1993), representing the median approval rating for all first-term presidents from Dwight Eisenhower through Ronald Reagan. According to this conceptualization, the expectations gap is not considered to be an unchanging constant, but rather an impediment to presidential leadership that increases over time, ameliorating only in the re-election year and then only for successful presidents (neither Johnson nor Carter saw an upturn in their fortunes in their fourth year in office, and George H. W. Bush saw a precipitous decline in his ratings during that year).

1-2b Another Way of Thinking about the Expectations Gap

The second and most common method presidential scholars use to conceptualize the expectations gap is as the difference between a hypothetical or ideal president and a real incumbent—that is, the difference between what we expect from an ideal president and what a real incumbent actually can do. This conceptualization of the gap is derived from the tendency of presidential scholars to compare all presidents to Franklin Delano Roosevelt (e.g., Neustadt 1960).

The idea was that Roosevelt created the modern presidency and that all of his successors pale in comparison. Whereas the expectations gap is expected to widen

Honeymoon: The period after the presidential inauguration, usually the first four or five months of a new president's term, when the new president receives generally positive press and muted criticism from the political opposition.

Rally round the flag effect:
During a crisis, the effect seen when the public supports the president as the symbol of the nation. The president's popularity often increases suddenly as a result, though the effect is generally limited over time.

over time in the first formulation, with the ideal/incumbent comparison the gap is more of a constant; that is, it does not increase or decrease over time. While the honeymoon and crisis events (promoting a "**rally round the flag**" effect) may give the president advantages for limited periods of time, in general, the gap is hypothesized to be a constant that undercuts the ability of all presidents to succeed (Lowi 1985).[4]

Presidential scholars also have identified four possible ideas they believe are related to both conceptualizations of the expectations gap:

1. Expectations are connected to presidential performance (e.g., on important issues such as the economy).
2. Expectations are generated by the greater propensity (since the days of Franklin Roosevelt) for individuals to look to the White House for leadership. This is often encouraged by presidents themselves.
3. At the same time that expectations are increasing, the public has excessive, contradictory, and hence unrealistic expectations of what presidents actually can do.
4. As a result, most presidents will fail.

Whatever way we conceptualize the expectations gap, or for whatever reason scholars believe the gap exists, all agree that the gap has had a devastating impact on the presidency.

Hence, the argument that public expectations are unrealistic has important practical political consequences for the presidency; for *perceptions* of presidential power often end up defining the *reality* of presidential power. As Wayne (1982: 185) writes,

> How Americans view the president affects what he does, how he does it, and whether he is thought to have succeeded or failed. It affects the scope of his job, the extent of his power and ability to lead or be lead. It influences his appearance, his manner, and evaluations, in turn, affect the capacity [of presidents] to get things done.

Thus, the paradox of the expectations gap is that it offers presidents increased power in the short term, while in the long term, it threatens to leave behind one failed presidency after another. With the perceived failures of the Johnson, Nixon, Ford, Carter, and George H. W. Bush presidencies, and with the scandals of the Nixon, Reagan, and Clinton presidencies in mind—as well as the Enron debacle of the Bush-Cheney years—scholars wonder if the presidency has become too big for any one individual to handle (Buchanan 1978). What then can presidents do to deal with the expectations gap?

1-2c What Can Be Done about the Expectations Gap?

To address this question, I introduce what I call the six political resources of the presidency. A *political resource* is designed to advance the policy interests of presidents and to maintain their power position (relative to other political actors) within the national and international political arenas. I will argue throughout this book that as the *traditional political resources* have become less useful to presidents in recent decades, they have turned instead to the development of **new political resources.** This is a development that goes back, at least, to 1937, when Franklin Roosevelt's Committee on Administrative Management, also known as the *Brownlow Committee,* identified a presidential need for new political resources. The Brownlow Committee reported,

New political resources:
Resources that consist of the president's internal and informational resources.

While in general principle our organization of the presidency challenges the admiration of the world, yet in equipment for administrative management our Executive Office is not fully abreast of the trend of our times, either in business or in government. . . . The president's administrative equipment is far less developed than his responsibilities and . . . a major task before the American government is to remedy this dangerous situation.

The report concluded that "the president needs help." Each of Roosevelt's successors reiterated this sentiment, expanded the presidential bureaucracy, or created other innovations (e.g., expanded use of executive orders and bureaucratic rule-making) to increase presidential influence over the policy-making process. Aware that their future electoral success and historical ranking, as well as current job approval ratings, depend on their ability to satisfy escalating expectations, Roosevelt's successors identified a variety of new political resources designed to promote their own political influence.

Consequently, rather than viewing the expectations gap as a source of the ultimate failure of the modern presidency, I will view it throughout this book as a changing construct. Expectations change over time, and this influences the power of the presidency. Since political resources are a central construct I will use to analyze changing expectations over time, I next turn to a more detailed examination of the concept of political resources.

1-3 Political Resources

Presidents have a wide variety of political resources at their disposal. According to Light (1983: 15), there are two basic categories of political resources: internal and external. Internal resources include such factors as time, information, expertise, and energy. External resources include party support in Congress, public approval, the breadth of a president's electoral margin of victory, and patronage.

Rose (1988: 77-92) discusses three other political resources: laws, money, and public employees. Presidents depend on the law to justify or legitimize their actions. Money is a resource that allows presidents to pursue their policy objectives. Presidents also have the necessary personnel to actually implement their policy initiatives.

These approaches provide a useful starting point in terms of conceptualizing what we mean by a political resource. They do not, however, directly focus on a number of important presidential resources, particularly those related to the centralization of authority directly in the White House that has been a major trend over the past century (see Hess 1976; Arnold 1986; Hart 1987). I argue that an explication of these centralized resources is essential to our understanding of how and why the modern presidency has evolved. I therefore formulate a typology of six resources: personal, legal, electoral, external, internal, and informational, the latter two dealing with the trend to centralize resources directly within the White House.

1-3a Personal Resources

Personal resources are those that presidents bring with them when they enter the presidential office. These resources include the tools that Neustadt (1960) discussed, including reputation and bargaining skills. But they also include a president's rhetorical skills (or lack thereof), his or her ability to manipulate the media, his or her ability to deal with a crisis situation, his or her moral proclivities, and the image presented to the public. Some of these factors can be altered; that is, presidents can become better public speakers, find friendly venues for communicating with the

Personal resources: The resources (speaking ability, personal likeability, intelligence, ability to compromise, experience, etc.) presidents bring with them when they enter the presidential office.

Legal resources: Resources that derive directly from the Constitution (e.g., the president's enumerated power) or indirectly from it (inherent powers). They also derive from Supreme Court (and other court) decisions and legal precedent that define the parameters of presidential power, from congressional delegation of authority, treaties, defense pacts, and other agreements with other nations and international organizations.

Electoral resources: Resources that derive from elections and include such elements as how presidents are nominated (King Caucus, party conventions, presidential primaries), how presidents campaign, the technologies (radio and television) and political organizations (parties, independent committees) they use to present themselves to the public, whether the president is a lame duck or faces competition in his or her re-election campaign, the scope of the president's margin of victory, the accompanying "mandate," the so-called "honeymoon" period, the presidential coattail effect, and the midterm penalty effect.

External resources: Resources that relate to the exogenous political environment and consist of such diverse entities as public opinion, the media, Congress, political parties, interest groups, the courts, state and local governments, foreign governments, international organizations, and the bureaucracy. These are various actors and institutions that presidents must interact with on a regular basis, but they are actors or institutions over which the president does not have direct hierarchical authority.

Political ecosystem: The political system as a whole, rather than its individual components (president, Congress, courts, public, interest groups, etc.). The focus is on where the public and other political actors look for leadership (or aim their demands for leadership) in the governmental system. The idea is that the political ecosystem is constantly changing or evolving over time, as individual institutions gain or lose influence, as public expectations of these institutions change, and as demands for action are aimed at different political actors.

media, learn more about foreign policy, or change their public image. But if a president has limited skill in a certain area (e.g., public speaking), then his or her personal resources may present more of a problem than an opportunity for promoting presidential influence. As I argue in Chapter 3, finding ways to promote the best qualities of a particular president is consequently critical to presidential success.

1-3b Legal Resources

Legal resources are a second type of political tool. They can derive directly from the Constitution (e.g., the president's enumerated power) or indirectly from it (inherent powers). They also can derive from Supreme Court (and other court) decisions and legal precedents that define the parameters of presidential power. Congressional delegation of authority (such as through the passage of the Budget and Accounting Act of 1921) can expand presidential power, or reduce it (as in the case of the War Powers Resolution of 1973). Presidents also derive legal authority from treaties, defense pacts, and other agreements with other nations and international organizations. As I argue in Chapters 4 and 5, presidents have derived power from changing perceptions of their legal political resources in both domestic and foreign affairs.

1-3c Electoral Resources

Electoral resources derive quite naturally from elections and include such elements as how presidents are nominated (King Caucus, party conventions, presidential primaries), how presidents campaign, and the technologies (radio and television) and political organizations (parties, independent committees) they use to present themselves to the public. Whether the president is a lame duck or faces competition in his or her re-election campaign from within his or her own party is also an electoral factor that can greatly affect the level of a president's political influence. The president's electoral resources also include such factors as the scope of the president's margin of victory, the accompanying "mandate," the so-called "honeymoon" period, the presidential coattail effect, and midterm penalty effects. These factors are discussed in Chapter 6.

1-3d External Resources

External resources relate to the exogenous political environment, or as I will call it, the **political ecosystem,** and consist of such diverse entities as public opinion (Chapter 7), the media and political parties (Chapter 8), Congress (Chapter 9), bureaucracy (Chapter 10), interest groups, the courts, state and local governments, foreign governments, and international organizations (Chapter 11). These are various actors and institutions that presidents must interact with on a regular basis, but they are actors or institutions over which the president does not have direct hierarchical authority. Even the bureaucracy, technically in the Executive Branch, is not directly under the president's control. As Neustadt (1960) famously warns, presidents must learn to bargain and compromise with these actors for they cannot rule them. Yet, many of these actors and institutions became more difficult to manage over time. This development led many presidential scholars to lament the failure of the **modern presidency.** Since Rose (1988) in his writings on the **post-modern presidency** suggests that recent presidents have even fewer resources to deal with these external actors/institutions, the long-term prognosis for the presidency could look dismal indeed. That is why presidents create their own political resources.

1-3e Internal Resources

As a result of the decline in the utility of the president's electoral and external political resources (and the limited potentials offered by his or her personal and legal resources), presidents turned to two new types of political resources. The first is **internal resources.** Rather than using the Cabinet (Chapter 12), presidents in recent decades increasingly turned to both formal and informal mechanisms developed directly within the White House itself. As will be discussed in Chapter 13, they include the creation of organizations and staff within the White House that are directly under the president's hierarchical control; that is, the president is in a stronger position to give commands to these individuals and to then expect them to respond accordingly. Presidents are also using old resources in new ways, such as the vice presidency (see Chapter 14). Internal resources also include a variety of techniques, such as the development of the "administrative presidency strategy," for increasing bureaucratic influence (see Nathan 1983; Waterman 1989) and the expanded use of executive orders (a legal resource) to accomplish what presidents believe they cannot do legislatively (see Chapter 15).

1-3f Informational Resources

Finally, presidents can resort to **informational resources.** As also discussed in Chapters 13 and 15, these types of resources consist of intelligence the president alone can acquire. Many agencies are involved in collecting information for the presidency (from the Central Intelligence Agency, or CIA, to the National Security Council, or NSC). Presidents also use White House organizations (an internal resource) to acquire information (e.g., the Legislative Liaison Office provides the president with information on vote counts in Congress). These sources of information place presidents in a more advantageous bargaining position with other external political actors, both in domestic and foreign affairs.

Table 1-1 summarizes all the resources described in sections 1-3a to 1-3f.

Because there has been a decline in the utility of many of the president's traditional political resources, especially their electoral and external ones, presidents, with increasing frequency have adopted a wide variety of internal and informational resources in an attempt to increase their influence and thereby satisfy public expectations. To understand why presidents have done so, we begin with an examination of how changes in the nation's economy and military (contextual factors) have encouraged changes in public expectations toward the presidency. That is the subject of the next chapter.

Modern presidency: A concept used to describe the period in which the presidency has assumed dominance in our governmental system. Most scholars begin the modern presidency with Franklin Roosevelt, although others have argued that the roots of the modern presidency were laid by presidents such as Theodore Roosevelt and Woodrow Wilson.

Post-modern presidency: Richard Rose's idea that the United States is no longer capable of leading the world on its own, but now is but one of the world leaders. The idea is that the presidency, in this age, is constrained by various resource limitations.

Internal resources: Formal and informal mechanisms that have been developed directly within the White House itself. They include the creation of organizations and staff within the White House that are directly under the president's hierarchical control.

Informational resources: Resources that consist of intelligence the president alone can acquire. Many agencies are involved in collecting information for the presidency (from the Central Intelligence Agency, or CIA, to the National Security Council, or NSC). Presidents also use White House organizations (an internal resource) to acquire information (e.g., the Legislative Liaison Office provides the president with information on vote counts in Congress). These sources of information place presidents in a more advantageous bargaining position with other external political actors, both in domestic and foreign affairs.

TABLE 1-1 Terms and Definitions

Term	Definition	Example
Personal Resources	Attributes or skills that presidents bring with them to office	Good speaking style
Legal Resources	Justifications for presidential power, such as the Constitution, treaties, laws, precedent, and Supreme Court decisions	The Constitution
Electoral Resources	Legitimacy is provided by the president's election to the highest office in the land. Other types of elections, including primary and congressional elections, also affect presidents.	Primary elections
External Resources	Presidents daily must deal with a variety of other political actors, including the Congress, the courts, special interest groups, state governments, foreign governments, and so on. These actors are external because none is under the direct control of the president.	Congress
Internal Resources	Institutions created within the White House itself that provide the president with help in running the functions of the government	The National Security Council
Informational Resources	Internal resources often provide the president with vital information on such factors as how the budget works, how members of Congress will vote, or national security data.	Data on how members of Congress intend to vote on a security bill

Chapter Summary

In recent decades, presidential scholars have identified nothing less than a fundamental transformation in the structural dynamics of American politics. In the twentieth century, as public attention and demands for governmental action shifted toward the federal level, the presidency became the most powerful office in the American governmental system. This was quite a change from the eighteenth and nineteenth centuries, when Americans focused their attention primarily on state and local officials or the U.S. Congress. Today, with ever increasing frequency, the public, the media, and elites focus their demands and expectations directly on the presidential office. In short, public expectations of the presidency expanded and with them the power of the presidential office. What accounts for this radical transformation in public expectations of the presidency? That is the question raised in this chapter and then addressed throughout the book.

Review Questions

Review Questions

1. When did a radically different view of our constitutional system begin to emerge?
   a. during the nineteenth century
   b. during the early twentieth century
   c. during the mid twentieth century
   d. during the late twentieth century

2. Incoming mail to the White House increased rapidly under which of the following presidents?
   a. Theodore Roosevelt
   b. Franklin Roosevelt
   c. Dwight Eisenhower
   d. John Kennedy

3. A short-term effect of increased public expectations was
   a. a decrease in presidential power.
   b. an increase in presidential power.
   c. no change in presidential power.
   d. various random fluctuations.

4. The long-term effect of increased public expectations
   a. increased the prestige of the presidency.
   b. threatened to decrease the power of the presidency.
   c. increased the power of the presidency.
   d. threatened to alter Congress's constitutional powers.

5. The utility of the president's traditional resources has
   a. increased over time.
   b. remained unchanged over time.
   c. decreased over time.
   d. fluctuated randomly over time.

6. The expectations gap is the idea that
   a. the nation expects more from its presidents than they can possibly do.
   b. the nation expects more from members of Congress than they can possibly do.
   c. the nation expects more from the courts than they can possibly do.
   d. the nation expects more from all three constitutional actors than they can possibly do.

7. The expectations gap is the difference between
   a. what the president and Congress can do.
   b. what the public expects government to do and what it can actually do.
   c. what the public expects the Congress to do and what it can actually do.
   d. what the public expects the president to do and what he or she can actually do.

8. About five or six months into most presidents' terms of office,
   a. their popularity begins to decrease.
   b. their popularity begins to increase.
   c. they give their state of the union address.
   d. they begin to think about re-election.

9. One way to think about the expectations gap is the difference between
   a. an ideal president and a real incumbent.
   b. two ideal presidents.
   c. an ideal president, an incumbent, and a failed presidential candidate.
   d. an ideal candidate and a real incumbent.

10. Presidential scholars have argued that most presidents
    a. succeed.
    b. fail.
    c. neither fail nor succeed.
    d. get reelected.

Discussion Questions

Discussion Questions

1. Some presidential scholars argue that the presidency is doomed to failure. Do you agree with this statement? If you do, then does it matter at all who is elected president?

2. Do you personally think there is a gap between what you expect of the president and what the president actually can do?

3. If there is an expectations gap, what can be done to overcome it?

Notes

1. On this point, see Reedy (1970), Buchanan (1978), and Lowi (1985).

2. Some have argued that Clinton did not get a honeymoon period.

3. But this fourth-year process does not work for all incumbents. Jimmy Carter and Lyndon Johnson, for example, saw no such upturn in their political fortunes.

4. Recently, the expectations gap was empirically tested by two groups of scholars. Kimball and Patterson (1997) found that the expectations gap was related to public evaluations of members of Congress, while Waterman, Jenkins-Smith, and Silva (1999) found that the expectations gap did lead to lower presidential job approval ratings and an increased propensity to vote against the incumbent at re-election time.

The Contextual Revolution in America: The Economy, Foreign Affairs, and Changing Public Expectations

Key Terms

commander-in-chief
expectations
isolationism
laissez-faire
militia system

national security
realignment
Shays's Rebellion
White Fleet

2-1 The Contextual Revolution in America: The Economy, Foreign Affairs, and Changing Public Expectations

In 1819, the Bank of the United States abruptly called in outstanding loans and demanded the immediate redemption of state bank notes. This drastic retrenchment policy proved to be a serious economic miscalculation, bringing a sudden end to the economic boom that followed the War of 1812 and providing the catalyst for the Panic (a bank panic usually followed by an economic recession or depression) of 1819. While the nation's economy floundered, President James Monroe argued that Congress was responsible for the state of the economy, not the president. The public apparently agreed. Despite deteriorating economic conditions, Monroe ran unopposed for re-election in 1820, receiving every electoral vote but one.[1]

Today we expect our presidents to provide us with a strong and healthy economy. Those presidents who cannot are likely to suffer lower approval ratings and defeat in their re-election contest. In this chapter, we ask, What has changed since Monroe's time? Why does the American public have different **expectations** of presidential performance today than they did in 1819 and 1820? One factor is the changing nature of the U.S. economy. Beyond that, however, we also need to examine how and why expectations of presidential performance in the area of national defense changed over time. Why does the presidency today exert vastly greater authority as commander-in-chief than it did in the nineteenth century?

To answer these questions, we must look at how changes in the historical context of the United States led to a new set of public expectations—in other words, how the economy was transformed from a rural to a mass industrial state and how America became a dominant world power had implications for the way Americans perceive the power of the presidency. We first turn to an examination of how perceptions of the economy changed over time.

Expectations: A central concept in the presidential literature. The idea is that how we perceive the presidential office, what we demand from it, and where we look for leadership have a direct impact on the extent of presidential power. In short, the greater our expectations of the presidency, the greater is the potential for increased presidential power. Since expectations can change more quickly than constitutional provisions, laws, or the president's legal authority, it is also a central concept explaining change in the American presidency over time.

2-2 A Rural Nation

According to the 1790 census, the first conducted by the government of the new republic, 3,929,214 people lived in the United States (a number that clearly does not adequately include the number of Native Americans living in America), 681,834 of whom were slaves; see Figure 2-1. In fact, only twenty-four communities had populations of 2,500 or more and only five cities had populations in excess of 10,000 (Rossiter 1966: 25).

Furthermore, "perhaps eight in ten Americans dug their living in the dirt; one in ten worked in a closely allied extractive industry such as fishing or lumbering; one in ten had a place, whether as merchant, lawyer, sailor, clerk, or cartman, in the scheme of commerce. . ." (ibid., 33). And of the fifty-five delegates to the 1787 Constitutional Convention in Philadelphia, only three "had invested in manufacturing enterprises" (ibid.). Not only was the nation rural, it was even anti-urban. As historians Elkins and McKitrick (1993: 168) write,

> At the time of the republic's founding, there was little room in the American imagination for the idea of a metropolis as the mirror of a national civilization. On the contrary, the anti-urban, anti-metropolitan component of the Revolutionary mentality would prove to be one of its most persistent and durable features. . . . [T]he metropolis was London, a place out of sight and out of reach, where corruption permeated everything, and where everyone knew, all the schemes for abridging colonial liberties had been hatched. One of the earliest decisions of the fathers of the new republic was made with more or less clear purpose not to have that kind of metropolis in America.

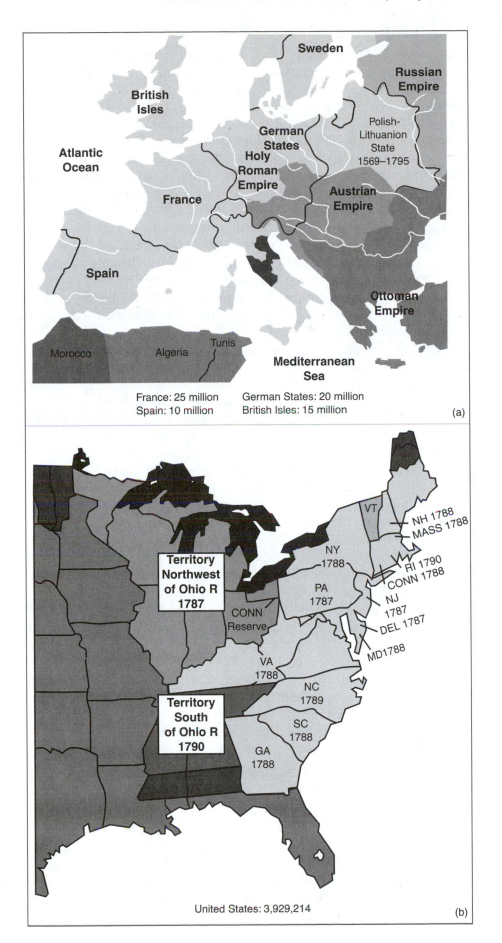

France: 25 million   German States: 20 million
Spain: 10 million   British Isles: 15 million

(a)

United States: 3,929,214   (b)

Figure 2-1
**Population Change:
A Growing Nation**

(a) Populations of countries
in western Europe, relative
to *(b)* U.S. population, 1790.

2-2a Rural Virtue

To many of the Founders, rural America signified virtue. It suggested self-reliance, where the "poorest immigrant could soon earn enough to buy his plot of ground, cut down his trees, erect his log hut and plant his seeds against the coming spring" (Bowen 1966: 70). While, as Bowen (1966: 164) writes, "America in 1787 was on the verge, the very brink of industrial and scientific expansion," to most Americans this was not a welcome development. The Federalist Party, following the leadership of Secretary of the Treasury Alexander Hamilton, did actively support a pro-industrial, pro-British, pro-metropolitan agenda. Yet, while the Federalist Party controlled the agenda during the administrations of George Washington and John Adams, Thomas Jefferson soundly rejected the party's vision in the election of 1800. The Federalist Party then declined until its ultimate extinction in the mid-1810s.

Like many of the Founders' visions, Jeffersonian democracy actively promoted the ideal of rural life. In fact, Jefferson's decision to purchase a large tract of land from Napoleon (the Louisiana Purchase) was premised on the belief that it was necessary to provide room for rural expansion westward, which would in turn delay the advent of industrialization, containing its deleterious effects along the eastern seaboard.

Why did Jefferson and many of the Founders support a rural vision of America? As Stuckey (1991: 16) notes, "The Founders were profoundly suspicious of popular leadership as a means of soliciting power and sought to establish a forum of leadership that depended on character rather than personality. This is, of course, entirely dependent on a polity that is small enough to allow an individual's character to be well known." A rural America, then, would provide the best means of developing character and leadership, while Europe and particularly England already demonstrated that industrialization provided the basis for corruption and abject poverty.[2] In essence, a small, rural polity was closely associated with the Founders' notions of governance. Additionally, since the federal government in a rural nation would have relatively little to do, it fostered limited public expectations of governmental action. With little commerce to regulate, with an ocean separating the new nation from Europe (and therefore little need for self-defense), a spirit of isolationism (of which more will be said later in this chapter) would further promote ideas of limited (or small) government.

Therefore, when George Washington first assumed the presidential office, his power derived not merely from constitutional provisions (the subject of Chapters 4 and 5), but also from the rural nature and limited expectations (public and elite opinion) of the nation he served. How the nation subsequently changed and how expectations of presidential leadership were altered by these changes create one of the central pieces of a puzzle that help us to explain the growth of presidential power. To better understand this point, we need to see how the national economy and our relationship with other nations changed over time.

2-3 Nineteenth Century Views of the Presidency and the Economy

During the Panic of 1819, James Monroe argued that the president was not responsible for the state of the nation's economy. To understand Monroe's claim, we must remember that America was a far different nation then than it is today. Not only was it a rural nation, it remained one throughout the nineteenth century: As late as 1880, almost 75 percent of Americans lived in communities of fewer than 25,000 people (Rossiter 1966). Largely as a result of the relative isolation of nineteenth century rural life, the federal government in Washington was a distant entity (not just in terms of geography, but also in the minds of most Americans). The majority of Americans were either self-reliant or dependent on state and local governments. Most Americans even identified themselves as citizens of their own state rather than as citizens of the United States.

Consequently, when the national economy declined in 1819, many Americans were not immediately affected, and many of those who were constituted unpopular segments of American life (e.g., urban dwellers, big city bankers, and industrialists). The fact that James Monroe did not vigorously respond to the economic tumult precipitated by the Panic should not, however, be interpreted as evidence that there was no public concern over its effects. In May 1820, Secretary of War John C. Calhoun expressed his concern that the depression was undermining public confidence (Schlesinger 1945: 35). But as the election results in 1820 suggest, the public apparently did not look to the president for economic leadership. Rather, when it looked to the federal government for action, it was more likely to look to Congress. As Monroe argued, the Constitution delegated the power to deal with the economy to the legislative branch, not to the executive. Since Congress jealously guarded its power, this left presidents with greater freedom to remain aloof from economic matters, but it also gave them less responsibility to act (and hence, less real power).

2-3a The Panic of 1837

It is important to emphasize that Monroe's view of presidential responsibility was shared by many of his contemporaries and by various presidents throughout the remainder of the century. During the Panic of 1837, for example, President Martin Van Buren concluded that the Constitution did not allow the president to "interfere" with "the ordinary operations of foreign or domestic commerce." He further stated, "all communities are apt to look to government for too much . . . especially at periods of sudden embarrassment and distress. . . . This ought not to be" (quoted in Sundquist 1981: 61).

Still, Van Buren played a more active role in dealing with the Panic of 1837 than had his predecessor James Monroe, but not by choice. When Van Buren assumed the presidency, there was intense pressure for him to rescind Andrew Jackson's "Specie Circular," which stated that only specie and not bank notes could be received as payment for government lands (Wilson 1984: 49); see Figure 2-2. The newly inaugurated president considered the matter for two months, largely on his own, without even the advice of his Secretary of the Treasury. In New York on

Figure 2-2
The Specie

The Specie was issued on July 11, 1836, by the Treasury Department, but represented the will of then-President Jackson. Although bank notes were issued by the Bank of the United States, the Specie Circular required that only specie and not bank notes be accepted as payment for government lands.

This material is copyrighted by, and used with permission of, the Independence Hall Association. For further information, visit the Independence Hall Association's home page on the World Wide Web at www.ushistory.org

May 4, 1837, he then announced that he would retain the Specie Circular, thus continuing Jackson's policy. When the bank panic began shortly after Van Buren's decision, Van Buren's political opposition, the Whig Party leaders, criticized the president for supporting the Specie Circular.

2-3b Van Buren Refuses to Act

Again, as with the Panic of 1819, there were palpable demonstrations of public displeasure, much of it centered in the nation's major cities, such as New York, where high inflation led to flour riots (Schlesinger 1945: 219). As a result of these riots, a Committee of Fifty was selected by New York merchants and eventually met with President Van Buren to express their concerns. The meeting was not a success, with the president reluctant to intervene. Eventually, the depression provoked strong business opposition to Van Buren's administration and prompted the president to offer a controversial proposal to create an independent Treasury that would require payments in legal tender (ibid., 215–41). As Wilson (1984: 55) writes, "In its political effects . . . the Panic of 1837 had a great impact. Party debate over who was to blame for the crisis reached a new level of intensity. Whigs triumphantly announced the bankruptcy of Jackson's 'experiments' of the currency. . . ."

The policy, and Van Buren's support of it, were called "the great fundamental error" or, as Wilson (1984: 56) describes it, the "original sin" of "executive usurpation." Interestingly, however, "Van Buren did not enter directly into this debate . . ." (ibid.). The economic issue, however, dominated American politics for the rest of the decade, though the economy revived in 1839, just prior to the next presidential election.

While the economy improved, Van Buren was defeated in his re-election bid in 1840. Is this evidence that public expectations already had begun to change? There is some evidence to support an affirmative answer to this question. Van Buren was preceded in the presidency by the first truly activist president, Andrew Jackson. Jackson adopted a presidential leadership style that emphasized aggressive action and even presidential intervention in economic affairs. His attack on the Bank of the United States was one of his administration's major political accomplishments. His subsequent decision to transfer funds from the Bank of the United States to state banks likely contributed to the Panic of 1837. Hence, presidential fingerprints—if not Van Buren's, then his mentor's—could be traced to the Panic's genesis. As a result, Van Buren was in a more politically vulnerable position than was Monroe.

Still, if the Panic was a primary reason for Van Buren's defeat in 1840, it is not readily apparent in the campaign rhetoric from that year. As Riccards (1995: 153) writes, that year "the Whigs ran the first successful image, nonissue campaign for the presidency in American history." The Panic did not dominate the campaign of 1840. Rather, the election was about personality, with Van Buren portrayed as an aristocrat and the aristocratic Harrison ironically presented as a man of the people. Log cabins and hard cider were used to portray Harrison as a common man. Even his ornate house was refitted with a log cabin exterior to perpetuate the newly created image of him. Image dominated the 1840 campaign, not a discussion of the issues or of the Panic of 1837 (see Waterman, Wright, and St. Clair 1999).

Did Van Buren's defeat and the Panic of 1837 promote long-lasting changes in public expectations of presidential leadership? The answer here appears to be no. Van Buren was defeated in 1840, but not by an advocate of increased presidential power and authority over the economy, but rather by William Henry Harrison, who espoused perhaps the most limited constitutional vision of presidential power of any president (see section 3-2g, "William Henry Harrison and the Whig

Conception of the Presidency"). Furthermore, the reaction to the next major economic dislocation, the Panic of 1857, does not suggest that the American public or presidents themselves expected a more activist approach to presidential leadership in economic affairs.

2-3c The Panic of 1857

The Panic of 1857 was precipitated by the financial collapse of the Ohio Life and Trust, to which most of the New York banks were creditors. By late August, banks in New England, Virginia, upstate New York, Missouri, and Nebraska Territory had either failed or suspended payments on their notes. There was a fear that "the fragile American banking system could not withstand the pressures suddenly placed upon it" (Stampp 1990: 223). Secretary of the Treasury Thomas Cobb responded, but his actions had little effect. Yet, as Stampp (1990: 224) notes, ". . . the financial panic, though severe, was soon over. . . . However, the accompanying economic recession was equally severe and much longer. Eventually, it resulted in more than 5,000 business failures, as well as disastrous losses to countless investors in farmlands, town properties, and other securities."

Through it all, President James Buchanan continued the practice of presidential passivity in the face of an economic calamity. In his first annual message to Congress, he did express the opinion that the panic was caused "solely from our extravagant and vicious system of paper currency and bank credits exciting the people to wild speculations and gambling in stocks." He also agreed that banks and their paper currency "might continue with advantage to the public" if properly regulated (quoted in Stampp 1990: 232). But Buchanan did little else to deal with either the panic or the resulting recession. While the opposition Republican Party was critical of the Buchanan administration and even raised the Panic as an issue in the election of 1860,[3] Republicans blamed the Panic not on the president, but rather ". . . on the individual shortcomings of Americans, particularly their speculation in land and stocks which had reached 'mania' proportions in the years preceding the crash, and on generally extravagant living" (Foner 1970: 24).

What is most interesting about the Panic of 1857 is not changes in public expectations but rather which part of the country was most affected by it. While Stampp (1990) argues that all sections of the country were affected, according to Nevins (1947: 466–67), "The South [with its more rural economy] breasted the financial collapse much better than the [industrial] North . . ." (see also Randall and Donald 1969: 107). Hence, by as early as the 1850s, prior to the Civil War, as the nation's rural/industrial divisions were becoming more evident, differential impacts to the panic and recession were experienced by rural and industrial segments of the nation. The lesson from the Panic of 1857, then, was not that the public expected the president to be more assertive in dealing with an economic crisis, but rather that as the nation industrialized, more people directly experienced the negative impacts of it.

2-3d The Panic of 1873

With the Panic of 1873, President Ulysses S. Grant largely followed the pattern of his predecessors and played only a limited role in formulating economic policy. He did allow his Secretary of the Treasury, William A. Richardson, to reissue about $26 million in greenbacks and called for resuming species repayments. In addition, he vetoed a currency bill designed to limit inflation, an anti-depression measure supported by Congress. Generally, however, Grant left economic policy making to the legislative branch (McFeely 1981: 393–98).

According to Schlesinger, Jr. (1986: 235), Grant at one time did consider supporting a program to assist the unemployed. But when Grant proposed it, congressional leaders restrained him. Representative James A. Garfield, who would himself be elected to the presidency (in 1880), argued, "We had somewhat of a struggle to keep [Grant] from drifting into that foolish notion that it was necessary to make large appropriations on public works to give employment to laborers" (ibid.). Grant backed down and no further presidential action was forthcoming.

Unlike the Panic of 1857, however, the effects of the depression of 1873 were long lasting, experienced well into the year 1879, when the country returned to the gold standard, thus stabilizing prices and restoring public confidence (Fels 1951). Industrialization was a key factor in the increased longevity of the economic decline. According to Randall and Donald (1969: 662), the depression was, at the time, the longest on record and "had calamitous consequences for every segment of the American economy." They continue:

> Businessmen were badly hurt. Shaky banks collapsed; sound ones were wrecked by "runs"; currency payments were generally suspended; hundreds of factories closed; "indescribable" scenes were witnessed in financial marts; railroad building came to a halt; stock quotations fell; the "whole business of iron making" was deranged; bankruptcies multiplied. Commercial failures for the year 1873 exceed five thousand, with liabilities of $228,000,000. These losses outnumbered those of 1872 by more than a hundred million; yet, there was worse to follow. Failures in 1876 numbered nine thousand, those of 1877 about the same, those of 1878 over ten thousand.

In addition, wages fell and there were bread lines in the streets of many major cities. In fact, the economy was so bad that the decade was known as the "black seventies" (Vanderbilt 1989: 56). Why was the impact of the Panic of 1873 so much more severe than the effect of earlier panics? One reason is that the national economy was becoming more integrated; that is, the various segments of the economy came to depend upon each other. For instance, farmers became increasingly dependent on the railroads to get their goods to market and then on the people in the city to buy their products. Hence, whereas farmers in the past had been at least somewhat isolated from the effects of panics, by the 1870s they experienced extended hard times. Farm prices declined and did not move up again until the first decade of the twentieth century (Schlereth 1991: 35).

2-3e The Political Effects of the Panic of 1873

Given these continuing economic problems, did an angry and dissatisfied public punish the governing Republican Party? They did with regard to the Congress. In the 1874 midterm election, the Republican Party lost eighty-five seats in the House of Representatives and an additional four seats in the Senate. Unlike later periods in American history, however, the president's party made a quick comeback in Congress, gaining thirty-one seats in the House in 1876 and eventually regaining control of both Houses of Congress in 1880. Thus, even with a depression as devastating as the Panic of 1873, the public's rebuke of the ruling Republican Party in Congress was only temporary.

But in presidential elections, there is no evidence of a public desire to punish the incumbent party. In 1876, Rutherford B. Hayes and Samuel Tilden contended in one of the closest elections in presidential history. Like the election of 2000, its conclusion was controversial. Hayes was selected in a deal that put an end to the Reconstruction period. As a result, Republicans retained control of the presidency.

The effects of the depression then continued throughout Hayes's four years in office. Did an angry public take electoral revenge against the Republican Party in

1880? It did not. James A. Garfield, a congressional leader and a Republican, was elected president. Thus, the public did not use the state of the economy as a reason to punish the party of the president. Rather, the Republican Party continued in office until the election of 1884, after the worst effects of the Panic had ended. These election results provide evidence that the public did not hold Presidents Grant or Hayes personally responsible for the depression and its devastatingly long-lasting effects. In fact, if there was any retribution at all, it was against Congress in 1874. Congress was still considered as the most influential of the three branches of government, particularly on economic matters. Hence, if the public in the 1870s expected governmental action, it still looked first to Congress. But this public expectation was about to change.

2-4 Changing Public Expectations

As devastating as was the Panic of 1873, the Panic of 1893 and the depression that lasted from 1893 to 1897 was worse. Describing the effects of the Panic of 1893, Greenberg (1995: 62) writes,

> By June 1894, 192 railroad companies were in receivership, representing a quarter of all rails. Unemployment reached 17 to 19 percent in 1894. By some estimates, 2 to 3 million people were out of work; 100,000 of the unemployed walked the streets of Chicago. Farm incomes and prices hit their lowest point in 1896.

The Panic also involved a number of strikes. The Pullman Strike of 1894, which resulted in the intervention of federal troops, was one of many: "thirteen hundred . . . in 1894 alone" (Vanderbilt 1989: 266). The impact of the panic was broad, then, with most segments of society affected. As a broader spectrum of Americans directly experienced the deleterious consequences of a panic and its long-term economic effects, the public began to alter its own expectations regarding the legitimate role of government in times of economic crisis. As Hofstadter (1955: 166) writes, the Panic of 1893 and the depression that followed it initiated a change in public expectations:

> During the depression of 1893–7 it was clear that the country was being profoundly shaken, that men everywhere were beginning to envision a turning-point in national development after which one could no longer live within the framework of the aspirations and expectations that had governed American life for the century past. Americans had grown up with the placid assumption that the development of their country was so much unlike what had happened elsewhere that the social conflicts troubling other countries could never become a major problem here. By the close of the century, however, young Americans began to feel that it would be their fate to live in a world subject to all the familiar hazards of European industrialism.

In response to the policies of President Grover Cleveland, who was serving the first year of his second nonconsecutive term in 1893, a special session of Congress was convened in an attempt to repeal the Sherman Silver Purchase Act. Cleveland's call for repeal divided his party, costing him the political support of congressional leaders such as William Jennings Bryan "who resented the president's aggressive intervention in domestic policy" (Milkis and Nelson 1994: 196). The political repercussions of the Panic and the split within the Democratic Party would be profound. Remember that in 1874, the public punished the governing Republican Party in Congress, but its political retribution was only short-lived. In 1894, however, electoral retribution against the governing Democratic Party would be swift, severe, and long lasting.

2-4a Political Retribution

In 1894, the first midterm election following the commencement of the Panic was conducted. The Republicans gained more than 100 seats in the House of Representatives as well as control of the Senate. Although the ruling party had suffered losses during previous decades following economic declines, the losses sustained by the Democrats in 1894 were different: these losses would be sustained over time as the Republicans became the dominant political party in both the House and the Senate for most of the first three decades of the twentieth century.

Furthermore, the presidential election of 1896 pitted Democrat William Jennings Bryan (representing the nation's rural interests) against Republican William McKinley (representing the big cities and newly developing suburbs). Not only did McKinley win the election, only one Democrat would be elected president during the elections conducted from 1896 to 1928 (Woodrow Wilson in the three-way election contest of 1912 and then again in a very close re-election contest in 1916). Democrats lost seven out of the nine presidential elections from 1896 to 1928, and they lost most of them by overwhelming margins.

In essence, the election of 1896 represented a **realignment** in which the urban and industrial interests moved behind the Republican Party, while the Democrats dominated the rural and southern vote. Burnham (1970: 38–39) argues that the catalyst for this electoral realignment was the Panic of 1893.

Realignment: The idea that there are certain elections in American history in which the electorate (or important segments of it) change or realign from one party to another. Most scholars argue that there were realigning elections in 1828, 1860, 1896, and 1932. Some have argued that 1964 and 1980 were also realigning elections, though there is lesser consensus regarding the long-term electoral implications of these latter two elections.

2-4b What Accounts for This Political Change?

Why did the Panic of 1893, and the long-lasting depression that followed it, have such a critical impact on the electorate, while previous depressions had not? What happened between 1873, where the president's party suffered only temporary losses in Congress and where there was no electoral retribution against the Republican presidential candidates, and the elections of 1894 and 1896? One can argue that the change in public attitudes, powerfully expressed at the polls, was the direct result of the metamorphosis of the economy and the industrialization that drove that transformation. With increased industrialization, by the dawn of the twentieth century, a greater number of Americans than ever before resided in cities representing the nation's expanding industrial base. In this setting, people were more likely to directly experience the effects of the economic depression (e.g., bankruptcy and unemployment). In fact, the period from 1870 to 1920 witnessed a massive migration of Americans from the farms to the cities.

In addition, millions of immigrants came to America buoyed by promises of freedom and opportunity. Most of them settled in urban areas. The population of cities all over America increased dramatically during the late nineteenth and early twentieth centuries, so much so that by 1920 for the first time urban dwellers represented a majority of the nation's population (Still 1974: 206). According to Still (1974: 228), this "increasing concentration of populations in cities and especially large cities was primarily a consequence of the industrialization of the United States."

In fact, a nation "that was only a quarter urbanized in 1880 (28.2 percent) was approaching an urban majority by 1910 (45.7 percent)" (Greenberg 1995: 62). Additionally, "the population of the United States doubled between 1870 and 1900. . . . These changes were accompanied by a shift in the economy from local, small-scale manufacturing and commerce to large-scale factory production and mammoth national corporations" (Milkis and Nelson 1994: 204). Hence, between "1880 and 1910, the United States emerged as a manufacturing and industrial society." As Greenberg (1995: 62) notes, "National wealth increased 275 percent, and the manufacturing of finished products by 250 percent." Among the developments of the time, the "steel industry introduced the Bessemer and open-hearth processes; conveyors and hoists became standard in manufacturing; shoe production was taken over completely by machines; refrigeration changed meat packing and created a food industry."

When we add to this the invention and application of electric lighting, the telephone, and motion pictures, plus the development of a national transportation infrastructure and an emerging national media, it is clear that by the 1890s America was in no sense the same country it had been when the Founders created the presidency in 1787. It was even far different from the nation that existed in 1857 or even 1873. As historian Frederick Jackson Turner proclaimed the frontier's end in 1890, it was also clear that America was re-creating itself into a new industrial nation and soon a world power, as well.

Along with this transformation came a decline in rural political and economic influence. As Greenberg (1995: 62) writes, "Between 1870 and 1900, farmers found themselves in a vice, pressed on the one side by declining prices and on the other by new monopolies in marketing and transportation that pushed their costs up. More and more farmers found themselves surviving as tenants rather than as freeholders; a crushing debt and sharp downturns in prices produced a rising desperation across the Great Plains and the South."

Rural areas were once insulated from the cities and the depressions they fostered. By the 1870s, that isolation had declined. By the 1890s, there was no isolation; as the economy became steadily more integrated, particularly with the development of the national railroad transportation system, farmers found their economic fate tied to the interests of the cities. Furthermore, as the cities prospered, the rural interests suffered. They did not do so without a fight, however. In so doing, rural interests through such organizations as the Grange and the Populist Party called on local, state, and federal governments to play a more active political role. These demands for increased governmental action eventually translated into a larger governmental role to meet changing economic needs. It in turn led to an expansion in the size of the government. In "1881 there was one federal employee per 502 people of the total population, compared with one per 237 people in 1911. Similar figures record the parallel expansion of government workers in state capitols and cities" (Schlereth 1991: 75–76). Thus, by 1910 the size of the federal government had increased to 373,379 federal civilian employees, an approximate increase of 300% since 1878. Peri Arnold (1986: 26–27) attributes this expansion to the "transformation of a decentralized agricultural republic into an expansive, industrial republic." As the public expectations changed, as the public looked more and more to government for solutions, the size of government increased. Over time, changing expectations also would contribute to the growth of presidential power and a decline in the relative influence of Congress.

2-4c The Limitations of Congressional Leadership

As the population of the cities increased, so did the problems associated with urbanization and industrialization. "Muckrakers," writers, who chronicled the details of urban conditions, soon wrote powerful exposes on life and poverty in the cities. These exposes shocked the nation and increased demands on all levels of government to do something to ameliorate the newly developing urban problems. In sum, the days of a purely *laissez-faire* (hands-off) economy and a passive federal political system were coming to an end. But who would provide leadership in this changing economic environment? As it turned out, Congress was particularly ill equipped to deal with this more activist political environment.

Laissez-faire: A central concept of economic theory. It is the idea that the government should take a hands-off approach to economic policy.

While Congress was able to deal with the nation's economic problems in a time when the tariff was the biggest economic issue, it struggled to provide leadership and direction in an era of developing industrialization. Congressional decision making was decentralized through an elaborate committee system. This organizational system was adequate so long as the nation itself was largely decentralized. But as the economy integrated, as power within and across corporations became more centralized, and as demands on government increased, Congress's decentralized decision-making process became an impediment to swift and bold action. Citing these flaws, one of Congress's most prominent critics, a young political scientist and future president named Woodrow Wilson, scathingly attacked the congressional committee system and the separation of powers. In his classic book *Congressional Government,* he also provided an intellectual basis for a new interpretation of the U.S. Constitution, one in which the president could play a more active policy role.[4] The model for a new, more active presidency first derived, perhaps ironically, from the new chief executive officers of the nation's newly created corporations. These so-called captains of industry provided a model of active executive leadership, one that the newly evolving field of Public Administration took to heart and advocated with great zeal throughout the first decades of the twentieth century.

In this and other ways, the centralization of business (and with it the greater integration of the U.S. economy) was to have a considerable impact on the development of presidential power, providing both a rationale and a blueprint for it. To understand this point, we can look at the centralization of business, which came first to the railroad industry. Faced with the problem of coordinating management over a widely dispersed geographical area, the railroad industry devised a new hierarchical system for controlling business practices, a system that proved to be so successful that it was soon employed by other industries. According to Chandler (1977: 345–46), "after 1900 the modern multiunit industrial enterprise became a standard instrument for managing the production and distribution of goods in America. Hundreds of such companies came into existence." With a proliferation in the number of corporations, the economy itself became more centralized, with giant corporations dominating markets that had previously been controlled by small, local, or regional businesses.

Thus, centralization developed on two levels, each with consequences for the evolution of the modern presidency. On one level, centralization created new management techniques with a strong corporate leader in charge—a new prototype for the modern presidency. On a second level, centralization created a more integrated and interdependent economy, where the effects of economic changes in one area of the country could have an almost immediate impact on conditions in other regions (making rural areas more vulnerable to national economic conditions), thus creating a greater need for executive leadership. Hence, by the birth of the twentieth century, the basic contextual building blocks were in place to construct a new presidency. What was now required was an individual with the vision and willingness to seize the presidency's new potential.

2-4d Theodore Roosevelt

The first man to adopt the new leadership model in the White House was a young, energetic, progressive politician who was elevated to the White House in 1901 by an assassin's bullet: Theodore Roosevelt. He believed that the power of the federal government was required to offset the growing power of the corporations. According to Roosevelt, increased governmental activity did not represent centralization, but rather "it represent[ed] merely the acknowledgment of the pattern fact that centralization [had] already come in business. If this irresponsible outside power [was] to be controlled in the interest of the general public, it [could] be controlled in only one way—by giving adequate power of control to one sovereignty capable of exercising such power—the National Government" (quoted in Schlesinger 1986: 237).

In many respects, and as we will discuss throughout this book, it is Teddy Roosevelt who first introduced many of the innovations that eventually led to the development of what presidential scholars call the *modern presidency*. It is not a coincidence that he, and not one of his predecessors, was able to do so. As noted, various contextual changes in the nature of the U.S. economy created the opportunity, the rationale, the public demands, and the model for an increased presidential role. While that development was by no means pre-ordained, it is unlikely that the first Roosevelt in the White House would have been able to initiate increased presidential power without a growing perceived need for it. As Louis Brownlow (who served Franklin Roosevelt) writes (1969: 41),

> ...I think I am on safe ground in saying that not until the time of Theodore
> Roosevelt did the people of the country consciously expect the President to take the
> leadership in minimizing the detrimental effects on the public welfare.... There had
> been occasional demands for Presidential action and occasional compliance with
> those demands, but they seem to have been exceptional....

Teddy Roosevelt both responded to the public's demands for action and encouraged the public to look to the White House for leadership. Using the newly evolving national media (see Chapters 7 and 8), he placed himself and the presidency at the center of the governmental system, or at the center of what I will later call the political ecosystem (see Chapter 11). In dealing with the Anthracite coal strike, advocating progressive legislation for food and drug safety, and attacking the power of the trusts, he began the creation of a new, more activist presidential model. According to Roosevelt biographer William Draper Lewis (1919: 281), the president played an active role from the commencement of the Panic of 1907: "The President and Secretary Cortelyou of the Treasury kept in hourly communication with New York and from time to time took such action as they thought might serve to allay the panic." As these early efforts failed, and as the magnitude of the crisis became more apparent, Roosevelt again responded by providing federal aid to banks, expanding the currency, and moving to reduce interest rates (see Romasco 1974; Schlesinger 1986: 237; though for a different view, see Morris 2001).

2-4e Institutionalizing Expectations

While some of Roosevelt's successors, especially Warren G. Harding in the economic recession of 1921, disavowed an active presidential role in the face of a fairly mild economic downturn, the presidential leadership model, and rationale for it, was firmly established following Theodore Roosevelt's presidency. As the economy further expanded and integrated, twentieth century presidents were expected to act even more aggressively in the face of an economic calamity. Those who did not, or those who were not perceived as doing enough (such as Herbert Hoover with the Crash of 1929 and the depression of the 1930s), would be rejected by the American public at the polls or would see their public approval ratings decline, often precipitously. As Tufte (1978) demonstrated, the fate of presidents is therefore inextricably linked to the state of the U.S. economy. As a result, those who run for re-election in good economic times (e.g., Reagan and Clinton) are rewarded, while those who do so during recessions or tough economic times (e.g., Ford, Carter, George H. W. Bush) are rejected at the polls.

Legislation further institutionalized these public expectations. In 1921, a federal budget was created and the president was delegated authority to take the lead in presenting it to Congress. Much of the New Deal legislation of the 1930s and the war legislation of the 1940s increased the president's control over the economy. The Employment Act of 1946 essentially made the president the nation's main economic policy maker. The creation of the Bureau of the Budget (later to be renamed the Office of Management and Budget) and the Council of Economic Advisers gave the president institutional tools to influence economic policy. In short, as expectations changed, the president's new, more activist economic role was institutionalized by Congress and by various presidents of both major political parties.

2-4f Summary: Economic Expectations

In summary, while the development of the modern presidency was not institutionalized until the 1930s and the arrival of Franklin Delano Roosevelt, its genesis can be seen in the presidency of Teddy Roosevelt. The expanded federal role he initiated, along with the introduction of an even more active presidential role during Woodrow Wilson's two terms in office, provided the basis for the development of a new activist model of presidential leadership. In this development, contextual changes in the nation's economy played a vital role. They provided the basis for presidential activism in the area of domestic policy, as well as a practical model for presidential leadership. Concomitantly, contextual changes also promoted a more active presidential role in foreign affairs. We turn to these developments next.

2-5 The Changing Role of the President as Commander-in-Chief

Public expectations of presidential performance in domestic affairs changed as the economy developed from rural to urban/industrial and as new economic realities created increasing demands for federal governmental action. The new economy, however, was not the only contextual factor that directly impacted presidential power. Another major contextual factor was America's developing role in world affairs.

In Federalist #69, Alexander Hamilton states the president as **commander-in-chief** was to be nothing more than the supreme commander of the military and naval forces, "as first General and Admiral of the confederacy." To have real influence, then, presidents must first have an army and a navy over which they can serve as first General or Admiral. Second, circumstances need to exist in which the president is commander-in-chief on a permanent, full-time basis—circumstances that require a continuous external threat to the nation's security.

Over the first 225 years of our nation's history, changes in the perceptions and expectations of policy makers and the public occurred that allowed presidents to play a more active role in foreign affairs. These changes can be placed in four categories.

These categories include

1. Whether there should be a standing army
2. Which military resources are available to presidents
3. America's entry on the world stage
4. The emergence of a permanent threat to national security

2-6 A Standing Army

On May 2, 1783, in response to a request from a committee headed by Alexander Hamilton, George Washington, the commander-in-chief of the American Revolutionary forces, released his now famous "Sentiments on a Peace

Commander-in-chief:
A constitutional role of the presidency. As commander and chief, the president, as a nonmilitary official, is the head of the military. This was part of the Founders' intent to limit the power of the military by placing it under civilian control.

Establishment." In it, Washington revealed how he thought the newly formed nation should organize its military. Washington wrote (Fitzpatrick, ed., 1932: 374–75, vol. 26),

> A Peace Establishment for the United States of America in my opinion [should] be classed under four different heads:

> First. A regular and standing force, the Garrisoning West Point and such other Posts upon our Northern, Western, and Southern Frontiers, as shall be deemed necessary. . . . Secondly. A well organized Militia; upon a Plan that will pervade all the States, and introduce similarity in their Establishment Manoeuvres *[sic]*, Exercise, and Arms. Thirdly. Establishing Arsenals of all kinds of Military Stores. Fourthly. Accademies *[sic]*, one or more for the Instructions of the Art Military; particularly those Branches of it which respect Engineering and Artillery, which are highly essential, and the knowledge of which, is most difficult to obtain. Also Manufactories of some kinds of Military Stores.

Washington's recommendations may not seem controversial to our twenty-first century eyes, but to Americans in the late eighteenth century, they were highly revolutionary, particularly the call for a "regular and standing force." The fear of a standing or regular army was as deeply imbedded in American political thought as was the idea that there should be "no taxation without representation." It was indeed a fundamental and widely held belief. Today, most Americans perceive their military in positive terms, usually equating it with such values as freedom, courage, and patriotism. In stump speeches, politicians freely invoke the U.S. military as the defenders of our freedoms. While there is inevitable controversy regarding the size of the defense budget, the utility of specific weapons systems, and the advisability of deploying troops in particular hostile situations, a majority of Americans today perceive the U.S. military in highly positive terms. This was not always the case.

2-6a The Fear of Standing Armies

One of the dominant ideas in early American thought was that a standing army is dangerous to the public's civil liberties, which were defined by English radical Richard Price as "the power of a Civil Society or State to govern itself by its own discretion; or by laws of its own making" (Wood 1969: 24). In fact, the fear of standing armies appears to have been an integral part of early America's psychological profile and certainly a basic component of the Whig philosophy of rebellion. In part, this fear related to the nature and organization of early standing armies. As Wood (1969: 30) writes, "Politics in the jaundiced eyes of the radical Whigs had always been a tale of 'bloodshed and slaughter, violence and oppression,' where the 'Monarchs of every age . . . surrounded by a banditti which they call a standing army' had committed havoc on the liberty, property, and lives of hapless people." The reference to a "banditti" signified that many of the armies of the seventeenth and eighteenth centuries consisted of hired soldiers. These army regiments often acted as a private business enterprise, with monarchs contracting them out for service in foreign wars.

Consequently, the objective of these private armies was profit, rather than the present military goal of protecting our nation's national security. As Millis (1956: 15) writes, "Venal and callous as this system may seem, it obviously arose from the fact that in the absence of effective administrative techniques private enterprise was the only available recourse." This system, however, "was considerably modified as the eighteenth century advanced and as a more competent bureaucracy began to take over a more centralized control of military operations." Still, at the commencement of the American Revolution, George III attempted to secure troops from Russia and, when that failed, hired Hessian units to fight against the colonies. Hence, the practice of a hired—for profit—military was still very much alive in the late eighteenth century.

Beyond the for-hire aspect, the fear of a standing army also "followed directly from the colonists' understanding of power and of human nature." As Bailyn (1992: 63) writes, "Only too evidently was it justified, as the colonists saw it, by history and by the facts of the contemporary world. Conclusive examples of what happened when standing armies were permitted to dominate communities were constantly before their minds' eye." History, and in particular British history, was riddled with examples of the abuses of standing armies and of the demagogues who used them to advance their own personal political ambitions. History was neither an obtuse subject of study nor a mere abstraction to the colonists. They were generally well read, if not formally educated, and quite knowledgeable about British history. As Higginbotham (1971: 14) writes, "Americans were well versed on Parliament's confrontations with the Stuarts over military matters."

2-6b The Dangers of a Standing Army

The dangers of a standing army had first become apparent during the British Civil War. That war pitted the royalist army of Charles I against Parliament's army. After assuming the throne in 1625, Charles asked Parliament for loans to pay for the conduct of his wars with France and Spain. When Parliament refused, Charles retaliated. When his soldiers returned from "the wars with Spain and France in 1625 and 1626, instead of being discharged, [they] were billeted on the citizens" (Higginbotham 1971: 14). The "greatest numbers of armed men seemingly" were "placed in the homes of those who had most resisted the loans." Consequently, the "seeds of implacable resistance to a standing army were sown by that decision."

Later, after Parliament had temporarily gained an advantage over the King, it forced Charles to accept a Petition of Rights "that included prohibitions on billeting soldiers in private houses and restrictions on the peacetime grant of military commissions" (Palmer 1994: 95). But Parliament's advantage over the monarchy proved to be short-lived and by 1642 a state of total civil war existed. In this conflict, "the most outstanding battle leader . . . was Oliver Cromwell, who skillfully commanded and trained an effective [military] force known as the 'Ironsides'" (Palmer 1994: 95). When the Parliamentary forces, based on the model of the Ironsides, were reorganized by ordinance on February 17, 1645, into the New Model Army, Cromwell became a lieutenant general.

As Smith (1974: 331) writes, "The New Model Army became a formidable and efficient military machine, the first national standing army." By the end of 1645, the army had increased to 80,000 men. In 1647, Parliament issued an order to disband the army without pay. Cromwell, who had tried to negotiate a compromise between the army and Parliament, eventually announced that he would support his soldiers (Smith 1974: 331–33). A second civil war then ensued, after which Britain experienced "the full impact of military rule" (Higginbotham 1971: 14). "Military leaders quickly consolidated power, purging Parliament of all but those supporting the army" (Palmer 1994: 95). The King was beheaded, an act which "Englishmen would forever afterwards remember that the army had done. . . ." Hence, as Palmer (1994: 95–96) notes, in the future, while "there would be a Royal Navy . . . , and one day a Royal Air Force, there would never again be a Royal Army. An English army, or a British army, but not a royal one."

Meanwhile, under Cromwell's leadership as "Lord Protector of the Commonwealth of England, Scotland, and Ireland," a written constitution was established which "mandated a standing army of thirty thousand soldiers" (Palmer 1994: 96). As Palmer (1994: 97) writes, under Cromwell's leadership, "the English people got a thorough taste of government by a man on horseback. And they did not like it." Following Cromwell's death in 1658, the "nation was sick of military rule" (Smith 1974: 349). When Charles II was restored to power, Parliament disbanded the New Model Army, this time "wisely" approving separation pay for the soldiers (Palmer 1994: 97). Still, an army of 7,000 to 9,000 men was retained, which further exacerbated the English citizenry's suspicions. As Higginbotham (1971: 14) notes, it was Charles II's rule that "witnessed the birth of classic English ideological opposition to militarism." Higginbotham continues, "The obsession was not to be simply a distrust of armies in general . . . but especially of 'standing armies,' permanent establishments maintained by government and regularly supplied by the public treasury in peace as well as war."

2-6c The Founders' Concerns with Defense

Americans shared this fear of standing armies through a common ancestry. As Palmer (1994: 100) writes, "Americans of the late seventeenth century understood fully the philosophy behind the Declaration of Rights imposed upon William and Mary. Indeed, they probably approved of provisions limiting royal military power even more overwhelmingly than did their countrymen in England." Evidence for this point is provided by the fact that Oliver Cromwell "led the list of men whose names surfaced most often" in the notes from the Constitutional Convention of 1787. As Palmer (1994: 94) states, "His was a prominent presence the framers could not ignore."

That these thoughts were very much on the minds of the Founders is evidenced by Edmund Randolph's opening statement to the Constitutional Convention on May 29, 1787. According to Madison's Record of the Convention, Randolph observed the character of the "foederal [sic] system we ought to inquire" into should "secure 1. against foreign invasion; 2. against dissentions between members of the Union, or seditions in particular states; 3. to p[ro]cure to the several States various blessings, of which an isolated situation was i[n]capable; 4. to be able to defend itself against incroachment; & 5. to be paramount to the state constitutions."

Madison notes that Randolph "proceeded to enumerate the defects: 1. that the confederation produced no security agai[nst] foreign invasions; congress not being permitted to prevent a war nor to support it by th[eir] own authority—Of this he cited many examples; most of whi[ch] tended to shew [sic], that they could not cause infractions of treaties or of the law of nations, to be punished; that particular states might by their conduct provoke war without controul; and that neither militia nor draughts being fit for defence on such occasions, enlistments only could be successful, and these could not be executed without money" (Farrand 1966: I: 18-19).

2-6d How to Defend the Nation?

With security such a paramount concern, the question before the convention was how the nation could best provide for its defense. As John Randolph later remarked, "there was not a member in the federal Convention who did not feel indignation" at the prospect of a permanent standing army (Huntington 1956: 680). Yet, standing armies already existed in America. The Articles of Confederation did not prohibit their establishment, and several states, including some with provisions condemning standing armies, employed them to put down local insurrections. For

Shays's Rebellion: A farmers' rebellion that was led by Revolutionary War veteran Daniel Shays in rural western Massachusetts to oppose higher taxes. The rebellion forced several courts to close, thus preventing them from conducting foreclosure proceedings against farmers. An attack on the federal arsenal at Springfield also occurred. Although unsuccessful, the rebellion sent a shockwave through the new nation and was an important factor leading to the replacement of the Articles of Confederation with a new Constitution.

example, both Pennsylvania and Massachusetts raised and employed armies. As Madison asked the Convention on June 19, "Has not [Massachusetts] . . . the most powerful member of the Union, already raised a body of troops [in response to **Shays's Rebellion**]? Is she not now augmenting them, without having even deigned to apprise [Congress] of Her intention?" (Farrand 1966: I: 316).

The idea that individual states were raising armies was of particular concern to Madison. On June 29, he noted, "Let each State depend on itself for its security, & let apprehensions arise of danger from distant powers or from neighboring States, & the languishing condition of all the States, large as well as small, wd. soon be transformed into vigorous & high toned Govts." Madison continues, "The same causes which have rendered the old world the Theatre of incessant wars, & have banished liberty from the face of it, wd. soon produce the same effects here. The weakness & jealousy of the small States wd. quickly introduce some regular military force agst. sudden danger from their powerful neighbors. The example wd. be followed by others, and wd. soon become universal."

He then reminded the delegates, "A standing military force, with an overgrown Executive will not long be safe companions of liberty" (Farrand 1966: I: 464-65). Yet, this scenario was more likely if the states decided to go their own way or if "partial confederacies" of several states each was established. Clearly, according to Madison, a federal government established under republican principles would provide the best security against the threat of a standing army.

2-6e Should There Be a Standing Army?

Despite this concern, the convention's report of the Committee of Detail did not mention standing armies. The omission of a reference to standing armies and provisions related to the militia drew scathing comment from several members of the Convention. One of the most vociferous critics of a standing army was Elbridge Gerry. As Bowen (1966: 218) writes, "Gerry trotted out the timeworn arguments against a standing army; all summer he . . . used them." On August 18, Gerry noted, "there was [no] check" in the Constitution "agst. standing armies in time of peace." Madison, in describing Gerry's comments, then continued, "He thought an army dangerous in time of peace & would never consent to a power to keep up an indefinite number. He proposed that there shall not be kept up in time of peace more than _____ thousand troops. His idea was that the blank should be filled with two or three thousand" (Farrand 1966: II: 329).

Farrand (1966: IV: 229) notes, "In response to Gerry's motion . . . that no standing army exceed 3,000 men, Washington is alleged to have suggested a counter-motion that 'no foreign enemy should invade the United States at any time, with more than three thousand troops.'" Whether Washington actually made this comment to another delegate is not known. But it is clear that other delegates quickly assailed Gerry's proposal.

General Pinckney "asked whether no troops were ever to be raised until an attack should be made on us?" Gerry responded, "if there be no restriction, a few States may establish a military Govt." Mr. Williamson reminded Gerry "the appropriation of revenue" was "the best guard in this case." Mr. Dayton then responded, "preparations for war are generally made in peace; and a standing force of some sort, for ought we know, become unavoidable." The proposal by Gerry and Luther Martin was then rejected (Farrand 1966: II: 330).

A proposal for limiting the necessity of standing armies was then discussed. Earlier in the day, George Mason declared that the general government should be responsible for regulating the militia. Madison, describing Mason's statement, then added, "He hoped there would be no standing army in time of peace, unless it might be for a few garrisons." Instead of a standing army, the "Militia ought therefore to be the more effectually prepared for the public defence. Thirteen States will never concur in any one system, if the displining [sic] of the Militia be left in their hands." Mason therefore recommended "a power to regulate the militia" to the Committee of Detail (Farrand 1966 II: 326).

2-6f The Founders Revisit the Issue

On September 14, the delegates again revisited the issue of a prohibition on standing armies. Mason, "being sensible that an absolute prohibition of standing armies in time of peace might be unsafe, and wishing at the same time to insert something pointing out and guarding against the danger of them, moved to preface the clause (Article I section. 8) 'To provide for organizing, arming and disciplining the Militia &c' with the words 'And that the liberties of the people may be better secured against the danger of standing armies in time of peace.'"

Madison favored this motion noting, "It did not restrain Congress from establishing a military force in time of peace if found necessary; and as armies in time of peace are allowed on all hands to be an evil, it is well to discountenance them by the Constitution, as far as will consist with the essential power of the Govt. on that head" (Farrand 1966: II: 616–17). Gouvenor Morris and Charles Pinckney then opposed the motion, and when it was voted upon, only Virginia and Georgia supported it, with nine votes against it. Commenting on this vote, Anderson (1993: 76) writes, "In England in the 1690s the Country opposition had fought hard to reduce William's armies in time of peace; in the Convention of 1787, on the other hand, the Court view had overwhelming support."

It is important to cite these debates at some length because in the end, the members of the Constitutional Convention, while they feared it, did not prohibit or limit a standing army, except by appropriation and then to a two-year period. This meant that while the nation was not inclined toward the establishment of a large standing army in the late eighteenth century, or for that matter throughout most of the nineteenth century, it did leave open the possibility that a large standing army might eventually be needed, thus allowing for its establishment in the twentieth century.

Still, as Huntington (1956: 681) writes, "Few provisions in the Constitution were agreed to with more reluctance; some delegates most vehemently against standing forces refused to sign the Constitution." Most prominent among them was Elbridge Gerry, who ironically would later serve as James Madison's Vice President during the War of 1812. In refusing to sign, he objected to the provisions granting "the general power of the Legislature . . . to raise armies and money without limit" (Higginbotham 1971: 456).

2-6g Opening a New Door

Fear of standing armies was the prevalent expectation at the time of the nation's founding. Even as late as 1907, Boughton (1907: 128) wrote, "It does not require a close study of the military policies of the American people to discern that they are by tradition and custom opposed to a large standing army. . . ." Hence, a decade prior to America's entry into the Great War, or World War I, America's distrust of standing armies was still evident. So long as Americans feared a standing army, they were not likely to create a large, permanent one.

While the size of the U.S. regular army expanded during the nineteenth century, it would take the new international political realities of the twentieth century, two world wars, an abiding fear of communism, the development of nuclear weapons, and America's entry onto the world stage to establish a widely shared expectation that the United States needed a standing army. While skepticism of the military would continue to exist and play an important role in such conflicts as Korea and particularly Vietnam, the general public and policy elites overwhelmingly agreed that a strong military was vitally important to America's national security interests. With this change in expectations, a new door was opened that provided the presidency with vastly increased power.

2-7 Military Resources

Related to the fear of a standing army is the level of military resources available to presidents as commander-in-chief. The more one fears a standing army, the smaller the existing army is likely to be—except that is, in times of war or when war is imminent. Such expectations also can result in a smaller navy, since there is a general suspicion of military power. These expectations are important because if virtually no army or navy exists, then presidential power is greatly constrained. For much of the nation's first century, presidents had access to only very limited military resources (see Table 2-1). With the American Revolution finally at an end, as Lloyd (1988: 31) writes, "The need for a large standing army ceased with the signing of the Treaty of Paris in 1783, and immediate steps were taken by Congress to reduce the size of a force which was rapidly becoming a burden on the economy."

Likewise, as Higginbotham (1971: 438) writes, "The American Experience ran counter to trends found elsewhere in the past and present. The end of the Revolutionary War and the end of the army were virtually synonymous." In June 1784, with the war at an end, the Continental Congress established a regular army consisting of only 700 men and just 46 officers (Lloyd 1988: 31; Skelton 1992: 5). The state militias continued to be responsible for most security issues. As during the war, Congress periodically requested troops from the states, and more often than not, the states turned a deaf ear to such requests (Higginbotham 1971: 446). In so doing Congress observed, "Standing armies in time of peace are inconsistent with the principles of republican governments" (ibid.).

This practice continued throughout the nineteenth century. "Instead of building a small but effective standing army buttressed by a large, well-trained reserve of citizen-soldiers, as advocated by Washington, [the United States] virtually disbanded the army after each war and never developed a satisfactory reserve system, with the result that every subsequent conflict has found the United States sorely unprepared at the outset" (ibid., 442–43).

The fear of standing armies translated into a small regular (or standing) army for much of the nation's first century. In addition, while there was no concomitant fear of a navy (navies rarely oppressed the rights of citizens but rather sailed away to distant lands, unlike the army which could be deployed on American soil), the size of the U.S. navy was also greatly constrained. As a result, among the early presidents, the commander-in-chief could not call upon either an army or navy of great size or capabilities to promote his foreign policy.

2-7a Hamilton's Vision

In 1798, during the presidency of John Adams, events did contribute to a sudden expansion of the army. With a renewed threat of war with France, the army was abruptly increased to more than 13,000 men, and the officer corps expanded to almost 800 men. This period represented the last chance for the Federalists to build a standing army, based on the British model. As Skelton (1992: 7) notes, "Conservative Federalists—including Alexander Hamilton, the inspector general and dominant figure in the army of the Quasi-War period—hoped to make this enlarged

TABLE **2-1** **Total U.S. Military Personnel for Presidents through Nixon**

President	Military Personnel
George Washington	718
John Adams	Not available
Thomas Jefferson	4,051
James Madison	6,977
James Monroe	8,446
John Quincy Adams	5,903
Andrew Jackson	6,332
Martin Van Buren	17,449
William Henry Harrison	Not available
John Tyler	11,319
James K. Polk	8,509
Zachary Taylor	10,744
Millard Fillmore	10,929
Franklin Pierce	10,572
James Buchanan	15,918
Abraham Lincoln	186,845
Andrew Johnson	1,000,692
Ulysses S. Grant	36,953
Rutherford B. Hayes	24,140
James Garfield	Not available
Chester A. Arthur	25,842
Grover Cleveland	27,157
Benjamin Harrison	27,759
Grover Cleveland	27,830
William McKinley	27,865
Theodore Roosevelt	85,557
William Howard Taft	84,971
Woodrow Wilson	92,756
Warren G. Harding	230,725
Calvin Coolidge	148,763
Herbert Hoover	139,118
Franklin Roosevelt	136,547
Harry S. Truman	8,267,958
Dwight Eisenhower	1,533,815
John Kennedy	858,622
Lyndon Johnson	975,716
Richard Nixon	1,512,169

army permanent and thus provide the United States with the equivalent of a European standing army."

If realized, Hamilton's vision would have introduced professionalism through the expansion and improved training of the officer corps. Legislation enacted on March 3, 1799, established a "uniform structure for regiments" and defined "the army pay scale." It also provided for a "clothing allowance" and established "an elaborate staff apparatus." Additionally, it "authorized a quartermaster general with the rank of major general," as well as "a number of deputy quartermasters general and brigade quartermasters attached to lesser commands." Most importantly, "the act set up a network of inspection officers who would be appointed by Hamilton . . ." (Skelton 1992: 96–97).

If successful, Hamilton's reforms "would have converted the officer corps from a disorganized collection of individuals into a cohesive and professionally trained cadre of regulars" (Skelton 1992: 97). The army therefore would have taken a major step toward professionalization. But Hamilton's vision of a European-style standing army remained just that—a vision. As the threat of war with France receded, and with a president—John Adams—who did not trust either Hamilton or standing armies (McCullough 2001), both perhaps with good reason, Hamilton's grand design was quickly dismantled (Miroff 1988: 311). Thus, even under a Federalist president, the movement toward the development of a professional standing army was thwarted. On May 14, 1800, "Congress abolished the additional army, including Hamilton's office of inspector general, ending Federalist hopes of building a European-style standing army" (Skelton 1992: 98).

2-7b Jefferson's Reductions

Still, when John Adams's term of office expired, the peacetime army consisted of more than 5,000 men and the U.S. Navy had thirteen frigates in service, plus six additional ships-of-the-line that were then under construction (Hickey 1989: 6). Following the election of 1800, however, the newly elected president, Thomas Jefferson, commenced a massive downsizing of the army and navy. By 1802, the army consisted of just over 3,000 men. By 1805, it had been further reduced to just 2,732 men scattered over forty-three posts. The largest single aggregation of men was 375 at New Orleans; the smallest, 3 at Fredericktown, Maryland (Millis 1956: 59).

As Skelton (1992: 39–40) notes, "In this situation, the influence of the army's central bureaucracy was minimal. The primitive state of communication, especially west of the Appalachian Mountains, kept small garrisons isolated from army and regimental headquarters. . . ." Hence, not only was the army diminutive in size, but its dispersion over thousands of miles of frontier land impeded any movement toward professionalization. As a result of Jefferson's downsizing, the army lost many of its most qualified officers. By 1802, there were just 191 men in the officer corps. Thirty of those who departed had ten or more years of military experience (Skelton 1992: 61). Thus, the quality of the officer corps was utterly obliterated.

Jefferson also virtually eliminated the U.S. Navy. He canceled the construction of the ships-of-the-line, while unceremoniously decommissioning most other ships. Jefferson informed Congress that seven frigates would be "laid up," to be "preserved in such condition . . . as to be at all times ready for sea on a short warning" (Foner 1944: 340). Of the thirteen ships that had existed at the end of the Adams administration, six subsequently rotted or otherwise were destroyed during the intervening twelve years, so that by the time of the commencement of hostilities with Britain in 1812 only the seven "laid up" frigates remained.

As for the naval officer corps, it too was reduced. The Naval Act of 1801 abolished nineteen captains. Then, in October 1801, Jefferson met with his Cabinet Secretaries and voted on each of the remaining fifteen captains, eventually eliminating six more captaincies (Malone 1970: 103). Consequently, not only was the number of ships reduced, but the officer corps and number of sailors were diminished, as well, steps that further undercut the long-term professionalism of the naval corps.

Jefferson's actions in downsizing the military were consistent with his view of Republican government, as well as with the nation's expectations regarding the nature of standing armies. The practical effect, however, was to force presidents to rely on the militia system. This was also consistent with the expectations of the time. As McDonald (1976: 21) writes, "The American Republicans' fear of standing armies was largely abstract, since they believed that the traditional American reliance on militias would prevent the rise of dangerous armies. . . ."

2-8 The Militia System

In this spirit, Jefferson wrote Congress (Foner, ed. 1944: 339),

> For defense against invasion, their number [the present military establishment] is as nothing; nor is it conceived needful or safe that a standing army should be kept up in time of peace for that purpose. Uncertain as we must ever be of the particular point in our circumference where an enemy may choose to invade us, the only force which can be ready at every point and competent to oppose them, is the body of neighboring citizens as formed into a militia. On these, collected from the parts most convenient, in numbers proportioned it threatens to be permanent, to maintain the defence until regular may be engaged to relieve them.

While the size of the U.S. army and navy would vary over time, and the army would be a factor precipitating the Mexican War of the 1840s, the idea that the true American soldier was a citizen soldier gave rise to the myth that the nation could defend itself solely on the basis of the **militia system.** While this belief was rudely shattered during the War of 1812, Americans continued to espouse the militia system as a real alternative to a standing army long after that war ended largely because it was consistent with their expectations that standing armies were dangerous.

In this regard, then, it is important to note that while the Constitution stated that "the president shall be the Commander in Chief of the Army and Navy of the United States, and of the Militia of the several states, when called into the actual Service of the United States," a question remained over the extent to which the president really controlled the militia forces.

Instead of relying on a permanent military, the Militia Act of 1792 gave presidents the right to call forth the militias of the various states "whenever the United States shall be invaded or in imminent danger of invasion." Under these circumstances, there would be dual control of the militia. When the militia were not actually called forth by the president to meet an invasion or imminent danger, the act provided that the militia would be under the control of the various states. Thus, control of the militia was purposely diffused (Huntington 1956: 684). Although this coincided with the Founders' concern for limiting the power of the national government, it greatly constrained presidential power.

2-8a The War of 1812

State and national prerogatives came into conflict during the War of 1812. On June 22, 1812, Brigadier General Henry Dearborn requested forty-one companies of militia from Massachusetts, four from Rhode Island, and five from Connecticut. The governors of the three New England states refused to provide troops. Governor John Cotton Smith of Connecticut wrote General Dearborn that his request for the militia was unconstitutional because the president had not indicated that any one of three constitutional stipulations justified calling forth the troops (i.e., an invasion of the nation, an actual insurrection, or a combination designed to break the law) (Mahan 1972: 32).

Smith also asserted that the militia could not be placed under the authority of federal officers when state-level officers already were designated for that purpose. When the Secretary of War, William Eustis, responded that an invasion either did exist or was imminent, Smith responded that neither a declaration of war nor the cruising of a hostile fleet represented an invasion or the threat of one (ibid.).

Governor Caleb Strong of Massachusetts likewise hesitated to provide troops in response to Dearborn's call for militiamen. He waited until July 3 to respond with the issuance of a general order for his state militia. When Dearborn arrived to

Militia system: An alternative to a standing army. The militia system created by the Constitution gave primary control for creating a militia (similar to today's National Guard) to Congress. Congress also had the authority to provide regulations for the new militia. The militias would then be under the control of the state governors except in times of war or when war was imminent. Then the president as commander-in-chief could ask the governors to call forth the militias of the several states in defense of the nation. The militias, in theory, were meant to be the "bulwark of democracy." In reality, while some states had "well regulated militias," most state militias were not efficient or competent. During the War of 1812, governors of several states refused President James Madison's request to call up the militias. Hence, over time, the nation turned from the militia as the primary method of defense to a professional, standing army.

take command, however, "he met with inertia and hostility" (ibid.). At a town meeting in Boston in August, Governor Strong rejected the president's request to use the Massachusetts militia for an invasion of Canada (Rutland 1990: 116). On August 5, Strong wrote that the president's request for militiamen was unconstitutional: His reasoning was that the determination of whether an invasion existed or not rested with the governors, as well as with the president. Seeing no evidence of an invasion, Strong refused to release his militia to federal officials (ibid., 32–33). As a result of these decisions, the United States was denied the services of a militia of some 70,000 "well-armed, well-drilled" men (Adams 1986b: 1063).

2-8b Who Controls the Militia?

While the Supreme Court in *Martin v. Mott* [19 Wheat. 19 32–33 (1927)] upheld the president's right to call forth the militia, a right that was reserved only for emergencies and circumstances threatening the security of the nation, it did not definitively settle the question over who controls the militia once it is called forth. Although the president serves as commander-in-chief, Huntington (1956: 684) asks,

> . . . how could [the president] function [as commander-in-chief] when his officers, in war as in peace, were appointed by state governments? In the war . . . state governors challenged the authority of the President to subordinate militia units to the command of Regular Army general officers. State officials removed their troops from national service as they saw fit and upset the lines of command by appointing militia officers to higher rank than the regular officers to whom the militia units were theoretically subordinate.

As a result, Madison found it excruciatingly difficult to command the war effort. That history has labeled him an ineffective commander-in-chief is thus somewhat unfair. Congress tied his hands by only reluctantly providing troops and supplies, and the state governors often refused to release their militia forces. The result was that Madison as commander-in-chief had relatively little authority at his command.

2-8c The Potential for Presidential Power

We can contrast Madison's experiences with those of Polk in the Mexican War and Lincoln during the Civil War. Both presidents had vastly greater military resources than did Madison, principally because they had access to an evolving and growing professional regular army and a larger navy. Hence, the power of the presidency was already changing, not because of any alteration in the wording of the Constitution, but because the president requires military resources in order to have authority as commander-in-chief. Without an army, navy, or reliable militia, Madison was in a most unenviable position. As Alexis de Tocqueville wrote in the 1830s (1945: 130–31),

> It is chiefly in its foreign relations that the executive power of a nation finds occasion to exert its skill and its strength. If the existence of the Union were perpetually threatened, if its chief interests were in daily connection with those of other powerful nations, the executive government would assume an increased importance in proportion to the measures expected of it and to those which it would execute. The President of the United States, it is true, is the commander-in-chief of the army, but the army is composed of only six thousand men; he commands the fleet, but the fleet reckons but few sail; he conducts the foreign relations of the Union, but the United States is a nation without neighbors. Separated from the rest of the world by the ocean, and too weak as yet to aim at the dominion of the seas, it has no enemies, and

its interests rarely come into contact with those of any other nation of the globe. . . . The President of the United States possesses almost royal prerogatives, which he has no opportunity of exercising; and the privileges which he can at present use are very circumscribed. The laws allow him to be strong, but circumstances keep him weak.

As the size of the U.S. army and navy expanded over time, with the creation of the Air Force and Marines, the ability to deploy troops quickly all over the world, the development of institutional resources such as the Central Intelligence Agency, the National Security Council, and the Department of Defense, as well as the most sophisticated weapons systems imaginable, presidents today have a vast array of military resources at their disposal. As such, they exert considerable authority as commander-in-chief.

2-9 America as a World Power

Another factor constraining presidential power was the concept of **isolationism.** Throughout most of the nineteenth century, America embraced the idea that it was physically separated from Europe and thus did not need a permanent standing army. As the European powers competed for colonial prizes, the United States originally was willing to sit back and watch. As the United States frontier began to disappear, however, as historian Frederick Jackson Turner famously proclaimed in 1890, Americans began to look elsewhere, first haltingly and then with greater vigor and consensus (see Figure 2-3).

Interestingly, it was Congress that first provided the impetus for this overseas expansion. During President Grover Cleveland's second term in office, a delegation from Congress informed him that it decided to declare war against Spain over Cuba. Cleveland responded that there would be no war so long as he was president. When reminded that it was Congress that had the power to declare war, Cleveland reminded the members that it was the president as commander-in-chief who was charged with fighting the war. This he would not do (Fisher 1978: 214).

Isolationism: The idea that America was isolated from Europe by a great ocean and hence was largely invulnerable to foreign attack. As a result, America could (and should) try to stay out of European politics (that is, to isolate itself from Europe). Interestingly, although the Pacific Ocean also separated the nation from Asia, isolationism would be used more often as an argument for staying out of European affairs than Asian politics. Isolationism was the framework of American foreign policy throughout most of the nineteenth century and even well into the twentieth century. Indeed, a consensus did not exist to replace isolationism with internationalism until after World War II.

Figure 2-3
Settlement of the United States Circa 1890

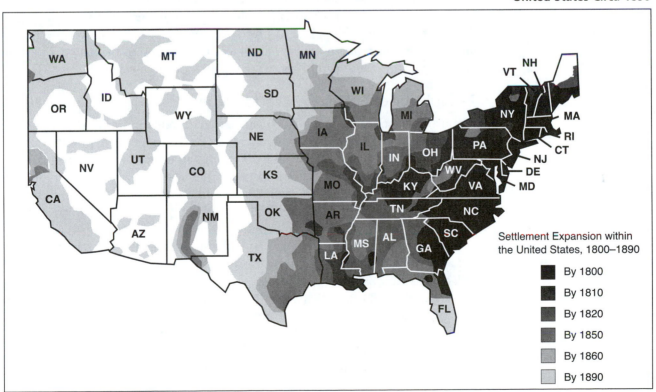

Settlement Expansion within the United States, 1800–1890

- ■ By 1800
- ■ By 1810
- ■ By 1820
- ■ By 1850
- ■ By 1860
- ☐ By 1890

2-9a Theodore Roosevelt and the World Stage

A few years later, another reluctant president, William McKinley, again prompted by Congress, led the nation into war against Spain. This war provided America with its first colonial conquests. According to Schlesinger (1973: 82), the war provided an impetus for the expansion of presidential power. America now had overseas possessions that it could not ignore, especially the continuing problems associated with management of the Philippines. To meet these needs, the navy was expanded, thereby increasing presidential military resources. Likewise, as it did in economic affairs, a new expectation evolved as the public began to look to the White House for leadership in foreign affairs.

While McKinley was hesitant, his successor was not, aggressively taking advantage of the newly evolving military resources and public expectations. Once again, as he had in domestic affairs, Theodore Roosevelt was eager to expand presidential power. He did so in myriad ways: advocating construction and deployment of a larger navy, proclaiming the Roosevelt Corollary to the Monroe Doctrine, interfering in the affairs of the sovereign nation of Colombia in order to secure land for the construction of the Panama Canal, sending the **White Fleet** around the world (which he forced upon a reluctant Congress), and negotiating a peace treaty between Russia and Japan. In all these ways, Roosevelt thrust himself and the nation prominently onto the world stage.

Of course, Roosevelt's enthusiasm for expanding the U.S. role in world affairs did not occur in a vacuum. The world itself was a considerably different place in the first decade of the twentieth century than it had been at the founding. Urbanization and industrialization also encouraged greater trade with foreign nations, thus bringing America into more frequent contact with the other nations of the world. Technological developments (improvements in overseas communications, faster ships such as the ocean liner, and later air travel) and better communications made America more accessible to the rest of the world and vice versa. Thus, a variety of forces (i.e., new expectations, economic factors, and new technologies) were propelling the nation onto the world stage.

Roosevelt's foreign policy adventures also provided his successors with precedents for increasing the president's role in foreign affairs. Perhaps more importantly, his enthusiasm captured the spirit and imagination of the nation and made an expanded presidential role in foreign affairs more acceptable.

2-9b America Enters the World Stage

Woodrow Wilson further expanded the nation's foreign policy role. The nation's entry into World War I in 1917 promoted not only a more active presidential role in foreign affairs, but also encouraged Congress to delegate considerable military authority to the presidency. For instance, the National Defense Act of 1916 (preparing the nation for the possibility of war) provided the president with the unprecedented authority to order and procure weapons in time of war or when war was imminent. The president could also cancel or modify existing contracts dealing with the production of ships and other war materials. The Selective Service Act also provided the president with the military resources necessary to fight a war (a large standing army).

While the 1920s and 1930s saw the nation return to a policy of isolationism, the nation did not fully recede from its foreign policy role. Warren G. Harding oversaw the Washington Disarmament Conference, and Calvin Coolidge committed U.S. forces to Central America. In 1941, while the nation was still reluctant to enter the war in Europe, Pearl Harbor smashed the last vestiges of isolationism.

White Fleet: A fleet (painted white and therefore called the White Fleet) that Theodore Roosevelt sent around the world in the early 1900s as a symbol of America's growing military prominence. Roosevelt considered his decision to send the White Fleet around the world as the most significant of his administration.

America entered World War II united behind the war effort, and presidential power further expanded. While there would be a call for a return to isolationism after the World War II, it was quickly muted, as America, faced with the threat of international communism, assumed primacy on the world stage. Hence, without a change of one single word to the Constitution, the president's role as commander-in-chief was completely transformed. Instead, expectations changed: All presidents now would be expected to lead the nation as commander-in-chief. But one final building block was needed for presidents to take on this responsibility on a full-time (24-by-7) basis: the introduction of a constant threat. Communism and nuclear weapons technology provided it in the 1940s, while in the twenty-first century, international terrorism provides a similar rationale.

2-10 A Permanent Threat to National Security

Throughout the nineteenth and even well into the twentieth century, the president's role as commander-in-chief was greatly constrained by the fact that an aggressor did not consistently threaten the United States. According to Hess (1976: 40), prior to World War II, most presidents focused their attention on domestic affairs. Foreign affairs and questions of what, after World War II, became known as **national security** were critical only during actual wartime or when war was imminent.

This part-time concern with national defense promoted a pattern in which an army was raised when the nation's security was at risk and then largely disbanded afterward. Although a small regular army and navy were maintained, both were severely limited in terms of size and capability throughout the nineteenth century. This pattern continued well into the twentieth century. Following World Wars I and II, the size of the U.S. army and navy was again slashed.

2-10a What Changed?

Even at the end of World War II, there was considerable support in the U.S. for a return to isolationism. Before his death in April 1945, even President Franklin Roosevelt was convinced there would be no public support for continued involvement in European affairs after the war was over (Robinson 1987: 136). But the political environment in the post–World War II period was different than with past wars. Although there would be a lively debate about the nature of the United States' role in world affairs, this time the nation would reject isolationism and adopt an activist, internationalist posture.

What changed? Why did the U.S. finally become an active participant on the world stage, and what implications did this step have for the growth of presidential power? As to the first question, technology changed. Air transportation and communications (contextual factors) put the U.S. in immediate contact with nations all over the world. Even more important was the development of nuclear weapons that could be launched without warning from a distance of thousands of miles or from directly offshore via submarine.

These technological developments, combined with the hostile relationship with Russia and other communist nations that developed into the Cold War, meant that the U.S. was vulnerable to a sudden, unprovoked attack and had an enemy perceived of being capable of continuing aggressive tendencies. As a result, expectations regarding the nation's defense changed. Instead of a periodic threat to national security, the nation was now threatened twenty-four hours a day, seven days a week. With this threat, the role of the president as commander-in-chief was utterly transformed, and the power of the presidency greatly expanded with it, again without the need to change one word of the Constitution.

National security: This is actually a term of fairly recent usage. Although security was an issue that the Founders were concerned with (note that the first several *Federalist Papers* deal primarily with security issues), they did not refer to a concept of national security until after World War II. Since then, the national security state (including the Department of Defense, the National Security Council, the Central Intelligence Agency, etc.) has been established, and the president's authority as commander-in-chief has greatly expanded. In this book, I refer to a national security presidency, which combines the president's role as commander-in-chief with the national security machinery and the goal of national security.

2-10b New Political Resources

The Cold War also provided greater political resources—in particular, legal resources. A series of treaties and defense pacts with various nations around the world provided a legal justification for the U.S. role in international relations, as well as the president's role in this process. In 1947, Congress also created the Department of Defense, the National Security Council, and the Central Intelligence Agency, providing presidents with new and powerful institutional tools (internal resources) to conduct foreign policy. These developments helped to create the *national security presidency*—a full-time job devoted to protecting the nation from foreign threats.

With this development and the expansion of the U.S. military's size and capabilities, the president as commander-in-chief finally became an integral part of the president's job description, which was not the case at most times during the eighteenth or nineteenth century. While various presidents have exhibited different levels of interest in foreign affairs since World War II, the president's authority as commander-in-chief remains as one of the presidency's defining powers and characteristics. All presidents, whether they are popular or not, share this awesome power and responsibility.

Associated with the development of the national security presidency, the public came to expect presidents to provide peace, as well as prosperity. Those presidents who failed, especially those who involved the nation in protracted conflicts, such as Harry Truman with Korea or Lyndon Johnson with Vietnam, saw their poll ratings and electoral viability decline. Those who were seen as weak on national defense, such as Jimmy Carter, likewise suffered the public's wrath. While the collapse of the Soviet Union and the decline of the communist threat temporarily reduced public interest in foreign affairs, presidents such as George H. W. Bush with the Persian Gulf War and Bill Clinton with military engagements in the Balkans and elsewhere, demonstrated that the president still played a primary role in foreign affairs. Then, following the terrorist attacks on September 11, 2001, President George W. Bush found a new and potent permanent enemy: international terrorism. Like Communism, it provides both a rationale for the expansion of the military and for military action in various locations around the world. As such, it further increases the prominence of the president's authority as commander-in-chief.

Chapter Summary

This chapter examined how contextual factors influenced the growth of presidential power, with a particular emphasis on the president's role as economic manager and commander-in-chief. It should also be noted that as the presidency took a more prominent place on the world stage, its authority as chief diplomat also expanded. While I only alluded to that role here, I do examine the president and the treaty-making power in more detail in Chapter 5. Likewise, while the president's war power has increased, there have been congressional attempts to limit presidential war power, such as the passage of the War Powers Act of 1973. I

will present a more extensive examination of congressional-presidential relations in foreign affairs in Chapter 9.

Here I examined the metamorphosis of the U.S. economy from a rural to an urban, industrial one and the ways that change played a major role in altering the expectations of presidential performance in the area of domestic policy. Likewise, the president's role as commander-in-chief was transformed, not by changes in the Constitution, but by changes in America's relationship with the rest of the world, the development of new technologies, and a permanent threat to national security. Directly associated with these contextual changes were changes in public expectations of the presidency itself. The public came to expect the president to deliver both prosperity and peace. Those presidents who failed to deliver on these expectations were much more likely to face rejection at the polls.

What is most interesting about the changes delineated in this chapter is that they did not require a change in the Constitution. While the American presidency has changed, the Constitution remains virtually unchanged. Rather, contextual factors and expectations changed, and with it, the power of the presidency was transformed. While the president did derive additional legal resources (through treaties and defense pacts) and new internal resources (the Bureau of the Budget, the Council of Economic Advisers, the Department of Defense, the National Security Council, the Central Intelligence Agency), they were not the cause of the growth of presidential power but rather followed developments already in progress. Hence, in America, the power of the presidency is not dependent solely on the Constitution. Nor is the power of the presidency etched in stone. It changes over time and likely will continue to do so as events, circumstances, and other contextual factors continue to change our expectations of presidential leadership.

Review Questions

1. At its founding, America was essentially
   a. a rural nation.
   b. a rural and industrial nation.
   c. a nation at war with Canada.
   d. an urban nation.

2. Which of the following presidents had a vision of America as an industrial and urban nation?
   a. Thomas Jefferson
   b. George Washington
   c. James Madison
   d. Alexander Hamilton

3. At the founding of America, Americans expected the president to
   a. be responsible for the nation's economy.
   b. provide leadership on the domestic agenda.
   c. defer to Congress on foreign affairs.
   d. defer to Congress on domestic affairs.

4. The region of the country that suffered the least during the Panic of 1857 was
   a. the North.
   b. the South.
   c. the West.
   d. All regions suffered equally.

5. Who of the following presidents was re-elected despite governing during an economic panic?
   a. James Monroe
   b. Martin Van Buren
   c. James Buchanan
   d. Herbert Hoover

6. Which of the following was the worst panic of the nineteenth century?
   a. the Panic of 1817
   b. the Panic of 1857
   c. the Panic of 1873
   d. the Panic of 1893

7. America emerged as a manufacturing society during the period from
   a. 1840 to 1850.
   b. 1860 to 1870.
   c. 1880 to 1910.
   d. 1920 to 1950.

8. Congress struggled to provide leadership in an era of
   a. ruralism.
   b. industrialism.
   c. isolationism.
   d. militarism.

9. Congressional decision making was
   a. centralized through a committee system.
   b. decentralized through a committee system.
   c. unable to deal with the tariff.
   d. strong and effective in the face of changing contextual factors.

10. Centralization created
    a. new management techniques.
    b. a more integrated economy.
    c. a new corporate model of leadership.
    d. all of the above.

11. Which of the following did the Founders fear and mention often at the Constitutional Convention?
    a. invading armies
    b. standing armies
    c. retreating armies
    d. armies and navies

12. To the Founders, the proper defense of the nation should be in the hands of the
    a. army.
    b. navy.
    c. marines.
    d. militia.

13. The president as commander-in-chief has little real authority without which of the following?
    a. a war
    b. an impending war
    c. military resources
    d. domestic resources

14. The idea that America was physically separated from Europe by two oceans and hence did not need a strong military is called
    a. isolationism.
    b. internationalism.
    c. interventionism.
    d. nation building.

15. A permanent threat to the nation's security
    a. helped to overcome isolationist sentiment in the nation.
    b. encouraged further isolationist sentiment in the nation.
    c. encouraged a need to further expand the militia system.
    d. directly led to the creation of the U.S. Air Force.

16. One effect of the development of the national security presidency is that the public now expects it to provide
    a. prosperity.
    b. peace.
    c. interventionism.
    d. isolationism.

Discussion Questions

1. Should nineteenth century presidents have been more attentive to the state of the nation's economy?
2. How are changes in contextual factors (such as urbanization, industrialization) related to changing expectations of presidential leadership?
3. What impact did the fear of standing armies have on the development of presidential power?
4. What impact did isolationism have on the development of presidential power?
5. What factors encouraged the expansion of the president's role as commander-in-chief?

Notes

1. One elector decided that George Washington should be the only unanimously elected president and thus cast his electoral vote for John Quincy Adams, Monroe's Secretary of State.
2. Of course, the Founders conveniently overlooked the point that a rural America would also be more open to the need for slavery than would an industrial America. In fact, as the North industrialized and the South remained largely rural prior to the Civil War, this provided the basis for different views on the issue of slavery.
3. While Buchanan did not run for re-election in 1860 and his party suffered electoral defeat, the defeat is more a function of the developing tensions between the north and south and the slavery issue. There is no evidence that the economic decline of 1857 and continuing recession had an impact on the outcome of the 1860 election.
4. In this work, Wilson expressed a preference for a prime ministerial form of government, but in later writings, he would advocate a more powerful and active presidency instead.

Active Presidents:
The Path to Presidential
Greatness

Key Terms

activist presidency
executive privilege

3-1 Active Presidents:
The Path to Presidential Greatness

In 1933, Franklin Roosevelt became the nation's thirty-second president. His presidency is generally considered a key moment in American history, for many scholars contend that FDR created the modern presidential office. But what if Roosevelt had not been president? Would the presidency have developed the same way as it did? This is not merely a hypothetical question, for Roosevelt was nearly assassinated shortly after his election (see Burns 1984: 147). Had Roosevelt been killed, John Nance Garner of Texas would have been president. Few doubt that American history or the history of the presidency would be the same today had Garner served instead of FDR.

Roosevelt's close brush with death and his activist New Deal approach to the Great Depression, his leadership in World War II, and the concomitant transformation of the presidential office remind us that when it comes to the presidency, the personality, background, and skills of the man (and someday the woman) in the Oval Office have much to do with the development and growth of the presidency itself. Personality and the individual president's personal views of the presidency matter. Therefore, we need to examine them. We do so in this chapter. We begin by examining what various presidents thought about the presidency and presidential power.

3-2 Different Perceptions of the Presidency

To understand the importance of personal political resources, we need look no further than our first president, George Washington. Had Washington announced at the Constitutional Convention in Philadelphia in 1787 that he would not serve as president, it is unlikely that the presidency would even faintly resemble its present-day contours. The delegates to the Constitutional Convention felt comfortable creating a potentially more powerful office than any of them could have imagined at the beginning of the convention, partly because they knew that George Washington would be the first president. As Bowen (1966: 190–91) writes,

> After the Convention [Founding Father Pierce] Butler wrote his son that the powers of the President have been made "full and great"—greater than he himself had been disposed to make them. It was his private opinion that these powers would have been less extensive had not many members looked to General Washington as their first President. "So that" Butler concluded, "the man, who by his patriotism and virtue, contributed largely to the emancipation of his country, may be the innocent means of its being, when he is laid low, oppressed."

3-2a An Outline for an Office

While the Founders invested the presidential office with greater powers than they had originally intended, the office was still, at the Convention's conclusion, only an outline for a presidency. According to Phelps (1989: 259),

> When George Washington arrived in New York [the temporary Capitol] in 1789 to take his oath of office, no one doubted that he was president of a newly constituted United States. There remained much doubt, however, as to what this presidency was. . . . Ambiguity reigned . . . when the political character of the presidency was considered. What should be the relationship between the president and the other branches of the national government? Between the president and the states? Between

the president and the people? What were the president's responsibilities to the Constitution itself? For Washington, then, the problem of the first presidency was not so much defined by the desire to fulfill a personal policy agenda as it was by the need to define the powers of the office and the role of the person who occupied it. Washington was aware of both the ambiguity of the constitutional text and his own potential as an explicator of that text.

The Founders believed they could trust George Washington with the potentially treacherous task of filling in the details of the new presidential office. Washington also understood this point, saying early in his first term, "Few who are not philosophical spectators can realize the difficult and delicate part which a man in my situation has to act. . . . I may use the expression, I walk on untrodden ground. There is scarcely any part of my conduct which may not hereafter be drawn into precedent" (quoted in Milkis and Nelson 1994: 71). Because of the important role Washington played in creating the presidency, it is therefore important to examine his personal views on the presidential office.

3-2b George Washington

First and foremost, Washington was keenly aware that virtually everything he said or did could create precedents for future presidents, thereby beginning the process of defining the presidential office. He therefore entered the office with a few clear goals in mind. Principally, he wanted to guard the powers of the presidency, particularly those in the realm of foreign affairs, while concomitantly deferring to Congress in areas he felt the legislative branch should control. As a result, he played a less active role in domestic affairs. In this regard, Washington was dedicated to the rule of law; that is, he was committed to constitutionalism.

As Phelps (1989: 263) writes, "What is remarkable about Washington's commitment to the rule of law was his willingness to subordinate other firmly held political sentiments to that standard. He had confided that 'there are some things in the new form [Constitution], I will readily acknowledge, [that] I never did, and I am persuaded never will, obtain my cordial approbation.'" For example, he had little enthusiasm for the concept of separation of powers and checks and balances. According to Phelps, "His own vision of republicanism emphasized the idea of mixed government," which in its British manifestation included representation of the three segments of society—the monarchy, the aristocracy, and the people—all of which were to cooperate for the public good (ibid., 262–63).

Despite his own preferences, Washington followed what he considered to be the intent of the Constitution, deferring to Congress on many occasions and protecting the powers of the presidency only when he believed there were sound constitutional grounds to do so. Through this process, Washington came to endorse the separation of powers in practice, even if he did not personally espouse it. Washington made no stronger statement of this belief than in his Farewell Address of September 19, 1796, in which he stated,

> It is important . . . that the habits of thinking in a free Country should inspire caution in those entrusted with its administration, to confine themselves within their respective Constitutional spheres; avoiding in the exercise of the Powers of one department [or branch of government] to encroach upon another. The spirit of encroachment tends to consolidate the powers of all departments in one, and thus to create whatever the form of government, a real despotism. A just estimate of that love of power, and proneness to abuse it, which predominates in the human heart is sufficient to satisfy us of the truth of this position. (Quoted in Allen 1988: 520–21)

3-2c Mere Mortals

In addition to the separation of powers, Washington also tried to bring a spirit of dignity, comity, and nonpartisanship to government, in particular eschewing both partisanship and faction. He did not, however, succeed in all these objectives. While he certainly brought dignity to the office, partisanship and faction developed in domestic and foreign affairs (e.g., Secretary of the Treasury's Hamilton's economic program; the Jay Treaty). Nevertheless, while partisanship emerged in the form of the Federalist and Democratic-Republican parties, each represented by a member of his own Cabinet (Treasury Secretary Alexander Hamilton and Secretary of State Thomas Jefferson), Washington was able to establish a precedent for a presidency of energy, dispatch, and vigor—qualities identified by Hamilton in the *Federalist Papers* as necessary for good government.

Once Washington's two terms were completed, however, it was understood that mere mortals would take his place in the presidential office, men who might not put their personal views aside and govern in what they considered the best interests of the country. There were serious doubts as to whether these men would be capable of finishing the job that Washington had begun.

Each of the forty-one men who followed Washington to the presidency have brought not only their own unique skills and political proclivities, but also their own interpretation of what it means to be president. Some believed in an **activist presidency**, motivated by the goal of accomplishing domestic and/or foreign policies while increasing the power of the presidency, while others believed that the president should be a manager or magistrate rather than an activist initiator of policy. Still others believed that presidents should be purely passive, leaving the heavy governmental lifting to the legislative branch. How each individual perceived the presidential role is important, for it helps us to understand not only how an individual is likely to govern once he or she is in office, but also how the presidential office has evolved from its narrow constitutional framework into the most powerful political office on earth.

Activist presidency: A presidency motivated by the goal of accomplishing domestic and/or foreign policies while increasing the power of the office. The alternatives are the idea that presidents should be managers or magistrates rather than activist initiators of policy or that they should be purely passive, leaving responsibility for policy making to the legislative branch.

3-2d John Adams

The personal viewpoint of the nation's second president, John Adams, for example, played a critical role in the history of his presidency and set important precedents for the development of the office. Adams had thought about executive power for quite some time. In his *Thoughts on Government,* published in pamphlet form prior to the issuance of the Declaration of Independence, Adams "had the clearest idea of anyone in Congress of what independence would actually entail, the great difficulties and risks, no less than the opportunities" (McCullough 2001: 102). Long before others considered the possibility, Adams's thoughts also moved to the kind of government the new nation should have once it declared independence. It should be republican, Adams's wrote, "an empire of laws and not of men." With regard to the executive, McCullough (2001: 103) writes, summarizing Adams's thought,

> [He should] be chosen by the two houses of the legislature, and for not more than a year at a time. Executive power would include the veto and the appointment of all judges and justices, as well as militia officers, thus making the executive commander-in-chief of the armed forces.

That Adams had such a fully developed idea of the presidency is remarkable, since the first U.S. Constitution, the Articles of Confederation, contained no independent executive office, and since many of the Founders (including James

Madison, the father of the Constitution) did not have a clear concept of the office and its powers even as the Constitutional Convention was set to convene in 1787.

Once the office was established, Adams, like Washington, advocated a strong presidency. He realized that while the president was limited to just a four-year term, the president's power "during those four years is much greater than that of an avoyer, a consul, a podesta, a doge, a stadholder; nay a king of Poland; nay, than a king of Sparta" (quoted in Bowen 1966: 189). As president, Adams used his authority energetically, even when his actions were not popular with the public or among members of his own party. For example, while he was slow to realize that Alexander Hamilton's influence had a deleterious impact on his presidency, Adams eventually boldly excluded pro-Hamiltonians from his Cabinet, decreased the size of the U.S. military (which Hamilton was also using to advance his power and reputation as a possible successor to George Washington), and averted what would likely have been a devastating war with France.

Adams also believed that a strong presidency was required to provide balance to the political system. To Adams, balance did not mean a balance of power between institutions, but rather, as Washington conceived in his notion of a mixed government, a balance between various segments of society: the common man and the aristocracy (see Elkins and McKitrick 1993: Chapter XII). As president, Adams was determined that neither segment should have too much power (Miroff 1989: 309). Still, for his own part, Adams's demeanor tended to be monarchical and aristocratic, leading him at times to favor policies (such as the Alien and Sedition Acts) that later would be considered as violations of basic First Amendment free speech rights, thereby placing his administration in strict opposition to the emerging Democratic-Republican Party of Thomas Jefferson and James Madison. By often framing the political world in black-and-white terms, and using (or some might say misusing) the power of the presidency to limit free speech, even imprisoning his political enemies, Adams sowed the seeds of his own political destruction and raised concerns about the viability of the strong presidency model.

3-2e Thomas Jefferson

While historians have identified Jefferson as an activist president, his political philosophy favored limited government and a strict or narrow interpretation of the U.S. Constitution. Yet, despite these views, Jefferson did not undertake to reduce the power of the presidency once he was elected. As Milkis and Nelson (1994: 104) write,

> [O]ne might have expected important changes to occur in the presidency when Jefferson and his party took control of the government. But the Democratic-Republicans did not undertake the sort of wholesale dismantling of executive power that would have made governing virtually impossible. Jefferson, with able support from his Secretary of the Treasury, Albert Gallatin, exercised as much control of domestic policy as Hamilton had during the Washington administration. Hamilton's assurances to his Federalist colleagues in 1801, that Jefferson was "no enemy to the power of the executive" predicted accurately how Jefferson would act as president. . . . Jefferson used those powers with the kind of energy that he once denounced as the mark of tyranny.

Why did Jefferson maintain a strong presidency in spite of his strict interpretation of the Constitution? The primary reason was that Jefferson found a new source of power for the presidency in its unique relationship with the American people. As Milkis and Nelson (1994: 104) continue,

Jefferson's presidency marked an important change in the relationship between the president and the people. His predecessors, Washington and Adams, had believed that the power of the presidency derived from its constitutional authority. Jefferson, although not rejecting this view, maintained that the strength of the office ultimately depended on the "affections of the people." He strongly implied in his first inaugural address that the program of the Democratic-Republican party should be enacted simply because a majority of the people had endorsed it in the 1800 election.

Hence, Jefferson derived a new justification for presidential power, albeit one constrained by the constitutional limits. Yet, there was an inherent tension in Jefferson's view of the presidency, one that offered the presidency newly found power and another that narrowly defined the scope of presidential power. Jefferson's presidency often represented a struggle between these two conceptualizations of the presidency.

For example, when Jefferson agreed to purchase the Louisiana Territory from France, he initially believed that the president lacked the authority to do so and that only Congress could proceed with the purchase. But when Jefferson's political philosophy came face to face with political reality, he proved willing to compromise. When it became apparent that Napoleon was having second thoughts and that Congress could not provide its imprimatur with sufficient haste, Jefferson went forward with the purchase, leaving its legality to be decided at a later date by Congress. Jefferson also greatly expanded the presidential power in the Embargo Crisis of 1807, moving well beyond the parameters of limited executive leadership. He also was the first president to offer a legislative agenda to Congress.

Jefferson, then, was at heart a practical and pragmatic man who was willing to compromise on his political philosophy when necessary. This is in stark contrast to other early presidents, who often believed that they did not have the power to act affirmatively under the Constitution without congressional authorization. James Monroe, for instance, blocked federally funded internal improvements at least in part because he thought the government did not have the power to act. Likewise, when pirates attacked American shipping interests off the coast of Florida, Monroe referred the matter to Congress, rather than taking the initiative as commander-in-chief (Adler 1989: 136). In fact, the presidencies of Madison, Monroe, and John Quincy Adams represent a retreat from an activist presidency, both in conception and execution.

3-2f Andrew Jackson

An activist model of presidential leadership was soon reasserted, however. Among the early presidents, no one more strongly rejected the passive presidential model than did Andrew Jackson. Jackson re-introduced Jefferson's rationale for presidential power (the public), though his inaugural address suggested a more traditional approach. In it, he stated, "In administering the laws of Congress, I shall keep steadily in view the limitation as well as the extent of the executive power, trusting thereby to discharge the functions of my office without transcending its authority" (quoted in Hunt 1995: 88). In reality, Jackson did not pay close attention to the constitutional and legal limits of his office. Instead, he adopted the idea that the president's power derived from elections, and the president was therefore the "tribune of the people." As had Jefferson, this idea allowed Jackson to extend presidential power beyond a narrow reading of the Constitution, though Jackson would move much further than Jefferson ever contemplated.

Unlike Jefferson, Jackson's view of the presidency was not counterbalanced by a narrow interpretation of the Constitution. Without this counterbalance, since he believed his legitimacy derived from election by the people, Jackson also threatened to ignore Supreme Court decisions and refused to enforce congressionally enacted legislation. Such a justification for ignoring the "take care" clause of the Constitution (for more on this, see section 4-5, "The Take Care Clause") could not be derived from even the most expansive reading of the Constitution. By claiming that the president was the only individual elected by the people, however, and thus the true representative of its will, Jackson found a new and near boundless rationale for presidential power.

Jackson's opponents considered the president's views as pure despotism. Yet, Jackson's view of the presidency eventually did much to transform the office and its powers. While his view of presidential power was considered radical in the 1830s, today politicians of both political parties cite public opinion, election results, and the will of the people to justify their actions. In the 1830s, however, there was a backlash against Jacksonian activism. While Jackson's handpicked successor, Martin Van Buren, was elected president in 1836, the opposition Whig Party, so named because the Whig Party of England opposed the power of the British monarchy, was established. It argued that presidential power should be greatly constrained.

3-2g William Henry Harrison and the Whig Conception of the Presidency

In 1840, the Whig Party's candidate for president, William Henry Harrison, defeated Van Buren in an election that ironically appealed directly to the public, just as Andrew Jackson had successfully done (see section 6-1c, "When the Election Goes to the House"). In his inaugural address, Harrison expressed a detailed description of his concept of the presidency. He noted that the "Constitution of the United States is the instrument containing this grant of power to the several departments composing the government. On an examination of that instrument, it will be found to contain declarations of power grants and of power withheld" (quoted in Hunt 1995: 113). He referred to his position not as the *presidency* but as *chief magistrate*, a term that suggested more of a clerical or managerial function, rather than activist presidential leadership: It is a term that was commonly used in the nineteenth century but is rarely used today to describe the presidency.

Noting that the Founders were afraid of the possibility of monarchy, Harrison discreetly criticized Andrew Jackson when he said, "I sincerely believe that the tendency of measures and of men's opinions for some years past has been in that direction, it is, I conceive strictly proper that I should take this occasion to repeat the assurances I have heretofore given of my determination to arrest the progress of that tendency if it really exists and restore the government to its pristine health and vigor, as far as this can be effected by any legitimate exercise of power placed in my hands" (ibid., 115). Harrison, however, had little chance to do so in practice. The day of his inaugural was cold and wet, and the nearly seventy-year-old president refused to wear a coat. He contracted pneumonia and died a month later.

Harrison identified what he considered to be the "evils" of the present system: the ability of presidents to serve a second term (he vowed not to seek one under any circumstances); the ability of presidents to make recommendations, which he said any citizen could do; the power of the negative or veto which should be used only sparingly "first, to protect the Constitution from violation; secondly, the people from the effects of hasty legislation; and thirdly, to prevent the effects of combinations violative or the rights of minorities" (ibid., 119). Believing that the president had too much authority over the nation's finances, he promised "never to remove a secretary of the treasury without communicating all the circumstances attending such a removal to both houses of Congress" (ibid., 122). It was a remarkably detailed inaugural address that can best be described as an attempt to put the genie of presidential power back in the bottle.

3-2h The Pre-Civil War Presidents

John Tyler, a member of Jackson's Democratic Party who was elected vice president, replaced Harrison. Tyler opposed most of the Whig policy agenda as well as Harrison's view of the presidency; for example, Tyler vetoed more legislation than any of his predecessors. "Like Jackson . . . Tyler argued that when a conflict developed between the president and congress, it was for the people to decide who was right" (Milkis and Nelson 1994: 138).

Tyler's successor, James Polk, was a direct follower of Jacksonian Democracy. He governed not only as an activist president, becoming the first president to use a budget, but as commander-in-chief, he also closely supervised U.S. involvement in the Mexican War. Upon entering office, he also identified a clear political agenda, which he largely achieved during his four years in office.

Polk's influence on the development of the presidential office, however, was not as long lasting as Jackson's, and he was followed in the presidential office by a series of passive-minded presidents. Zachary Taylor used his inaugural address to articulate a philosophy of limited executive leadership. While he held a more active view of the presidency's role than Harrison—for example, he said he would "recommend such constitutional measures to Congress as may be necessary and proper to secure encouragement and protection" of the nation's great interests—Taylor believed that "all legislative powers are vested by the Constitution" in Congress "to regulate these and other matters of domestic policy" (ibid., 157).

In short, Congress was expected to play the primary role, with the president in a subordinate one. Ironically, Taylor's one major policy contribution was to oppose the Compromise of 1850, brokered by the Great Compromiser Senator Henry Clay of Kentucky. Only Taylor's premature death in 1850, and the ascension of his vice president, Millard Fillmore, allowed the compromise to be enacted. But while Taylor had shown an inclination to block legislation he did not favor, he did not restore an activist bent to presidential leadership.

In fact, with the exception of Polk, the presidents between Andrew Jackson and Abraham Lincoln mainly extolled the virtues of limited presidential power. Fillmore stated, "The government of the United States is a limited government. It is confined to the exercise of powers expressly granted, and others as may be necessary for carrying those powers into effect; and it is at all times an especial duty to guard against any infringement on the just rights of the states" (quoted in Nevins 1947: 152). The next president, Franklin Pierce, a Democrat, echoed a similar theme in his inaugural address, stating, "The dangers of a concentration of all power in the general government of a confederacy so vast as ours are too obvious to be disregarded. You have a right, therefore, to expect your agents in every department to regard strictly the limits imposed upon them by the Constitution of the United States" (quoted in Nevins 1947: 152–53).

3-2i Abraham Lincoln

Ironically, Lincoln, too, had been a loyal Whig. As a leader in the Illinois Whig Party, and in support of its candidate for president, Henry Clay, Lincoln on June 19, 1844, endorsed the practical restriction of the veto power, so that I may not be wielded to the centralization of all power in the hands of a corrupt and despotic Executive; the limitation of the presidential office to one term; the noninterference of all officers of the government as such, in the government as such, in elections; an economical faithful and impartial administration of the government—and reform of all those abuses which have sprung of the corrupt use of the power of appointments, are also objects that claim our approval, and challenge our untiring efforts to secure their accomplishment. (Quoted in Basler 1953: 339–40)

This statement was a direct rejection of Andrew Jackson's political philosophy. As president, Lincoln continued to express a view of limited presidential power, although one phrase in his first inaugural address is tantalizing: "The chief magistrate derives all his authority from the people, and they have referred none upon him to fix terms for the separation of the states" (Hunt 1995: 196). In this one sentence, while Lincoln disavows any power to "fix terms" for the states, he also invokes authority derived from the people. This sentence suggests a greater adherence to Jacksonian principles than to Harrison's constrained Whig philosophy.

It is also interesting, then, that as president Lincoln closely studied Jackson's response to the South Carolina secession crisis, using Jackson's words and actions as a model for his own initiatives. Lincoln also did more to centralize power in the hands of the executive than any president including Jackson and was active in his use of the appointment power. He even used (some have argued misused) executive power to influence the outcome of the 1864 presidential election (by allowing Union soldiers who were mostly loyal to his administration unprecedented opportunities to vote).

Lincoln was also an active war president, employing the powers of the office in ways that clearly increased the scope of presidential power. Yet, on January 12, 1848, as a member the U.S. House of Representatives, he had adamantly opposed James Polk's war policies on the basis of solid Whig principles of limited executive power. Declaring the war with Mexico unconstitutional and attacking Polk in personal terms: "He is a bewildered, confounded, and miserably perplexed man" (Basler 1953: 442–43).

Lincoln, like Jefferson, thus represents a strange political dichotomy. Even more so than Jefferson, his governing principles and his perception of the presidential office seem completely at odds with his governing approach. In the case of Lincoln, however, the commencement of the Civil War and the powers he needed to wage the war and preserve the union explain why he was so willing to violate long-held views of presidential power. It also raises a series of interesting questions. Had the Civil War occurred at a later time, after Lincoln's presidency, would he be remembered today for his reticence to act, for his adoption of the Whig philosophy of limited presidential government, and for his ultimate failure as president, or would Lincoln, like Jefferson, have been a more activist president than his prior rhetoric and writings suggest? We have no definitive answer to this question, though Lincoln's long and detailed dissertations on the nature of presidential power show he believed that many of the powers he employed during the Civil War eventually should revert to Congress, the states, and the people once the conflict ended. That he helped to transform both the nation and the presidency, then, is perhaps one of the great ironies of American history. Like Jefferson, inevitably, Lincoln was willing and capable of setting aside his own political philosophy when the needs of political reality demanded it.

But Lincoln's political activism did not bring with it a transcending change in popular perceptions of presidential power, at least not at first. As was the case following Jackson's presidency, the post Civil War/Reconstruction period and beyond brought to the executive mansion (not yet officially called the White House until Teddy Roosevelt's presidency, although it was commonly called so by the public) a series of presidents who espoused a political philosophy of limited presidential power. Ulysses Grant deferred to Congress, as did Benjamin Harrison, the grandson of William Henry Harrison. As a member of the Senate, the second Harrison had opposed what he considered to be the more activist leanings of President Grover Cleveland. When Harrison defeated Cleveland in the election of 1888, he did not argue with Senator John Sherman's advice that the president should "touch elbows with Congress." He should have no policy distinct from his own party's, which is best represented by Congress, not the president (Milkis and Nelson 1994: 193).

3-2j Theodore Roosevelt and William Howard Taft

The man who came to characterize the energy of the new twentieth century quickly challenged the rationale for the dominant nineteenth century model of presidential passivity. Theodore Roosevelt, who rose quickly from Assistant Secretary of the Navy, to war hero, to Governor of New York, to Vice President and then to President, brought with him an entirely novel conception of presidential power. In his autobiography, Roosevelt (1913: 357) wrote that he

> [d]eclined to adopt the view that what was imperatively necessary for the nation could not be done by the President unless he could find some specific authorization to do it. My belief was that it was not only his right but his duty to do anything that the needs of the Nation demanded unless such action was forbidden by the Constitution or by the laws. . . . I did not usurp power, but I did greatly broaden the use of executive power.

As president, Roosevelt initiated policy, though he was not yet ready to take the lead in proposing a fully developed legislative agenda (Woodrow Wilson would do that). He also played a dominant role on the newly emerging world stage, and intervened in labor problems, economic panics, and business affairs in an unprecedented manner for a U.S. president. Interestingly, the public approved. While we cannot measure Roosevelt's opinion poll ratings, historians widely believe that he was one of the most popular men to hold the presidential office (see section 7-4, "The Birth of the Rhetorical Presidency"). The vigor that Roosevelt brought to the White House, then, changed the way many people thought about the presidency and presidential power.

Ironically, it did not change the views of Roosevelt's own hand-picked successor, William Howard Taft, who held a more traditional view of presidential power. Taft argued,

> The President can exercise no power which cannot be fairly and reasonably traced to some specific grant as proper and necessary to its exercise. Such specific grant must be either in the Federal Constitution or in an act of Congress passed in pursuance thereof. There is no undefined residuum of power which he can exercise because it seems to him to be in the public interest. . . . My judgment is that the view of Mr. Roosevelt . . . is an unsafe doctrine and that it might lead under emergencies to results of an arbitrary character, doing irremediable injustice to private right. The mainspring of such a view is that the Executive . . . is to play the part of a Universal Providence and set all things right. (Quoted in Sundquist 1981: 31)

But as Milkis and Nelson (1994: 229) note, "Taft, his narrow construction of executive power notwithstanding, was sensitive to the new public demands" or expectations for executive leadership. Ironically, in many respects, Taft actually was more active than Roosevelt—e.g., as evidenced by his aggressive record as a trust-buster and his support for a formal budget. Taft then espoused a traditional view of presidential power, but he did not retreat to a nineteenth century model of presidential passivity, as had most presidents following an activist administration. As such, Taft remains today one of our most misunderstood presidents, in part because his political philosophy is remembered more so than his occasional bursts of presidential activism.

3-2k Woodrow Wilson

Of all of our presidents, none came to the White House with a more intellectually derived model of presidential leadership than did Woodrow Wilson. Wilson was an academic, a political scientist, also known as the Father of Public Administration. In his dissertation, published as a book in 1885 (*Congressional Government*), Wilson criticized the presidency for its inherent weakness while also attacking the constitutional concept of the "separation of powers."

Wilson (1981: 186) wrote, "There is no one supreme, ultimate head—which can decide at once and with conclusive authority what must be done at those times when some decision there must be, and that immediately." He continued, "The best rulers are always those to whom great power is intrusted [sic] in such a manner as make them feel that they will surely be abundantly honored and recompensed for a just and patriotic use of it. . . . It is therefore, manifestly a radical defect in our federal system that it parcels out power and confuses responsibility as it does" (ibid., 187).

In 1908, during Theodore Roosevelt's presidency, however, Wilson developed a more positive and activist conceptualization of presidential power in his book *Constitutional Government in the United States*. In this book, he wrote (1964: 57), "The presidency has been one thing at one time, another at another, varying with the man who occupied the office and with the circumstances that surrounded him." Sounding Jacksonian, Wilson continued, the president "is the political leader of the nation, or has it in his choice to be. The nation as a whole has chosen him, and is conscious that it has no other political spokesman. His is the only national voice in affairs" (ibid., 68). Wilson then added, "He may be both the leader of his party and the leader of the nation, or he may be one or the other. If he leads the nation, his party can hardly resist him. His office is anything he has the sagacity and force to make it. That is the reason why it has been one thing at one time, another at another" (ibid., 69).

With regard to the president's constitutional authority, Wilson wrote, "Some of our Presidents have deliberately held themselves off from using the full power they might legitimately have used, because of conscientious scruples, because they were more theorists than statesmen. . . . The President is at liberty, both in law and conscience, to be as big a man as he can. His capacity will set the limit. . . ." (ibid., 70). From his prior criticism of the presidential office as a largely inconsequential office, Wilson by 1908 had devised a governmental model that placed the president at the center of the American political system. No longer was it the right of Congress to predominate. Now the president, by the force of his personality and the will of the people, could seize politics' center stage.

As president, Wilson practiced what in his academic career he had merely preached. He transformed the presidency into an active participant in the legislative process, initiating policy and then building support within his own party to enact legislation. As such, the president at times acted more like a prime minister than a modern president, but Wilson, like Theodore Roosevelt before him, laid the intellectual basis for the birth of the modern presidency. He also added legal precedent while Congress passed legislation further expanding presidential power.

While Wilson's presidency was in many respects largely successful, his failure to secure the senate's acquiescence of the Treaty of Versailles and eight years of activist presidential leadership had its consequences. There was a backlash against Wilson's presidential activism, but again, as with the Taft presidency, there would be no return to the nineteenth century model of presidential passivity. While Harding, Coolidge, and Hoover were more passive than is expected of presidents today, and more so than either Theodore Roosevelt or Woodrow Wilson had been, they were far more active than their nineteenth century counterparts. As Sundquist (1981: 33) notes,

> When Wilson left the White House, the public mood was ready for a less assertive presidency, and the course of evolution was halted for a decade. But even so, the three Republican presidents of the 1920s did not go all the way back to the nineteenth century Whiggery. In fact, they appear ambivalent, consciously trying to steer a middle course between the extreme activism of Wilson and the passivity that had destroyed Taft.

Harding, for instance, denounced Wilson's "executive dictatorship," but he played a more active role legislatively (particularly with his direct intervention on behalf of the bonus bill legislation) than had most prior presidents. Likewise, Coolidge, while saying after he left office that he "never felt it was my duty to attempt to coerce Senators or Representatives or to take reprisals," submitted a legislative program to Congress and made liberal use of his veto power (ibid.). Likewise, Herbert Hoover was a more activist president in the face of a panic than any previous president, including Theodore Roosevelt, had been (see Stein 1969). While these three presidents are rarely given credit for activism today, it is clear that although they did not espouse the Theodore Roosevelt/Woodrow Wilson model of presidential activism, they did not practice the Whig philosophy of the presidency either.

In fact, in some regards, they anticipated the modern conceptualization of the presidency that in the 1920s was just around the corner, though they could not have known it. Calvin Coolidge, for instance, "had a keen understanding of the public's interest in the human side of the presidency." He was therefore convinced "that news about his personal activities would pave the way for popular acceptance of his more serious pronouncements. . . ." As a result, "the shy Coolidge threw open his private life to unprecedented public gaze." As with Theodore Roosevelt, he became one of the most photographed presidents in American history, to his time. "He was never too busy to be photographed; nor is it recorded that he ever resented any revelation as to his personal habits" (Milkis and Nelson 1994: 267).

3-2l Franklin Roosevelt

In this regard, Coolidge foresaw the politics not of his politically shy successor, Herbert Hoover, but of Hoover's successor, the man who transformed the presidency, Franklin Delano Roosevelt. The second Roosevelt was a practical political man. He was not wedded to one particular approach, but rather was willing to try different policies. If one succeeded, he would continue with it; but if another failed, he would jettison it and try another. What Roosevelt understood was that the president needed the power to act. In his inaugural, Roosevelt stated,

It is to be hoped that the normal balance of executive and legislative authority may be wholly adequate to meet the unprecedented task before us. But it may be that an unprecedented demand and need for undelayed action may call for temporary departure from that normal balance of public procedure. I am prepared under my constitutional duty to recommend the measures that a stricken nation in the midst of a stricken world may require. These measures, or such other measures as the Congress may build out of its experience and wisdom, I shall seek, within my constitutional authority, to bring to speedy adoption. But in the event that the Congress shall fail to take one of these two courses, and in the event that the national emergency is still critical, I shall not evade the clear course of duty that will then confront me. I shall ask the Congress for the one remaining instrument to meet the crisis—broad executive power to wage a war against the emergency, as great as the power that would be given me if we were in fact invaded by a foreign foe. (Hunt 1995: 382)

It was a remarkable presidential declaration. Given the crisis the nation faced and the perception that Roosevelt's predecessor, Herbert Hoover, had not done enough to deal with the depression, it is perhaps not surprising that Roosevelt's request was met with thunderous applause. But far from being a temporary transfer of power from the legislative to the executive branch, the powers delegated to Franklin Roosevelt reshaped the nation's constitutional balance of power. With Roosevelt, and the birth of what came to be called the *modern presidency*, the president was now the seat of power in Washington, not Congress.

From Franklin Roosevelt's time onward, Congress would more often respond to presidential initiatives than set the political agenda. The public, the press, the pundits, even legislators themselves, began to look first to the White House for political leadership. Franklin Roosevelt, like Theodore Roosevelt before him, ardently encouraged these altered expectations and the power that came with them. In fact, the passive presidential model seems to have largely fallen out of favor with FDR's presidency. As Barber (1992: 169) writes, "The passive Presidents may be a vanishing breed. By my estimation, there has been only one passive President since Calvin Coolidge and his case is a mixed one [Eisenhower]. Possibly the public senses that rapid change requires an active President."

3-2m Too Much Power?

Certainly, FDR's successor, Harry Truman, shared the view that the presidency should be active. As Truman biographer Alonzo Hamby (1988: 60) writes,

As a boy [Truman] had been a hero-worshiper of Andrew Jackson; throughout his life he admired strong presidents. His reading of the Constitution reinforced his belief that the presidency was a position of power. The example of his predecessor underscored all these lessons and left him with a determination to defend his office against all encroachments. . . . If at times he overreached himself, as in the steel seizure of 1952 he was largely successful in his objection of passing the presidency on to his successor unimpaired.

While Eisenhower represented a temporary break from the activist presidential model, he did not restore the nineteenth century conceptualization of a weak presidency. In fact, as Greenstein (1982) argues, Eisenhower practiced a skilled "hidden hand" form of presidential leadership, manipulating events from behind the scenes, while portraying an amiable face to the public. While he was not particularly active in domestic affairs, certainly his use of the Central Intelligence Agency to foment rebellion in several foreign nations is indicative of an activist behind-the-scenes presidential approach in foreign affairs.

METHODIST COLLEGE LIBRARY
FAYETTEVILLE, NC

Still, many scholars including Neustadt (1960) found Eisenhower's more passive leadership style to be anathema to the new demands of the presidential office and thus criticized his leadership approach. But the subsequent political overreaching of a Democratic (Lyndon Johnson) and Republican (Richard Nixon) president raised questions about the accountability of the activist presidential model. With these two presidencies, the political philosophy of a powerful presidency seemed to tip the constitutional scales out of balance. Both men desired power, often for its own sake. Johnson and his subordinates misled Congress and the nation with regard to the conduct of the Vietnam War and its domestic impact on the budget.

Nixon invaded the sovereign nation of Cambodia without informing Congress, the press, or the public. According to Assistant to the President, Leonard Garment, "Over the years, Nixon observed politics very closely; it's not a tea party or a love match, but a form of combat. Part of what fueled him to be effective was anger, ambition, and the appetite for revenge—the knowledge that unless you made yourself fearful to your enemies, they would savage you." Garment acknowledges, the "tendency to pursue these instincts" had "self-damaging consequences" (quoted in Strober and Strober 1994: 56).

Also destructive was Nixon's perception of the legality of his presidential actions. After leaving the White House, Nixon told journalist David Frost that if the president did something, it was legal. It was an astonishing declaration of unbounded presidential power. While Johnson did not go quite that far, both presidents raised questions about the propriety of presidential power. In so doing, they also raised serious questions about the ethics and trustworthiness of our nation's highest official. As historian Stanley Kutler (1997: xxii) writes, "When Nixon expressed concern for his public image, he also was aware of the president's symbolic place in the popular mind as the 'government.' Moral legitimacy is the chief prop for that role, and Nixon realized that his actions compromised the canons of civility that sustained such legitimacy."

3-2n A New Moral Tone?

It is not surprising, then, that following Johnson's prevarications regarding the Vietnam War (as documented in the *Pentagon Papers* and his White House tapes) and Nixon's role in both the Vietnam War and the Watergate-related scandals, Gerald Ford and then more prominently Jimmy Carter's presidencies brought a new moral tone to the White House. Carter's vision of the presidency was strikingly different from Johnson's and Nixon's:

> There is only one person in this nation who can speak with a clear voice to the American people. There's only one person who can set a standard of ethics and morality and excellence and greatness and call on the American people to make a sacrifice and explain the purpose of the sacrifice, or answer difficult questions or propose and carry out bold programs, or to provide for the defense posture that would make us feel secure, a foreign policy that would make us proud again, and that's the President. (Quoted in Stuckey 1991: 91)

The idea that the president should provide a moral example did not long survive the Carter presidency, however, as the Iran-contra scandals of the Reagan years and more prominently the Monica Lewinsky sex scandal and subsequent impeachment of Bill Clinton raised additional questions about morality, trust, and the legitimacy of presidential leadership. While there was no return to presidential passivity, although George H. W. Bush's domestic policy certainly exhibited a wide degree of *seeming* or *perceived* presidential indifference (e.g., to the recession of 1990–1991), it was clear that the presidential office would continue to embrace activism, but in a somewhat different way. While presidents were still expected to be powerful, they were not expected to be too powerful or imperial (see Schlesinger 1973).

The events of September 11, 2001, again altered the political equation and the president's role in our political system. With the attacks on the World Trade Center and the Pentagon, George W. Bush unexpectedly was thrust into the position of a war president, defending the nation against international terrorism. The overthrow of the Taliban government in Afghanistan was merely the beginning of a wide-ranging war on terrorism that identified some 60 potential countries where terrorists might be in hiding.

With this powerful new justification, Bush moved quickly to assert presidential power. Furthermore, though it did not use the word **executive privilege**, a term made unpalatable by the Nixon administration, the second Bush administration also took several actions to limit congressional and other public scrutiny of its actions (e.g., Vice President Richard Cheney's meetings with energy executives, the availability of presidential documents, and even the availability of then-Governor George W. Bush's documents were shielded from public and congressional oversight). Hence, the stage was set for yet another confrontation between Congress (in the Enron case, through a lawsuit initiated by its General Accounting Office) and the White House. The question of accountability and the proper scope of presidential power once again was an issue.

> **Executive privilege:** The idea that presidents can keep certain information secret or privileged even from Congress.

As we move into the twenty-first century, one thing is clear. The presidency, which has evolved for more than two hundred years, will continue to do so, and the personal political philosophies of the various individuals who hold that office will provide a clear indication of how these men and women will both govern and are likely to alter the presidential office. They may also tell us which presidents are more likely to possess the quality of presidential greatness, a subject we turn to in the next section.

3-3 Presidential Greatness

It is interesting to note that of the forty-two men who have held the presidential office, those who have gone down in history as the great or even near-great presidents are the ones who generally believed in (Franklin Roosevelt, Theodore Roosevelt, Woodrow Wilson) and/or ultimately adopted (in the case of Thomas Jefferson and Abraham Lincoln) an activist presidential model. On the other hand, most of those who adopted a more passive presidential approach have not found favor in historical polls. In the appendix, "The Gallery of Presidents," I present several historical rankings of the presidents.

In the 1948 poll by Arthur Schlesinger, Sr. (see Box 3-1), activist presidents did very well. In the "great" category, historians ranked Lincoln, Washington, Franklin Roosevelt, Wilson, Jefferson, and Jackson. Teddy Roosevelt and James Polk ranked in the "near great" category, along with Grover Cleveland (who was considered at the time of his presidency to be more activist than his immediate successors) and John Adams. The two presidents ranked as "failures" are Grant and Harding, two passive presidents whose administrations were involved in scandals. In the "below average" category, we find such passive presidents as Tyler, Coolidge, Fillmore, Taylor, Buchanan, and Pierce. Even the "average" category is made up of mostly passive presidents, with the possible exception of McKinley, who like Cleveland was more active than most of his contemporaries, and John Quincy Adams, who proposed a full agenda at the beginning of his term, only to see Congress ignore it.

Box 3-1

1948 Schlesinger Poll

Great

1. Lincoln
2. Washington
3. F. Roosevelt
4. Wilson
5. Jefferson
6. Jackson

Near Great

7. T. Roosevelt
8. Cleveland
9. J. Adams
10. Polk

Average

11. J. Q. Adams
12. Monroe
13. Hayes
14. Madison

15. Van Buren
16. Taft
17. Arthur
18. McKinley
19. A. Johnson
20. Hoover
21. B. Harrison

Below Average

22. Tyler
23. Coolidge
24. Fillmore
25. Taylor
26. Buchanan
27. Pierce

Failure

28. Grant
29. Harding

Sources: Reuters; Murray and Blessing 1994: 16–17; and Stanley and Niemi 2000: 244–45.

3-3a Other Poll Results

By 1962, in the Arthur Schlesinger, Jr., poll (see Box 3-2), Jackson fell from the "great" to the "near great" category, but the same other five presidents were still ranked as "great." Likewise, Harry Truman had joined the ranks of the "near great," an activist president not evaluated in the 1948 poll. The other poll results again reflect the more passive presidents in the "average" (with Eisenhower ranked thusly) and "below average" categories, with the "failure" category reserved for Grant and Harding, again the two scandal presidents.

In the 1970 Maranell-Dodder poll (see Box 3-3), the first twelve presidents ranked were activist presidents. The more passive presidents, such as Eisenhower, are ranked lower overall. Again, along with the scandal presidents, some of the most passive presidents (Pierce, Coolidge, and Fillmore) are ranked toward the bottom of the list. Likewise, the 1977 DiClerico poll, which ranks only the top ten presidents, includes a list of ten activist presidents.

In the 1981 Porter poll (see Box 3-4), Teddy Roosevelt moved into the ranks of the "great" presidents, while his bitter political rival, Woodrow Wilson, fell to the "near great" category. Jackson and Truman remained in the "near great" category, joined by another activist president, Lyndon Johnson. Eisenhower, one of the more passive of the modern presidents, remained in the "average" category, along with Cleveland, whose historical stock fell, and two other modern presidents, Jimmy

Box 3-2

1962 Schlesinger Poll

Great

1. Lincoln
2. Washington
3. F. Roosevelt
4. Wilson
5. Jefferson

Near Great

6. Jackson
7. T. Roosevelt
8. Polk
9. Truman
10. J. Adams
11. Cleveland

Average

12. Madison
13. J. Q. Adams
14. Hayes
15. McKinley

16. Taft
17. Van Buren
18. Monroe
19. Hoover
20. B. Harrison
21. Arthur
22. Eisenhower
23. A. Johnson

Below Average

24. Taylor
25. Tyler
26. Fillmore
27. Coolidge
28. Pierce
29. Buchanan

Failure

30. Grant
31. Harding

Sources: Reuters; Murray and Blessing 1994: 16–17; and Stanley and Niemi 2000: 244–45.

Carter and Gerald Ford. Given the scandal-ridden nature of his administration and the fact that he was forced to resign from office, it is not surprising that historians rated Nixon in the "failure" category with Buchanan and Harding, although it is clear that Nixon (an activist president) had many more substantive accomplishments than either of these presidents.

A year later, in the 1982 *Chicago Tribune* poll (see Box 3-5), the ten best presidents were, in order, Lincoln, Washington, Franklin Roosevelt, Teddy Roosevelt, Jefferson, Wilson, Jackson, Truman, Eisenhower, and Polk. Except for Eisenhower, whose historical reputation has improved over time with the publication of works that argue that he was not quite as passive as scholars once thought (e.g., Greenstein 1982), the other nine presidents were activists who contributed to the growth of presidential power. Of the activist presidents who did not make the top ten list, Lyndon Johnson was ranked twelfth; Cleveland, thirteenth; Kennedy, fourteenth; and John Adams, fifteenth. Nixon, who was also an activist, ranked next to last, with only Harding behind him. In fact, the ten worst presidents included from the bottom up, Harding, Nixon, Buchanan, Pierce, Grant, Fillmore, Andrew Johnson, Coolidge, Tyler, and Carter. Of these, only Nixon and Carter can be considered activists, and Nixon had the Watergate scandals and Carter the hostage seizure in Iran. Both Nixon and Carter also governed during economic recessions.

Box 3-3

1970 Maranell-Dodder Poll		1977 DiClerico Poll
Accomplishments of Administrations	16. J. Q. Adams	**Ten Greatest Presidents**
1. Lincoln	17. Hoover	1. Lincoln
2. F. Roosevelt	18. Eisenhower	2. Washington
3. Washington	19. A. Johnson	3. F. Roosevelt
4. Jefferson	20. Van Buren	4. Jefferson
5. T. Roosevelt	21. Arthur	5. T. Roosevelt
6. Truman	22. Hayes	6. Wilson
7. Wilson	23. Tyler	7. Jackson
8. Jackson	24. B. Harrison	8. Truman
9. L. Johnson	25. Taylor	9. Polk
10. Polk	26. Buchanan	10. J. Adams
11. J. Adams	27. Fillmore	
12. Kennedy	28. Coolidge	
13. Monroe	29. Pierce	
14. Cleveland	30. Grant	
15. Madison	31. Harding	

Sources: Reuters; Murray and Blessing 1994: 16–17; and Stanley and Niemi 2000: 244–45.

The 1982 Murray-Blessing poll (see Box 3-6) ranked activists as the nation's ten best presidents, while the more passive Eisenhower ranked eleventh, and activists Polk and Kennedy ranked twelfth and thirteenth, respectively. Again, the scandal presidents hold up the rear, and the passive presidents are ranked lower than the activists ones.

3-3b The 2000 Presidential Poll

On February 21, 2000, Reuters reported a ranking of the forty-one men who had served to that date as president. This is not strictly a historian poll: Rather historians, politicians, pundits, and other knowledgeable individuals were asked to rank the presidents on the ten different dimensions shown in Figure 3-1.

Some changes are apparent in this poll, as you can see in Box 3-7. John Kennedy ranks among the top ten presidents, as does Eisenhower. Ronald Reagan—who despite his calls for limited government and his personal detachment from the details of government, had an activist political agenda—ranks eleventh. While Andrew Jackson's historical ranking declined, he still ranks with the active presidents, with John Adams also ranked somewhat lower at sixteenth.

While there are some differences in the results of the 2000 poll, generally, we find the activist presidents again ranked more highly than their passive counterparts. The examination of the various historical polls, then, shows that those presidents who expressed an active presidency in their political philosophy or who governed as activist presidents are generally ranked higher than are the passive presidents. This point is consistent with Barber's (1992) classic work, in which he

Box 3-4

1981 Porter Poll

Great

1. Lincoln
2. Washington
3. F. Roosevelt
4. Jefferson
5. T. Roosevelt

Near Great

6. Wilson
7. Jackson
8. Truman
9. Polk
10. J. Adams
11. L. Johnson

Average

12. Eisenhower
13. Madison
14. Kennedy
15. Cleveland
16. McKinley
17. Monroe
18. J. Q. Adams

19. Van Buren
20. Hayes
21. Taft
22. Hoover
23. Carter
24. Arthur
25. B. Harrison
26. Ford

Below Average

27. Taylor
28. Tyler
29. Fillmore
30. Coolidge
31. A. Johnson
32. Grant
33. Pierce

Failure

34. Nixon
35. Buchanan
36. Harding

Sources: Reuters; Murray and Blessing 1994: 16–17; and Stanley and Niemi 2000: 244–45.

identifies presidents with an "active positive" disposition as those most likely to achieve success, though it differs in that he also identifies "active negative" presidents as the most likely to fail.

3-3c Other Factors?

If activism is related to presidential greatness, which other factors are related to greatness? Landy and Milkis (2000: 2) make the interesting comment that, "Greatness is far more compatible with monarchy, in which a leader is required not to serve the people but to take care of them." It is clear that the activist presidents, while they certainly were not monarchists, were more likely to be accused of dictatorial ambitions by their political opponents than were the passive presidents. In addition, these presidents were more likely to leave a legacy behind: either of policy accomplishments, wars won, or the expansion of the presidential office. Those presidents who increased presidential power, and most of the activist presidents left the presidency more powerful (at least potentially) than they had found it, are generally ranked by historians as "great" or "near great."

Box 3-5

1982 Chicago Tribune Poll

1. Lincoln	20. Taft
2. Washington	21. Hoover
3. F. Roosevelt	22. Hayes
4. T. Roosevelt	23. Ford
5. Jefferson	24. Arthur
6. Wilson	25. B. Harrison
7. Jackson	26. Taylor
8. Truman	27. Carter
9. Eisenhower	28. Tyler
10. Polk	29. Coolidge
11. McKinley	30. A. Johnson
12. L. Johnson	31. Fillmore
13. Cleveland	32. Grant
14. Kennedy	33. Pierce
15. J. Adams, Monroe, Madison	34. Buchanan
18. Van Buren	35. Nixon
19. J. Q. Adams	36. Harding

Sources: Reuters; Murray and Blessing 1994: 16–17; and Stanley and Niemi 2000: 244–45.

As Landy and Milkis (2000: 3) continue, "The great presidents were great because they not only brought about change but also left a legacy—principles, institutional arrangements, and policies that defined an era." On the other hand, those presidents who damaged the office, through scandal or incompetence, tend to be ranked at the bottom of the various historical rankings (e.g., Harding, Grant, Nixon, Buchanan, Pierce, and Andrew Johnson; though not yet Reagan because of the Iran-contra scandal or Clinton because of his impeachment).

Which other factors are related to presidential greatness? Successfully governing during a period of crisis (such as a war or the Great Depression) is related to most of the presidents ranked as "great" or "near great" (see Genovese 1995). Of those ranked highest in the 2000 poll, for example, Lincoln governed during the Civil War, Franklin Roosevelt during the Great Depression and World War II. While George Washington did not have a crisis per se, he helped to create the presidency. Had he failed, the new government might not have survived. Truman dealt with the end of World War II, the Cold War, and the Korean War. Wilson governed during World War I or, as it was known then, the Great War. Kennedy had the Cuban Missile Crisis; Eisenhower, the end of the Korean War and the continuation of the Cold War; and Lyndon Johnson, the Vietnam War (though that hardly added to his historical prestige—Johnson is better remembered for his domestic accomplishments, particularly in the area of civil rights and Medicare). Of the top ten presidents, only Teddy Roosevelt and Thomas Jefferson did not govern during times of war, though war with Great Britain was on the horizon during Jefferson's presidency and Teddy Roosevelt expanded the scope of

Box 3-6

Murray-Blessing Poll 1982

Great

1. Lincoln
2. F. Roosevelt
3. Washington
4. Jefferson

Near Great

5. T. Roosevelt
6. Wilson
7. Jackson
8. Truman

Above Average

9. J. Adams
10. L. Johnson
11. Eisenhower
12. Polk
13. Kennedy
14. Madison
15. Monroe
16. J. Q. Adams
17. Cleveland

Average

18. McKinley
19. Taft
20. Van Buren
21. Hoover
22. Hayes
23. Arthur
24. Ford
25. Carter
26. B. Harrison

Below Average

27. Taylor
28. Tyler
29. Fillmore
30. Coolidge
31. Pierce

Failure

32. A. Johnson
33. Buchanan
34. Nixon
35. Grant
36. Harding

Sources: Reuters; Murray and Blessing 1994: 16–17; and Stanley and Niemi 2000: 244–45.

presidential power in foreign affairs. Of the top ten ranked presidents in the 2000 poll, then, most had an opportunity for presidential greatness thrust upon them.

One can wonder whether Lincoln would have been a great president without the Civil War or Truman without the Cold War. While one can question whether the Vietnam War actually added to Lyndon Johnson's reputation or served as a detriment that kept him from ranking even higher, it is clear that a crisis of some sort is often related to presidential greatness. Crises often provide the opportunity for presidential activism (as they did especially during the nineteenth century) and for the creation of new organizational arrangements or precedents that expand the scope of presidential power.

3-4 The President's Personal Resources

One of the personal resources that is most prized in the presidency today is communication skills. Historians and political pundits often speak glowingly of the rhetorical skills of presidents such as Franklin Roosevelt, John Kennedy, Ronald

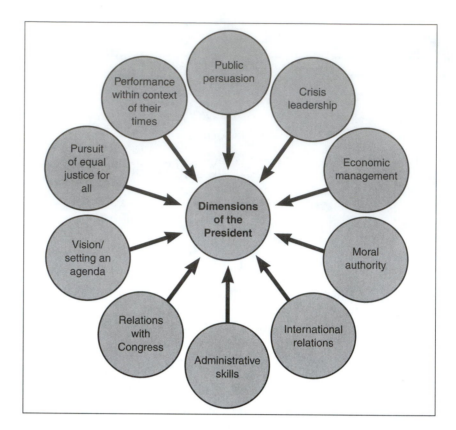

Figure 3-1
Dimensions on Which Presidents Were Ranked in the 2000 Presidential Poll

Reagan, and Bill Clinton, while simultaneously disparaging the often-garbled syntax of such men as Dwight Eisenhower, Lyndon Johnson, Gerald Ford, Jimmy Carter, George H. W. Bush, and George W. Bush.

There is some evidence in the 2000 poll that communication skills matter. Lincoln was considered one the great speakers of his age, though he spoke rarely as president, given the norms of the time (which did not include active presidential speaking). Teddy Roosevelt made great use of the "bully pulpit" and was instrumental in the creation of the "rhetorical presidency" (see Tulis 1987). Woodrow Wilson was the first president since John Adams to deliver his state of the union address directly before Congress and made considerable use of the president's rhetorical opportunities.

Likewise, Kennedy is often identified as the first TV president, and Reagan, who ranks eleventh, is called the "great communicator." On the other hand, Truman was an ineffective public speaker, as was Lyndon Johnson. Jefferson, who governed during a time when public speaking was not prized, had a stutter, and Washington was not fond of public speaking. If we exclude the eighteenth and nineteenth century presidents from our consideration, since public speaking was not considered as important a skill at that time, and look only at the twentieth century ones, the presidents known for their acumen as public speakers do appear to rank higher. This may not be, however, because they spoke more often, but because they had something to speak about; that is, they expressed a vision.

Franklin Roosevelt's rhetoric is filled with verbal images that we remember even today (e.g., "we have nothing to fear but fear itself" and America has a "rendezvous with destiny"). These were not merely empty words at the time; they signaled something palpable to the people of the Depression and World War II generation. Likewise, presidents like Truman and Johnson, while they did not have refined rhetorical skills, communicated a message and a vision that was clearly

Box 3-7

2000 Ranking of Presidents

1. Lincoln	22. Carter
2. F. Roosevelt	23. Ford
3. Washington	24. Taft
4. T. Roosevelt	25. Nixon
5. Truman	26. Hayes
6. Wilson	27. Coolidge
7. Jefferson	28. Taylor
8. Kennedy	29. Garfield
9. Eisenhower	30. Van Buren
10. L. Johnson	31. B. Harrison
11. Reagan	32. Arthur
12. Polk	33. Grant
13. Jackson	34. Hoover
14. Monroe	35. Fillmore
15. McKinley	36. Tyler
16. J. Adams	37. W. H. Harrison
17. Cleveland	38. Harding
18. Madison	39. Pierce
19. J. Q. Adams	40. Johnson
20. G. H. W. Bush	41. Buchanan
21. Clinton	

Sources: Reuters; Murray and Blessing 1994: 16–17; and Stanley and Niemi 2000: 244–45.

perceived by the people of their time: whether it was the Truman Doctrine or Johnson's idea of a "Great Society."

3-4a Rhetoric and Speaking

On the other hand, some of our modern presidents have been criticized for speaking too much and lacking a strategic vision. While Bill Clinton was a skilled orator, he often had little of substance to say (see Waterman, Wright, and St. Clair 1999). Jimmy Carter's rhetoric was often poorly chosen (e.g., his declaration that the energy crisis represented the "moral equivalent of war," or MEOW), and his top-heavy political agenda also did not send a clear signal of his intentions to either Congress or the American people. Likewise, George H. W. Bush was criticized for lacking what he himself called "the vision thing." In 1989 columnist Burt Solomon (*National Journal*, March 11, 1989: 603) wrote,

> Is anyone on the [Bush] staff minding the big picture? "There's no one whose job it is to keep hold of the agenda," [a] former transition official complained. "Absolutely nobody" is thinking about the long term "or is inclined to. . . . What's missing is that big thinker"—someone who ponders long-term strategy and decides how the President's political capital should be spent.

Box 3-8

Presidential Intelligence and Historical Ranking

Communication skill is but one resource that presidents bring to the White House. Intelligence varies across presidents. Some of our most intelligent presidents include Jefferson, Madison, Wilson, Hoover, Carter, and Clinton. Jefferson was a highly successful president. His successor, Madison, was undoubtedly a genius, but he is more remembered for framing the Constitution and the Bill of Rights, and not as president. Likewise, among the most intelligent presidents of the twentieth century, Herbert Hoover, Jimmy Carter, and Bill Clinton are rarely considered as great presidents.

Contrarily, Ronald Reagan, who was described by even many of his closest supporters as intellectually lazy, ranks high in the most recent historical poll. This does not mean that intelligence is irrelevant or

that it should not be prized in presidential candidates. What I mean to suggest is that it is not a sufficient condition for presidential greatness.

Likewise, possessing political skill is not sufficient to be a great president. As Genovese (1995: 36) writes, "Skill is of great importance, but it is not enough." Merely having the political skills of a John Quincy Adams, Martin Van Buren, or Richard Nixon is not sufficient to be a great leader. All three men are duly remembered for their political acumen. Yet, none ultimately succeeded as president, though Nixon has many important accomplishments that might have brought him greatness had it not been for Watergate. Personal resources, then, are important, but they are not the deciding factor determining whether one becomes a great or near-great president.

In sum, many political experts may be confusing communication skills with vision. Certainly, it helps to be a polished public speaker, but without a message, a president becomes more of a performer than a leader. It is strategic vision that gives the president both a short-term focus and a possibility for long-term meaningful achievements. As Genovese (1995: 59) notes,

> Beyond question, the most important "power" a president can have is the ability to present the public a clear and compelling vision. . . . Vision energizes and empowers, inspires and moves people and organizations. A president with a compelling vision can be a powerful president.

Obviously, vision also is related to presidential activism. Presidents who are passive rarely have a clearly expressed vision of where they want to lead the nation. Activist presidents, on the other hand, cannot lead without such a vision, unless they want to make the kind of sequential incremental changes that the Clinton administration favored. (See Box 3-8.)

3-5 Presidential Background

Presidents have held a variety of jobs prior to becoming president (see Figure 3-2). Prior to 2000, of those with previous legislative experience, sixteen served as state legislators, thirteen served in the House of Representatives, and nine served in the U.S. Senate. Since 1900, only five have served in the state legislature, five in the House of Representatives, and five in the U.S. Senate. Many presidents also had prior executive experience: of the pre-1900 cohort, seven served as vice president; seven, as a member of the Cabinet; eleven, as governor; two, as mayor; and seven, as diplomat or ambassador. Since 1900, seven have served as vice president; three, as a member of the Cabinet; eight, as governor; one, as mayor; and two, as diplomat or ambassador. The biggest difference over time, however, is related to military

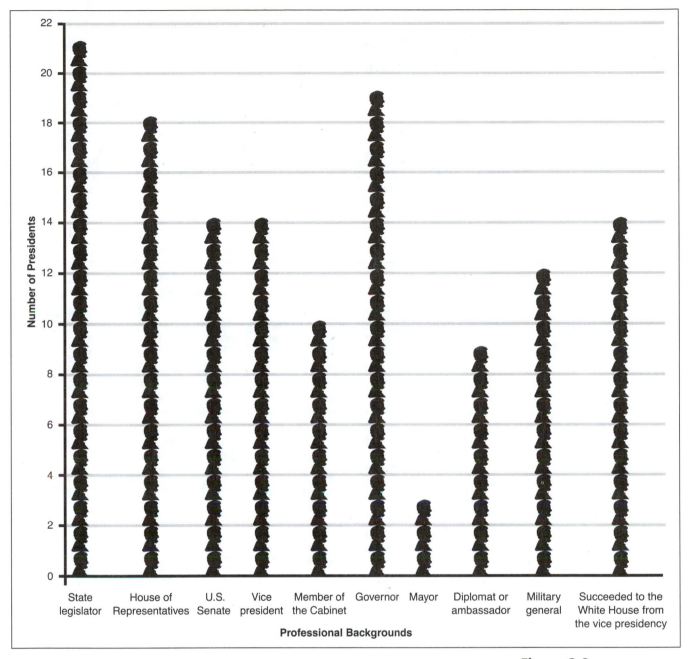

Figure 3-2
Jobs Held Prior to
Becoming President

experience. There were eleven military generals prior to 1900, but only one (Eisenhower) since then (see Stanley and Niemi 2000: 246). With regard to the last position prior to becoming president, fourteen have succeeded to the White House from the vice presidency.

According to Schlesinger (1973), the longer one has served as vice president, the less likely he is to be an effective president. Hence, Teddy Roosevelt and Harry Truman served for a relatively short time as vice president, while Nixon and Johnson were vice presidents for an extended period. Schlesinger's thesis, however, does not explain the low rankings of Andrew Johnson and John Tyler, who were

Box 3-9

More on Presidential Backgrounds

The utility of a legislative career seems to be less important today as a route to the White House. The last president to come directly from the legislature was John Kennedy, a senator. The last presidents with vast congressional experience were Lyndon Johnson and Gerald Ford (George H. W. Bush had served two terms in the House of Representatives, but many years prior to becoming president). This factor may explain why there is less comity between the legislative and executive branches and less understanding on each side of the two branches' unique responsibilities.

The main method by which presidents come to the White House today is through the governor's mansion. Of these presidents, there are some notable successes. Teddy Roosevelt (who served briefly as vice president) was governor of New York. Woodrow Wilson was governor of New Jersey. Franklin Roosevelt was governor of New York. Ronald Reagan was governor of California. But some presidents who have been ranked lower also had gubernatorial experience (e.g., Jimmy Carter was governor of Georgia). While the rankings of Bill Clinton (governor of Arkansas) and George

W. Bush (governor of Texas) are not yet firmly established, they too came to the White House with prior executive experience, but with little knowledge of the Washington political community. As a result, many of the governors must learn the Washington establishment, as well as the job of president simultaneously, a daunting, but obviously not impossible task.

In virtually every background category, then, we can find both good and bad, highly and lowly ranked presidents: Among the military generals are George Washington, but also Zachary Taylor. And some with the least prior Washington, D. C., experience (Lincoln served but two years in the House of Representatives) proved to be great presidents, while some with vast experience (Nixon served in the House, Senate, and as vice president) were less successful. Even prior political experience is not a measure of presidential success. Martin Van Buren was an acknowledged master of politics in his age, yet was not a successful president. James Madison is known as the Father of the Constitution and the Bill of Rights, yet did not distinguish himself as president.

vice president for a short period of time, or the high rankings for Lyndon Johnson, despite criticism of his administration's Vietnam War policies.

Six individuals have come from the Congress to the White House, ten from the governor's mansion, four from military office, five from the Cabinet, and two from ambassadorial posts (Stanley and Niemi 2000: 246). The Cabinet, and in particular the position of Secretary of State, used to be the position through which presidents anointed their successors (e.g., Jefferson and Madison, Madison and Monroe, Monroe and John Quincy Adams). In the twentieth century, this mechanism was less used, with Herbert Hoover as the last man to so rise to the White House from the Cabinet (he was Secretary of Commerce). While none of the presidents who came to the presidency in this manner are considered great, they did bring considerable executive experience to their administrations (see Box 3-9).

Chapter Summary

When we look at the determinants of presidential success, at least as measured by historians, we find that the following are likely the three most important qualities for a president to possess:

1. A propensity toward an activist presidency
2. Governing in a period of crisis
3. Having a strategic political vision

All three are related in that activism encourages a strategic vision, and a crisis situation certainly encourages presidential activism.

Activism in itself, however, is not sufficient to achieve greatness. As McDonald (1994: 470) writes, "Polls taken by the American Institute of Public Opinion since the 1930s have reflected two unchanging popular attitudes toward the presidency, namely that the people want strong, activist presidents and that they distrust and fear strong, activist presidents."

There is indeed a fascination and fear of activism in America. Many of the activist presidents have been derided as monarchs, tyrants, or dictators, and some have certainly overstepped the boundaries of constitutional propriety, thus, at times, raising concerns about the deleterious impact of an "imperial presidency" (Schlesinger 1973; see also Berger 1974). Still, as the various historical rankings indicate, it is the activist presidents, particularly those who have increased the power and influence of the presidential office, who are ranked most highly by historians.

There have been some exceptions to these criteria: Eisenhower is now ranked high despite his relative passivity, though, as noted, historians now contend that he was actually more active than historians once thought; likewise, Richard Nixon, who governed during crisis times and expressed a definite leadership vision is ranked toward the bottom of the historical lists, but almost exclusively because of the scandals that destroyed his presidency. Scandal is the strongest determinant of a historical perception that a presidency has failed. The presidents who did not handle crises well, such as Buchanan, Pierce, and Hoover, also rank low in various polls.

Hence, the one personal political resource that seems most closely associated with presidential success is the president's political philosophy. Those presidents who bring an activist bent and a clear policy vision to the White House are most likely to succeed. If they then face a crisis situation, particularly a foreign policy crisis, they then have the greatest opportunity to rise to the level of presidential greatness.

Review Questions

1. If George Washington had announced at the Constitutional Convention that he would not run for president,
   a. the presidency would likely be much the same as it is today.
   b. the presidency would likely be much different than it is today.
   c. the Founders would have increased the power of the presidency.
   d. Benjamin Franklin would have been our first president.

2. At the end of the Constitutional Convention, the presidency can best be described as
   a. a fully developed office.
   b. an office of substantial power and prestige.
   c. an outline.
   d. a battle plan.

3. President Washington was more careful to protect the president's power in the realm of
   a. domestic affairs.
   b. executive affairs.
   c. judicial affairs.
   d. foreign affairs.

4. Despite the fact that his political philosophy favored limited government and a strict interpretation of the Constitution, who of the following was an activist president?
   a. George Washington
   b. John Adams
   c. Thomas Jefferson
   d. James Madison

5. Whose presidency represented a retreat from an activist presidency?
   a. George Washington
   b. John Adams
   c. Thomas Jefferson
   d. James Madison

6. Who of the following argued that the president is the "tribune of the people"?
   a. George Washington
   b. James Madison
   c. Andrew Jackson
   d. Abraham Lincoln

7. Who of the following presidents argued for the Whig conception of the presidency, an argument for limited presidential power?
   a. James Madison
   b. William Henry Harrison
   c. Andrew Johnson
   d. Benjamin Harrison

8. Who of the following was the first president to use a budget?
   a. James Polk
   b. Abraham Lincoln
   c. Theodore Roosevelt
   d. William Taft

9. Who of the following came to the White House with the most intellectually derived conception of the presidency?
   a. Abraham Lincoln
   b. Theodore Roosevelt
   c. Woodrow Wilson
   d. Franklin Roosevelt

10. Who of the following presidents believed that "it was not only his right but his duty to do anything that the needs of the Nation demanded unless such action was forbidden by the Constitution or by the laws"?
    a. James Polk
    b. Abraham Lincoln
    c. Theodore Roosevelt
    d. William Taft

11. Who of the following presidents understood that news about his personal life could pave the way for popular acceptance of his more serious policy pronouncements?
    a. William Taft
    b. Woodrow Wilson
    c. Warren Harding
    d. Calvin Coolidge

12. With which activist president was a new modern presidential model set?
    a. Franklin Roosevelt
    b. Harry Truman
    c. Dwight Eisenhower
    d. John Kennedy

13. Who of the following presidents practiced a "hidden hand" style of presidential leadership?
    a. Franklin Roosevelt
    b. Harry Truman
    c. Dwight Eisenhower
    d. John Kennedy

14. Which two presidents raised questions about accountability and the dangers of an activist presidency?
    a. Theodore Roosevelt and Franklin Roosevelt
    b. Franklin Roosevelt and Harry Truman
    c. Lyndon Johnson and Richard Nixon
    d. Richard Nixon and Bill Clinton

15. Who of the following do historians most often rate as America's greatest president?
    a. George Washington
    b. Thomas Jefferson
    c. Abraham Lincoln
    d. Franklin Roosevelt

16. Presidents who govern at such times are often rated as great.
    a. good economic times
    b. times of peace and tranquility
    c. periods before and after wars
    d. periods of great crisis

Discussion Questions

1. Are great presidents activist presidents, or are historians biased (and therefore name activist presidents as the great presidents)?
2. Dwight Eisenhower and Calvin Coolidge were very popular presidents when they were in office. Yet, history does not regard them as highly as did their own contemporaries. Why do you think Eisenhower and Coolidge are not more highly regarded by historians? Do you think popularity should be related to the concept of presidential greatness?
3. What qualities do you think account for presidential greatness?

Chapter

4

Domestic Policy, Constitutional Ambiguity, and the Growth of Presidential Power

Key Terms

adjourn
convene
pocket veto
session

4-1 Domestic Policy, Constitutional Ambiguity, and the Growth of Presidential Power

In his seminal study of the presidency, Rossiter (1960) enumerates five constitutional roles of the president of the United States: chief of state, chief executive, chief legislator, chief diplomat, and commander-in-chief. See Figure 4-1.

Whereas the president as chief of state is largely a ceremonial function, similar to that performed by the English monarchy, the other roles derive their principal justification from the enumerated powers of the U.S. Constitution. For example, as the nation's chief executive, the president has supervisory authority over the activities of his or her own executive branch, and as chief legislator, the president participates in the law-making process. As the nation's chief diplomat, the president meets with foreign dignitaries and negotiates treaties. Finally, the president, as commander-in-chief, plays a principal role in the nation's defense.

In practice, each of these roles has proven to be a mixture of palpable presidential authority and pure symbolism. While the constitutional provisions agreed upon by the Founders in 1787 provided the basis for what Rossiter (1966: 221) calls an "office of unusual vigor and independence," they did not guarantee that presidents would have real influence. In fact, as we shall see in section 9-4, "Nineteenth Century Expectations of the Presidency," for much of the nineteenth century, the presidency was clearly subservient to the legislative branch and did not live up to Rossiter's characterizations of either "vigor" or "independence."

4-2 The Founding Fathers' Priorities

At the Constitutional Convention, the Founding Fathers' primary concern was the creation of a new covenant to replace the failed Articles of Confederation. In so doing, the Founders had to deal with complicated theoretical problems, such as how to design a government that would have all the power it needed to function, while at the same time providing a government that would not threaten the personal liberty of its citizens. The Founders also had to consider intricate practical questions, such as the southern interest in preserving slavery and the fear that large states would politically dominate small ones. Concomitantly, they also needed to identify the powers of various governmental institutions. This was a gargantuan task, one that the Founders performed with great skill, but which they failed to do with precision, a point that is particularly evident when we examine the powers of the presidential office.

Most of the presidency's authority is delineated in Article II of the Constitution, though the veto power is identified in Article I. As can be seen in Table 4-1, fully 46 percent of the words in Article II describe the various procedures and qualifications for selecting a president, another 8 percent are dedicated to the issue of presidential succession, 3 percent to presidential impeachment, and 5 percent to compensation. Only 38 percent of the words in Article II, then, deal with the actual enumerated powers of the presidency.

Clearly, the number of words in Article II is a *very* rough indicator of the Founders' interest in presidential power. Extraordinary powers can be delegated in only a few words such as identifying the president's role as "Commander-in-Chief of the Army and Navy," though I will have more to say on this power in section 5-6, "Commander-in-Chief." Yet, this analysis suggests that the Founding Fathers were more concerned with the method and qualifications for selecting presidents than they were with a delineation of the specific role of the president in the constitutional system.

Figure 4-1
Roles of the Presidency

T A B L E **4-1** Content Analysis of Article II of the Constitution

Provision	Words	Percentage
Executive vesting clause	15	1.5%
Election of president	463	46.0%
Succession	83	8.0%
Compensation	48	4.7%
Oath of office	54	5.3%
Commander-in-chief	34	3.4%
Opinion of department heads	28	2.8%
Pardons and reprieves	21	2.0%
Treaties	25	2.5%
Appointments	115	19.5%
State of the union	31	3.0%
Convene Congress	38	3.7%
Receive ambassadors	8	0.7%
Laws faithfully executed	20	2.0%
Impeachment	31	3.0%

4-2a A Plural Executive and Presidential Selection

An examination of the constitutional debate provides further evidence of the Founding Fathers' concerns described in section 4-2. Most of the debate about the presidency centered around two points: (1) whether the nation should have a plural or single chief executive and (2) the method for selecting a president. Both of these points tangentially relate to the issue of presidential power. The case for the single executive was based on two ideas. First, as Hamilton argued in Federalist #70, a single executive was required for effective administration of the laws: "Energy in the executive is a leading character in the definition of good government." Second, and of virtually equal importance to Madison and others at the Convention, was the idea that a single executive was required to provide an adequate check on the power of the legislative branch.

Both of these factors suggest the Founders wanted the presidency to have enough power and influence to provide for effective administration of the government. The fact that the president was to be a single individual, rather than a rancorous and divided council or cabinet, certainly provided a clear basis for the later expansion of presidential power. Likewise, by allowing the people to have a voice in the selection of the president, through the mediating influence of the electoral college, the Founders provided presidential autonomy from the legislative branch. As a result, presidents would not be the legislature's puppet. Furthermore, as Andrew Jackson did (see section 3-2f, "Andrew Jackson"), presidents (and their vice presidents) could argue that they alone among all federal actors were elected by and thus represented all the people (see Polsby 1978).

Along with the method of selection, the Founders also sought to guarantee the independence of the president from the legislative branch by specifying that presidential compensation would be fixed throughout each term of office. Hence, presidential pay could neither be reduced so as to punish a sitting president nor increased so as to bribe one.

4-2b No Clear Framework for Presidential Power

Aside from the abstract or indirect concerns with presidential power, the Founders spent relatively little time discussing the actual delegated powers of the presidency. The problem was that the Founders had few models upon which to base a new chief executive. They could look to past historical practice, including the crown of England, the royal governors of the colonies, or to the revolutionary-colonial governors. But neither method provided an acceptable model for executive leadership. The King had been too powerful, and the idea of a monarch for life was unrepresentative and, hence, not republican. The royal governors had been despised in their time for their corruption and overt loyalty to the King. As for the Revolutionary War state constitutions, they largely eliminated executive power.

As Forrest McDonald (1994: 130) writes, "All the states designed features to prevent executive abuse in [the] future." Excepting New York, only the governors of Massachusetts and South Carolina had the veto power, only Maryland's governor had an appointment power that carried with it any real influence, and only the governors of Delaware and North Carolina had the pardon and reprieve powers (while Virginia's governor could issue reprieves but not pardons). Of all the governors, only New York's had any real authority. The New York governor was elected by the people, could serve multiple terms in office, had a veto power through a council on revision, had the power to call the legislature into session, was charged with issuing a periodic report on the state of the state, could grant pardons and reprieves except in cases of treason and murder, execute the laws, correspond with the Continental

Congress, and command the armed forces (ibid., 133–34). While not as powerful, the governor of Massachusetts was also popularly elected (Thomas, Pika, and Watson 1993: 16). Still, even in Massachusetts, there had been considerable sentiment for creating a government without an executive (McDonald 1994: 135). Since the Articles of Confederation essentially did just that at the national level, the Founders had few role models for their new executive office.

Thus, many of the Founders came to the Constitutional Convention without a clear framework for an executive office. For example, James Madison, who developed an extensive plan for the new government, the Virginia Plan, arrived with only vague notions of what the executive branch should entail. Writing to George Washington on April 16, 1787, Madison stated, "I have scarcely ventured as yet to form my own opinion either of the manner in which [the executive] ought to be constituted or of the authorities with which it ought to be cloathed [sic]" (quoted in Thach 1969: 83). Likewise, most of the other delegates attending the Convention had only vague notions of how the executive branch should be constituted. One of the few delegates who did express a clear view of the executive's authority was Alexander Hamilton, but there is little evidence that his statements favoring a president for life made much of an impression on the convention's other delegates.

4-2c An Autonomous Executive

While the Founders did not have a clear vision of the executive office, the experience of the Articles of Confederation taught them that the creation of a weak chief executive could prove counterproductive and that a government dominated by a powerful legislative branch was unworkable. Consequently, there was support among the Founders for creating an autonomous executive. But how much power this executive should possess was uncertain.

The fact that the Founders chose the term "president" to describe the new executive is one indication of their perception of the office. The term derived from the Latin word meaning "to sit in front of or at the head of" and secondarily "to defend." It had been used by the Ancient Romans for a guardian office of a minor provincial outpost, by New Hampshire and South Carolina to refer to their executives, and to describe the weak presiding officer of the Confederation Congress. Minor social clubs and fraternal organizations also had presidents: In short, "the name was familiar and innocuous" (McDonald 1994: 157).

In addition to the lack of a clear conceptualization of the presidential office, there was also little time at the Convention to constructively debate the powers of the presidency. Some of the Founders did not believe it was necessary to delineate specific powers, preferring instead to leave this task to the legislative branch, an act that would have left the powers of the presidency at the whim of Congress. According to Thach (1969: 103–4), as the end of July approached "the truth is that, while the Convention thought itself ready to proceed to the business of drawing up a draft of a constitution on the basis of the general principles, so far as the executive was concerned they had settled practically nothing except the question of unity and the veto power." Nor was there much debate of the issue of presidential power in August.

Robinson (1987: 89) states, "During the month of August [1787], when so much time was spent devising the electoral scheme, there was little attention given to the question of presidential powers." Consequently, the task was turned over first to a Committee on Detail and then later to the Committee on Unfinished Business. Under the direction of the Committee on Detail, led by Charles

Pinckney, who had a "remarkably complete" concept of executive power, a list of enumerated presidential powers was finally identified (Thach 1969: 109–10). Despite this important accomplishment, the Committee spent no time discussing the "subject of [presidential] control of foreign policy" (ibid., 113–14).

4-3 Constitutional Ambiguity

Ambiguity was probably inherent in any attempt to write a Constitution. As Madison wrote in Federalist #37,

> All new laws, though penned with the greatest technical skill, and passed on the fullest and most mature deliberation, are considered as more or less obscure and equivocal, until their meaning be liquidated and ascertained by a series of particular discussions and adjudications. . . . Perspicuity therefore requires not only that ideas should be distinctly formed, but that they should be expressed by words distinct and exclusively appropriated to them. But no language is so copious as to supply words and phrases for every complex idea, or so correct as not to include many equivocally devoted different ideas. Hence, it must happen, that however accurately objects may be discriminated in themselves, and however accurately the discrimination may be considered, the definition of them may be rendered inaccurate by the inaccuracy of the terms in which it is delivered. And this unavoidable inaccuracy must be greater or less, according to the complexity and novelty of the objects defined.

Likewise, in *McCulloch v. Maryland* (17 U.S. 4 Wheat 406 1819), Chief Justice Marshall wrote,

> A Constitution, to contain an accurate detail of all the subdivisions of which its greatest powers will admit, and of all means by which they may be carried into execution, would partake of the prolixity of a legal code, and could scarcely be embraced by the human mind. Its nature, therefore, requires, that only its greatest outlines should be market, its important objects designated, and the minor ingredients which compose those objects, be deduced from the nature of the objects themselves.

But if ambiguity was more or less inherent in the writing of the Constitution, the presidential powers were clearly more nebulous than those identified for the legislative branch. In fact, by the time the Constitution was ready for presentation to the American people, the scope of the president's powers was still unclear. As Thach (1969: 140) writes,

> The completion of Article II of the Constitution seems, at first sight, a logical place for an evaluation of the work of the Convention and an interpretation of the executive established by it. A closer view reveals the fact that such an evaluation and interpretation is hardly possible. Rushed through in the last days of the Convention's being, as much of it was, the executive article fairly bristles with contentious matter, and, until it is seen what decision was given to these contentions, it is impossible to say just what the national executive meant.

4-3a The Powers of the Legislative and Presidential Branches

In Box 4-1 and Box 4-2, I present the constitutional powers of the Congress and the president. As is evident in Box 4-1, Congress's powers are quite specific. Congress is delegated the powers to lay and collect taxes, to borrow money, to regulate commerce, to establish uniform rules of naturalization, to coin money and regulate the

Box 4-1

Congress's Constitutional Power

Section 1. All legislative Powers herein granted shall be vested in a Congress of the United States, which shall consist of a Senate and a House of Representatives. . . .

Section 8. The Congress shall have Power To lay and collect Taxes, Duties, Imposts and Excises, to pay the Debts and provide for the common Defence and general Welfare of the United States; but all Duties, Imposts and Excises shall be uniform throughout the United States;

To borrow Money on the credit of the United States;

To regulate Commerce with foreign Nations, and among the several States, and with the Indian Tribes;

To establish an uniform Rule of Naturalization, and uniform Laws on the subject of Bankruptcies throughout the United States;

To coin Money, regulate the Value thereof, and of foreign coin, and fix the Standard of Weights and Measures;

To provide for the Punishment of counterfeiting the Securities and current Coin of the United States;

To establish Post Offices and post Roads;

To promote the Progress of Science and useful Arts, by securing for limited Times to Authors and Inventors the exclusive right to their respective Writings and Discoveries;

To constitute Tribunals inferior to the Supreme Court;

To define and punish Piracies and Felonies committed on the high Seas, and Offences against the Law of Nations;

To declare War, grant Letters of Marque and Reprisal, and make Rules concerning Captures on Land and Water;

To raise and support Armies, but no Appropriation of Money to that use shall be for a longer Term than two Years;

To provide and maintain a Navy;

To make Rules for the Government and Regulation of the land and naval Forces;

To provide for calling forth the Militia to execute the Laws of the Union, suppress Insurrections and repel Invasions;

To provide for organizing, arming, and disciplining, the Militia, and for governing such Part of them as may be employed in the Service of the United States, reserving to the States respectively, the Appointment of the Officers, and the Authority of training the Militia according to the discipline prescribed by Congress;

To exercise exclusive Legislation in all Cases whatsoever, over such District (not exceeding ten Miles square) as may, by Cession of particular States, and the Acceptance of Congress, become the Seat of the Government of the United States, and to exercise like Authority over all Places purchased by the Consent of the Legislature of the State in which the Same shall be, for the Erection of Forts, Magazines, Arsenals, dock-Yards, and other needful Buildings;—And

To make all Laws which shall be necessary and proper for carrying into Execution the foregoing Powers, and all other Powers vested by this Constitution in the Government of the United States, or in any Department or Officer thereof.

---

value thereof, to punish counterfeiters, to establish post offices and roads, to promote the progress of the sciences and the arts, to constitute courts inferior to the Supreme Court, to define and punish piracies, to declare war, to raise an army and navy, to make rules for each, and to provide for calling forth the militia of the several states. In sum, there is little doubt what the Founders expected the legislative branch to do.

In contrast to the legislative branch, the powers of the presidency are not clearly delineated, but rather in most cases are quite general. In Article I, the president is provided with the veto power, which is one of the clearest articulations of presidential power. The Article II powers delegate presidential authority as commander-in-chief of the army, navy, and militia. Also included are the appointment power, involvement in the treaty-making process, and the pardon/reprieve powers; each is a palpable designation of authority.

Box 4-2

President's Constitutional Power

Article I, Section 7. Every Bill which shall have passed the House of Representatives and the Senate, shall, before it come a Law, be presented to the President of the United States; If he approve he shall sign it, but if not he shall return it, with his Objections to that House in which it shall have originated, who shall enter the Objections at large on their Journal, and proceed to reconsider it. If after such Reconsideration two thirds of that House shall agree to pass the Bill, it shall be sent, together with the Objections, to the other House, by which it shall likewise be considered, and if approved by two thirds of that House, it shall become a Law. . . . If any Bill shall not be returned by the President within ten Days (Sundays excepted) after it shall have been presented to him, the Same shall be a Law, in like manner as if he had signed it, unless the Congress by their Adjournment prevent its Return in which Case it shall not be a Law.

Every Order, Resolution, or Vote to which the Concurrence of the Senate and the House of Representatives may be necessary (except on a question of Adjournment) shall be presented to the President of the United States; and before the Same shall take Effect, shall be approved by him, or being disapproved by him, shall be repassed by two-thirds of the Senate and the House of Representatives, according to the Rule and Limitations prescribed in the Case of a Bill. . . .

Article II, Section 1. The executive Power shall be vested in a President of the United States of America. . . .

Before he enter on the Execution of his Office, he shall following Oath or Affirmation:—"I do solemnly swear (or affirm) that I will faithfully execute the Office of President of the States, and will to the best of my Ability, preserve, protect, and defend the Constitution of the United States."

Section 2. The President shall be Commander in Chief of the Army and Navy of the United States, and of the Militia of the several States, when called into the actual Service of the United States, he may require the Opinion, in writing, of the principal Officer in each of the executive Departments, upon any Subject relating to the Duties of their respective Offices, and he shall have Power to grant Reprieves and Pardons for Offences against the United States, except in Cases of Impeachment.

He shall have Power, by and with the Advice and Consent of the Senate, to make Treaties, provided two thirds of the present concur; and he shall nominate, and by and with the Advice and Consent of the Senate, shall appoint Ambassadors, other public Ministers and Consuls, Judges of the supreme Court, and all other Officers of the United States, whose Appointments are not herein otherwise provided for, and which shall be established by Law: but the Congress may by Law vest the Appointment of such inferior Officers, as they think proper, in the President alone, in the courts of Law, or in the heads of Departments.

The President shall have Power to fill up all Vacancies that may happen during the Recess of the Senate, by granting Commissions which shall expire at the End of their next Session.

Section 3. He shall from time to time give to the Congress Information of the state of the union, and recommend to their consideration such Measures as he shall judge necessary and expedient; he may, on extraordinary Occasions, convene both Houses or either of them, and in Case of Disagreement between them, with respect to the Time of Adjournment, he may adjourn them to such Time as he shall think proper; he shall receive Ambassadors and other public Ministers; he shall take care that the Laws be faithfully executed, and shall Commission all the Officers of the United States.

But what is to be made of the provision stating that the president may ask the principal officers in each of the executive departments for their opinions in writing upon any subject? Likewise, what does it mean that the president will, from time to time, report on the state of the union or shall receive ambassadors and other public ministers? And finally, what is meant by the provision that the president shall take care that the laws are faithfully executed? Was the president to be a mere clerk, executing the will of the Congress and occasionally reporting to it and the public on the nation's business? Was the president to be a symbolic figurehead meeting with the leaders of other nations? Or were these provisions meant to signify the actual delegation of tangible power and authority to the presidential office?

As the Constitutional Convention came to a close and the ratification debate began, the answers to these questions were not evident. In fact, even such major powers as the president's authority as commander-in-chief were not clearly delineated, since it was Congress that would decide if there would be an army or navy and whether to declare war. What then was the president's role? To provide leadership in time of war or when war was imminent? Who would decide when war was imminent? Again, there was no clear answer to these questions in the Constitution.

According to Mezey (1989: 41), the Founders may have intentionally made the Constitution ambiguous. He argues, "It is possible that their vagueness about the presidency bespoke their desire for a much stronger presidency than the country at large would have been prepared to accept. The Founders may have assumed that presidents could interpret the general terms of Article II in an expansive way when that was necessary, whereas the more specific terms that the Founders used in their enumeration of congressional powers in Article I would restrict similar attempts by the legislature to expand its power."

Certainly, even among the Founders there was disagreement about the scope of presidential power, with some arguing for a strong presidency and others a more constrained model. While a few Founders may indeed have preferred intentional ambiguity, the likely cause of the president's vague powers is that the Founders wanted an executive office powerful enough to constrain the legislative branch (which they believed would dominate the governmental system), but not so powerful that it would diminish freedom. Given these contradictory goals, it is not surprising that the Constitution offers the possibility for both a strong and a weak executive office.

4-3b The Most Defective Part of the Constitution

Our understanding of the enumerated presidential powers does not end with the closing of the Constitutional Convention, but rather begins with it. Thus, as scholar Abel Upshur (quoted in Corwin 1984: 22) wrote in 1840,

> The most defective part of the Constitution beyond all question, is that which relates to the Executive Department. It is impossible to read this instrument, without being struck with the loose and unguarded terms in which the powers and duties of the President are pointed out. So far as the legislature is concerned, the limitations of the Constitution are, perhaps, as precise and strict as they could safely have been made; but in regard to the Executive, the Convention appears to have studiously selected such loose and general expressions as would enable the President, by implication and construction either to neglect his duties or to enlarge his powers.

This constitutional ambiguity has had important implications for presidential power throughout our nation's history. As the Founders expected, it allowed the legislative branch to dominate the governmental system throughout most of the nineteenth century. Then, during the twentieth century, this same ambiguity made it possible for such presidents as Theodore Roosevelt, Woodrow Wilson, and Franklin Roosevelt to adopt a broad interpretation of presidential power, thus allowing for the emergence of the modern presidency. It also opened the door for continuous conflict between the executive and legislative branches. As Milkis and

Nelson (1994: 70) write, "By stating that 'the executive Power shall be vested in a President of the United States of America' and that 'he shall take Care that the Laws be faithfully executed,' without in most cases stipulating what those executive responsibilities would be, the Constitution gave rise to two centuries of conflict about the proper extent of presidential authority."

How did this happen? According to Thomas, Pika, and Watson (1993: 12), ". . . the powers of the presidency are so vast and vague that incumbents have tremendous latitude in shaping the office to their particular desires." To illustrate the importance of constitutional ambiguity and how presidents have taken advantage of it, we need look no further than the vesting clauses of Articles I and II of the U.S. Constitution.

4-4 The Vesting Clause

One method presidents have used to justify their authority is the vesting clauses to Articles I and II. According to the introduction to Article II, Section I, "the executive Power shall be *vested* in a President of the United States of America." Uncertainty regarding the exact meaning of this clause emanated from the Constitutional Convention itself. A last-minute change in the Constitution by Gouvenor Morris, a leading advocate of a strong presidency, promoted considerable confusion over the exact interpretation of the vesting clause. In his capacity as chief draftsman for the Committee on Style, which had the duty of putting the Constitution into a final, polished written form, Morris altered the legislative vesting clause. He inserted the word "herein" as in "All legislative Power *herein* granted shall be vested in a Congress of the United States."

At the same time, he left the executive vesting clause unchanged. This subtle change allowed future presidents and advocates of a strong presidency model to claim that there is an executive power or presidential prerogative beyond that which is adumbrated in the Constitution (Hargrove and Nelson 1984: 41–44). As Thach (1969: 139) comments, Morris's change "admitted an interpretation of executive power which would give to the President a field of action much wider than that outlined by the enumerated powers. . . . The results of such a possibility were far reaching."

4-4a A Far-Reaching Interpretation

Many presidents adopted a far-reaching interpretation of the vesting clause, employing it as a confirmation of their legitimate authority over the administrative state, as well as a justification for exerting power in foreign policy, such as Washington's 1793 declaration of neutrality in conflicts between foreign nations. In this case, Alexander Hamilton, then serving as Washington's Treasury Secretary, defended the action on the basis of the president's authority under the vesting clause, an argument that was eventually rejected by Congress. Andrew Jackson also cited the vesting clause in defending his right to fire his Secretary of the Treasury, William J. Duane, and his decision to remove funds from the Second Bank of the United States.

Some constitutional scholars have questioned this broad interpretation of the vesting clause. Corwin (1984: 4) asked whether the clause was an additional grant of power or the mere designation of an office: "If the former, then how are we to explain the more specific clauses of grant in the ensuing sections of the same article?" Corwin further raised the question of whether the "President's executive power" is the "only executive power known to the Constitution?" He answered in the negative by stating that Congress was delegated certain executive power under the provisions of the "necessary and proper" clause (ibid.).

Further, the provision that the president "shall take care that the laws are faith-fully executed" suggests someone other than the president carries out the law (i.e., a presidential subordinate such as the Secretary of the Treasury). Thus, Corwin contends, the Constitution did not intend for all executive power to rest with the president. Rather, the vesting clause was merely an introduction to the office of the presidency and not an additional grant of presidential authority.

Other scholars agree with Corwin's interpretation. Berger (1974: 58) adds, "It is incongruous to attribute to a generation so in dread of executive tyranny an intention to give a newly created executive a blank check." And Adler (1989: 130) comments, "For the framers, the phrase 'executive power' was limited, as [James] Wilson said, to 'executing the laws, and appointing officers.'"

Not all scholars agree with this interpretation, however. Contrarily, McDonald writes, ". . . it seems evident that some of them [the Founders], at least thought of executive power as contingent and discretionary: the power to act unilaterally in cir-cumstances in which the safety or the well being of the republic is imperiled . . . power in sum, that extends beyond the ordinary rules prescribed by the Constitution and the laws."

It is clear that the Founders were well versed in John Locke's ideas about the power of *prerogative* or the existence of an inherent executive power (e.g., the exec-utive's right to protect the nation from an impending foreign attack). But while the Founders may have accepted prerogative in theory, did they really intend for the vesting clause to grant such broad authority to the presidency?

4-4b Contradictory Viewpoints on the Vesting Clause

While Corwin's intellectual argument is convincing, the vesting clause has indeed been widely interpreted as a constitutional justification for extending presidential influence in foreign policy crises and over the executive branch. But should presi-dents use the vesting clause as a source of additional presidential power? Even the Founders disagree on this point. In fact, they even expressed contradictory view-points on it. For instance, James Madison, in 1789, while defending the president's right to remove officials from the executive branch without Senate approval, stated (Goldsmith 1980: 184),

> The constitution affirms, that the executive power shall be vested in the President. Are there exceptions to this proposition? Yes, there are. The constitution says that in appointing to office, the Senate shall be associated with the President unless in the case of inferior officers, when the law shall otherwise direct. Have we a right to extend this exception? I believe not. If the constitution has invested all executive power in the President, I venture to assert that the Legislature has no right to diminish or modify his executive authority.

Madison's basic reasoning was that if the legislature infringed on the powers vested in the executive branch, then the doctrine of the separation of powers would be violated. The executive power would be unwisely commingled with that of the legislature to the detriment of both branches of government. This was Madison's argument in 1789. By 1793, however, in the debate over whether President George Washington had the right to proclaim neutrality in the war between France and England, Madison adopted a different point of view. He argued that the vesting clause was not a grant of presidential power at all.

At the urging of Thomas Jefferson, Madison challenged Hamilton's broad defense of the president's action in proclaiming neutrality. Hamilton had argued that the president's action was justified because of the broad executive power conferred upon the president by the vesting clause. Madison countered that Hamilton's defense was "no less vicious in theory than it would be dangerous in practice." If Hamilton's broad interpretation of the vesting clause prevailed, then "no citizen could any longer guess at the character of the government under which he lives; the most penetrating jurist would be unable to scan the extent of constructive prerogative" (quoted in Fisher 1978: 18).

Thus, even the so-called Father of the Constitution expressed different interpretations of the vesting clause within a brief four-year period. This ambiguity, then, provided presidents with one rationale for the broad exercise of executive power. Had the Founding Fathers provided a clearer statement of their intent, there would have been less room for interpretation. For example, if the original version of the vesting clause had remained in the Constitution, there would have been less room to argue that the clause provided additional authority for the presidential office: "The executive power shall be vested in a single person. His style shall be 'the President of the United States' and his title shall be 'His Excellency'" (Corwin 1984: 11–12).

This wording designated a person rather than an office and suggests nothing more than an introduction to the President of the United States. The introduction of the word "herein" in the Article I vesting clause and the change to the presidential vesting clause introduced ambiguity, thus planting the seeds for presidential power. Presidents such as Andrew Jackson and Richard Nixon were quick to take advantage of these ambiguities.

4-5 The Take Care Clause

Another constitutional provision that is widely cited as a justification for presidential influence is the specification that the president "shall take care that the laws are faithfully executed." Like the other presidential powers, this clause was little debated at the Constitution. As Cronin (1989: 188–89) notes, "Presumably there was little to debate. State governors were similarly charged with faithfully executing the law, and the framers were convinced that Congress could no longer both make and administer the laws [as they had done under the Articles of Confederation]." As a result, a "clearly defined division of labor was necessary." While Cronin believes the take care clause was "reasonably straightforward," like the vesting clause, it too introduced considerable ambiguity into later interpretations of the Constitution.

The take care clause has been interpreted as meaning that presidents must have direct supervisory influence over the executive branch and the conduct of executive branch officials, since it is this branch of government and these officials that execute the laws. During the presidencies of Andrew Jackson and Richard Nixon, however, the take care clause took on a broader interpretation, justifying a wider variety of presidential activities. But was it the intent of the Founding Fathers to interpret the take care clause as conferring such power on the presidency?

4-5a The Founders' Intent: The Take Care Clause

James Madison argued in the House debates over the establishment of the new executive departments that the take care clause meant only that the president should be responsible for the executive departments and that this authority carried with it the power to "inspect and control" the conduct of presidential subordinates (Corwin 1984: 96). Despite Madison's strong statement in support of presidential responsibility, when the departments were first created, Congress did not follow through on this expansive theory of presidential power. Whereas the officials of the Departments of War and State were responsible to the president, the head of the Treasury Department was required to "perform all services relative to finances as he shall be directed to perform." Directed by whom? The clear inference from the legislation is that the new Treasury Secretary would be under the jurisdiction of Congress (ibid.).

When Congress later established the Post Office and the Interior Department, they were likewise placed under the direct control of Congress, though the Navy Department was not. The distinction that Congress drew in these cases was between questions of foreign affairs, where the president was seen as having control, and domestic politics, where authority came from Congress. President James Monroe's Attorney General advanced this narrow interpretation of the president's authority. According to William Wirt in 1823, the president's authority under this provision required only that he bring a criminally negligent official to task for his behavior by either removing him or setting into motion the machinery for impeachment (Corwin 1984: 97).

According to McDonald (1994: 280), "The president's responsibility to 'take care that the laws be faithfully executed' . . . has turned out to be among the least important of his functions." This is true because at "the beginning and through much of the Nineteenth Century, Congress chose to rely upon state and local sheriffs and police to enforce its legislation rather than create a federal enforcement role."

Still, some presidents took their responsibility under this clause quite seriously. For instance, Andrew Jackson adopted a broad interpretation of the take care clause (along with the vesting clause) in defending his decision to remove funds from the Second Bank of the United States. When his Secretary of the Treasury, William Duane, refused to remove the funds, Jackson argued that, "A Secretary, sir, is merely an executive agent, a subordinate. . . ."

Duane countered that, "In this particular case, congress confers a discretionary power, and requires reasons if I exercise it [alluding to the original act establishing the Treasury Department]. Surely this contemplates responsibility on my part" (quoted in Goldsmith 1980: 204).

Jackson removed Duane from office and eventually replaced him with Roger B. Taney, whom Congress refused to confirm. Since the funds were indeed removed, Jackson was victorious in this battle between the executive and legislative branches, but the question of the intent and meaning of the take care clause was not settled.

The essential question in the disagreement between Jackson and Duane was over who was legally charged with taking care that the laws were faithfully executed? Jackson's contention was that he, as president, had that ultimate authority, while Duane argued that Congress placed that authority in the position of the Secretary of the Treasury. Therefore, did ultimate authority reside with the president or with his subordinate?

In 1839, the courts addressed this question in the case of *Kendall v. United States*. The case involved a man who was owed a sum of money by the United States. President Jackson ordered Postmaster General Kendall not to pay the amount owed. This led the man to file suit. In deciding the case, the lower court ruled that the take care clause gave the president "no control over (his subordinate) officer than to see that he acts honestly, with proper motives." It did not give the president the "power to construe the law. . . ." (Corwin 1984: 99). The court also argued that "it would be an alarming doctrine that Congress cannot impose upon any executive officer any duty they may think proper, which is not repugnant to any rights secured and protected by the Constitution; and in such cases, the duty and responsibility grow out of and are subject to the control of the law, and not to the direction of the President" (ibid., 100). The Supreme Court later upheld the lower court's ruling.

Thus, the president's authority under the take care clause was constrained by the courts. As Fisher (1986) argues, "if a statute creates an independent officer and makes the officer's judgment final and conclusive, and the officer faithfully executes the assigned statutory duty, the President's responsibility is at an end." Although the evidence seems to suggest that there are real limits to the president's authority under the take care clause, at least in domestic affairs, the case is not as clear in the realm of foreign affairs.

4-5b The Take Care Clause and Foreign Policy

Accompanying the president's constitutional responsibility as the commander-in-chief of the army and navy is the duty to take care that international laws are faithfully executed. According to Corwin (1984: 224), "From the first . . . it devolves on [the president] to protect American rights and to discharge American duties under the law of nations; and, as commonly happens, the path of duty became in time a road to power."

Thus, as the president's authority as commander-in-chief expanded, the president's authority to "take care that the laws are faithfully executed" likewise increased. Whereas one can argue in the domestic sphere that Congress can delegate authority to a subordinate, and therefore the president's role is at an end, this same argument cannot be as easily advanced with respect to foreign affairs. In that realm, the president holds the ultimate responsibility. No subordinate can have power and authority to disrupt the chain of command in military or diplomatic affairs. As a result of the stronger emphasis on a hierarchy of command in foreign affairs, the presidential claim of authority to "take care that the laws are faithfully executed" is both a potential and real tool for advancing presidential power.

As Robinson (1987) argues, with the expansion of defense and other international pacts following World War II, presidents came to be responsible for taking care that a growing number of international agreements were faithfully executed, thereby providing a greater opportunity for the expansion of presidential power.

Thus, in understanding the scope of the president's authority under the take care clause, it is important to draw a distinction between domestic and foreign affairs. In domestic affairs the power of the president to "take care that the laws are faithfully executed" is more constrained than it is in foreign affairs, though presidents such as Andrew Jackson, and modern presidents like Richard Nixon, adopted a broad interpretation of this authority in domestic as well as foreign affairs. Still, in the area of foreign affairs, presidents clearly have much greater latitude.

4-6 The Presidential Oath of Office

Presidents find power in the most unusual constitutional provisions. For instance, most people see the presidential oath of office as nothing more than an affirmation that presidents must take assuring the public that they will indeed uphold their presidential duties and responsibilities. In this view, the oath is a measure of accountability, of officially accepting duties and responsibilities, rather than a grant of power. But there is another way to interpret the presidential oath.

The oath requires that the president "preserve, protect and defend the Constitution of the United States." Does this provision grant the president additional authority to defend the nation and to make sure that the laws are faithfully executed, or is it simply an affirmation that presidents will not violate their electoral trust with the American people, subject to the sanction of impeachment?

Conservative constitutional scholar Edward Corwin (1984: 69) argues that the oath does not confer any additional authority on the presidency. Not a word was spoken at the Convention, "or afterwards while ratification of the Constitution was pending, so far as I have discovered, that lends any countenance to the idea that the oath would increase presidential powers."

Still, Abraham Lincoln employed the oath as a justification for presidential power. In fact, Lincoln cited the oath as an excuse for *not taking care* that certain laws were faithfully executed—in particular his suspension of the writ of habeus corpus. Lincoln argued that it would be a violation of his oath of office "if the government were overthrown, when it was believed that disregarding the single law, would tend to preserve it" (Basler 1953: Volume IV: 430). Lincoln's argument is given force by the fact that the nation was in the midst of the greatest constitutional crisis in its history, one that threatened its very existence.

4-6a The Oath of Office in Less Dangerous Times

Lincoln's interpretation of the presidential oath of office provided a rationale for his successors to make similar claims in less dangerous times, both with regard to foreign and domestic policy matters. In fact, Lincoln's unfortunate successor similarly employed the oath as a rationale that the Tenure of Office Act should not be carried out (that is, he should not faithfully execute the law). During the impeachment trial of Andrew Johnson, one of his defense attorneys argued that if the president enforced a law which was clearly unconstitutional, and which would have the effect of improperly removing power from the presidency, he would violate the intent of the Founding Fathers; that is, his oath of office would require him to protect the Constitution by not enforcing the law. According to this argument, "The president . . . is bound to execute no such legislation; and he is cowardly and untrue to the responsibilities of his position if he should execute it" (Corwin 1984: 71). The phrase "untrue to the responsibilities of his position" meant among other things, untrue to his oath of office.

Thus, Lincoln and Andrew Johnson provided a clear precedent for their successors, in both war and peace time, in both foreign and domestic affairs. They

President Bill Clinton taking the oath of office in 1997

Clinton Presidential Materials Project.

provided the means for presidents to cite their oath of office as a justification for presidential action or even inaction, to counteract other presidential responsibilities (e.g., the take care clause). Despite the fact that the Founders apparently did not intend for the oath to confer any additional authority on the presidency, it came to be interpreted, at least by some presidents, as a grant of authority.

4-7 Appointment and Supervisory Power

Not all of the powers in the Constitution derive from obscure origins. A more substantial, and certainly a clearer grant of presidential authority than the vesting clause, the take care clause, or the presidential oath of office is the president's appointment power. This provision represents a major grant of authority to presidents, since it allows them to nominate officials who will support their programs and policies. As has been argued elsewhere (Nathan 1983; Waterman 1989; Wood and Waterman 1991), the power of appointment represents the president's greatest single source of potential influence over the bureaucracy and can be of invaluable assistance in promoting the president's political agenda. With the growth of the bureaucratic state, it is a power that has become even more important over time.

The president today nominates approximately 3,000 officials, although presidents usually play a critical role in the nomination of only about 600 of them (see Mackenzie 1981: 5). In addition, Congress over the years augmented presidential appointment power by increasing the size of the federal judiciary and the number of judges that presidents can appoint (Carp and Rowland 1983), as well as establishing new agencies and new positions in existing agencies.

Although some scholars, such as Pfiffner (1986) and Light (1987), argue that this escalation in the number of appointed positions has provided an added burden on the presidency, it also provides presidents with the opportunity to increase their influence over the judiciary and the myriad executive branch agencies, departments, boards, and commissions.

The appointment power does, however, involve some ambiguity. Fisher (1991: 51) notes that it "operates in a framework of studied ambiguity. . . ." This ambiguity derives from the fact that the power is divided between the president and Congress. As Fisher (1991: 52) continues, while the "Senate is often hesitant in challenging and rejecting the names submitted by the President . . . [e]ach Senator has widely different interpretations of the degree of deference that is appropriate." In addition, the legislative branch can place constraints on the positions the president can appoint. In short, the appointment provision can open the door for some ambiguity.

4-7a A Broad but Not Unconstrained Power

Although the president's appointment power is broad, it is not unconstrained. As the Constitution prescribes (see Box 4-2), appointments are to be made subject to the "Advice and Consent of the Senate." Although the Senate has rejected relatively few presidential appointees, this does not mean that the confirmation process is perfunctory or irrelevant. The Senate plays an active role in the confirmation process (Mackenzie 1981; King and Riddlesperger 1987), though as Deering (1987) warns, the Senate's role has been far from systematic with a great deal of variation between congressional committees regarding the amount of time and effort devoted to the confirmation process. Why is there variation?

Fisher (1991: 40) notes, "The Senate's responsibility for confirming presidential nominees, although fixed firmly in the Constitution, remains unsettled in its application." In fact, "for the most part" the Senate "has acted cautiously, uncertain of the scope of its own constitutional power." While Fisher contends that the "source of this uncertainty is not the Constitution," it is clear that the Senate's role in the confirmation process is not clearly delineated, thus leaving open the possibility of considerable flexibility in the implementation of the confirmation phase.

Since the Senate rejected Ronald Reagan's appointment of Robert Bork to the U.S. Supreme Court in the 1980s, the confirmation process has become more political and confrontational. Still, at the same time presidents have derived an even greater power to appoint individuals by avoiding the Senate's "Advice and Consent" role entirely. Presidents Clinton and G. W. Bush and others have used recess appointments, which can be made for limited periods of time to avoid the confirmation process. Furthermore, the establishment, by Congress, of the Executive Office of the President (EOP) and the almost continuous growth since 1939 of the White House Staff provide presidents with considerable influence by increasing the number of important executive positions that can be made without Senate confirmation.

For example, presidents have the power to name a Chief of Staff, one of the most powerful officials in the executive branch, without Senate confirmation. Likewise, the President's Adviser for National Security Affairs does not require senatorial action. Thus, with the development and expansion of the institutional presidency, the president's appointment power was greatly expanded.

On the other hand, Congress has the power to limit presidential discretion in the appointment process. Congress can decide whether certain so-called "inferior" positions are subject to the presidential appointment process. Congress may by law vest the appointment of such inferior officers, as they think proper, in the president alone, in the courts of law, or in the heads of departments. But what is meant by the term "inferior?" Corwin (1984: 91) suggested that it relates to officials who are "subordinate to those whom their appointment is vested." Still, there have been intense debates over which positions Congress can legitimately place in the hands of the Courts or the heads of the Departments.

During the Reagan administration, the so-called Independent Counsel or Special Prosecutor law (for more information, see section 11-5, "The Independent Counsel") was attacked for placing the appointment of this official in the hands of the courts and for not placing the removal power in the president's hands. The Supreme Court ruled that Congress acted properly in placing the appointment authority in the courts. But the case did not definitively define the term "inferior officer."

4-7b Recess Appointments

In addition to the president's appointment of inferior positions, there is also disagreement over the president's authority to make recess appointments. While the Constitution grants the president the authority "to fill up all Vacancies that may happen during the Recess of the Senate, by granting Commissions which shall expire at the End of their next Session" the application of this power has not occurred without controversy. Presidents have used this provision not only to name individuals during the recess of the Senate, but also when the Senate is still in session, thus avoiding the Senate's legitimate confirmation role.

For example, in 1863 Congress rebelled against such practices employed by Abraham Lincoln when it passed legislation prohibiting the use of funds for recess appointments to fill vacancies that exist "while the Senate was in session. . . ." On this point, Senator Fessenden stated, "It may not be in our power to prevent the [recess] appointment [made by Abraham Lincoln], but it is in our power to prevent the payment; and when payment is prevented, I think that will probably put an end to the habit of making such appointments" (quoted in Fisher 1991: 42). Presidents, however, continued to use the practice. For example, Bill Clinton used it when he named a controversial selection (a gay man) to be his Ambassador to Luxembourg.

In short, the presidential appointment process, while clearly less ambiguous than the vesting or take care clauses, has not been implemented without controversy. Interestingly, ambiguity opened the door for both a more active presidential and congressional role.

4-7c The Opinion, in Writing, of the Principal Officers and the Removal Power

Even greater confusion surrounds the question of whether the president's appointment power invests the president with supervisory authority over his subordinates once they assume office. This point is critical because it raises a serious limitation with regard to the president's appointment power. While the president has the authority to appoint individuals to government, the Constitution does not unambiguously provide the president with the power to supervise these individuals once they take office. As Fenno's (1959) study of the president's cabinet demonstrates, the lack of an adequate supervisory power can be a major constraint, limiting presidents in their efforts to control the political agenda.

In section 4-5, "The Take Care Clause," we examined one constitutional provision relating to the president's supervisory powers, the take care clause. Another is the provision that the president "may require the Opinion, in writing, of the principal Officer in each of the executive Departments, upon any Subject relating to the Duties of their respective Offices. . . ." Under this provision, presidents can constitutionally request information from their subordinates, but cannot constitutionally control these very same officials. In short, there is no constitutional stipulation that presidents have the right to set priorities or otherwise direct their officers to obey their will.

In the case of *Kendall v. United States*, the Supreme Court ruled that for an executive official to follow the president's intent in clear contradiction of congressional intent would provide the president with a power entirely to control the legislation of Congress, which in turn would "paralyze the administration of justice" (Corwin 1984: 420). Hence, following the will of the president was not a sufficient reason for presidential subordinates to disobey the will of Congress. Under this more restricted view, the idea that presidents can acquire the written comments of subordinates merely seems to suggest that presidents can require their subordinates to consult with them. As Corwin (1984: 97) argues, there is no suggestion that this consultation was to be done in a joint session, such as through the Cabinet, or that it was to involve a strict hierarchy of presidential control.

To secure the cooperation of executive branch officials after appointment then, presidents were forced to cite their constitutional authority under the executive vesting and take care clauses. But as we saw in sections 4-4 and 4-5, these clauses themselves are open to widely different interpretations. Given the president's weak constitutional supervisory power over subordinate officials, it was thus necessary that presidents have the power to remove recalcitrant appointees from office; for this would provide presidents with a powerful sanction over subordinates who would not follow the will of the president. But with regard to the president's removal power (the obverse of the appointment power), the Constitution was silent. In Federalist #77, Alexander Hamilton stated,

> The consent of [the Senate] would be necessary to displace as well as to appoint. A change of the chief magistrate therefore would not occasion so violent or so general a revolution in the officers of the government, as might be expected if he were the

sole disposer of offices. Where a man in any station had given satisfactory evidence of his fitness for it, a new president would be restrained from attempting a change, in favour [sic] of a person more agreeable to him, by the apprehension that the discountenance of the senate might frustrate the attempt, and bring some degree of discredit upon himself.

Hamilton's narrow interpretation of the president's removal power was soon challenged. The first Congress of the United States, in deciding the structure and scope of the first executive departments, squarely addressed the question of the president's removal authority. James Madison argued that presidents should be able to remove appointed officials: If the removal power was vested jointly in the Senate and the presidency, it would destroy the "great principle of unity and responsibility in the Executive department, which was intended for the security of liberty and the public good" (quoted in Fisher 1978: 53).

Congress agreed and provided the president with the authority to remove appointed officials from the executive departments. Alexander Hamilton, who was a supporter of the strong presidency model, later came to agree with this position. In a memorandum to President George Washington, he argued that the "executive power of the United States is completely lodged in the President . . . of which the power of removal from office is an important instance" (quoted in Goldsmith 1980: 182).

Despite Hamilton's change of heart, the question of the extent of the president's removal authority has been debated throughout our nation's history. Congress rebelled when Andrew Jackson became the first president to extensively employ this power. On several occasions, Congress passed legislation specifically designed to limit presidential removal power. In the most notorious case, the Tenure of Office Act of 1867, congressional displeasure with Andrew Johnson led to his impeachment, though not his removal from office.

4-7d Challenging the Removal Power

Although Rossiter (1960: 20) characterized the president's removal authority as the "gun behind the door," it is a gun that has been periodically unloaded and reloaded by Congress and the courts. Far from being a clear delegation of supervisory authority to the president, it often has been a hotbed of contention between the executive and legislative branches.

The Supreme Court did not address the removal question in depth until 1926, when former President, and then Chief Justice, William Howard Taft, in the case of *Myers v. United States* [272 U.S. 52 (1926)], provided a broad rationale for the presidential removal of subordinates. In 1935, however, the Supreme Court greatly angered President Franklin Roosevelt by recapturing some of this power in the case of *Humphrey's Executor v. United States* [295 U.S. 602 (1935)], thus allowing Congress to set the terms for certain appointees and prevent the president from removing them before the end of their term (the case involved the Federal Trade Commission; presidents cannot summarily remove commissioners).

In sum, the president has expansive authority to nominate individuals to the executive branch, with some important constraints, but does not possess a clear constitutional supervisory authority over them once they assume office. This fact can greatly constrain presidential influence over the bureaucracy. Since Richard Nixon's presidency, however, with the evolution of the "administrative presidency" (Nathan 1983), based on a broad interpretation of the president's appointment power (see section 13-6, "Declining Political Party Influences and New Structures for Presidential Transitions," and section 15-1, "How Internal and Informational

Resources Can Increase Presidential Influence: The Case of Presidential Appointments"), presidents exerted increased supervisory influence over the administrative state and a more prominent, even strategic role in the removal of subordinates. Hence, the ambiguity of the president's authority as chief executive promoted alternate interpretations of presidential power at different times in our history. Under such administrations as Richard Nixon and Ronald Reagan, however, the broadest possible interpretation of these constitutional powers was adopted.

4-8 Chief Legislator

In domestic affairs, the Constitution also provides for the president to play a legislative role. According to Wayne (1978: 2), "The Constitution requires the president to perform only a few legislative duties. Designing an annual legislative program and exerting influence to get it adopted were not part of these original responsibilities. . . . The framers of the Constitution did not envision the president as chief legislator." Rather, the Founders intended for the presidency to provide a check on the power of the legislative branch. Consequently, the presidency was delegated little constitutional authority to initiate legislation, although it was granted broader power to negate congressional activity through the presidential veto.

4-8a State of the Union

Beyond the negative role of a veto, presidents partake of an active role in the legislative process only by claiming the broadest possible interpretation of the few provisions that relate to presidential authority in legislative matters. In the area of law making, it is clear that the Constitution intended that Congress should assume the primary role. This did not mean, however, that presidents would have no authority or input in legislative matters. Just as the legislature exerted some executive power, such as the Senate's role in the appointment process, the president was granted some limited legislative authority. These constitutional delegations of authority did not allow presidents to make laws, but rather provided them with the ability to recommend legislation to Congress and to negate legislative action through the veto process.

The fact that the Constitution granted the president only a limited role in the legislative process greatly explains why the presidential role in legislative matters was so constrained throughout most of the nineteenth century. Presidents simply did not perceive their job description as including the task of proposing legislation or advocating a specific presidential agenda. When a few early presidents attempted to do so, such as John Quincy Adams, Congress largely ignored them.

The Constitution does not grant presidents extraordinary power to initiate legislation or to promote a presidential agenda. Two sections of the Constitution do provide presidents with some potential influence: the provisions that the president shall report on the state of the union and that the president can recommend to the legislative branch "such measures as he shall judge necessary and expedient. . . ."

The requirement that presidents shall report on the state of the union was not principally employed as a means of promoting presidential authority until Grover Cleveland advanced his views on the tariff question. Later, Woodrow Wilson became the first president since John Adams to personally present the state of the union message directly to Congress. Prior to Wilson's presidency, a clerk read the address aloud. With Wilson's innovation, both the president and his speech received greater media and public visibility. As such, the state of the union address had a much greater potential to impact the views of the members of Congress, as well as the American public (see section 7-6, "Woodrow Wilson's Innovations").

4-8b Recommending Legislation

A more substantial grant of presidential authority than the state of the union was the provision that presidents have the right to recommend legislation to Congress, a right that could be interpreted broadly to mean that presidents have a constitutional right to propose legislative initiatives of their own—that is, in effect, to propose a legislative agenda to Congress. But the power to recommend legislation does not guarantee influence, and Congress can simply ignore presidential requests, as they often do. Furthermore, there was nothing inherent in the clause that forced presidents to adopt a broad interpretation of presidential power. In fact, until the dawn of the twentieth century, most presidents adopted a limited view of the president's authority to make recommendations to Congress.

The most extreme view was espoused by William Henry Harrison, one of the principal purveyors of the Whig philosophy of limited presidential power (see section 3-2g, "William Henry Harrison and the Whig Conception of the Presidency"). In his 1841 Inaugural Address, Harrison stated that the power to recommend was "a privilege which [the president] holds in common with every other citizen, and although there may be something more of confidence in the propriety of the measures recommended in the one case than in the other, in the obligations of ultimate decision there can be no difference" (quoted in Fisher 1981: 22).

Harrison's narrow view of the president's authority ignores the fact that the president, by the very virtue of his propinquity to Congress, is likely to have much greater potential influence with the legislative branch than any other citizen outside Congress. Harrison's view also is not fully consistent with precedent established up till his own time, as several presidents already had adopted an active role in recommending legislation to Congress.

President George Washington expressed his ideas for a national militia to Congress through his intermediary, Secretary of War Henry Knox. Washington also on occasion met personally with members of Congress to discuss pending legislation, often inviting them to dine with him. Thomas Jefferson also drafted legislation, which was then introduced by friendly members of Congress who often had been wined and dined at the White House. Additionally, Andrew Jackson played an active role in the fight over the renewal of the charter for the Second Bank of the United States. Consequently, presidents before Harrison occasionally played an active role in the legislative process. Still, it was not until Woodrow Wilson that the president emerged as a real chief legislator.

Because the recommending provision is not specific, presidents were able to interpret it either broadly, as Woodrow Wilson and most of his successors did, or narrowly, as William Henry Harrison did. The recommending provision thus provided a rationale for the more active presidential role in the legislative process during the twentieth century, just as it had justified a more limited role during much of the nineteenth century. The recommending function took on an even greater role following major congressional delegations of authority to the president, such as the Budget and Accounting Act of 1921, which requires that the president report a budget to Congress each year. The Employment Act of 1946 also required that the president report on the state of the economy each year. Hence, with congressional acquiescence the president's recommending function expanded over time.

4-8c Convening and Adjourning Congress

In addition to the constitutional provisions related to the state of the union message and the president's right to make recommendations to Congress, presidents also have the constitutional authority to force Congress to **convene** when it has adjourned, a provision that has become less influential over time, as Congress now meets throughout most of its two-year session. Harry Truman took advantage of this provision to call the so-called "Do Nothing Congress" back into session in the summer of 1948, a tactic to advance his re-election chances.

Abraham Lincoln delayed the convocation of Congress from April 12 to July 4, 1861, thus providing himself with a twelve-week period of "executive grace" in which to initiate his war preparation agenda (Schlesinger 1973: 58). Related to the power to convene is the constitutional authority to **adjourn** Congress, which the president can do when there is a disagreement between the House of Representatives and the Senate regarding the time of adjournment. As with the power to convene Congress, this provision has been little used.

4-8d The Veto Power

A much more substantial enumeration of legislative authority is provided in Article I, Section 7 of the Constitution, which grants the president the power to veto legislation (see Box 4-2). Although it is primarily a negative power—that is, it is the power to negate action and not to initiate it—the veto power is one of the president's most effective legislative tools. It is much more clearly delineated than most of the Article II powers. Still, even here ambiguity exists. For much of our history, there was considerable debate over the legitimate extent of the president's veto authority, and many presidents as a result were reluctant to employ it.

At the Constitutional Convention, the Founding Fathers debated three options (see Figure 4-2):

1. to deny the president any veto;
2. to have the president share the veto with a council of judicial officials; and
3. to grant the president alone the veto power.

According to Wayne (1978: 7), "The . . . history of legislative dominance [under the ineffective Articles of Confederation] made the first and second alternatives unacceptable."

The framers did not want to replicate the mistakes of the Articles, in which an ineffective legislature dominated. Consequently, many of the men at the Constitutional Convention came to believe that a strong independent executive was vital to the operation of the new government and to the protection of basic freedoms. A president denied the power to veto legislation would be at the mercy of Congress. By granting presidents the veto power, the framers placed a valuable tool for constraining legislative initiative. But the Founders felt that an unlimited veto power was unacceptable. As a result, the framers adopted a limited veto, where presidents could veto legislation subject to a two-thirds override in each House. The courts later interpreted this to mean two-thirds of all members present and not two-thirds of all congressional members.

The fact that the Founders considered the veto to be an important tool in the president's legislative arsenal does not mean that they intended presidents to employ the technique frequently. In fact, the opposite conclusion seems to be supported from an examination of the Federalist papers. In Federalist #73, Alexander Hamilton wrote, "If a magistrate, so powerful and so well fortified as a British monarch, would have scruples about the exercise of the power under considera-

Convene: To bring Congress back into session after it has adjourned. Presidents have the constitutional authority to use this provision, which has become less influential over time, as Congress now meets throughout most of its two-year session.

Adjourn: When Congress ends a session. Presidents have this constitutional authority when there is a disagreement between the House of Representatives and the Senate regarding the time of adjournment. As with the power to convene Congress, this provision is little used.

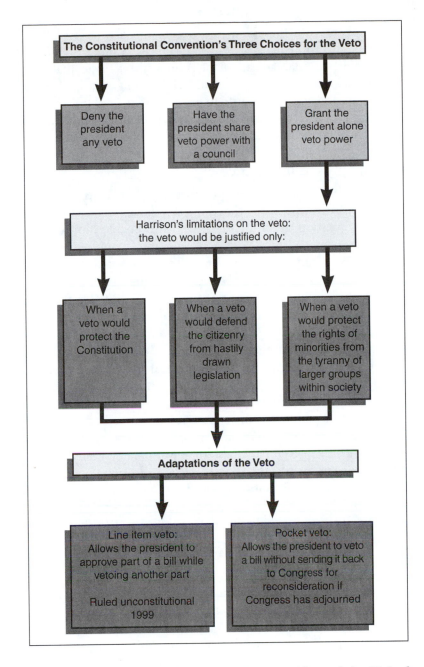

The Constitutional Convention's Three Choices for the Veto

Deny the president any veto

Have the president share veto power with a council

Grant the president alone veto power

Harrison's limitations on the veto: the veto would be justified only:

When a veto would protect the Constitution

When a veto would defend the citizenry from hastily drawn legislation

When a veto would protect the rights of minorities from the tyranny of larger groups within society

Adaptations of the Veto

Line item veto: Allows the president to approve part of a bill while vetoing another part

Ruled unconstitutional 1999

Pocket veto: Allows the president to veto a bill without sending it back to Congress for reconsideration if Congress has adjourned

Figure 4-2
Three Choices for the Veto

tion, how much greater may be reasonably expected in a President of the United States, cloathed *[sic]* for the short period of four years with the executive authority of a government wholly and purely republican?"

If the Founding Fathers did not intend for presidents to make unlimited use of the veto power, when did they believe presidents would use it? This question has promoted considerable debate over the past two centuries. William Henry Harrison explained the Whig philosophy on the president's veto power. It was "preposterous" to believe that presidents better understood the needs and wishes of the citizenry than the members of Congress. The presidential veto power was therefore justified only under certain limited circumstances:

1. when a veto would protect the Constitution,
2. when it would defend the citizenry from hastily drawn legislation, and
3. when a veto would protect the rights of minorities from the tyranny of larger groups within society (Fisher 1978: 86).

Another Whig President, Zachary Taylor, also argued that the veto power should be used only in extreme circumstances (Sundquist 1981: 23–24).

Such presidential claims, and the Founders' clear belief that the veto power would not be employed extensively, led some scholars (e.g., Black 1976) to argue that presidents should mainly use the veto to protect and defend the integrity of the presidential office. But is this interpretation appropriate? To answer this question we can look for guidance to the Founders and to the experience of the first several presidents.

4-8e The Veto in Practice

In Federalist #73, while arguing that the president's veto power would be seldom used, Alexander Hamilton stated, "The primary inducement to conferring the power in question upon the executive, is to enable him to defend himself. . . ." Hamilton expressed the fear that a legislature could emasculate the president's authority by a mere one-vote majority. The veto would protect the presidency from legislative encroachment. This defense of the veto power is consistent with Harrison's narrow constitutional interpretation. But Hamilton did not stop there. He also stated that a secondary reason for employing the veto power "is to encrease [sic] the chances in favor of the community, against the passing of bad laws, through haste, inadvertence [sic], or design." This too is consistent with Harrison's reasoning, though the practical questions of when law is hastily drawn and when the citizenry requires defending are more ambiguous points.

The experience of the first six presidents also provides evidence regarding the intent of the Founding Fathers, particularly since both George Washington and James Madison were present at the Constitutional Convention. Washington was the first president to employ the veto power. The first bill he vetoed was on constitutional grounds, while the second was issued on the basis that the bill was carelessly drawn, unwise in substance, and thus not worthy of becoming a law (Fisher 1978: 86). This second veto extended the veto power beyond a narrow focus on protecting the presidential office.

The next president to employ the veto power and another Founding Father, James Madison, also expressed policy concerns. Of the five bills that he vetoed, four were rejected because of constitutional concerns, while one (a bill relating to the national bank) was rejected because Madison felt it was so poorly designed as to be incapable of accomplishing its purpose (ibid.).

According to Fisher (1978: 87), "During this initial period of twenty-eight years, covering four presidents and seven administrations, there were seven regular vetoes, five of them for constitutional reasons. Only one affected the independence of the executive: the district courts bill, which Madison vetoed in part because he thought it usurped his appointment powers." Thus, the record of the early presidents, while supporting the belief that presidents would not often employ the veto power, does not entirely support the conclusion that vetoes would be justified on the basis of protecting the integrity of the presidential office. Early presidents made judgments regarding the quality of legislation as well, and they were clearly concerned with "preventing bad laws."

4-8f A Broader Interpretation over Time

Over time, presidents did come to employ the veto technique more often than the Founders originally had intended. As can be seen in Table 4-2, following the Civil War, Andrew Johnson, in his attempts to halt the Radical Republican's Reconstruction program, employed the technique almost 30 times. Ulysses S. Grant, Grover Cleveland, and their immediate successors made regular use of their

T A B L E **4-2** Presidential Vetoes from 1789 through 1998

President	Regular Vetoes	Vetoes Overridden	Pocket Vetoes	Total Vetoes
Washington	2	0	0	2
Adams	0	0	0	0
Jefferson	0	0	0	0
Madison	5	0	2	7
Monroe	1	0	0	1
J. Q. Adams	0	0	0	0
Jackson	5	0	7	12
Van Buren	0	0	1	1
W. H. Harrison	0	0	0	0
Tyler	6	1	4	10
Polk	2	0	1	3
Taylor	0	0	0	0
Fillmore	0	0	0	0
Pierce	9	5	0	9
Buchanan	4	0	3	7
Lincoln	2	0	5	7
A. Johnson	21	15	8	29
Grant	45	4	48	93
Hayes	12	1	1	13
Garfield	0	0	0	0
Arthur	4	1	8	12
Cleveland	304	2	110	414
B. Harrison	19	1	25	44
Cleveland	42	5	128	170
McKinley	6	0	36	42
T. Roosevelt	42	1	40	82
Taft	30	1	9	39
Wilson	33	6	11	44
Harding	5	0	1	6
Coolidge	20	4	30	50
Hoover	21	3	16	37
F. Roosevelt	372	9	263	635
Truman	180	12	70	250
Eisenhower	73	2	108	181
Kennedy	12	0	9	21
L. Johnson	16	0	14	30
Nixon	26	7	17	43
Ford	48	12	18	66
Carter	13	2	18	31
Reagan	39	9	39	78
G. H. W. Bush	29	1	17	46
Clinton	25	2	0	25

Source: Stanley and Niemi. 2000. *Vital Statistics on American Politics 1999–2000*, p. 256.

veto power, with Franklin Roosevelt employing it the most—635 times in just over twelve years. While presidents since FDR's time have not employed it as often, Truman did exercise his veto power 250 times; Eisenhower, 181; Ford, 66; and Reagan, 78 times. Likely, the Founders did not envision such a frequent use of the veto power. But then the Founders could not have fully envisioned the industrialization of America and the changing demands on government that occurred in the late nineteenth and early twentieth centuries. As Fisher (1978: 84) states, with regard to the use of the veto power, "the framers could not have anticipated the vast range of activities to be carried out by the federal government, the outpouring of legislation that resulted, and the great mass of private bills."

The Founding Fathers also did not envision the evolution of political parties, which have provided major organized support and resistance to the president in Congress. Nor did they conceive of the possibility that Congress would place extraneous matter within bills (riders), that is, legal non sequitors, as a means of forcing presidents to adopt measures they believed were inappropriate. The framers also did not envision the possibility that presidents would employ variations on a line-item veto, such as signing legislation while sending a separate message to Congress in which they disagree with a particular section of the bill (Andrew Jackson was the first president to do this) or simply refusing to perform a particular function incorporated in a bill (a seeming violation of the take care clause). The line-item veto itself, enacted by Congress in 1996, was ruled unconstitutional by the Supreme Court in 1999. As the nature of our *political ecosystem* changed (see section 11-1, "The Presidency and the Political Ecosystem"), both the legislative and executive branches designed new mechanisms in an attempt to increase their influence over the legislative process. This altered the manner in which the veto power is employed beyond anything the Founders originally envisioned.

4-8g The Pocket Veto

Pocket veto: A president's ability to veto a bill without sending it back to Congress for reconsideration if Congress has adjourned.

Session: The two-year time period in which Congress meets. Every two years, a new House of Representatives is elected, as well as one-third of the Senate. The newly elected Congress then governs within a two-year session.

Beyond the debate over the questions of how often, when, and how the Founders intended the president to employ the veto power, there also has been debate over one other aspect of this authority: the **pocket veto.** Under which circumstances could a president pocket veto a bill—that is, veto a bill without sending it back to Congress for reconsideration if Congress has adjourned? But what does adjournment mean? Does adjournment mean the end of a congressional session or merely a short period in which Congress is not currently in **session?** If the latter, then could presidents pocket veto a bill when Congress is on a break, such as at Christmas or Easter vacation?

The first use of the pocket veto (see Table 4-2) was by James Madison, who used it twice. Andrew Jackson then used it 7 times. The first president to make extensive use of the pocket veto was Ulysses S. Grant, who exercised it 48 times. Cleveland had 238 pocket vetoes in his two nonconsecutive terms as president, while Franklin Roosevelt used it 263 and Eisenhower 108 times.

In issuing pocket vetoes, several presidents tried to determine what exactly constitutes an adjourning Congress. Franklin Roosevelt pocket vetoed a bill when Congress was on adjournment for only three days. In the case of *Wright v. United States*, the Supreme Court ruled that a pocket veto could be employed only if the Secretary of the Senate did not have the authority to receive the president's message. This interpretation concluded that a three-day adjournment was not sufficient for a president to employ the pocket veto, but it failed to provide an exact demarcation point. Thus, it was possible that the president could pocket veto a bill during a thirty-day inter-session adjournment (Schlesinger 1973: 242–43). In the mid-1970s, the courts finally settled the question by deciding in the case of

Kennedy v. Sampson that a pocket veto could be employed only during the final adjournment of Congress—that is, following the end of the second congressional session (Fisher 1981: 25). This decision provided an unambiguous definition and a clear boundary for the president's pocket veto authority.

4-8h A Powerful Tool

The veto power is a powerful presidential tool. Congress overrides relatively few vetoes. In sum, as this examination of the provisions dealing with the president's constitutionally delegated legislative authority suggests, presidents have little affirmative constitutional authority to promote their legislative initiatives. Their greatest single power is a negative one, the veto power, which can block congressional action. Real presidential authority over legislative matters has come, not from the Constitution, but from congressional delegations of authority to the executive branch, particularly through the Budget and Accounting Act of 1921 and the Employment Act of 1946.

Recent broad interpretations of the president's legislative role, such as Kernell's (1986) idea of presidents "going public"—that is, over the heads of the members of Congress—derive not from any specific constitutionally enumerated power but from the idea that presidents can speak directly to the people (a democratic notion the Founders found most unacceptable). Hence, the development of an active presidential role in legislative affairs derives more from extra-constitutional presidential powers and the use of the negative power of the veto, than from any positive powers enumerated in the U.S. Constitution.

Chapter Summary

In this chapter, we examined the ambiguity of the president's constitutional authority, primarily in the area of domestic policy. Constitutional ambiguity is an important subject because without it there would be little potential for a changing presidency over time, that is, without fundamental constitutional amendment. As the level of ambiguity increases, however, it is possible to change the power of the presidency without constitutional amendment. All that is required are new perceptions of presidential power—that is, new expectations regarding what presidents should or should not be able to do—and a creative interpretation of the existing, nebulous constitutional provisions. We have seen that this informal revision of the Constitution has occurred continuously throughout our nation's history, and we can speculate that it is likely to continue.

Hence, *while the actual words related to the presidency in the Constitution have changed very little over time, our perceptions of them have been greatly altered.* We now perceive the meaning of the president's constitutional powers in vastly different ways than did the Founders in 1787 or for that matter the politicians of 1887. *Our perception of the Constitution is in a state of constant change, always evolving, always providing opportunities for the development of new presidential powers.* This is a point we will address as well in the next chapter as we turn our primary focus to the president's foreign policy constitutional powers.

Review Questions

1. Which of the following presidential roles is largely ceremonial?
   a. chief of state
   b. commander-in-chief
   c. chief of staff
   d. chief diplomat

2. Presidential power is discussed in
   a. Article I.
   b. Article II.
   c. Article III.
   d. Article's I and III.

3. Most of the debate about the presidency surrounded which two issues?
   a. presidential power and the method of selection
   b. presidential power and a plural presidency
   c. the method of selection and impeachment
   d. the method of selection and a plural presidency

4. The Virginian Plan
   a. had a detailed plan for presidential power.
   b. had only vague notions of what the presidents would do.
   c. had only vague notions of what the Congress would do.
   d. had a detailed plan for the powers of the president and Congress.

5. In comparison to the powers of Congress, the president's powers are
   a. more detailed.
   b. about as detailed.
   c. more ambiguous.
   d. about as ambiguous.

6. The most defective part of the Constitution relates to
   a. the method of presidential selection.
   b. the powers of the legislative branch.
   c. the powers of the judicial branch.
   d. the powers of the executive branch.

7. Which of the following is an introduction to the powers of the executive branch?
   a. the preamble
   b. the vesting clause
   c. Genesis
   d. the Prologue

8. The take care clause provides
   a. that presidents will faithfully execute the law.
   b. that presidents will execute the law subject to review by the cabinet.
   c. that presidents can be impeached and removed from office.
   d. that presidents have great latitude in carrying out the law.

9. Which of the following requires presidents to preserve, protect, and defend the Constitution?
   a. the law
   b. the preamble
   c. the vesting clause
   d. the oath of office

10. In which case did the Supreme Court rule that for an executive official to follow the president's intent in clear contradiction of congressional intent would provide the president with a power entirely to control the legislation of Congress, which in turn would "paralyze the administration of justice"?
   a. *Kendall v. United States*
   b. *Madison v. Maybury*
   c. *Humphrey's Executor v. United States*
   d. *Gore v. Bush*

11. In 1926, in the case of *Myers v. United States*, the Supreme Court provided a broad rationale for the presidential removal of subordinates. In 1935, however, the Supreme Court greatly angered President Franklin Roosevelt and recaptured some of the president's removal power in the case of _____ [295 U.S. 602 (1935)], thus allowing Congress to set the terms for certain appointees and prevent the president from removing these officials before the end of their term.
   a. *Kendall v. United States*
   b. *Madison v. Maybury*
   c. *Humphrey's Executor v. United States*
   d. *Gore v. Bush*

12. Who of the following presidents became the first president since John Adams to deliver the state of the union address in person?
   a. Thomas Jefferson
   b. Theodore Roosevelt
   c. William Howard Taft
   d. Woodrow Wilson

Discussion Questions

1. Why are the provisions related to the power of the presidency ambiguous?
2. How could the Founders have made the presidential powers less ambiguous and more concrete?
3. What is the effect of having ambiguous presidential power?
4. Does the ambiguous power of the presidency provide an opportunity for increasing presidential power, or does it serve to limit presidential power?

Chapter

The Constitution and Foreign Policy

Key Terms

chief diplomat
extra-constitutional powers

5-1 The Constitution and Foreign Policy

Which branch of the United States government has primacy in the field of foreign affairs? Corwin (1984: 201) writes,

> Where does the Constitution vest authority to determine the course of the United States as a sovereign entity at international law with respect to matters in which other similar entities may choose to take an interest? Many persons are inclined to answer offhand "in the President"; but they would be hard put to it, if challenged, to point out any definite statement to this effect in the Constitution itself. What the Constitution does, and all that it does, is to confer on the President certain powers capable of affecting our foreign relations, and certain other powers of the same general kind on the Senate, and still other such powers on Congress; but which of these organs shall have the decisive and final voice in determining the course of the American nation is left for events to resolve.

In this chapter, we examine the question of who, under the Constitution, controls foreign policy. We begin with an examination of the constitutional authority of the U.S. Congress.

5-1a Congress, the Constitution, and Foreign Policy

In Box 4-1, "Congress's Constitutional Power," we found that the Constitution grants Congress considerable and detailed authority in the realm of domestic affairs. The same is true of Congress's foreign policy powers. The Constitution grants Congress the following authority in foreign policy: Congress has the authority to regulate commerce with foreign nations, to "define and punish Piracies and Felonies committed on the high Seas, and Offences against the Law of Nations; To declare War, grant Letters of Marque and Reprisal [a form of small or limited war], and make Rules concerning Captures on Land and Water; To raise and support Armies . . ." and "To provide and maintain a Navy" (see Figure 5-1).

Congress also has the authority to call "forth the Militia to execute the Laws of the Union, suppress Insurrections and repel Invasions," as well as organize, arm, and discipline the militia and govern "such Part of them as may be employed in the Service of the United States. . . ." Congress also has the power of the purse. It can approve or deny funding for presidential initiatives in foreign affairs. It can make new laws or change existing ones, subject, of course, to a presidential veto. In addition to these powers, the Senate also shares certain authority with the president, particularly with regard to the making of treaties and appointments.

Taken together, these enumerated powers represent a potentially greater amalgam of authority than do the enumerated presidential powers. Indeed, some members of the Constitutional Convention feared that the legislative branch would dominate foreign affairs. As a result, additional authority was added to the presidency at the last minute (e.g., the treaty-making power). Furthermore, by dividing foreign policy authority between the president and Congress, the Founding Fathers created a constitutional system that Corwin (1984: 201) called "an invitation to struggle for the privilege of directing American foreign policy." Initially, it was a struggle that favored the legislative branch.

5-1b Congress Dominant in the Nineteenth Century

Schlesinger (1973) argues that Congress was the dominant player in foreign policy during the nineteenth century. A bellicose Congress, spurred on by Representative and perennial presidential hopeful Henry Clay, forced a reluctant President James Madison into open conflict with the British in 1812. Congress also exerted pressure

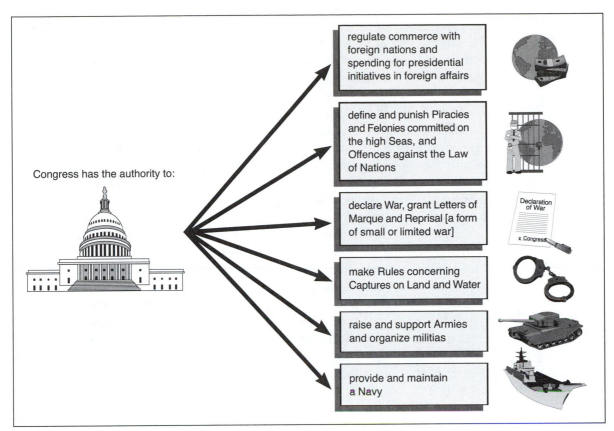

Congress has the authority to:

- regulate commerce with foreign nations and spending for presidential initiatives in foreign affairs
- define and punish Piracies and Felonies committed on the high Seas, and Offences against the Law of Nations
- declare War, grant Letters of Marque and Reprisal [a form of small or limited war]
- make Rules concerning Captures on Land and Water
- raise and support Armies and organize militias
- provide and maintain a Navy

Figure 5-1
The Authority of Congress in Foreign Policy

on William McKinley to go to war with Spain in 1898. Congress played an active role in the treaty-making process and dominated the major foreign policy issue of the century: the tariff. In fact, Congress jealously guarded its power to set tariff rates.

There were, however, important exceptions. In 1798, John Adams ignored pressure from congressional partisans in the Federalist Party to go to war with France. Grover Cleveland likewise refused to go to war with Spain over Cuba, despite pressure from Congress to fight. On the other hand, James Polk initiated war without congressional approval between the United States and Mexico and threatened to go to war with Great Britain over Canada during the 1840s. Abraham Lincoln provided additional precedents for the accretion of presidential war power: Though it was a civil war and not a war with a foreign foe, the president acted as commander-in-chief for three months without calling Congress into session. But even after Polk's and Lincoln's presidencies, Congress quickly reasserted its domination of both domestic and foreign policy.

Even during the twentieth century, Congress played a primary role in formulating foreign policy. Following the Senate's rejection of Woodrow Wilson's Treaty of Versailles, Congress dominated foreign policy throughout the 1920s and 1930s (see section 9-6c, "Presidential Influence Further Expands"). Even as powerful a president as Franklin Roosevelt was forced to compromise with an isolationist Congress in order to advance such key programs as Lend-Lease. Thus, while today's presidents have great power in foreign policy, this has not always been the case. How then did the president emerge as the dominant player in foreign policy? As I argued in section 4-3, "Constitutional Ambiguity," the very ambiguity of the Constitution has contributed to periods of congressional and presidential dominance. Because there is ambiguity in the Constitution's provisions, there is ample room for the actual influence of Congress and the president to be altered by changing expectations of both the public and political elites. This is so because the few constitutional provisions that deal directly with presidential authority can be interpreted narrowly or broadly.

5-1c The Sole Organ of the Federal Government

Should the president play the dominant role in foreign policy? This question has been much debated and often vastly misunderstood. In 1799, in congressional debate, then Representative and future Chief Justice of the Supreme Court, John Marshall, stated that the president was the sole organ of the United States in dealings with other nations. Corwin (1984: 208) interprets Marshall's comment as meaning only that the president was the sole "instrument of communication with other governments." But in a 1936 Supreme Court case, the *United States v. Curtis-Wright Corporation et al.* [299 U.S. 304 (1936)], Justice Sutherland invoked Marshall's phrase. He drew a fundamental distinction between the powers of the presidency in the area of foreign and domestic affairs. In so doing, he provided the presidency with new and expanded power. Sutherland wrote, "The broad statement that the federal government can exercise no powers except those specifically enumerated in the Constitution and such implied powers as are necessary and proper to carry into effect the enumerated powers, is categorically true only in respect of our internal affairs." Sutherland concluded that the powers of external sovereignty passed from the British crown to the U.S. government as a collective entity, rather than to several states. As a result, the government spoke with one voice, with the president as the sole organ of the government in its relations with other nations. Sutherland concluded, the "President alone has the power to speak or listen as a representative of the nation." Since the president has superior information and confidential sources, it is the president who is best equipped to deal with foreign nations.

Sutherland's conclusions were based on a dubious reading of British and American history. For example, he mistakenly claims that President Washington "refused to accede to a request to lay before the House of Representatives the instructions, correspondence and documents relating to the negotiation of the Jay Treaty"—Washington, in fact, did turn over the documents to the House. As Schlesinger (1973: 103) notes, while Sutherland's opinion was grossly at odds with the intent of the Founding Fathers and the historical record, the opinion itself has been misinterpreted by later scholars and political officials, of whom Iran-Contra conspirator Oliver North may be the most famous example. *Curtis-Wright* involved only "the power to act under congressional authorization, not the power to act independently of Congress." Furthermore, the individual case involved "the power over foreign commerce, not the power over war." Thus, many modern interpretations of the president's authority under the *Curtis-Wright* decision, like the decision itself, have involved an exceedingly broad interpretation or misinterpretation of presidential power. To better understand this point, we need to examine the constitutional provisions related to the president's role in foreign affairs.

5-2 Chief Diplomat: To Receive Ambassadors and Other Public Ministers

Several constitutional provisions relate to the president's role as **chief diplomat**. The Constitution states that the president shall "receive Ambassadors and other public Ministers. . . ." This function can be largely ceremonial, a mere "formality" as Thach (1969) argues it was intended to be, or it can involve tangible influence.

Chief diplomat: One of the "hats" or tasks of the presidency, as identified by historian Clinton Rossiter. It involves the president's diplomatic functions, including those functions covered by the Constitution involving treaty making and receiving foreign dignitaries.

In Federalist #69, Alexander Hamilton stated that the provision that the president should meet with foreign ambassadors is "more a matter of dignity than of authority." Rather than envisioning this role as a foundation for real influence and power, Hamilton argued that the Founders assigned this role to the president for the sake of convenience: "[I]t was far more convenient that it should be arranged in this manner, than that there should be a necessity of convening the legislature, or one of its branches, upon every arrival of a foreign minister; though it were merely to take the place of a departed predecessor."

Although it may have been meant as a mere convenience, the specification that the president is the sole organ of the American government authorized to meet with foreign dignitaries carries with it potentially greater authority than the Founders may either have intended or understood. Yet, the fact that the Constitution is not specific is of critical importance. In the modern world, the fact that presidents meet with foreign leaders provides them with information, prestige, a prominent place on the world stage, and ultimately considerable power and influence.

Clarification of the Constitution's meaning began with our first president. According to historian James Flexner (1970: 215), when the French King notified Washington and Congress of the death of the Dauphin, Washington responded that "the honour of receiving and answering" such communications no longer involved the Congress, but was the president's duty alone. By this act, Washington protected his right to receive information from foreign dignitaries, as well as the dignitaries themselves, and provided a precedent for the later claim that the president was the "sole organ" of the nation in its communications with foreign nations.

Thus, inadvertently or not, by specifying the president as the sole individual who would meet with the representatives of foreign nations, the Founders provided a rationale for the later argument, expressed in *Curtis-Wright*, that the president is the only official under the Constitution who is provided with the authority to communicate with other nations. Although members of Congress meet with foreign leaders on a regular basis, they do not speak for the nation as a whole when they do so. Only the president is perceived to have that right.

5-2a Recognizing Other Nations

The provision that the president shall receive ambassadors and other foreign dignitaries also means that presidents have the right to decide whether to recognize foreign dignitaries and thus the governments that they represent. This interpretation of the president's duty to receive foreign dignitaries provides presidents with tangible authority. Presidents can threaten to remove ambassadors or to cut diplomatic ties with foreign nations, a sanction that can give a president considerable leverage diplomatically.

In sum, though the provision that the president has the right to receive ambassadors and other foreign dignitaries may at first glance appear to be mere matter of convenience, it sets the president aside as the only member of the U.S. government constitutionally endowed with the right of communication with foreign nations. Because the Founders were not careful in specifying exactly what they intended by this provision, they established a potent rationalization for the expansion of presidential power.

5-3 Pardons and Reprieves

Another presidential power that was in part designed for negotiating purposes is the power of pardons and reprieves. According to Hamilton writing in the *Federalist Papers*, the principal justification for placing the pardon power in the presidency was that "in seasons of insurrection or rebellion, there are often critical moments, when a well timed offer of pardon to the insurgents may restore the tranquillity of the commonwealth; and which, if suffered to pass unimproved, it may never be possible afterwards to recall." Since the legislative branch is not always in session, it might miss this brief opportunity to grant a pardon. The president, thus, can perform an important function that could keep the nation at peace.

Thus, one reason the Founding Fathers decided to place this power in the presidency, as with the rationale for placing the president's authority to receive foreign dignitaries, was based more on convenience than an active presidential role in foreign affairs. Despite this limited rationale, presidents have exerted their pardon power on many occasions, for both domestic and foreign policy purposes. Presidents can provide full pardons, conditional pardons, clemency for a group of people, conditional amnesty, commutation of a sentence, conditional commutation, and the remission of fines and forfeitures (see Fisher 1981).

According to Fisher (1981: 9), "The pardon power is one of the few 'exclusive' powers available to the president," as Congress discovered when it investigated perceived improprieties in several of Bill Clinton's last-minute pardons in January 2001. Still, despite its exclusivity, this power is not without congressional influence. Congress can, in effect, pardon or provide amnesty for individuals by repealing legislation that imposes criminal penalties. Also, the president cannot use the pardon power to provide compensation to victims without congressional approval (Fisher 1981: 9–10). Unlike the president's other powers, the pardon power is clearly stated and unambiguous in nature. As we shall see in section 5-4, "Treaty Making," however, the president's treaty-making power has been the subject of considerable debate.

5-4 Treaty Making

The centerpiece of the president's authority as chief diplomat is the treaty provision. According to the Constitution, "the president shall have the power, by and with the Advice and Consent of the Senate, to make Treaties, provided two thirds of the Senators present concur. . . ." Hamilton in Federalist #75 referred to this provision as "one of the best digested and most unexceptionable parts of the plan." Yet, the president's treaty power has not been "unexceptionable." In fact, there are many questions about the provision's precise meaning.

The most important question relates to which branch has the right to make treaties. Does the president have the sole right to make treaties? In the *Curtis-Wright* case, Justice Sutherland stated that the president "alone negotiates. . . . Into the field of negotiation the Senate cannot intrude; and Congress itself is powerless to invade it." If, indeed, the Founding Fathers intended for the president alone to be the sole organ of communication with foreign nations, then the president alone, or a presidential subordinate, would negotiate treaties with foreign nations.

Further support that the president alone can negotiate or make treaties is provided by Hamilton's statement in Federalist #72 that the "actual conduct of foreign negotiations" would be included under the category of "administration of government." He goes on to state that "the persons therefore, to whose immediate management these different matters are committed, ought to be considered as the assistants or deputies of the chief magistrate; and on this account, they ought to derive their offices from his appointment, at least from his nomination, and ought to be subject to his supervision." This statement can be inferred to mean that the Senate would play a role in the appointment process and then again once the treaty was negotiated. But was this really the intent of the Founding Fathers?

According to Fisher (1981: 8), the "Constitution does not confer upon the president an exclusive role in negotiations." Fisher contrasted the treaty-making provision in the Constitution with the appointment provision. In the latter case, there is a strict hierarchy of activity. First, the president is charged with the sole duty of nominating an individual for a particular office, and then the Senate is charged with the sole duty of providing its advice and consent. Following these two phases, the president officially appoints the individual to office. No such strict hierarchical scheme exists, however, with regard to the treaty-making process. The power to make treaties is not meant to be performed by the president, to be followed by senatorial advice and consent. Rather, the Constitution states, "the president shall have the power, by and with the Advice and Consent of the Senate, to make Treaties, provided two thirds of the Senators present concur. . . ." By placing the words "to make Treaties" after the words "by and with the Advice and Consent of the Senate," the Founders, Fisher argues, clearly intended for the Senate to play an active role in the treaty-making process.

Is there evidence for Fisher's contention beyond the Constitution's actual wording? With regard to the treaty-making power, Hamilton stated in Federalist #75, "if we attend carefully to its operation, [the treaty process] will be found to partake more of the legislative than of the executive in character, though it does not seem strictly to fall within the definition of either of them." Hamilton continues, the treaty-making power "relates neither to the execution of the subsisting laws, nor to the enaction [sic] of new ones, and still less to an exertion of the common strength. Its objects are CONTRACTS with foreign nations, which have the force of law, but derive it from the obligations of good faith. . . . The power in question seems therefore to form a distinct department, and to belong properly neither to the legislative nor the executive."

The confusion over whether the treaty-making power is truly executive or legislative in nature, or a combination of both, further complicates the question of who should be charged with making treaties. Since it is not, as Hamilton states, a legislative power, though Wayne (1978) and Fisher (1981) assign it to this category, it is not the same thing as making a law, in which Congress or the president can initiate action. On the other hand, if it is not truly an executive function either, then there is no reason why the president should have hegemony over it.

5-4a The Evidence from the Washington Administration

A clearer understanding of the president's and the Senate's role in the negotiation process is provided by John Jay's analysis in Federalist #64 and by the experience of the Washington administration. According to Jay, the Senate and the president do share authority over the negotiation of treaties, but this authority does not appear to be equal. In situations in which secrecy and dispatch are required, the president has greater latitude. Under these circumstances, the president plays the primary role in the negotiation process, while the Senate's role is that of a secondary partner, providing advice only when the president requests it or when negotiations have been completed.

As Jay writes, in circumstances involving matters of secrecy and dispatch, "should any circumstance occur which requires the advice and consent of the senate, [the president] may at any time convene them. Thus we see that the constitution provides that our negociations [sic] for treaties shall have every advantage which can be derived from talents, information, integrity, and deliberate investigations on the one hand, and from secrecy and dispatch on the other." Corwin (1984: 237–38) interprets Jay's comment as meaning that cases of secrecy and dispatch represent the only circumstance in which the president has primary authority over negotiations. But since Jay intended for the president to be the sole judge over when this circumstance prevails, the president has significant practical advantages in controlling the negotiation process.

The evidence from the Washington administration further underscores this point. George Washington believed that the Senate should be included in the negotiation process, for he regularly sent propositions to the Senate for their consideration. He did not, however, treat the Senate as an equal partner. Washington wrote that since the Senate was acting as "a council only to the President," it was the President who should determine, in each individual case, the appropriate method for consultation (quoted in Flexner 1970: 216).

Early on, Washington tried to directly involve the Senate in negotiations. In August 1789, he went before the Senate to discuss a treaty involving the Creek Indian nation. Washington found this process of personal presidential participation to be demeaning and generally unproductive, and thus refused to ever go before that chamber again to discuss Senate business. Despite this fact, which is often misconstrued as evidence that Washington was determined to eliminate the Senate from negotiations, he did continue to send written communications to the Senate. Therefore, it is not true that Washington believed that the Senate should not play a role. As his term of office progressed, however, Washington did come to believe that the Senate should be involved in the treaty-making process only after negotiations were completed.

As Flexner (1970: 218) writes, after the incident involving the Creek Indian treaty,

> Washington still sometimes sent the Secretaries of War or Foreign Affairs to meetings of the Senate committees bearing documents that would help them "advise," but the idea seems to have already been growing in his mind that if there were to be any effective foreign negotiations, the prior advice of the Senate would have to be skimped in favor of ultimate consent. Otherwise, the negotiators' hands would be tied before the negotiations started.

In the case of the Jay Treaty, the Senate allowed the Washington administration to negotiate the treaty and then, after the treaty was submitted to it, proceeded to amend it. The Senate apparently accepted this as its constitutional function, and Washington, by failing to criticize the Senate for amending the treaty, at least implicitly concurred.

Therefore, although Fisher may be technically correct that the Constitution does allow the Senate to play a role in the negotiation of treaties, the presidency has played the primary role in this process since Washington's presidency. This does not mean, however, that the Senate has not played an active role in the treaty-making process or that presidents have not sought the Senate's "advice" during negotiations. Despite the president's clear advantages, the Senate has played an active role in providing its "advice and consent" on the question of whether a treaty should be ratified. As Sundquist (1981: 93) writes, "If the power of the president to negotiate treaties was exclusive, so was the authority of the Senate to reject them. Of the 786 treaties submitted to the Senate between 1778 and 1928, 15 were rejected—including the Treaty of Versailles—46 not acted on, and 51 nullified through unacceptable amendments. The Senate also has forced the president to clarify ambiguous language in treaties and has tacked on nonbinding amendments expressing its displeasure with one or another treaty provision.

As the case of Woodrow Wilson and the Treaty of Versailles demonstrates, one factor that may encourage presidents to allow the Senate to play a more active role at the negotiation stage is the very fact that an irascible Senate ultimately has the power to ratify treaties. Wilson's unwillingness to include senators in his negotiation team greatly angered members of Congress and may have doomed his treaty to defeat. This lesson was not lost on many of Wilson's immediate successors, who encouraged greater Senate participation in the negotiation stage as a means of building support for their treaties.

5-4b Terminating Treaties

The question of who has the constitutional authority to negotiate a treaty is not the only question raised about the treaty power. Also at issue is the question of who is responsible for terminating a treaty. Since treaties, as well as the Constitution, are considered the supreme law of the land, it could be argued that the Senate should also play a role in the cessation of a treaty agreement.

Although presidents played a role in canceling a number of treaties, this issue came to a head in December 1978, when President Jimmy Carter announced that the United States would recognize the People's Republic of China as the legitimate government of China, thus, in effect, unrecognizing Taiwan. Since this action violated an existing defense treaty with Taiwan, Senator Barry Goldwater (R-AZ) argued that the president had exceeded his authority by canceling an existing treaty. According to the senator, in cases in which a treaty is to be terminated, as well as in cases in which a treaty is formulated, the Senate has to be involved.

Goldwater and several other members of Congress filed suit to contest Carter's action. Although the court decided in Carter's favor, according to Fisher (1981: 27–28), "the decision left unclear how the courts might decide future treaty-termination cases." This point is still relevant: In 2001, George W. Bush unilaterally canceled the Anti-Ballistic Missile (ABM) Treaty with Russia.

5-5 Executive Agreements and Joint Resolutions

The fact that the Senate has the power to render the ultimate judgment on treaties, through its "advice and consent" function, has encouraged presidents to find other (nontreaty) means of reaching agreements with foreign powers. One such means is the executive agreement. Schlesinger (1973: 85) refers to the executive agreement as "one of the mysteries of the constitutional order," stating that the basis for them is loosely derived from Article 1, Section 10 of the Constitution; from the distinction "between treaties, which states of the union were forbidden to make, and agreements or compacts, which they make with the consent of the Congress."

Further underscoring the ambiguity of this technique, Fisher (1978: 205) found an entirely different source of constitutional authority for executive agreements. According to Fisher, the president's right to form executive agreements derives from four of the president's enumerated powers:

1. The president's "duty as chief executive to represent the nation in foreign affairs;
2. His authority to receive ambassadors and other public ministers;
3. His authority as commander-in-chief; and
4. His duty to 'take care that the laws be faithfully executed.'"

   With regard to the specificity of these constitutional foundations, Fisher states,

   These powers are so open-ended that Congress may find its own sphere of action constricted because of ambitious executive interpretations. Particularly nebulous are the first, second, and fourth constitutional sources. A more solid case can be made for the commander-in-chief authority, for surely a president may enter into an armistice or cease-fire agreement with a foreign power (subject to Senate action on a peace treaty at a later date).

Because of their fundamental ambiguity, executive agreements were relegated to mostly minor matters for much of our nation's history, with treaties employed when important issues were involved. The presumption was that executive agreements could be employed only when legislative authority for a presidential action already existed. Otherwise, presidents would resort to treaties.

This conception of the executive agreement began to change, however, with the presidencies of William McKinley and Theodore Roosevelt. McKinley employed an executive agreement to "lay down the terms by which the Spanish-American War was concluded" as well as to initiate the "Open Door Policy" (Schlesinger 1973: 87). Theodore Roosevelt then used the same authority to approve of Japan's military protectorate over Korea. Subsequent presidents made even greater use of executive agreements. In fact, since Truman, presidents have been more likely to resort to executive agreements than treaties in election years (King and Ragsdale 1988: 115). Over time, then, executive agreements came to supplement and, in some important cases, to supplant the treaty-making process as a means of making agreements with foreign nations.

What was the opinion of the Supreme Court with regard to the use of this constitutional technique? In the case of the *United States v. Belmont* [301 U.S. 324 (1937)], Justice Sutherland ruled that the president of the United States had the right to enter into executive agreements without the consent of the Senate. Sutherland, as he did in the *Curtis-Wright* case the year before, justified this expansion of presidential power on the basis that the president is the "sole organ" of the United States in its contacts with other nations. Thus, the Supreme Court, far from constraining the president's authority to issue executive agreements, provided presidents with broad support for continued and expanded reliance on it.

5-5a Joint Resolutions

Another deviation from the Constitution that weakened the Senate's diplomatic role was the invention of the joint resolution, which was first introduced by President John Tyler. After failing to secure two-thirds of the Senate in favor of the annexation of Texas, Tyler claimed that the same objective could be achieved through a joint resolution, in which only a majority of the Senate and House members would be required to support the measure. Despite the doubtful constitutionality of the technique, Congress acquiesced and Texas was added to the union via joint resolution. A precedent was established that provided yet another loophole for any president who could not count on the support of two-thirds of the Senate.

Later, William McKinley garnered the necessary majority in both houses to gain congressional approval for the acquisition of Hawaii, after he likewise failed to secure two-thirds support in the Senate for a treaty. In a variety of situations since McKinley's time, when two-thirds of the Senate could not be counted upon to support a treaty, presidents have employed joint resolutions.

In sum, the treaty-making provision involves a great deal of ambiguity and room for interpretation. Left open to interpretation are such questions as who shall negotiate, whether presidents can circumvent the treaty-making process, and when and whether presidents can terminate treaties unilaterally. These questions will likely promote additional political conflict and legal challenges to the president's treaty-making power in the future.

5-6 Commander-in-Chief

Along with the president's role as chief diplomat, the commander-in-chief clause provides a rationale for an active presidential role in foreign policy. As with the treaty-making function, however, there has been considerable disagreement as to the proper scope of presidential war-making power. According to constitutional expert Donald Robinson (1987: 120), "In the field of national defense the Constitution's provisions are brief and full of leeway." Nowhere is this "leeway" more evident than in the few words that refer to the president's authority as commander-in-chief. The Constitution states that the president is the "Commander-in-Chief of the Army and Navy of the United States, and of the Militia of the several States, when called into the actual Service of the United States. . . ."

Although presidents in the modern era interpret these few words as significant delegation of constitutional authority, the Founding Fathers may have had a more limited notion of what the president could do as commander-in-chief than we do today. According to Alexander Hamilton in Federalist #69, the president's power amounted "to nothing more than the supreme command and direction of the military and naval forces, as first General and Admiral of the confederacy. . . ." Since the president did not have the power to declare war, as the British Kings did, Hamilton assumed that this authority would be greatly constrained by the will of Congress.

There was very little discussion of the commander-in-chief clause at the Convention itself. The only real objection related to the question of whether the president could personally take command of the army and the navy. The Virginia Plan, introduced by James Madison, contained a restriction on the authority of the president to personally lead troops into the field of battle. But the Founders, most of whom anticipated that George Washington, the former commander-in-chief of the Continental Army, would be the first president, believed that the president should have this authority.

In fact, President Washington temporarily led the troops during the suppression of the Whiskey Rebellion, while James Madison played a role in organizing the defense of Washington, D.C., during the War of 1812. Later, James K. Polk personally formulated strategy during the Mexican War (Huntington 1956: 694), and Lyndon Johnson identified bombing targets during the Vietnam War. Consequently, the president's right to take personal command of the military to formulate war strategy is firmly established (see Table 5-1).

5-6a How Ambiguous Is the Commander-in-Chief Clause?

At first glance, the commander-in-chief clause appears to be clearly delineated: The president is the first general and the first admiral of the army and navy only

TABLE **5-1** The Commanders-in-Chief in Wartime

President	War
James Madison	War of 1812
James Polk	Mexican War
Abraham Lincoln	Civil War
William McKinley	Spanish-American War
Woodrow Wilson	World War I
Franklin Roosevelt, Harry Truman	World War II
Harry Truman, Dwight Eisenhower	Korean War
Lyndon Johnson, Richard Nixon	Vietnam War
George H. W. Bush	Persian Gulf War
George W. Bush	War on Terrorism

when a state of war exists, and the president can take personal command of the armed forces. But is this delegation of presidential authority really unambiguous? The answer appears to be no. According to Huntington (1956: 690), the commander-in-chief clause is

> unique in the Constitution in granting authority in the form of an office rather than in the form of a function. The president is not given the function "to command the Army and Navy"; he is given the office of "Commander in Chief." This difference in form is of considerable importance, for it left undefined the specific powers and functions [of the office]. This eased the approval of the Constitution in ratifying conventions, but it gave subsequent generations something to argue about. The powers of the Commander in Chief might range from the extremely broad power to conduct war to a narrow restricted power of military command.

The idea that the commander-in-chief is an office, rather than simply a function, provides presidents with a stronger rationale for expanded presidential power. For example, Huntington (1956: 690) states, "It could be argued that the office of commander in chief possesses authority to seize a strike bound war plant. It would be harder to argue that the function of commanding the Army and Navy implied such authority." Hence, presidents have attempted to justify such broad actions as issuing the Emancipation Proclamation (Lincoln) and the seizure of strike-bound steel plants (Truman) on the basis of the office of commander-in-chief.

One can legitimately ask if the Founders originally intended for the commander-in-chief clause to designate an office rather than a mere function. Evidence for this view can be found in George Washington's role as commander-in-chief of the armed forces during the American Revolution. His position appears to be more of an office than merely a personal power. But Washington's experience is of limited relevance since Washington was not also a chief executive, but rather acted as an agent of the Continental Congress.

The Constitution itself provides only limited evidence, stating that the president "shall be" commander-in-chief, as opposed to designating the president as having the power of commander-in-chief. This syntax can be interpreted as evidence that the Founders intended for the clause to designate an office rather than simply assigning additional functions to the president. But this is merely an inference. Unfortunately, we have little information regarding the exact intentions of the Founding Fathers with regard to this provision. Thus, the actual meaning of the clause must be derived, as with so many of the other enumerated presidential powers, from a review of precedent.

5-6b "Purely Military" Matters

One case that relates directly to the president's powers as commander-in-chief is the Supreme Court's decision in the case of *Fleming v. Page* [9 How. 603–618 (1850)]. The court concluded that the president's authority was strictly limited to matters that were "purely military" in nature. During the Civil War, Abraham Lincoln apparently concluded that the suspension of habeas corpus, the declaration of the Emancipation Proclamation, the suppression of free speech and free press, and a myriad of other similar activities designed to preserve the union were purely military in nature. What Lincoln's example demonstrates is that during a time of war, in which the nation's very existence may be threatened, the president undoubtedly will be able to develop an extraordinarily broad interpretation of the commander-in-chief powers.

Even if Congress or the courts challenge the president's authority, they do so post facto. Ambiguity regarding the president's authority as commander-in-chief goes beyond simply cases in which war has actually commenced. It also relates to the nebulous question of when a state of war exists. Does it exist only when Congress declares it, or can it exist independent of congressional action? These questions involve one of the most debated areas of constitutional interpretation—the question of the Founder's intent with regard to *presidential prerogative*.

5-7 Presidential Prerogative and the Role of Precedent

Philosopher John Locke addressed the concept of prerogative in his *Second Treatise on Government*. He stated that prerogative power involved "nothing but the power of doing public good without a rule." More generally, prerogative involves giving the president the authority to deal with those emergencies without prior congressional approval, but subject to later congressional scrutiny. In an emergency situation the president may not be able to secure an *a priori* congressional declaration of war because Congress might, for example, be adjourned. Under these circumstances, it could be dangerous for the president to do nothing while he or she waits for constitutional authority. It is therefore understood that presidents have the prerogative to act in what they feel is the nation's best interest, subject to later investigation, and if necessary, a later sanction (impeachment), by Congress.

The question of whether the Founders intended for the president to exercise prerogative power is unclear, although most scholars agree that the Founders, who were well versed in the writings of Locke, clearly understood the concept. Likewise, many scholars agree that presidents can exercise prerogative power in extraordinary circumstances.

5-7a Is Prerogative an Extra Constitutional Power?

Despite the scholarly consensus that the president does have a right to use prerogative, there is considerable disagreement whether the president's prerogative power derives directly from the Constitution or if it represents an extra constitutional grant of authority. Sorenson (1989) argues that an analysis of the Constitution and the *Federalist Papers* demonstrates that the Founders clearly intended for the president to exercise prerogative; thus, it is a constitutional power. Sorenson finds constitutional support for this argument in the "necessary and proper" clause.

Bessette and Tulis (1981) also argue that the prerogative power derives from the Constitution, but they do not place that power exclusively in the hands of the executive. Meanwhile, Schlesinger (1973) determines that the power is extraconstitutional; that is, the power is neither enumerated nor directly encouraged by the Constitution. Such diverse scholarly interpretations suggest that there is ample room for presidential interpretation of this power. In fact, various presidents have come to extraordinarily different interpretations of the prerogative power.

In the case of the pirates of Tripoli, for example, Thomas Jefferson adopted a narrow interpretation of the president's powers during a time of enemy attack. Jefferson directed that American naval vessels in the Bay of Tripoli only had the right to defend themselves against enemy attacks until Congress formally declared war. Hamilton, writing as Lucius Crassus, bitterly attacked Jefferson's narrow interpretation:

> [I]t is the peculiar and exclusive province of Congress, when the nation is at peace to change that state into a state of war . . . in other words it belongs to Congress only to go to war. But when a foreign nation declares, or openly and avowedly makes war

upon the United States, they are then by the very fact already at war, and any declaration on the part of Congress is nugatory, it is at least unnecessary. (Quoted in Corwin 1984: 229)

This point has important implications. For example, in 1846 James Polk asked Congress to recognize that a state of war already existed with Mexico, rather than asking Congress to declare war. Woodrow Wilson followed the same strategy at the commencement of World War I. During the Civil War, the Supreme Court, in the *Prize Cases*, ruled that in cases involving an invasion of U.S. territory or the existence of hostilities, the president did not have to wait for a congressional declaration of war. Since Congress's role was to recognize that a state of war already existed, and since the circumstances involved insurrection and invasion of U.S. territory by hostile forces, the president had not exceeded his authority in defending the nation.

Whereas a convincing case can be made for presidential prerogative in those instances in which the nation is already threatened, if we extend the logic of prerogative power to simple acts of defense, ample room is created for presidents to provoke a conflict which then can force Congress to recognize that a state of war exists, thus essentially usurping Congress's right to declare war.

This is precisely what happened in the case of the Polk administration and the Mexican War. By sending U.S. troops into a disputed area claimed by both Texas and Mexico, Polk encouraged an enemy attack. He then asked Congress to recognize that a state of war existed. With hostilities under way, Congress was not in an enviable position, politically speaking, to say no to the president. By denying funds for the conflict, Congress would place itself in the unenviable position of refusing necessary arms and supplies to American military personnel already in battle. Such an action would be politically damaging and could have serious repercussions for the security of the nation. Thus, Polk was able to force Congress's hand by provoking an enemy attack and then requesting congressional recognition that hostilities existed.

5-7b A Dangerous Precedent

Polk's aggrandizement of presidential power under the commander-in-chief clause set an important and potentially dangerous precedent for his successors. Lincoln then established further precedent for prerogative during the Civil War. According to Randall and Donald (1969: 295), "Lincoln's view of his own war powers was most expansive. He believed that in time of war constitutional restraints did not fully apply, but that so far as they did apply they restrained the Congress more than the President."

There is no doubt that Lincoln adopted a broad interpretation of the prerogative powers. Lincoln called forth the militias of the several states on April 15, 1861, approximately three months before Congress convened. In taking this action, Lincoln initially did not refer to his authority as commander-in-chief, but rather to the "power vested in me by the Constitution," which, of course, among other powers included the commander-in-chief clause (Basler 1953: Volume IV: 332).

Lincoln did, however, later make direct references to his authority as commander-in-chief. In announcing the Emancipation Proclamation, he referred to the "power in me vested as Commander-in-Chief, of the Army and navy of the United States in time of actual armed rebellion against authority and government of the United States. . . ."

Since Lincoln considered the proclamation to be "a fit and necessary war measure for suppressing said rebellion," he interpreted it as a justifiable assertion of presidential authority (Basler 1953: Volume VI: 30). In a letter to James C.

Conkling, written shortly after he announced the proclamation, Lincoln wrote, "You say [the Emancipation Proclamation] is unconstitutional—I think differently. I think the constitution invests its commander-in-chief, with the law of war, in time of war" (ibid., 408).

Although Lincoln adopted a broad interpretation of the commander-in-chief clause, his experience must be evaluated on the basis of the prevailing circumstances. Many of Lincoln's successors have cited his actions as precedents for their own broad interpretation of the clause. But is it justifiable to apply Lincoln's actions during a civil war as a precedent for presidential action in Korea or Vietnam?

The argument in these latter cases, in which the nation's survival was not immediately at stake, is less obvious. But what about World War I or II? It can be argued that these wars, particularly the latter one, presented a palpable threat to the nation's survival. And what about the current war on terrorism? Is the nation's survival at risk, and does terrorism represent a continuing threat to the nation's survival? If so, how much power should the president have to fight international terrorism? As these questions suggest, although Lincoln's use of prerogative was designed to preserve the nation, it did indeed open Pandora's box, thus providing future presidents with myriad precedents for future armed conflicts (see Figure 5-2).

Figure 5-2
The President as Commander-in-Chief

Presidents have often used their authority as commander-in-chief to take military action in other parts of the world, as well as closer to home.

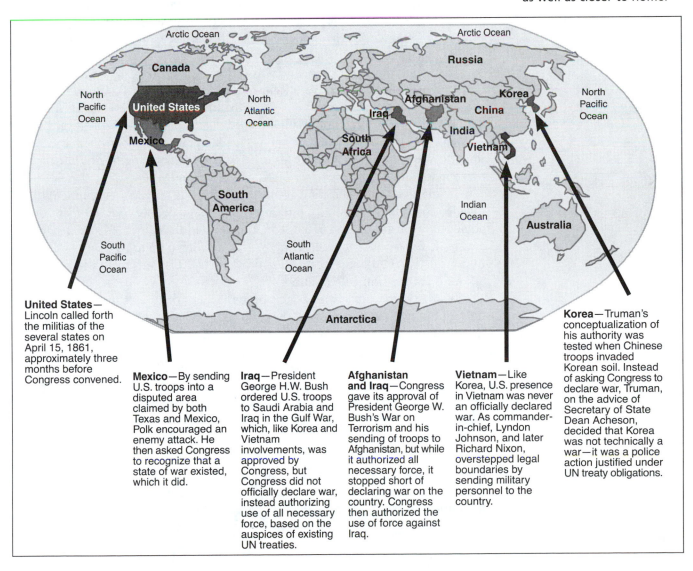

United States—Lincoln called forth the militias of the several states on April 15, 1861, approximately three months before Congress convened.

Mexico—By sending U.S. troops into a disputed area claimed by both Texas and Mexico, Polk encouraged an enemy attack. He then asked Congress to recognize that a state of war existed, which it did.

Iraq—President George H.W. Bush ordered U.S. troops to Saudi Arabia and Iraq in the Gulf War, which, like Korea and Vietnam involvements, was approved by Congress, but Congress did not officially declare war, instead authorizing use of all necessary force, based on the auspices of existing UN treaties.

Afghanistan and Iraq—Congress gave its approval of President George W. Bush's War on Terrorism and his sending of troops to Afghanistan, but while it authorized all necessary force, it stopped short of declaring war on the country. Congress then authorized the use of force against Iraq.

Vietnam—Like Korea, U.S. presence in Vietnam was never an officially declared war. As commander-in-chief, Lyndon Johnson, and later Richard Nixon, overstepped legal boundaries by sending military personnel to the country.

Korea—Truman's conceptualization of his authority was tested when Chinese troops invaded Korean soil. Instead of asking Congress to declare war, Truman, on the advice of Secretary of State Dean Acheson, decided that Korea was not technically a war—it was a police action justified under UN treaty obligations.

5-7c A Remarkable Transformation

Schlesinger (1973: 132–33) comments that, beginning with Harry Truman, there was a remarkable transformation in the way presidents invoked the commander-in-chief clause. Previously, the clause was invoked sparingly and usually only in wartime. After World War II, presidents relied on this authority on a regular basis, in peacetime as well as wartime. The principal justification was the existence of a permanent threat to the nation's security: the "communist menace."

Thus, beginning with the presidency of Harry Truman, the interpretation of the president's authority as commander-in-chief expanded well beyond anything the Founders had intended. Truman himself discusses this broad interpretation of the commander-in-chief clause in his memoirs (1955: 478):

> In this day and age, the defense of the nation means more than building an army, navy, and air force. It is a job for the entire resources of the nation. The President, who is Commander in Chief and who represents the interests of all the people, must [be] able to act at all times to meet any sudden threat to the nation's security. A wise President will always work with Congress, but when Congress fails to act or is unable to act in a crisis, the President, under the Constitution, must use his powers to safeguard the nation.

Because actions anywhere in the world could presumably threaten the security of the nation, Truman believed an expanded interpretation of the president's authority as commander-in-chief was required. Thus, even when Congress failed to act in the time of a crisis, the president, "under the Constitution, must use his powers to safeguard the nation."

This is an important presidential assertion of constitutional authority, potentially threatening Congress's very right to declare war: For if Congress fails to act, presumably "under the Constitution," Truman believed the president could act on his own. George H. W. Bush made much the same statement with regard to the Persian Gulf War, saying that if Congress failed to grant him the necessary authority to go to war, he would act under his existing constitutional authority. Other presidents made similar claims.

Truman's conceptualization of his authority was tested when Chinese troops invaded Korean soil. Instead of asking Congress to declare war, Truman, on the advice of Secretary of State Dean Acheson, decided that Korea was not technically a war—it was a police action. Since America was living up to its treaty obligations, under the North Atlantic Treaty Organization (NATO) pact, there was no need to ask for a congressional declaration.

Truman's interpretation of the president's authority as commander-in-chief did not end with an assertion of the right to go to war without a formal declaration. Truman also justified the decision to increase the number of U.S. forces in Europe without congressional approval and attempted to seize the strike-bound steel industry under his authority as commander-in-chief (an act later reversed by the Supreme Court). Although Truman's two immediate successors adopted a more modest interpretation of their authority, Lyndon Johnson and Richard Nixon further expanded presidential authority under the clause.

5-7d Justifications for a Stronger Commander-in-Chief?

Modern-day interpretations of the commander-in-chief clause exceed anything the Founders ever intended or imagined. Yet, this statement should not be viewed as an indictment of the modern presidency. There are justifications for expanding presidential authority. Although Truman's statement is expansive, it is not without merit.

As we saw on September 11, 2001, American interests and lives can be threatened at a moment's notice. In a world in which terrorists can strike against American citizens abroad or at home, do we want to tie the hands of the president with an eighteenth century conceptualization of presidential power? On the other hand, do we want to give presidents a broad grant of power? The ambiguity of the commander-in-chief clause thus serves a useful function in allowing the power of the presidency to expand in order to deal with these unexpected exigencies, but it does not set useful parameters that tell us when presidential power is too expansive.

The ambiguity of the Constitution thus also means that unwarranted and dangerous assertions of presidential power can be justified on the basis of the same clause. Since so much of the precedent for presidential power has been misquoted and misunderstood by the courts and by scholars, ample (and often unjustified) precedents abound for the further accretion of presidential authority. For example, the Greytown incident is perhaps the most famous and infamous example of *bad precedent*. In this case, Lieutenant Hollins of the U.S.S. Cyane exceeded his orders from President Franklin Pierce and the Navy Department and bombarded the village of Greytown, Nicaragua, as retribution for an apparently minor affront to a U.S. citizen. The president and his advisors were furious, but they did not publicly acknowledge that Hollins had exceeded his authority, lest the president's prestige be damaged.

Unaware that Hollins had exceeded his authority, the courts then used the merits of this case to argue that the president has the right to protect U.S. interests abroad, including property and lives (Schlesinger 1973: 56). Thus, from the Greytown incident, presidents derived an important justification for the use of their authority as commander-in-chief: to protect the lives and property of Americans abroad. Unfortunately, the Greytown incident is not the only example in which precedents derived power from a judicial misreading of the events.

Therefore, the ambiguity surrounding the president's authority as commander-in-chief, while providing a useful tool that allows modern presidents to deal with the realities of a more dangerous world, also threatens to break down the constitutional balance between executive and legislative authority.

5-8 Constitutional Ambiguity, Expectations, and Extra-Constitutional Powers

According to Schlesinger (1973: 297),

> The vital difference between the early republic and the Imperial Presidency resides not in what Presidents did but in what Presidents believed they had the inherent right to do. Early Presidents, even while they circumvented the Constitution, had a cautious and vigilant concern for consent in a practical if not a formal sense. . . . In the late twentieth century, Presidents made sweeping claims of inherent power. . . .

The ambiguity of the Constitution certainly provided opportunities for presidents to adopt an expanded interpretation of their war power. Hence, while the words contained in the Constitution were not changed, their meaning and our expectations of presidential leadership changed radically over time. A number of factors helped to alter the perceptions of policy makers and the public regarding the legitimate role of the presidency (e.g., the development of a constant threat and new technologies following World War II). But the ambiguity of the Constitution itself also opened the door for the growth of presidential power.

Had the Constitution been more specific, and thus required an amendment in order to expand the role of the presidency in the political system, it is unlikely that the power of the presidency would have expanded as rapidly as it did. The amendment process is lugubrious and would have provided a major obstacle to the growth of presidential power. But because the Founders failed to precisely define what they meant by the enumerated powers of the Constitution, all that was required was a reinterpretation of existing provisions.

This is not to suggest that the Constitution provided no useful guidance in interpreting the powers of the presidency or that it has not constrained presidential power. Although the Constitution is vague, it does provide some boundaries for presidential power. But what I have argued here is that those boundaries are exceedingly broad, that there is ample wiggle room for expanding presidential power. Furthermore, presidents have taken full advantage of the Constitution's ambiguity to advance their power and influence over time.

The Constitution's ambiguity also was critical in the development of extra-constitutional presidential roles. These roles have proven to be as important, if not more important, than the constitutional roles of the president. For example, Rossiter (1960), besides identifying the president as chief of state, chief executive, chief legislator, chief diplomat, and commander-in-chief, also identifies the president as the "Party Chief" and the "Voice of the People." Although the Constitution says nothing about the power of the political parties or the president's relationship to them, the role of "Party Chief" provides the president with extraordinary influence over the electoral process.

Because the Constitution does not deal with this issue, it was not necessary to alter the Constitution in order to create party nominating conventions or presidential primaries. Similarly, the president's role as the "Voice of the People" greatly advanced presidential power and influence. In fact, it may be the greatest of the extra-constitutional presidential roles. Thus, perhaps the most important means of transforming the presidency has been extra-constitutional. In so doing, it should be noted that the decision to incorporate the presidency in one person, rather than in a council, and to free the presidency from selection by the legislature provided a sound constitutional basis for the growth of each of these **extra-constitutional powers**.

Extra-constitutional powers: The roles, identified by Rossiter, as Party Chief and Voice of the People, which are not identified in the Constitution but are important roles that presidents now play nonetheless.

Presidential power also has expanded as a result of the use of other legal resources, such as the president's use of executive orders, which, like the executive agreements discussed in section 5-5, are now more commonly used by presidents to circumvent the legislative process (see Mayer 2001). Executive orders and executive agreements have been used in recent decades as part of a new presidential strategy to internalize presidential resources in the White House, thus obviating the need to deal with external actors like Congress. In short, the battle over the president's legal resources, their meaning, and the ways they should be used continues to be fought in the political system.

Chapter Summary

In Chapter 4, "Domestic Policy, Constitutional Ambiguity, and the Growth of Presidential Power," we found that the Constitution grants Congress considerable and detailed authority in the realm of domestic affairs. The same is true of Congress's foreign policy powers. Yet, the political system that exists today is much different from the one the Founders delineated. While the words in our Constitution are the same as they were in 1787, our interpretations of them are vastly different today. As our expectations related to the president's role in foreign affairs changed over time, presidential power likewise changed. Hence,

George W. Bush's role as commander-in-chief is nothing like that of our first president, George Washington. Not only does the president have a larger military at his disposal today, but expectations of what the president can do militarily are also vastly different. Whether this development is for good or ill is one that has kept scholars busy for many decades and likely will for many more. What is certain, however, is that the foreign policy presidency is much more powerful than it once was, all without the revision of one single word of constitutional text.

Review Questions

1. According to the Constitution, which branch of the U.S. government has primacy in the field of foreign relations?
   a. legislative
   b. executive
   c. judicial
   d. all of the above

2. In the Supreme Court case the *United States v. Curtis-Wright Corporation*, Justice Sutherland invoked Marshall's phrase:
   a. We have only begun to fight.
   b. Fourscore and seven years ago . . .
   c. Read my lips, no new taxes.
   d. The president is the sole instrument of communication with other governments.

3. The provision that the president shall receive ambassadors and other foreign dignitaries also means that presidents have the right to
   a. decide whether to recognize foreign dignitaries and thus the governments that they represent.
   b. unilaterally declare war.
   c. declare war only if attacked.
   d. none of the above.

4. In "seasons of insurrection or rebellion, there are often critical moments, when" this "may restore the tranquillity of the commonwealth; and which, if suffered to pass unimproved, it may never be possible afterwards to recall."
   a. a well-timed offer of pardon to the insurgents
   b. a declaration of war
   c. a diplomatic visit
   d. all of the above

5. The president shall have the power to make treaties, by and with the advice and consent of the
   a. Supreme Court.
   b. House of Representatives.
   c. State Department.
   d. Senate.

6. Which of the following presidents canceled a treaty, thus raising the question of whether the president alone can terminate a treaty?
   a. Richard Nixon
   b. Gerald Ford
   c. Jimmy Carter
   d. Ronald Reagan

7. Schlesinger refers to these as "one of the mysteries of the constitutional order."
   a. pardons
   b. reprieves
   c. vetoes
   d. executive agreements

8. Which of the following presidents was the first president to use a joint resolution instead of a treaty?
   a. Andrew Jackson
   b. John Tyler
   c. James Polk
   d. Abraham Lincoln

9. Constitutional expert Donald Robinson states, "In the field of national defense, the Constitution's provisions are brief and full of leeway." What is he speaking about?
   a. the treaty-making power
   b. the commander-in-chief clause
   c. the pardon and reprieve clause
   d. the foreign policy powers in general

10. Lincoln considered this to be "a fit and necessary war measure for suppressing said rebellion."
    a. the Emancipation Proclamation
    b. the Gettysburg Address
    c. the battle of Gettysburg
    d. none of the above

Discussion Questions

1. Which branch of government should have primacy in the field of foreign relations?
2. Should the president be the "sole organ" in communication with other nations?
3. How active should the Senate's role be in the treaty-making process?
4. Does the presidency have too much power in foreign affairs? If so, should we go back to a strict construction of the U.S. Constitution in foreign affairs? Is that even possible?

Presidential Elections in a Constitutional Framework

Key Terms

dark horse candidate
favorite son

6-1 Presidential Elections in a Constitutional Framework

In section 3-3, "Presidential Greatness," we examined the historical rankings and backgrounds of the forty-two men who thus far have held the office of president of the United States. As noted, our presidents have come from various backgrounds. While the Founders did not believe that any one job would prepare an individual for the presidency, they did have a particular quality in mind for presidential candidates: *virtue.* They wanted to create an electoral scheme that would promote virtuous men, preferably men of vast experience and high moral character (and limited personal ambition). At the same time, they feared demagogues, like Oliver Cromwell, and thus wanted a representative electoral system, yet one that would limit the direct participation of the American voter.

But how could they create an electoral scheme that would be representative and yet at the same time limit the direct influence of the people? It is not surprising that the "question that had the delegates running around in circles" was how the executive should be elected. This question was "impervious to easy solution...." It was, however, "one of the keys to the future of republican government . . ." (Rossiter 1966: 198). For this reason, the Founders considered and rejected many options on their way to a decision.

6-1a Different Electoral Ideas

The Founders first considered the possibility of a plural presidency or a presidency in the hands of more than one individual (see Figure 6-1). While the concept of a plural executive had its adherents, the limitations of the Articles of Confederation were firmly in the Founders' minds, and the idea of creating yet another committee system to govern the nation was a less attractive option than it might have been had it been proposed a mere ten years before. Having witnessed firsthand the inertia of the Articles of Confederation, many Founders came to Philadelphia convinced that a government of greater vigor and energy was needed. As Hamilton later wrote in the *Federalist Papers,* the presidency as proposed in the Constitution provided an office that promised those very qualities. As the Founders sat in the

Figure 6-1
The Types of Presidencies That the Founding Fathers Considered

Plural Presidency
A plural presidency would have given us more than one president. What would happen if they couldn't decide? What would happen if they argued all the time? On the other hand, what if they worked well together? What would the benefits of a plural presidency have been?

Legislatively Elected Presidency
A president elected by and dependent on the legislature wouldn't be the kind of strong president the Founders wanted. What kinds of pressures would such a president be under? How might the legislators push and pull him or her to act?

?

One-Term Limit Presidency
Proponents of election by national legislature wanted to limit the president to one long term in office. Some feared, perhaps, that a president elected to a long-term presidency might become unreliable with the trust placed in him or her, could abuse his or her power, or could do the opposite and be a much-admired figure. Knowing what you do about the uses and abuses of power, why do you think the Founders hesitated in creating a presidency with a long term?

Short-Term Presidency with Term Limits
Those who favored election by other means (nonlegislative) preferred to allow the president to serve two or more shorter terms. How would a president manage the duties of the office while thinking about re-election more often? What are the benefits of shorter terms with limited or unlimited terms?

sweltering Philadelphia summer heat in 1787, however, they were faced with yet another apparent conundrum: How could they create an office of vigor and energy without introducing the potential for demagoguery?

Another alternative was presented by the Committee of the Whole. It provided for the election by the national legislature of an "executive to consist of a single person" who was to serve a seven-year term and then be "ineligible" for a second one (see Figure 6-1). The Founders, however, were not comfortable with this electoral option (Rossiter 1966: 198). Having the president depend on the national legislature for election meant that the presidency would not be a strong, independent office. Many Founders believed that an independent presidency was necessary to counterbalance the influence of the legislative branch, which the Founders believed would be the dominant branch of government.

As Rossiter (1966: 198) writes, "Although most delegates were now persuaded of the impropriety of election by the legislature, they were persuaded for quite different reasons. Some were determined to reinforce the independence of the executive, others to bring the states into the process, still others (with eyes turned toward the man who was expected to fill this post under the new constitution [Washington]) to find a way of rendering the executive eligible for two or more terms."

There was even disagreement with regard to how long the president's term of office should be. Proponents of election by national legislature wanted to limit the president to one long term in office, while those who favored election by other means preferred to allow the president to serve two or more shorter terms (see Figure 6-1). Rossiter (ibid.) continues, "The questions of length of term, reeligibility, and method of election were, in truth, so thoroughly mixed up that the debates on this resolution still read . . . like a running account of three-dimensional chess." Yet, as the delegates struggled for a solution, none appeared in sight.

Late in the Convention's deliberations, however, a solution finally was identified. The solution, the Electoral College, is a somewhat convoluted system whereby presidents are not elected directly by popular vote, but rather by a majority of the electors. In fact, several candidates who received the most popular votes subsequently were not rewarded with the presidency (Jackson in 1824, Tilden in 1876, Cleveland in 1888, and Gore in 2000). Instead, the Electoral College system provides for election of the president to be determined by the results in each state.

While the Electoral College system continues to befuddle us today, as McDonald (1994: 163) writes, with the decision to employ it, "[s]uddenly the constitutional order clicked into place. All that remained was to transfer a few powers from the Senate to the executive, and the presidency had been born." What, however, was the attraction of the Electoral College, a system that many critics today consider to be obsolete?

6-1b The Electoral College

Pfiffner (2002, forthcoming) writes that while there were problems with the idea of directly electing a president, the Founders did not create the Electoral College because they were afraid of democracy. Rather, they were concerned that in all probability "most citizens would not be personally familiar with all of the most qualified potential candidates." At the Constitutional Convention, George Mason expressed the opinion that "it would be unnatural to refer the choice of proper character for chief Magistrate to the people, as it would, to refer a trail of colors to a blind man." The size of the country made it impossible "to judge the respective pretentions of the Candidates" (ibid.). Hence, judging virtue was very much on the Founders' minds. The Electoral College dealt with this concern because the

Favorite son: A candidate who runs for president essentially because he or she represents a particular state or sometimes region of the country.

Founders believed that rather than candidates running in national elections (as they do today), there would be a greater propensity for **favorite son** candidacies from individual states.

The Founders also wanted to create an electoral system in which the small states would not be disadvantaged and slave states would be able to count three-fifths of their slave population toward the presidential vote (ibid.). The number of electors was based on the population of the state: The ratio of each state to the Electoral College was the same as its ratio to the legislature, with the number of electors equaling the number of Representatives and Senators to each state (ibid.). The College also preserved states' rights since electors would be chosen by state legislatures, and it protected against demagoguery and dictatorship by ensuring that electors could not be members of the national government and would meet only for the purpose of selecting the new president and then disband (ibid.). Furthermore, since the electors could vote for two persons, with only one from their home state, and since a majority was required for the election of a new president, there were further protections against the possibility of cabal and continued geographical dominance of the presidential office. Hence, the Electoral College was an ingenious scheme that allowed the Founders to deal with a wide variety of practical concerns.

In addition, some of the Founders believed the Electoral College would seldom result in a clear outcome. They specified that the

> [p]erson having the greatest Number of [electoral] Votes shall be President, [but] if there shall be more than one who have such Majority, and have an equal Number of Votes, then the House of Representatives shall immediately chuse [sic] by Ballot one of them for President; and if no Person have a Majority, then from the five highest on the List the said House shall in like manner chuse the President.

Furthermore, in this process each state would have but one vote, a quorum of two-thirds of the states being required, and "a Majority of all the States shall be necessary to a Choice." If a president could be chosen, but two or more candidates had an equal number of ballots for vice president, then "the Senate shall chuse from them. . . ." Mistakenly, many Founders assumed that the presidential choice, in most cases, ultimately would rest with the legislative branch.

6-1c When the Election Goes to the House

The House of Representatives rarely decided the outcome of a presidential election. In 1824, the House acted much as the Founders intended, refusing to select the popular vote winner, Andrew Jackson, whom many considered to be demagogic. Instead, the electors chose the more qualified candidate, former Secretary of State John Quincy Adams, but they did not act out of magnanimity. Rather, the stain of a "corrupt" political bargain between Adams and losing candidate Henry Clay raised serious questions about the legitimacy of the electors' choice.

Likewise, in 1876, the Democratic-controlled House and Republican-controlled Senate became involved in the most corrupt of all presidential elections: the Hayes-Tilden contest. After questions were raised about the electoral outcomes in several southern states, including Florida, a special joint committee was created to decide the election result. Still Hayes's legitimacy was questioned throughout his term.

It appears that Democrat Samuel Tilden should have won the election. For instance, in Louisiana a Republican election board threw out the votes of whole parishes where there was any evidence that violence or intimidation had affected the results. This changed a "Tilden majority into a Hayes margin of some 3,500 votes. . . ." (Roseboom and Eckes 1979: 94). In the other contested southern states, all of the electoral votes were eventually assigned to Hayes, giving him a one-vote majority in the Electoral College and the presidency.

6-1d Alternatives to the Electoral College

On the rare occasions described in section 6-1c, the Electoral College did not operate as the Founders had intended. Consequently, there have been periodic calls to abolish it and replace it with a direct popular vote election. While this change would be more democratic and would eliminate what is generally considered an antiquated electoral mechanism, it is unlikely to occur for two basic reasons. First, smaller states benefit from the Electoral College in several ways. Each state, no matter what its size, has two electors simply because it has two senators. Hence, smaller states have greater representation than is justified on the basis of their population.

Also, smaller states are more likely to receive greater attention from presidential candidates under an Electoral College scheme. If we moved to a popular vote system, there would be little incentive for presidential candidates to visit a less populous state such as New Mexico. But with five electoral votes in a close election, such as 2000, the state had numerous visits from the presidential candidates, vice presidential candidates, their spouses, and other prominent party officials. Under a popular vote scheme, the incentive would have been for presidential candidates to skip New Mexico and to go instead where the large population base is: the big cities and the suburbs.

The second reason why we are unlikely to abolish the Electoral College is that a two-thirds majority of the states is required in order to pass an amendment to the Constitution. Since small states benefit from the Electoral College, they are unlikely to act against their own self-interests by abolishing it.

There are other alternatives to amendment, however. One would be for the states themselves to adopt a district plan for allocation of electors. Under this system, used in the past by many states and still used in Maine and Nebraska, the candidate who wins a House district in a state also wins its elector, while the popular vote winner in the state wins the two Senate electors. This system might provide greater democracy, but it could benefit the Republican Party by splitting the electoral vote in Democratic strongholds such as California and New York. Since it would likely benefit one political party at the expense of another, this reform too is unlikely to gain national acceptance. In short, the electoral scheme created by the Founders is likely to remain with us for the foreseeable future. There is no serious movement to replace it, even after the 2000 election result, in which the man who won the most popular votes was denied access to the White House.

6-2 Constitutional Qualifications for President

Another issue related to the selection of a president is qualifications for the presidential office. The Constitution provides little detail regarding presidential qualifications. It simply says, "No Person except a natural born Citizen, or a Citizen of the United States at the time of the Adoption of this Constitution, shall be eligible to the Office of President. . . ." Next, the Constitution proscribes, "neither shall any Person be eligible to that Office who shall not have attained to the Age of thirty five Years, and been fourteen Years a Resident within the United States" (see Box 6-1).

Beyond these general criteria, no other qualifications were identified limiting a citizen from running for president. The Founders did not see fit to identify prior political office as a prerequisite to the presidency, nor did they specify any other

Box 6-1

When Is Fourteen Years Fourteen Years?

It was not clear whether the Constitution's requirement of fourteen years meant that a presidential candidate had to be a resident for fourteen years or for the past fourteen years. In 1908, when William Howard Taft was elected president, this question arose. He had been out of the country serving in the Philippines. Since he had not been in the country for fourteen consecutive years, was he eligible to be president? It was decided that the fourteen years of residence did not have to be consecutive. Hence, Taft was eligible to be president.

---

criterion that might limit the potential pool of presidential candidates. This may seem peculiar since most professional jobs today require certain specific qualifications or training (degrees, licenses, certificates, etc.) before one can assume them. Yet, the qualifications for president are less confining than those for a plumber, electrician, teacher, or real estate agent. One must merely be thirty-five years old, have lived fourteen years in the country, and be a natural-born citizen.

Since the Founding, the voting franchise has been considerably extended (property requirements and poll taxes were removed; women, African Americans, Native Americans, and other groups were given the right to vote), meaning that an even larger percentage of Americans today are qualified to run for president. Hence, as one of my elementary school teachers used to say, "In America, anyone can be president." In theory, that is true. In reality, of course, few of us have any realistic chance of ever being elected president.

6-2a Where Are the Great Presidents?

Have you ever wondered why such great Americans as Daniel Webster were never nominated for president of the United States or why such lesser individuals as Franklin Pierce and Rutherford B. Hayes were? In the late 1800s, Lord Bryce of Great Britain did. In 2000, the respected publication the *National Journal* asked the same question. Likewise, Landy and Milkis (2000) argue that the last "great" president was Franklin Roosevelt—meaning we have gone well over half a century since the last great president occupied the Oval Office (Roosevelt died in office in 1945).

Other scholars disagree with Landy and Milkis, ranking such presidents as Truman, Kennedy, and Johnson (see section 3-3, "Presidential Greatness,") among our best presidents. Still others ask whether Bill Clinton, George H. W. Bush, George W. Bush, Ronald Reagan, Jimmy Carter, and Gerald Ford are the very best, most qualified individuals that America has to offer. Are there no more Lincolns, Washingtons, or Roosevelts (Teddy or Franklin) left in America?

The answer to these questions is multifaceted, but one major explanatory factor is the system we have in place for electing presidents. As King and Ragsdale (1988: 28–29) write, "The electoral process defines the types of people who will and will not be elected president and the resources and perspectives they bring to the office." It is therefore important for us to examine the electoral system and its changing nature. While the Electoral College remains intact, the method of presidential selection has changed over time, as has the way candidates present themselves to the American people. Besides determining the kinds of individuals who will run for president, these changes also have had important implications for the development of presidential power. In section 6-3, we discuss four different periods or electoral orders and their impact on presidential selection.

6-3 The Four Electoral Orders

In a recent work on elections, Menefee-Libey (2000: 11) identifies four electoral orders in American politics:

> a pre-party era from colonial times into the 1830s; an intensely partisan era from the 1830s until the turn of the century; a transitional, reformed but still party-centered era from the 1890s until the 1950s; and a dealigned, fragmented, nearly postpartisan period since the 1950s.

In Table 6-1, I identify the four electoral orders, based loosely on Menefee-Libey's typology. I begin the second electoral order with the election of Andrew Jackson, rather than with his re-election (as Menefee-Libey does), though the latter election represents the first use of the Party Convention nomination process. I do so because Jackson's first election involved the popular electorate in an unprecedented manner. I also mark the beginning of the fourth electoral order with the election of Dwight Eisenhower in 1952 because he was the first president to use the primary process to run a successful insurgency campaign to unseat the party favorite. He also was the first president to use his own personal organization, rather than the party's organization, in the fall campaign, and was the first to use television to advertise his candidacy.

Each electoral order has its own unique characteristics. The first electoral order was characterized by the legislative branch's nomination of the president, with the president therefore greatly dependent on the Congress. The second order reflected the wider participation of the political parties in the nomination process through the rise of the party conventions. The third order reflected the rise of personal presidential campaigning and a move toward greater presidential control of the nominating process. It also reflected greater independence from the political parties. Finally, the fourth order (the present one) reflects the ascendancy of individual candidates in the nomination process, the presidential candidates' use of personal organizations (rather than party organizations), and greater reliance on presidential primaries (rather than conventions) to nominate candidates. As we shall discuss, each of these four orders and the electoral systems applied during them have important implications for the development of presidential power.

Some evidence for that point is evident in the results presented in Table 6-1. Of the six presidents elected during the first electoral order (1789–1824), four were elected twice. On the other hand, during the second electoral order (1828–1892), re-election was a rare accomplishment, happening but three out of fourteen times. In addition, Grover Cleveland was elected to two nonconsecutive terms in 1884 and 1892, but lost to Benjamin Harrison in 1888. In fact, relatively few of these presidents were even renominated by their parties. In the third electoral order (1896–1948), three men (out of nine) were re-elected (FDR four times). Theodore Roosevelt, Calvin Coolidge, and Harry Truman also became the first vice presidents to be elected to the presidential office in their own right after succeeding to the presidency upon the death of their predecessor. Hence, six out of nine presidents were either re-elected or elected after serving as vice president. In our current electoral order (1952–present), four presidents have been re-elected, while one vice president succeeding to the office upon the death of a president (Lyndon Johnson) was elected in his own right. Since George W. Bush has not yet had the chance to run for re-election, if we add Gerald Ford, who lost his election bid in 1976, this means five out of nine were re-elected or were vice presidents elected after the death of their predecessor. In terms of stability (defined as the percentage of presidents winning re-election and succeeding vice presidents winning

TABLE **6-1** The Four Electoral Orders and the Presidents Elected

I. Pre-party into the 1820s	George Washington*
	John Adams
	Thomas Jefferson*
	James Madison*
	James Monroe*
	John Quincy Adams
II. Partisan Era from 1828 till the 1890s	Andrew Jackson*
	Martin Van Buren
	William Henry Harrison (John Tyler)
	James K. Polk
	Zachary Taylor (Millard Fillmore)
	Franklin Pierce
	James Buchanan
	Abraham Lincoln* (Andrew Johnson)
	U. S. Grant*
	Rutherford Hayes
	James Garfield (Chester Arthur)
	Grover Cleveland
	Benjamin Harrison
	Grover Cleveland
III. Transitional Period from the 1890s till the 1950s	William McKinley* (Theodore Roosevelt)
	Theodore Roosevelt
	William Howard Taft
	Woodrow Wilson*
	Warren Harding (Calvin Coolidge)
	Calvin Coolidge
	Herbert Hoover
	Franklin Roosevelt* (Harry Truman)
	Harry Truman
IV. Post Partisan Period since the 1950s	Dwight Eisenhower*
	John Kennedy (Lyndon Johnson)
	Lyndon Johnson
	Richard Nixon* (Gerald Ford)
	Jimmy Carter
	Ronald Reagan*
	George Herbert Walker Bush
	William Clinton*
	George Walker Bush

*Indicates that a president was re-elected. In the case of Grover Cleveland, his re-election was not consecutive. In the case of Franklin Roosevelt, he was elected four times.

Note: The names of vice presidents who finished a presidential term appear in parentheses next to the names of the presidents whose terms they completed.

re-election in their own right), the first, third, and fourth electoral orders are the most stable, with the second order the least stable.

Beyond re-election, what can we say about the various men who have been elected in each electoral order? Of the top ten presidents as ranked in the 2000 poll (see section 3-3b, "The 2000 Presidential Poll"), two are from the first electoral order (George Washington and Thomas Jefferson), one is from the second electoral order (Abraham Lincoln), four are from the third electoral order (Theodore Roosevelt, Woodrow Wilson, Franklin Roosevelt, and Harry Truman), and three are from our present electoral order (John Kennedy, Dwight Eisenhower, and Lyndon Johnson).

In short, there are variations in both the re-election prospects and the historical ranking of presidents between the four electoral orders. This result suggests that we need to examine the four electoral orders to (1) determine how they differ in terms of the methods used to nominate and elect presidents and (2) determine how these procedures add to or constrain presidential power.

6-4 The First Electoral Order: The Move toward Contentious Campaigns

As I discussed in Chapter 3, "Active Presidents: The Path to Presidential Greatness"; Chapter 4, "Domestic Policy, Constitutional Ambiguity, and the Growth of Presidential Power"; and section 6-2, "Constitutional Qualifications for President," the U.S. Constitution is often vague, leaving the door wide open for radical changes in our governmental system without need for amendment to the Constitution. Often, all that is required is a new and innovative interpretation of a constitutional provision. Even the president's electoral political resources are not clearly identified in the U.S. Constitution. For instance, there is no mention of the method for nominating candidates. There is no discussion of the expected duration of presidential elections, how they are to proceed, or who is to be in charge of them. Again, as with the powers of the presidential office, only the most rudimentary of outlines is provided. As a result, the presidential election process that we have today is totally unlike the one that elected our first president, George Washington. Given changes in public expectations, technology, and contextual factors (see section 2-1, "The Contextual Revolution in America: The Economy, Foreign Affairs, and Changing Public Expectations"), it is likely that the system we use today will be revised again in future years. In short, the presidential election process has and will continue to evolve over time.

This evolutionary process is important, not simply because the methods we use to elect our presidents change over time, but also because it can impact the power and prestige of the presidential office. I argue that the method we use to select our presidents has much to do with the types of individuals who will be elected, as well as the influence they exert in the larger political system once they assume office. To understand these points, we need to examine how the electoral system has changed across the four electoral orders and its consequences for presidential power.

A good beginning point is the first presidential election in 1789. It occurred much as the Founders intended. There was no presidential campaign. No candidates announced their intention to run for president. There was a consensus that George Washington, a man of considerable virtue with a demonstrated disdain for political ambition, should be the president. While there was some disagreement over the choice of vice president, the election proceeded expeditiously and without partisan rancor. Furthermore, the people's role was greatly constrained, with direct popular election offered in only four states (Pennsylvania, Delaware, Maryland, and Virginia), with two (Massachusetts and New Hampshire) adopting a mixture of state legislative and popular elections, and four others choosing their electors via the state legislature.

New York, North Carolina, and Rhode Island did not participate in the first election—the latter two because they had not yet joined the union, the former because the upper and lower houses of its legislature could not yet agree on an electoral system (Schlesinger 1994a: 4).

Hence, "candidates were not nominated in any formal sense, and there was none of the public hoopla of later elections" (ibid., 5) nor was there much interest around the country. "The haste in which the election was organized, the lack of parties, the lack of any general popular vote, and the assumption that Washington was to be President meant that there was little grass-roots interest in the first presidential election" (ibid., 6). Consequently, while there was no precedent for the first election and procedures had to be invented as it unfolded, the result must have been comforting to the Founders. They were not to be comforted for long, however. The reason was the development of faction in the form of political parties.

The Founders believed they had created a system that would not encourage faction. As Madison wrote in the *Federalist Papers* (#10 and #51), faction would be controlled under the new Constitution. But Madison's essays failed to appreciate the deep ideological divisions that existed within the country. Even before Washington left the presidency, proto-parties, an early formulation of political parties, already had developed.

The election of 1796, the first without Washington as a candidate, also was the first in which parties played a significant role. The duration of the election process was still limited, with Washington officially declaring only in September that he would not run for a third term. Informal meetings among leaders of the proto-parties widely agreed that Vice President John Adams would represent the Federalist Party, while Thomas Jefferson would be the candidate for the Republican/Democratic Party (Sharp 1993: 138).

As Sharp (ibid.) writes, "Finally caught up in the fever of partisanship, both the Federalists and Republicans engaged in activities that led to the alienation of important factions within their proto-parties. In both cases the wounds would not be easy ones to heal." Adams was elected as the nation's second president, but only by three electoral votes over Thomas Jefferson. Jefferson, though he represented a rival political party, by a quirk of the Constitution, was elected as the nation's second vice president. Jefferson finished second in the vote rather than Adams's vice presidential candidate, because there were divisions in the Federalist Party—encouraged by Alexander Hamilton—regarding who should be elected vice president. Thus, because the Constitution prescribed that the two top finishers were to be president and vice president, the third election resulted in a most untenable result: The president and vice president were from different political parties. This handicap haunted Adams throughout his four years in office, with Jefferson often working behind the scenes to thwart administration policy.

6-4a The Election of 1800

The election of 1800 represented a bitter rematch between Adams and Jefferson. By 1800, the parties were more firmly established. According to the expectations of the time, direct presidential campaigning was evidence of ambition, a quality to be strictly avoided in presidential candidates. Hence, neither candidate publicly campaigned. Meanwhile, surrogates representing the two parties took up the case for their candidates. More importantly, each party's machinery in newspapers and pamphlets vehemently attacked the personal integrity and character of the opposition candidate. Adams and Jefferson were scurrilously attacked in a generally vituperative campaign. As McCullough (2001: 543–44) writes, "In the summer and fall of 1800, the question of who was to lead the nation rapidly became a contest of personal vilification surpassing any presidential election in American history."

The result was a narrow victory for Thomas Jefferson, by just eight electoral votes over Adams. But, as had been the case in 1796, the existing constitutional provisions created a strange result involving the vice presidency. This time Jefferson's vice presidential candidate, Aaron Burr, had the same number of electoral votes as Jefferson. With each man receiving the same number of votes, the Constitution dictated that the choice of president be decided by the House of

Representatives. There the matter remained stalemated until February of 1801, with Federalists holding the power to choose either Jefferson or Burr.

In the end, Alexander Hamilton, convinced that Burr was the far more dangerous man, encouraged Federalists in the House to throw their support to Jefferson, thus ending the constitutional crisis. But in two successive elections, the constitutional process had resulted in unexpected and potentially disastrous consequences. It was clear that something needed to be done to prevent a reoccurrence in 1804. The result was the Twelfth Amendment, which provided that the electors "shall name in their ballots the person voted for as President, and in distinct ballots the person voted for as Vice President, and they shall make distinct lists of all persons voted for as President, and all persons voted for as Vice President, and of the number of votes of each. . . ."

While it is still possible for electors to switch their votes (in 1988 a Democratic elector voted for vice presidential candidate Lloyd Bentsen for president and presidential candidate Michael Dukakis for vice president; in 2000 a Gore elector refused to cast her ballot in protest), the possibility that a candidate for vice president actually could be elected president had been essentially eliminated. In addition, the Twelfth Amendment made another important change: In case no one received a majority of the Electoral College votes, it limited the number of names to be sent to the House of Representatives to three instead of the original Constitution's designation of five. As we shall see, this change had important implications for the election of 1824.

6-4b The Rise and Fall of King Caucus

By 1800, presidential campaigning already had diverged from the Founders' ideal. Rather than a sedate, rational process, campaigns already had become boisterous political events. By 1800, another feature of the electoral era was also set. With partisanship now a fixture in presidential contests, candidates for president were predominantly nominated not as favorite sons, as the Founders had thought, or by reason of each candidate's personal virtue, but by the parties through a congressional caucus system; the Federalists had used a similar device to nominate Adams in 1796. As Thomas, Pika, and Watson (1993: 45–46) write, "Because legislators were familiar with potential presidential candidates from all parts of the new country, they were logical agents for choosing candidates for an office, with a nationwide constituency. Caucuses provided a peer review of candidates' credentials, with one group of politicians assessing another's skills, abilities, and political appeal."

The caucus system, sometimes ridiculed as "King Caucus," was a system employed to nominate candidates through the election of 1824. The system had a direct impact on the extent of presidential power. First, as many of the Founders feared, it made the president dependent on the legislative branch of government. Jefferson actually adapted to this system quite well, using it to his advantage as he wined and dined legislators at the Executive Mansion, subtly convincing them to support his administration's agenda. But following Jefferson, with Madison, Monroe, and Adams, the nomination system undercut presidential power, encouraging candidates to defer to the legislature's will. One can argue that Madison's presidency was largely shaped by his method of selection. To secure nomination and re-election, Madison needed to curry favor with his party's leaders in Congress. Congressional "war hawks" (led by young Henry Clay) induced the president to lead the nation ill prepared into a war against England in 1812. Throughout their presidencies Madison and then Monroe deferred to the will of the legislature, rather than advancing their own political agenda. As Milkis and Nelson (1994: 110) write,

The decline of presidential influence was especially evident during James Madison's administration. . . . Although Madison was duly nominated and elected, the promises he had to make to win support from his party's members in Congress suggested that subsequent presidential nominations might well become occasions "to make explicit executive subordination to congressional president-makers."

While the second Adams did enter office with a clearly delineated policy agenda, his party ignored it and Adams did not fight for it. Hence, after a promising start, Adams ceded political control to the legislative branch.

6-4c The Loyalty of the President's Cabinet

A second consequence of the caucus system was that it also encouraged obsequious behavior toward the Congress by members of the president's Cabinet, thus dividing the loyalty of Cabinet secretaries. Once a Cabinet was named, the secretaries curried favor with congressional leaders in an attempt to build support for their party's subsequent presidential nomination. This often made Cabinet secretaries more responsive to Congress than to the president who had nominated them (see Hargrove and Nelson 1984: 130). Consequently, the caucus system encouraged competition between Cabinet members, disloyalty to the president, and obsequiousness to Congress.

Presidential power, then, was constrained by the congressional caucus method of presidential selection, though two factors were working to unseat King Caucus. First, by 1828 most state constitutions allowed citizens to vote directly for president. Second, the election of 1824 showed that the caucus system was no longer tenable.

In the 1824 election, candidates were nominated by regional factions of the Democratic/Republican Party. The Federalist Party essentially had ceased to exist after the Hartford Convention of 1815, when its members discussed the possibility of New England's secession from the union.

With expanding internal divisions within the Democratic/Republican Party, John Quincy Adams was nominated to represent the North; Henry Clay, the West; and William Crawford, the South. Meanwhile, the Tennessee state legislature nominated Andrew Jackson. At first, Jackson's candidacy was not taken seriously, even by the people who had nominated him. But then Crawford's supporters made a strategic mistake. They used the caucus system to nominate their candidate. Supporters of Adams, Clay, and Jackson, however, did not participate. Instead, Adams and Clay attacked the caucus system in an attempt to damage Crawford's candidacy.

The issue caught on, but not in the manner the two candidates had expected. Rather, Andrew Jackson, who was the only candidate clearly not associated with the party, reaped the electoral benefits. In the end, Jackson won both the most electoral and popular votes. He did not, however, win a majority of the electoral votes; thus, the contest was decided by the House of Representatives. Since only the three top finishers now qualified for consideration (instead of the Constitution's original provision of five—a change made effective by the Twelfth Amendment), Clay, who finished fourth, was no longer in the running. Clay, angry with Jackson for usurping his role as the western candidate in the race and possibly tempted by the offer of being Secretary of State, threw his support behind Adams.

Jackson's supporters characterized the election as a "corrupt bargain" between Adams and Clay. Without a united party and with Jackson's supporters raising a rallying cry against the new president's legitimacy, Adams's presidency was essentially doomed from the start. Likewise, a discredited King Caucus system unceremoniously was dethroned. With its demise, a second order in electoral politics was about to be established.

6-5 The Second Electoral Order: Party Control from 1828–1892

During the first electoral order, presidential nominations were decided by the caucus system and the legislative branch. In the second electoral era, the political parties dominated the nomination function through a new innovation: the political convention. The political parties also controlled the partisan press, thus allowing them to convey their message directly to voters. Political campaign events, such as public speeches, parades, picnics, and barbecues, also developed as standard campaign techniques, as did more structured campaigns with catchy slogans (e.g., "Tippecanoe and Tyler Too") and a reliance on image building (e.g., Honest Abe, the rail splitter) to sell presidential hopefuls (see Waterman, Wright, and St. Clair 1999) to the American public.

These innovations were made possible (or made necessary, depending on one's perspective) because by 1828, American voters played a larger role in the electoral process than they had in 1789 when George Washington was first elected. Laws had been liberalized to increase the number of eligible voters, and by 1828, all but one state allowed its voters, rather than the state legislature, to select its electors to the Electoral College.

Various factors, then, encouraged changes in the electoral process. Andrew Jackson took advantage of these changes as the first candidate to directly appeal to the voters. As Jackson's preeminent biographer, Robert Remini (1972: 89–90) writes,

> The election of 1828 was in some respects the first modern presidential election. Democrats [the new name for Jackson's new political party] launched a national campaign of song, slogan, and shouting to attract the largest possible number of votes. It was the first campaign which witnessed a concerted effort to manipulate the electorate on a mass scale. Hereafter the major parties sought presidential candidates with wide popular appeal—frequently war heroes—then backed them with an engine of ballyhoo in order to create the numbers which would provide success.

By appealing to the public, Jackson's election both added to his political prestige and raised concerns about his fitness for office. As Sundquist (1981: 23) writes, Jackson "came to office with both a program and a popular mandate, and as he set out to execute them he aroused both passionate devotion and fierce enmity." Jackson's critics accused him of despotism and demagoguery. But despite the opposition's fears, there would be no turning back to the old electoral order. A precedent had been established for the popular election of the president. It would lead to the formulation of new organizational structures and provide a powerful rationale for increased presidential power.

6-5a The Nominating Convention

Organization was of critical importance to the new electoral order. Remini (1972: 90) notes that "Jackson's impressive showing was not so much the result of campaign ballyhoo as it was the organization that provided it. . . ." With the death of King Caucus, new organizational techniques were needed to nominate candidates. Jackson's re-election in 1832 witnessed the birth of such an important organizational innovation: A new nominating system, the political convention, was employed. The technique involved each state sending delegates (usually party regulars) to a national convention where the delegates (and hence, the political parties) would select candidates for president and vice president (see Box 6-2). They also would write the party platform to inform the voters about the candidate's governing intentions. Hence, to a great extent, the parties controlled both the nomination choice and the candidate's political message.

Box 6-2

Early Conventions

The Anti-Masonic Party (so named because Jackson was a Mason) used a nominating convention to select candidates in 1831, and as early as the turn of the nineteenth century, many states used it to nominate candidates (Roseboom and Eckes 1979: 50). In December 1831, the newly formed National Republican Party (later to be called the Whig Party after they joined with members of the Anti-Mason Party and disgruntled "bank" Democrats) met in Baltimore and nominated Henry Clay of Kentucky as its presidential candidate. In May 1832, the Democrats also met in Baltimore and re-nominated Jackson for president. They also used the occasion to dump the disloyal incumbent vice president, John C. Calhoun, in favor of Jackson's former Secretary of State, Martin Van Buren, a man who had played a critical role in creating the nominating convention in his home state of New York.

With the election of 1832, the nominating convention was established as the primary means of nominating candidates (see Hargrove and Nelson 1984). As Roseboom and Eckes (1979: 49) write, "It was representative in character; it divorced nominations from congressional control and added to the independence of the executive; it permitted an authoritative formulation of a party program; and it concentrated party strength behind a single ticket, the compromise of personal rivalries and group and sectional interests."

Delegates were selected using various methods: "by state conventions, district conventions, local meetings, informal caucuses—dependent on the organization and strength of the party in each state; a national convention might even recognize as delegates visitors in attendance from a state that sent no delegates" (Roseboom and Eckes 1979: 49).

For example, "Edward Rucker cast the entire vote of unrepresented Tennessee" to nominate Van Buren for president "because he happened to be in Baltimore and was a Van Buren man." Likewise, in "the Whig national convention of 1848, the Louisiana delegates cast their own votes and those of Texas because a Texas Whig convention had given them its proxies" (ibid.).

Each state delegation was polled, sometimes voting unanimously, sometimes splitting its votes among different candidates, with surrogates for the various candidates working behind the scenes in an attempt to build support for their candidate. In the second electoral order, it was rare for a presidential candidate to secure nomination on the first ballot. In fact, on many occasions balloting continued over a period of days, as the political fortunes of particular political candidates waxed and waned.

6-5b The Influence of Party Leaders

During the nominating process, party leaders met, often behind closed doors (in what later came to be known as infamous "smoke-filled rooms") to discuss, politick, compromise, and play hardball with supporters of various candidates. Negotiations took place, with supporters of a candidate whose political fortunes were in retreat often joining forces with another candidate, sometimes to support a **dark horse candidate.** Other times, as one candidate's support grew, there was a groundswell of support for him.

The power brokers in this process were no longer the members of Congress, but rather the leaders of the respective political parties in the various states. Candidates thus had every incentive to show deference to these party officials.

Dark horse candidate:
A candidate who has come out of nowhere to secure a party's nomination. This person is often a little-known candidate who gets the nomination because of political compromises.

They did so by promising them partisan favors; one such favor was established by Andrew Jackson after his election in 1828: the spoils system. Based on the idea that to the victor go the spoils, Jackson advocated replacing bureaucrats through a process of rotation in office.

Through this process, the sinecures that had existed under the first electoral order were replaced by the placement of political partisans in a variety of government jobs. Presidents could build party support for their candidacy by promising to use their patronage power in ways that would favor particular state delegations. As such, "[t]he president found himself the chief dispenser of favors for his party. . . ." As a result, "the presidency became a political office, with its control the great aim of each party" (ibid.). Hence, governing and electioneering were joined, thus opening the door for political abuse and corruption, as occurred to an unprecedented extent during the Grant administration.

Importantly, because presidential candidates were dependent on the party machinery for nomination, the convention system, like its predecessor, did not encourage the nomination of independent-minded candidates. As King and Ragsdale (1988: 28–29) note,

> Presidential candidates of the nineteenth century were chosen from negotiations among political machines within the two parties largely on the criterion of how well the candidates could award patronage to major local elements of the party. Often those with strong national reputations aspiring to the office were passed over because the state parties feared the loss of control. Thus, the elections were frequently battles between relatively weak or unknown candidates who, once in office, served the patronage needs of state parties, not the policy needs of the nation. Weak candidates became weak presidents who could be controlled by strong state party organizations. The electoral arrangements by which the person entered office were not suited to producing a chief executive who would assume a policy-making role and would enjoy significant public prestige.

In short, while the legislative branch no longer controlled the nomination process, the presidency itself was still controlled by an external political actor—the political parties—and it would remain so for another hundred years. Because the presidency was subordinate to the political parties, presidential power was greatly constrained. Hence, Franklin Pierce, an undistinguished man with few (if any) political accomplishments and an equally undistinguished military record, could still appeal to different factions of the Democratic Party.

Likewise, James Buchanan's principal political advantages in 1856 were that he (1) was from the swing state of Pennsylvania and (2) had been out of the country as Minister to Great Britain and, hence, had made relatively few political enemies. Even the Republican Party's choice of Lincoln in 1860 seems curious. Other individuals who were considered to have more political clout vied for the office, but Lincoln was the more acceptable compromise candidate because he (1) represented Illinois, which the Republicans needed to win the election, and (2) was perceived to be more moderate than either Chase or Seward on the issue of slavery's abolition.

Yet, while the second electoral order ultimately constrained presidential power, it also provided a powerful rationale for increasing it. Now, for the first time, presidents could claim that they were the only individuals in the national government elected by all the people. A rationale for presidential power therefore was established, but before it could be fully exploited, a closer relationship first had to develop between the presidency and the public. This would occur in the third electoral order.

6-6 The Third Electoral Order: Out of the Shadow of the Parties

The methods candidates use to present themselves to the American public have important consequences for presidential power. By appealing directly to the public, presidential candidates can promote their own personal political agenda, can build personal support, and can develop rhetorical skills they can later use if they choose a strategy of "going public" over the heads of Washington insiders. We see these trends develop during the third electoral order.

6-6a Direct Campaigning

Despite the possibilities described in section 6-6, few presidential candidates initially appealed directly to the public, either in writing or by giving speeches, largely because the Founders greatly feared demagogues. This fear of dictatorship was so prevalent that the presidential candidates of the first electoral order rarely expressed a public interest in the presidency, lest it be perceived as a sign of ambition. For this reason, the early presidents also did not campaign for office. Even Andrew Jackson, who claimed to be a "tribune of the people," did not often speak publicly or actively campaign.

Yet, public campaigning was important. Not only did it have a democratizing impact by involving more Americans in electoral contests (e.g., by building enthusiasm, encouraging people to join and work for campaigns, etc.), but it also provided the public with a chance to see, hear, and evaluate the presidential candidates for themselves. This innovation also was important because it brought the president directly into contact with the American public, thus fostering a relationship that allowed presidents to make promises directly to the public and encouraging both more active presidential involvement in the governing process and increasing public expectations of presidential performance. Most importantly, it provided an opportunity for presidents to step out of the shadows cast by the political party organizations and to emerge as leaders in their own right.

6-6b Harrison and Other Candidates Campaign for Office

Despite the potential for direct campaigning, throughout the nineteenth century, the practice of public campaigning was largely disdained. Ironically, then, the first candidate to actively campaign for president was the man who appears to have been most interested in constraining the power of the presidency: William Henry Harrison. As the Whig Party candidate for president in 1840, Harrison campaigned on the theme of limiting the power of the presidency.

Yet, in 1840, he delivered several speeches on behalf of his candidacy (McDonald 1994: 431). As Schlesinger (1945: 292) writes, Harrison's "public appearances were infrequent, vague and highly effective." Still, other candidates did not immediately follow his example. By the 1850s, the public was an integral part of the election process. Even if the candidates themselves were not present on the campaign trail, party "managers made industrious use of mass meetings, barbecues, open-air speeches, debates, and torchlight processions, while they freely employed newspaper editorials, pamphlets, and handbills" (Nevins 1947: 183). In short, while the candidates did not yet appeal directly to the public, the parties did.

Eventually, however, Harrison's campaign innovation was employed by a number of unsuccessful presidential candidates. In 1860, Stephen Douglas stumped the country in his losing campaign (Foote 1958: 33–34). Likewise, Horatio Seymour campaigned against Ulysses Grant in 1868 (Roseboom and Eckes 1979: 85). In 1872, Horace Greeley, who likewise lost to Grant, "went on the stump for several weeks in a remarkable oratorical campaign before large crowds" (ibid., 88).

(a)

(b)

(c)

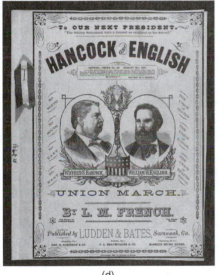

(d)

(e)

Presidential Campaign Materials
(a) Buchanan campaign flyer.
(b) Cleveland scarf.
(c) McKinley blanket.
(d) Hancock-English flyer.
(e) Tilden campaign card.
Reprinted with permission from Duke University, Rare Book, Manuscript and Special Collections Library.

6-6c The Front Porch Campaign and Beyond

In 1884, Grover Cleveland became the first successful presidential candidate since Harrison in 1840 to publicly campaign, making "two formal speeches" and attending "a great celebration in Buffalo." Likewise, Cleveland's opponent, James G. Blaine, publicly "preached on the benefits of the protective tariff and dilated on his favorite theme, the dangers of rebel rule" (ibid., 104, 106).

A low profile by the candidate was still preferred, however, to such an extent that when James Garfield introduced the modest innovation of a "front porch" campaign in 1880, some pundits were initially disconcerted (Tulis 1987: 84). Other candidates, however, adopted Garfield's innovation, particularly William McKinley in 1896, who dutifully campaigned from his home porch, meeting with supporters and the public alike. McKinley felt that "a presidential candidate . . . must remain in dignified waiting until the voters made their decision." Roseboom and Eckes (1979: 118) continue,

He then devised a curious compromise. He might not go to the people, but the people might come to him. The idea of delegations and committees calling upon the candidate was familiar enough, but the excursions of 1896 amounted to mass pilgrimages. People came by the thousands in special trains—farmers, merchants, GAR posts, railroad workers, religious and racial groups, and many others, often with their expenses paid—to see McKinley and to listen to a few, well-chosen remarks or, in the case of large delegations, a formal address of some length.

Ironically, McKinley had built support for his 1896 presidential bid by delivering a number of speeches during the 1894 congressional elections. "Not a candidate himself, he was free to accept invitations that took him from New England to Kansas, and even into the Deep South. In one day of speaking in Iowa and Minnesota, he made twenty-three appearances. . . ." (Fite 1972: 237). Once he was a candidate for president, however, McKinley campaigned from his front porch, while his opponent, Democrat William Jennings Bryan, actively campaigned across the nation. "All together, by his own estimates" Bryan "covered 18,009 miles and made some 600 speeches to possibly 5,000,000 persons" (Roseboom and Eckes 1979: 121).

In the 1900 presidential election, Bryan again campaigned actively against President McKinley. Again McKinley remained far from the campaign trail, though Theodore Roosevelt, his vice presidential candidate, actively campaigned. Roosevelt's "tours were a grand success. In part, he followed Bryan's trail, and the duel of these two rabble-rousers gave color to a campaign that was otherwise apathetic. Bryan preached—Roosevelt shouted" (ibid., 126). Interestingly, when Roosevelt himself ran for president in 1904, he did not campaign.

By 1908, both candidates for president campaigned for office. William Howard Taft, "burdened with his judicial temperament, would have preferred a front-porch affair but was persuaded that stumping was necessary to counteract the appeal of [his opponent, William Jennings] Bryan," who was running in his third and last unsuccessful presidential campaign (ibid., 134). Four years later, in 1912, all three presidential candidates again campaigned for office. That the Democrat Woodrow Wilson and the insurgent Progressive/Bull Moose Theodore Roosevelt would was not surprising, but the incumbent president, Taft, also chose to campaign. It did Taft little good; he finished third in the popular vote and the Electoral College.

As for Theodore Roosevelt, not only did he campaign enthusiastically, he also became the "first [candidate] in history" to appear and speak at his own convention. His fifty-two minute speech roused the crowd to a standing ovation (Milkis and Nelson 1994: 236). Roosevelt then actively campaigned for president, even giving a lengthy speech after a would-be assassin shot him in the chest.

While Harding tried to revive the McKinley front porch campaign in 1920, the new precedent was set. Presidential candidates had stepped out of the shadows cast previously by King Caucus and the political party organizations and into the light of public and media scrutiny. With it, and a greater propensity for presidents to speak once in office as well, the public presidency was born, a vitally important step in changing public perceptions of the presidency and in expanding presidential power.

6-6d Radio and Going Public

Contextual factors made public campaigning possible and also encouraged a closer relationship between presidents and the public. A truly national media had begun to develop in the late nineteenth century, and Teddy Roosevelt made great use of it to appeal directly to the American public. But his ability to use the presidency as a "bully pulpit" was greatly constrained by the technologies of the day.

In 1924, however, presidential communication entered a new era when radio was first used in a presidential campaign. Early presidents and presidential candidates, speaking in sonorous tones, made poor use of the new technology. While the largest item in Herbert Hoover's 1928 campaign budget was money for radio (Altschuler 1991: 43), he was not an effective speaker on the radio. Still, it was apparent to politicians that "radio was creating the instant national community that has been an American experience ever since" (Schlesinger 1994b: 125). What was needed was a politician with the skill to effectively use the new technology.

Franklin Roosevelt understood the new technology in a way other politicians had not. During the 1932 campaign, when he spoke into the radio microphone, he envisioned himself speaking directly to ordinary citizens. His speech patterns were thus more relaxed and his syntax less formal and more conversational. Sometimes, Roosevelt would purposely include grammatical mistakes, such as changing "isn't" to "ain't," because he believed it sounded more genuine to his radio audience. "The deep mellow tones of his voice, a cheerful warmth of personality, and a skill in interjecting light, humorous touches into his speeches made his broadcasts the most effective type of propaganda the Democrats used." In contrast, the "heavy monotonous seriousness of Hoover's speeches made listening an effort" (Roseboom and Eckes 1979: 162).

Roosevelt demonstrated the power of radio to connect a politician to his or her audience. He also used grand gestures, such as flying to Chicago to personally deliver his acceptance speech before the Democratic National Convention, the first candidate since Teddy Roosevelt in 1912 to do so. But it was radio that defined Roosevelt to most Americans. In his 1932, 1936, 1940, and 1944 campaigns, he relied on radio to take his case for election/re-election directly to the voters. As Stuckey (1991: 31) notes, an "overwhelming amount of the speeches [Roosevelt] addressed to the public" were delivered "during election years." It was one of his primary means of getting his message directly to the public and thus avoiding the filter of media coverage. Indeed, in 1936, the "power of radio to overcome unfavorable newspaper publicity was clearly shown. . . . In the fifteen largest cities, the newspaper alignment was 71 percent for [Republican Alf] Landon, as measured by circulation figures" (Roseboom and Eckes 1979: 172). Roosevelt went around the print media, and in this process the print media began to see its influence decline as presidents used radio and later television to take their case directly to the American public.

Radio was the dominant communications technology throughout the 1930s and 1940s. By 1948, however, a new technology was emerging, one that would bring presidents and the public even closer together. It would also be one of the key contextual factors defining the politics of the fourth electoral order.

6-7 The Fourth Electoral Order: The Post Partisan Era

Like radio, only more so, television transformed the face of presidential politics. Its introduction is also one factor that marks the beginning of the fourth electoral order, along with the expanded use of presidential primaries and the introduction of independent presidential political organizations. We examine each of these factors in sections 6-7a, 6-7b, 6-8, and 6-9.

6-7a Television's Impact

The first television station took to the air in 1947 (in Pittsburgh, Pennsylvania). Just five years later, in 1952, television "was still very much in its infancy." As of July 1952, there were only "108 stations on the air, almost all in large cities, thereby depriving much of rural, small-town America of real access to the medium." But an estimated 19 million television sets were in America's homes, "a majority of the electorate" (Schlesinger 1994b: 260).

Despite the limited number of Americans owning TV sets, the new technology played an integral role in a presidential election for the first time. First, it saved Richard Nixon's place on the Republican vice presidential ticket. When the *New York Post* accused Nixon of financial improprieties, he took to television to make his case directly to the American people. His "Checkers" speech, so called because he referred to his dog Checkers, was both a defense of his ethics and an appeal to the public to support his candidacy. The appeal was so astonishingly successful that Dwight Eisenhower, who had been wavering in his support for his running mate, decided to keep Nixon on the ticket. "The big winner," as Halberstam (1993: 242) comments, "in the whole episode was not Nixon but television." It "highlighted the real movement of television into politics" (Stuckey 1991: 81).

Television also proved to be an important development undermining the strength of the political parties. Stuckey (ibid.) notes, "What it taught Richard Nixon was that he now had a way to circumvent the party politicians and reporters who were opposing him. He could go straight to the people, with the kinds of appeals the people could understand and support."

Second, in the fall campaign of 1952, Eisenhower himself became the first presidential candidate to run televised campaign commercials. "The emergence of television coincided with and fostered an important development—the movement of professional advertising into television campaigns" (Schlesinger 1994: 260–61). Eisenhower was a revered figure, but on the political stump he was ineffective. As Halberstam (1993: 227–28) writes, "when a group of Texas oilmen . . . who supported Eisenhower asked him to come up with a retaliatory slogan to the Democrats' 'You Never Had It So Good,' [ad man] Roser Reeves told them that what they needed was not a slogan but a campaign of quick television spots, featuring the general speaking to the American people on a vast range of issues—in short, punchy, unanswerable takes." A plan called "How to Insure an Eisenhower Victory in November" recommended "$2 million be spent in the last three weeks

Republican vice presidential candidate Richard M. Nixon giving his "Checkers" speech on television, September 23, 1952:
"I should say this, that Pat doesn't have a mink coat, but she does have a respectable Republican cloth coat. And I always tell her that she'd look good in anything. . . . We did get something, a gift after the election. It was a little cocker spaniel dog, black and white spotted. And our little girl Tricia, the six-year-old, named it Checkers. And you know, the kids, like all kids, love the dog and I just want to say this right now, that regardless of what they say about it, we're going to keep him."

GEORGE SILK/TIMEPIX

on spots, 'the quickest, most effective and cheapest means of getting across a message in the shortest possible time'" (ibid.). Interestingly, in 1948, Reeves had recommended that Republican Thomas Dewey do a series of similar radio spots. Dewey rejected the idea as undignified (ibid.). In 1952, however, Eisenhower agreed, and presidential politics was forever altered.

Television advertising further undercut the power of the political parties in presidential election campaigns. As Stuckey (1991: 54) notes, "Before Eisenhower, unpopular individuals could be elected because of their ties to a popular party or to a popular party platform. As Eisenhower discovered, and candidates since Eisenhower have realized, strong candidates need television more than they need parties." Hence, the 1952 election demonstrated not only the power of television, but also a weakness in political party control.

6-7b Presidential Debates

In 1960, television's power was again showcased in a presidential election—this time with the Kennedy-Nixon debates. A series of debates ensued, though most remember only the first one. Nixon, having been ill, refusing to wear makeup, and wearing a gray suit that blended into the stage's background, looked haggard and untrustworthy. Further underscoring this impression, his eyes darted from side to side as he listened to Kennedy speak. On the other hand, Kennedy, tanned, wearing a blue suit, and looking confident both when he spoke and when he listened to Nixon, projected an image of strength.

After the first debate, the crowds following the Kennedy campaign became larger and more enthusiastic. Even Nixon realized that the debates had not helped him. He would later write (Nixon 1979: 423), "Looking back now on all four of them, there can be no question but that Kennedy had gained more [politically] from the debates than I had." Still, Nixon recognized that "joint TV appearances of candidates at the presidential level are here to stay, mainly because people want them and the candidates have a responsibility to inform the public on their views before the widest possible audience." Interestingly, though, when he ran for president in 1968 and 1972, Nixon eschewed further presidential debates.

While no debates were held between 1964 and 1972, beginning with the 1976 Carter-Ford election, at least one televised presidential debate has been conducted in each successive election. Rather than focusing the public's attention on the issues, however, the debates, beginning with the 1960 ones, have tended to focus scrutiny on cosmetic concerns, gaffes, and snappy one-liners. As Jamieson and Birdsell (1988: 98) write, "The televised debates . . . have been shaped by the assumption that their audience has a short attention span and is drawn to the event by the prospect of clash." Hence, television has changed the focus to the candidate and personality issues rather than the political party and substantive issues. It appears to have devalued the importance of issues in presidential campaigns.

6-8 Presidential Primaries

A second innovation diminished the political parties' influence even more so than television: the presidential primary. Primaries actually were an innovation initiated early in the twentieth century by the Progressive Party movement in an attempt to clean up and democratize the political process. The idea is that the people, not party leaders, should directly nominate candidates in a primary election (occurring before the secondary fall election that actually elects the president). "In 1912, a dozen states, mainly in the middle west, adopted the primary system" (McDonald 1994: 436).

Theodore Roosevelt entered all of the primaries, as did the Progressive Party candidate Robert M. LaFollette and President William Howard Taft. As McDonald (1994: 436–37) notes, "Roosevelt mopped up, carrying states with a total of 278 delegates, as opposed to 48 for Taft and 36 for LaFollette." But during the third electoral order, the party machinery was still dominant. Since Taft still controlled it, he was renominated for president. A bitter Roosevelt then bolted his party, running under the Progressive mantle, where he finished second to Woodrow Wilson in the fall presidential election. Embarrassingly, Taft, the incumbent president, finished third.

While presidential primaries continued to be conducted in subsequent elections, it was another sixty years before they became the dominant method of nominating presidential candidates. In the meantime, they were not entirely irrelevant. From time to time, a particular presidential challenger would try to make his name by showing the party faithful that he was of presidential timbre; that is, he could attract votes. Still, it was the party organizations that made the final decision regarding the nomination. Primaries remained but a tool to speak to the party leaders.

Primaries were still a political sideshow, but they often were an interesting sideshow. For instance, in 1940, Thomas E. Dewey first came to the attention of national party leaders when he "showed surprising strength in several state primaries . . ." (Roseboom and Eckes 1979: 177). In 1944, Dewey was able to secure his party's nomination, in part, by defeating the 1940 standard bearer, Wendell Willkie, in the Wisconsin primary. Willkie's defeat forced him to withdraw from the contest, thus ending his hopes of again securing the Republican nomination (ibid., 193). Dewey got the nomination and, though he lost to Franklin Roosevelt in November, earned a reputation as an up-and-coming star in the Republican Party.

Again, in 1948, primaries played an interesting role. With a weak incumbent, Harry Truman, running for president, just about everyone considered it to be New York Governor Thomas Dewey's year. But in the Republican primaries, Harold Stassen of Minnesota emerged as a potentially viable alternative after he captured nineteen of twenty-seven delegates in the Wisconsin primary and polled more than 40 percent of the vote in Nebraska. On the other hand, General Douglas MacArthur's poor showing in these two states effectively dashed his presidential ambitions. Dewey was then forced to confront Stassen in the Oregon primary, where he decisively defeated him, thus clearing the way for his own nomination. While the frontrunner and the choice of the Republican Party establishment did get the nomination, he was forced to do so by confronting his main opponent in a primary election (ibid.).

6-8a The Presidential Primaries of 1952

In 1952, the party's favorite presidential candidate was Senator Robert Taft of Ohio. But Taft was too conservative and isolationist for the internationalist wing of the Republican Party. The party's only hope of stopping Taft was to convince General Dwight D. Eisenhower to seek the nomination. Ike had turned down invitations from both parties to run in 1948. In 1952, however, he agreed to run as a Republican, but he entered the race as an underdog, with Taft already having secured the critical backing of Republican Party insiders.

Eisenhower therefore had but one option: to run as an insurgent in the presidential primaries. He won in New Hampshire, New Jersey, Massachusetts, and Oregon; though he lost to Taft in Nebraska and South Dakota, Eisenhower "demonstrated heavy vote-getting firepower" (Davis 1967: 78). In the Pennsylvania primary, Eisenhower startled party insiders by pulling 847,420 votes to 176,000 for

Taft's write-in campaign (ibid., 78–80). After a bitter convention fight, in which television played a key role, Eisenhower secured the Republican Party nomination. In so doing, he demonstrated one of the principal dangers (to party insiders) of the primary system: It could take the nomination choice out of the hands of the political party leaders and, hence, weaken and undermine their influence.

6-8b Kennedy in the 1960 Primaries

In 1960, John Kennedy used the primaries in the traditional manner—to show the party insiders that he could get votes. He used the West Virginia primary to show Democratic "big city party professionals" who considered "his youth, Roman Catholicism, and his position in the U.S. Senate as almost insurmountable barriers to his nomination" that he was in fact a viable candidate (Davis 1969: 82, 84). By defeating Minnesota Senator Hubert Humphrey in West Virginia and confronting the Catholic issue directly, Kennedy advanced his candidacy among party insiders. On the other hand, Lyndon Johnson, the favorite of many party insiders, irreparably damaged his campaign by deciding not to compete in the primaries. Kennedy secured the nomination and the presidency.

6-8c The 1968 Election

The amazing presidential election of 1968 provided the catalyst for changing the nomination system. The 1968 campaign unfolded dramatically, with one astonishing event after another shaking the political world. First, Lyndon Johnson, the incumbent president, decided not to seek re-election after he won only a narrow victory in the New Hampshire primary against an underfinanced and little-known U.S. Senator, Eugene McCarthy. With Johnson's withdrawal, Robert Kennedy and Hubert Humphrey announced their intentions to run for president, though Humphrey decided not to compete in any of the primaries; on the other hand, Kennedy actively participated in them. The assassination of Martin Luther King, Jr., followed within two months by Kennedy's own assassination after his victory in the California primary, presaged the most destructive political convention in American history. As a television audience at home watched images of the Chicago police beating anti-Vietnam war protestors in the streets outside the convention hall, the Democratic Party nominated Vice President Humphrey. Many Democrats were outraged. To them, the will of the people—as expressed in the primaries—had been ignored.

6-8d The McGovern-Fraser Committee Reforms

As an attempt to mollify dissidents within the Democratic Party and to present a united front against the Republicans in the 1968 fall election, the Democrats agreed to create a commission that would establish new rules to govern the 1972 delegate selection process. When Humphrey was narrowly defeated by Richard Nixon, the dissidents within the party were suddenly in a strong position to rewrite the party's nomination rules.

By opening the process to a greater number of women and minorities, the 1970 McGovern-Fraser Committee advocated a more democratic selection process. The committee may not have anticipated that its recommendations would encourage most states to adopt the primary election nominating method, but most Democratic state officials, after deciding that the new procedures were too complex to use other selection methods, decided to use primary elections. Republican state officials, though they were not bound by the McGovern-Fraser Committee recommendations, soon followed suit. Consequently, the number of states using primaries expanded rapidly. As it did, the influence of individual candidates increased, while the political parties' influence concomitantly decreased.

A palpable demonstration of this shift occurred in 1976, when Jimmy Carter used the Iowa caucus and the New Hampshire primary to advance his candidacy for the Democratic nomination over party favorite Scoop Jackson. Carter then defeated the incumbent president, Gerald Ford, who had faced formidable opposition from the insurgency candidacy of Ronald Reagan in the Republican primaries.

6-8e Primaries Are Damaging to Incumbent Presidents

In 1980, the tables were turned in the primaries: Carter, the incumbent, faced a challenge from within his own party from Senator Edward Kennedy of Massachusetts. While the challenge failed, it divided the Democratic Party, and Ronald Reagan, now the Republican Party favorite, was elected that fall. A new pattern was thus established. Not only did the primaries advance the prospects of personal candidates for president over the party leaders, but they also proved severely damaging to incumbent presidents if they were challenged in the primary process. In 1992, for example, conservative candidate Patrick Buchanan challenged incumbent George H. W. Bush for the Republican Party nomination. Buchanan received more than 30 percent of the vote in a number of primary elections, thus forcing the incumbent to actively fight for the nomination, dividing the Republican Party and making Bush a more vulnerable candidate in the fall election. He was subsequently defeated by Bill Clinton. Hence, incumbents such as Ronald Reagan in 1984 and Bill Clinton in 1996, who faced no credible primary challengers, have a major advantage going into the fall campaign: a united party.

While political parties still exert influence in American political elections today, they no longer play the premier role in it (which is why the fourth electoral order is called the post partisan order). In reality, there is considerable partisanship, but the political parties do not orchestrate it, as was the case in the second and third electoral orders. Television and primary elections clearly weakened the role of the parties. A third factor further contributed to this process: independent presidential campaign committees.

6-9 President Campaign Committees

The 1952 election played another important role in the introduction of the fourth electoral order. Dwight Eisenhower employed his own presidential committee separate from the Republican national committee to campaign for president. As Lowi (1985: 73–74) writes,

> Presidential candidates before Eisenhower had made some use of "citizen politics." For example, there had been hundreds of Willkie Clubs during the 1940 campaign. But not until Eisenhower had there been an effort to form these citizen groups into a national organization for the purpose of running a campaign independent of the political party. Out of this effort came Citizens for Eisenhower (CFE)....

In 1960, John Kennedy further developed Eisenhower's innovation. As Weko (1995: 24) writes, "Kennedy relied heavily upon personal emissaries to supervise and coordinate his campaign...." He also "assembled his own organization to manage the national campaign.... The party's national committee, meanwhile, was 'relegated to a poor place in the shadows.'" After the election, Kennedy "brought his campaign people en masse into the top positions in government" (Hess 1976: 80), thus merging electioneering and governing. Kennedy also extensively used polling during the campaign. He had Louis Harris conduct nearly 50 polls between the Democratic Convention and Election Day, and he used these polls "to make decisions about his campaign itinerary, advertising, campaign speeches, and policy positions" (Weko 1995: 23). These innovations likewise would make their way into the governing sphere, thus narrowing the difference between running for president and governing as president.

Still, it was up to Richard Nixon to essentially divorce the Republican Party from his own campaign. In 1972, with the establishment of the Committee to Re-Elect the President or, as it became more infamously known during the Watergate hearings, CREEP, the party's role was relegated to a clear secondary status. Presidents had once depended on the party for their nomination and election. Now, the parties depended on how extensively the presidential candidates decided to use them in the electoral and governing processes. In the fourth electoral order, the parties therefore moved to the political shadows.

6-10 Implications for Presidential Power

The decline of the political parties in the electoral process has important implications for presidential power. It now often makes the process of running for president and governing indistinguishable. The Clinton White House seemed to stay in campaign mode after its election in 1992, immediately beginning the process of running for re-election in 1996, thus giving birth to what is called the "permanent campaign" (see Ornstein and Mann 2000). Since the primary process and the preparation for it (including raising campaign funds and putting together a national organization) have elongated the election process to up to two years, this means there is less time for presidents to govern. Hence, unless presidents "hit the ground running," as Pfiffner (1988) recommends, they may have little time to accomplish their major policy goals.

Yet, it is more difficult to "hit the ground running" because by reducing the role of the political parties, presidents have less organizational support or support in Congress than they once did when they take office. In the third electoral order, presidents could build an electoral coalition (such as Roosevelt's New Deal coalition), which then would help them to govern. Now, presidents must build multiple and shifting coalitions. They build one to secure their party's nomination (often by appealing to liberals in the Democratic primaries or conservatives in the Republican primaries). They then must begin to move toward the center for the fall campaign, thus building a broader electoral coalition. Then, having won the election, they need to build a series of governing coalitions, often on each individual issue, as the electoral coalitions begin to collapse. This is a daunting task for even the most skilled politician (see Seligman and Covington 1989).

6-11 The Effect of Presidential Elections
on Congressional Elections

The declining influence of the political parties in the fourth electoral order is relevant to the presidency (and presidential power) in yet another way: There has been a decline in the presidential coattail effect, or the propensity of members of Congress to secure election because they coast to victory on a popular president's electoral coattails. During past electoral orders presidents secured influence with many members of Congress because they helped to elect them in the first place. Loyalty to the president therefore carried over to the governing process. For instance, numerous House Democrats owed their electoral success to Franklin Roosevelt in 1932 and 1936, as did many House Democrats to Lyndon Johnson in 1964. But this was an era in which voters were more likely to take their cues from the political parties and, hence, to vote for the entire Democratic or Republican ticket.

By 1968, however, and increasingly thereafter, more people cast "negative votes" for president; that is, they voted for the presidential candidate they least disliked instead of one they most liked (Gant and Davis 1984; Gant and Sigelman 1985; Sigleman and Gant 1989; Gant and Richardson 1993). Under these circumstances, these voters were more likely to split their votes in presidential and congressional contests (Gant, Richardson, and Waterman 1992). As the propensity toward split-ticket voting increased, the impact of the coattail effect diminished over time (see Calvert and Ferejohn 1983; Ferejohn and Calvert 1984; Oppenheimer, Stimson, and Waterman 1986; Waterman, Oppenheimer, and Stimson 1991; though for another view see Campbell 1986). Edwards (1980: 73) found no evidence of a coattail effect after 1968, and Jacobson (1990: 10) writes, "Certainly, if coattails are measured by the capacity of winning presidential candidates to pull their party's other candidates into office along with them, the data are reasonably persuasive: Presidential coattails have indeed atrophied."

Hence, with the decline of the political parties, presidents have lost another valuable electoral resource. At the same time, however, the so-called midterm penalty effect continues to undercut presidential influence with Congress. That is, the propensity for the public to penalize the president's party in Congress in midterm elections continues. Since the size of the House was set at 535 members in 1914, the party of the president lost seats in all but three of the midterm House elections (1934, 1998, and 2002). Thus, the decline of the parties has decreased presidential influence in other important ways.

An early explanation for this phenomenon was the theory of "surge and decline." According to Campbell (1960), there is a surge of voters participating in presidential election contests, and this surge results in increased support for congressional candidates of the president's political party (hence, a coattail effect occurs). At midterm, however, with the members of the House running for re-election, and the president not on the ballot, there is a decline in voter turnout, with opponents of the president more motivated to vote. Consequently, the pattern at midterm is that the president's partisans lose seats roughly in percentage to gains made in the past presidential contest; that is, the decline depends on the level of the surge (Campbell 1960). While Campbell proposed the thesis in 1960, in 1990, Jacobson (1990: 19) wrote, "Tides of *surge and decline* still occur; the more seats a party wins in one election, the more seats it is likely to lose in the next election. The difference is that the individual seats lost in the *decline* are far less likely to be seats won in the prior *surge* than they were before" (italics in original).

An alternative explanation for the midterm loss phenomenon was based on the idea that presidents prime the economic pump in order to get elected, thus improving their and their House partisans' electoral fortunes in presidential election years. Economic downturns and less pump priming are common at midterm, the reason why so many presidential House partisans are defeated at midterm. Kramer (1971); Jacobson and Kernell (1983); Lewis-Beck and Rice (1992); Oppenheimer, Stimson, and Waterman (1986); and Gaddie and Bullock (2000) provided additional support for this thesis, demonstrating that the state of economy was related to the midterm loss phenomenon. Meanwhile, Campbell (1985) combined both the "surge and decline" and economic models and showed that they were not inconsistent. Still another explanation for the midterm loss phenomenon is Erikson's (1988) presidential penalty thesis. According to Erikson, voters at midterm consciously cast a vote to penalize the party of the president. Yet, in the last two midterm elections, the party of the president actually has gained seats. It is too early to tell, however, if the midterm loss phenomenon has ended.

6-12 Personality over Policy Substance

Without the political parties, one can argue that presidents no longer consistently convey a clear message or political vision. Campaign advertisements that stress personality over substance greatly undercut the ability of presidents to develop or express a governing vision. Since McGinniss (1970) first compared the selling of Richard Nixon to the American voters of 1968 as comparable to selling a pack of cigarettes, the marketing of the presidency has received increasing criticism. A quarter century later, Newman (1994: xvii) writes, "We have entered a new era in American politics. . . . Bill Clinton was 'marketed' to the American electorate in much the same way as a product or service is marketed to a consumer, and we are seeing the Clinton administration relying on these same tactics to win approval for their programs." In other words, the marketing of presidents, like other electoral innovations, may further obfuscate the difference between elections and governing.

Such marketing may also be devaluing the role of substance in presidential elections. As Waterman, Wright, and St. Clair (1999) argue, the result of these various campaign innovations, as well as the propensity of presidents to speak more often (see section 7-13, "Speaking Often"), is that the presidency is becoming less substantive and more image driven. Campaigns are offering us a choice only of competing personalities and symbols, not competing governing strategies (see Box 6-3).

Additionally, while presidents are less dependent on the parties than they once were, they are not entirely independent. Today, they appear to be quite dependent on the people who provide money for their campaigns. In 2000, George W. Bush and Al Gore scared away many potential rivals for the nomination by raising huge sums of money in advance of the presidential primaries. Once Bush was elected, he rewarded many contributors with ambassadorships and other influential positions in his administration. Bill Clinton had done the same thing in 1992. After the Enron scandal of 2002, new campaign finance legislation was approved, but realistically, money will continue to talk and those who raise the most money in campaigns will have the loudest voice, though they may not have the best message.

Hence, the fourth electoral order raises serious questions about whether elections adequately prepare presidential candidates for presidential leadership. Building independent campaigns (then hiring professionals—handlers, pollsters, image makers, strategists, and fund-raisers—to run them), looking good on television, and raising large sums of money are the qualities that are needed for a *good* presidential candidate today. Do these same qualities, however, lead to good presidents? As Neustadt famously declared in his classic work *Presidential Power,* the White House is "no place for amateurs." Instead, one can argue that what we are getting today are professional campaigners—not quite amateurs, but perhaps not experienced men or women of presidential timbre, either.

Box 6-3

How to Run an Issueless Campaign

Step 1

To run for president, you first have to get your party's nomination. This is a long process. Today, many candidates literally begin to unofficially campaign for president up to four years before they actually run for office. Most candidates begin by raising money. If they raise enough money, it is possible for them to be credible candidates. Raising literally tens of millions of dollars from campaign contributors allows a candidate to run a national campaign and also to scare off other candidates who cannot raise money, as well as set up a campaign organization, which is very expensive. The nomination generally is awarded to the person who is able to win a majority of his or her party's convention delegates. Each state's number of delegates is related to the number of people who live in that state. However, Iowa generally holds the first presidential caucus and New Hampshire the first presidential primary, so you would visit these states first.

The road to getting your party's nomination includes speeches, fund-raising, and trips to states with early primaries and caucuses.

Step 2

Let's say that you won the Iowa caucus and finished a respectable second in New Hampshire. You now have to run in primary elections in several states at the same time, especially on Super Tuesday when most southern states hold their primaries. Television is by far the most important medium for communication with voters. Everyone complains about commercial advertisements, but they work. Your advertising team has come up with commercials that are likely to portray you as patriotic, religious, or caring, but, surprisingly, not focusing on the issues! Candidates who concentrate on the issues tend to divide the electorate, but candidates who depend on symbols and images tend to be able to connect to a larger percentage of the voters. But you cannot totally ignore the issues because voters in primary elections tend to be more politically active and tend to be more liberal or conservative than average voters. You must perform a balancing act, talking about the issues enough to get primary voters excited, but not enough to enrage them. Your safest choice, therefore, is to run as a religious, patriotic, and caring American, and pour lots of money into issueless campaign commercials.

In this stage of your campaign, you'll portray yourself on TV as kind, patriotic, and/or religious, while avoiding divisive issues.

Step 3

You have now won the next primary, and all candidates have dropped out of the race but you and one other. You now must face off against your opponent in a debate. Past experience shows that the public generally tends to favor a candidate if they like him or her. Likability is therefore VERY IMPORTANT. Very intelligent

After appearing likable and winning debates, you want your former opponents to endorse your candidacy.

candidates have lost because they were not considered likable enough. So you have to be concerned with likability. You dazzle the audience in the debate, and you win the next several primaries. A teary-eyed opponent you vanquished in the primaries is now conceding defeat. Now you must reach out to your opponent for an endorsement because you want the voters who supported him or her to support you now. A photo opportunity with you and the vanquished candidate holding hands above your head shows that your party is indeed united.

Step 4

It's April, and you have the nomination wrapped up. Now you need to keep raising money, begin to plan your convention, and formulate strategy for the fall campaign. At the convention, you will run a multi-day infomercial, largely devoid of content, with some clever one-liners aimed at your fall opponent, and best of all, lots of praise for you and your lovely family. Smiles and hand-waving are important, plus lots of flags and patriotic symbols. The media will be bored, but who cares? The public needs to see that you are presidential and likable. In your convention speech, you'll set a campaign theme, which is largely meaningless but catchy and memorable. You are now ready to run for the presidency itself. It's time for some math: Each state has 2 electoral votes, representing its two senators, and then 1 electoral vote for each member of the House of Representatives. The District of Columbia also has 3 electoral votes. Thus, there are 538 electoral votes, so 270 represent a majority. That is what you need to win the presidency.

After you have the nomination and have set a theme, it's time to look at numbers.

Step 5

You can then divide the states into those that you are likely to win, those that you are likely to lose, and those that are competitive. You will find that the competitive states, the so-called swing states, will determine your political future. These are states that swing back and forth from election to election and states that can swing either way in the current election. You will want to examine how these states have voted in the past and do intensive polling to determine how they stand at present. If you are ahead in the polls, you begin to look presidential, but if you are behind in the polls, you can look desperate or, worse yet, like a loser. If you are behind in the polls, your message is not resonating with voters. But you tell pundits that you have never been a believer in polls, even as you pay for new ones. You change your message. The polls show that people are interested in leadership, so you begin to say things like "Leadership for a New America." Your pollsters test the new message. It appears to work: You are moving up in the polls. Your opponent is trying to belittle your new theme, claiming you are untrustworthy because you change your message from week to week, but your supporters lash back that your campaign has always been about leadership. You never tell pundits that you do believe in the polls. You do tell them, "Look, I didn't pay attention to the polls when I was down, and now that I am moving up, I still don't pay attention to them." That reminds everyone that you are moving up. Your pollsters meanwhile continue to run additional polls. You breathlessly await these results.

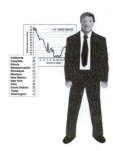

Your campaign becomes caught up in studying swing states and keeping track of public opinion through polls.

Step 6

Now you prepare for debates. You work on developing snappy one-liners and avoiding mistakes rather than developing a real theme. If you are smart, you will mention leadership over and over again, as in "as Governor I have provided leadership." Or you say things like "that is what leadership is all about." You, of course, have memorized a couple of clever one-liners that you will use when given the opportunity. "You're no John Kennedy" is a good one, but I wouldn't mention "lock boxes." In the debate, the media will be looking to see whether you came across well on TV. This is sad but true. Many pundits who listened to the debate on the radio thought Nixon won the first debate over Kennedy, but Nixon did not come across well on TV. Likewise, it can be argued that Gore bested Bush on substantive matters, but Gore looked stiff, untrustworthy and, most damaging of all, uncomfortable on TV, while Bush looked likable.

Likability and clever remarks are more important at debates than the issues, at least in the eyes of the media.

Step 7

The debates are over and the polls have not moved much. You are leading by five points going into the last week of the campaign. If you are ahead, you will generally get better press than your opponent, but the reality is that while the media concentrate on who is up or down by five or ten points, the real mathematics is 270. You are now racing to go to undecided states, and since you have a five-point lead, you may want to spend a day visiting some of the states

your opponent once considered safe but now needs to win. You run a blitz of media ads, most of them stressing your theme of leadership and portraying you as a likable family man/woman. You and your opponent do a series of around-the-clock campaign stops. Your voice is hoarse. You have repeated your basic campaign speech a couple of thousand times, and the media are talking about a narrowing of the polls as Election Day approaches. You return to your home state and vote for president; that is, you vote for yourself. Your spouse and children accompany you. You wave to the camera and perhaps do a few last-minute satellite interviews in close states. But your task is done. It is now time to count the votes. At eight o'clock eastern time, the networks make their first projections. Projections are based on actual votes counted, exit polls, and expert opinion. "We have a winner. CNN now projects that [your name] has been elected as the 44th President of the United States." Your picture surrounded by the presidential seal and flags appears on TV screens all over America.

Your quest for the presidency, which under the best of circumstances has consumed only four years of your life, is over. You have run a largely issueless campaign, based on personality and slogans. Now, you face the questions Robert Redford's character confronted in the movie *The Candidate*. Now what do I do? The election has won you the White House, but did the campaign lay the groundwork for how your new administration actually will govern the nation?

After all that campaigning, are you ready to govern the United States?

Chapter Summary

The Founders wanted to create an electoral scheme that would promote virtuous men, preferably men of vast experience and high moral character (and limited personal ambition). At the same time, they feared demagogues, like Oliver Cromwell, and thus wanted a representative electoral system, yet one that would severely limit the direct participation of the American voter. But how could they create an electoral scheme that would be representative and yet at the same time limit the direct influence of the people? This chapter examined this question.

Review Questions

1. Which of the following institutions was created by the Founders because it was feared that most people would not be familiar with all of the presidential candidates?
   a. the presidential primary
   b. the caucus system
   c. the Electoral College
   d. the presidential debates

2. If no candidate for president receives a majority of the Electoral College vote, then
   a. a run-off election is held.
   b. the Senate decides who the next president will be.
   c. the House of Representatives decides who the next president will be.
   d. the Supreme Court decides who the next president will be.

3. To be president, one must be
   a. a naturalized citizen.
   b. at least forty years of age.
   c. a resident within the United States for fourteen years.
   d. all of the above.

4. Who of the following was the first president to use the primary process to run a successful insurgency campaign to unseat the party favorite?
   a. Franklin Roosevelt
   b. Dwight Eisenhower
   c. John Kennedy
   d. Ronald Reagan

5. Who of the following was the first president of the "partisan era" of presidential elections?
   a. George Washington
   b. Thomas Jefferson
   c. John Quincy Adams
   d. Andrew Jackson

6. The Founders believed they had created a system that would not encourage
   a. faction.
   b. slavery.
   c. compromise.
   d. all of the above.

7. By which election year were political parties firmly established in the electoral system?
   a. 1792
   b. 1800
   c. 1828
   d. 1860

8. By which election year did American voters play a much larger role in the electoral process than they had in 1789 when George Washington was first elected?
   a. 1800
   b. 1808
   c. 1818
   d. 1828

9. Jackson's re-election in 1832 witnessed the birth of which important organizational innovation?
   a. the presidential primary
   b. the Electoral College
   c. the party caucus
   d. the presidential debate

10. Who of the following was the first president to understand the power of radio?
    a. Theodore Roosevelt
    b. Franklin Roosevelt
    c. John Kennedy
    d. Ronald Reagan

Discussion Questions

Discussion Questions

1. Should we abolish the Electoral College and make the popular-vote winner the president? If we did so, would there be any implications for the way presidential candidates run for office?

2. The Constitution includes very few requirements for president. Should the Constitution include higher standards in order for someone to qualify to run for president?

3. What are the four electoral eras, and why are they important?

4. Do we need a new system for nominating presidential candidates? What are the pros and cons of the current system?

5. How have various communications technologies impacted the presidential election process?

The Presidency and the Public: A Double-Edged Sword

Key Term

fireside chats

7-1 The Presidency and the Public: A Double-Edged Sword

Perhaps the best way for us to understand how the presidency has changed over the past two hundred plus years is to examine its relationship with various external political actors in the policy process. Such actors as the public, the media, the political parties, the Congress, the courts, interest groups, the bureaucracy, the states, other national governments, and international organizations (to name but a few) are *external political resources* because the president regularly interacts with them but does not have hierarchical control over them.

Among these external actors, the president's relationship with the public is of particular importance. Perhaps *the* distinguishing characteristic of the presidency is its evolving relationship with the American public. As I noted in section 6-4c, "The Loyalty of the President's Cabinet," and section 6-6c, "The Front Porch Campaign and Beyond," during the nineteenth century, presidents depended and largely interacted with the legislative branch and the political parties. While they did not ignore the public, they were not overly dependent on them. Since the birth of the twentieth century, however, presidents have developed a powerful symbiotic relationship with the public to such an extent that today presidents derive enhanced power and authority from this continuing relationship, such as by regularly invoking the public's name to legitimize presidential actions. The fact that the public *expects* the president to lead the nation is another source of presidential power and prestige. This relationship also impacts presidential interactions and influence with other external political actors, particularly Congress.

Yet, the relationship between the president and the public also can be described as a *double-edged sword* because it provides the presidency with greater independence from Congress and the political parties, provides an important constituency for presidents and their programs, and expands public expectations of the presidency, thus placing the presidency at the center of the American political system. It also has turned the presidency into a veritable public relations operation, ardently selling its product (either a program or more often the personality or an image of the president) to the public. How successful a president and his or her staff are at this task often determines how popular that president is, which in turn can determine whether other Washington insiders perceive a particular president as having the ability to exert real influence and power. It also can promote an expectations gap. Hence, the president's relationship with the public can provide the president with increased or decreased power and prestige, depending on how other elites view the president's relationship with the public.

7-2 The President and the Public in the Nineteenth Century

The Founders did not foresee a close political relationship between the public and the presidency, and the early presidents did not see popularity as an important political resource. After his election to the presidency in 1796, John Adams wrote to his daughter, "If the way to do good to my country were to render myself popular, I could easily do it. But extravagant popularity is not the road to public advantage" (McCullough 2001: 471). In fact, few nineteenth century presidents cultivated a close relationship with the American public. While Washington and Jefferson were popular presidents, in part because of their past achievements (Washington as the hero of the American Revolution and Jefferson as the author of the Declaration of Independence), neither curried public favor during their terms of office. Likewise, while by all accounts, James Monroe was popular—he governed during what became known as the "Era of Good Feelings"—his popularity did not translate into real presidential influence. On the other hand, James Polk, who has been rated as a successful president by historians, was a rather "[d]rab, secretive, hard-working" man who "was not a popular president" though he "left behind him a record of accomplishing every one of his major objectives" (Roseboom and Eckes 1979: 60).

Likewise, the man usually ranked as our greatest president, Abraham Lincoln, was highly unpopular during his presidency. Vilified by the press and virulently scorned by other politicians and even members of his own Cabinet, literally portrayed in cartoons as a man of great physical awkwardness and limited intelligence, many Americans apparently thought that Lincoln was not qualified to be president. Yet, Lincoln is rated by most historian polls as our greatest president (see section 3-3, "Presidential Greatness").

The presidents of the nineteenth century, then, were neither overly concerned with public approval nor was their perceived success or failure evaluated with reference to it. Stuckey (1991: 133) writes, "During the early days of the Republic, the president's role was purely administrative. The president was less of an active participant in public debates, but communicated primarily to other elites." Hence, there was little incentive for presidents to curry favor with the public. On the other hand, during the first electoral order (1789–1824) the legislative branch, through the caucus system, nominated presidents. Presidents therefore had a real incentive to defer to Congress. In the second electoral order, the political parties played the dominant role in both the nomination and general election process. Presidents thus were most accountable to the political parties. Consequently, due to "the nature of the presidential selection process," presidents "communicated with those by whom they were held accountable" (ibid., 133–34).

Since securing the nomination did not depend on a direct relationship with the public, presidents were not concerned with their public standing. The parties therefore could nominate relatively bland and colorless individuals such as Franklin Pierce, James Buchanan, Rutherford B. Hayes, and Benjamin Harrison for president. It was not yet necessary for a presidential candidate to be a good public speaker, to photograph well, or to have charisma. In fact, given the expectations of the nineteenth century, these very qualities generally proved detrimental to a prospective presidential candidate.

Since oratorical skills were not important, few of the early presidents displayed skill or interest in public speaking. Summing up the oratorical skills of the early presidents, Stuckey (ibid., 14–15) writes,

> George Washington maintained a low public profile. He spoke only rarely and then only on ceremonial occasions and in muted tones. John Adams . . . was also a reluctant public speaker. The only speeches recorded during his presidency are the annual addresses required by the Constitution. . . . Partly this may have been a result of his shyness, and partly a reflection of his lack of oratorical ability. . . . Jefferson is said to have been "one of the least effective public speakers to hold the nation's highest office." . . . In fact, Jefferson thought so little of his oral persuasive abilities that he discontinued the practice of reading his annual address to Congress personally and had them delivered by someone else. . . . Clearly, Jefferson's prose was better read than heard. . . . The same might be said of James Madison, who "rated rather poorly as a platform orator." . . . All of which reveals an interesting trend among the first presidents—none of them was an able speaker. This is a reflection of the low premium the founders placed on popular rhetoric and the "popular arts."

7-3 Presidential Speaking during the Nineteenth Century

Presidential speaking ability did not improve much throughout the nineteenth century. As Stuckey (ibid., 24) writes, "The speeches of [the post Civil War presidents] are colorless, terse, and without vision. None of the presidents of this era earned a reputation for their oratorical skills." As can be seen in Table 7-1, nineteenth century presidents made little attempt to speak directly to the American public. Only eight out of twenty-four presidents (33 percent) averaged more than 10 speeches per year. Only one of the first fifteen presidents, Zachary Taylor, averaged more than 10 speeches per year. Eight presidents averaged fewer than 2 speeches per year, seven if we drop William Henry Harrison, who lived only one month after taking office, from the analysis. There was, however, an increase in public speaking from Lincoln's presidency onward, with Hayes delivering 31.5 speeches per year; Benjamin Harrison, 74; and William McKinley, 32.5. Yet, while presidents were beginning to speak more often in public by the end of the century, they were not using these speeches for policy purposes. As Tulis (1987: 67) notes, only four of the twenty-four presidents "attempted to defend or attack a specific bill or law" in their speeches.

Hence, while Lincoln was known in his time as a great orator, he is remembered as president for only a few of his speeches (the Gettysburg Address). As Stuckey (1991: 21) comments, "After his nomination . . . Lincoln greatly reduced

T A B L E **7-1** Speeches Delivered by Eighteenth and Nineteenth Century Presidents

President	Total Number of Speeches	Average per Year
George Washington	25	3.1
John Adams	6	1.5
Thomas Jefferson	3	0.4
James Madison	0	0.0
James Monroe	42	5.3
John Quincy Adams	5	1.3
Andrew Jackson	9	1.1
Martin Van Buren	27	6.8
William Henry Harrison	0	0.0
James Tyler	5	1.3
James Polk	15	3.8
Zachary Taylor	22	16.9
Millard Fillmore	20	7.4
Franklin Pierce	20	5.0
James Buchanan	9	1.1
Abraham Lincoln	78	19.5
Andrew Johnson	70	17.5
Ulysses S. Grant	25	3.1
Rutherford B. Hayes	126	31.5
James Garfield	10	14.0
Chester A. Arthur	40	12.1
Grover Cleveland*	51	6.4
Benjamin Harrison	296	74.0
William McKinley	130	32.5

Source: Tulis (1987: 64).

*Both nonconsecutive Cleveland administrations are included here.

his public appearances, since he was now a sitting president endowed with the dignity of that office, not a mere presidential aspirant." Rather than public speaking, presidents mostly communicated via written correspondence, either letters or through surrogates who wrote articles for the partisan press. Still, while they seldom spoke publicly, in another way, nineteenth century presidents were more accessible to the public than presidents are today. A nineteenth century citizen had a better chance of actually meeting a president than a twenty-first century citizen does. As Nevins (1947: 41) writes, presidents "spent an undue amount of time in the favorite American pastime of shaking hands. . . ." On "stated days the White House was thrown open" and ordinary Americans could walk through and shake hands (and even speak briefly) with the president. This practice, which many presidents detested, continued until Franklin Roosevelt (due to the fact that he was physically challenged) ended it.

Another way presidents met with the public in the eighteenth and nineteenth centuries was by domestic travel: No president prior to the twentieth century left the boundaries of the United States. Still, Washington considered it important to travel about the country "to gather information, particularly concerning the 'temper and disposition of the people toward the new government. . . .'" But for "these purposes, public speaking was not as important as public appearances" (Tulis 1987: 69).

Initially, Washington was leery of traveling to see the public. The "adulation of the crowds had frightened him" when he visited New York for the inauguration, "as presaging a catastrophic comedown if the new government did not please the people." As his presidency unfolded, however, "he interpreted the galloping of horses, the delegations of grave officials, the cheers, and the jerry-built triumphal arches as demonstrations that the people *were* pleased" (Flexner 1970: 229; italics in the original). Thus, Washington made two major trips, or "tours" as he called them, during his two terms in office. The first tour, from New York to New England, lasted about a month (Elkins and McKitrick 1993: 74). It proved so successful that Washington later made a second tour through the South.

Following Washington's example, other early presidents also "made grand tours throughout the country one of the chief events of their terms in office" (King and Ragsdale 1988: 249). Like Washington's trips, however, these were not partisan affairs.

In fact, the practice of making tours was not controversial until the administration of Andrew Johnson. In August 1866, Johnson embarked on a major tour of the country that he called "the swing around the circle." In his speeches, Johnson "compared himself to Jesus Christ and explained that like the Savior, he too, liked to pardon repentant sinners." As Trefousse (1989: 263) notes, "These set statements were not always in the best of taste, but they were nothing compared to his impromptu replies to hecklers, who became ever more challenging as he traveled west. The result was a series of confrontations that greatly hurt the president's cause." In fact, the partisan tone of his rhetoric was later identified in one of the Articles of Impeachment against him. The Article read,

> Andrew Johnson, President of the United States, unmindful of the high duties of his office and the dignity and propriety thereof . . . did . . . make and deliver in a loud voice certain intemperate, inflammatory, and scandalous harangues, and did therein utter loud threats and bitter menaces as well against Congress as the laws of the United States. . . . Which said utterances, declarations, threats, and harangues, highly censurable in any, are peculiarly indecent and unbecoming in the Chief Magistrate of the United States, by means whereof . . . Andrew Johnson has brought the high office of the President of the United States into contempt, ridicule, and disgrace, to the great scandal of all good citizens. (Quoted in Tulis 1987: 91)

After Johnson's experience, presidents continued to travel throughout the nineteenth century, but they were less likely to use the occasions for overtly partisan purposes.

While making broad appeals to the public was not a common characteristic, this does not mean that nineteenth century presidents were entirely unmindful of the public; they did have to face them on Election Day. Importantly, they were more dependent on the political parties and Congress. Hence, until "the end of the nineteenth century, presidents had no need for direct communication with voters. Strong parties and a partisan press successfully communicated party positions to voters, and vigorous party loyalties undergirded a system in which voters judged candidates primarily on the basis of party labels" (Gamm and Smith 1998: 90).

7-4 The Birth of the Rhetorical Presidency

Before Theodore Roosevelt, presidents occasionally reached out to the public, but usually tentatively. Roosevelt understood that the power of the presidency depended far more on public approval than it did on a strict constructionist reading of the Constitution. As Grossman and Kumar (1981: 3) write, "A president requires popular support to obtain political influence because his office's constitutional and institutional prerogatives are insufficient for him to achieve many important objectives." Roosevelt understood this point better than any president before his time and arguably better than many since then. The connection he created between the presidency and the American public went beyond even Andrew Jackson's idea of the president as "tribune of the people." Under Roosevelt, the public began to emerge as a constituency.

Roosevelt understood that not only did the president derive authority as the "tribune of the people" (because he was the only politician elected by the entire nation), but he also derived authority continuously over time as a result of popular support from the people. Roosevelt recognized the synergy between the presidency and the public, which in turn changed—one might even say revolutionized—the presidency. As Cornwell (1965) notes, from Roosevelt's presidency onward, one of the primary goals of all presidents would be to find new ways to reach out and communicate with the public.

One major innovation was combining rhetoric with policy-related appeals. Tulis (1987: 85) writes, "Teddy Roosevelt doggedly pursued a strategy of appealing to the people regarding specific legislative matters." When Congress appeared ready to oppose the Hepburn Act, which gave the Interstate Commerce Commission authority to fix limits on railroad rates, Roosevelt attempted to "influence public opinion with speeches" (Miller 1992: 457). An expert on presidential speechmaking, Jeffrey Tulis (1987: 19) writes, Roosevelt was the "first president" to reach over the heads of Congress to secure legislation. As a result, "Roosevelt can lay some claim to being the father of the rhetorical presidency." Not only did he endorse the Hepburn Act, the "core of his argument was that a change in authorized practices was necessary to fulfill the purposes of the underlying founding theory of governance."

In this regard (see section 3-2j, "Theodore Roosevelt and William Howard Taft"), Roosevelt had a unique interpretation of the president's constitutional powers. The presidency was not limited to the powers specifically delineated in the Constitution. Rather, Roosevelt (1913: 357) wrote in his autobiography, "My belief was that it was not only his [the president's] right but his duty to do anything that the needs of the Nation demanded unless such action was forbidden by the Constitution or by the laws." By combining that expansive constitutional philosophy with a new constituency, the public, Roosevelt provided a new rationale for presidential power. It is a rationale that has become familiar to his presidential successors, but it was a radical break from the past. It succeeded because the American public embraced Roosevelt as they had few other presidents. Other politicians took notice of Roosevelt's popularity and influence. While many no doubt feared him, others saw the political benefits of this new governing approach and sought to emulate it.

7-5 Not a Revolutionary

Teddy Roosevelt was not a revolutionary. He was successful in part because he used the Founders' very own arguments to justify a closer presidential relationship with the public. As Tulis (1987: 95) notes, "If popular rhetoric was proscribed in the nineteenth century because it could manifest demagoguery, impede deliberation, and subvert the routines of republican governance, it could [by the dawn of the twentieth century] be defended by showing itself necessary to contend with these very same political difficulties. Appealing to the founders' general arguments while abandoning some of their concrete practices, Roosevelt's presidency constituted a middle way between the statecraft of the preceding century and the rhetorical presidency that was to follow."

Roosevelt's success in passing the Hepburn Act thus "signaled a change in the executive: the president's most important political relationship soon would be with the public rather than with his party or with Congress" (Milkis and Nelson 1994: 213). Ironically, Roosevelt's bitter political rival, Woodrow Wilson, continued and expanded Roosevelt's innovation. As Greenstein (1988: 3) writes, "The activist presidents of the early twentieth century, Theodore Roosevelt and Woodrow Wilson, established a precedent by appealing directly to the public, in contrast to the eighteenth and nineteenth century practice of directing persuasive communications mainly to Congress."

7-6 Woodrow Wilson's Innovations

Wilson not only used presidential rhetoric to promote his policy agenda, as Roosevelt had done, but he also created new venues for presidential communication. One of the most prominent and controversial was his use of the state of the union address as a public forum to promote the president's policies. On April 6, 1913, the White House announced that the president himself would deliver the state of the union in person before Congress and would use the address to talk about tariff reform. Though Washington and Adams had delivered this speech in person, Jefferson (who was shy and had a stutter) had ended the practice. All of Jefferson's successors followed the new precedent and sent a written transmittal to Congress, which was then read to the members by a clerk.

Confronted with Wilson's announcement, more than a dozen senators voted to adjourn the Senate in an attempt to prevent the new president from delivering the speech in person. When that attempt failed, Senator John Sharp Williams of Mississippi, who was a Wilson supporter, hoped the tariff message "would be the only instance of the breach of the perfectly simple, democratic and American custom of messages in writing which Thomas Jefferson instituted" (quoted in Milkis and Nelson 1994: 241). It was not, and for good reason: The reaction to the speech was immediate and positive. "Newspapers across the country carried the speech, whereby millions of Americans also 'heard' what Wilson had said. No previous speech had reached so many people" (Gelderman 1997: 7). On a personal level, Wilson and his wife were also secretly pleased that he had thought of presenting the state of the union address in person while Theodore Roosevelt had not.

Go to the online version of the text to hear Woodrow Wilson give a speech.

With one speech, Wilson mightily contributed to the transformation of presidential rhetoric. Wilson joined rhetoric with policy making, something that Theodore Roosevelt had initiated, but that Wilson and his successors would do with increasing regularity. According to Tulis (1987: 133), "Wilson altered the two principal nineteenth century prescriptions for presidential speech. First, policy rhetoric, which had formerly been written and addressed principally to Congress, would now be spoken and addressed principally to the people at large." Furthermore, from now on, really "important speeches would be delivered orally, where the visible and audible performance would become as important as the prepared text."

The real significance of Wilson's innovation may not have appeared obvious to his contemporaries. Why would public speaking enhance the power and prestige of the presidency? It did so by (1) bringing policy discussion and debate directly before the people. The public might previously have read about policy debates in the paper and even have read written correspondence from the president. Now, however, it was the president standing alone, on a stage, articulating a message. It therefore not only made the president a serious policy player, but it (2) also made people aware of the personal presence and personality of the president. As I noted in section 6-6, "The Third Electoral Order: Out of the Shadow of the Parties," the third electoral order reflected a process whereby presidents stepped out of the shadows of the political parties. One way they did so was by speaking more often in presidential election campaigns. They also brought rhetoric to the presidency in another way: They used what Teddy Roosevelt called the "bully pulpit" to make a case for *their* program. It was no longer a congressional program or a party platform; it was now Theodore Roosevelt's Square Deal, Woodrow Wilson's New Freedom, Franklin Roosevelt's New Deal, Harry Truman's Fair Deal, John Kennedy's New Frontier, and Lyndon Johnson's Great Society.

This development made presidents more potent political forces in Washington politics. As Stuckey (1991: 25) notes, "Where early presidents had led through example and policy, the presidents following [Theodore] Roosevelt would increasingly rely on the arts of [verbal] persuasion." Stuckey (1991: 26–27) continues that Wilson built on a "'visionary rhetoric'" that "articulated a vision of the future and sought to propel the people toward that vision. Wilson and Roosevelt provided a view of the world and of the presidency that was profoundly to influence the rhetoric of the presidents who followed them."

Yet, if Wilson showed future presidents the power of the bully pulpit, he also showed them its limitations. In his second term, following the end of World War I, Wilson stumped the country and "sought to force the Senate to accept his version of the League [of Nations]," a forerunner of today's United Nations. Despite an extensive speaking tour, "Wilson failed miserably" and Congress rejected the Treaty of Versailles and with it U.S. membership in the League of Nations (Kernell 1997: 26). Verbal persuasion might promote an idea, but it was not sufficient to guarantee presidential success. In other words, presidential speechmaking would not be translated automatically into political influence.

Yet, despite Wilson's failure, a new pattern of presidential communication with the public was established. While all presidents did not use the same techniques, they all began to reach out to the public. For instance, Harding "was the first president to recognize that public opinion could be courted through leisurely as well as through formal and ceremonial events . . ." (Milkis and Nelson 1994). He therefore played golf with members of the press and was photographed in relaxed settings (an early form of the photo opportunity). "Silent Cal," the nickname for Calvin Coolidge, likewise used photography rather than rhetoric as a primary means of communicating with the public.

7-7 Franklin Roosevelt and Radio

Radio was invented at perhaps the perfect time with regard to the needs of the presidency. Presidents, especially since Theodore Roosevelt, had begun to reach out to the public, but they had limited technological means to do so. Photography, motion pictures, and the national media could get a president's image and message across, but not the president's voice. As Lowi (1985: 65) notes, radio was of great importance to presidents seeking to communicate with the public because of both the "increasing responsibility of the presidency and the severe difficulty of reaching the masses" individually or through the political parties. While Harding and Coolidge were the first presidents to use the radio, it was Franklin Roosevelt who mastered the new technology.

Roosevelt could now talk directly to the American people, tell them of his programs and, more importantly, of his vision for the country. In his inaugural and state of the union addresses, and then through a series of **fireside chats,** Roosevelt communicated directly with the public, talking to them as individuals in their homes and building a personal bond with them. Roosevelt was so effective with the radio that, like Teddy Roosevelt and Woodrow Wilson before him, he contributed in a major way to a re-invention of both presidential practices and public expectations. Public speaking now became a central tool of the presidency. Those who excelled at it would have advantages over those who could not. As Stuckey (1991: 35) states, "Presidents through [Franklin] Roosevelt were able to choose whether they would engage in mass appeals, and such appeals were generally confined to election years. No president after Roosevelt had such a choice: Presidential leadership became, by definition, public leadership." Yet, there was a cost to this new public leadership. As Stuckey (ibid., 36) continues, "while Roosevelt reaped many benefits from this style of leadership, it also put a certain amount of pressure on him to perform up to expectations."

By personally addressing the public and making promises of presidential and programmatic leadership, Roosevelt created a closer relationship with the public and increased public expectations of presidential performance. Since, however, it was now the president's program, there would be less room for presidents to hide if the program did not work, if Congress did not adopt it, or if the public did not like it. Furthermore, as Roosevelt and his successors promised the American public jobs and a sound economy, they were increasingly held accountable for delivering on these promises. Rhetoric thus provided the basis for increased presidential power at the very same time it increased public expectations of the presidency.

The question since Franklin Roosevelt's presidency has been how can presidents satisfy expanding public expectations? Just as radio provided Franklin Roosevelt with a powerful new technology for communicating with the public, another innovation provided him (and his successors) with a window into the minds of the American people. But like presidential speechmaking, it proved to be a double-edged sword that could cut both ways.

Fireside chats: Franklin Roosevelt's radio communications with the public. He talked to the American public via radio as individuals in their homes and built a personal bond with them.

7-8 The Emergence of Presidential Polling

In the 1920s and again in 1932, the highly respected publication the *Literary Digest* conducted presidential polls and correctly predicted the winners. The polls, however, were not scientific, a fact that became important with the 1936 *Literary Digest* poll. "In 1936, the *Literary Digest* sent out more than 10 million questionnaires, primarily to people listed in telephone directories or on automobile registration lists. More than 2 million people returned the questionnaires. In October, the *Literary Digest* published its final results—which indicated that Roosevelt would lose by a landslide. In fact, Roosevelt won by a landslide" (Corbett 2001: 93).

That same year, using a scientific poll of about 2,000 people, a young pollster by the name of George Gallup predicted the winner correctly (ibid.). In addition, his projection was extremely accurate. Political pundits were amazed, and Franklin Roosevelt was intrigued.

What if a politician could find out what the people were actually thinking before he had to create a policy agenda? This information could help a president to identify which issues to adopt and which to avoid, even which words and themes to use in speeches. Public approval was not only a political commodity to be courted, but it was now something that could be identified and measured. Presidents could find out what the public thought of them and then use that information to shape a new image or program. The political possibilities were endless. Roosevelt understood this opportunity and was quick to act on it. Consequently, he became an "avid reader of polls" (Barnet 1990: 197). As Barnet (ibid.) writes,

> [T]he White House began receiving in advance of publication confidential analyses of Gallup polling data from Dr. Hadley Cantril, who ran the Office of Public Opinion Research at Princeton. Later, the president was even invited to submit his own question in secret, and through an intermediary, his friend Anna Rosenberg, he did. . . . Roosevelt saw the possibilities at once. Polling could take some of the risk out of politics.

Soon Roosevelt hired his own pollster, a practice followed by each of his successors (Thomas, Pika, and Watson 1993: 111). While some presidents, particularly Harry Truman, found the polls distasteful, many other politicians, like Roosevelt, found them indispensable. Still, while polling provided obvious benefits, it also introduced new potential costs, as well (see Box 7-1). Would the polls promote presidential leadership, or would presidents obsequiously follow the will of the polls (the possible antithesis of leadership)? The answer to this question varies with each president and sometimes within presidencies themselves. As for Roosevelt, the evidence indicates that he used them to govern. For example, when "he received a report from his pollsters on the public's lack of understanding" regarding the "Lend-Lease policy toward Great Britain," he went out of his way to clarify this issue "in a public message to Congress." A subsequent survey showed that public understanding of the program had increased (Edwards 1983: 17). Hence, Roosevelt used the polls to find out where the country was and then used this information to lead the country in the direction he preferred.

This use of polls was not the practice with all presidents, however. As Edwards (1983: 18) writes, "Nixon at times waited for public opinion to coalesce before he took a stand." Jimmy Carter and Bill Clinton were often accused (fairly or unfairly) of the same behavior. What is clear is that very few of the modern presidents ignored the polls. When the polls speak, presidents and other politicians generally listen. Yet, as Stuckey (1991: 140) notes, "Public opinion polls cannot tell politicians which actions are 'right' only which actions are popular." Hence, mere governing by the polls can be fraught with peril.

7-9 Presidential Popularity

Another problem created by the polls is one that even the master politician Franklin Roosevelt may not have intuitively understood: Public opinion polls can be both a blessing and a curse for a politician. As Jones (1994: 112) notes, it is common wisdom that high presidential approval "ratings represent power, which should be used to enact programs: low ratings suggest failure, which should encourage a president to reorient his leadership practices. . . ." While Jones disagrees with this prescription, it is evident that many political scientists, Washington insiders, and pundits believe that there is a clear connection between *perceived* presidential approval and *actual* presidential influence. Buchanan (1987: 7) even refers to it as the president's "core resource."

In part, this relationship derives from a question that the Gallup organization began asking while Roosevelt was president: "Do you approve or disapprove of the way [president's name] is handling his job as president?" For many Washington insiders, the public's response to this question would define presidential influence. Consequently, if the aggregate response to this question is favorable, with poll ratings in the 60 or 70 percent range, then a president is assumed to have influence. If the president's ratings fall below the 50 percent mark, or more disastrously into the 30 or even 20 percent range, no matter what else that president brings to office (e.g., experience, integrity, honesty, intelligence, prestige, reputation), he or she is perceived by the press and Washington insiders as weak and ineffectual, perhaps even mortally politically wounded.

There is empirical evidence that these polls indeed do have a real impact on presidential influence. Table 7-2 presents the combined presidential success scores in Congress for each president from 1953–1998. "Percentages [are] based on the number of congressional votes supporting the president divided by the total number of votes on which the president had taken an actual position" (Stanley and Niemi 2000: 253). Victory percentages for votes in the House and Senate are presented for each presidency, as well as a combined victory percentage. While there are different means of measuring presidential success with Congress, the point here is to show that there is considerable variation in an individual president's ability to influence Congress.

Can we explain these variations? Two early studies found that presidents had very little ability to influence congressional voting decisions (Kingdon 1973; Clausen 1973). Other studies, however, found a link between the president's popular standing and congressional voting behavior. Ostrom and Simon (1985: 349) found that "the cumulative rate of roll-call victories will decline by three points for every ten-point drop in [presidential] approval." Rivers and Rose (1985) likewise found a correlation between presidential approval ratings and presidential success in Congress, as did Edwards—though he argues presidential influence occurs at the margins (1989: 118). Brace and Hinckley (1992: 81) also note, "public approval clearly increases the chances of congressional success. Presidents gain 7.5 percent in victories for every 10 percentage points more of approval they receive in the polls." Consequently, as Spitzer (1993: 65) writes,

T A B L E **7-2 Presidential Victories on Congressional Votes, 1953–1998**

President	Percent of House and Senate Victories	Percent of House Victories	Percent of Senate Victories
Eisenhower	69.9	68.4	70.7
Kennedy	84.6	83.7	85.2
Johnson	82.2	85.9	79.7
Nixon	64.3	68.2	61.5
Ford	58.3	51.0	65.0
Carter	76.6	73.1	79.7
Reagan	62.2	45.6	77.9
G. H. W. Bush	51.8	40.2	65.6
Clinton	59.9	53.4	68.5

Source: Stanley and Niemi (2000: 252–53).

Box 7-1

How Polling Is Done

Pollsters decide what questions to ask of the public they will sample. Pollsters working for or against a cause or individual may create questions that will cause the respondents sampled to think of issues or people in a certain way. Nonpartisan polls ask questions that are as neutral as possible in order not to influence the answers they get.

Polling banks use computers to generate random phone numbers and then call those numbers to get a random sampling of the American population. Numbers that belong to businesses, fax machines, and pay phones are removed from the lists. The callers ask the poll participants the questions written by the polling experts, and statisticians collate the data.

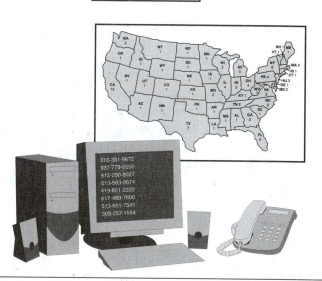

When the president's standing is high, members of Congress are likely to interpret this positive support as either direct or indirect evidence of a popular mandate for the President. Fearing a popular backlash, Congress is less likely to buck presidential preferences under these conditions. . . . Continued public approval is a sign of success (or, to be more precise, perceived success); declining public approval signals an ebbing mandate.

Why are members of Congress so concerned about the president's popular standing? Edwards (1989: 105) writes, "The president's standing in the public provides members of Congress with a guide to the public's views." It is also more difficult for a member of Congress to openly oppose a popular president. On the other hand, "low presidential approval ratings free members of Congress from supporting the president if they are otherwise inclined to oppose him." Thus, the

Presidential polls conducted during times of crises often show ratings boosts.

The poll results in the table show changes to presidents' approval ratings after times of crisis.

esident	Event	Change in Approval Polls
nnedy	Bay of Pigs invasion	+5%
nnedy	Cuban Missile Crisis	+13%
on	Vietnam peace accord	+16%
d	Mayaguez rescue	+11%
rter	Iran hostage crisis	+6%
agan	Invasion of Grenada	+4%
orge H. W.Bush	Start of Gulf War	+23%
orge W. Bush	September 11	+35%

evidence suggests that public approval is a valuable political resource presidents can use to increase their influence.

The evidence then tells us that the polls define what we think of our presidents and tell other policy makers whether to take presidents seriously or not. This is an important alteration in the concept of presidential power. Now, for the first time, we can put a number on presidential influence. For many of Roosevelt's successors, this numbers game proved politically damaging. To understand this point, try to imagine what would have happened if scientific polling had existed in Abraham Lincoln's time: If polls had measured his approval ratings in the 20 or 30 percent range in 1864, would he have been renominated? Would Congress have been even more obstreperous in its relations with him? If so, American history might very well be much different. Since their approval ratings are so important, what control do presidents have over them?

7-10 Patterns of Presidential Approval

In general, there is a pattern to presidential ratings. They are generally high (above 50 percent, often in the 60 and 70 percent range) during a president's first months in office—the honeymoon period (an electoral resource). Newly arrived presidents are given a short period, usually four or five months, in which the public, the media, and the political opposition are generally muted in their opposition. All presidents do not, however, have a honeymoon. Gerald Ford's honeymoon period ended abruptly when he pardoned Richard Nixon, and Bill Clinton, who raised the controversial issue of gays in the military prior to his inauguration, entered office under a critical microscope. Even when presidents get a honeymoon, however, it generally is brief.

After the honeymoon, however, presidential poll numbers typically begin to decline slowly and consistently (though George H. W. Bush and George W. Bush are clear exceptions to this pattern) throughout their first and second years in office (see Figure 7-1). The president's approval ratings generally hit bottom at the time of the midterm election. At this point, the president is most vulnerable to political attack by the opposition party, since he or she is not actually on the ballot. Still, all over the country, members of the opposition party running for Congress and governorships question the president's policies and competence.

After the midterm election, the focus begins to turn to the next presidential election, and one of two patterns is evident: (1) In cases such as Eisenhower, Nixon, Reagan, and Clinton, we then see a sharp increase in their popularity as the excitement of the next presidential campaign and the reality of a weak challenger boost their popular image, or (2) there is a continued decay in the polls, as was characteristic of Johnson, Ford, Carter, and George H. W. Bush, as the public questions their competence to deal with the nation's problems. Most often, those presidents who face the second pattern are running for re-election in poor economic times. Ford, Carter, and George H. W. Bush ran during or just after an economic recession. On the other hand, Eisenhower, Nixon, Reagan, and Clinton ran in better economic times. As Tufte (1978) argues, the state of the economy is a powerful determinant of re-election success.

Stimson (1976; 1976/1977) empirically identified this pattern of decline in approval ratings over a series of presidencies. Mueller (1973: 205) tried to explain this pattern, writing, "An administration, even if it always acts with majority sup-

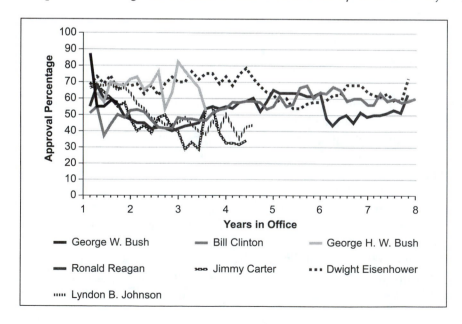

Figure 7-1
Presidential Approval Ratings

port on each issue, can gradually alienate ... minorities ... [until] the minority on each issue feels so intensely about its loss that it is unable to be placated by administration support on other policies it favors ... this concept would predict that a president's popularity would show an overall downward trend as he is forced on a variety of issues to act and thus create intense, unforgiving opponents of former supporters." Meanwhile Brody (1991: 23) argues, "Incremental weaknesses in public support strengthen the opposition of political elites." This in turn weakens a president's ability to influence opposition members of Congress, which in turn increases opposition and leads to "increased public disappointment at the president's inability to fulfill expectations." The process continues with the president's approval ratings moving further downward.

7-11 The State of the Economy

A variety of research on presidential approval ratings (e.g., Mueller 1973; Tufte 1978; MacKuen 1983; Ostrom and Simon 1985) demonstrates that the state of the economy is an important determinant of the public's assessment of a president's job performance. As Brace and Hinckley (1992: 165) write, "Economic circumstances ... can be powerful conditioning factors."[1] Hence, individuals expect presidents to provide the nation with a sound and healthy economy. Those presidents who govern during good economic times are more likely to be rewarded with higher approval ratings and re-election success. Those who do not are more likely to face declining approval ratings, election defeat, and a widening expectations gap.

MacKuen (1983) found national economic factors are important determinants of presidential popularity, though inflation's impact is of a longer duration than that of unemployment. Ostrom and Simon (1985: 351) came to a different conclusion, arguing, "It is noteworthy that high unemployment or inflation are not, in and of themselves, necessary conditions for the erosion of popular support. .... Instead, high levels of the two measures and a substantial degree of public concern with economic problems are required." Furthermore, in an analysis of presidential voting behavior, Erikson (1989) found that the change in per capita income was the best predictor of vote choice.

Another factor that is obvious from the polling data is that Vietnam and Watergate and the Johnson and Nixon presidencies fundamentally altered the way the public evaluates presidents. The level of public trust in government plummeted from the early 1950s to the 1970s, and these patterns continued until the September 11, 2001, terrorist attacks on the World Trade Center and the Pentagon. As can be seen in Table 7-3, fewer Americans came to identify themselves as trusting government to do what is right. Evidence of lower trust in government began to emerge in the late 1960s and continued through to 2000.

These altered perceptions had an impact on the evaluations of the presidents who followed Johnson and Nixon into the White House. Generally, what we see is lower ratings for Presidents Ford and Carter. Even Reagan has lower approval ratings than Eisenhower or Kennedy. While George H. W. Bush was initially very popular, his approval ratings collapsed over time, and while Clinton was very popular throughout his second term in office, with his highest poll ratings ironically coming during his impeachment trial, his first term ratings were not impressive until his re-election year. Even George W. Bush's approval ratings were not extraordinarily high before September 11, with ratings in the mid to high 50 percent range, again far lower than Eisenhower or Kennedy at a comparable period.

Citrin and Green (1986) found that presidential approval ratings and perceptions of the character of presidents have an impact on trust in government (see

TABLE **7-3** **Response to Gallup Question:** "How much of the time do you think you can trust government in Washington to do what is right—just about always, most of the time, or only some of the time?"

Year	Just about Always	Most of the Time	Only Some of the Time	Never	No Opinion
1958	16	57	23	0	4
1964	14	62	22	—	2
1966	17	48	28	3	4
1968	7	54	37	—	2
1970	7	47	44	—	2
1972	5	48	44	1	2
1974	2	34	61	1	2
1976	3	30	62	1	4
1978	2	27	64	4	3
1980	2	23	69	4	2
1982	2	31	62	2	3
1984	4	40	53	1	2
1986	3	35	58	2	2
1988	4	37	56	2	1
1990	3	25	68	2	2
1992	3	26	68	2	1
1994	2	19	74	3	0
1996	3	30	66	1	0
1998	4	36	58	1	1
2000	4	40	55	1	1

Source: Gallup Poll, October 12, 2001, "Trust in Government Increases in Wake of Terrorist Attacks," Gallup web site.

also Hetherington 1999). Hence, empirical analysis indicates that there is a relationship between trust in government and presidential approval ratings, though it may not be entirely clear which one promotes the other.

In summary, as Edwards (1983), Brody (1991), and Brace and Hinckley (1992) argue, presidents may have limited ability to alter their poll ratings. While Tufte (1978) and Ostrom and Simon (1985) are more optimistic, it is clear that for presidents to be popular, they generally must govern in good economic times, though there are rare exceptions, such as George W. Bush's extraordinary popularity in 2001 and 2002 in the face of an economic downturn. Presidential approval also is related to overall trust in government and to other exogenous factors largely beyond any president's direct control.

7-12 Excessive Expectations?

Presidents do attempt to influence their poll ratings. Major public addresses and foreign travel are more likely to follow drops in approval ratings, while domestic travel is related most closely to poor economic conditions (Brace and Hinckley 1992: 152). Likewise, the use of military force is "significantly more likely to occur following negative dramatic events—scandals in the White House, strikes, and other signs of domestic disarray." It is also "more likely to occur when economic conditions are worsening" (ibid., 97). As a result of their concern with the polls, presidents are more likely to concentrate on short-term goals rather than long-term planning (ibid., 113).

The evidence, however, suggests that presidents have only limited ability to influence their poll ratings. Even speeches, travel, the use of force, and foreign policy crises positively impact the president's approval ratings in the short term, generally only a few months at the very most. The harsh reality for most presidents is that their approval ratings will follow the pattern described in section 7-10, "Patterns of Presidential Approval": a brief honeymoon, better ratings in the first year followed by a decline and a nadir toward midterm, and either a move upward in the polls in the third and particularly fourth year or further decay, largely dependent on external factors such as the state of the economy.

Light (1983) combined this pattern of public opinion with a presidential learning curve and suggested that as presidents' approval ratings decline, they become better equipped (e.g., more experienced and knowledgeable) to actually govern in the White House. Unfortunately, by the time they develop these skills, their lower approval ratings strip them of the ability to get things done. Consequently, Light argues, most presidents do not succeed.

The problem is no better for second-term presidents. These presidents have even less ability to influence the polls than do first-term presidents. Speeches, domestic travel, and foreign travel either have no impact or a negative impact on their approval ratings (Brace and Hinckley 1992: 60–61). Likewise, they are much less likely than first-term presidents to have a honeymoon after they are re-elected (Brody 1991: 35).

Given these dynamics, some scholars argue that the problem is not with the polls so much as it is with the effect excessive and unrealistic public expectations have on the presidency itself (see section 1-1, "Public Expectations and the Political Resources of the Presidency"). If only the public had more realistic expectations, presidents would be in a better position to govern. As Stuckey (1991: 140) argues, "We must hold presidents accountable for what they can control, and not expect them merely to present reassuring images in the face of complex, and often disturbing social events. Presidents control only a limited part of the world; to expect them to do more is to create a fiction that contributes little to our communal life and actively detracts from our ability to engage in meaningful politics." Likewise, Brace and Hinckley (1992: 44) state, "People should . . . realize that the polls are not accurate reflections of the job a president is doing. A good part of the fluctuation is beyond the scope of White House influence."

The problem here, of course, is that presidents and other politicians themselves elevate the perceived importance of the polls by strategically citing them whenever it is convenient to do so. They also tend to fuel public expectations at election time, promising a wide variety of panaceas for the nation's ills, and then often proving incapable of ameliorating these problems once they are elected. All presidents promise economic good times, but they usually have little control over whether the economy is growing or not. Presidents promise a higher moral ground, a more secure world, and a variety of platitudes, but they do not control events (domestically or internationally) and often are swept along by them. When George H. W. Bush tried to lower public expectations about domestic affairs, he was criticized and widely perceived as being out of touch with the needs of ordinary citizens and highly passive in his governing approach. Consequently, while public expectations are no doubt too high, it is difficult to determine how we can change them, how we can make them more realistic, and how we can restore some balance to the governing process (see Table 7-4). As a result, we have a conundrum: If presidential success is related to public approval ratings and presidents cannot control these ratings, how then can presidents increase their chances of success, which would then increase their poll ratings? Most recent presidents have attempted to do so by speaking more often.

T A B L E **7-4** Presidents and Public Perceptions

President	Historical Perception	Contemporary Opinion
Abraham Lincoln	Today, Lincoln ranks as one of the greatest presidents of all time. Lincoln is called "The Great Emancipator," and without his presidency, the United States as we know it would be a very different place today.	During his presidency, Lincoln's intellect and physical appearance were ridiculed. The public thought him dim-witted, and political cartoonists portrayed him as an orangutan.
Grover Cleveland	Cleveland is remembered best for his illegitimate child. His opponents' chant, "Ma, Ma where's my pa?/gone to the White House ha ha ha," is to many people Cleveland's only legacy.	Widely recognized for his stubborn honesty and anticorruption stances, Cleveland was widely admired and was the only president to serve two nonconsecutive terms.
William Howard Taft	Taft angered members of both his own party and the opposition, and seemed weak in the face of bitter partisan fighting. Far happier as a jurist than president, Taft is generally ranked as an "average" president.	Taft led the way in promoting a formal budget and was more aggressive in antitrust matters. Yet, he was regarded as Roosevelt's puppet: A common joke was that T.A.F.T. stood for "Take Advice From Theodore."
Chester A. Arthur	Arthur was something of a surprise to presidential scholars, who expected him to be part of the New York political machine. While relatively uncelebrated, Arthur rates in the middle of the pack in presidential rankings.	Known as "The Gentleman Boss" and "Elegant Arthur," Arthur's early reputation was marred by rumors of corruption, but during his term as president, he vetoed legislation favoring his own party's bosses.
Martin Van Buren	Today, Van Buren is considered an average president, hardly a failure but not a great success either.	Van Buren was viewed as an upper-class snob, vain, and effeminate by many of his contemporaries.
John Quincy Adams	Adams is thought of primarily as a failure as president. Seen as out of touch with the country, his experience as a secretary of state did nothing to help him become the kind of leader people wanted.	Adams and Henry Clay were accused of manipulating the election of 1824 to gain Adams the White House. During the following election, Adams also vilified Andrew Jackson's wife as an "American Jezebel," a tactic that backfired and contributed to his overwhelming loss of the presidency to Jackson.

7-13 Speaking Often

Stuckey (1991: 136) writes, "Presidents now talk to us more than ever before." In so doing, presidents want to show us that they either care about an issue or that they are doing something about it, even if there is no real substantive proposal associated with the speech. As Stuckey notes (ibid., 127), "Presidents may increasingly believe that they can substitute speech for action, but speaking on an issue implies that action on it should be forthcoming." Often, however, it is not. Yet, merely having the president condemn racism or bespeak the need for a sound economy often is presented by administrations as evidence of presidential action!

Speeches also have short-term political benefits. Brace and Hinckley (1992: 56) write, "Each major address adds on average about 6 percentage points in the polls." While this bump is temporary, it is important for presidents because it is evidence for other political elites that the public is responding positively to a particular presidential initiative. Since the increase in the polls is temporary, the game becomes one of short-term stimulus to the polls.

In Table 7-5, I present data on presidential speechmaking for some of the presidents of the present (or fourth) electoral order. The data indicate that presidents are indeed speaking more often. The monthly average increased with Kennedy and, with the exception of Nixon, remained at more than 20 speeches per month. Ford spoke most often, delivering an incredible 42.6 speeches on average per month. The data also reveal an increase in the number of televised addresses over time, and an exponential increase in the number of televised speeches during the Reagan presidency.

Along with an increase in the total number of speeches, presidents have appeared at public events more often. In Table 7-6, we show that John Kennedy conducted approximately nineteen public activities on average per month throughout his presidency, while Johnson conducted twenty-four such activities. While there was a decline in public activities under Nixon, his successors appeared in public quite frequently. From the data, it is apparent that presidents increased their number of foreign appearances, particularly since Gerald Ford's presidency. The most striking finding, however, is the increase in the number of "political" appearances since Lyndon Johnson's presidency. Furthermore, the data in Table 7-7 indicate that the number of speeches is increasing in both election and nonelection years. We therefore cannot merely attribute increased presidential propensity to increased speaking in election years.

With reference to Table 7-8, the number of major speeches (which usually occur before a national audience) delivered by the presidents has not changed much over time. Of those presidents who served a full term in office, Carter spoke the least, with seventeen. On the other hand, Nixon, who did not appear as often in public, was more likely to deliver major speeches (twenty-three of them). While the evidence on major speeches does not suggest that presidents are speaking more often, presidents are delivering fewer news conferences over time. Table 7-8 also reveals considerable variation in the number of minor speeches delivered. From Gerald Ford's presidency onward, presidents have delivered a larger number of

T A B L E **7-5** Frequency of Presidential Speechmaking, 1953–1985

President	Total Speeches	Monthly Average Percent	Number of National Addresses per Year on Radio and Television
Dwight Eisenhower	925	9.6	9.6
John Kennedy	771	22.0	13.3
Lyndon Johnson	1,636	26.8	12.9
Richard Nixon	1,035	15.2	19.8
Gerald Ford	1,236	42.6	22.5
Jimmy Carter	1,322	27.5	23.0
Ronald Reagan*	1,637	27.3	52.8

Source: Hart (1987: 8 and 53).

*Speeches through 1985.

TABLE **7-6** Levels of Public Activities of Presidents, 1953–1984

President	Total Activities	Yearly Average	Monthly Average
Dwight Eisenhower, first term	330	83	6.9
Dwight Eisenhower, second term	338	85	7.0
John Kennedy	658	219	18.8
Lyndon Johnson	1,463	293	24.0
Richard Nixon, first term	634	159	13.2
Richard Nixon, second term	204	113	10.2
Gerald Ford	756	344	26.0
Jimmy Carter	1,047	262	22.0
Ronald Reagan*	1,194	299	24.9

Source: King and Ragsdale (1988: 275).

*Reagan's activities are counted through 1984.

TABLE **7-7** Presidential Speaking in Election Versus Nonelection Years, 1953–1985

President	Average Number, Nonelection Years	Average Number, Election Years
Dwight Eisenhower	108.0	123.3
John Kennedy	236.5	298.0
Lyndon Johnson	280.0	347.1
Richard Nixon	182.3	203.3
Gerald Ford	396.0	542.1
Jimmy Carter	281.5	379.5
Ronald Reagan*	293.7	382.0

Source: Hart (1987: 157).

*Reagan through 1985

minor speeches (which usually occur before smaller, specialized audiences). Over one-third of all presidential speeches occurred at ceremonies honoring some group or individual. Another 15 percent occurred at political rallies. In fact, over one-half of all speeches occurred in these two types of settings. These findings suggest that presidents are speaking more, but not to a national audience. Rather, they are speaking more often before local audiences, special interest groups, and invited guests. Here, they can tell a specialized audience what it wants to hear, far from the glare of the national media or the broader American public.

In sum, presidents are trying to appeal to local and more specialized audiences so that they can tailor their messages directly to these audiences. This means greater specialization and also that presidents are becoming more likely to reach out to special interests or specific interest groups they believe they will need for re-election, to donate campaign funds, or to support administration policy (or all three). Hence, presidents are fine-tuning the way they approach public opinion. Rather than trying to influence all voters, presidents, their pollsters, and their political handlers identify key constituencies they will need to either maintain or build political support. For example, Bill Clinton appealed to so-called "Soccer Moms" as he geared up for his re-election campaign in 1996, while George W. Bush made outreach to Latinos and Catholics, a central component of his presidency.

T A B L E **7-8** **Presidential Speeches and Appearances, 1953–1984**

President	Major Speeches	Minor Speeches	News Conferences	Foreign Appearances	Public Appearances	Political Appearances
Eisenhower, first term	21	11	99	11	75	66
Eisenhower, second term	20	18	94	18	43	45
Kennedy	15	30	65	30	97	49
Johnson	23	49	132	49	244	131
Nixon, first term	23	25	30	25	166	102
Nixon, second term	13	22	9	22	38	11
Ford	12	77	41	77	183	409
Carter	17	82	59	82	172	234
Reagan, first term	20	78	23	78	260	206

Source: King and Ragsdale (1988: 262–74); Reagan had 53 total news conferences, Bush had 64, and Clinton had 41 through 1998 (Stanley and Niemi 2000: 170).

What is interesting about this approach is that presidents are less likely to appeal to the mass public, but rather carve out segments of the electorate they believe they will need in the future. This process increases the likelihood that presidents will represent specific interests instead of the national interest.

7-14 Television and the Presidency

As presidents have spoken more often to the public, they have relied on yet another technology—television. Television is yet another contextual factor that has transformed the presidency. Its invention had an even greater influence on the presidency than did radio, and radio's influence, as we have noted, was profound. As Grossman and Kumar (1981: 21) write, "The most conspicuous changes in the relationship between the White House and news organizations since the 1950s can be traced to the growing perception by the White House that television is the most important medium for the President to dominate." Since the first television station took to the air in 1947, its influence has expanded. As noted in section 6-7a, "Television's Impact," in 1952 Dwight Eisenhower was the first president to run advertisements in a political campaign. Yet, it was John Kennedy who first realized the full political potential of television.

Kennedy instinctively understood the power of television, just as Franklin Roosevelt had understood radio. While Eisenhower had allowed segments of his press conferences to be taped and televised, Kennedy performed live on TV. His personality, his humor, and his natural political skills were perfectly suited to this new technology. Television helped Kennedy to forge a closer relationship with a broader public, but more importantly, it helped him to look presidential. The images that we have of Kennedy (speaking on civil rights, the decision to send a man to the moon, the Cuban Missile Crisis) are still powerful today. That television made John Kennedy look presidential was no small accomplishment. Coming into office after a narrow electoral victory, Kennedy faced serious questions about whether he was too young and sufficiently qualified to be president. Television removed all doubt. As Americans watched the young president, he looked calm, composed, and competent. Most importantly, he looked in charge and presidential. In short, it is impossible to understand the presidency of John Kennedy without watching his various speeches and press conferences on television. Television helped to define Kennedy in his time and for all time.

Television helped John
Kennedy to forge a
closer relationship with
a broader public and
made him look
presidential.

Television also had a profound impact, for both good and bad, on all of Kennedy's successors. Not only do presidents speak more often today, but increasingly, they are evaluated on the basis of how well they can deliver a speech, particularly on television. Televised speeches have become the central moments in a presidency. George W. Bush's presidency was as much transformed by the reaction to his televised speech to Congress after the terrorist bombings on the Pentagon and the World Trade Center as it was by those events. Pundits noted how the president had sounded the right note, how he had showed confidence and commitment, and how he had been transformed; in other words, he was now perceived to be presidential! It also was noted that in earlier speeches he had looked uncomfortable (a sign that he was not presidential). One could argue that cosmetics and presentational skills are becoming as important as (some might argue even more important than) the message the president is delivering. For example, Bill Clinton is remembered as a great public speaker; yet, it is hard to remember anything that he said other than his denial that he had sex, that he did not inhale marijuana, or his answer to the question, do you wear boxers or briefs?—not exactly momentous presidential pronouncements! His state of the union addresses are perhaps as memorable for their impact on his approval ratings as they are for any individual lines that he uttered. In this type of political environment, where appearances and even perceptions of appearances are of critical importance, it is not surprising that Walter Mondale, Jimmy Carter's vice president, after he had lost his own presidential bid to Ronald Reagan in 1984, told reporters, anyone who looks and sounds like me should not run for president. It was a telling indictment of television's impact on presidential politics.

Lyndon Johnson was the first president to learn this lesson. He had extraordinary political skills, but his presentational skills on television were, to be kind, lacking. In the age of radio, Johnson's larger-than-life physical features would have been less apparent or important. Yet, on television, they helped to create a negative image of him. People saw Johnson on television, and many Americans simply did not like him. He was not as telegenic as Kennedy. He did not have a smooth delivery. While Johnson certainly did much else to undermine his relationship with the American public, television was a factor. It was a lesson that Johnson's successor understood.

Richard Nixon owed his political career to television. The "Checkers" speech in 1952 had saved his political career and his debate performances with John Kennedy in 1960 may have contributed to his narrow loss in his first bid for president. When Nixon ran for president in 1968, he therefore worked hard to use television effectively. After his narrow election, he then made public relations a keystone of his administration. As we will discuss in section 13-4d, "Nixon's Staff and Its Legacy," Nixon created a sophisticated public relations operation in the White House. Presidential events were now orchestrated so that they could be broadcast on television. His trip to China, for example, was a television event, with visuals (Nixon on the Great Wall) specifically chosen because they would look good to television audiences at home. While Nixon was not a naturally gifted speaker, he worked hard to project an image of confidence in his televised appearances. His approval ratings increased substantially following his "Silent Majority" speech on the war in Vietnam (Waterman, Wright, and St. Clair 1999: 145). Still, television continued to be a double-edged sword for Nixon. While he used it masterfully during his first term, particularly during his re-election campaign in 1972, the televised Watergate hearings, his famous televised encounter with Dan Rather at a press conference, as well as his televised declaration that he was "not a crook" (along with the sordid revelations in the Watergate case) irreparably damaged his presidency.

Bill Clinton learned this lesson. When he was faced with the specter of scandal and impeachment, he used TV to project an image of confidence. Others might wallow in the sordid details of the Monica Lewinsky scandal, but he would be seen as hard at work, doing his best for the American people. Unlike Nixon, Clinton thrived politically (securing some of his highest approval ratings), even as he faced his greatest political challenge. Television was his ally in this process—making him look presidential, while Independent Counsel Kenneth Starr was shown talking to reporters as he took his garbage to the curb. The contrast was clear and the White House loved the juxtaposition of these two images.

Presentational skill therefore was more important than ever. Those presidents who excelled at it (John Kennedy, Ronald Reagan, Bill Clinton, and George W. Bush) had tremendous political advantages over those who did not (Gerald Ford, Jimmy Carter, and George H. W. Bush). Being a "Great Communicator," as Reagan was called, was now of vital importance to a perception of presidential success and competence. Again, when Reagan was elected, there were serious questions about his competence. Was he too old? Was he too reactionary? Could a former actor be the commander-in-chief? Television provided the perfect stage for Reagan. Whether it was his speech to Congress following the assassination attempt in 1981 or his televised speech about Grenada, he projected a reassuring quality, as well as toughness (another quality associated with looking presidential).

There was a lesson: Those presidents who did not look comfortable or did not speak firmly might be perceived as weak and ineffectual. It was important to be able to stare into the camera and to show strength and determination. While Ronald Reagan was criticized by nations around the world for referring to the Soviet Union as "the evil empire," this comment helped project an image of leadership to many Americans. Likewise, when George W. Bush referred to Iran, Iraq, and North Korea as the "axis of evil," foreign governments chastised him, while opinion polls showed that a large majority of Americans responded favorably. Perhaps, however, a new lesson was raised by these comments: While television allows presidents to reach a domestic audience, it also places the president front and center on the world stage, as well. With CNN and other all-news networks broadcasting around the world (twenty four hours a day, seven days a week), the president now performs on a world stage. This may make it harder for future presidents to communicate with the American public, knowing that what they say also has direct implications for America's prestige and power, as well as its leadership role around the world. In short, television is further expanding the presidency's reach, beyond our borders and around the world.

Chapter Summary

Chapter Summary

Twentieth century presidents reached out more to the public than did their nineteenth century counterparts. As they did so, a new presidential constituency was born—one that offered a new rationale for the accretion of presidential power. It also provided a new political resource, allowing presidents to tie their elections, their policies, and their political fortunes more closely to the American people. At the same time, however, the new emphasis on public approval proved to be a double-edged sword. It meant that lower approval ratings, whatever the cause, would be interpreted as a lack or decline of presidential influence. While the factors that determine a president's poll ratings are largely beyond his or her control, presidents have attempted to manipulate the polls. In section 13-1, "The Search for New Political Resources," and section 16-3, "The Six Political Resources," we will examine how new political resources were created over time to deal with the new issue of public relations. In this chapter, we also saw that presidents are speaking more often, usually to specialized audiences, in an attempt to improve their poll ratings. In Chapter 8, "A New Intermediary: The Decline of the Political Parties and the Rise of the Media," we will examine another external political actor, the media, which has become an important intermediary between the public and the presidency. As presidents realize that their political fortunes depend to a large extent on how they are perceived by the public, they have expended vastly increased time and resources in an attempt to control or manipulate how they are portrayed by the media. As the public is a new presidential constituency, the media is now a new intermediary, replacing in many ways the political parties that once performed this vital function.

Review Questions

Review Questions

1. The relationship between the president and the public is a *double-edged sword* because
   a. it provides the presidency with greater independence from Congress and the political parties.
   b. it provides an important constituency for presidents and their programs.
   c. it expands public expectations of the presidency thus placing the presidency at the center of the American political system and turning it into a veritable public relations operation.
   d. all of the above.

2. Which of the following is *true*?
   a. The Founders did not foresee a close political relationship between the public and the presidency.
   b. The Founders foresaw a close political relationship between the public and the presidency.
   c. The Founders foresaw a close political relationship between the public and the political parties.
   d. None of the above.

3. Which of the following is *true*?
   a. The presidents of the nineteenth century were overly concerned with public approval, and their perceived success or failure was evaluated with reference to it.
   b. The presidents of the nineteenth century were not overly concerned with public approval, nor was their perceived success or failure evaluated with reference to it.
   c. The presidents of the twentieth century were not overly concerned with public approval, nor was their perceived success or failure evaluated with reference to it.
   d. The presidents of the nineteenth century were overly concerned with raising campaign funds for their re-election campaigns.

4. Presidential speechmaking in the post Civil War period can best be described as
   a. "occasionally brilliant and usually insightful."
   b. "defining the issues of the day in clear and crisp fashion; remarkable and insightful!"
   c. "brilliant oratory unmatched in our present era."
   d. "[c]olorless, terse, and without vision. None of the presidents of this era earned a reputation for their oratorical skills."

5. Which of the following nineteenth century presidents spoke the most often?
   a. Andrew Jackson
   b. Abraham Lincoln
   c. Ulysses Grant
   d. Benjamin Harrison

6. Which of the following presidents "doggedly pursued a strategy of appealing to the people regarding specific legislative matters"?
   a. Abraham Lincoln
   b. Theodore Roosevelt
   c. Warren Harding
   d. Harry Truman

7. Which of the following presidents was the first to communicate with the American public via radio?
   a. Warren Harding
   b. Franklin Roosevelt
   c. Harry Truman
   d. Dwight Eisenhower

8. The president's popularity at midterm
   a. is usually among his highest ratings.
   b. is usually among his lowest ratings.
   c. varies considerably from president to president.
   d. ranges from very high to very low ratings.

9. Which of the following is an important determinant of presidential approval ratings (meaning that it is an important factor related to a president's public standing)?
   a. the economy
   b. the number of speeches a president gives
   c. the amount of money a president raises in fundraisers
   d. all of the above

10. Before September 11, 2001, public trust in government was
    a. high.
    b. low.
    c. patriotic.
    d. unmeasurable.

Discussion Questions

1. What are the implications of the president's changing relationship with the American public? What impact has it had on presidential power?
2. Presidents speak more often today with the American public than ever before. Do they actually communicate more with the public, or do they simply talk more?
3. What effect has the measurement of public opinion had on the presidency? Is this a positive or negative development?
4. Would we be better or worse off without public opinion polling?
5. Do we expect too much from our presidents?

Note

1. The analysis of election data also shows that different ways of looking at the economy (or what scholars call sociotropic and pocketbook attitudes) are related to electoral outcomes. *Sociotropic* attitudes exist when "political judgments are shaped by evaluations of the *nation's* economic health, and not by" an individual's perceptions of his/her "own" economic situation. On the other hand, those manifest pocketbook attitudes "whose support for the incumbent or his party varies directly with their personal financial well-being" (Markus 1988: 138). For more on this subject, see the following research: Kinder and Kiewiet 1979, 1981; Kinder, Adams, and Gronke 1989; Markus 1988, 1992; Abramowitz, Lanoue, and Ramesh 1988; Erikson 1989.

Chapter 8

A New Intermediary: The Decline of the Political Parties and the Rise of the Media

Key Terms

linkage mechanisms
national party chairman
patronage system

photo opportunities (photo-ops)
press conference
spin control

8-1 A New Intermediary: The Decline of the Political Parties and the Rise of the Media

Presidents cannot reach out to the American public entirely on their own. As we shall see in section 13-2a, "Innovations in the Transitional Era," and section 13-3, "Centralization in the Modern Presidential Era," the modern presidents have created a number of organizations located in the White House providing outreach to various segments of the American public. Even with the development of these internal political resources, however, presidents need additional help from other external political actors to be able to forge a closer relationship with the American public. In section 8-2, "The Dominant Political Parties," and section 8-7, "A New Intermediary: The Media," we examine two **linkage mechanisms** (the political parties and the media) and how their relationship with the presidency has changed over time.

8-2 The Dominant Political Parties

Historian Clinton Rossiter (1960) notes that one of the hats (or roles) of the president is to be the Party Chief (an extra-constitutional responsibility). This designation suggests that the president is the head of the party. Yet, during the nineteenth century (particularly from 1828 on), the parties (the Democrats, the Whigs, and later the Republican Party) played the dominant role in the nomination and election process. As a result, they exerted considerable influence over individual presidents. To exert real influence within and beyond the parties, presidents needed to control the partisan press's message and the **patronage system.** Yet, according to Pious (1996: 162–63), "Of all the nineteenth-century Democratic Presidents, only Jefferson, Jackson and Polk were effective in using patronage to build up their party organizations or carry out party principles in their platforms." Pious notes, "Republican presidents in the nineteenth century fared no better than Democrats in handling divisions within their party." In sum, most nineteenth century presidents found themselves dependent on the parties for their political survival, instead of being party leaders. In fact, Woodrow Wilson (first elected in 1912) was the first president to choose the **national party chairman** (ibid., 166). In the nineteenth century, the party chose the presidential candidate; the president did not choose the party leader.

Figure 8-1 provides a model of nineteenth century outreach to the public by the political parties, the media, and the presidency. Since the parties controlled the nomination of the presidency, as well as the parties' message through the party platform and partisan press, the model represents the parties (combined with the partisan press) as being closest to the public. For the presidency to communicate with the public, it had to go through the parties and the press. Presidents' ability to directly communicate with the public depended on how much they controlled the party machinery and the partisan press. But as noted, only Jefferson, Jackson, and Polk of the nineteenth century presidents really exhibited this level of control and/or influence. Most presidents of the time were dependent on the party to reach out to the American public.

Hence, as noted in section 6-5, "The Second Electoral Order: Party Control from 1828–1892," section 6-5a, "The Nominating Convention," and section 7-2, "The President and the Public in the Nineteenth Century," nineteenth century presidents did not depend on the will of the people as much as they depended on the will of their own parties. For example, since presidents had no independent means of securing their party's nomination (they could not run in primaries or

Linkage mechanisms: The various policy actors that link constitutional political actors to the American public. The media and political parties, plus interest groups, perform these functions in the American political system.

Patronage system: A system whereby jobs in bureaucratic agencies were made generally on the basis of whether a job candidate worked for and supported a particular political candidate and/or political party.

National party chairman: The head of the Democratic or the Republican national committee, which is the national (as opposed to state or local) organization for each party.

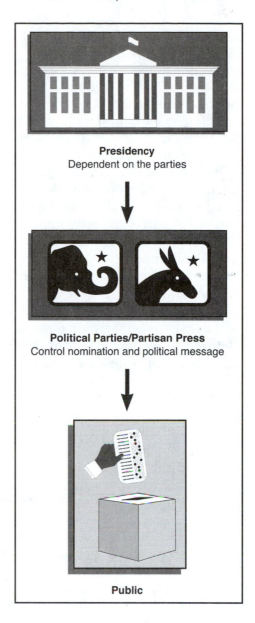

Presidency
Dependent on the parties

Political Parties/Partisan Press
Control nomination and political message

Public

Figure 8-1
Nineteenth Century
Outreach to the
American Public

appeal directly to the media and/or the public), they had to get the support of party leaders to earn the right to run for re-election. Several presidents who wanted to do so were denied the opportunity by their own parties. The fact that relatively few presidents from the second electoral order (1828–1892)—the period of the greatest party control—actually ran for re-election is therefore further evidence of the party's control over the presidents of the time.

8-3 The Decline of the Political Parties

The parties' control over the presidents began to change slowly only after the Civil War. As we shall see in section 8-9, "The Decline of the Partisan Press," first the partisan press was replaced by the development of a new independent national press corps. Grover Cleveland was the first president to reach out (though reluctantly) to this new press. Second, as noted in section 7-4, "The Birth of the Rhetorical Presidency," beginning with Theodore Roosevelt, presidents began to develop a closer relationship with the American public. Consequently, by the dawn of the twentieth century, the groundwork was laid for the development of a new presidential constituency (the public) and a new intermediary to it (the media). The parties also had begun to lose control over one of their main functions: patronage. The passage of Civil Service reform in 1883, following the assassination of James Garfield by a disgruntled office seeker, threatened to limit the two parties' control over patronage, a system whereby party loyalists are rewarded with jobs after the election. Individuals therefore had strong incentives to support and work hard for the election of party candidates.

Patronage reform proved to be an incremental process. It would take time for various presidents to extend civil service protection to a wide array of federal employees. Reform presidents in both political parties, Grover Cleveland and Theodore Roosevelt, played an important role in this process. Thus, slowly over time, as the scope of civil service protection was expanded, patronage, the mother's milk of the political parties, was constrained, and with it, so was the two parties' political influence.

A series of Progressive Era reforms also threatened to weaken the parties, though many did so only incrementally.[1] The primary role of a political party is to nominate and elect candidates to office. Parties that do not elect candidates, no matter how compelling their message, will have limited political influence. Yet, reforms such as primary elections, the direct election of senators, and the initiative and referendum process, combined with civil service reform, further eroded the influence of the parties, particularly the large inner-city political machines. If candidates could run on their own in primaries and secure nomination without the blessing of the parties, if U.S. senators and other state officials could do the same thing, and if individuals could force votes on specific policy issues (thus removing to some extent the parties' control over the political agenda), what role was left for the parties?

In sum, a variety of reforms threatened the two parties' influence as the new century dawned. As I will argue in section 11-1, "The Presidency and the Political Ecosystem," where I introduce the concept of *political ecosystems*, power in our political system does not exist in a vacuum. When one political actor loses power and influence, another political actor (or set of actors) assumes that power. Consequently, as the parties' power declined, there was a potential for the growth of presidential power. This process, however, was far from predestined. The flow of political power could have evolved in a different way, one that would have increased the influence of both the parties and the presidency.

8-4 A New Model of Political Party Leadership

For a brief period at the beginning of the twentieth century, it appeared that the power of the political parties and the presidency could move in a different direction. After his election in 1912, Woodrow Wilson resurrected the idea (dormant since the days of Thomas Jefferson) of using party government to enact his political agenda. Even more so than Jefferson, who informally met with party leaders and members of Congress to advocate his political agenda, Wilson established a leadership model that was more like a prime ministership than a modern president. Wilson was elected in 1912 with a large number of progressive Democrats. They looked to him as their leader, "while the minority of conservative Democrats went along at the outset in the interest of making a party record after their long period out of power" (Sundquist 1981: 32). Wilson therefore was able to use the Democratic Party as a viable governing mechanism: pushing issues through Congress on party line votes, rather than working with the opposition to negotiate an acceptable compromise. Using this model, Wilson and the congressional

Democrats enacted a broad-based reform agenda that included the creation of the Federal Reserve System, the Federal Trade Commission, and tough new anti-monopoly legislation. A series of reforms protecting the rights of working women and children also were enacted. In essence, Wilson and the Democrats enacted much of the Progressive Party agenda that Theodore Roosevelt had espoused in his 1912 third-party campaign for president, thus co-opting the progressive movement.

Given Wilson's political success, why then was this governing model abandoned? Pious (1996: 163) writes, "Woodrow Wilson was unable to hold his congressional party together in the years prior to the U.S. entry into World War I, as the Democratic Speaker Oscar Underwood actively opposed the possibility of U.S. involvement. . . ." As Sundquist (1983: 32) argues though, while party cohesion and "discipline broke down later" in his second term, "Wilson remained dominant over his party in Congress until his incapacitation late in 1919" (ibid.).

The Wilson record is indeed impressive, but the task of combining presidential and party leadership is exceedingly difficult in a system of separated powers, though it is interesting to speculate what might have been possible had Congress continued to nominate presidents through the King Caucus system. Since the president and members of Congress are elected separately, however, they often represent vastly different policy and ideological viewpoints. They also have different political incentives. What is good for the president may not be good for his or her party. For example, Democrats criticized Bill Clinton for signing the Kennedy-Kassenbaum Health Care Bill in 1996 and the Welfare Reform Act because they wanted to use these issues in the fall congressional campaigns. By signing these bills, though, Clinton achieved two of his main campaign promises and removed two potentially divisive issues from his own re-election campaign. Thus, Clinton's incentives were far different from those of his own party.

There are other problems with the move toward a prime ministerial system. Given the difficulties in enforcing party discipline in Congress, a prime ministerial system is not really feasible. The sanction of losing power, of a call for new elections, provides a palpable means of controlling party faction in many parliamentary systems. Since American elections occur at regular and predictable intervals, this threat does not exist.

Wilson's experiment also demonstrated both the potential and the limitations of working closely with the parties. Accomplishments were impressive, but many contemporaries judged his presidency a failure (he has done much better in historical rankings), and the Republicans resumed power in 1920 and held it for twelve years. Consequently, there was little incentive for Wilson's successors to adopt his leadership model. The stage therefore was set for a new model of presidential party relations, one in which the parties would watch as their functions incrementally were co-opted by various presidents.

8-5 Franklin Roosevelt and the Decline of the Parties

I will not delineate the full transformation of the party system in the twentieth century or the ways that transformation increased presidential power at the expense of the parties (see Milkis 1993 for a detailed treatment). A few examples, however, will show how a variety of different presidents, of both political parties, aggressively co-opted the functions of the political parties.

Even before his election, Franklin Roosevelt, a Democrat, believed that the existing party system was not conducive to executive-oriented leadership. Rather, he believed the localized nature of the parties (they were principally organized at the state and local levels) was more conducive to congressional primacy. Thus, in his Commonwealth Club speech in San Francisco during the 1932 campaign, Roosevelt discussed "an economic declaration of rights" and "an economic constitutional order" that required a shift in the American party system from localized to national party control (Milkis 1988: 332). Roosevelt's instrument for performing this transformation was the remnants of the old patronage system and newly evolving patronage opportunities (jobs) created by the federal government to combat the depression.

During the first 100 days of his new administration, Roosevelt withheld the distribution of thousands of patronage jobs (Kennedy 2000: 139), thus forcing both the Congress and his own Democratic Party to defer to him legislatively. He also used the jobs created by agencies such as the Works Progress Administration (WPA) and the Civilian Conservation Corps (CCC) to build political support in states where he needed to secure re-election, thus essentially using federal programs to dispense patronage. After his re-election in 1936, he used his appointment power to further diminish the power of local and state parties. As Milkis (1988: 333) notes,

> Beginning in 1938, especially, as Ed Flynn, who became Democratic chairman in 1940, indicated in his memoirs, "The president turned more and more frequently to the so-called New Dealers," so that "many of the appointments in Washington went to men who were supporters of the President and believed in what he was trying to do, but who were not Democrats in many instances, and in all instances were not organization Democrats."

Roosevelt therefore used his appointment power to promote his policy agenda rather than his political party's objectives. In so doing, he challenged such traditional party instruments as *senatorial courtesy,* whereby presidents generally defer to senators on appointments that will affect a senator's home state and sometimes even their home region. As with patronage, the parties long had played a major role in determining who presidents appointed. Roosevelt's successor, Harry Truman (a Democrat), also would wrestle with the Democratic Party for control of the appointment process. While Truman was not entirely successful in his efforts (see Weko 1995), his struggle was further evidence that the presidency was attempting to assume functions long controlled by the political parties.

In addition to his attempt to control appointments, Franklin Roosevelt declared open warfare on his own political party. Roosevelt intervened "in a dozen congressional campaigns in 1938 in an effort to unseat entrenched conservative Democrats." By attacking Democrats who did not support his New Deal, Roosevelt "made no attempt to work through the regular party organization" (Milkis 1988: 333). The result was politically disastrous. Only one of the senatorial candidates Roosevelt opposed was defeated. His efforts divided the Democratic Party and likely contributed to Republican gains in House, Senate, and gubernatorial positions in the fall elections (Pious 1996: 161–62).

While his electoral intervention in 1938 proved unsuccessful, Roosevelt continued to use other techniques to weaken the party's grip on the presidency, such as providing federal unemployment insurance to replace functions long provided by the political parties. Parties had long provided services for the poor, using patronage and public works projects to build direct support for their local and state organizations. Now the federal government provided these services, plus unemployment insurance and social security, thus removing valuable resources from the parties' control while concomitantly shifting the focus of public expectations to the national level. As Milkis (1988: 334) writes, "Presidential leadership during the New Deal helped to set the tone for the post-1950 resumption of party decline by preparing the executive branch to be a government unto itself, and establishing the presidency rather than the party as the locus of political responsibility."

8-6 Roosevelt's Successors and the Decline of the Parties: A Bi-Partisan Effort

As noted in section 6-2a, "Where Are the Great Presidents?," a Republican, Dwight Eisenhower, also did much to undercut the influence of the political parties. He was the first president to use his own political organization rather than the party's to run for election, he used television to communicate directly with the public during the 1952 campaign, and he secured the Republican nomination over the party favorite by running as a candidate in several presidential primaries. Likewise, Eisenhower's second term witnessed an even greater decline in the influence of the parties. Eisenhower

> campaigned in 1956 as he had governed earlier—as a politician above party—and he began his second term with relatively few obligations to his party's organization. For the Eisenhower administration, these changes meant that the party constraints that had initially hemmed in the White House appointment staff were eroding and that costs of enlarging personnel staff and increasing its capabilities to act as an instrument of administrative leadership were diminishing. (Weko 1995: 107)

Party decline continued unabated in the 1960s. John Kennedy, a Democrat, established a White House system for identifying appointees rather than relying on the party to perform this traditional function (see section 15-2, "BOGSAT!"). The result was that presidents secured greater control over the appointment process, while the parties' influence declined. Presidents also increased their control over the national party organization. They often purposely named party chairmen of lesser ability to ensure greater White House control of the political process. For example, "Lyndon Johnson [a Democrat] tolerated the ineffective John Bailey because he had no intention of revitalizing the Democratic party organization, which he thought might interfere with his own prerogative to conduct White House patronage politics" (Pious 1996: 166).

Richard Nixon, a Republican, then made the Republican Party organization completely subservient to the White House, running his election campaign through the Committee to Re-Elect the President and often cutting the Republican party machinery entirely out of the decision-making loop. By Nixon's presidency, then, the transformation essentially was complete. The parties were now in the shadows of the presidency, not the other way around.

Why was this the case? Basically, the parties no longer provided a service that presidents needed. Presidents no longer needed the parties to secure the nomination or to run for president. Presidents could raise their own campaign funds. They benefited politically from their control over appointments and patronage. They could now use various White House units instead of the party organization to reach out directly to the American public. In short, there was little incentive for presidents to have strong parties. In fact, power tended to flow more easily to the White House in the absence of strong parties. As Burns (1989: 126) writes, "In the absence of broadly organized, programmatic, membership-rooted parties, channels of public opinion and political influence tended to center in political offices and their incumbents, from village fence viewer to President." The decline of the parties therefore opened the door for increased presidential power.

By the mid-1980s, some "interesting signs of party renewal" began to emerge, especially at the state level. Yet, the national parties that rose "from the ruins of traditional state and local organizations failed to reach beyond the Washington Beltway and influence the perceptions and habits of the American people" (Milkis 1993: 300). While the decline of the parties did have consequences for presidential leadership—particularly a loss of political vision (see Lowi 1985; also see section 6-6, "The Third Electoral Order: Out of the Shadow of the Parties")—once the parties began to lose their grip on the presidency, presidents had real incentives to expedite this process. Since a prime ministerial system was not feasible, largely due to the constitutional separation of powers, a decline of the parties' influence can be seen as an important precondition to the expansion of presidential power. It also opened the door for a new intermediary: the media.

8-7 A New Intermediary: The Media

As the political parties' influence over the presidency declined, the influence of another external political actor increased. As the presidency once depended on the political parties to be its intermediary to the public, by the early twentieth century, it began to develop a similar relationship with the media. There was a difference, however: The political parties and the presidency had the same basic incentives (to get elected and to govern successfully), while the media had no such similar incentive. Rather, their focus on subscriptions and later ratings would mean that stories favorable to or critical of the presidency were acceptable so long as they were profitable. As presidents moved outside the parties' shadows, the presidency moved into a potentially more hostile political environment because it now operated through an independent intermediary that did not share its basic electoral or policy objectives.

Because the media do not share the president's incentives, presidents quickly realized that they would have to expend considerable political resources to control the media's message. On the other hand, the media would resist such manipulation, unless it was to their mutual advantage (that is, unless the manipulation produced good copy). If it did not, the media could be counted on to resist efforts at manipulation and to dig deeper for the real story. Hence, the seeds for a new adversarial relationship (one that could be either mutually beneficial or highly destructive to presidential influence) were planted. But how did this new relationship come about?

8-8 The Early Presidents and the Press

To some extent, the relationship between the president and the media always has been adversarial. Even George Washington, who was the unanimous choice for president in 1789 and 1792, dealt with negative press coverage. As a result, he wrote to friends expressing his view that the press was disturbing the "peace of the community." He also believed that press coverage was polarizing the nation and contributing to faction. Still, Washington was a believer in "managed news" as well, or the art of presidential manipulation of the news to get the president's message across. Accordingly, he used the media to his own political advantage whenever possible (Tebbel and Watts 1985: 10).

Consequently, from our nation's very beginnings, three basic attributes of the presidential-press relationship existed:

1. Presidents were concerned about the way the press portrayed them,
2. presidents used the press, whenever possible, to put their own spin on political events, and
3. there was potential for conflict between the president and the press.

These three attributes define presidential-press relations, though in other important ways, the relationship between the president and the press fundamentally has changed.

Vituperative press stories were common during the days of our early presidents, and Presidents Adams and Jefferson were certainly the victims of negative press coverage (including allegations that Adams was mad and that Jefferson had several children by one of his slaves, Sally Hemings). The press was hardly neutral in its reporting of these events. Federalist newspapers were highly critical of Jefferson and his policies, while Democrat/Republican newspapers tended to take a dim view of Federalist policies and personalities. In an attempt to combat negative press, and to provide a more reliable mouthpiece for the administration, party control of the partisan press increased over time. As Thomas, Pika, and Watson (1993: 113) write, "The partisan press reached its peak during the presidency of Andrew Jackson when federal officeholders were expected to subscribe to the administration organ, the *Washington Globe,* which was financed primarily by revenues derived from the printing of official government notices."

Despite the lack of objectivity, the partisan press was of extraordinary importance to candidates interested in winning the presidency. As Barnet (1990: 79) writes,

> In the 1830s every serious candidate [for president] had to have at least one newspaper editor in his pocket, for most of the country read nothing but newspapers, and generally a single newspaper at that. Buying editors, as John Quincy Adams discovered to his disgust, was expensive. Jackson had a coterie of sympathetic editors around the country, "a chain of newspaper posts, from the New England states to Louisiana, and branching off through Lexington to the western states." . . . His closest political advisers were all newspapermen.

8-9 The Decline of the Partisan Press

Although the press played an important role in a presidential candidate's campaign, it was not just speaking to the public: As noted, it was also speaking on behalf of the political parties. The parties controlled newspapers and consequently what they reported. In the first decade of the nation's history, a Federalist press emerged, reporting events from the Federalist's point of view. Likewise, papers supportive of Jefferson and later Jackson supported their administrations' political perspectives and often vehemently attacked the political opposition, as later did newspapers for the Whig and Republican Parties. In essence, then, the media represented the party line and reporting was biased toward the views of each party.

There was one advantage to this system. Someone picking up a particular newspaper would be aware in advance that it was an anti-Jacksonian publication, for example, and thus not likely to report favorably on the president or his administration's record. Likewise, in reading the *Washington Globe,* readers could be assured of a pro-administration bias.

Another characteristic of the media was that it was local. While materials reported in one paper might be reprinted in others, presidents did not have a national megaphone to speak to the American public. The nation itself also had a limited national identity. Thus, there was no real national press.

An independent national press did not begin to develop until the latter half of the nineteenth century. A necessary precondition for this development was the decline of the partisan press. That process had begun as early as 1860 when the Government Printing Office (GPO) was established. The GPO destroyed the "contract patronage that had supported former administration organs." The partisan press further declined during Lincoln's presidency: "Lincoln felt that tying himself to one newspaper would limit his relationships with others" (Thomas, Pika, and Watson 1993: 113–14).

Technological developments also contributed to the decline of the partisan press. "The invention of the telegraph led to the formation of wire services. Information distributed by wire to all parts of the country tended to be standardized and politically neutral to avoid antagonizing the diverse readership of the various subscribing newspapers" (ibid., 114). A combination of factors, then, contributed to the decline of the partisan press; yet, presidents were not quick to realize the possibilities created by the newly evolving national media.

8-10 Presidents and the Evolving Media

Press conference: A meeting of the president and various members of the press. The basic purpose is for presidents to communicate a desired message to the media so that the press can report it to the public.

One way that presidents communicate with the media is through the **press conference.** This can be a structured or informal meeting of the president and various members of the press. The basic purpose, however, is the same: for presidents to communicate a desired message to the media so that the press can report it to the public. Presidents, of course, want this coverage to be positive, thus portraying the president in the best possible light.

The "progenitor of the presidential press conference was the private interview, offered first by President Andrew Johnson to select reporters" to rebuke charges in his impeachment trial (Kernell 1997: 73). While Johnson had an incentive to reach out to friendly members of the press, most presidents of this era tended to distance themselves from it. If a president thought it wise, he would issue a statement to the entire press. Correspondents could submit questions through a presidential secretary, but the president would answer only those questions he desired. Interviews "were infrequent, and anything approaching an off-the-record conversation was rare" (Tebbel and Watts 1985: 270).

Grover Cleveland reluctantly reached out to the press during his second nonconsecutive term in office. Cleveland was deeply disturbed by press reporting about his personal life, which included his marriage to a much younger woman who had been his legal ward. While the public responded favorably to the Cleveland wedding, the first president to be married in the Executive Mansion, Cleveland did not enjoy reading about his personal life in the papers. His relationship with the press was therefore stormy throughout his first term (see Jeffers 2001).

At the beginning of his second term, Cleveland was advised to improve his press relations. He therefore became the first president to name a liaison for press relations, the progenitor of the modern press secretary (see Nelson 1998; Grossman and Kumar 1981: 20). Despite this decision, Cleveland continued to be suspicious of the press and did not develop a close relationship with its members (Jeffers 2001). Still, another precedent that could be used by Cleveland's successors was established.

McKinley was the first president to understand the political possibilities of a more intimate presidential-press relationship. According to Barnet (1990: 126),

> McKinley was the first president to understand the power of the mass media. . . .
> Unlike his predecessors, McKinley cultivated the press. He attended the press corps'
> annual Gridiron Dinner, invited editors and reporters to receptions, and encouraged

them, particularly the Washington representatives of the newly expanded national wire services, to call on him and his cabinet for information. The White House put out regular press releases.

William McKinley thus expanded the relationship between the president and the press. During McKinley's presidency, Dan Lamont, the White House secretary, "realized that to reach the public on behalf of the President he had to find ways to provide the press with a continuous flow of news. He needed to supply reporters with appropriate information in time for the deadlines, and to do so in a way that would help the President" (Grossman and Kumar 1981: 21). Lamont's efforts, however, were hampered by McKinley's rather colorless personality. Still, even if he did not take full advantage of it, McKinley understood the connection between media coverage and public opinion.

8-11 Theodore Roosevelt's Media Image

McKinley's successor, Theodore Roosevelt, also was concerned with his media image. As Kernell (1997: 74) writes, he "was probably the first president to appreciate the value of public opinion in leading Washington. Certainly, he was the first to cultivate close ties with Washington correspondents and consequently the first important transitional figure in presidential-press relations."

In addition, as Waterman, Wright, and St. Clair (1999: 142) note, "he was certainly newsworthy. A still small but growing Washington press corps was hungry for news about the president, and Teddy Roosevelt was smart enough to realize that he could use his favorable press coverage to advance his political aspirations." His secretary, William Loeb, Jr., thus "continued the practice of providing 'guidance' for reporters by issuing statements and press releases, answering questions at regular but informal meetings, and providing reporters with stories when their deadlines required that they have something" (Grossman and Kumar 1981: 22).

As McDonald (1994: 436) notes,

> Roosevelt talked with reporters endlessly. He used them to float trial balloons and to leak information for political purposes, he held informal press conferences, and he regularly invited a handful of reporters to chat while he had his daily shave, just after noon. Furthermore, his personal secretary, William Loeb, Jr., was "in all but name the President's press secretary," feeding the reporters colorful anecdotes about Roosevelt's family as well as serious information. By such means, the people could feel for the first time that they really knew their president. . . . These doings were part of a shrewdly calculated agenda to win the presidency for Roosevelt "in his own right" in 1904. . . .

Roosevelt also used the press for policy purposes. As Milkis and Nelson (1994: 212) write, "Roosevelt's remarkable victory in the battle for the Hepburn Act [reforming railroad rates] was helped considerably by the press." Roosevelt, following McKinley's lead, was again establishing another central tenant of the modern presidency: using the relationship between the media and the presidency to build popularity, advance his electoral fortunes, and promote his legislative program.

To do so, he manipulated the media for his own political advantage. He set the ground rules for the press, promising unprecedented access in return for control of the message. Roosevelt was able to control the rules because "he was working with a still poorly professionalized press. Washington correspondents had neither a strong sense of their rights nor any means for enforcing them" (Kernell 1997: 74–75). As time passed, however, presidents would find that they had less ability to manipulate the press as Roosevelt had.

8-12 Woodrow Wilson and the Professionalization of the White House Press Corps

Following Theodore Roosevelt's lead, his successors tried to develop an even closer relationship with the press. As the press became more professionalized, however, presidents found it more and more difficult to control the message the press reported. Woodrow Wilson is an early example of this phenomenon. "Like Roosevelt..., he also recognized the value of public opinion and sedulously set out to establish favorable relations with the press" (Kernell 1997: 75). But Wilson "distrusted the press and was by temperament and philosophy unable to cultivate reporters personally" (Milkis and Nelson 1994: 241). He "considered reporters dullards, and they sensed his condescension" (Kernell 1997: 75). Still, Wilson became "the first president" to have formal press conferences, "which he held frequently during his first two years in office" (Milkis and Nelson 1994: 241). The press, however, never warmed to Wilson's personality and after "two years of discomfort for all involved, Wilson quietly abandoned the weekly gatherings" (Kernell 1997: 75).

An important institutional development also occurred during the Wilson presidency. In 1913, Wilson presented his views on conditions in Mexico *off the record*. The next day the story appeared on the front pages of several different newspapers. A meeting was held between James Tumulty, the president's secretary, and members of the press. As a result, the press agreed to regulate its own behavior. To accomplish this goal, the White House Correspondents Association was formed "with the mandate to establish standards of professional behavior and to regulate attendance at the conferences" (Kernell 1997: 76).

Consequently, a formal White House press corps was developed. An independent and more politically objective press also was established. As Kernell writes (1997: 72),

> In the past when newspapers were as much party organs as they were business enterprises, correspondents served the party in the news they wrote. Absolute fidelity to the editorial position of the home paper was a prerequisite to assignment. Client relationships, however, required flexibility on the part of reporters. While they perhaps had to be willing to color reports with whatever slant a paper's editor wanted, correspondents could ill afford to be too partisan lest they lose their appeal to other current and potential clients. Too close an association with a particular line reduced correspondents' marketability. The more neutral the stance reporters could maintain, the better their market position.

In addition, by the early 1900s, "reporters viewed Washington as an attractive assignment." From the days in which an assignment in Washington was essentially a career burial ground, it now became a stepping-stone to career advancement, a prerequisite for positions such as the paper's managing editor (ibid.). There also was an increase in the number of correspondents, and as the Washington beat became more prestigious and newsworthy (largely because of increased access to the presidency), the level of turnover of Washington correspondents also declined. Consequently, by the early twentieth century, reporters had less incentive to follow any particular party line (and in fact a real disincentive to do so), they had greater access to the presidency, the job was more prestigious, turnover was down, the number of correspondents was up, and a formal White House Correspondents Association was formed.

These developments represented an opportunity for presidents to reach out directly to the American people. As the White House press corps became more

TABLE **8-1** Points in the Evolution of Presidential Use of Mass Media

President	Use of Mass Media
Grover Cleveland 1885–1889	Named a liaison for press relations, an informal forerunner of the modern White House press secretary.
William McKinley 1897–1901	First president to hold regular press conferences.
Theodore Roosevelt 1901–1909	Used the press to advance his career and for policy purposes.
Woodrow Wilson 1913–1921	Following a news leak, Wilson's rules for press behavior led to the professionalization of the White House press corps.
Warren Harding 1921–1923	Invented the position of White House spokesperson, which became today's press secretary.
Franklin D. Roosevelt 1933–1945	Met with the press on a regular basis; used radio and television to reach millions.
John F. Kennedy 1961–1963	Kennedy's photogenic looks and ease of speaking made him a media star, and his knowledge of how to use the media helped construct his image.
Richard M. Nixon 1969–1974	Hostile to the press, Nixon tried to revoke TV licenses for stations covering the Watergate affair. Nixon's distrust of the press created an antagonism between presidents and the press.
Ronald W. Reagan 1981–1989	A former movie star, Reagan knew how to charm the media and play to the cameras, resulting in positive coverage for the president even during scandals like the Iran-Contra affair.
William J. Clinton 1993–2001	Clinton's spin-control on the media left the media feeling manipulated even as it manipulated Clinton's image. Throughout the Clinton presidency, the media remained hostile to the president and first lady.

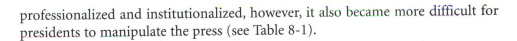

professionalized and institutionalized, however, it also became more difficult for presidents to manipulate the press (see Table 8-1).

8-13 Three Republican Presidents and Their Relationships with the Press

By the 1920s, the relationship between the president and the media had developed to such an extent that at the White House there "was a growing recognition . . . of the need to delegate more press duties to the staff" (Grossman and Kumar 1981: 22). Warren Harding continued the practice of delivering the state of the union address in person before Congress. He also held regular press conferences and invented the "White House spokesman" position "to convey information from the administration to the public without attributing it to the president" (Milkis and Nelson 1994: 264). His successor, Calvin Coolidge's popularity was reinforced by his shrewd sense of public relations. During his term, he held "520 press conferences . . . more each month than even the gregarious Franklin D. Roosevelt." He also provided provisions for the press's comfort. Coolidge's "concern for the press corps won him a considerable measure of favorable coverage in the press" (ibid., 267).

The next president, Herbert Hoover, became the first to limit his assistant's duties to "making appointments and maintaining press relations." Still, his secretary's duties were not to be a spokesman for the administration, but rather to provide information to the press about administration activities (Grossman and Kumar 1981: 22). But Hoover also had a highly confrontational relationship with the press. He was accused by the press of using the secret service to "stop leaks and launching a campaign of 'terrorism' to get publishers to fire certain newspapermen" (Leuchtenburg 1988: 17).

Consequently, by the time Franklin Roosevelt was elected, the basic building blocks of the modern presidential-press relationship were in place:

1. presidents understood the need for good press,
2. they worked hard to manipulate the press for their own benefit,
3. they assigned administration officials the task of doing so, but
4. they often had a confrontational relationship with the press. Wilson had had much less success with the press than had Theodore Roosevelt, and as Kernell (1997: 76) notes, Harding, Coolidge, and Hoover experienced difficulties in their press relations. It was therefore apparent that
5. good press relations could not be counted on as a given, but rather required considerable presidential skill.

In the modern presidency, those presidents who had good press skills would have a considerable political advantage over presidents who lacked this ability. Consequently, just as speaking ability is important for the modern presidents, skillful press relations are another significant leadership attribute.

8-14 Franklin Roosevelt and the Power of the Media

Franklin Roosevelt understood the power of the media and used it for precisely the first three purposes described in section 8-13, "Three Republican Presidents and Their Relationships with the Press," and to avoid as much as possible the fourth one. He also demonstrated considerable skill in his press relations. After his first press conference, "the correspondents applauded, the first time ever according to some veterans" (Kernell 1997: 79). While his relationships with the press were not always so congenial (see Best 1993), over his twelve-plus years in the White House, Roosevelt demonstrated that good press relations were vital to effective presidential leadership.

Roosevelt met with the press on a regular basis, usually every Tuesday and Friday of each week: 998 times in all. Most importantly, he provided reporters with hard news items. As a result, reporters arrived "expecting hard news" (Kernell 1997: 79). By meeting with reporters often, by taking them into his confidence (or at least appearing to), and by giving them hard news, Roosevelt built a close relationship with the White House press corps. This was particularly important to FDR, because most of the editorial boards of the papers were more conservative than their reporters (ibid., 80). Consequently, even if Roosevelt were excoriated in a paper's editorials, the front page would likely express a more favorable image of his leadership.

Roosevelt's personality was also perfectly suited to these occasions. They provided "ample opportunity to employ his considerable interpersonal skills." He was cordial to reporters, and whenever he "complained about a particular article, he would frequently blame the paper's editor, who he tactfully asserted must have put the correspondent up to it. This technique reduced tension and gave the reporter a convenient way of dissociating himself from his paper's editorial stance" (ibid., 80).

There was more to Roosevelt's strategy than merely increased use of press conferences. Roosevelt essentially "reinvented press relations" (Waterman, Wright, and St. Clair 1999: 142). As Richard Stout is quoted saying, "The whole administration was a public relations effort, and [Press Secretary Stephen] Early was right in the middle of it" (Grossman and Kumar 1981: 22). Public relations was now a central concern of the presidency. Presidents actively cultivated the media in order to influence the opinions of the Washington elite and the public.

As Grossman and Kumar (1981: 8) write, "By the middle decades of the twentieth century, the role played by the media had become crucial to the success of the President's efforts to bring about most significant changes in policy or even to administer existing policies." Consequently, they continued to develop innovations for dealing with the media. Truman created a pre-briefing process to prepare him for press conferences, with portions of his conferences recorded and played on the radio (Hess 1976: 51). Eisenhower's press secretary emerged as the administration's principal spokesperson, and press conferences were taped for use on television (ibid., 71). Eisenhower's press secretary, James Hagerty, also was effective at managing the news. As Stuckey (1991: 58) writes, "He was especially adept at releasing big, favorable stories to blanket the bad news." Kennedy then became a master of the press conference and was the first to televise them live.

While presidents continued to deal with the press, not all of the modern presidents fully appreciated the need to reach out to it. Truman, Ford, and Carter (all presidents with relatively low public approval ratings) were slow to learn that they needed the press to govern affectively, and in particular, they needed the press to communicate with the public. "It was not until after he had been in office for eighteen months that Jimmy Carter recognized the relationship between his lack of attention to political communication and his political weakness." On the other hand, "Truman never learned" and Ford only "grasped the lesson once he selected an able group of assistants to coach him"(Grossman and Kumar 1981: 24).

Other presidents—Eisenhower, Kennedy, Johnson, Nixon—however, better understood "the importance of White House publicity operations" (ibid.). The same can be said for Reagan, Clinton, and George W. Bush. George H. W. Bush masterfully used the press during the Gulf War but was less effective in getting his message across in other situations (e.g., the recession that followed the war).

It would be important for presidents to understand their new relationship with the press. To a large extent, it is the press that defines a new president to the American public. How the press covers a president has much to do with how people (including Washington insiders) perceive that president (e.g., as a tough, determined, focused, natural leader or as a detached, unfocused, overwhelmed, incompetent president). Since the press can do much to establish an image (good or bad) of a particular president's leadership abilities (see Waterman, Wright, and St. Clair 1999), presidents have an even greater incentive today to control the media's message. The political world has changed considerably since the days of Franklin Roosevelt, however. Then, the president did not have to be concerned with the omnipresent 24–7 saturation news coverage on cable television, and with it, a more confrontational political environment. The rules of political gamesmanship were still more civilized. As Kernell (1997) argues, however, the political world today is vastly more complex than it was in Theodore or Franklin Roosevelt's time. One characteristic of this new political world is increased competition and, on occasion, even open hostility between the White House and the press.

8-15 A New Political World

As discussed in section 7-14, "Television and the Presidency," the presidencies of Lyndon Johnson and Richard Nixon raised fundamental questions about trust in government. They also altered the relationship between presidents and the press. A new adversarial relationship emerged in the wake of their presidencies. Johnson was a classic insider politician, but he did not appear to fully understand the dynamics of press relations in the age of television, a point Kennedy appears to have instinctively understood. As the Vietnam War exacerbated cleavages in society and raised questions about Johnson's veracity, his relations with the press deteriorated. According to Stuckey (1991: 74), "The press found Johnson 'unpresidential' and did not hesitate to tell him so." Johnson responded to poor press coverage by firing his press secretary, George Reedy. As Hess (1976: 99) notes, "For the first time, a Press Secretary's downfall was based not on his performance, but on the performance of a President."

Nixon was every bit as controversial as Johnson, and his relationship with the media likewise deteriorated over time. Nixon was deeply suspicious of the Washington elite and considered the media to be liberal and biased. Lacking Roosevelt's or Kennedy's natural charm, as had Johnson, Nixon nevertheless worked hard to control the media's message. While he succeeded quite remarkably at this task during his first term in office, greatly expanding the presidential focus on public relations, Nixon's suspicious nature also led him to bug reporters' telephones. The Nixon administration also tried to revoke the licenses for TV stations owned by the *Washington Post* as a means of punishing them for their coverage of the Watergate affair. Eventually, Nixon's hostility toward the press spilled out into the open. Dan Rather wrote a book about how the White House "palace guard" insulated Nixon from other members of his administration and the public. He also was one of the reporters who was most critical of Nixon's administration. At a press conference, when reporters applauded Rather after he had been criticized by Nixon administration officials, Nixon asked, "Are you running for something?" Rather responded that he was not and then asked, "Are you?" The hostility between the press corps and the presidency was televised across the nation. Unfortunately for the presidency, the hostility of the Johnson and Nixon presidencies would set the stage for continued suspicion between the presidency and the press.

Thus, in 1981 Grossman and Kumar (10) wrote, "Former and current officials of the White House Press Office agree that both the tone of the relationship with the media and the scale of White House press operations have changed dramatically since the early 1960s." Various officials referred to "simpler relations of a different era." They continued, "The relationship between the White House and the news media since 1965 might appear to demonstrate three points: first, that the relationship is characterized by an underlying antagonism; second, that it is subject to dramatic and unpredictable changes; and third, that it is still affected by the traumas of Watergate and Vietnam."

While press relations improved dramatically following the terrorist attacks of September 11, 2001, by the summer of 2002, President George W. Bush once again was struggling with a recalcitrant press. In fact, the history of presidential-press relations in the decades following Vietnam and Watergate cannot be described as sanguine. While Ford initially was treated well by the press, following the pardon of Nixon, his relations with the press deteriorated (DeClerico 1993). Carter's coverage was, if anything, even more negative than Ford's. As Brody (1991: 151) notes, "the public received a large proportion of negative results during the Carter presidency. More than half (56 percent) of the results of stories from 1977 though 1980 were classified as negative. This means that, from the perspective of a consensus on desirable results or expectations that President Carter had set, Americans were getting a lot of bad news."

After Ford and Carter, neither of whom exhibited great skill in media relations, the Reagan administration made controlling the media's message one of its central concerns. Using techniques such as the line or message of the day (a prearranged decision to stay on focus by talking about one and only one political talking point each day) and the use of **photo opportunities (photo-ops)** (events at which the president would be photographed in a setting that emphasized a particular policy or pre-selected image of the president—president as leader, president as concerned American, president as patriot), Reagan took full advantage of television's potential. To reduce the level of confrontation with the press, the White House limited the number of presidential press conferences. In addition, the president was not encouraged to respond to reporters' questions at photo-ops (though he often did), and bad news was reported to the media not by the president but by another administration official. On the other hand, good news almost always was reported by the president, often without follow-up questions from the media. Given his cordial personality, rhetorical and telegenic skills, and a favorable public mood (many people wanted Reagan to succeed because the four presidents before him—Johnson, Nixon, Ford, and Carter—were perceived as failures), Reagan had better press relations than most of the modern presidents since Kennedy. While the press was critical of his administration during the Iran-Contra affair, Reagan received more positive press coverage than his immediate predecessors.

Whether a president received good press coverage depended on the president's personal resources as well as the ability of administration officials to initiate an effective public relations operation. While George H. W. Bush had good press relations throughout much of his presidency, during his failed re-election campaign, media bias became an issue. Bumper stickers reading "Annoy the Media, Reelect President Bush" were unveiled.

The Clinton presidency then witnessed a level of presidential-press hostility not prevalent since the days of Richard Nixon. Even before the Monica Lewinsky scandal, Bill and Hillary Clinton distrusted the media. Even during the 1992 presidential campaign, their relations with the media were not cordial. During and after the election, the media, for its part, seemed quite disturbed by Clinton's efforts at **spin control,** even though many of the techniques Clinton used had been established during the Nixon and Reagan presidencies. The press seemed to resent the fact that Clinton was trying to manipulate it, though this had been a common presidential practice throughout the twentieth century. Whatever the root causes, media relations during the Clinton years remained quite hostile (see Kurtz 1998). Still, given the importance of good press coverage, it is understandable why presidents and their aides continue to spend an inordinate amount of time trying to influence and manipulate the media and to transmit a positive image or self-serving political message to the American people.

Photo opportunities (photo-ops): Events at which the president is photographed in a setting that emphasizes a particular policy or pre-selected image—president as leader, president as concerned American, president as patriot.

Spin control: The effort made by presidential officials and other political actors to create (for the media) a positive spin or interpretation on a presidential speech or decision.

George H. W. Bush signing the Martin Luther King, Jr., Holiday proclamation, May 17, 1989

Chapter Summary

According to an empirical study by Brody (1991: 137), the percentage of negative news stories has increased over time in relation to the number of positive stories. Still, most presidents consider the media to be vital to their eventual success. The reason is obvious: As Newman (1994: 46) writes, "Most . . . [pundits] agree that the mass media have gradually replaced party organizations as the principal conduits between the voters and the candidates." Making a connection with voters is important. As Grossman and Kumar (1981: 30) write, "White House officials expect that their regulation of the flow of information to the media will provide such benefits to the President as a higher standing in the polls, greater success in his policy initiatives, and reelection."

The stakes, therefore, are high. Presidents need good media coverage to be able to reach out to the American public. They do not control the media or its message, however, as was the case during the days of party dominance. Consequently, as the presidency reached out to a new constituency, the public, it traded one intermediary that shared similar incentives (election and policy objectives) for another that often has vastly different incentives from the president. The result is a high stakes poker game. Winners can walk away from the table rich beyond their wildest dreams, but losers can lose it all. It therefore is a dangerous political game.

What makes this relationship even more perilous is that, in an age of divided government, presidents must struggle with an often recalcitrant Congress. The adversarial relationship between the president and the media has important implications not only for how the public perceives the president, but also how other Washington elites will interact with the president.

Review Questions

1. Nineteenth-century presidents did not depend on the will of the people as much as they depended on the will of
   a. the media.
   b. their own parties.
   c. the courts.
   d. interest groups.

2. Which reforms eroded the influence of the political parties?
   a. primary elections
   b. the direct election of senators
   c. the initiative and referendum process
   d. all of the above

3. Which of the following presidents briefly provided a prime ministerial model for the presidency and the parties?
   a. Theodore Roosevelt
   b. Woodrow Wilson
   c. Franklin Roosevelt
   d. Lyndon Johnson

4. Which of the following presidents ran his election campaign through the Committee to Re-Elect the President and often cut the party machinery entirely out of the decision-making loop?
   a. Franklin Roosevelt
   b. Lyndon Johnson
   c. Richard Nixon
   d. Ronald Reagan

5. As a direct result of the decline of the political parties' influence, the influence of which other external political actor increased?
   a. interest groups
   b. Congress
   c. the bureaucracy
   d. the media

6. The partisan press reached its peak during the presidency of
   a. Andrew Jackson.
   b. Abraham Lincoln.
   c. Andrew Johnson.
   d. Theodore Roosevelt.

7. What particular technological developments also contributed to the decline of the partisan press?
    a. wire services
    b. telephone
    c. airplane
    d. air conditioning

8. Which of the following presidents was the first to name a liaison for press relations?
    a. Abraham Lincoln
    b. Rutherford Hayes
    c. Grover Cleveland
    d. William Howard Taft

9. Which of the following presidents met with the press on a regular basis, usually every Tuesday and Friday of each week: 998 times in all?
    a. Theodore Roosevelt
    b. Franklin Roosevelt
    c. Ronald Reagan
    d. Bill Clinton

10. An adversarial relationship between the president and the press developed after
    a. the Kennedy assassination.
    b. Watergate.
    c. Iran-Contra.
    d. the Monica Lewinsky scandal.

Discussion Questions

1. Should the political parties have more influence in American politics today? Why? How could their influence be increased?
2. Do the media have too much influence in American politics today?

3. Do presidents need the media?
4. Can presidents discuss a substantive political agenda with the media as its main intermediary, or is the media interested only in gossip and stories that highlight personality?

Note

1. A number of scholars have examined the causes and consequences of the decline of the political parties, including Broder 1972, Scott and Hrebenar 1979, Crotty and Jacobson 1980, Sorauf 1980, and Sundquist 1983.

An Invitation to Gridlock or to Govern? The Presidency and Congress

Key Terms

congressional hegemony
divided government
executive hegemony
Watergate

9-1 An Invitation to Gridlock or to Govern? The Presidency and Congress

In the 1830s, Alexis de Tocqueville (1945: Volume 1: 126) wrote, "Yet, the struggle between the President and the legislature must always be an unequal one, since the latter is certain of bearing down all resistance by persevering in its plans." Later, in his classic study of the presidency, Edward Corwin (1984) similarly wrote, "The Constitution is an invitation to struggle for the privilege of directing American foreign policy."

Language that emphasizes conflict between the executive and legislative branches is common in the political science literature. Not only are words such as "conflict," "gridlock," and "deadlock" commonly employed, books have such titles as *Invitation to Struggle* (Crabbe and Holt 1989), *Politics of the Budget: The Struggle Between the President and the Congress* (Shuman 1992), *The President and Congress: Collaboration and Combat in National Policymaking* (LeLoup and Shull 1999), and *Divided Government: Cooperation and Conflict Between the President and Congress* (Thurber 1991). Outside academia, journalists also use military metaphors. For instance, journalist Hedrick Smith (1988: xviii) in his book *The Power Game* refers to Congress as "the principal policy arena of battle." In this chapter, therefore aptly titled "An Invitation to Gridlock or to Govern," I examine how the president's relationship with Congress has changed over time. We begin with a discussion of the constitutional basis upon which presidential-congressional relations are based.

9-2 The Separation of Powers

Why do scholars write about conflict between the president and the Congress? To answer this question, we must first understand that nowhere in the Constitution did the Founders make the presidency the preeminent branch of government, nor did they even believe it would play the primary role in our governmental system. As Tocqueville's quote in section 9-1 suggests, the Founders created a constitutional system in which the legislative branch was expected to dominate. To limit its power, they consequently divided the legislature into two houses: a House of Representatives and a Senate. They then provided different electoral schemes for each and the proviso that both houses must agree in order for most business of government to occur (with some exceptions, such as the treaty process, which resides with the Senate and not the House). The Founders also provided other constitutional actors with the ability to check the power of the legislative branch (such as the presidential veto power) and also gave the legislature the power to keep a watchful eye on the other two branches.

In so doing, the Founders were guided by the writings of such political philosophers as Charles Montesquieu.[1] "By establishing separate government institutions, assigning them specific and distinct powers, and finally safeguarding these powers from usurpation, Montesquieu hoped to preserve constitutional liberty, to keep government free" (Wayne 1978: 4). The Constitution thus enacted a form of separation of powers, but not an absolute one; that is, the executive power was not delegated exclusively to the executive branch, the legislative power solely to the legislative branch, and the judicial power only to the judicial branch. Rather, the Constitution attempted to control political power by creating a system of overlapping authority whereby one branch could check and constrain the power of another branch, that is, a system of checks and balances.

9-2a Separate Institutions Sharing Power

Separation of power combined with checks and balances creates what Neustadt (1980: 26) calls "a government of separated institutions sharing power."[2] This is a more complex relationship than a mere separation, for it means that power is blended or intermingled. The president therefore has the power to sign or veto legislation, the ability to recommend legislation, and to make treaties. The president also influences the courts by nominating judges. Congress has the power to confirm judges and can create courts inferior to the Supreme Court, changing their size and composition and providing funding for them. It also has executive authority in that it can declare war—previously a function held by kings—as well as to confirm appointments. Congress also has the power to impeach and remove the president, with the Chief Justice of the Supreme Court presiding. It also can impeach other executive officials (e.g., cabinet secretaries), as well as judges. These are but some examples of the overlapping constitutional authority—so that no one branch ultimately can have too much power without the cooperation of the others. The genius of this system, as Madison famously declared in the *Federalist Papers,* was that ambition was designed to check ambition.

Hence, the relationship portrayed at the top of Figure 9-1, the basic model of a separation of powers, does not really exist in American politics. Rather, power is blended and shared. The resulting system, however, is highly inefficient, creating multiple veto points in which government action can be brought to an abrupt halt.

As a result, some scholars characterize the constitutional framework as promoting stalemate, deadlock, gridlock, and an ongoing struggle or conflict between the legislative and executive branches of government. For example, then political scientist Woodrow Wilson (1908: 60) believed that the separation of powers was a detriment to sound government, even stating, "You cannot compound a successful government out of antagonisms." More recently, Mezey (1989) refers to the present system of government as "the Constitution against government" because it encourages stalemate and deadlock. Not all scholars agree with this characterization, however. Tulis (1987: 45) argues, "Viewed at particular moments the system may appear deadlocked: considered over time substantial movement becomes apparent."[3] Still, deadlock, gridlock, stalemate, conflict, and struggle have become keywords in the discussion over presidential-congressional relations. To better understand this point, we need to examine how the presidential-congressional relationship has changed over time.

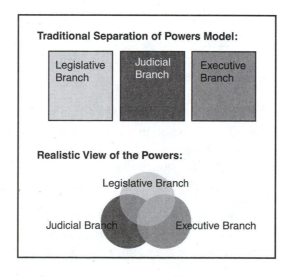

Figure 9-1
Separation of Powers: Traditional View Versus Reality

9-3 Congressional or Presidential Dominance: Why Does It Matter?

One of the basic questions in the study of American government is which branch of government controls the policy process? Over time, however, as Sundquist (1981) argues, congressional influence declined while that of the presidency increased. Likewise, Spitzer (1993) contends that what was once a system of **congressional hegemony** is now one of **executive hegemony.** Others disagree with this description. Jones (1994: 15) describes the presidential-congressional relationship as a continuing competition. While "occasionally one or the other institution is dominant [more] typically the White House and Congress must 'act in tandem.'" Hence, "there is nothing automatic about conferring of power to presidents in a separated system" (ibid., 41; see also Peterson 1990; Bond and Fleisher 1990).

But why does it matter whether the president or Congress is dominant in our political system or whether they struggle in tandem? To answer this question, just think of the differences between the war presidencies of James Madison and Franklin Roosevelt. We cannot understand the differences merely by examining the Constitution or the two presidents' respective leadership styles. We also need to understand the power of the presidential institution at the time they governed. Likewise, in understanding the influence of Congress in 1812–1815 and 1941–1945, we need to understand its institutional strengths and weaknesses, as well as the views of its individual members. This helps us to explain why Madison struggled to exert authority as commander-in-chief while FDR soared.

Likewise, initially, in terms of presidential leadership in congressional affairs, the powers of the executive were "as bare as Mother Hubbard's kitchen" (Young 1966: 158). On the other hand, Congress's constitutional role was delineated in considerable detail. Hence, Congress had a clear advantage after the Founding in terms of providing leadership and extending its hegemony over the American political system. To use Pfiffner's (1988) famous phrase in a different context: after the Founding, Congress was better prepared to "hit the ground running" than was the presidency.

As a result, Congress was able to play a critical role in defining the parameters of presidential power. For example, Congress created the first cabinet departments and defined the relationship between these departments, the president, and Congress. In creating the Secretary of the Treasury, Congress required the secretary to report directly to it, rather than to the president. Spitzer (1993: 22) writes, "The purpose was to limit executive power in the realm of financial affairs in order to secure congressional control of taxing and spending." While the plan backfired by paving "the way for a strong treasury secretary" capable of co-opting "the congressional agenda" (ibid., 22–23), it was Congress that played an important role in defining the parameters of presidential power. As such, it could promote its own institutional dominance.[4]

9-3a Washington and Congress

Given the discussion in section 9-3, it is not surprising, then, that initially presidents deferred to Congress. As Elkins and McKitrick (1993: 59) note, "Washington, ever sensitive to the possibility that he might be accused of overstepping his powers (such as presuming to initiate legislation), forbode in his inaugural address from telling Congress what measures he thought it ought to take. . . ."

Washington, then, provided a means for regularized contact between the president and Congress. While his early decision to seek "advice and consent" directly from the Senate regarding a treaty with the Creek Indians did not prove workable,

---

Congressional hegemony: A system in which the Congress dominates the political system.

Executive hegemony: A system in which the president dominates the political system.

he established a "special chamber where the Senate could meet on a regular basis for consultation, especially about appointments and treaties" (Phelps 1989: 269). While this idea was eventually abandoned, he regularly invited legislators to dine with him to communicate with individual members of Congress. While developing a relationship with Congress was therefore important to Washington, he did not take the policy lead in domestic affairs.

Washington did, however, carve out a more active role for the presidency in foreign affairs. For instance, "Washington wrote down his ideas for a bill on the national militia and sent them to Henry Knox, his secretary of war, for legislative action." He also conferred in 1790 with "two senators in an effort to reverse an action the House had taken on appropriations with the foreign service" (Fisher 1981: 33–34). In another case, when opponents in Congress appeared to have a majority to enact legislation that, among other sanctions, would suspend imports from Britain, Washington named Chief Justice John Jay to negotiate any grievances.[5] Thus, Washington created different leadership expectations on domestic and foreign policy: expectations that would provide the basis for what is called the "Two Presidencies" (Wildavsky 1969) or the idea that there is both a foreign and domestic policy presidency.[6]

9-3b Jefferson and the Democratic/Republican Presidents

Spitzer (1993: 25) notes, "Adams continued Washington's practice of avoiding direct involvement in legislative matters, and no members of Adams' cabinet adopted Hamiltonian aggressiveness toward Congress." Jefferson's presidency, however, developed a model for presidential-legislative relations that might have set a standard for nineteenth century presidents, had others had the skill to implement it. By the time Jefferson was elected, the political parties had formed (see section 8-2, "The Dominant Political Parties"). Consequently, Jefferson was the first president who was "primarily a party leader. The chief instruments of his leadership were the party caucus, which enabled the party membership to present on the floor [of Congress] a united front" (Corwin 1984: 18–19). In fact, by "the time Jefferson was ensconced in office, the party apparatus had so joined the other branches that he could draft bills and give them to friendly members of Congress for action" (Fisher 1981: 35).

The political model that Jefferson employed was a variation of a prime ministership, similar in many ways to the leadership style that Woodrow Wilson later employed (see section 8-4, "A New Model of Political Party Leadership"). Whereas Wilson was an aggressive leader, proposing a detailed policy agenda, Jefferson, following the political norms of his time, provided leadership subtly behind the scenes. As had Washington, Jefferson dined with legislators at the Executive Mansion. In this setting, he was able to discuss issues and even suggest policy options.

The historical record indicates that Jefferson had considerable success with this leadership model. Yet, Jefferson had advantages that his successors did not have. He was the intellectual leader of his political party. His election in 1800 also provided unified Democratic/Republican Party control of the presidency and both branches of Congress, replacing the Federalist Party, which controlled the executive and legislature during John Adams's presidency. While unified party control would continue for some time, the Democratic/Republican Party would become more fractured over time. Therefore, although he was nominated by his party's congressional caucus, Jefferson had considerable influence over his party and Congress. Like Washington, then, he had substantial independent standing.

As Fisher (1981: 37) writes, however, "Jefferson's persuasive innovations did not survive his administration." Instead, "President James Madison and his immediate successors in the White House lacked the personal qualities and political skills that Jefferson had used to maintain party unity and executive legislative-cooperation." While Madison was the Father of the Constitution and another intellectual leader in the Democratic/Republican Party, he did not enter office as Jefferson had, leading his party to power over the opposition Federalist Party. Members of Congress did not depend on Madison for their election, but rather the reverse was true. Owing his office to the congressional caucus, and needing their approval to run for re-election, Madison found himself in a much less enviable political position than his predecessor. The political situation was no better for James Monroe or John Quincy Adams.

Beyond the method of presidential nomination, other newly formed institutions also constrained executive power (Fisher 1981: 37). The executive departments, as they grew in number, responsibility, and complexity, drifted beyond the president's immediate control. Members of the Cabinet who had presidential ambitions often were more attentive to Congress (which controlled the nomination process) than they were to the presidents they ostensibly served.

In addition, Congress developed its present system of standing committees, dispersing power away from congressional leaders to "little legislatures." It was therefore more difficult for a president to dine with party leaders for there were many more of them and each had less overall authority. As a result, presidents after Jefferson dealt with an increasingly decentralized Congress with independent blocks of power. This made it more difficult for presidents to exert formal or informal control of Congress.

By the time of Madison's presidency, then, Congress dominated the political process. Congress then further constricted presidential power by reducing the utility of the president's recommending function, as McDonald (1994: 355) notes, to "little more than a ritual." Hence, when, in 1817, James Monroe "announced that Congress lacked constitutional authority to appropriate money for internal improvements" a House committee "expressed shock that a president would try to interfere with the ability of Congress to express its will" (Fisher 1981: 24). While John Quincy Adams was "not content to remain in the Shadow of Congress," the legislature simply ignored his attempt to present a detailed legislative program (Milkis and Nelson 1994: 117).

9-4 Nineteenth Century Expectations of the Presidency

As noted in section 6-4c, "The Loyalty of the President's Cabinet," Andrew Jackson came to the presidency with greater political influence within the developing party system: The rise of the Democratic Party is associated with his election and administration. During his presidency a new rationale for presidential leadership was provided: The president is the "tribune of the people"—see section 7-4, "The Birth of the Rhetorical Presidency." A new nomination system was established: the political convention through the political parties. Jackson was therefore able to more aggressively flex presidential power over Congress. For example, he was more active in vetoing legislation than his predecessors: issuing twelve vetoes (five regular vetoes and seven pocket vetoes). He reclaimed control of the Cabinet by freely removing those Cabinet secretaries with whom he disagreed. He initiated the practice of the spoils system to expand presidential and party control over patronage. He challenged and eventually destroyed the Second National Bank, ignored the advice of his own Treasury Secretary, and dispersed federal funds to state banks.

Box 9-1

Expectations and Contours of the Nineteenth Century Presidency

1. Most nineteenth century presidents were weak, and almost all deferred to the will of Congress, particularly on domestic policy matters.

2. Most nineteenth century presidents had relatively little to do in the realm of foreign policy, and hence could not develop a reputation in this realm either.

3. Even active presidents, like Jackson, *rarely* initiated legislation. That was the role of Congress, not the president.

4. Nineteenth century presidents, when they did challenge Congress, were more likely to do so with the presidential veto.

5. When nineteenth century presidents did challenge Congress, they were called a dictator or a demagogue and there was a backlash (often a severe one) against that president's successor.

6. Since presidents were nominated by the congressional caucus and later by the political party conventions, other external actors (Congress and the parties) had considerable influence over the president's cabinet, often much more so than the president. Consequently, the use of the word "administration" is a bit of a misnomer, since it was not really the president's administration.

7. Since presidents owed their election to Congress or the parties (and not the public), they did not need to develop a colorful public persona. Thus, many nineteenth century presidents were rather colorless individuals, administrators or magistrates rather than leaders.

8. Nineteenth century presidents rarely spoke or campaigned in public. Hence, they did not have the means of developing a constituency that would allow them to challenge congressional or party dominance.

Despite the evidence of greater vigor and energy in the executive, Jackson's dealings with Congress were "chiefly negative, being confined for the most part to a vigorous use of the veto power" (Corwin 1984: 23). When Jackson did try to confront Congress directly, by firing several Treasury Secretaries who refused to transfer deposits from the national bank to state banks, Congress censured him, though it retracted its censure just before he left office (Milkis and Nelson 1994: 129–30). Consequently, while Jackson represented a temporary increase in presidential power, Congress still dominated the political system. Furthermore, once Jackson retired from the political scene, there was a political backlash against his immediate successor—Martin Van Buren.

A pattern for nineteenth century presidents was therefore established. Most would be weak and would willingly defer to the will of Congress. When a strong president emerged, however, and temporarily challenged congressional dominance, not only would he be attacked as a dictator or a demagogue, there also would be a powerful backlash against his successor. Congress then quickly would reestablish its influence over the political system. As is summarized in Box 9-1, by Jackson's presidency, then, a number of expectations and contours of nineteenth century presidential life firmly were established. Even though occasional strong presidents—in particular, Jefferson, Jackson, Polk, and Lincoln—would emerge, most nineteenth century presidents would fit the pattern of mediocrity.

9-4a Backlash

To understand the points presented in Box 9-1, let us look at what happened after Andrew Jackson retired from the presidency. While his handpicked successor was elected in 1836, Martin Van Buren's presidency was characterized by a palpable political backlash from Congress. Van Buren was then defeated in his 1840 re-election bid by William Henry Harrison, who as we noted in section 3-2g, "William Henry Harrison and the Whig Conception of the Presidency," and section 4-8b, "Recommending Legislation," developed a rationale for a weak strict construc-tionist presidency: a president who would rarely use the veto, never initiate legisla-tion, and would willingly defer to Congress. Harrison died a month after his inauguration and his vice president, John Tyler, became president.

Tyler's presidency is interesting. Presidential-congressional relations were highly conflictual during Tyler's presidency. First, Tyler angered many members of Congress by declaring that he was in fact president of the United States, rather than acting president. Many members of Congress believed that an election should have been held to select a new president. Tyler insisted, however, that he was president in his own right. Congress deferred, but not for long.

Over time, "Tyler progressively enraged supporters and opponents in Congress, by assuming full presidential duties instead of acting as a caretaker, breaking with members of his party in Congress over the national bank issue, and using his veto power ten times" (Spitzer 1993: 27). The latter issue, the use of a constitutionally enumerated power, proved to be the most controversial of all. After twice vetoing the national bank bill in 1842, Congress debated the "extent and scope of presiden-tial powers, particularly the veto. Most speakers argued that vigorous use of the veto represented an improper, even unconstitutional intrusion by the President into the legislative realm." When Tyler used the veto power again in 1842, one Whig news-paper referred to him as a "corrupt fool and knave who pretends to act as President" and "ought to be shot down in his tracks, as he walks along." In congressional debate, he was compared to "Judas Iscariot" (ibid., 28–29). Spitzer (1993: 29) writes, "This was incredibly venomous rhetoric to be directed against a President whose sin was the exercise of three lawful vetoes!" In 1843, Representative Botts introduced a nineteen-count charge of impeachment against Tyler. While the motion was defeated by a margin of 83–127, it tangibly demonstrated the low standing of the presidency in relation to the legislative branch (ibid.).

The important point here is not that Tyler's presidency was perceived as a fail-ure, or that he was not perceived as a great leader: These are characteristics shared by many nineteenth century presidents. What is important is that once Jackson left the presidency, there was a backlash against the presidency. It was clear that in the nineteenth century there would be a price to be paid for strong presidential leader-ship. If it was not paid by a strong president like Jackson, then it certainly would be paid by his successors. The same pattern would replay itself throughout the century.

9-4b Polk, Lincoln, and Two More Backlashes

James Polk governed in the Jacksonian tradition (Skowronek 1993). While he is often overlooked today, he "offered the most detailed list of policy objectives" of any president prior to the Civil War, "urging a lower tariff, no third Bank of the United States, and the annexation of Texas and Oregon" (Tulis 1987: 49). He also developed a budget for the nation's expenses, the first president to do so, and was a hands-on commander-in-chief, actively planning military strategy. Polk ran on a promise not to seek re-election. In the twentieth century, this would greatly under-cut presidential influence, since a president who did so would be a lame duck from his first day in office. In the nineteenth century, however, one can make the case that this promise actually advanced presidential power. Since he was not going to seek re-election, Polk could be more aggressive in his political dealings with Congress and his party. They did not hold the ultimate sanction: the threat of denying him re-nomination to keep him in his place.

Whatever the reason (personal skill or his close association with Jackson), Polk was an activist president. Like Jackson, he was derided for overstepping his constitutional authority. Yet, despite abuses of presidential power (such as provoking military action in disputed territory with Mexico), Polk was a successful president if we evaluate him by his accomplishments. All of his priorities were accomplished by the time he left office (see Skowronek 1993). One could argue, then, that Polk should have been a role model for his successors.

Once Polk passed from the political scene, however, his successors were hardly distinctive: Zachary Taylor, Millard Fillmore, Franklin Pierce, and James Buchanan were all weak presidents. While Pierce actually played an activist role in passing the ill-fated Kansas-Nebraska Act, and James Buchanan urged the Supreme Court to rewrite the Dred Scott decision (encouraging them to rule the Missouri Compromise unconstitutional), both actions that history condemned, these four presidents left a sparse record of achievement. They certainly were not leaders of Congress in any sense of the word.

Again, there was a backlash against a strong presidency. It did not involve the controversy associated with the Tyler presidency, but it did witness the ascension of four undistinguished presidents who generally were willing to defer to Congress. Taylor, like William Henry Harrison, was a Whig who believed in a limited presidency. Like Harrison, he died in office. His vice president, Fillmore, did not make the same mistakes as Tyler but did little else to distinguish his presidency, beyond his support for the Compromise of 1850. While Pierce was a member of Jackson's and Polk's political party, he did not emulate their leadership approach. In fact, there is ample historical evidence that Pierce was nominated because he lacked those leadership qualities; he was a relatively minor political figure even at the time of his election. While Buchanan had more political stature than Pierce, his presidency rates with Pierce toward the bottom of the historical rankings (see section 3-3, "Presidential Greatness").

It is tempting to identify Lincoln as a break from the nineteenth century tradition of a weak presidency. We can concentrate on Lincoln's many accomplishments and forget that he was a former Whig who espoused a passive presidential model. He criticized Polk's involvement in the Mexican War. In his campaign for president, he did not advocate an activist presidency. If the Civil War had been delayed another decade, would Lincoln today be remembered as a great president? While the question is impossible to answer with certainty, it is likely, given his predilection for a weak presidency, that he would not have distinguished himself and thus today we might speak of Taylor, Fillmore, Pierce, Buchanan, and Lincoln as if they all were weak presidents. The circumstances of the Civil War encouraged Lincoln to be an activist president. There is no doubt that he rose to the occasion.

Still, Lincoln faced considerable opposition from Congress. For example, toward the end of the Civil War, he used "all of his resources to help Congress pass the Thirteenth Amendment" (Palludan 1994: 302). Yet, as Wayne (1978: 12) writes, "With the exception of the first years of the Lincoln presidency, Congress grew to dominate relations with the president until the end of the century. Most successful political initiatives emanated from within the Congress. Presidents could muster little support for their proposals." Following Lincoln's presidency, as had occurred after Jackson's, there was a palpable rejection of presidential leadership. In fact, most scholars agree that the presidencies of Andrew Johnson and Ulysses Grant represent the nadir of presidential leadership in general and presidential-congressional relations in particular.

Andrew Johnson, unlike Lincoln, appears to have had few political skills. Furthermore, he aggressively courted hostile relations with Congress. Not only did he use the veto more than any of his predecessors, he vetoed significant legislation, which greatly angered members of Congress. Johnson even defied nineteenth century tradition by speaking out publicly, not only against Congress, but against specific individual members of it. This became the basis for one of the articles of impeachment against him in 1864. Johnson was the first president to be impeached, an effort that failed by only one vote in the Senate.

Following Johnson's contentious presidency, "President Grant was happy to leave reconstruction policy to the Congress" and declared that he was a "purely administrative officer" (Sundquist 1981: 27). Under Grant, Congress assumed direction of important presidential functions, such as the choice of important presidential cabinet secretaries. The president's inattentiveness manifested itself in one of the most scandal-ridden administrations in U.S. history. Of equal importance, the presidency reached its lowest point in relationship to the power of Congress. By the 1870s, it appeared that the presidency was largely irrelevant and that congressional dominance would continue unabated. Yet, several contextual factors already were working against this historical trend.

9-5 The Building Blocks for the Resurgence of the Executive

By the 1870s, America was about to undergo a demographic revolution that would transform it from a rural, decentralized, agricultural economy to an urban, centralized, industrial one. New technologies were helping to reshape the nation, as well, including the railroad, which provided the first practical national transportation system and new communications technologies (the telegraph and later the telephone) that would contribute to the development of a national media. These contextual factors (see section 2-4b, "What Accounts for This Political Change?") would not only exert a profound influence on the nation, but ultimately on its governing institutions, as well.

As noted earlier, Congress had developed a decentralized standing committee system during the early decades of the nineteenth century. That decentralized system provided an appropriate organizational model for a governing body consisting of the many members of the House and Senate. It allowed Congress to specialize by function and issue such as agriculture, trade, and appropriations committees. Over time, special interests developed around the various congressional committees, what later would be called special interests and "iron triangles," providing subsystem government in each issue area. This was a governing system that served the interests of various segments of American society, though not always the national interest. More importantly, it represented a decentralized decision-making structure that was better suited to a rural, agricultural nation with a decentralized economy. It would not, however, be as effective in dealing with the abruptly changing needs of an urban and industrial nation with a centralizing economy.

The presidency, on the other hand, had been created by the Framers as a single executive. While the concepts of energy and dispatch were often more theoretical than real presidential attributes during the nineteenth century, the presidency had greater potential than Congress to reach across special or particularized interests and to represent the national interest; its more centralized leadership model also made it more capable of dealing with the evolving problems of a centralized economy. Consequently, at the very time that the presidency reached its nadir under Johnson and Grant, economic, technological, and demographic forces were transforming the country and with it providing new (though as yet unrealized) potential for the growth of presidential power. This was likely not apparent to the individuals of the time, however. What they saw was an emasculated presidency and a dominant Congress. For example, writing in the 1880s, political scientist Woodrow Wilson referred to the relationship between Congress and the president as one of "Congressional supremacy" (Wilson 1981). He criticized Congress for its labyrinth of committees and the presidency for its utter ineffectiveness. Likewise, Lord Bryce (1908) openly pondered why so few great men became president.

As for the presidents themselves, just "about the only effective tool" they had was the veto. "Its use increased sharply" in the period following the Civil War (Wayne 1978: 13), as its legitimacy was at last grudgingly accepted. Presidents still had little role as the initiators of policy, though Grover Cleveland did advance tariff reform as an issue after he was elected in 1884; in fact, some scholars think it may have contributed to his defeat in the election of 1888 (Jeffers 2001). For most presidents though, "The expression of his [the President's] wishes conveyed to Congress in messages has not necessarily any more effect on Congress than an article in a prominent party newspaper" (Bryce 1908: Volume 1: 230).

Presidents were about to reassert and reclaim authority from Congress, however. As Sundquist (1981: 27) writes,

> [F]rom the pitiable state to which the presidency sank under Johnson and Grant it could only rise, and it began to do so as soon as their successors in the White House were ready to assert a greater degree of authority. Presidents Hayes, Garfield, and Cleveland all battled the Senate to a series of showdowns over patronage, and Hayes fought with his veto the House's attempt to control policy and administration through riders on appropriations bills. The presidents won these contests and succeeded in checking the erosion of the office, when it became clear to the legislators that public opinion overwhelmingly supported the executive. . . . But rejuvenation of the presidency did not extend to legislative leadership. The years from Grant to the end of the century saw in the White House an unbroken line of staunch conservatives . . . and their messages are singularly barren of major program proposals.

A war with Spain and a new presidential leadership style, however, were about to transform the presidential office and its long-term relationship with Congress (see also Table 9-1).

9-6 The Transitional Presidential Era

William McKinley may have been the first president to sense the changing political tides and to begin, if only tentatively, to respond to them. McKinley was more active than most of his predecessors in dealing with Congress. To some extent, his "style of influence in Congress resembled that of Jefferson, who had quietly used the congressional caucus to enact the Democratic-Republican program nearly a century before" (Milkis and Nelson 1994: 198). The expectations of the time, however, limited McKinley's activism. Writing in his autobiography, Senator George F. Hoar (1903: Volume 2: 46), a Republican from Massachusetts, wrote, "The most eminent Senators would have received as a personal affront a private message from the White House expressing a desire that they should adopt any course in the discharge of their legislative duties that they did not approve. If they visited the White

TABLE **9-1** Presidential Versus Congressional Power Struggle during the Eighteenth and Nineteenth Centuries

President(s)	Political Circumstances	Advantage: President or Congress
Washington	Washington subtly promotes legislation by using proxy proposers of bills and speaks with Congressmen personally to advance his concerns.	Congress
Jefferson	Jefferson leads a united party and, like Washington, drafts bills to be proposed by a friendly member of Congress. He maintains cordial relations with Congress throughout his presidency.	None/consensual
Madison, Monroe, J. Q. Adams	In debt to members of Congress for getting them elected, and hoping to have second terms, these presidents rely heavily on Congress for support.	Congress
Jackson	Jackson challenges Congress's control of the political system through veto use and removal of appointees but can't entirely rein in the congressional power apparatus.	None/confrontational
Van Buren, Harrison, Tyler	Hit by backlash from Congress in response to Jackson's tactics, all three are known for having deferred to Congress.	Congress
Polk	Polk's aggressive dealings with Congress differentiate him from his predecessors, and since he isn't seeking a second term, he is less beholden to Congressmen for future support.	President
A. Johnson	Openly hostile to Congress and its power plays, Johnson frequently uses his veto power, speaks out against Congress, and is the first president to be impeached.	Congress

House, it was to give, not to receive advice." This had been the expectation from the nation's Founding, but it was an expectation that was about to change, even if it did so incrementally.

Ironically, Congress contributed to this change when it pressured the executive branch to go to war against Spain in Cuba. Initially, McKinley (like his predecessor Grover Cleveland) was reluctant to go to war. After the sinking of a U.S. battleship, the *Maine*, Congress declared war with McKinley's support. The war placed the United States prominently onto the world stage for the first time, thus laying the groundwork for a fundamental transformation in the foreign policy power of the presidency. While the conflict was of short duration, by the war's end the United States had new foreign policy responsibilities: the need to manage colonial possessions in Cuba and the Philippines. Therefore, the presidency now had a palpable continuing role in international relations. While McKinley did not live long enough to develop this new political resource—he was assassinated in 1901—his successor played a key role in the development of the power of the presidency in foreign affairs.

9-6a Theodore Roosevelt and the Rise of the Legislative Presidency

Theodore Roosevelt expanded America's international commitments; he promised to "walk softly and carry a big stick" in foreign affairs. His administration introduced the Roosevelt Corollary to the Monroe Doctrine. Roosevelt personally intervened in the Russo-Japanese War, earning the Nobel Peace Prize for his mediation efforts. He also became the first president to promise U.S. military intervention if another nation was attacked (when he promised U.S. recognition of Japan's claim to Korea) (Milkis and Nelson 1994: 223). Roosevelt urged Congress to expand the size of the navy and then defied Congress by sending the so-called "White Fleet" on a journey around the world. When Congress had told him there wasn't enough money to do so, he had sent the fleet anyway, and Congress eventually acquiesced. Perhaps most prominently, Roosevelt encouraged Panama to break from Colombia and then quickly recognized the new government and negotiated a treaty with it to build the Panama Canal (see McCullough 1977). He was also the first president to leave U.S. territory and travel to another country, personally visiting Panama to oversee the canal's construction.

In all of these foreign policy actions, it was Roosevelt who took the lead. Roosevelt also moved the presidency toward the center stage in domestic affairs, but more tepidly. He played an active role in the passage of such legislation as the Pure Food and Drug Act of 1906 and the Hepburn Act. More so than his predecessors, Roosevelt also used the state of the union address to identify his priorities in domestic and foreign policy (Light 1983: 160). He even identified a domestic policy agenda—the Square Deal. As Milkis and Nelson (1994: 215) write, "However defined, Roosevelt's enunciation of the Square Deal [his domestic political agenda] was important to the development of the modern presidency because it invoked the principles of fairness as he, rather than his party or Congress understood them." Because Roosevelt enunciated a programmatic agenda, separate and distinct from Congress, "a new style of presidential leadership" was created. "In this new style, the executive, not the Congress, assumed the major burden of formulating policy" (ibid., 216). As Fisher (1981: 38) notes, Congress, for the first time, "explicitly acknowledged the president's role as legislative leader" (see also Binkley 1956: 93). To put it another way, the president was playing an important role in setting the policy agenda.

As McDonald (1994: 358) writes, "Roosevelt's showmanship in pretending to be the fountain of reform legislation transformed the expectations Americans had for their presidents and thus opened the door for the emergence of the legislative presidency." Roosevelt even articulated a need for a new legislative presidency. In his autobiography, Roosevelt (1913: 292) wrote,

> In theory, the Executive has nothing to do with legislation. In practice, as things are now, the Executive is or ought to be peculiarly representative of the people as a whole. Therefore, a good Executive under present conditions of American life must take a very active interest in getting the right kind of legislation in addition to performing his Executive duties.

His justification for this more active role, as discussed in section 2-4d, "Theodore Roosevelt," and section 3-2j, "Theodore Roosevelt and William Howard Taft," was the rise of the centralized economic state (a contextual factor). As the economy became more centralized, as the power of the corporations and the monopolies became more prevalent, as the externalities from industrialization and urbanization required a more active response from the federal government,

Roosevelt viewed the presidency as the appropriate vessel for a new leadership role. It is, of course, interesting to speculate what would have happened had Congress stepped boldly into this changing contextual environment. It did not and some might argue that its decentralized committee structure and its dependence on special interests made it difficult for Congress to respond to the changing nature of American politics. The presidency, with its potential for energy and dispatch, however, was much more readily poised for action. What it needed was a president with a vision and the ability to carry it out. Theodore Roosevelt provided both of these.

It is important to note that although he provided greater leadership, Roosevelt rarely challenged Congress directly. "Although Roosevelt was the first president to successfully appeal 'over the heads' of Congress, he did so in a way that preserved, and did not preempt, Congress's deliberative capacities and responsibilities" (Tulis 1987: 106). As Sundquist (1981: 30–31) writes, "Because the strong president had to deal with a Congress dominated by entrenched conservatives and also strong in leadership and organization, his legislative requests were modest. He did not challenge the ideologically hostile Republican leadership of the Congress until near the end of his second term, at which point executive-legislative relations disintegrated."

9-6b No Turning Back!

Following Roosevelt, there would be no turning back. Even the passive presidents of the next two decades—Taft, Harding, Coolidge, and Hoover—were more active in legislative affairs than their nineteenth century counterparts. This point is usually raised in studies of the presidency (e.g., Milkis and Nelson 1994) but is seldom explained. Why were even these passive presidents unwilling or incapable of taking the presidency back to the days of the nineteenth century? Why didn't the political parties and Congress, once they were threatened with the accretion of presidential power, strike back against an activist presidency as they had done so often in the nineteenth century? The answer is that the economy, demographic factors, and demands on government were changing, and with them, public expectations of the governmental system. In addition, once presidents began to develop their own political constituencies separate and distinct from the parties and the legislative branch, the presidency was on the road toward greater power and influence.

At the same time, congressional power was under assault from inside the organization. The Speaker of the House long had dominated the national political scene, exerting almost dictatorial powers over legislative matters. A revolt, however, against the leadership of House Speaker Joseph Cannon radically altered the internal dynamics of Congress. In March 1910, an unprecedented coalition of Democrats and Republicans passed a resolution making the Speaker ineligible for membership on the committee on rules, thus sharply circumscribing the Speaker's power. The House of Representatives, with its power already dispersed through its committee system, now lacked the commanding power of the Speaker's office. The power in Congress was therefore even further diffused. At almost the same time, the method of selecting U.S. senators changed. The Seventeenth Amendment provided for the direct election of senators. Consequently, senators would be more responsive to the public and less so to the political party establishment.

As noted in section 8-3, "The Decline of the Political Parties," the Progressive Era reforms also challenged the influence of the political parties and the rise of a national media, and new technologies (still photography and the movies) allowed presidents to reach out to the American public. A number of factors then combined to provide a potential for the growth of presidential power.

9-6c Presidential Influence Further Expands

Woodrow Wilson was well poised to contribute to the evolution of congressional-presidential relations. As a scholar, he had criticized Congress for its decentralized committee structure and its inability to lead. At first, he was equally critical of the presidency (Wilson 1885), but after witnessing Roosevelt's presidency, he realized there were new possibilities for presidential leadership (Wilson 1908). Elected in 1912 with a Democratic-controlled Congress, Wilson "had no qualms about dominating Congress." As Sundquist (1981: 32) writes, "He had written much of the need for leadership in the American system, and he sought the presidency explicitly for purposes of leading." Wilson resurrected the idea of combining presidential leadership with party control of Congress.

Wilson and the Democrats in Congress had a number of major legislative achievements. The Federal Reserve Board and the Federal Trade Commission were established. Essentially, his first administration enacted Theodore Roosevelt's Progressive Party agenda from the 1912 "Bull Moose" campaign. In so doing, Wilson's New Freedom provided an even clearer example than Roosevelt's Square Deal of effective presidential leadership of Congress.

The Wilson presidency, however, showed both the potential benefits and the costs of active presidential leadership of Congress. While his first-term domestic policy achievements were indeed impressive, his presidency is remembered as well for the Senate's rejection of the Treaty of Versailles. Congress perceived it as "a political device to circumvent" its "role in foreign affairs" (Barnet 1990: 183).

What is interesting is not simply that Congress rejected the Treaty of Versailles and with it Wilson's cherished League of Nations, but rather that Congress then proceeded to delegate additional authority to the presidency rather than seeking to constrain the presidency, as it had throughout the nineteenth century. With a more passive president in the White House, Warren G. Harding, and a Congress and president of the same political party, Congress in 1921 delegated extraordinary new authority in domestic affairs to the presidency with the enactment of the Budget and Accounting Act. The act made the president responsible for developing a budget and submitting it to Congress. To help in this task, Congress established the Bureau of the Budget (BOB), one of the first major elements of what would later be called the Institutional Presidency. This new delegation of authority provided a prominent and institutionalized presidential role in setting the domestic policy agenda. As Representative Garner argued when the bill was considered by Congress, "tell me of a single appropriation that does not involve a question of public policy" (quoted in Sundquist 1981: 45). While Garner clearly understood the possibilities inherent in the legislation, "Congress did not see their delegation of authority under the Budget and Accounting Act of 1921 as giving the president any additional power. The president had only the power to make estimates, but Congress had the full power to increase or decrease presidential estimates" (Fisher 1981: 39). The House Select Committee on the Budget even stated, the law "does not change in the slightest degree the duty of Congress to make the minutest examination of the budget. The bill does not in the slightest degree give the Executive any greater power than he now has over the consideration of appropriations by Congress" (quoted in Fisher 1981: 39).

History would demonstrate that the committee was wrong. The Budget and Accounting Act provided the presidency with considerable new authority and, more importantly, institutionalized the president's role as an active legislative leader (Arnold 1993: 227). One of the president's major responsibilities today is to act as the nation's economic manager. Congress itself provided a justification for this new presidential role.

Another factor that is often overlooked, which helped change the relationship between the president and Congress, is the Twentieth Amendment to the U.S. Constitution. It synchronized the presidential and congressional terms of office. Prior to its ratification in February 1933, the president and Congress were elected in November, but the new president did not take office until March 4 of the following year (or four months later), while the Congress often was not seated until the following December (a full thirteen months after its election). Consequently, a new president would have limited opportunities to govern with the new Congress during his first year in office. Thus, the idea of taking advantage of the honeymoon period to "hit the ground running" was not a feasible option. The Twentieth Amendment, combined with a congressional tendency to convene for longer periods of time (Congress had previously met for as little as three months in a year), promoted increased political interaction between the president and Congress in the modern presidential era. In many ways and for many reasons, then, by the 1930s the political stage was set for the arrival of a new relationship between Congress and the president.

9-7 The Great Depression and Changing Public Expectations

The Great Depression, which began in 1929 and would not end until the dawn of World War II, played a critically important role in altering public expectations of the legitimate role of the federal government in domestic affairs. It also changed expectations of the president's role, thus providing a basis for a change in the relationship between the presidency and Congress. Although Herbert Hoover was much more politically active in dealing with the slowly unraveling economy between 1929 and 1932 than any of his predecessors had been in previous times of economic crisis (see section 2-4e, "Institutionalizing Expectations"; also see Kennedy 2000; Stein 1969; though also see Schlesinger 1957 for an alternative view), he was generally perceived as ineffectual in dealing with the effects of the depression. By 1933, there was greater public demand for the federal government and the presidency to play an active role in combating the depression.

This new demand was a significant change in prior expectations, exemplified by Calvin Coolidge's comment: "If the Federal Government should go out of existence, the common run of people would not detect the difference in the affairs of their daily life for a considerable length of time" (quoted in Schlesinger 1957: 57). In the 1920s, relatively little was expected from the federal government. The Great Depression shattered the public expectations of the old political order. As a result, the public began to look to the federal government and the White House for leadership. When they did, they saw in Herbert Hoover a man who was overwhelmed by events and unwilling to aggressively use the federal government to create jobs or provide unemployment compensation.

Roosevelt's election thus occurred in tumultuous political times. The old order in American politics was under siege (see Romasco 1974) and a partisan *realignment* was underway that would alter the way various constituencies would vote for decades to come.[7] Economically, by 1933 gross national product stood at half its 1929 value. "Businesses invested only $3 billion in 1933, compared with $24 billion in 1929." Iron and steel production were down 60 percent. Thirteen million Americans, or about 25 percent of the labor force, were unemployed, many for extended periods of time (Kennedy 2000: 162–63).

Consequently, when Roosevelt declared in his inaugural address that if Congress did not act, he would ask "for the one remaining instrument to meet the crisis—broad Executive power to wage a war against the emergency, as great as the power that would be given to me if we were in fact invaded by a foreign foe," few dissented. It was a remarkable presidential declaration, but even more so because it engendered so little controversy and so much political support. Throughout the country people listened to the president's speech on the radio. "Nearly half a million of them wrote letters to the White House in the next few days." People wrote, "It was the finest thing this side of heaven." "Your human feeling for all of us in your address is just wonderful." "People are looking to you almost as they look to God" (Schlesinger 1958: 1). As Davis (1986: 34) writes,

> It would be difficult to exaggerate the extent of the change in national mood which took place during Franklin Roosevelt's first thirty-six hours in the White House. The gloomy compound of fear, anger, disgust, cynicism, and despair which had been as a lowering cloud upon the mind and spirit of the Republic at high noon on Saturday March 4, rendering all hope defiant and desperate, was by the morning of March 6, greatly qualified by new confidence, new determination, a "warm courage of national unity." And for this dissipation of gloom, this sudden focus of resurgent energies in the light of renewed optimism, the tone of the inaugural address and the image projected by the new President of the United States were largely responsible.

9-7a Roosevelt and the First 100 Days

After FDR's inaugural address, the mood on Capitol Hill was also framed by the public's mood, the apparent confidence of the new president, and the sense that action was required lest a critical opportunity to deal with the economic crisis be lost. As Leuchtenburg (1963: 43) notes, "On March 9, the special session of Congress convened in an atmosphere of wartime crisis." Under these circumstances, with both the public and Congress looking to him for leadership, Roosevelt was able to move quickly to secure passage of key ameliorative legislation. The Emergency Banking Act "furnished a startling demonstration of Roosevelt's penchant for action and of the Congress's willingness, at least for the moment, to submit to his leadership" (Kennedy 2000: 136). As is generally noted, the first 100 days of Franklin Roosevelt's presidency not only provided a laundry list of ameliorative legislation but also a fundamental change in the relationship between the president and the Congress. This is a bit of an overstatement, however.

The idea that Congress ceased to function as an active legislative body and simply acquiesced to the will of a new, untested president is either myth or radical exaggeration. On March 10, when Roosevelt sent his second emergency measure to Congress, requesting some $500 million in budgetary cuts, the bill ran into considerable opposition, and "carried in the House only with heavy conservative support. It moved swiftly through the Senate only because the Democratic leadership had adroitly scheduled just behind it on the legislative calendar a popular measure to legalize beer, thus forestalling extended debate" (ibid., 138). Congress was in a mood to act in consort with the president, but not to follow the president blindly.

Still, Roosevelt was politically astute enough to understand that the economic crisis provided him with a unique opportunity to address numerous legislative proposals. Though he had initially called Congress into session only to deal with three legislative proposals, all passed with such lightning speed he sensed "the unexpected pliancy of Congress" and "determined to hold it in session to forge ahead with additional proposals, proposals that would begin to fulfill liberal expectations and give meaning and substance to the New Deal" (ibid., 139). In this process, twelve more major pieces of legislation (three of which Congress initiated and Roosevelt reluctantly supported) were enacted before Congress adjourned.

The first 100 days therefore witnessed a milestone in American politics. While Congress was far from obsequious, the balance of power had begun to shift toward the presidency. Most importantly, it now was expected that the president would initiate the policy agenda, with Congress generally following the president's lead. As Thomas, Pika, and Watson (1993: 192) write, FDR's "major contribution was to establish the expectation that the president would be actively involved at all stages of the legislative process by submitting a legislative program to Congress, working for its passage, and coordinating its implementation." As Leuchtenburg (1988: 21) adds, "Although he was not the first chief executive in this century to adopt the role of chief legislator, he developed its techniques to an unprecedented extent." Congress contributed to this process. Congress had delegated authority to the presidency with the Budget and Accounting Act of 1921; in the 1930s, it would continue to delegate additional authority to the presidency (e.g., the Reciprocal Trade Act of 1934—see Sundquist 1981: 99).

Throughout Roosevelt's first two terms in office, as Barone (1990: 95–96) writes, "The New Deal changed American life by changing the relationship between Americans and their government. In 1930, the federal government consumed less than 4% of the gross national product; except for the Post Office, it was remote from the life of ordinary people. By 1936, the federal government consumed 9% of the work force; it was a living presence across the country." The scope of the American government would further expand and with it the power of the presidency.

9-7b The Presidency and Foreign Policy

The Great Depression and the New Deal largely changed perceptions of the president's role in domestic policy. Still largely unchanged, however, was the president's role in foreign affairs. While the potential for presidential leadership certainly had been demonstrated by Theodore Roosevelt and Woodrow Wilson, since the end of Wilson's presidency, Congress had dominated foreign policy.

When Franklin Roosevelt became president, the U.S. military consisted of fewer than 200,000 personnel, and one of Roosevelt's first actions was to reduce it even further. In 1935, Congress then adopted neutrality legislation designed to prevent the United States from becoming involved in the growing conflagration in Europe. The act greatly constrained the president's foreign policy authority. While Roosevelt did not support the goals of the legislation, he endorsed the bill only because he feared his opposition would provide a reason for conservative Democratic members of Congress to oppose his New Deal policies. "The bill that finally emerged required the president, after proclaiming that a state of war existed between foreign states, to impose an embargo on the shipment of arms to all the belligerents. It also empowered the president to declare that all American citizens traveled on belligerent vessels at their own risk. It sought to avoid the perceived mistakes of Woodrow Wilson by removing the possibility that either the economic or emotional provocations of 1914–17 could be repeated" (Kennedy 2000: 394).

Throughout the remainder of the decade, Congress continued to tie the president's hands in foreign policy. As a European war became apparent, Roosevelt had to find increasingly clever means of getting around the "cash and carry" provisions of congressional arms legislation (such as his idea for Lend-Lease). But despite his few successes, Roosevelt found that he did not have the authority to send convoys to protect U.S. shipments of arms to Europe. Roosevelt faced a palpable isolationist sentiment in Congress and among the American electorate. By 1937, Congress enacted a fourth neutrality act. As Kennedy (ibid., 401) writes, "With stout legal thread, Congress had spun a straightjacket that rendered the United States effectively powerless in the face of the global conflagration that was about to explode."

Roosevelt made an abortive attempt to challenge isolationism in a major speech delivered on October 5, 1937. When the public did not respond to his interventionist declarations, Roosevelt allegedly said, "It is a terrible thing to look over your shoulder when you are trying to lead—and find no one there" (ibid., 406). Instead of moving linearly forward, "Roosevelt marched forward two paces, retreated one, and side-stepped, meantime indulging in moral rhetoric and vague threats that unduly raised his followers' expectations while markedly inflaming his isolationist opposition" (Burns 1989: 157). With Congress in charge of foreign policy, and no mandate from the public, Roosevelt was forced to bide his time, hoping that events would nudge public opinion away from isolationism. It would take the attack at Pearl Harbor on December 7, 1941, to change public and congressional sentiment. Once expectations were altered, Roosevelt played an active role as commander-in-chief. After World War II, the Cold War then provided a basis for the continued decline of isolationist sentiment, the rise of internationalism, and with it, an active, continuing presidential role in foreign affairs.

Hence, by time of the Korean War, Harry Truman did not ask Congress for a declaration of war. The war would be legally justified under United Nations charter, not the U.S. Constitution. No war has been declared by Congress since World War II. While Congress would reassert its authority from time to time, in foreign affairs, the presidency was now in ascendancy, and the public expected the president to provide strong leadership in international affairs (see Box 9-2).

9-8 The Presidency and Congress in the Modern Presidential Era

Describing the presidency in the modern presidential era, Neustadt (1980: 27–28) writes,

> A President's authority and status give him great advantages in dealing with the men he would persuade. Each "power" is a vantage point for him in the degree that other men have use for his authority. From the veto to appointments, from publicity to budgeting, and so down a long list, the White House now controls the most encompassing array of vantage points in the American political system. With hardly an exception, the men who share in governing this country are aware that at some time, in some degree, the doing of their jobs, the furthering of their ambitions, may depend upon the President of the United States. Their need for presidential action, or their fear of it, is bound to be recurrent if not actually continuous. Their need or fear is his advantage.

Changing economic conditions and demographic factors (which placed new demands on the federal government for policy action); the inability of a decentralized Congress to deal with these demands; the decline of political parties' influence; the inherent potential for energy and dispatch in a single executive; the willingness of Theodore Roosevelt, Woodrow Wilson, and Franklin Roosevelt to exploit this potential for new power; plus the Great Depression and America's new place on the world stage all fueled changing expectations of presidential leadership. As a result, over a period of half a century, a new or modern presidency was established, one that scholars view as fundamentally different from the presidency that preceded it.

While the presidency has greater power in the modern presidential era, it is tempting to suggest that the power of Congress has diminished. As Thomas, Pika,

Box 9-2

Evolution of Presidential Power in Foreign Relations

Cuba

In conflict over Cuba, Congress seeks McKinley's support for declaring war on Spain. For the first time, the United States is involved on the world stage. McKinley's involvement begins a trend in the growth of presidential power in foreign affairs.

Panama

Theodore Roosevelt bucks Congress and acts on his own initiative to increase the size of the navy, promises U.S. intervention if another country is attacked, encourages Panama to break away from Colombia, and negotiates a treaty with Panama for the building of the Panama Canal.

Europe

Although Wilson's Treaty of Versailles and League of Nations proposals are rejected by Congress, the legislative body nonetheless gives the president extensive power and authority during World War I to conduct foreign affairs and construct foreign policy as he sees fit.

Japan

Congress passes several neutrality declarations despite Franklin Roosevelt's apprehensions that war will be inevitable. However, when Pearl Harbor is attacked by Japan, Roosevelt's concerns are proven correct, forcing Congress to concede its erroneous appraisal of the situation and give him full support in conducting the war.

Korea

By the time Truman needs to send troops to Korea, he can do so without having to ask Congress, using instead the United Nations charter. Congress has lost much of its power over foreign affairs.

and Watson (1993: 193) observe, however, Congress also has more power today than it did prior to the creation of the modern presidency, though the "power of Congress as an innovator of public policy has declined relative to that of the presidency." While the presidency was clearly subservient to Congress in the traditional presidential era (1789–1898), it is not correct to characterize Congress as subservient to the presidency in the modern era. Instead of a pure model of presidential hegemony, as recommended by Spitzer (1993), other scholars write of a "tandem institutions" model (see Jones 1994; Peterson 1990; Bond and Fleisher 1990) in which the presidency and the Congress compete for power.

In this new relationship, the presidency has certain advantages, particularly in the realm of foreign affairs. As noted, Congress has not declared a war since World War II. Presidents often act unilaterally to commit U.S. forces to overseas locations and even to overseas conflicts. Congress is often at a disadvantage in terms of the information it receives and has a lesser ability to initiate foreign policy. Still, it does have the power to rein in presidential power and does use this power, such as when it passed the War Powers Resolution in 1973 (see Fisher 1995).

Congress also has considerable influence in domestic policy matters. Congress has multiple means to block presidential initiatives. Members can bury them in committees or subcommittees, attach riders and amendments to dilute the intent of the legislation, and they can filibuster legislation in the Senate (thus blocking its enactment). Hence, as Neustadt (1960) famously recommended, for presidents to succeed in an era of separate institutions sharing power, they must develop the ability to bargain, compromise, and persuade. More recently, Cameron (2000) developed a rational choice model of presidential-congressional behavior. His "veto bargaining" model is one in which presidents use the threat (and sometimes the practice) of their veto power to induce Congress to move toward the president's preferred policy outcome. Whether through persuasion or veto bargaining or a strategy of "going public" over the heads of the members of Congress (Kernell 1997), it is understood that presidents share power with Congress. Thus, the period of the modern presidency is characterized by a focus on intense competition or a struggle between the two branches of government.

9-8a New Expectations for Presidential-Congressional Relations

In the modern presidential era, we generally evaluate presidential success on the basis of specific criteria. As noted in section 7-8, "The Emergence of Presidential Polling," public approval ratings are a means of evaluating presidential influence and success. The president's popular standing is then related to his or her ability to influence Congress (see also section 7-9, "Presidential Popularity"). As the presidential success scores in Table 7-2 suggest, there has been considerable variation in presidential ability to influence Congress. Some presidents (Franklin Roosevelt and Lyndon Johnson) have been more successful in getting legislation they prefer through Congress than have others (Jimmy Carter and George H. W. Bush).

While variations in ability and success rates are evident, all presidents are expected to be able to work with Congress. When respondents to two surveys conducted in 1996 were asked to rate on a scale from 0 (not at all important) to 10 (very important) how important is it for an excellent or ideal president to have an ability to work well with Congress, the mean scores were 8.17 and 8.45 (Waterman, Jenkins-Smith, and Silva 1999: 952). This is evidence that the public expects presidents to be effective leaders of Congress.

Elite expectations also have changed. As noted in section 9-6a, even as late as the presidency of Theodore Roosevelt, it was expected that presidents should not take the lead in initiating legislation. Woodrow Wilson provided a new leadership model, and Franklin Roosevelt further developed it. Thus, there was little controversy when Harry Truman became the first president to use his state of the union address to submit a legislative agenda to Congress; in fact, the greatest criticism came from his own Democratic Party. Each of Truman's successors followed his example (King and Ragsdale 1988: 21–22). Further indicating how much public and elite expectations of presidential leadership had changed, Dwight Eisenhower was openly criticized when he did not include legislative proposals in his first state of the union address. Thereafter, he "ritualistically followed the Truman formula" and submitted policy proposals to Congress (McDonald 1994: 368), and in time the Eisenhower administration came to dominate economic policy (Sundquist 1981: 76).

But while Truman ritualized the submission of a legislative agenda to Congress, it was the legislative branch itself that may have contributed the most to changing public expectations of presidential-congressional relations. In 1944, Franklin Roosevelt proclaimed a "Second Bill of Rights," demanding economic security and prosperity for all Americans. It included such proposals as "the right to a useful and remunerative job in the industries or shops or farms or mines of the Nation." In 1946, Congress enacted the Employment Act committing the government to a continuous and activist economic policy, primarily through an aggressive fiscal policy, to assure "maximum employment, production and purchasing power." As Sundquist (1981: 62–63) notes, the act also "assigned to the President the role of initiator and leader and created institutional facilities to enable him to serve in that capacity." The act thus "magnified the stature and importance of the presidency and the public dependence on presidential leadership." It also provided yet another means of evaluating presidential success: By requiring the collection of data on various economic indicators, it provided a measure of the president's success as steward of the nation's economy. Therefore, while expectations of presidential performance were increasing, a significant change also was occurring that would affect the ability of presidents to work with Congress: the measurement of presidential success.

9-8b Divided Government

Following a period of virtually unprecedented accomplishment between Congress and the president from 1964–1966 (landmark legislation was enacted in the realm of civil rights, the war on poverty, education, health care for the poor and elderly), presidential-congressional relations deteriorated, in large part because of divergent opinion about the Vietnam War. Urban violence, the cost of the Great Society programs, questions about their effectiveness, and the proper scope of government action, combined with questions about Lyndon Johnson's veracity, and his declining approval ratings, also promoted a more hostile relationship between the president and Congress. While Johnson's relations with Congress deteriorated over time, he had the political advantage of sharing the same party affiliation as the majority Democratic Party in both the House and the Senate. In the 1968 election, however, a new pattern of presidential-congressional relations commenced.

As Cameron (2000: 11–12) demonstrates, prior to 1968, divided government was relatively rare. From the late 1840s to the election of 1896, the probability of divided government was 50 percent, but after 1896, the probability dropped to 20 percent. For the first half of the twentieth century, only Taft (a Republican with a Democratic-controlled Congress from 1911–1912), Wilson (a Democrat with a Republican-controlled Congress from 1919–1920), Hoover (a Republican with a Democratic-controlled Congress from 1930–1932), and Truman (a Democrat with a Republican-controlled Congress from 1947–1948) confronted divided government. In the 1950s, Dwight Eisenhower then dealt with divided government for six of his eight years in office. Into the 1960s, though, no twentieth century president had faced divided government at the beginning of his term of office. Then, in 1968, Richard Nixon, a Republican, was elected president while the House and Senate were controlled by the Democratic Party. Though it was not apparent at the time, a new era of **divided government** had been born.

The probability of divided government is now 80 percent (Cameron 2000: 12). Since Nixon's presidency, only Jimmy Carter (1977–1981) governed exclusively with a Congress of his own political party. Nixon, Ford, and George H. W. Bush entered office with the opposition party in control of both houses of Congress. Reagan (a Republican) assumed the presidency with a Republican-controlled Senate and a Democratic-controlled House. Bill Clinton (a Democrat) was elected with a Democratic-controlled Congress. After the 1994 midterm elections, however, the Republicans controlled both the House and Senate for the remaining six years of his presidency. George W. Bush (a Republican) was elected with a Republican-controlled House and Senate. The Senate, however, was evenly divided between Democrats and Republicans. When Senator James Jeffords of Vermont left the Republican Party in May 2001 to become an independent, the Democratic Party gained control of the Senate. Consequently, six out of seven presidents since the election of 1968 have had to deal with some form of divided government. Of the modern presidents (Franklin Roosevelt to George W. Bush), eight out of twelve have experienced divided government.

> **Divided government:** When different political parties control the presidency and at least one branch of Congress.

This political relationship makes it more difficult for presidents to rely on the bargaining approach Neustadt (1980) recommended and, hence, more likely to use other leadership approaches, such as "going public" over the heads of members of Congress (Kernell 1997) or "veto bargaining" (Cameron 2000). In part because presidents are more likely to use the media to go over the heads of Congress or to threaten to use their veto power, divided government increases the likelihood of conflict between the president and Congress. As a result, such words as "gridlock," "deadlock," "conflict," and "struggle" have become common adjectives describing presidential-congressional relations. In practical terms, this means that while the public expects presidents to work well with Congress (see Waterman, Jenkins-Smith, and Silva 1999), the political arena is characterized by greater conflict between the two branches of government. Presidents therefore find themselves in an often unenviable situation: How can they satisfy public expectations by working with Congress when Congress and the president are more often than not of different parties? Unfortunately, there is no simple answer to this question. Presidents must combine political skill, a favorable public image, high approval ratings, a positive media presence, and a bit of good luck in order to lead an often obstreperous Congress. Under these circumstances, it is not surprising that many presidents do not succeed.

9-8c Why Does Divided Government Exist?

Prior to 1969, divided government was a fairly rare political phenomenon. Jacobson (1990: 5) writes, "Only once in the twenty-five presidential elections between 1856 and 1952 did the party winning a majority of the popular two-party vote for president fail to organize the House (it happened in 1888)." Why, then, does divided government now exist? Cameron (2000: 12) writes, "the source of the system's potential for divided government is quite clear: it is an inevitable by-product of the Founders' design. It is quite literally built into the system." Unlike a parliamentary system, in which governments are organized on the basis of political parties, the U.S. government's system of separated institutions and elections creates the potential for divided government. Yet, why has it been more or less prevalent at different times in U.S. history and why is it particularly prevalent today?

One explanation is that there has been a disassociation between presidential and House seat outcomes since the end of World War II. In fact, "the progressive dissociation of election results across both offices and election years is among the most striking and fundamental postwar electoral developments" (Jacobson 1990: 7). Likewise, "House and Senate results have become increasingly disconnected regardless of House incumbency" (ibid., 12). In fact, "State-level results for simultaneous Senate and gubernatorial contests are no longer related" (ibid., 14). What accounts for this disassociation? According to Jacobson (1990: 20),

> Its immediate source is the decline in party loyalty among voters. This, in turn, is usually traced to two other major developments. One is the increased ability of candidates and elected officials to communicate directly with voters without relying on party organizations or a partisan press to get the message across. The advent of television as a campaign medium and the growth of resources available to elected officials to communicate with constituents are the most prominent developments of this sort. Of greater importance, however, have been changes in the utility of party cues to voters. As long as electoral politics were given focus by New Deal issues, partisan lines were reasonably clear: Democrats were for New Deal policies, Republicans opposed them. The party label thus gave voters adequate information for expressing their preferences on the dominant political issues. The party label became less informative and thus less useful to voters as a shorthand cue for predicting what elected officials would do once in office. Information about individual candidates became more important.

The declining utility of party cues also promoted a decrease in the coattail effect and a continuing propensity to punish the party of the president at midterm (see section 6-11, "The Effect of Presidential Elections on Congressional Elections"). Voters may even consciously decide that they prefer to vote for a president of one party and members of Congress from another, so as to build accountability into the system. Thus, it is apparent that there is a relationship between the decline of the political parties' influence and the increase in the likelihood of divided government. Until a stronger party system is established, divided government is likely, though not certain (see the 2002 elections), to continue.

What, then, is the effect of divided government on presidential-congressional relations? According to one prominent scholar, it has had relatively little impact. Mayhew (1991: 198) concludes, "Surprisingly, it does not seem to make all that much difference whether party control of the American government happens to be unified or divided." Later studies, however, disagree with Mayhew's conclusion. For example, Epstein and O'Halloran (1999: 11) argue that it is not sufficient to look at the quantity of legislation enacted under unified and divided government, as Mayhew did, but also the substance of that legislation. When they re-analyzed Mayhew's data, they found "Congress delegates less and constrains more under divided government. Thus, split partisan control of our national policy-making, even if it does not lead to legislative gridlock, may result in procedural gridlock— that is, producing executive branch agencies with less authority to make well-reasoned policy and increasingly hamstrung by oversight from congressional committees, interest groups, and the courts."

Likewise, Cameron (2000) found that during "unified government, the probability of a veto was very low regardless of the bill's legislative significance. But a remarkable change occurred under divided government." The probability of a president vetoing a landmark bill was 20 percent, or one in five. Hence, for "landmark legislation during divided government, vetoes are not rare events at all."

Cameron also found that presidents are more likely to employ the techniques of veto bargaining, that is, to use the veto threat to gain legislative concessions from Congress. There is also evidence that Congress is more likely to override presidential vetoes. From 1789–1998, a period of more than 200 years, only 107 presidential vetoes were overridden out of 2,540 exercised by presidents—or just 4 percent of all presidential vetoes. Among these, the largest number of overrides occurred while Andrew Johnson was president. Twelve each also occurred during the presidencies of Harry Truman and Gerald Ford. In recent years, however, as relations between the executive and legislative branches have become been characterized by greater conflict, Congress has overridden a larger percentage of presidential vetoes. Of the 289 issued by presidents from Nixon through Clinton (during his first six years), 11.4 percent were overridden, compared to 4 percent for all presidents. Even if we take out the 12 vetoes overridden during the post-Watergate Ford presidency, the percentage of overrides is 8.7 percent, or more than twice the percentage for the period from 1789–1998. In short, during the current period of divided government, congressional overrides have become more common. This trend, however, may be changing: Only two of Clinton's vetoes were overridden during the first six years of his presidency and only one of George H. W. Bush's vetoes.

During the present era of divided government, scholars also have increasingly identified the existence of an expectations gap and have openly discussed the possibility of presidential failure as the norm (see Lowi 1985; Rose 1997). The evidence: one president was impeached (Clinton), while another resigned rather than face impeachment (Nixon); Reagan's presidency was rocked by revelations from the congressional hearings into the Iran-Contra scandal; and Ford, Carter, and G. H. W. Bush failed in their election/re-election bids. There appear, then, to be important negative factors related to the greater propensity for divided government.

9-8d Greater Hostility!

Another manifestation of divided government is an increase in the level of hostility between the president and Congress. This hostility is part of the change in the larger political environment and is not simply related to divided government. Presidential media relations also are more conflict ridden, single-issue interest groups are more demanding, campaigns are nastier, and even the courts have been politicized. Hostility, then—at least until the events of September 11, 2001—became a common characteristic of the larger political environment, not just the relationship between Congress and the president; and by the summer of 2002, the political environment returned to normal—that is, with greater open criticism of the president, harsher media coverage, and congressional opposition to the president (even from members of George W. Bush's own party).

In practical terms, however, over time presidential-congressional relations have changed significantly. It is harder for presidents to sit down, as Franklin Roosevelt once did, with the leadership of the Congress or a small number of committee chairmen/women and come to agreement on a grand policy design. Party members in Congress are more independent and, hence, less likely to follow policy direction from not only the president, but even their own party leadership. As noted in section 6-8, "Presidential Primaries," candidates can run in primaries and are not as beholden to the parties as they once were. Hence, we have a new breed of independent-minded members of Congress, a greater potential for intra-party disagreements, and a much higher level of hostility between the two political parties. Gone are the days when congressmen/women of both parties could disagree on Capitol Hill and then go to dinner together afterward. Real friendships across party lines could be cultivated because members generally remained in Washington during a congressional session. Now, with the klieg lights of CSPAN, members use downtime to pontificate to an empty chamber and, more importantly, to viewers at home. They then fly in and out of town, visiting their districts, raising funds for their next campaign, and doing other political events. The result is that members of Congress now have less time to get to know each other and to build the kinds of personal relationships that can mitigate (at least to some extent) the hostility prevalent within the Washington beltway (see Gergen 2000).

A more hostile political environment, then, whether directly related to divided government or another outgrowth of it, has made it considerably more difficult for presidents to work with Congress. It is important to remember that, when the 1960s began, we were in a period of high expectations of presidential performance and high levels of trust in the presidency. Historian Clinton Rossiter (1960: 15–16) wrote of the "veneration, if not exactly reverence, for the authority and dignity of the Presidency." Likewise, James MacGregor Burns (1965: 330) wrote, "the stronger we make the Presidency, the more we strengthen democratic procedures." Other scholars likewise hailed a new era of presidential dominance (Finer 1960; Schlesinger 1957, 1958, 1960). On the other hand, a 1957 edition of Edward Corwin's classic *The President: Office and Powers*, with its warnings about the dangers of presidential power, seemed sadly out of date.

The 1960s, however, witnessed the beginning of a fundamental transformation in the way the public views its political institutions. I present data documenting a pattern of declining trust in government in Table 7-3. It is relevant because, as Charles O. Jones (1995: 107) writes, there has been a "decline in trust and respect for governmental institutions" and this is one of the reasons for the greater difficulty in conducting presidential-congressional relations. For many individuals, the beginning of this process, the end of governmental innocence, began with the Kennedy assassination and the subsequent charges that the CIA, the FBI, and other government agencies and officials were behind the young president's assassination. The main catalysts for change, however, were the presidencies of Lyndon Johnson and Richard Nixon, the Vietnam War, and the **Watergate** political scandal.

Watergate: A political scandal precipitated when officials of the Nixon administration broke into the Democratic Party headquarters in the Watergate building in Washington, D.C. The Watergate scandals represented a wide assortment of abuses of government by the Nixon administration.

Questions were raised about the veracity of both Presidents Johnson and Nixon. Their respective administrations were periods of great political accomplishment, but also increased concern that the presidency had grown too powerful, even imperial (see Schlesinger 1973). Both exhibited highly partisan and paranoid personalities that exacerbated tensions between the president and Congress. Johnson was less than candid about America's role in the Vietnam War. By the end of his presidency, a vocal anti-war movement existed, strongly represented by members of the president's own party in Congress.

Presidential-congressional relations deteriorated even further during the Nixon presidency. Even before Watergate, there was conflict. For example, Congress was infuriated when the Nixon administration refused to spend appropriated funds, impounding them without congressional approval. As a result, Nixon's impoundments were challenged in court, and Congress eventually enacted the Budget and Impoundment Act of 1974, limiting the president's ability to legally impound funds, while creating new resources for congressional oversight of the budget (e.g., the Congressional Budget Office). The act also specified a mechanism for limited legal impoundments: the rescission and deferral process (see section 10-8, "Budgetary Power").

Likewise, conflict between the Nixon administration and Congress over Vietnam War policy (including the administration's decision to expand the war into Cambodia without congressional knowledge and/or authorization) resulted in passage of the War Powers Resolution of 1973, limiting the period that presidents can commit U.S. troops overseas without prior congressional approval. At the same time, however, the resolution gave the president the authority to commit troops without congressional authorization. Both the Budget and Impoundment Act and the War Powers Resolution were enacted over presidential vetoes.

There were other sources of conflict between Congress and President Nixon. Members of Congress also were outraged when they discovered that the Nixon administration had prepared a "145-page kit of materials to be used against Congress in the 'Battle of the Budget.' The kit consisted of guidelines for speeches, 'one-liners,' and 'horror stories' about wasteful federal programs—all to be used as part of a coordinated attack on the 'spendthrift' Democratic-controlled Congress" (Fisher 1981: 57). Congressional investigations of the Nixon presidency therefore were conducted on a wide array of fronts, many of them beginning before the sordid details of the Watergate political scandal began to emerge.

Some people date the changed relationship between the president and Congress and the lower levels of public trust to Lee Harvey Oswald's (left) assassination of John F. Kennedy and the Johnson (lower left) and Nixon (lower right) presidencies.

Photo of Oswald: © CORBIS.

What became apparent through these investigations and the later release of Nixon's recorded tapes of presidential conversations was that the Nixon White House had been involved in a wide series of "abuses of power" (see Kutler 1997). A delineation of these many abuses is beyond the scope of this book, but it is fair to say that the paranoia of the Nixon administration extended well beyond Congress and included a war on the media, a war on the "liberal" bureaucracy, and a war on U.S. citizens deemed enemies of the administration.[8] In short, it was no longer possible to ignore Corwin's warnings about the unbridled growth of presidential power. Even Arthur Schlesinger, Jr. (1973), who once supported the growth of presidential power, now added an important codicil, warning of the dangers of the "imperial presidency."

9-9 Presidential Victories with Congress: Eisenhower through Clinton

To further examine the effects of divided government and the increasingly hostile world in which presidential-congressional relations operate, we need to look at presidential success rates with Congress. Table 9-2 presents aggregate annual data on the percentage of presidential victories in the House and Senate for all modern presidents from Eisenhower (1953) through Clinton's sixth year (1998). We can therefore view presidential relations with Congress both across time within a presidency and across time for different presidencies.

Within presidencies, presidents generally have their greatest level of success with Congress early in their term. Eisenhower's highest victory percentage was in his first year. Johnson had his highest in his second and first years. Nixon had his in his first three years, Reagan and G. H. W. Bush in their first years, and Clinton in his first two years. The percentage of presidential victories then declines as each president's administration continues. While some presidents exhibited high levels of success even late in their terms, particularly Lyndon Johnson and, more surprisingly, Jimmy Carter, other presidents had little success over time: Reagan's and G. H. W. Bush's victory percentages fell below 50 percent over time, and Clinton's hovered around 50 percent by his sixth year in office. Therefore, Table 9-2 provides more evidence for Pfiffner's (1988) thesis that presidents should indeed "hit the ground running." The best time for presidents to get legislation passed is early in their first term.

We also can look across presidencies to determine how presidential relations with Congress have changed over time. When we do so, we can see that

TABLE **9-2** Percentage of Presidential Victories in the House and Senate, 1953–1998

	Eisenhower	Kennedy	Johnson	Nixon	Ford	Carter	Reagan	G. H. W. Bush	Clinton
First Year	89.2	81.5	87.9	74.8	58.2	75.4	82.4	62.6	86.4
Second Year	82.8	85.4	93.1	76.9	61.0	78.3	72.4	46.8	86.4
Third Year	75.3	87.1	78.9	74.8	53.8	76.8	67.1	54.2	36.2
Fourth Year	69.2		78.8	66.3		75.1	65.8	43.0	55.1
Fifth Year	68.4		74.5	50.6			59.9		53.6
Sixth Year	75.7			59.6			56.5		50.6
Seventh Year	52.9						43.5		
Eighth Year	65.1						47.4		

Eisenhower, Kennedy, and Johnson were quite successful in dealing with Congress throughout their terms (Eisenhower's success percentage falls to 52.9 in 1959 but rebounds to 65.1 in 1960). Even Nixon had victory percentages in the 70 percent range prior to 1973, the year that the Watergate scandal erupted. In his last two years Nixon's success percentage declined to 50.6 and 59.6, but even here the latter percentage is more than respectable given that he was forced to resign the presidency that year.

Ford's interregnum presidency is characterized by percentages considerably below those of Nixon, but given the difficult circumstances under which he governed (he was not even an elected president or vice president, he followed a disgraced president into office and then pardoned him), these lower victory percentages are understandable, as is Ford's increased use of the veto. Carter's percentages are all in the 70 percent range, which is surprising since he had, according to most accounts, an abysmal relationship with Congress (see Gergen 2000). Even members of Carter's party were dissatisfied with his liaison efforts; see section 13-4d, "Nixon's Staff and Its Legacy," and section 13-5c, "Specific Areas of Presidential Interest." Carter did, however, govern only during a period of united government; that is, both the White House and Capitol Hill were controlled by the Democratic Party. He therefore had an advantage that no president had enjoyed since Lyndon Johnson, and no president since has enjoyed.

The last three presidents in the series all have had widely varying victory percentages. Reagan started out quite strong with percentages in the 70s and 80s. By his second term, however, his victory fell to the 50 percent range, and by his last two years, to the 40 percent range. The relationship between George H. W. Bush and Congress was even less amenable. His highest percentage was 62.6. His victory percentages then declined to the 40 percent range in two of his next three years.

For Clinton, the first two years (in which he enjoyed united party control) were his best in terms of victory percentages: 86.4 percent for both years. Once, however, the Republicans gained control of Congress, his victory percentage plunged to 36.2, the lowest in the series for any president. While his victory percentages improved to the 50 percent range prior to the impeachment crisis, there is a stark difference between his early and later term victory percentages.

These results indicate that presidential success with Congress has declined over time. The results also suggest that Watergate, and the high level of distrust it created between the two branches of government, played a role in this decline. The data also suggest that divided government played a role. Carter, who was not particularly adept at dealing with Congress, nonetheless had higher ratings than any president since Lyndon Johnson because he enjoyed the political advantage of united party government. On the other hand, Ford and G. H. W. Bush, who ruled exclusively in periods of post-Watergate divided government, had the lowest average victory percentages in the series. Clinton's ratings plummeted once the Republicans secured control of Congress, and Reagan's lowest percentages occurred in his last two years, when Democrats regained control of the Senate.

The figures in Table 9-2 therefore provide further evidence that it is becoming more difficult for presidents today to successfully govern with Congress. Victory percentages are, of course, but one measure of presidential success, and there are controversies involved over which votes should be counted in calculating the scores (see Spitzer 1993 for an excellent discussion). Also, while presidential victory scores declined, various presidents have signed landmark legislation during their terms. Clinton's relationship with Congress deteriorated after the Republicans gained control of Capitol Hill; yet, he signed some of his most important legislation during this period of divided government, including welfare reform and the Kennedy-Kasenbaum Health Care Bill. George H. W. Bush also signed the Clean Air Act of 1990 and the Americans with Disabilities Act, despite working with a Democratic-controlled Congress. Reagan signed a major Tax Reform Bill during his second term, as well as other major legislation during his first term (a three-year tax cut).

Hence, while the victory percentages are one measure of presidential success with Congress, we also need to look at presidential victories on important pieces of legislation. Each of our recent presidents has key legislative achievements. In 2001, George W. Bush and Congress agreed to a sizeable tax cut and education reform, and in 2002, Congress gave him "fast track" trade authority. All of these bills were priorities of the Bush administration.

Chapter Summary

Although it may indeed be harder for presidents today to work with Congress, it is not impossible. Words such as "gridlock," "struggle," "deadlock," and "combat" may describe the ongoing relationship between the two branches of government, and the political environment is certainly more hostile today than it was in the pre-Watergate days. Yet, it is important to note that the two branches still have a functional relationship: Most presidents do have achievements, and Congress does still work with the president. Their relationship may then be a modified form of gridlock. Both sides are willing to stare each other down when it is convenient to do so, to threaten gridlock and deadlock when they see advantages in the polls. When, however, there is an incentive to act, presidents and Congress still do so. This was palpably demonstrated in 1996 when a Republican Congress and a Democratic president agreed on a series of major legislation, largely because each political actor needed evidence of legislative success going into the fall elections. Likewise, Democrats and Republicans worked together during the harrowing days following September 11, 2001, passing major legislation that provided aid to New York City and an airline security bill, as well as other legislation dealing with the terrorist threat. Presidential-congressional relations today, then, may offer an invitation to gridlock, but the good news is that such relations also offer an invitation to govern when it is in the political interests of actors on both sides of Capitol Hill to do so. The most successful presidents, then, will be those who govern in politically propitious times (see Lammers and Genovese 2000) and those who have the skill to either persuade Congress (Neustadt 1980) or go over its head (Kernell 1997), or to use the skills of veto-bargaining (Cameron 2000) to get what they want.

Review Questions

1. The Constitution enacted a form of separation of powers, but not an absolute one. It also included
   a. checks and balances.
   b. judicial power.
   c. legislative power.
   d. executive power.

2. The separation of powers and checks and balances set up a system of
   a. separate institutions.
   b. balanced institutions.
   c. balanced institutions sharing power.
   d. separate institutions sharing power.

3. After the Founding, which branch of government was best suited to "hit the ground running"?
   a. the legislative branch
   b. the executive branch
   c. the judicial branch
   d. all were ready to do so

4. Washington was more protective of presidential power in which of the following areas?
   a. domestic affairs
   b. foreign affairs
   c. economic affairs
   d. regulatory affairs

5. Who of the following was the first president to govern with his own political party leadership?
   a. George Washington
   b. Thomas Jefferson
   c. Andrew Jackson
   d. Abraham Lincoln

6. John Tyler angered members of Congress
   a. by vetoing three bills.
   b. by recommending legislation.
   c. by line-item vetoing three bills.
   d. by naming his own successor.

7. Congress was best able to dominate American politics in
   a. a decentralized economic era.
   b. a rural, agricultural era.
   c. an era in which the public had few demands for governmental action.
   d. all of the above.

8. Following the activist presidency of this individual, there would be no turning back to the old relationship between Congress and the presidency. Presidential influence was on the ascendancy.
   a. Theodore Roosevelt
   b. Woodrow Wilson
   c. Franklin Roosevelt
   d. Harry Truman

9. Which of the following events led to changed public expectations about the president's role in the world?
   a. World War I
   b. the Great Depression
   c. World War II
   d. the Cold War

10. Divided government, as a nearly continuous practice, commenced with which of the following presidents?
    a. Richard Nixon
    b. Jimmy Carter
    c. Ronald Reagan
    d. Bill Clinton

Discussion Questions

1. Why do we use military metaphors to describe the relationship between the president and the Congress?
2. Why did the legislative branch dominate the political system throughout the nineteenth century?
3. Why does the presidential branch dominate the political system today? Or does it?
4. Is divided government good for the country?

Notes

1. Charles Montesquieu, 1748, *The Spirit of the Laws.*
2. Other scholars including Peterson (1990), Bond and Fleisher (1990), Jones (1994), and Cameron (2000) also view the president and the Congress as sharing power.
3. Cameron (2000) likewise argues that the veto, an obvious executive check on the legislative power, is part of an ongoing process between the president and Congress, veto bargaining, and that one cannot understand this system and its policy results unless one examines a time sequence of congressional-presidential bargaining.
4. Another example is the integral role Congress played in deciding whether the president could remove appointees from office without congressional approval; see section 4-7, "Appointment and Supervisory Power."

5. After the controversy engendered by the Jay Treaty, and the Chief Justice's role in negotiating the treaty, members of the court moved to a position of greater independence from the presidency.
6. There has been much debate as to whether two presidencies actually exist. For more on this debate, see LeLoup and Shull 1979; Sigelman 1979; Cohen 1982; Edwards 1989; and Shull 1991.
7. There is, however, disagreement over when the realignment began and which factors triggered it (see Erikson and Tedin 1981; Sundquist 1983).
8. The charges against the Nixon administration continue to mount. Using newly released evidence, Berman (2001) charges that Nixon and Kissinger prolonged the war in Vietnam until after the 1972 election because they knew that in the end the North Vietnamese forces would prevail. They did not want this to happen, however, until after the 1972 election.

Chapter

10

The Bureaucracy:
The New Kid on the Block

Key Terms

capture theory
iron triangle theory

10-1 The Bureaucracy: The New Kid on the Block

Other than rewarding party loyalists with patronage appointments, during the nineteenth century, presidents rarely exhibited an interest in the bureaucracy. The federal bureaucracy was small and its policy scope and influence limited. Even though, historically speaking, the bureaucracy is one of the oldest political institutions, I call it the "new kid on the block" because its relationship with the presidency really did not begin to develop until the twentieth century. Furthermore, although the federal bureaucracy is part of the executive branch, I treat it as an external political actor because under the Constitution the Congress has greater authority over it than does the president.

10-2 The Constitution and the Bureaucracy

Who controls the bureaucracy? Since the federal bureaucracy is housed in the executive branch, the answer seems quite apparent: The president should control it. Yet, as Peri Arnold (1986: 7) writes,

> The formal mandate of agencies, their organization, their funding and subsequent discretion in spending, the specification of the number of positions they might fill, the qualifications attached to those positions, and the precise definition of the actual jurisdiction of that agency all rest upon congressional will. If anything, it is Congress and not the presidency that is the institution intended by the Constitution to exert predominant responsibility over administration.

Congress has extensive potential influence over the bureaucracy through its ability to appropriate funds. R. Douglas Arnold's (1979) analysis of congressional-bureaucratic relations demonstrates that agencies often adapt their programs to the needs of key congressmen (and their districts) and committees in order to ensure continuous funding. Such activity makes executive branch agencies more responsive to Congress and less alert to presidential cues.

Congress also draws authority over the bureaucracy from several sections of the Constitution. Article I, Section 8 grants Congress the power "to regulate commerce with foreign Nations, and among the several States" (the commerce clause). This provision allows Congress to play a vital role in the management of the economy and the control of business practices. Congress's greatest constitutional authority over the bureaucracy comes from the implied powers of the "necessary and proper" clause of the Constitution. This is particularly true with regard to the organizational structure of the executive branch, for Congress has the authority to "create, alter, or abolish departments, agencies, commissions, and bureaus within the executive branch and to determine the powers of each" (Redford and Blisset 1981: 2). Congress can delegate specific or broad grants of authority. It also can specify the functions of the officers of the agency. Congress also can play an active role through direct oversight (McCubbins and Schwartz 1984; Aberbach 1990) and by enacting legislation that can force executive branch agencies to comply with its will (McCubbins 1985). In other words, Congress has tremendous potential to influence the activity of the executive branch agencies it creates.

10-3 The Emergence of the Bureaucracy

Given Congress's inherent constitutional advantages in controlling the bureaucracy, it is perhaps ironic that one of the distinguishing characteristics of the rise of the modern presidency is the concomitant establishment of a large federal bureaucracy. This occurred because as the public demanded increased federal

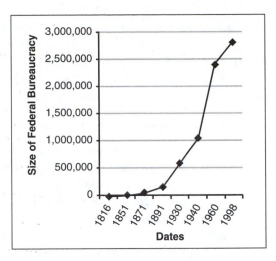

Figure 10-1
The Growing Bureaucracy

action on a variety of issues, Congress and the president created various bureaucratic institutions with the power to satisfy these demands. Throughout most of the nineteenth century, with its rural economy and limited urban population, there was little need for government regulation. While there were limited attempts at government control of private interests, such as the short-lived regulation of the steamboat industry, regulation was not widely used as a public policy tool throughout the nineteenth century (Lowi 1964).

As a result, the federal bureaucracy was relatively small; there were only 4,837 civilian federal government employees in 1816; 26,274 by 1851; and 157,020 in 1891 (see Figure 10-1). This contrasts with 601,319 in 1930 (before the New Deal); 1,042,420 in 1940 (before World War II); and 2,798,992 by 1998 (Stanley and Niemi 2000: 259).

Another reason the bureaucracy expanded is that the U.S. government adopted a broader role in regulating the nation's economy. A Supreme Court decision in 1877 opened the door for a larger federal regulatory role. In the case of *Munn v. Illinois*, the court ruled that the state government of Illinois could regulate business "affected with the public interest." Later, however, the courts limited state power by ruling that the states could not regulate interstate commerce. Since the federal government possessed this authority under the commerce clause of the U.S. Constitution, public demands for government regulation of the railroads and monopolies suddenly were directed toward the federal government.

10-3a Changes in Bureaucracy

The industrial revolution and the trend toward increased urbanization led broad-based and varied political interests to lobby the federal government to play a more active regulatory role. The predominant engines of this movement were the Populist (in the late 1800s) and Progressive (in the early 1900s) parties. As Hofstadter (1955: 231) writes, "The Progressives were . . . haunted by the specter of private power far greater than the public power of the state." The men who led these movements represented a cross-section of American politics: "Theodore Roosevelt, with his leisure-class background and tastes, [Woodrow] Wilson with his professional reserve, [Robert] La Follette with his lonely stubbornness and his craftsmanlike interest in the technical details of reform . . . ," and William Jennings Bryan, who "did not merely resemble that average man, he was that average man" (Hofstadter 1973: 241).

The reaction against private power and the need for the federal government to do something about it was not a movement specific to any one political party or region of the country. It was not advocated by one segment of the population. It was a broad-based if far from united movement that promoted a new way of thinking about economic matters: a model that mixed capitalism with democratic control. It began with rural criticism of the railroad industries and the growing number of monopolies, then moved to the Progressive era calls for urban reform, and proceeded to Franklin Roosevelt's New Deal and Lyndon Johnson's Great Society policies.

10-3b The Emergence of a Federal Bureaucracy

As demands on the federal government for a more active economic or regulatory role expanded, the federal bureaucracy emerged slowly, at least at first. In 1887, Congress enacted the Interstate Commerce Act, which tentatively extended government regulation to the railroad industry (see Kolko 1965). It also established the first continuous federal regulatory agency, the Interstate Commerce Commission. Other acts followed, each increasing the federal government's regulatory role: the Sherman Anti-Trust Act of 1890 (limited monopoly control), the Pure Food and Drug Act of 1906 (created the Food and Drug Administration), the Federal Trade Act of 1914 (created the Federal Trade Commission), and the Federal Reserve Act (created the Federal Reserve Board and system). Kolko (1963) argues that many of these acts served the interests of business rather than the public interest. Even if these initial regulatory structures were largely symbolic, however, they did establish a precedent for creating bureaucratic agencies to regulate the economy.

While these new agencies did not directly and immediately increase presidential power, they did provide that potential, since they placed authority previously held by the legislative branch or the states into the executive branch. They created a precedent for future delegations of authority and, more importantly, placed functions in the executive branch that could be exploited by a more active presidency.

10-3c Changing Perceptions of the Bureaucracy

As noted, the road toward modern perceptions of the bureaucracy was incremental. While the administrations of Republican Theodore Roosevelt and Democrat Woodrow Wilson saw an initial expansion in bureaucratic functions, the 1920s witnessed a period of limited bureaucratic growth. The Federal Radio Act (later superceded by the Federal Communications Act) was passed to bring order to the myriad wave bands in the newly emerging radio industry, but until the Great Depression, there was little demand for new governmental agencies. Then, first Herbert Hoover (on a limited level) and Franklin Roosevelt (on an unprecedented level) created new federal agencies to respond to the depression's deleterious effects.

Not only were new organizations created, but of greater importance, the public came to look to these new federal agencies to provide leadership at a time of national crisis. Agencies such as the Civilian Conservation Corps, the Public Works Administration, the Works Progress Administration, and the Social Security Administration were seen as vital instruments in the fight against the depression and as a means of providing Americans with a better quality of life. The scope of the New Deal bureaucratic expansion was broad, influencing virtually all segments of the American economy. Within but a few years, a nation that had seldom looked to Washington before depended on the federal government for its very survival: It was now the economic manager; provider of unemployment benefits, relief and old-age benefit payments; and even employer (through the CCC and WPA). Government created a system for controlling farm prices and competition in the transportation industries; in addition, regulation of the financial and banking industries was vastly expanded. Virtually overnight, government involvement in the economy became the norm, rather than the exception. The public not only accepted this development, but encouraged further growth by demanding new benefits and new federal programs.

Throughout the remainder of the twentieth century, the bureaucracy grew even further. In 1947, there was a major expansion in the size and capabilities of the U.S. military forces with the establishment of the Department of Defense and other defense and security agencies (e.g., the Central Intelligence Agency). In the 1960s and 1970s, bureaucracies were created to safeguard the rights of the elderly and African Americans, to protect the environment, to ensure worker and product safety, among a variety of other reforms (see Box 10-1): these reforms, generally popular with the American public, often placed additional costs on business, thus engendering increased hostility between the business sector and the federal government. As business became more concerned, however, the public continued to clamor for additional governmental programs and agencies such as the Environmental Protection Agency. As a result, as Greenberg (1995: 127) writes, "Nixon [a Republican] topped every other postwar president on the number of new statutes and new agencies created to regulate business," though most of these "broad regulatory initiatives came mainly from the Democratic Congress."

As the scope and functions of the bureaucracy expanded, public perceptions of it finally began to change. In the 1930s, the public perceived bureaucracy as a savior, providing jobs and opportunities during the worst years of the depression. By the 1960s and 1970s, many considered the bureaucracy to be a vital ally in the war against racial prejudice and environmental degradation, among other societal problems. At the same time, other segments of the public began to perceive Washington as an obstacle and the bureaucracy as a purveyor of an irrational way of thinking. Beginning with the third-party campaign of George Wallace in 1968, candidates began to campaign against the bureaucracy, increasingly portraying it as the problem, not the solution, as Reagan would later famously declare. By the 1980s, the backlash against the bureaucracy was in full force.

Still, while the perception exists that we hate bureaucracy and big government, the public continues to demand more action from the government and its institutions. When tainted grapes from South America, *E. coli* in hamburgers, terrorist attacks, or toxic waste threaten the nation's health and security, the public demands that the government do something about it. Hence, it was not surprising that after the September 11, 2001, terrorist attacks on the World Trade Center and the Pentagon, the response was the creation of various new bureaucracies. Congress created the Department of Homeland Security, while George W. Bush established an Office of Cyberspace Security. Airport security was federalized. The lesson is clear. As the public demands action from its government, government invariably responds by creating new bureaucracies to handle these functions. Unless the public is willing to demand less from its government, bureaucracy will not only continue to exist, but it also will continue to expand. Given this reality, what can presidents do to control the bureaucracy?

10-4 Presidents and the Bureaucracy

In 1887, Woodrow Wilson (1987 edition: 18) wrote, "administration lies outside the proper sphere of politics." Goodnow (1900) then identified the need to separate politics from administration: the politics-administration dichotomy. The idea was that politics should be limited to the policy formulation and adoption stages, but should not continue in the implementation or administration stages. In other words, bureaucrats should not play politics, politicians should.

Box 10-1

Government Agencies

USAID

"USAID is an independent federal government agency that receives overall foreign policy guidance from the Secretary of State. The agency works to support long-term and equitable economic growth and advancing U.S. foreign policy objectives by supporting: economic growth, agricultural and trade; global health; and, democracy, conflict prevention and humanitarian assistance." (from www.usaid.gov)

Central Intelligence Agency

"CIA's mission is to support the President, the National Security Council, and all officials who make and execute the U.S. national security policy by:

- "Providing accurate, comprehensive and timely foreign intelligence on national security topics.

- "Conducting counterintelligence activities, special activities, and other functions related to foreign intelligence and national security, as directed by the President." (from www.cia.gov)

Equal Employment Opportunity Commission

"EEOC was created in the historic Civil Rights Act of 1964. This Act was an omnibus bill addressing not only discrimination in employment, but also discrimination in voting, public accommodations, and education as well." (from www.eeoc.gov)

Federal Communications Commission

"The FCC was established by the Communications Act of 1934 and is charged with regulating interstate and international communications by radio, television, wire, satellite and cable. The FCC's jurisdiction covers the 50 states, the District of Columbia, and U.S. possessions." (from www.fcc.gov)

Securities and Exchange Commission

"The primary mission of the U.S. Securities and Exchange Commission (SEC) is to protect investors and maintain the integrity of the securities markets." (from www.sec.gov)

National Endowment for the Humanities

"NEH is an independent grant-making agency of the United States government dedicated to supporting research, education, preservation, and public programs in the humanities." (from www.neh.gov)

Peace Corps

"The Peace Corps' three goals: To help the people of interested countries in meeting their need for trained men and women; To help promote a better understanding of Americans on the part of the peoples served; To help promote a better understanding of other peoples on the part of Americans." (from www.peacecorps.gov)

Smithsonian Institution

"The [Smithsonian] Institution is as an independent trust instrumentality of the United States holding more than 140 million artifacts and specimens in its trust for 'the increase and diffusion of knowledge.' The Institution is also a center for research dedicated to public education, national service, and scholarship in the arts, sciences, and history. The Smithsonian is composed of sixteen museums and galleries and the National Zoo and numerous research facilities in the United States and abroad." (from www.si.edu)

United States Customs Service

"The United States Customs Service ensures that all imports and exports comply with U.S. laws and regulations. The Service collects and protects the revenue, guards against smuggling, and is responsible for the following: Assessing and collecting Customs duties, excise taxes, fees and penalties due on imported merchandise; Interdicting and seizing contraband, including narcotics and illegal drugs; Processing persons, baggage, cargo and mail, and administering certain navigation laws; Detecting and apprehending persons engaged in fraudulent practices designed to circumvent Customs and related laws; Protecting American business and labor and intellectual property rights by enforcing U.S. laws intended to prevent illegal trade practices, including provisions related to quotas and the marking of imported merchandise; the Anti-Dumping Act; and by providing Customs Recordations for copyrights, patents, and trademarks; Protecting the general welfare and security of the United States by enforcing import and export restrictions and prohibitions, including the export of critical technology used to develop weapons of mass destruction, and money laundering; Collecting accurate import and export data for compilation of international trade statistics." (from www.customs.gov)

Voice of America

"The Voice of America (VOA) is an international multimedia broadcasting service funded by the U.S. Government. VOA broadcasts over 900 hours of news, informational, educational, and cultural programs every week to an audience of some 91 million worldwide. VOA programs are produced and broadcast in English and 52 other languages through radio, satellite television, and the Internet." (from www.voa.gov)

To some extent, the idea was not new, even in 1887. Congressional enactment of the Pendleton Act of 1883, which established the U.S. Civil Service Commission and merit system, attempted to promote expertise over patronage (a political consideration) in hiring decisions. Likewise, though it was initially created within the Interior Department, the Interstate Commerce Commission was re-established by Congress as an independent regulatory commission. "In so doing, Congress's clear intent was to limit presidential influence over commission activities. Although presidents were granted authority to appoint the commission's members, they were not delegated authority to remove these members from office. In addition, until 1969 presidents did not have the authority to designate the commission's chair" (Wood and Waterman 1994: 33).

Two fundamental views therefore developed early on with regard to the bureaucracy: It should be nonpolitical, and while the president would have some limited authority (primarily through appointments), constitutionally it was Congress that would oversee and control the bureaucracy. These initial beliefs have had continuing effects on scholarly perceptions of bureaucratic politics.[1]

10-4a Interest Groups and Political Influence

In 1952, Samuel Huntington discussed a new theory of bureaucratic politics: the **capture** of regulatory agencies by the interest groups—later called the **iron triangle theory** (see Cater 1964; Freeman 1965). This subgovernmental politics consisted of an iron triangle: the regulated industry (an interest group), the regulatory agency (the bureaucracy), and the relevant committees of Congress. Not included in the iron triangle were presidents, the courts, public opinion, or the media.

Capture theory/Iron triangle theory: A theory describing the relationships of regulatory agencies, regulated interest groups, and congressional committees. The idea is that regulated agencies are captured by the groups they are supposed to regulate. Therefore, the public interest is not protected.

With the development of the capture and iron triangle theory, scholars argued that the president was incapable of controlling the bureaucracy. For example, Rossiter (1960: 19–22) asserts that the most difficult task a president faces is trying to sell his program, not to Congress, but to the bureaucracy. This is the case even when an official selected by the president heads an agency. A number of scholars then argued that the president had little influence over the bureaucracy and made little attempt to influence it (Koenig 1975: 184; Cronin 1980: 333; Noll 1971: 36; Dodd and Schott 1979: 42; Bryner 1987: 66). A few studies (Beck 1982; Yandle 1985; Cohen 1985) provided empirical evidence that presidents were unable to influence the policies of the Federal Trade Commission, the Interstate Commerce Commission, and the Federal Reserve Board.

On the other hand, a number of empirical works under the umbrella of the "congressional dominance theory" argued that the Congress, not the president, was most capable of controlling the bureaucracy. Using a new theoretical perspective, the principal-agent model, Weingast and Moran (1983) and Weingast (1984) provided evidence that Congress controlled bureaucratic institutions. Other scholars, such as McCubbins and Schwartz (1984) also convincingly argued that Congress had influence. In so doing, they superceded a long tradition in the congressional literature. Previously, scholars had argued that Congress had little interest in or ability to influence the bureaucracy (see Bibby and Davidson 1972; Ogul 1976; 1981; Katzman 1980a; 1980b; Sundquist 1981).

By the mid-1980s, then, the case seemed to have been made that the president had limited interest and ability to influence, while Congress could control the bureaucracy: Whether one applied the politics-administration dichotomy, the capture/iron triangle model, or the principal-agent model, the evidence was the same. It was conventional wisdom within the presidential literature, as well. But when Richard Nixon declared war on the bureaucracy, and later when Ronald Reagan did the same, scholars took another look at presidential influence over the bureaucracy

(Nathan 1983); Waterman 1989). The results of the empirical work from the 1980s and 1990s provides convincing evidence that Nixon, Reagan, and other presidents were indeed capable of influencing the bureaucracy. In particular, the works of Terry Moe (1982; 1985a; 1985b) and others (Brigman 1981; Stewart and Cromartie 1982; Menzel 1983; Wood 1990; Wood and Waterman 1991; 1993; 1994; Wood and Anderson 1993) empirically demonstrate that presidents not only could but indeed did influence bureaucratic behavior across a wide variety of federal agencies.

10-5 The Tools of Presidential Control of the Bureaucracy

One of the first scholars to argue that presidents can influence the bureaucracy was Richard Nathan (1983). He identified the various strategies and tools of an "administrative presidency" approach or a series of specific techniques presidents use to influence the bureaucracy. They include the president's powers of appointment, removal, and reorganization, together with the presidential budgetary authority. Presidents also can transfer program authority to the states. Presidents such as Richard Nixon, Jimmy Carter, and Ronald Reagan also used two more sources of presidential influence—administrative central clearance and the use of cost-benefit analysis—in their attempts to control the bureaucracy. In sections 10-6 through 10-12, I will examine each of these techniques, looking, when possible, at the available empirical evidence to see how and if presidents actually secure increased influence when they employ these techniques.

10-6 Appointment Power

Why do presidents use the appointment power to influence the bureaucracy? Of the various tools of Nathan's (1983) administrative presidency strategy, the power of appointment is the most prominent. It is the first among equals—a necessary but not a sufficient means of influencing agency goals and behavior—for, unlike the other tools of the administrative presidency, the president's appointment power is derived directly from the Constitution (see Box 4-2, "President's Constitutional Power"). In addition, there is evidence that presidents derive considerable authority from the use of this constitutional power. In an empirical analysis of eight federal agencies, Wood and Waterman (1994: 73) find, "In six of the eight programs, agency outputs [e.g., various enforcement actions conducted by the agencies to carry out their legal mandate] shifted immediately after a change in agency leadership." The authors continue, "The responses reveal that political appointments dominate the dynamic of institutional political control."[2]

Not only have political scientists demonstrated that influence derives from the political appointment power, but bureaucrats themselves also perceive presidential appointees as exerting considerable influence. Table 10-1 presents the responses of EPA bureaucrats to the following question: "On a scale from 1 to 5 where 1 is no influence and 5 is a great deal of influence, how much influence do the following (actors) have over how your office enforces the law?" Two different types of appointees, Regional Administrators (who are in charge of the ten EPA regional offices) and the EPA Administrator (who is in charge of the entire agency), are ranked first and second, respectively, with mean influence scores of 4.04 and 3.99. On the other hand, the president is ranked much lower, seventh overall, with a mean influence score of just 2.84. Since the president appoints the EPA Administrator and the regional directors (the latter with the help of members of Congress, through the practice of senatorial courtesy), it is interesting that EPA bureaucrats did not draw a direct connection between the influence of the president's appointees and the president's influence. Elsewhere (Waterman 1999: 156),

TABLE **10-1** Perceptions of Environmental Protection Agency Enforcement Personnel Regarding the Influence of Various Political Actors

Actors	Rank	Mean	Standard Deviation
Regional administrator	1	4.04	0.95
EPA administrator	2	3.99	0.97
Federal courts	3	3.44	1.10
Congress	4	3.36	1.30
Environmental groups	5	3.09	1.10
Public opinion	6	2.97	1.10
President	7	2.84	1.40
Permittees/regulated industry	8	2.83	1.03
Media	9	2.72	1.10
Governors	10	2.71	1.00
Business groups	11	2.59	1.10
State courts	12	2.50	1.10
State legislatures	13	2.31	0.90
Agricultural groups	14	2.21	1.00

Source: Waterman (1999: 156).

I called this the "president-appointee dichotomy." There I wrote, "There may be some advantage in this dichotomy. If presidents name appointees to represent them in the bureaucracy, and if bureaucrats perceive them as exerting influence (but not the president), then presidents may develop an aura of 'plausible deniability' if the actions of their appointees should be perceived in a negative light. In other words, the dichotomy may insulate presidents from negative fallout deriving from their appointees."

Despite this evidence of a dichotomy, it is clear that bureaucrats in an important federal agency perceived the influence of two different types of presidential appointments. They also ranked them as having more influence than Congress, the federal courts, interest groups (such as environmental, business, and agricultural ones), the public, the media, and even the regulated industry (the permittees) itself.[3]

What is particularly interesting is that even state-level bureaucrats rank the president's appointees high in terms of perceived influence over the bureaucracy. Officials working for the New Mexico Environment Department rank the EPA Administrator third out of a list of seventeen political actors it deals with on a regular basis. These same bureaucrats also ranked the EPA Regional Director for Region VI, the region that oversees environmental issues in New Mexico, as ranking sixth out of seventeen actors (Waterman 1999: 157). Consequently, whether we look at federal or state bureaucrats, we have evidence that they perceive presidential appointments as having considerable influence over the way their office enforces the law.

The combined evidence then tells us why presidents use their appointment power to influence the bureaucracy. How then do they use it? One characteristic of the modern presidency is a greater trend toward appointing individuals who share the president's political philosophy and programmatic goals. Also, personal loyalty to the president is prized. There are benefits to naming loyalists. According to Cohen (1986), loyal appointees tend to stay in office longer and consequently provide presidents with more stable bureaucratic structures. Presidential influence is advanced because presidential appointees are no longer constantly coming and going (the average tenure for appointees is approximately two years). Hence, they can learn the intricacies of their jobs. They can then use the knowledge they derive to be a better advocate for the president's programs.

Although the appointment of loyal individuals can be helpful, it alone does not guarantee expanded presidential influence. First, loyalists sharing the president's political philosophy are more likely to perceive the bureaucracy, and particularly the civil servants who work in it, as the enemy. Since they share the president's policy goals, they are skeptical or even hostile to civil servants who are not as enthusiastic about the president's agenda. As Michaels (1997), in her detailed analysis of George H. W. Bush's appointments shows, however, over time Bush's appointees came to recognize the value of the expertise civil servants provide. The longer appointees stay in office, the more likely they are able to work with the bureaucracy. Still, in the short run, there is much suspicion and even open hostility between appointees and the bureaucracies they head.

Additionally, as Linda Fisher argues, "appointing people who support the president's philosophy is not enough to ensure presidential control of the bureaucracy." Loyal individuals who lack political experience can do the president more harm than good (Lynn 1984). Fisher recommends that presidents should be concerned with the competence of their nominees as well as their loyalty to the president.

10-6a Competence and Qualifications

What is competence? Individuals who are substantively competent (that is, technically well trained) may not be politically competent. As Fenno (1959: 225) notes, "An expert in terms of substantive knowledge may turn out to be a very poor departmental administrator." More than substantive knowledge is necessary to manage a bureaucracy in Washington. Fenno recommends that presidents should also look for individuals who have management experience. In addition, they should seek individuals with prior experience in the federal government (see also Hess 1976). Appointees without prior governmental experience require a great deal of time to learn the important details of governmental management, such as how to deal with Congress, how the budgetary process works, what to say and not to say to the press, and how to deal with interest groups and the public (Pfiffner 1987). Because of these many factors, presidents who can appoint experienced and loyal individuals are at a distinct political advantage.

Unfortunately, it is often difficult to locate qualified individuals who not only share a president's personal political philosophy, but also are willing to serve in government. The trials and tribulations associated with governmental service scare many qualified individuals away. Many turn down service because of financial considerations; the remuneration is quite low compared to that in the private sector. Moreover, the hours of work are long: In one survey of presidential appointees, 73 percent of all respondents reported working 61 hours or more per week (Brauer 1987).

In addition to inadequate pay and long hours, reporting requirements under the 1978 Ethics in Government Act also kept many qualified individuals from accepting appointments. The act demands that appointees provide detailed information regarding their finances and severely limits their post-government employment options. More critically, since appointees are often forced to sell stock and other holdings that might be considered a conflict of interest, they may suffer severe financial losses on stock sales and extremely high capital gains taxes (Mackenzie 1987).

Because of all of these factors, a president is often forced to nominate a candidate who is neither his or her first nor even second choice. The lack of a constant pool of qualified potential candidates is thus a factor that can constrain presidential influence because presidents often are unable to get the people that they really want. This has increased the need for new institutional mechanisms that can identify potential candidates for appointive office (see Chapter 13, "The Search for New Political Resources," and Chapter 15, "How Internal and Informational Resources Can Increase Presidential Influence: The Case of Presidential Appointments").

10-6b Other Factors in Appointment Power

Factors other than those mentioned in section 10-6a also constrain the president's appointment power. For example, appointments are subject to confirmation by the Senate. Although most presidential appointees are routinely confirmed, the confirmation process is by no means a rubber stamp (King and Riddlesperger 1987). Presidents therefore must consider potential Senate opposition when nominating individuals for office. In this process, according to Gerhardt (2000: 103), "a president's popularity or unpopularity . . . might incline some if not many senators to oppose nominees who can be closely associated with the president personally or with unpopular policies." Committees also have increased the amount of time they spend on nominations and are holding hearings for a greater number of positions. There are still no uniform rules for the nomination process, and wide variations exist across committees regarding the times dedicated to presidential appointments (Deering 1987).

Even when presidents are able to name individuals that they most prefer for particular positions, presidential influence still can be constrained. Appointed officials do not owe their loyalty solely to the president. Once they assume office, appointed officials must perform certain legally mandated functions that are enumerated in detail in congressional legislation. Appointed officials cannot simply do as the president wishes. Rather, they have an obligation to enforce the law consistent with congressional intent (see section 4-5, "The Take Care Clause").

Still, while presidents cannot expect their appointees to enforce the law without regard to statute and the will of Congress, presidents need a measure of loyalty from their appointees in order to govern effectively. Presidential influence is undercut when, rather than openly challenging the president on policy matters, appointed officials drag their feet to stall the implementation of the president's program. In such cases, the need for presidential followup can be crucial (e.g., to make sure that his or her actions are being carried out, including removing officials who do not act in accordance with the president's wishes).

10-7 Reward or Remove

In section 4-7c, "The Opinion, in Writing, of the Principal Officers and the Removal Power," I discussed the president's removal power. As I noted, considerable ambiguity exists with regard to the scope of this presidential power. While it is now understood that presidents can remove cabinet secretaries, sub-cabinet appointments, appointees to executive branch agencies such as the Environmental Protection Agency, as well as sundry other executive positions, it is also understood that presidents can remove members of the independent regulatory commissions only under limited circumstances (see section 10-7a). Otherwise, commissioners remain in office until their term of office expires.

As noted in section 4-7d, "Challenging the Removal Power," when Franklin Delano Roosevelt fired Commissioner William Humphrey of the Federal Trade Commission (FTC), he challenged the constitutionality of regulatory statutes that limit a president's removal power. Roosevelt justified his action on the basis that Humphrey's philosophy was not in accord with his administration's policy. In the case of *Humphrey's Executor v. United States* [295 U.S. 602 (1935)], the Supreme Court ruled unanimously that an FTC Commissioner could be removed from office by the president only for malfeasance in office, neglect of duty, or inefficiency.[4]

10-7a The Pendleton Act

By far the largest category of federal employees protected from presidential removal is the civil servants. After the assassination of President James Garfield by a disgruntled job seeker, Congress passed the Pendleton Act of 1883. The act created the Civil Service Commission, established the merit system as a means of selecting and promoting administrative employees, and also limited removal from office to certain specific violations such as malfeasance in office. It also "empowered the president to extend the 'classified service' by executive order. Every succeeding president for some time, except McKinley, did extend the coverage, from about one-seventh of the total in 1883 to about one half in 1901" (McDonald 1994: 325). By 1928, about 80 percent of all bureaucratic positions below the policy-making level were covered (ibid., 326).

The civil service system was an attempt to separate administration from politics by limiting the direct influence of the president over the bureaucracy (Mosher 1982). Although it did not succeed in this objective, it did greatly limit the presidential use of patronage and with it the spoils system—instituted by Andrew Jackson—that allowed presidents to remove large numbers of government employees. This step was usually taken when a new president, particularly of a political party different from his predecessor, assumed office. Still, as the experiences of the Nixon and Reagan administrations attest, it has not prevented presidents from removing individuals from office. Nixon skirted—and even may have violated—the provisions of the original civil service act. Reagan, on the other hand, used the new provisions of the Civil Service Reform Act of 1978, particularly those relating to the new Senior Executive Service (SES), to transfer civil servants from offices in Washington, D.C., to remote locations around the country (Nathan 1983; Waterman 1989).

10-7b The Civil Service Reform Act

The Civil Service Reform Act of 1978 was designed to increase presidential influence over the bureaucracy by creating a new level of civil servants, the Senior Executive Service. Approximately 7,000 positions were created throughout the government. Presidents were also granted the authority to appoint an additional 800 or so individuals from outside the government to serve within the bureaucracy (Sanders 1988: 393). In addition, the act replaced the Civil Service Commission with the Office of Personnel Management (OPM), which is headed by a single executive appointed by the president. This latter reform was similar to the one requested by Franklin Roosevelt and the Brownlow Committee Report in the late 1930s (U.S. Government 1937).

The new provisions of the 1978 act provided presidents with greater influence over the civil service, just as Eisenhower's innovation of creating Schedule C appointees allowed him to appoint a counter bureaucracy loyal to his policies. The act increased the president's ability to transfer and even terminate civil servants. It did not, however, extend total control to the president. The Merit Systems Protection Board also was created to investigate alleged abuses of the civil service system and to air employee grievances (ibid., 392–93). Presidential influence over career civil servants who do not hold SES rank is still strictly limited, however. Therefore, though presidents do have more influence over civil service employees, they are still greatly constrained in terms of their direct influence over the career bureaucracy.

In the debate over its creation, George W. Bush argued that the employees of the Department of Homeland Security should be subject to less protection than employees in other agencies. The idea is that the president should be able to transfer and even fire individuals when national security is at risk. Hence, the debate over the proper scope of civil service protection in relationship to presidential power continues to unfold, even as new agencies and departments are created.

Overall, then, the president's removal power is limited. So how much real influence does the president have to influence the bureaucracy (see Figure 10-2)? There is some empirical evidence on this point. Wood (1990) examined the politics of the Equal Employment Opportunity Commission (EEOC) and found that Reagan's appointment of Michael Connolly as its General Counsel had a direct impact on agency activity: a sharp and precipitous drop in the number of cases litigated by EEOC. Democrats in Congress were particularly dissatisfied with this result and placed considerable pressure on the Reagan administration and its General Counsel. In 1983, Connolly was removed from office and the number of litigation actions conducted by the EEOC increased dramatically. The removal of a presidential appointment thus had a major impact on the agency's behavior. Yet, the actual winner in this case was Congress, which had forced the removal. Thus, while there is empirical evidence that the removal changed the agency's behavior, the removal was forced on a reluctant president by a truculent Congress. It is therefore not evidence that removal increases presidential power, but rather that it can increase congressional influence.

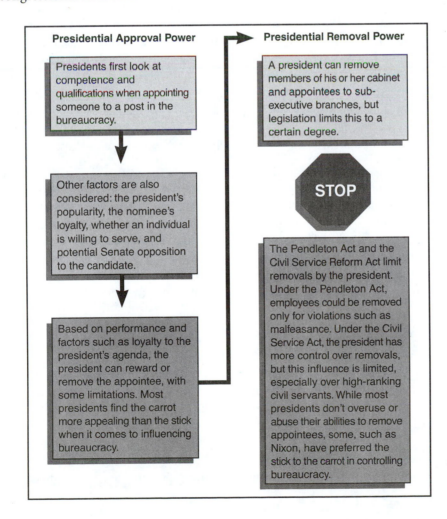

Presidential Approval Power

Presidents first look at competence and qualifications when appointing someone to a post in the bureaucracy.

Other factors are also considered: the president's popularity, the nominee's loyalty, whether an individual is willing to serve, and potential Senate opposition to the candidate.

Based on performance and factors such as loyalty to the president's agenda, the president can reward or remove the appointee, with some limitations. Most presidents find the carrot more appealing than the stick when it comes to influencing bureaucracy.

Presidential Removal Power

A president can remove members of his or her cabinet and appointees to sub-executive branches, but legislation limits this to a certain degree.

STOP

The Pendleton Act and the Civil Service Reform Act limit removals by the president. Under the Pendleton Act, employees could be removed only for violations such as malfeasance. Under the Civil Service Act, the president has more control over removals, but this influence is limited, especially over high-ranking civil servants. While most presidents don't overuse or abuse their abilities to remove appointees, some, such as Nixon, have preferred the stick to the carrot in controlling bureaucracy.

Figure 10-2
Presidential Means of Controlling the Bureaucracy through Appointment Power

Likewise, when Anne Gorsuch Burford, Reagan's first Administrator of the Environmental Protection Agency, was cited for contempt of Congress (for refusing to turn over subpoenaed information), EPA hazardous waste litigations increased sharply and Burford left office shortly thereafter (Wood and Waterman 1991). Again, Congress forced the removal of a presidential appointee, reducing the president's influence and increasing its own. Hence, two available empirical studies suggest that the removal power actually increased congressional influence, not the president's.

These findings are consistent with my earlier admonishment that (Waterman 1989: 175–76), "Presidential use of the removal power can be a costly strategy at best. The Nixon and Reagan administrations made extensive use of this approach. In both cases, the strategy resulted in congressional investigation and highly critical media exposure." The lesson is that the removal strategy should be used with great caution.

10-7c Reward Strategies

The reward strategy may prove more useful for presidents than the removal strategy. In a controversial 1970 document prepared by Frederick Malek for H. R. Haldeman, Richard Nixon's first Chief of Staff, the relative cases for reward and removal were openly discussed. In the document, called the "Management of Non-Career Personnel: Recommendations for Improvement," Malek (quoted in Mackenzie 1981: 47) wrote,

> In the two years of the Nixon administration, the difficulty in effectively managing the Federal Government has become increasingly apparent. The Executive Branch has not galvanized sufficiently as a team implementing Presidential policy. In some cases, Presidential directives have not been carried out, and counter-productive efforts have taken place within a number of Departments. While the causes of this problem are varied and complex, the President can do much to solve it by increasing his direct management control over appointees to noncareer positions in the Executive Branch. Such management control can be achieved by attracting the best qualified individuals who are philosophically compatible with and loyal to the President and placing them in leadership positions, motivating them by recognizing and promoting outstanding performers, and removing any whose performance is poor.

While the Malek report was strongly criticized for politicizing the bureaucracy, it does raise an interesting point. Presidents can benefit by rewarding "outstanding performers" with positions of greater influence and authority, so long, that is, as the word "qualified" is not lost in defining an outstanding performer. In Nixon parlance, this often was used as a surrogate for loyalty. Yet, both loyalty and competence are required in a good appointee. Rewarding individuals who meet these two criteria may be an effective means of promoting presidential influence.

10-8 Budgetary Power

Beyond the appointment and removal power, the budget is another means of influencing the bureaucracy. In his memoirs, Gerald Ford wrote, "A president controls his administration through the budget. The document reflects his basic priorities" (Ford 1979: 352) Budget expert Lance LeLoup (1980: 126) also stated, "the budget offers the President promising opportunities to achieve his policy goals."

The budgetary process gives the president tangible powers and real influence over the administrative state. The fact that the president submits the budget to Congress is in itself a major agenda-setting power. Presidents can set the tone for the budget, such as increasing defense spending, reducing allocations for social welfare programs, and so forth. They also can influence the fate of a particular agency by proposing increases or decreases in funding, initiating new programs, or vetoing appropriations.

Of course, in using these powers, presidents must be aware that Congress plays an active role in determining the final budgetary figures. Many presidents have discovered this as their budgets arrived DOA—Dead on Arrival—on Capitol Hill. On the other hand, as Clinton demonstrated in his first term budget wars with House Republicans and later in his second term as a lame duck president, skilled presidents can use the threat of a presidential veto to exert considerable influence over the budgetary process (see Cameron 2000).

Consequently, even after Congress appropriates funds, there are a number of techniques available to presidents. Presidents can impound funds. This practice, which "gained momentum particularly under Franklin D. Roosevelt, allowed presidents to negate part of an appropriations act. Most of the impoundments by Roosevelt, Truman, Eisenhower, and Kennedy were directed at military programs. Lyndon Johnson moved against domestic programs, but only temporarily, for he backtracked in the face of opposition from Congress and the states" (Fisher 1978: 91). It was Richard Nixon's unprecedented use or misuse of this authority, however, that led Congress to enact the Budget and Impoundment Act of 1974, which created a process of rescissions and deferrals subject to congressional action.[5]

Spitzer (1993: 72) writes, "When the veto [as opposed to the legislative veto] is used often, it usually means that the President has not succeeded in establishing a pattern of positive leadership based on the presidential legislative program." The same point can be made with regard to a presidential strategy that relies on the use of recissions and deferrals. While it is a tool in the president's budgetary arsenal, regular use of the technique is evidence of the president's precarious influence in the budgetary process. As Nixon learned with his broad use of the impoundment technique, it also can inflame congressional opposition and create hostility toward other elements of the president's political agenda (see Fisher 1975).

Beyond recissions and deferrals, presidents also can transfer funds across or within agencies. Since Congress is often limited in its ability to force agencies to spend funds exactly as specified in the budget, presidents and their subordinates have a great deal of freedom to determine how funds will be allocated after the budget has officially been set (Fisher 1975).

10-8a Presidential Commitment

Perhaps the greatest source of presidential budgetary power is the personal commitment presidents themselves make to this process. LeLoup (1980: 149) writes, "The greater the personal involvement of the President [in the budgetary process], the greater the constraints on subsequent decisions in the bureaucracy. On the other hand, the less active the President's role, the greater the discretion of other actors." But presidential interest in the budgetary process varies according to who is in the White House. Richard Nixon initially had little interest in budgets. As inflation came to dominate the domestic political agenda, however, he adopted a much more vigorous role in the budgetary process. Jimmy Carter's interest was precisely the opposite: He had a quite substantial interest in the beginning, but it waned over time. On the other hand, Gerald Ford and Bill Clinton were intensely interested in the budgetary matters. George W. Bush has demonstrated a lesser interest in budgets than his predecessor.

Even though presidents have a great deal of influence over the budgetary process, it is not easy for them to use the budget as a means of influencing administrative behavior. A large and growing percentage of the federal budget is made up of entitlements (such as Social Security and Medicare), which can be cut only if legislation is adopted to change the basic requirements and benefit levels. Many programs, particularly defense systems, are framed with multi-year appropriations; accordingly, it is more difficult to substantially alter the budgets for these programs. Finally, there are programs that, for political reasons, are virtually untouchable. These programs have the strong support of powerful interest groups. Presidents attack these programs at their own peril. Jimmy Carter's ill-fated decision to scrub several ongoing dam and water projects demonstrated what can happen to presidents who attempt to cut such programs from the budget: This decision greatly weakened Carter's future bargaining strength with Congress.

10-8b Other Factors in Presidential Budgetary Influence

Factors other than those described in sections 10-8 and 10-8a also can constrain a president's influence over the budget. A sudden downturn in the economy, a poor wheat crop, an oil embargo, or a crisis such as the terrorist attacks on the World Trade Center and the Pentagon can force a president to radically alter budgetary priorities. Economic trends such as rising deficits also can limit a president's discretion. For example, it is more difficult to advocate new social welfare programs in the face of a widening budget deficit or to advocate cutting them during a recession.

Schick (1981) argues that due to these various constraints, presidents have actually lost much of their power and influence over the budgetary process. In a period of retrenchment politics, the opposite argument may be advanced. Record high budget deficits increased the Reagan administration's ability to demand cuts in the programs that it opposed. When surpluses were available in the Clinton years, the president had greater flexibility to call on Congress for new spending initiatives. When budget deficits re-emerged in the early 2000s, George W. Bush promised greater fiscal responsibility (meaning tighter budgets). Therefore, presidential budgetary proclivities and influence can wax and wane according to prevailing budgetary and economic conditions.

As with presidential removal power, then, using the budgetary process as a means of promoting presidential objectives at the administrative level can entail political risks. Proposed reductions in popular programs can increase congressional oversight as well as bureaucratic resistance to presidential initiatives. The question therefore is, Do they actually increase presidential influence? Again, we have some empirical evidence on this point. The Reagan administration used the budget as one of its principal means of controlling the bureaucracy (see Shuman 1992: Chapter 10). In a time series analysis that spanned most of the Carter and Reagan presidencies, Wood and Waterman (1993; 1994) found that EPA enforcement activity, across four of the agency's divisions, varied over time in response to changes in the agency budget. They noted, "[T]he most important tools of political control are the shared tools of the president and Congress. The budget and political appointment variables explain most of the variation in EPA enforcements; they also produce the fastest responses" (Wood and Waterman 1994: 101).

Likewise, Wood (1988) found that EPA clean air enforcement declined precipitously after the Reagan administration secured severe cuts in the agency's budget. On the other hand, when Congress later restored these funds, EPA Hazardous Waste enforcement activity increased. Wood and Waterman (1994: 74) add, "It took the budget increases of fiscal year 1984 to move hazardous waste enforcements to significantly higher levels."

While Nathan (1983) was enthusiastic in touting the budget as a means of political control, and the Reagan administration made major use of it during its first two years in office, slashing the budgets for a variety of federal agencies (see Waterman 1989: 122–24; see also Vig 1984), and while the budget cuts had the desired impact in the short term (reducing the ability of agencies to regulate), in the long term, presidential influence often was not advanced. Congress reacted to the Reagan budget cuts by later restoring funding in some agencies. As with the removal power, then, presidents are best served when they do not make heavy-handed use of this technique, but rather use it selectively and, if possible, in conjunction with Congress. Otherwise, they increase the likelihood of a congressional counter-reaction.

10-9 Reorganization

The president's reorganization authority is another potential source of political influence. Organizational structure is not neutral. How an agency is organized can have a major impact on policy outcomes. In a highly decentralized agency, it can be very difficult for a president to extend personal influence over the agency's policy actions. Centralized agencies tend to be more amenable to presidential influence because greater authority rests with the agency's head, and potential sources of opposition within the organization thus are easier to circumvent or remove entirely. In a centralized agency, a president's appointees are in a stronger position to advance the president's program at the administrative level.

Whether an agency shares jurisdiction for a certain program with other agencies also can have an impact on presidential influence. If an agency has sole jurisdiction over a program, rather than sharing responsibility with several other agencies or departments, it has greater freedom to initiate a policy without being constrained by its external political environment. If, on the other hand, an agency must share program responsibility with one or more other agencies or departments, it must negotiate and compromise before decisions can be reached. This can slow progress toward policy change. As each of these organizational factors suggests, the structure of an agency can "help or hinder the president in performing his pivotal role within our constitutional system" (Seidman 1980: 38).

The reorganization authority is thus important, dating back to Woodrow Wilson, who received temporary reorganization authority during World War I (Sundquist 1981: 50). Herbert Hoover was then the first president to receive reorganization authority in the executive branch in June 1932, an authority Hoover and later Franklin Roosevelt held until March 1935 (ibid.). Fisher (1989: 146) writes,

> President Herbert Hoover wanted to reorganize the executive branch without having to pass a bill through Congress. He realized that Congress would never consent to delegating that authority without being able to check his actions with something short of passing a law. Thus, a pact was born: Hoover could submit a reorganization plan that would become law within sixty days unless either house of Congress approved.

According to Mezey (1989: 168), although forerunners of the legislative veto appeared in various statutes in the nineteenth century, its origin can be traced to the 1932 bill.

10-9a Presidential Reorganization Authority

The president's reorganization authority was expanded, and the legislative veto used again, on the basis of the recommendations of Franklin Roosevelt's Committee on Administrative Management, better known as the Brownlow Committee. The Reorganization Act of 1939 gave the president the further power to transfer, consolidate, or abolish governmental agencies unless both Houses of Congress vetoed the president's plan within a period of sixty days after it was submitted to Congress (Sundquist 1981: 54). Since 1939, presidential reorganization authority has been extended and redefined on a number of occasions, including the Legislative Reorganization Act of 1946.

Presidential reorganization authority, when established by Congress, existed only for a specified period of time, after which the reorganization authority had to be renewed. The provisions of the various reorganization authorizations changed over time. Presidents were granted the authority to establish new units within the Executive Office of the President and to create new departments subject to congressional disapproval, usually within a period of sixty days. Congressional disapproval varied from a one-house to a two-house legislative veto. In 1964, Congress amended the president's reorganization authority to prevent the president from creating or abolishing cabinet-level departments (DeClerico 1979: 118). In 1977, presidents were excluded from reorganizing the independent regulatory commissions (Seidman 1980: 262). In 1984, following the Supreme Court's 1983 *Chadha* decision, in which the legislative veto was ruled unconstitutional, the president was given the right to reorganize subject to congressional approval, rather than disapproval. Later, Congress allowed the president's reorganization authority to expire.

These latter constraints on presidential authority, along with Congress's eventual decision to let it expire, demonstrate how fluid the president's reorganization authority has been. Rather than giving presidents a fixed and permanent power, Congress has consistently changed the rules under which presidents can seek reorganizations. These changes have reflected not only the president's need to control the organization of the executive branch, but also Congress's unwillingness to grant presidents too much power.

Presidents do have other options beyond congressional reorganization authority. They also can reorganize the executive branch by submitting legislation directly to Congress and can make organizational changes via Executive Order. The latter was the means by which the Nixon administration created the Environmental Protection Agency in 1970. The use of Executive Orders is constrained by the fact that future presidents can change or even abolish the reorganization by issuing a new Executive Order. To create a permanent structure, George W. Bush asked Congress to pass legislation creating a new Department of Homeland Security. The new department consists of agencies from a variety of different existing departments, thus establishing the largest reorganization of the federal government since the creation of the Defense Department in 1947.

Given its limitations and constraints, why have presidents sought to reorganize the executive branch? They have initiated reorganizations for a variety of reasons. Salamon (1981) identifies three types of reorganization goals: economy and efficiency, policy effectiveness, and tactical political advantage. Provisions of law often have required presidents to defend reorganizations on the basis of economy and efficiency; that is, reorganization should result in net budgetary savings over the existing organizational structure by removing duplication and unnecessary programs (waste and red-tape). The first Hoover Commission, headed by former president Herbert Hoover, espoused the idea that programs should be structured so as to promote maximum efficiency. Although economy and efficiency are the legally sanctioned reasons for presidential reorganizations, the goal of much reorganization actually is policy effectiveness or tactical political advantage (Benze 1985). Often these last two goals are interrelated.

Franklin Roosevelt's Brownlow Committee believed that reorganization should improve the president's ability to manage the government; that is, economy and efficiency should not be the only legitimate goals for a presidential reorganization. The Committee's report stated, "Managerial direction and control of all departments and agencies of the Executive Branch . . . should be centered in the President; that while he now has popular responsibility for this direction . . . he is not equipped with adequate legal authority or administrative machinery to enable him to exercise it" (quoted in Arnold 1986: 103).

Congress in 1937 did not greet the unabashedly pro-executive power views of the Brownlow Committee's report with great enthusiasm. Although Congress in 1939 did create the Executive Office of the President, congressional dissatisfaction with the Brownlow report underscores a major limitation of the presidential reorganization strategy: Reorganizations can and often do provoke deep hostility from congressional committees and from various affected interest groups. As DeClerico (1979: 121) writes, "Any time a President seeks to transfer, abolish, or consolidate government agencies, he is likely to face formidable opposition from three sources; those within the agency, those congressional committees exercising oversight over the agency, and finally, those clientele groups served by the agency." Bureaucratic employees may see their interests threatened. Reorganization could weaken their program authority or even force lay-offs. Interest groups may see their interests threatened by the elimination of a favorably disposed agency and its replacement by a less sympathetic entity.

Congressional interests also can be threatened. Executive branch reorganization often is accompanied by reorganizations in congressional committee jurisdiction because changes in the structure of the executive branch force Congress to adopt a new committee structure that is consistent with the new goals and programs of the new executive units. This was a major problem Congress faced in creating the Department of Homeland Security. When reorganizations of this type occur, they can threaten long-entrenched relationships between congressional committees, interest groups, and agency officials. Presidential reorganizations that entail congressional committee reorganizations have thus long been met with intense resistance. Reorganizations that do not require congressional committee reorganization usually have a much higher probability of receiving congressional approval.

In an analysis of the president's reorganization authority, Fisher and Moe (1981: 302) argue the reorganization process tends to "degrade the institutional relationship between the president and Congress." According to this view, not only can the president's reorganization authority increase conflict between the president and Congress, but also there are few benefits derived from the use of the strategy.

What, then, is the empirical evidence on this point? One study examined a reorganization initiated by the Reagan administration at the Office of Surface Mining (OSM). "The reorganization plan involved structural changes to facilitate returning 'primacy' to the states. It eliminated field enforcement offices. It also reduced the number of OSM personnel from about one thousand to around six hundred. . . . Perhaps most important, the reorganization plan stripped field personnel of discretionary authority to write notices of violation, issue cessation orders, or initiate litigation without prior approval from central offices" (Wood and Waterman 1994: 64). What effect did the reorganization have? It "produced a decline of about 68 in the number of notices of violation per month, followed by a continuing decline to a new level that was about 220 notices lower than prior" to the reorganization (ibid., 65). In sum, the reorganization authority worked. It provided the Reagan administration with the result it desired: a reduction in regulatory enforcement by the OSM. While this is but one empirical study, it suggests why presidents may be willing to take the risk of antagonizing Congress, interest groups, and other political actors. The Reagan administration got the policy result it desired.

Reorganizations initiated by the president often receive the most attention in textbooks on organizational structure. Often overlooked is administrative-level reorganization or reorganizations initiated by a president's subordinates within the bureaucracy. Administrative reorganization is an important tool for promoting presidential influence over the bureaucracy, particularly within the independent regulatory commissions, where presidents lack reorganization authority. Yet, even this source of reorganization authority has been constrained, as Congress has at various times limited the ability of the independent regulatory commissions to reorganize their internal units without congressional approval. Still, administrative reorganization authority can be effective. In his study of the federal regulatory commissions, Welborn (1977) found only one case in which commissioners rejected a reorganization plan initiated by an agency's chairman. In this case, involving the Federal Communications Commission, the chairman himself expressed ambivalence about the reorganization plan at a crucial juncture, thus dooming the proposal.

Administrative reorganization can promote presidential objectives since the president appoints the chairmen of the regulatory agencies. A president can count on an agency's chairman to remove sources of administrative opposition to the president's program. This can pave the way for administrative action that promotes the president's program. If the appointee's action is controversial, as was the case with the Environmental Protection Agency under Anne Gorsuch Burford, administrative reorganization can threaten to reduce presidential influence by increasing interest group and congressional opposition to the president's program. Thus, administrative reorganization, like its presidential counterpart, is not risk-free.

10-10 Delegation of Program Authority

The delegation of program authority to the states is another means presidents can use to increase their influence over the administrative state. Program delegation advances presidential influence by limiting an agency's ability to initiate policies that are detrimental to a president's program. Both Presidents Nixon and Reagan advanced "New Federalist" proposals transferring various federal functions to the states.

Walker (1981) provided a strong justification for program delegation. His idea of "sorting out" federal activities is a means of determining which programs should be implemented at the national level and which can best be administered at the state or local level. The criteria for sorting out are based on cost considerations and whether a function can better be handled at the federal or local level. The Reagan administration endorsed the idea of sorting out federal activities as a justification for its delegation of various programs to the states. Yet, the administration did not always delegate authority on the basis of cost or an evaluation of which function can and should be handled by local governments. Rather, decisions were often made on the basis of whether the administration supported a particular program. Such considerations invite congressional intervention as well as criticism from state governments and sometimes the affected industries. In the case of the Office of Surface Mining (see section 10-9a), while the Reagan administration's reorganization transferred enforcement authority to the states, the OSM eventually was forced to intervene when two states did not enforce the law. While the intervention was temporary

(Wood and Waterman 1994: 65–66), it shows that even when authority is delegated to the states, the federal government still retains an important oversight function. This is so because the transfer of program implementation to the states can promote considerable variations across the states in terms of their commitment to enforcement (see Hunter and Waterman 1996: Chapters 6 and 7).

Consequently, the strategy of delegating program authority to the states for political reasons can run the risk of increasing opposition to presidential initiatives. Further, the delegation of program authority can have unanticipated consequences. Although a particular delegation of authority may be intended to reduce the level of governmental oversight, it may actually increase it. Since program delegation means that at least fifty functional units of government will be involved in the development of policy, rather than one, there are new opportunities for various state agencies to enact stronger restrictions than the federal government previously required. Under such circumstances, the relevant industries may actually find themselves in a less advantageous position. In fact, when the Reagan administration broadly delegated authority to the states, some industries, particularly in the transportation field, found the complex series of new state rules and regulations (which varied considerably from state to state) to be more perplexing than the previously existing federal system.[6]

10-11 Central Clearance

Besides their administrative activities, departments and agencies also prepare legislative proposals. Most of them are rather mundane matters, requiring only minor modifications in existing law. On occasion, however, bureaucratic units prepare major legislative proposals. To increase their knowledge and control over such administrative initiatives, presidents long have used a process known as central clearance.

Central clearance is a means of reviewing all department, agency, and commission legislative proposals before they are transmitted to Congress. The old Bureau of the Budget (BOB) performed clearance of administrative proposals for many years. When the Nixon administration reorganized the Bureau in 1970, its successor, the Office of Management and Budget (OMB), assumed this responsibility. The central clearance technique was first instituted, following congressional passage of the Budget and Accounting Act of 1921, as a means of keeping track of agency legislative proposals. It also ensured that these proposals were in accord with the Harding administration's budgetary goals.

The first presidents to employ the technique extensively were Calvin Coolidge and Herbert Hoover, who used central clearance solely as a means of keeping track of appropriations bills. Franklin Roosevelt became the first president to employ the technique as a means of providing greater presidential control over all legislative initiatives (Neustadt 1954). Not only did he ask the Bureau of the Budget to examine all proposals dealing with appropriations, but he also asked that purely policy-related bills be reviewed. This practice was followed by Roosevelt's immediate successors, Harry Truman and Dwight Eisenhower. John Kennedy and Lyndon Johnson also employed central clearance, but in a slightly different manner from their predecessors. Rather than using the BOB to review agency legislation, Kennedy and Johnson relied on their own White House staffs to perform the clearance function. Nixon later placed central clearance under the watchful eye of his Domestic Council (Gilmour 1976). The experiences of Kennedy, Johnson, and Nixon indicate that like many other sources of presidential influence, each president is likely to employ the central clearance technique differently.

Another example of this variation from president to president was established in January 1985 when the Reagan administration adopted a new central clearance technique to screen all ongoing administrative rule-making procedures. Executive Order #12498 required that the Office of Management and Budget ensure that the new rules and regulations were consistent with the goals of the Reagan administration. Consequently, OMB reviewed all department and agency rule-making proceedings, with the exception of the independent regulatory commissions. Some members of Congress, who were concerned that the president was intruding on the independence of the regulatory agencies and other bureaucratic entities, greeted this innovation with a great deal of skepticism. The Clinton administration later backed away from use of the technique. Since the system of administrative central clearance depends on who is in the White House, presidents elected with the support of organized labor and environmental groups may be less likely to use these techniques.

10-12 Cost-Benefit Analysis

Another means of controlling the bureaucracy is through the use of cost-benefit analysis. Although it been utilized for many years by various government agencies, particularly the Army Corps of Engineers, it did not achieve prominence until the 1960s, when the Johnson administration institutionalized a variation of the technique (cost-effectiveness analysis) within the Defense Department. Cost-effectiveness analysis is designed to help administrators to choose the best, most monetarily efficient alternative from the options available. Later, Johnson attempted to expand the employment of cost-effectiveness analysis to the government as a whole through the Planned Program Budget System (PPBS). PPBS was not successful, largely due to bureaucratic confusion over how the technique was supposed to work, but also because of strong resistance from career civil servants.

With the failure of PPBS, cost-benefit analysis did not again achieve prominence until Richard Nixon instituted the "Quality of Life" review process in 1971. Under the review, agencies were instructed to submit a comparison of the anticipated costs and benefits of proposed regulations, particularly those dealing with the environment, safety, and health.

In 1974, President Ford institutionalized the use of cost-benefit analysis within the Office of Management and Budget and the Council on Wage and Price Stability (CWPS) via Executive Order #11821. The order required agencies of the executive branch to file Inflation Impact Statements (IIS) for all new regulations. Although the administration's experience with cost-benefit analysis was checkered (see Fuchs 1988), Ford reauthorized the technique's employment before he left office when he issued Executive Order #11949. Carter and Reagan then continued to use cost-benefit analysis as a means of controlling regulatory spending. According to Fuchs (1988: xii), "The use of cost-benefit analysis as a management tool was an attempt to alter the institutional framework of regulatory decision making to broaden presidential discretion. It evoked an intense political struggle both because of the important interests involved and its economic consequences."

If cost-benefit analysis were value-free (that is, if no bias was involved in determining the costs and benefits involved), then it could be argued that the technique does not really promote presidential influence or constrain bureaucratic activity. Rather, it would simply promote cost-consciousness at the administrative level. There are, however, questions about whether cost-benefit analysis is really value-free. Indeed, the problem of adequately quantifying costs and benefits has led critics to charge that cost-benefit analysis is a weapon designed to prevent bureaucratic entities from adopting pro-safety and pro-environmental regulations (see Tribe 1972).

As these criticisms suggest, cost-benefit analysis has the strong potential for increasing conflict among the White House, the bureaucracy, and Congress. It has also led to a number of court challenges. The courts have been forced to determine whether presidents can avoid implementing certain safety requirements on the basis of cost. The courts also have been asked how much influence the president legally has over certain regulatory agencies, in particular the independent regulatory commissions. Thus far, the courts have ruled that presidents cannot use cost-benefit analysis to avoid rulemaking required by congressional legislation. The employment of cost-benefit analysis therefore also raises the question of who should control the bureaucracy—the president or the Congress, or in some cases, the courts (see Figure 10-3).

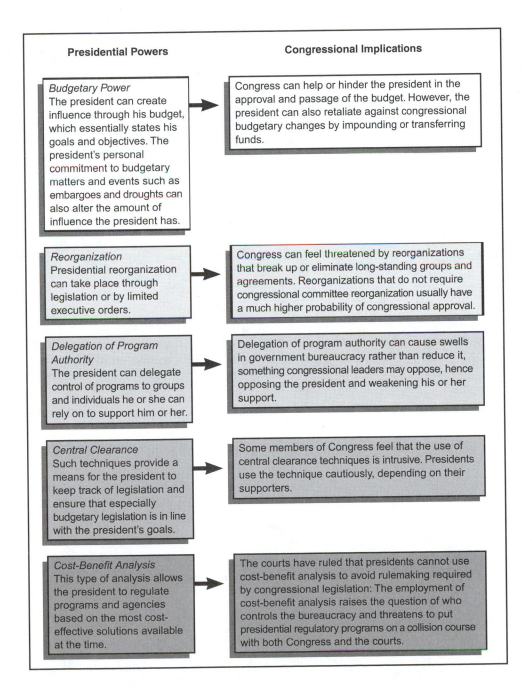

Presidential Powers	Congressional Implications
Budgetary Power The president can create influence through his budget, which essentially states his goals and objectives. The president's personal commitment to budgetary matters and events such as embargoes and droughts can also alter the amount of influence the president has.	Congress can help or hinder the president in the approval and passage of the budget. However, the president can also retaliate against congressional budgetary changes by impounding or transferring funds.
Reorganization Presidential reorganization can take place through legislation or by limited executive orders.	Congress can feel threatened by reorganizations that break up or eliminate long-standing groups and agreements. Reorganizations that do not require congressional committee reorganization usually have a much higher probability of congressional approval.
Delegation of Program Authority The president can delegate control of programs to groups and individuals he or she can rely on to support him or her.	Delegation of program authority can cause swells in government bureaucracy rather than reduce it, something congressional leaders may oppose, hence opposing the president and weakening his or her support.
Central Clearance Such techniques provide a means for the president to keep track of legislation and ensure that especially budgetary legislation is in line with the president's goals.	Some members of Congress feel that the use of central clearance techniques is intrusive. Presidents use the technique cautiously, depending on their supporters.
Cost-Benefit Analysis This type of analysis allows the president to regulate programs and agencies based on the most cost-effective solutions available at the time.	The courts have ruled that presidents cannot use cost-benefit analysis to avoid rulemaking required by congressional legislation: The employment of cost-benefit analysis raises the question of who controls the bureaucracy and threatens to put presidential regulatory programs on a collision course with both Congress and the courts.

Figure 10-3
Other Presidential Means of Controlling the Bureaucracy

Chapter Summary

Of the various tools of the "administrative presidency" strategy, the power of appointment stands out as the president's most potent weapon. Presidents can use their constitutional authority to influence administrative behavior by appointing loyal but competent individuals to the bureaucracy. Although taking such action does not guarantee presidential influence, it is an important first step.

Other tools of the "administrative presidency" strategy can also increase presidential influence, though at the same time they have the potential for increasing congressional, bureaucratic, and interest group opposition, as well as promoting court challenges that permanently can limit presidential discretion. As the empirical evidence shows, the budget can be a powerful contributor to presidential influence, but it also can promote congressional opposition. The president's reorganization authority, by limiting or removing authority from the various competing factions within the bureaucracy, can increase presidential influence (as shown in the case of the Office of Surface Mining), but by challenging entrenched interests, it also can create opposition to the president's program. The same can be said of the president's ability to delegate program authority to the states. It also can lead to wide and unexpected variations in program implementation. Other tools of the administrative presidency strategy, particularly the president's removal power, threaten to reduce presidential influence, often without palpable benefits. Hence, presidents must be careful which techniques they use in their attempts to influence the bureaucracy. Most importantly, however, and contrary to common wisdom, as the mounting empirical evidence demonstrates, while there are palpable constraints on presidential influence, *presidents can and have exerted considerable influence over the bureaucracy.*

Review Questions

1. Which political actor has more constitutional authority to control the bureaucracy?
   a. the president
   b. the Congress
   c. the courts
   d. all of the above

2. Why did a large federal bureaucracy emerge?
   a. The president mandated it.
   b. The courts mandated it.
   c. It was a response to public demands for governmental programs and action.
   d. None of the above

3. As a scholar, which of the following presidents wrote of a politics-administration dichotomy?
   a. Theodore Roosevelt
   b. Woodrow Wilson
   c. Jimmy Carter
   d. Bill Clinton

4. Of the various tools of political control of the bureaucracy, which of the following is the most important?
   a. the appointment power
   b. the budgetary power
   c. the removal power
   d. central clearance

5. Who do bureaucrats see as exerting the most influence over their agencies?
   a. presidents
   b. presidential appointments
   c. Congress
   d. interest groups

6. In which of the following cases did the Supreme Court rule unanimously that the president could remove an FTC commissioner from office only for malfeasance in office, neglect of duty, or inefficiency?
   a. *Curtis Wright*
   b. *Humphrey's Executor v. United States*
   c. *Marbury v. Madison*
   d. *Bush v. Gore*

7. Gerald Ford wrote, "A president controls his administration through the _____."
   a. appointment power
   b. budget
   c. reorganization power
   d. removal power

8. Which of the following is a means of reviewing all department, agency, and commission legislative proposals before they are transmitted to Congress?
   a. reorganization authority
   b. budgetary power
   c. removal power
   d. central clearance

Discussion Questions

1. Who should have primary control over the bureaucracy? Is presidential control of the bureaucracy necessary?
2. What can presidents do to increase their influence over the bureaucracy?
3. What can Congress do to increase its influence over the bureaucracy?
4. What techniques do presidents use to control the bureaucracy?

Notes

1. As a result, many presidential textbooks still portray the president as having only a limited role in overseeing the bureaucracy, a view I will challenge in section 10-4a, "Interest Groups and Political Influence."
2. Moe (1982), Stewart and Cromartie (1982), Wood and Anderson (1993), and Wood and Waterman (1993) provide additional empirical evidence demonstrating that agency outputs are sensitive to political appointments, particularly at the beginning of a new administration.
3. This latter finding is particularly interesting, for if the iron triangle or capture theory's basic assumptions were supported, the permittees would have been seen as having much more influence.
4. Since Roosevelt had not justified the termination on the basis of any of these criteria, the removal of William Humphrey was overturned. This decision provided a strong precedent limiting presidential removal power. The decision was later reaffirmed in the case of *Weiner v. United States* [357 U.S. 249 (1980)]. Nonetheless, the *Humphrey* decision placed restrictions only on presidential removal of executive branch officials who exerted "quasi-legislative" or "quasi-judicial" functions. The president could still remove, for any reason, other appointed officials serving in the executive branch.
5. In the case of deferral (which delays an expenditure for a period of time), Congress must vote to override, or the deferral is implemented. In the case of a recission (which, like an impoundment, prevents a congressional appropriation from being spent), congressional approval is necessary before the recission can be implemented. Since congressional approval is necessary for rescissions, most presidents have made more extensive use of deferrals as a means of slowing congressional spending. While the Supreme Court ruled the legislative veto unconstitutional in the *Immigration and Naturalization Service v. Chadha* [462 U.S. 919 (1983)] case, and Congress did move to repeal some legislative veto provisions, the technique is still used (Spitzer 1993: 123), as is the deferral and recission process. "The reason why presidents have quietly acquiesced to the quasi-legal devices that have, after *Chadha*, provided functional equivalents to the legislative veto: a requirement for affirmative legislation action on all measures now subject to the veto" would be required to replace it (Mezey 1989: 171). Hence, while all presidents since Hoover have questioned the legality of the legislative veto, they have not been eager to challenge it directly.
6. Along with the traditional notion of delegating program authority to states or local governments, recent presidents also have recommended privatization of federal functions or shifting governmental authority to private enterprises. This idea of privatizing federal functions derived from experiences on the state and local level in privatizing such functions as garbage collection. While there have been some successes with this approach at the federal and state levels, such as private postal services, the concept remains controversial.

The Presidency and the Political Ecosystem

Key Terms

borked
overload
political ecology/political
  ecosystem

11-1 The Presidency and the Political Ecosystem

While the study of institutions is important, over the past several decades, political science has concentrated its primary attention on the behavior of individuals (e.g., how can individual presidents be more effective leaders?). At the same time, the study of political institutions fell into disrepute. This happened because earlier studies of institutions generally were perceived to be descriptive and therefore atheoretical.[1] Yet, institutional power and design does matter! To understand this point, we need only look at the difference between the power of various political institutions when they were first established and their actual influence today. For instance, when the presidency and the courts were first created, they were defined only in the broadest of possible parameters. Their power and responsibilities today are far greater than they were in 1789 when George Washington became our first president.

In addition, Fisher (1987: ix) writes, "To study one branch of government in isolation from the others is usually an exercise in make-believe." In this chapter, I will extend this logic even further: To understand the institution of the presidency, we must understand its relationship with a variety of external political institutions. To do so, I introduce the concept of **political ecology** and **political ecosystems.** Ecology is defined as branch of biology dealing with the relations between living organisms and their environment. In the past decade, the study of ecosystems has moved beyond the natural to the social sciences. For example, the study of "industrial ecology" is a multidisciplinary study of factors related to the environment (see Allenby 1999). "Business ecology" involves an analysis of how businesses operate in a symbiotic fashion; that is, one company is likely to bring in market trade for another business located nearby (e.g., McDonald's at WalMart).

Like the environment or businesses, political institutions function together with (as we already have seen) changes in the power of one institution having a profound impact on the power and influence of other institutions. As Kennedy (2001: 227) notes, "Politics, no less than nature, abhors a vacuum." As one institution loses power and influence (e.g., the political parties) in our governmental system, its power does not disappear; it goes somewhere else, to another political actor or set of actors (e.g., the political parties lose power and the media and the presidency gain it).

Furthermore, expectations and demands for governmental action are constantly changing, often driven by changes in various contextual factors. This change also impacts multiple institutions of government. We often do not see this process when we examine the political world in the traditional fashion—that is, when we examine one or maybe two political institutions at a time. Rather than focusing on each institution separately, then, political ecology allows us to examine how institutions depend on and interact with each other, how power and influence flow from one institution to another over time, and how public demands for policy action and public expectations concomitantly shift from one institution to another. Consequently, for political ecosystems, instead of economic growth and markets, the concept of interest is power, as well as demands and expectations for political action.

11-2 Who Are the Actors in the Political Ecosystem?

A large and growing number of policy actors interact or compete in the political ecosystem. They compete for power and political influence, sometimes narrowly on particular issues, sometimes in a broader context with turf battles determining larger power-sharing relationships. In this process, over time, new political actors

Political ecology/political ecosystem: The political system as a whole, rather than its individual components (president, Congress, courts, public, interest groups, etc.). The focus is on where the public and other political actors look for leadership (or aim their demands for leadership) in the governmental system. The idea is that the political ecosystem is constantly changing or evolving over time, as individual institutions gain or lose influence, as public expectations of these institutions change, and as demands for action are aimed at different political actors.

are introduced, the influence of various existing actors changes, all generally occurring without formal constitutional amendment. Like an organism, the American political ecosystem evolves continuously. It has changed considerably from the days of the Founders to the dawn of the twenty-first century.

Figure 11-1 presents a rough approximation of nineteenth century political relationships, emphasizing the presidential separation from and dependency on other external political actors. Particularly with regard to domestic affairs, the presidency was subservient to the legislative branch and the political parties. Additionally, the political parties operated as a bridge between the presidency and various other external actors, including the media (with the parties controlling the partisan press), the public, and interest groups (relatively few of which were organized nationally). In this state of the political ecosystem, presidents had difficulty developing a direct constituency with the public. The presidency also was dependent on and subservient to Congress. Hence, institutionally, the presidency was most often a weak institution.

The arrows in Figure 11-1 (as well as in Figure 11-2) represent where demands (from both the public and elites) and expectations are aimed. In the nineteenth century, relatively few demands were aimed at the presidency. The office was more likely to respond to its constituencies (the parties and/or the Congress), rather than the public and the media. Relatively few policy demands were placed on the presidency, and it therefore had much less to do than it does today, both in domestic and foreign policy.

In contrast, in the twentieth and twenty-first centuries, the picture is much different. Admittedly, the many arrows represented in Figure 11-2 make it appear somewhat messy. That, in part, is the point. Almost all arrows now are aimed directly at the White House, meaning that expectations and demands for policy action are more likely to end up on the president's desk than on the desk of any other government official. Furthermore, these expectations and demands come from a wide array of policy actors. This can lead to **overload,** a situation in which too many demands and expectations are aimed at the presidential office. As the presidential office is overloaded, it is more difficult for all presidents to respond to growing demands for action. As a result, at least some of the policy actors delineated in Figure 11-2 are likely to be dissatisfied.

As can be seen in Figure 11-2, the presidency is now at the fulcrum, or center, of the American political system. While Congress may actually have more power and influence than it did in the nineteenth century, it does not dominate the presidency as it once did. In fact, some scholars, such as Spitzer (1993), describe it as

Overload: A situation in which too many demands and expectations are aimed at the presidential office. As the presidency is overloaded, it is more difficult for presidents to respond to growing demands for action.

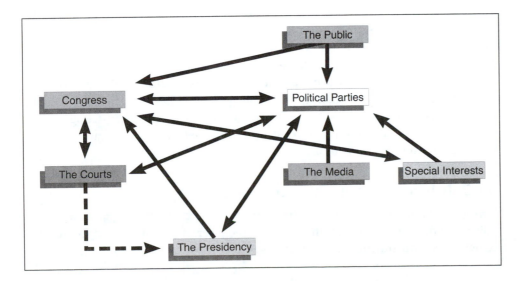

Figure 11-1
The Political Ecosystem in the Traditional Era, 1789–1898

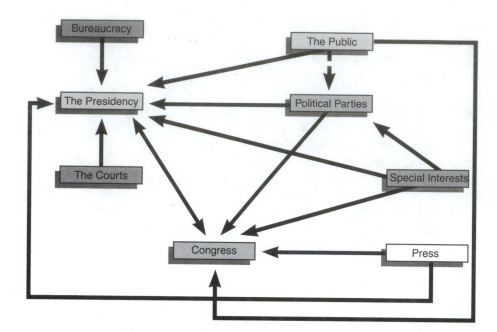

Figure 11-2
The Political Ecosystem in the Modern Political Era

subservient to the presidency; i.e., Congress waits for the president's budget and for the president to initiate legislation. Likewise, the power of the political parties has declined palpably. No longer do the parties provide an intermediary function between the president and the public. Rather, the parties, particularly at the national level, have become fundraisers and look for policy direction to the president (or if a party is out of power, it looks for ways to raise money and oppose the policies of the incumbent president).

The public, the media, special interests, and the political parties now interact directly with both the president and Congress. In addition, a new external political actor, the bureaucracy, is now an active participant in the political ecosystem. Other actors can be included as well, although they are not all represented in Figure 11-2, including state and local governments, foreign nations, and international organizations. Even interest groups and the courts are more dependent on the presidency today, as we shall see in sections 11-3 and 11-4.

11-2a How Does Overload Occur?

In section 11-2, we saw some examples of how overload can occur. As the influence of the political parties declines, presidents must take a more active role in cultivating public opinion and in establishing a workable relationship with the media (see section 7-7, "Franklin Roosevelt and Radio," section 7-14, "Television and the Presidency," section 8-1, "A New Intermediary: The Decline of the Political Parties and the Rise of the Media," and section 8-10, "Presidents and the Evolving Media"). Furthermore, as the Congress looks to the White House for policy leadership, the president must initiate policy, rather than wait for Congress to do so (see section 9-8a, "New Expectations for Presidential-Congressional Relations"). To understand this point more fully, let's take a look at some additional external political actors.

11-3 Interest Groups and the Presidency

Despite the Founders' concern with faction, interest groups have played a political role since our nation's beginning. While some interest groups looked to the presidency for action, during the nineteenth century, most turned their attention to the center of gravity in the political system: the U.S. Congress. Presidents were more likely to be lobbied by job seekers than they were by organized interest groups. As the influence of various actors in the political ecosystem changed over time, however, the interest groups began to broaden their lobbying effort. While they still concentrate much of their attention on Capitol Hill, they now are more active in lobbying the president, as well.

The expansion of federal programs during the New Deal, the Great Society, and the expansion of social regulatory agencies during the Nixon years encouraged the participation of new interest groups at the federal level, expanded the size of the bureaucracy, and provided a new pattern of relationships between interest groups and the federal government. The iron triangle relationships that developed in the 1930s brought interest groups into a politically intimate relationship with the executive branch, but not necessarily with the presidency (see Cater 1964; Freeman 1965). Over time, as the iron triangles weakened (Noll and Owen 1983; also see section 10-4a, "Interest Groups and Political Influence"), the president came to play a more active role in bureaucratic politics. In so doing, interest groups looked not only to the bureaucratic agencies and congressional committees, but also increasingly to the presidency (Waterman 1989). Thus, one effect of the growth of the federal government's role in domestic affairs has been to promote a more active presidential interaction with interest groups.

Beyond the growth of the federal bureaucracy, the decline of the parties also impacted presidential-interest group relations. As Pika (1993: 145) writes,

> Early in Franklin D. Roosevelt's third term in office, a cadre of White House aides was given the part-time assignment of maintaining liaison with organized interest groups. This new channel of interaction supplemented the traditional avenues of exchange between groups and presidents that had operated for nearly a century—political parties and government agencies.

In other words, as the influence of the political parties declined and as their ability to function as an intermediary was impaired, these functions were co-opted by the presidency. In turn, presidents found new ways to reach out to important interest groups. Hence, interests that once focused their attention toward the parties now looked directly to the White House instead (see section 13-5, "Internal Resources and the Changing Political Ecosystem").

As the number and variety of interest groups expanded over time, the tone of their political relationship changed, as well. In the past, interest groups represented broader coalitions of interests; e.g., labor unions, business organizations, civil rights groups. A president could oppose an interest group on one particular issue and yet continue to curry its favor by supporting something else that the group wanted. Interest group politics was therefore one of negotiation and compromise across a broader spectrum of issues, similar to the leadership model Neustadt (1980) describes between the president and Congress.

The rise of single-issue groups, however, made interest group demands more inflexible, leaving presidents with less room to compromise. Interest groups that represent only one issue, such as abortion or gun control, are less willing to compromise on their fundamental beliefs. Since there generally are different single-issue interest groups representing different sides of each controversial political issue (e.g., pro-choice and anti-abortion groups, pro- and anti-gun control groups), it often is impossible for presidents to satisfy all groups interested in a particular issue. The resulting opposition can translate into independently financed issue ads attacking the president, campaign contributions for the president's political opponents, and an organized effort on Capitol Hill to thwart the president's legislative initiatives.

The practice of lobbying also has changed. In the past, interest groups lobbied for political favor on Capitol Hill or in private with the president or more commonly with presidential subordinates. Some interest groups (e.g., labor or business) then threw their support behind a particular party or candidate in the primary or general presidential elections. Now, in their struggle for power, present-day political forces are "as likely to employ judicial and investigatory proceedings as presidential elections" (Ginsberg, Mebane, and Shefter 1995: 341). These venues (congressional hearings, court cases) bring interest group disagreements with the presidency out into the open. While backroom lobbying is still employed, interest groups are now willing to use more overt political methods when necessary. In summary, single-issue interest group politics focuses greater attention and criticism on presidents, leaves presidents with less room to compromise, and aims a variety of often conflicting demands for action directly at the White House. This is a fundamental change from the nineteenth century when presidents had limited interactions with interest groups.

11-4 The Courts

Interest groups are not the only political actors to become more politicized over time. While the judicial temperament of the courts would seem to guarantee a more objective legalistic approach, the courts too have become more politicized. The politicization of the courts is not entirely new. Washington was criticized for using Chief Justice John Jay to negotiate a treaty with England: the Jay Treaty. John Adams named a number of "midnight" judicial appointments after he lost his re-election bid to Thomas Jefferson in 1801. The purpose of these appointments, at least according to Jefferson and his supporters, was to stock the courts with Federalist judges. The Jeffersonians particularly were furious with the Adams appointment of John Marshall as Chief Justice of the Supreme Court. Jefferson urged his party in Congress to impeach a number of Adams's appointees. The emphasis on impeachment generally was not successful, however, and Jefferson and his party eventually abandoned the approach.

At least one nineteenth-century president even intervened to influence a Supreme Court decision. On February 3, 1857, President-elect James Buchanan wrote Supreme Court Justice John Catron and asked when the court would issue its opinion in the *Dred Scott v. Sanford* case. Seven days later, Buchanan wrote again, suggesting that some of the judges should write opinions mentioning territorial issues. Catron responded, telling Buchanan that the court would rule on the constitutionality of the Missouri Compromise. Buchanan wrote to other justices, as well, including a possible dissenter in the case (Stampp 1990: 91–92). Consequently, Buchanan knew what the court would decide prior to his inauguration and may even have influenced the scope of that decision. The independence of the judiciary was therefore compromised.

11-4a FDR and Court Packing

Politicization, as the examples in section 11-4 demonstrate, therefore existed in the nineteenth century, but it became more prevalent in the twentieth century. The most prominent case involved Franklin Roosevelt and his attempt to pack the Supreme Court. FDR's New Deal created a political backlash, first from the courts and later from Congress. On May 6, 1935, the Supreme Court declared the Railroad Retirement Act of 1934 to be unconstitutional. Then, as Kennedy (2000:

273) writes, "on May 27 a unanimous Court nullified the National Industrial Recovery Act, in terms so sweeping as to put at risk virtually all the New Deal legislation of the preceding two years." Kennedy continues (2000: 325), "[On] February 5, 1937, Roosevelt struck back with a special message to Congress. He asked for a statute that would allow the president to appoint one additional justice to the Supreme Court, up to a total of six new appointments, for every sitting justice who declined to retire at the age of seventy." It was a bold political act. While Roosevelt initially tried to justify it on efficiency grounds, the independence of the federal judiciary clearly was under assault.

After some initial indications that it would support the president's proposed amendment, Congress, including many of the president's most loyal partisans, rebelled. Whether Roosevelt knew it or not, he had declared open warfare on the judiciary.

As for the public, from the beginning, it was not enamored with the proposal. In the second week of February 1937, Gallup pollsters first asked, "Are you in favor of President Roosevelt's proposal regarding the Supreme Court?" In response, 45 percent said yes, 45 percent said no, and 10 percent were undecided. Within two weeks, support for the proposal declined to 41 percent, with 48 percent opposed. Roosevelt then delivered a Fireside Chat to explain the proposal on March 9, but the speech had little impact on public opinion. Once again, 45 percent favored it, 45 percent opposed it (Davis 1993: 75). Without congressional or public support, the court-packing legislation was not enacted.

Still, as Kennedy (2000: 331) writes, what became disparagingly known as the court-packing proposal "was a calculated risk, and not an unreasonable one." Roosevelt "was wagering a modest challenge to the tradition of an independent judiciary against the prospect of the entire New Deal's extinction." In the end, Roosevelt won at best a Pyrrhic victory. Whether as a result of intimidation, reflection, or other factors, Justice Robert Owens shifted and voted with the liberal justices—the famous "switch in time that saved nine"—thus upholding New Deal initiatives, including, importantly, the Wagner Act and the unemployment provisions of the Social Security Act of 1935. Shortly thereafter, Justice Van Devanter announced his retirement. In the end, Roosevelt made eight appointments to the Supreme Court, thus entirely altering its focus. As a result, "for at least half a century thereafter, the Court did not overturn a single piece of significant state or national socioeconomic legislation" (ibid., 337).

11-4b The Warren Court

Following Roosevelt's court-packing initiative, the battle for the soul of the Supreme Court turned to constitutionally prescribed mechanisms—in particular, the appointment power. As noted in section 11-4a, Roosevelt named eight justices who shared his basic political philosophy. Yet, it was Dwight Eisenhower, a Republican, who inadvertently initiated the most liberal era in the court's history when he named Earl Warren, the Republican governor of California, as Chief Justice. The Warren Court issued a number of controversial decisions. In a series of cases, it applied the Bill of Rights to the states and decided on behalf of expanded civil liberties and civil rights. Conservatives complained that the Warren Court was more concerned with the rights of offenders than with the rights of victims and ignored states rights. Then-Representative Gerald Ford became the leader of a movement to impeach Earl Warren, but the court continued to issue liberal opinions that outraged conservatives.

11-4c *Roe v. Wade* and the Politicization of the Appointment Process

The Supreme Court case that most angered conservatives was decided at the beginning of the era of Chief Justice Warren Burger, Earl Warren's replacement. In 1973, the Supreme Court issued an extremely controversial decision in the case of *Roe v. Wade*. Not only did the Supreme Court's decision legalize abortion, but it also ignited a political firestorm that continues to burn to this day and now extends well beyond the abortion issue. With a wide variety of controversial issues winding their way to the Supreme Court, the media and interest groups are more attentive to the court's activities. The public is asked its opinion on controversial court cases. Members of Congress are critical of the court and its liberal or conservative bias. As a result, the nomination process for judges, particularly to the Supreme Court but even to the District and Appellate courts, has been politicized.

While presidents regularly disavow using a litmus test (such as naming only pro-choice judges to the courts), an increasingly important criterion for nomination is the ideology of the judge (see Box 11-1). This is the case even at the district court level (see Carp and Rowland 1983). With ideology and politics playing a more important role, there have been a number of high-profile battles over court nominees since the Johnson and Nixon presidencies. Lyndon Johnson's decision to elevate his friend and political adviser, Supreme Court Justice Abe Fortas, to Chief Justice foundered as allegations were raised about various ethical improprieties.

The real fight for the court's soul, however, appears to coincide with the beginning of divided government. Richard Nixon failed in his attempts to appoint two justices who had expressed pro-segregationist views. Jimmy Carter made no Supreme Court appointments, but controversy erupted again during Ronald Reagan's presidency—in particular, Robert Bork's nomination to the Supreme Court. Whereas Fortas had been opposed, ostensibly for ethical reasons, and while Nixon's nominees had been opposed for holding segregationist views, the argument now was that Bork was unqualified because he was too extreme politically. As an academic, Bork had a voluminous publication record, thus providing a chart of his political transformation from liberal to conservative. When the Senate failed to confirm Bork, a new verb was added to the political lexicon: Getting **borked** meant that one's fate had been deleteriously determined by political considerations.

Bork was but the first of several nominees for various positions to get borked. George H. W. Bush's nominee for Secretary of Defense, John Tower, was rejected by the Senate because he was alleged to have drank too much. Bush's later appointment of Clarence Thomas to the Supreme Court engendered passionate support and opposition. Thomas, like Bork, was considered by some groups to be too conservative to be on the court. Opposition to the Thomas nomination exploded, however, when Anita Hill accused him of having made unwanted and inappropriate sexual comments. Overnight, the Thomas nomination became a media circus, with liberals arguing that Thomas was unfit, not because of his views, but because of his behavior. Conservatives countered that the charges were baseless and that the real reason Thomas was under attack was that he was a die-hard conservative. In the end, the Senate narrowly confirmed Thomas, but political fights over select judicial nominees' political views continue to be a relevant criterion in the confirmation process.

Borked: A term that refers to a political appointee's fate being deleteriously determined by political considerations.

11-4d *Bush v. Gore*

Charges that the courts have been politicized may have reached their zenith with the decision in the case of *Bush v. Gore*. In December 2000, by a five-to-four deci-

Box 11-1

Filling a Vacancy on the Supreme Court

If you were the president, how would you select a new justice for the Supreme Court? Answer the poll choices below on three current controversial issues and overall political position, and then see how your answers compare with those of your classmates.

My nominee would be:

Issue 1: Abortion

Pro-choice	Yes	No
Anti-abortion	Yes	No

Issue 2: Gun Control

Anti gun control	Yes	No
Pro gun control	Yes	No

Issue 3: School Vouchers

For school vouchers	Yes	No
Opposed to school vouchers	Yes	No

Overall Political Position:

Very conservative	Yes	No
Somewhat conservative	Yes	No
Moderate/a possible swing voter, depending on the issue involved	Yes	No
Somewhat liberal	Yes	No
Very liberal	Yes	No

sion, the Supreme Court decided to stop the recount in the contested state of Florida, essentially awarding the presidency to George W. Bush. The Florida Supreme Court had issued several rulings favorable to Al Gore, thus creating the impression that both candidates had their own loyal courts in the case. Later, *Newsweek* magazine revealed that on election night Supreme Court Justice Sandra Day O'Connor, a former Republican officeholder, had been very upset when the television networks erroneously announced that Al Gore had won Florida. Her husband, *Newsweek* alleged, explained to startled onlookers that his wife had hoped to retire, but that now with a Democrat in the White House, she would be unable to do so.

This allegation suggested a possible political motivation for the court's decision, not a legal one. In addition, conservative members of the court, who generally ruled in favor of states rights, had intervened on behalf of the federal government over the state of Florida. By basing the decision on the equal protection clause of the Constitution, a provision the same members had regularly ignored when raised in other (civil rights) cases, and by declaring that the decision was not meant to create a precedent, the justices raised further questions about their political motives. In the end, the independence of the judiciary was questioned. Whether the decision was, in fact, made on political grounds or not, there was a broad perception that the court had indeed voted for president. Many Democrats believed, then, that Al Gore had been borked. The politicization of the courts is therefore likely to continue. Thus, the relationship between the president and the courts is far different today than it was in the nineteenth century.

11-5 The Independent Counsel

Another way in which the judiciary has been politicized was via the establishment of the Office of the Independent Counsel. This Watergate era reform was designed to ensure that presidents could not name their own prosecutors when they were accused of a crime. The fact that Richard Nixon had fired Special Prosecutor Archibald Cox, when Cox pursued the Nixon tapes too aggressively, raised fundamental questions. How can we fairly investigate executive branch officials, and how can we ensure that the investigators have the necessary resources to follow through with an independent investigation?

Congress responded by establishing the Independent Counsel. According to the law, once the Attorney General determined that an independent counsel was needed, a three-judge panel of the special division of the District Court of Columbia federal court of appeals selected the Independent Counsel. The counsel then was provided with the necessary staff and resources to conduct an investigation (see Johnson and Brickman 2001). The process seemed logical, especially in the wake of the Watergate scandals. The problem was that Independent Counsels virtually had open-ended authority, meaning investigations expanded and the investigations often extended beyond the president's term of office.

At first, Republicans argued that the Independent Counsel had too much authority, as Republican presidents were the first to be impacted by the act's provisions. The Iran-Contra investigation during the Reagan presidency raised questions about President Reagan's conduct and his qualifications (was he too detached from the decision-making process to continue as president?). It also raised questions about Vice President George H. W. Bush. A number of administration officials were later indicted, though some of the convictions were later overturned (e.g., Oliver North's conviction). As president, George H. W. Bush even pardoned former Secretary of Defense Caspar Weinberger, even though it was possible that Weinberger may have had evidence that could have implicated Bush in the Iran-Contra investigations. Democrats cried foul.

Yet, Democrats too joined the chorus of critics of the Independent Counsel law when Bill Clinton became its target. The Whitewater investigation was ostensibly designed to examine Bill and Hillary Clinton's business investments in a Whitewater real estate development. It ended up raising questions about whether the president lied to a grand jury about sexual matters. While the president was impeached (though not convicted) and ended up accepting a modest deal with the Independent Counsel's office (admitting that he had not been entirely truthful, while his law license was suspended), both political parties had had enough. The Independent Counsel law was allowed to expire. Consequently, for the time being, there is one less external actor in the president's political ecosystem.

11-6 Other External Actors

As can be seen in Figure 11-2, presidents interact with a wide variety of external political actors. Providing a detailed analysis of each of these actors is clearly beyond the scope of this book. It is clear that demands for presidential action emanate from a variety of new political venues. Presidents today must be aware of the demands and policy expectations of mayors, governors, and other state-level actors. Presidents now regularly interact with other foreign leaders and with a wide range of international organizations (the Organization of American States, the North Atlantic Treaty Organization, the United Nations, etc.). Presidents are subject to lobbying by foreign-based investors and companies. In summary, throughout the twentieth century not only did the presidency take on greater prominence in the political ecosystem, but the number of external political actors that presidents deal with also expanded. How did these demands/expectations change over time, and how and why did the political ecosystem change? The answer to these questions not only allows us to synthesize much of the material from the first ten chapters of this book, but it also provides a more theoretical answer to the question of why the presidential office has changed over time.

11-7 Why Do Political Ecosystems Change?

Why do political ecosystems change? The examination of contextual factors and four political resources (personal, legal, electoral, and external) suggests there are two primary explanations. First, changes occur incrementally but continuously over time. Often, these changes occur in response to changing contextual factors (see section 2-1, "The Contextual Revolution in America: The Economy, Foreign Affairs, and Changing Public Expectations"). For instance, from 1890 to 1920, the nation's population doubled, and by the 1920s, for the first time, more people lived in the cities than anywhere else; by 1930, only 44 percent of the nation's population lived in rural areas (Kennedy 2000: 16).

Accelerated industrialization and urbanization created new demands for federal governmental action (e.g., regulation of the food and drug industries, the railroad industries, and the trusts). This, in turn, altered public expectations of the presidency and the federal system: People now began to look to Washington, rather than their individual states, for policy action. Congress, with its deliberative and highly decentralized decision-making system, was far less capable of responding quickly to these demands than was the presidency, with its energy invested in a single executive. When Theodore Roosevelt introduced a new, more vigorous model of presidential leadership, the public was further encouraged to look to the White House for leadership.

11-7a Institutional Developments

The development of a national media also played a critical role in the evolution of the presidency. Media reporting of the externalities generated by industrialization and urbanization created increased public demands for action and altered public expectations. Likewise, the media provided a new intermediary for presidents to communicate directly with the public, thus allowing presidents to develop a new and powerful constituency beyond the political parties and Congress (their traditional constituents of the nineteenth century). Concomitantly, the power of the political parties was undermined because presidents no longer had to rely on them to interface with the public.

Hence, multiple institutional factors contributed to the increased prominence of the presidency. This is an important point. If we focus on the presidency alone, we get a distorted view of how the power of the presidency changes over time. We tend to see it as initiated by innovative presidents who struck out in bold directions, taking advantage of the circumstances of the time to create a new presidential office. While certain presidents did innovate, the rise of the presidency to a position of increased power is also intricately related to changes in other political institutions and trends that occur more slowly over time. For example, despite Theodore Roosevelt's interest in strengthening the presidency, it is doubtful he could have done so without at least a nascent national media. The evolution of the media, then, is an important factor promoting the growth of presidential power. Over time, the decline of the political parties also was a critical prerequisite to the accretion of presidential power. Had the parties remained strong and vigorous, had the presidential primaries not been established, it would have been much more difficult for presidents to reach out directly to the American public. As we shall see in section 15-4d, "Party Decline and a New Appointment Process," the parties also would have continued to fight to control important presidential functions, such as the appointment process, and a prime ministerial type of government may have been more likely to emerge.

Changes in other political institutions also were relevant to the growth of presidential power. Conflict within Congress (as exemplified by the 1910 revolt against the Speaker of the House) contributed to further decentralization of the legislative branch to the committee level. As Congress became more decentralized, the presidency was moving in the opposite direction—toward greater centralization of authority. These dual developments provided an opportunity for presidential power to expand. Had Congress found organizational mechanisms to centralize authority, rather than continuing to decentralize, the political system today might be far different in practice than the one we have.

Therefore, to chart the rise of the presidency in our governmental system, we need to examine the history of the presidency's relationship with a variety of other political institutions. Their rise and fall also are directly related to the president's place in our governmental system. An examination of the political ecosystem allows us to examine presidential power in an institutionally comparative context.

11-7b New Issue Areas

In addition to institutional change, new issue areas also increased the possibility of increased presidential power. As Lowi (1964) notes, in the nineteenth century, most policies were distributive and, hence, were more likely to involve congressional action. In the twentieth century, there was more of an emphasis on regulatory and redistributive policies, which are more conflictual. The latter policy type promoted a more pluralist political environment, one in which the president often was intricately involved.

In addition, as the nineteenth century ended, there was a new focus on foreign policy. This too contributed to an expansion in the president's role as commander-in-chief. As this foreign policy role further expanded during the twentieth century, it provided the president with greater visibility and more important functions. Likewise, it further focused expectations directly toward the White House and its primary inhabitant.

11-7c Shocks to the Ecosystem

As section 11-7b describes, change occurs continuously, often incrementally, but there is another way that political ecosystems change: A major event can alter a political system's equilibrium. A powerful event (or shock) can suddenly and radically alter public and elite expectations. For instance, the Great Depression of 1929 through roughly 1941 provided a shock, creating new public expectations of government's proper role, as well as accentuating changes already underway (the decline of the parties, the increased prominence of the media, the prominence of the president as initiator of legislation, and Congress's greater proclivity to defer to the White House). It also promoted a sudden expansion in the size and functions of the bureaucracy and, as noted in sections 11-4 through 11-4d, contributed to the politicization of the courts. As David Kennedy (2000: 10) writes in his Pulitzer Prize–winning study of the depression and World War II, "The tumult of crisis and reform in the ten depression years massively enlarged and forever transformed the scanty Jeffersonian government over which Herbert Hoover had been elected to preside in 1928." An event, a crisis, a stimulus, a shock promoted a permanent change in the American political ecosystem.

Figure 11-3 presents a time line identifying various shocks to the political ecosystem that impacted the power of the presidency. I identify four in the nineteenth century, five in the twentieth century, and one, thus far, in the twenty-first century.

Nineteenth Century				
1789	**1800**	**1824–1844**	**1860–1868**	**1898–1901**
	Jefferson's revolution of 1800	Jacksonian democracy and the backlash against Van Buren and John Tyler	Lincoln, the Civil War, Reconstruction, and the impeachment of Andrew Johnson	The Spanish-American War and the assassination of William McKinley

Twentieth Century				
1918–1921	**1929–1941**	**1941–1945**	**1946–1952**	**1966–1974**
The League of Nations and Budget and Accounting Act	The Great Depression and the New Deal	World War II	The beginning of the Cold War	Vietnam and Watergate

Twenty-First Century
2001
War on terrorism

Figure 11-3
Shocks to the Political Ecosystem Affecting the Presidency

In the nineteenth century, the Jeffersonian revolution of 1800 first altered the political ecosystem. As a result of the election, the party system was reaffirmed—ironically, even as the Federalist Party began its descent into oblivion. The presidency developed, even if it was for a short time period, a close relationship with both Congress and the Democratic/Republican Party. In this relationship, the president was virtually an equal partner. Jeffersonian democracy, including his views about the role of government (smaller government, a smaller military), was therefore combined with a more active presidency. While the Jeffersonian presidency was followed by the ascension of the political parties and Congress, and the decline of the presidency (setting a precedent for the rest of the nineteenth century), a preliminary model of active presidential leadership also had been introduced.

The second and third shocks to the political ecosystem in the nineteenth century were the result of strong presidential leadership followed by a powerful congressional backlash against the presidency. In both cases, the ultimate result was a weakened presidency (though an occasional strong president, such as James Polk, was able to emerge). In the period from 1829–1837, Jacksonian democracy emerged, and the presidency again, as it had with Jefferson, stepped to the center of the governmental process. When Jackson retired, however, Congress reasserted itself, first against Martin Van Buren and then more palpably against John Tyler. The threat of impeachment was even raised against Tyler for issuing three constitutionally legal vetoes (see section 9-4a, "Backlash").

In the next shock, impeachment actually occurred. Lincoln again raised the prominence and power of the presidency. His reconstruction policies proved particularly controversial, and after Lincoln's assassination, Andrew Johnson struggled (often ineptly) with Congress for control of the policy process. The House responded by impeaching Johnson, and the Senate came within one vote of convicting him. As a consequence, the power of the presidency reached its nadir under the next president, Ulysses Grant.

The final shock to the political ecosystem in the nineteenth century, however, began the trend toward increased presidential power. Congress induced a reluctant president, William McKinley, to go to war against Spain. The resulting war, though brief, provided a rationale for a continuing role for the president as commander-in-chief. With territorial possessions, temporarily in Cuba and over a longer period in the Philippines, presidents now had a continuing foreign policy role. The assassination of William McKinley in 1901 (actually at the beginning of the twentieth century) then brought Theodore Roosevelt, an advocate of strong presidential leadership, to the White House. A fundamental transformation in the presidency was about to occur.

In the twentieth century, the first shock to the ecosystem, the Senate's fight over the League of Nations treaty, following World War I, is important for what it did not do. While the Senate struck back against a powerful president, this time the backlash was limited only to the incumbent. Once Wilson was gone from the scene, Congress actually delegated greater authority to the presidency in 1921 with the Budget and Accounting Act. Hence, the pattern of the nineteenth century was broken. Rather than constraining the power of the presidency, Congress actually increased presidential power.

The Great Depression then transformed public and elite expectations of the domestic policy presidency, increasing presidential power and responsibility, as well as further expanding the size and functions of the bureaucracy. During this period, the modern presidency was institutionalized. Franklin Roosevelt also built strong constituencies with the public through the media, while further reducing the influence of the political parties. Most important of all, the idea that the president should initiate policy, which Jefferson and Wilson had introduced, was never again challenged. From then on, it was the president who proposed and the Congress that disposed.

The Great Depression and the New Deal did little to alter the president's power in foreign affairs, however. Following the presidencies of Theodore Roosevelt and Woodrow Wilson, Congress had reasserted its influence in this policy domain. The League of Nations treaty fight, then, did represent a backlash against the presidency in foreign affairs. World War II, however, provided an opportunity for Roosevelt to take the presidency onto the world stage. It also provided the basis for a buildup of the American military, brought the world into the nuclear age, and raised questions about the viability of an isolationist foreign policy.

It is unclear whether isolationism would have reasserted itself after the war, as Roosevelt believed it would. We are unsure because the Cold War immediately followed the Second World War. With the Cold War America now had a continuous military threat, the Soviet Union, China, and international communism. Presidents now had a reason to be commander-in-chief twenty-four hours a day, seven days a week. While the debate over isolationism continued into the early 1950s, ultimately resolved with the so-called Great Debate in Congress, both political parties eventually rejected isolationism in favor of an internationalist approach to foreign policy. The continuing use of power by the presidency in foreign affairs was now assured.[2]

Presidential power continued to grow throughout the next decades until the experiences of Lyndon Johnson and Richard Nixon raised questions about the threat of an "imperial presidency" (see Schlesinger 1973). As noted in section 7-11, "The State of the Economy," the Vietnam War and the Watergate scandal fundamentally changed public attitudes about the federal government. From high levels of trust, solid majorities soon said they did not trust their own government. The scandals also changed the tone of Washington politics. The politics that had encouraged Neustadt's (1980) bargaining presidency were replaced by more aggressive politics that forced presidents to go over the heads of elected officials directly to the public (Kernell 1997). Facing a more hostile political environment, a number of presidents found it difficult to succeed. Scholars began to talk about excessive and unrealistic expectations and the ultimate failure of the modern presidency (Lowi 1985).

The twenty-first century already has experienced a shock to the political ecosystem. The terrorist attacks on September 11, 2001, had an immediate impact on presidential power. Not only did the nation look to the White House for leadership, as it does in all crises, solid majorities suddenly expressed trust in their government. Congress quickly enacted legislation that delegated broad power to the presidency. Most importantly, the end of the Cold War in 1989 had robbed the presidency of a constant foreign threat: Communism. As of September 11, however, presidents had a new reason to be aggressive in foreign affairs: the war on terrorism. Thus, the power of the presidency, once again, was in ascendancy.

A brief note should be made about a few events that I do not list as shocks to the political ecosystem. World War I can be included as a continuation of the Senate's rejection of the League of Nations treaty. The end of the Cold War may have encouraged the development of a post-modern presidency (Rose 1991) in which the resources available to the presidency are in decline (as well as ultimate presidential power). Presidents of the late 1980s and 1990s, however, found new military adventures in Panama, the Persian Gulf, Bosnia, and Kosovo. As noted, the events of September 11, 2001, have presented presidents with a new, continuing military threat: terrorism.

Finally, while the impeachment of Andrew Johnson witnessed a fundamental transformation in the power of the presidency, the impeachment of William Jefferson Clinton did not. Not only did Clinton survive the impeachment, he actually appeared to thrive politically. His approval ratings soared and his political influence developed even after impeachment, as he sent troops to Kosovo and bested Congress in its annual budget battles. Hence, Clinton's impeachment did not rise to the level of a shock to the political ecosystem because presidential power was not fundamentally transformed.

11-8 Dimensions of Presidential Leadership Prompting Changes in the Political Ecosystem

Another way to consider changes in the political ecosystem is with reference to three dimensions of presidential leadership (see Box 11-2).

11-8a The Legal Dimension

The first dimension of presidential leadership is constitutional or legal factors. As we discussed in section 4-3, "Constitutional Ambiguity," and section 5-8, "Constitutional Ambiguity, Expectations, and Extra-Constitutional Powers," there is a high level of ambiguity related to most presidential legal resources. Presidents, therefore, have been able to redefine their Article II powers without need for constitutional amendment. While this ability allows presidents to justify specific actions, it has not provided a broad resource base for increased presidential power. Rather, strictly interpreted, the constitutional and legal dimension tends to narrow the feasible set of presidential options. It alone does not provide an adequate explanation why the presidency has changed.

Box 11-2

Three Dimensions of Presidential Leadership

Dimension 1: Constitutional/Legal Resources/Constraints

1. Constitutional or legal factors narrow the feasible set of options, while ambiguity increases the ability of presidents to redefine their authority.
2. Constitutional or legal factors thus provide loose constraints on presidential power. They are not likely to lead to major changes in the power of the presidency unless fundamental changes are made to the Constitution itself.

Dimension 2: Expectations of the Public and Elites

1. Where do people look for leadership?
2. The expectations of the public and the elite define who has influence in our political system.
3. Unlike legal resources, these expectations are highly malleable, changing quickly and without need for constitutional amendment or new legislation.
4. These expectations provide greater uncertainty but greater potential as well.

Dimension 3: Contextual Factors

1. Contextual factors concern such demographic factors as the nation's urban/rural breakdown.
2. Industrialization, immigration, urbanization, and other contextual factors can create new demands for governmental action and can transfer demands from one level of government (local or state) to another (federal).
3. New demands for government action can also impact other institutions; centralization of economic power encouraged the development of centralized media power. On the other hand, the decentralized nature of Congress makes it is less likely to be able to deal with these centralizing tendencies.
4. New technologies, particularly in transportation and communications, can create new opportunities for presidential leadership (better communication with the public) and/or new demands on the presidential office (by introducing new issues such as stem cell research or cloning).

11-8b The Expectations Dimension

The second dimension presented in Box 11-2 relates to expectations, both public and elite. This involves the question, Where do people look for leadership? In part, expectations are constrained by the legal dimension. If the Constitution says that all appropriation bills commence in the House, then this conditions expectations. Yet, it does not always do so. The Constitution says that the Congress shall declare war; yet, today many people look first to the president, not to Congress, when war is on the horizon. The legal and constitutional dimension thus represents a loose constraint, rather than a firm one.

As we have seen throughout this book, expectations change over time. At the Founding, the legislative branch was expected to be the dominant political actor in the governmental system, and for more than 100 years, it was. While the Constitution does not deal with political parties, they quickly came to play an important organizing role in American politics. People came to expect them to nominate candidates, to generate policy ideas (platforms), to lead the political opposition, and so on.

Expectations are much more malleable than are constitutional and legal constraints. No amendment to the Constitution or new legislation is required to change expectations. Just as importantly, as expectations shift, the actual influence of political actors can shift, as well. If we expect the Congress to deal with an economic calamity, we look to the legislative branch for leadership, as Americans did throughout the nineteenth century. If, for whatever reason, people begin to look to the White House instead for leadership in hard economic times, then that places not only new burdens on the presidency (for, presumably, the president must deliver or will fail to satisfy expectations), but it also provides presidents with new opportunities to develop presidential power.

Changing expectations help explain why Congress has not declared a war since World War II. The Constitution still requires Congress to do so, but we now look to the White House for leadership on foreign affairs. If the commander-in-chief says that we need to commit U.S. forces in a far-away land, many people believe we should defer to the president's will. Expectations could change again, however. If the president commits the United States armed forces to another ill-considered military venture (many argue that Korea and Vietnam were ill-considered), then the public could alter their expectations yet again and focus instead on the more deliberative congressional setting. Again, no law will be needed to change public expectations.

Finally, increasing expectations also increase the level of political uncertainty. As expectations increase, there is a greater potential for an increase in presidential power, but presidents also must be successful in responding to these expectations. If an expectations gap is created, then presidents may find their power and influence threatened. Expectations thus provide both potential political benefits, as well as risks.

11-8c The Contextual Dimension

The third dimension in Box 11-2 consists of contextual factors. Whether the nation is predominantly urban or rural has an impact on the level of demands the public places on governments at various levels (local, state, and federal). Likewise, industrialization, immigration, threats to national security, the centralization of business (e.g., the rise of corporations), corporate crime (e.g., Enron), even new technologies (providing new means of transportation and communication) can have a direct impact on what government does and which political actor we expect to act; that is, do we look primarily to the local and state level, or do we begin to look to Washington? Do we look for action at the legislative or executive branch of government, or perhaps (as in the case of the civil rights movement), to the judiciary?

Contextual factors are of major importance in understanding the transformation of the political ecosystem and the presidency's place in it. Yet, most texts on the presidency examine contextual factors only peripherally. They often are worthy of mention, but not of an extended discussion. Few attempts are made to show how changes in our society (new business innovations such as the development of the corporation and the new leadership model it provided) are related to the rise of presidential power. Yet, the presidency, like other formal and informal governmental institutions, does not operate in a vacuum. It continuously responds to and is affected by changes in the political environment.

Various factors (industrialization, urbanization, immigration, technological development, new business leadership models, and many others) all contributed to the evolution of the presidency and the political ecosystem. Many of these factors contributed to a tendency to look first to the federal government, rather than the state and local governments, for policy action. Many also contributed to a tendency to look to the White House rather than to Capitol Hill. As a result, they help us to understand how and why expectations changed.

What is interesting is that most often scholars tend to focus on the first two dimensions in Box 11-2: constitutional/legal resources/constraints and expectations. Yet, unless we examine contextual factors, we have only a limited basis for understanding why expectations change, for an analysis of the constitutional/legal dimension mainly tells us why they do not change.

Chapter Summary

An analysis of contextual factors and their relationship to the political ecosystem provides a stronger theoretical basis for understanding the evolution of presidential power. Most importantly, it also tells us that the evolutionary process will continue. The presidency that we have at the beginning of the twenty-first century will likely be far different from the presidency at mid-century. As new contextual factors further alter public and elite expectations, the presidency and the other policy actors in the political ecosystem will continue to evolve. To better understand this point, we need to move beyond a focus on the president's external political resources. In Chapters 12 through 15, we turn our attention to the development of the president's new political resources.

Review Questions

1. Which of the following was the presidency's constituency in the nineteenth century?
   a. the public
   b. political parties
   c. the media
   d. the bureaucracy

2. Which of the following was a new constituency in the twentieth century?
   a. the public
   b. political parties
   c. the media
   d. the bureaucracy

3. Which of the following was a new participant in the political ecosystem in the twentieth century?
   a. the public
   b. political parties
   c. the media
   d. the bureaucracy

4. In the past, interest groups represented broad coalitions. Now they are more likely to represent
   a. single issues.
   b. multiple issues.
   c. bi-polar issues.
   d. tri-polar issues.

5. Which of the following presidents tried to pack the Supreme Court?
   a. Theodore Roosevelt
   b. Franklin Roosevelt
   c. Richard Nixon
   d. Ronald Reagan

6. As a member of the House of Representatives, which of the following future presidents led the movement to impeach Earl Warren?
   a. John F. Kennedy
   b. Richard Nixon
   c. Gerald Ford
   d. Bill Clinton

7. Which of the following shocks represented a congressional backlash against the presidency in the political ecosystem?
   a. the League of Nations and the Budget and Impoundment Act
   b. the Civil War
   c. Jacksonian Democracy and John Tyler
   d. the Cold War

8. Scholars have not paid sufficient attention to the effect of which of the following on presidential power?
   a. legal resources
   b. foreign policy conflicts
   c. contextual factors
   d. internal resources

Discussion Questions

1. Does it make sense to study political institutions only one at a time? What do we gain by examining them in a comparative context?

2. How do changes in the power and influence of one political institution impact the power and influence of other political actors?

3. How did the political ecosystem become more complicated for presidents in the twentieth and twenty-first centuries? What is overload, and why is it important?

Notes

1. Though over time, a theory of institutions, referred to as "neo-institutionalism," developed (see North 1981; Davis and North 1971), these approaches focused on how various economic incentives led to changes in the nature of institutions (e.g., the incentive structures that led to the formation of the corporate firm).

2. For an excellent analysis of this period, see Leffler 1992.

The President's Cabinet: An Internal or External Political Resource?

Key Terms

cabinet councils
kitchen cabinet
super-secretaries

12-1 The President's Cabinet: An Internal or External Political Resource?

Thus far in this book, we have examined the president's traditional political resources: personal, legal, electoral, and external. In this chapter, we examine the president's cabinet, an institution that is somewhat of a cross between an external and an internal resource (a formal or informal mechanism developed directly within the White House). The cabinet has the characteristics of an internal resource in that the president appoints its secretaries and other top officials and can remove recalcitrant members. The president can meet with department secretaries individually or as a group.

On the other hand, in addition to representing the president's interests, cabinet secretaries also are the heads of their respective departments (State, Defense, Treasury, Labor, etc.). In this capacity, at times, they have been more attentive to the needs of Congress, which provides the resources (budget and staffing) for their agencies, and the interest groups they represent (the Labor Department deals with organized labor, for instance). As Fenno (1959) writes,

> Cabinet members themselves are inextricably involved in the activities of the legislature, the bureaucracy, the political parties, and the political interest groups. The Cabinet, and especially its individual members, participates in a great multiplicity of external relationships which are not in the first instance matters of its internal characteristics nor of its presidential tie.

Consequently, the loyalty of a cabinet secretary can and often has been divided between what is best for the president and what is best for his or her own department and its external constituencies. In this regard, then, the cabinet represents an external political resource. In this chapter, we therefore ask a simple question: Is the president's cabinet an internal or external political resource, and can it serve the president's policy interests?

12-2 What Is the Cabinet?

The cabinet consists of a number of executive departments. Table 12-1 presents the various cabinet posts and the year they were created. The date of a department's creation is important, for it is related to presidential succession. The next in line behind the president is the vice president, the Speaker of the House, and then the President Pro Tempore of the U.S. Senate. After that, the Secretary of State is next in line, followed by the secretaries of the various departments in the order in which they were created. For instance, one of the cabinet secretaries traditionally does not attend the state of the union address so that someone in the presidential chain of succession is available to serve should, for example, there be a terrorist attack on Capitol Hill. Table 12-1 also presents the names of the initial appointees to George W. Bush's cabinet.

The cabinet also is informally divided into inner and outer cabinet positions, the former generally having the most prestige and influence. While the inner cabinet (the Secretaries of the State, Defense, Justice, and Treasury Departments) deals broadly with important issues that affect the nation (e.g., foreign policy, the economy, the law), the outer cabinet usually has more particularized interests and constituencies (e.g., agriculture, interior, labor, commerce, housing, etc.). At times, individual presidents elevate a particular cabinet secretary to inner cabinet status (e.g., at times, the Commerce Secretary or Trade Representative is elevated to this unofficial rank, depending on a particular president's interests and the important issues of the time). As the designations suggest, a member of the inner cabinet is

T A B L E   **12-1** **Cabinet Offices and the Years Established**

Cabinet Office	Year Established	Secretary as of 2001
State	1789	Colin Powell
Treasury	1789	Paul O'Neill
War	1789	(office no longer exists)
Navy	1798	(no longer cabinet department)
Interior	1849	Gale Norton
Justice	1870	John Ashcroft
Post Office	1872	(no longer cabinet department)
Agriculture	1889	Anne M. Veneman
Commerce and Labor	1903	(office divided in 1913)
Commerce	1913	Don Evans
Labor	1913	Elaine Chao
Defense	1947	Donald Rumsfeld
Health, Education and Welfare	1953	(office reconstituted in 1979)
Housing and Urban Development	1965	Mel Martinez
Transportation	1966	Norman Mineta
Energy	1977	Spencer Abraham
Education	1979	Rod Paige
Health and Human Services	1979	Tommy Thompson
Veterans Affairs	1989	Anthony Principi
Department of Homeland Security	2002	Thomas Ridge

Sources: Stanley and Niemi (2000: 248–49) and the White House website at www.Whitehouse.gov.

generally more influential than a member of the outer cabinet, though the influence of individual members and departments also varies over time. For example, during the Nixon presidency, the positions of Secretary of State William Rogers and Defense Secretary Melvin Laird had less real authority because the president and his National Security Council adviser Henry Kissinger conducted foreign policy out of the White House. Generally, however, being a member of the inner cabinet means having greater power and prestige.

In addition to these departments and offices, particular presidents often invite different appointees to join the cabinet (that is, they offer them cabinet rank). Hence, at times, the United Nation's Ambassador, the Director of the Central Intelligence Agency, and the Administrator of the Environmental Protection Agency have been invited to join the cabinet. As a result, the composition of the cabinet is fluid and changes from president to president, and sometimes even changes during presidential terms of office (see Table 12-2). For example, in the George W. Bush

T A B L E   **12-2** **The Presidents and the Departments Created during Their Administrations**

President	Department
George Washington	State Department, Treasury Department
John Adams	Navy Department
U. S. Grant	Justice Department, Post Office
Theodore Roosevelt	Commerce and Labor Department
Harry Truman	Defense Department
Dwight Eisenhower	Health, Education and Welfare
Lyndon Johnson	Housing and Urban Development
Jimmy Carter	Energy Department

presidency, other cabinet members have consisted of John Walters of the Office of Drug Policy Control; Tom Ridge when he was head of the Office of Homeland Security; Robert Zoellick, the United States Trade Representative; Mitchell E. Daniels of the Office of Management and Budget; Christine Todd Whitman of the Environmental Protection Agency; Andrew Card, the president's chief of staff; and Richard Cheney, the vice president.

As can be seen in Table 12-1, several departments no longer exist. The War Department was reconstituted as the Defense Department in 1947. At that time, the Department of the Navy also was eliminated from the cabinet. The Post Office Department, which was once a rich source of patronage for the political parties, is no longer a cabinet department. The Commerce and Labor Department was divided in 1913 into separate departments of Commerce and Labor. The education function was taken from the Department of Health, Education and Welfare (HEW) in 1979, and the new Department of Education was created. HEW then was re-designated as the Department of Health and Human Services.

While the individual departments are important, when we think of cabinet government, we usually think of the cabinet as a body, providing advice to the president. Yet, as with so many other presidential resources, the cabinet functions in a highly fluid and ambiguous political context. Why?

12-3 The Constitutional Derivation of the Cabinet

Cohen (1988: 8) writes, "The cabinet occupies an ambiguous position in the system of government in the United States. This ambiguity and complexity derive from the lack of constitutional provision for a cabinet, the separation of powers, and vagueness about the extent and limitations of presidential power and authority." Likewise, Schlesinger (1958: 518) notes, "In the American system" the Cabinet has "always been an ambiguous and unsatisfactory body." This is not because the founders overlooked the subject. Rather, as Warshaw (1996: 11) writes, "Of all the issues to be debated during the Constitutional Convention, the role of the president and his advisors proved to be the most volatile." The founders spent considerable time discussing the merits of a plural presidency, in which, as John Randolph recommended, chief executives would be "drawn from different portions of the Country" (quoted in Warshaw 1996: 13). Once the Founders decided on a single executive, the "architects of the Constitution endeavored to ensure that the president was not subject to collective decision-making" by making no mention of the cabinet (ibid., 14).

As a result, the Constitution provides little guidance regarding the president's relationship with the cabinet. Thus, while "the Constitutional Convention had numerous debates on the role of the president's Cabinet, it still failed to provide any specific guidance to the president in dealing with department heads" or the Cabinet as a collective entity (ibid.). It does advise that the president "may require the Opinion, in writing, of the principal Officer in each of the executive Departments, upon any Subject relating to the Duties of their respective Offices. . . ." According to Warshaw (1996: 16), "The implication of this section was that the president would not meet collectively with his department heads but would deal with each individually." Consequently, it was even unclear whether the Constitution intended for the presidents to employ a cabinet for advisory purposes.

Given its inherent constitutional ambiguity, Fenno (1959: 5) describes the cabinet as "a secondary political institution, understandable only in terms of a primary one. It lives in a state of institutional dependency to promote the effective exercise of the President's authority and to help implement his ultimate responsibilities." In this sense, it appears to be an internal resource. Yet, as Cohen (1988: 9) writes, "though the ties between the cabinet and the president are clearly the most important, the cabinet also has significant relations with other actors in the political system, including the Congress, the departments, and interest groups." Therefore, it also has characteristics of an external political resource. The cabinet's relationship is thus ambiguous, both in its constitutional formation and its relationship to the president (as an internal or external political resource).

12-4 The President's Cabinet?

The cabinet's designation as an internal or external resource is further complicated by its relationship to another constitutional actor: the U.S. Congress. Congress plays a role in the appointment of cabinet secretaries. As noted in section 6-4b, "The Rise and Fall of King Caucus," during the era of King Caucus, the cabinet was a primary road to the White House. Holding a top cabinet post was a virtually necessary prelude to the presidential nomination. James Madison, James Monroe, and John Quincy Adams all rose to the White House from such posts, and Thomas Jefferson had been Secretary of State. Since congressional caucuses decided who would be nominated, cabinet secretaries often showed greater loyalty to Congress than they did to their own president.

Following the decline of King Caucus, nomination was controlled by the political parties. As a result, presidents tended to defer to the parties in the nomination process. Presidential appointment of cabinet secretaries during the second and third electoral orders was generally for political purposes. Some appointments were promised to influential party members. In return, presidential candidates increased their chances of securing their party's nomination. Other cabinet appointments went to the defeated wings of the president's political party, and hence, brought the political opposition inside the cabinet. Other appointments represented different geographical locations or were made to promote politicians of different political backgrounds (members of Congress, governors, mayors, or businessmen) or as a consolation prize for failed candidates of the president's party. Thus, during these electoral orders a president's cabinet was constituted, for various political reasons, to reach out to various external constituencies, rather than to formulate a working group of individuals who could provide the president with useful counsel.

Thus, the appointment process did not necessarily result in the appointment of individuals who were loyal to the president and his policies (see Fenno 1959: Chapter 2; Polsby 1978; Cohen 1988). Rather, the strategy often encouraged party unity while increasing the probability that the president would bring into his governing family politicians who opposed him politically. This was certainly the case with the cabinets of such nineteenth century presidents as John Adams and Abraham Lincoln. In the case of Adams, his cabinet did much to undermine his presidency. As for Lincoln, he was more fortunate in controlling his political enemies, but struggled with them nonetheless.

Consequently, while it is often called the president's cabinet, throughout our nation's history, this has at times been a bit of a misnomer. Other external political actors have had considerable influence over it. In fact, the cabinet, or particular influential members of it, sometimes were among the president's most ardent detractors.

In the fourth electoral order, as presidents have eclipsed the power of the political parties and gained greater hegemony in the political system, presidents likewise have gained greater control over their cabinet appointments. Particularly since the 1970s, presidents consistently have made loyalty to the president a primary criterion for appointment to the cabinet, though external political considerations continue to be important, as well. While presidents now have greater control than ever over their cabinet appointments, they still must deal with the Senate in the confirmation process.

12-5 The Confirmation and Removal of Cabinet Secretaries

One way in which Congress can, at least theoretically, exert influence over the composition of the cabinet is through the confirmation process. The president nominates cabinet appointments and then the Senate confirms them (or rejects them or refuses to vote on them). The Senate therefore could play a critical role, though in reality it has deferred to the president's wishes and confirmed most cabinet nominees. Only twelve cabinet nominations have been rejected: Caleb Cushing, nominated for Secretary of the Treasury by John Tyler in 1853, was rejected three times in one day, and Coolidge's choice of Charles B. Warren was rejected twice in March 1925. If we allow for Cushing and Warren, nine cabinet nominations actually have been rejected. The first was Roger B. Taney, Andrew Jackson's choice for Secretary of the Treasury, and the last two were Eisenhower's choice of Lewis Strauss for Commerce Secretary (1958) and George H. W. Bush's choice of John Tower as Defense Secretary (1989) (Stanley and Niemi 2000: 258).

Of these rejections, the negative vote against Taney was in retribution for Andrew Jackson's decision to fire two previous Treasury Secretaries. John Tyler and Andrew Johnson were neither popular with members of Congress nor with their own political parties. Therefore, these cabinet rejections can be explained as a congressional attempt in the nineteenth century to limit presidential power. All three rejected twentieth century nominees were appointed by Republican presidents. These twelve rejections, however, are the exceptions. Most appointees are confirmed because "there is a general norm that the president should get the cabinet that he wants" (Cohen 1988: 9).

What is really important is that the Senate plays a role at all in the confirmation of cabinet secretaries. It does not have a similar role for most White House staffers (though a few positions, such as the Director of the Office of Management and Budget, are subject to Senate confirmation). For this reason, Hess (1988) argues that the cabinet is a more constitutionally accountable institution than the White House staff.

Congress also plays a role in the removal of cabinet secretaries, though again it rarely does so. The Tenure of Office Act of 1867 was a crude attempt to limit presidential power (during the presidency of Andrew Johnson) by requiring Senate approval before a cabinet secretary could be removed. The Supreme Court later struck down the law as unconstitutional. Congress also has the power to impeach and remove cabinet officers, that is, should the president not remove them first. Only one cabinet officer was impeached: William Belknap, Secretary of War in 1876. He was not convicted, though he later resigned. Impeachment proceedings also were commenced against Attorney General Harry Daughtery, who was implicated in the Teapot Dome scandal, but Calvin Coolidge forced Daughtery to resign. There also was a move to impeach Treasury Secretary Andrew Mellon on conflict of interest charges, but Herbert Hoover reappointed him as Ambassador to Great Britain, thus ending the conflict (Cohen 1988:10).

While members of Congress cannot serve as cabinet secretaries, Congress has other tangible means of controlling the various cabinet departments. As noted in section 10-8, "Budgetary Power," when we examined the president and the bureaucracy, Congress plays a major role in the budgetary process. It can eliminate departments, rewrite their enabling legislation, or reorganize them. It also maintains regularized oversight via congressional hearings. While members of the cabinet are expected to appear before Congress to testify on policy and political matters, members of the White House staff are not. Hence, once again, the cabinet is perceived as more constitutionally accountable to Congress than the White House staff.

Further blurring the distinction between internal and external resources, when cabinet secretaries testify before Congress, they serve as "an envoy from the administration to Congress" and engage "in what one could term executive lobbying of Congress" (ibid., 17). Alexander Hamilton initiated this process as Washington's Secretary of the Treasury. As Fisher (1989: 141) notes, "The journals of Senator William Maclay record the close contacts of Hamilton with legislative leaders. When his plan for a funding system was in jeopardy, Hamilton 'was here early to wait on the Speaker, and I believe spent most of his time in running from place to place among the members.'" Other Treasury Secretaries, including Jefferson's, Albert Gallatin, likewise stayed in close touch with members of Congress (ibid.). Congressional hearings therefore provide an opportunity for presidents to use their cabinet as a means of expressing their viewpoints on Capitol Hill, which is indicative of an internal political resource.

On the other hand, the cabinet secretaries also regularly deal with other external political actors. In particular, the interest groups that their executive departments oversee lobby cabinet secretaries. For example, the Secretary of Agriculture has to be attentive to farm interests, the Secretary of Labor (especially in a Democratic administration) needs to pay attention to organized labor, and so on. For this reason, one of Nixon's top domestic policy advisers, John Ehrlichman, said the problem with cabinet secretaries is that they end up "marrying the natives," meaning they are more loyal to the external interests they represent than they are to the president (quoted in Waterman 1989: 59). Consequently, one concern that presidents have with their cabinets is that departmental secretaries may be co-opted by members of Congress and other special interests, which makes them more of an external political resource. In fact, history shows that the cabinet often has been more interested in representing external interests rather than the presidents' agenda.

12-6 Historical Precedents for Cabinet Operations

Given its ambiguous nature, an examination of the way presidents use the cabinet may be useful in showing us what presidents expect from this institution. The first recorded meeting of the president's advisers took place in 1791, with the Secretaries of State, War, and Treasury, plus the vice president in attendance, but not the president or the Attorney General. Soon, the Attorney General was added to the group, "though not in pursuance of any policy other than convenience and expediency" (Fenno 1959: 17). In 1793, James Madison apparently was the first person to refer to this collection as a "cabinet." By this date, then, the president's advisers "were commonly referred to as the President's Cabinet" (Warshaw 1996: 17). Still, while the cabinet had an agreed-upon name, there was less agreement over precisely what the cabinet would do.

12-6a The Cabinet as a Voting Body

One possibility for the cabinet's role was that it would serve as an executive council, a voting body, in essence providing the basis for a plural presidency. In this process, as Jefferson put it, "the president counts himself but one" (quoted in Schlesinger 1958: 518). Another possibility was that the cabinet only would provide advice to the president. Presidents would then be free to take the advice but not obligated to act upon it. There is some controversy regarding which approach George Washington actually used.

Washington raised most important issues before the cabinet; yet, there is some disagreement as to what happened next. Warshaw (1996: 16) writes, "The Cabinet was never considered to have collective responsibility for policy-making, but rather was a forum for educated discussions on national policy issues." On the other hand, Schlesinger (1958: 518) writes, Washington used the "practice of deciding questions by a vote at the Cabinet meeting and announcing the decision on the spot. Of Washington's early meetings [his Secretary of State Thomas] Jefferson says: 'In these discussions, [Secretary of the Treasury Alexander] Hamilton and myself were pitted in the cabinet like two cocks'" (ibid., 518).

It is clear that most presidents have not used the cabinet as a voting body. While John Quincy Adams allowed himself to be overruled by a majority vote of his cabinet (Paludan 1994: 175), Andrew Jackson went so far as to decline to submit questions to his cabinet for a vote. He noted, "I have accustomed myself to receive with respect the opinions of others, but always take the responsibility of deciding for myself" (quoted in Schlesinger 1958: 518). Lincoln allowed the cabinet to vote but then made up his own mind, even going so far as to ignore a unanimous vote of his cabinet (Warshaw 1996: 20–21). On one occasion, Lincoln asked for a vote of the cabinet. All members disagreed with him. He then recorded the vote: "Ayes one, noes seven. The ayes have it" (quoted in Schlesinger 1958: 518).

While presidents have used the cabinet in different ways—some working closely with it and others virtually ignoring it —a norm was quickly established: The cabinet would provide advice to the president, if he wanted it, but the cabinet would not be a decision-making body. In sum, there would be no plural presidency.

12-6b Washington's Regular Meetings with His Cabinet

Washington began the practice of meeting regularly with his cabinet: He met once a week with it (Flexner 1968: 475). A precedent therefore was established for using the cabinet as an advisory mechanism. There has been wide variation, however, in terms of how often presidents meet with their cabinets. For example, Andrew Jackson rarely met with his cabinet, while James Polk met regularly with his (Warshaw 1996: 20). While there was variation, the early presidents could easily sit down and discuss issues with their cabinets because they consisted of just four advisers (the Secretaries of State, War, and Treasury and the Attorney General) plus the president. It was not difficult for five men to sit around a table and discuss the affairs of state, particularly at a time in which relatively few issues crowded the policy agenda.

As can be seen in Table 12-1, the president's cabinet today consists of fifteen different departments; the George W. Bush administration created the fifteenth department, the Department of Homeland Security, in 2002. When we add a wide range of other policy participants who have been given cabinet status, a cabinet meeting today consists of a large group of people, with many different interests, and representing an array of different policy constituencies. Since the president's policy agenda also has many more issues on it and since few of these issues are relevant to all members of the cabinet, there is less incentive to sit down with the entire cabinet. By George H. W. Bush's presidency, his vice president, Dan Quayle (1994: 100), could write, "The truth is, Cabinet meetings are an anachronism. Generations ago, the Cabinet was small, a handful of key individuals who would meet and quietly hammer out policy. Now it has swollen to the point where it can barely fit around its enormous table. . . ."

The cabinet secretaries today also manage giant departments, each with thousands of employees. In addition, they regularly testify before Congress, which is a highly time-consuming process (often requiring days of preparation). Consequently, cabinet secretaries have severe time constraints. The idea of regular cabinet meetings, especially where issues peripheral or irrelevant to their departments are discussed, is therefore much less attractive and useful than it was in Washington's time. During Eisenhower's presidency, when regular cabinet meetings were held, secretaries often sat for hours discussing issues that had no relevance whatsoever to their department's mandate (see Fenno 1959). As a result, most modern presidents since Eisenhower, while they might profess the need for more regular cabinet meetings, eventually turn to alternative mechanisms (greater use of the White House staff, meeting with subsets of the cabinet). Hence, presidents have created new internal political resources in part because the cabinet has not served their interests as an effective internal resource.

12-6c Side-Stepping the Cabinet

Because they could not use their cabinet as an internal resource, over time a number of presidents tried to develop alternatives to the cabinet. For example, Andrew Jackson rarely sought policy advice from his cabinet. Instead, he formulated what came to be known as a **kitchen cabinet** of advisers, most of them outside the administration (Warshaw 1996: 19). This informal advisory system provided Jackson with political advice that he could trust, since the kitchen cabinet was more loyal to Jackson than was his cabinet. A number of other presidents followed Jackson's example, and used informal advisory systems. Grover Cleveland used his "fishing cabinet," while Herbert Hoover relied on his "medicine ball cabinet" and Franklin Roosevelt his "brain trust" (ibid.).

Kitchen cabinet: Advisers outside the administration that some presidents use instead of or in addition to the cabinet for advice.

There were reasons why many presidents decided to form a separate group of advisers and use the cabinet essentially as administrative personnel. The main reason related to the cabinet's loyalty. Washington had noted the importance of loyalty, eventually constructing his cabinet on this criterion (Corwin 1984: 98).

Washington's successor, John Adams, learned the hard way that it was important to name loyal individuals to the cabinet. Adams retained Washington's cabinet when he assumed office. The cabinet members were, however, more loyal to Alexander Hamilton and the Federalist Party than they were to Adams. Though Adams eventually dismissed these members and named a cabinet more to his liking, considerable damage was done to Adams's political reputation, a contributing factor to his electoral defeat in 1800 (see McCullough 2001). Yet, by purging his cabinet and naming his own men, Adams set an important precedent for his successors (Sharp 1993: 213).

Other presidents, then, were concerned with the loyalty of their cabinets. Jackson, as noted, virtually ignored his cabinet. John Tyler, who inherited William Henry Harrison's cabinet, battled with it and watched as all but one member resigned during his first year in office. Even after Tyler named his own cabinet, constant turnover continued (Warshaw 1996: 19). Millard Fillmore likewise had a high turnover in his cabinet after the death of Zachary Taylor.

According to Schlesinger (1958: 518), Lincoln "found cabinet meetings so useless that he often avoided them and at one time seemed on the verge of doing away with them altogether." Lincoln used cabinet meetings "as a sounding board to discuss the timing or the language of statements or for actions he was about to take or messages he was about to issue." On the other hand, the "real business of government occurred when the cabinet members worked in their own domains and when Lincoln consulted with them one-on-one" (Paludan 1994: 180).

Lincoln was not the last president to ignore his cabinet. As Schlesinger (1958: 520) notes, "Theodore Roosevelt ignored his cabinet on important issues. Woodrow

Wilson did not even bother to discuss the sinking of the Lusitania or the declaration of war with it." As for Franklin Roosevelt, his Secretary of the Interior wrote, "For some weeks we have spent our time at Cabinet meetings largely telling stories" (quoted in Schlesinger 1958: 520). Cabinet Secretary Harold Ickes, likewise wrote, "Only the barest routine matters were discussed. . . . All of which leads me to set down what has been running in my mind for a long time, and that is just what use the Cabinet is under this administration" (quoted in Schlesinger 1958: 520).

Consequently, while an entity called the cabinet has existed in every single presidential administration, it has not been used in the same way by all presidents. There is considerable variation in how the cabinet has been employed. Still, as Warshaw (1996: 23) writes, "Although the Cabinet's advisory role fluctuated during the eighteenth and nineteenth centuries, in general the Cabinet remained the president's primary source of policy advice." However, this was "principally due to an absence of viable alternatives for policy development." Even while some presidents turned to informal advisers, "their members did not have the range of technical expertise to match that of the executive departments" (ibid.). Hence, prior to the creation of the Executive Office of the President (EOP) in 1939, other than an informal network of advisers, presidents did not have a viable alternative to the cabinet. No matter how little they trusted it, to some extent most presidents still were reliant on their cabinets.

As we will see in Chapter 13, "The Search for New Political Resources," this situation began to change in 1939 as presidents developed a variety of formal institutions within the White House. New internal resources that were much more responsive to a president's policy and political needs emerged, and with it, the cabinet's influence further eroded.

Still, presidents were reluctant to abandon the idea of cabinet government. Roosevelt, Truman, and Eisenhower greatly expanded the scope and functions of the White House staff, though Eisenhower continued to meet regularly with his cabinet throughout his eight years in office. Eisenhower even created the position of Cabinet Secretariat to provide a clear agenda for cabinet meetings. The Cabinet Secretariat also prepared a "Cabinet Action Status Report," which was circulated to all cabinet members to keep them up to date on "major administration issues and presidential decisions" (Warshaw 1996: 30).

12-6d A Major Change in the President's Relationship to the Cabinet

While the Kennedy and Johnson administrations represented a move away from the cabinet and toward greater use of the White House staff, Richard Nixon was elected in 1968 on a pledge of restoring cabinet government. Initially, Nixon appointed a number of individuals who were independent forces in the Republican Party and men of independent minds. They included a rival for the Republican nomination, former governor George Romney. Two other former governors, Walter Hickel and John Volpe, also were named to the Nixon cabinet. In the end, all three advocated policies long espoused by the civil servants serving in their respective departments of Housing and Urban Development, Interior, and Transportation. Soon a political disjuncture developed between the views of the president and those of his domestic cabinet advisers. "Nixon and Romney's views diverged on a variety of specific issues. George Romney supported the continuation of the Model Cities Program, while Nixon desired its termination" (Waterman 1989: 53). Walter Hickel eventually was fired because he criticized the president's Vietnam War policy.

Nixon had instituted a cabinet government on the rather naïve assumption that a hands-on president was required for foreign affairs, but the cabinet alone could run domestic affairs (ibid., 52). This view was surprising, given that Nixon had served in the House of Representatives, the Senate, and for eight years as vice president. Yet, domestic policy was not a Nixon priority. As Warshaw (1996: 54) writes, "Nixon failed to articulate a clear agenda for the administration during the campaign, and provided little direction from which to orient the administration's policies." Nixon therefore had "no specific program for domestic affairs" and little personal interest in it (Waterman 1989: 56–57).

Eventually, Nixon's "experiences with Romney, Hickel, Volpe and other first term cabinet secretaries led the administration to search for a new appointment strategy" (ibid., 58). According to Richard Nathan (1983), a former official in the Nixon administration, that strategy was premised on the idea that the president should select cabinet secretaries and even subcabinet appointees who reflect the president's policy positions. Naming loyalists to cabinet and subcabinet positions also offered the benefit of increasing presidential control of the bureaucracy.

Nixon also devised a new method for organizing the cabinet. In his first term, he used the Urban Affairs Council as a means of allowing cabinet participation, not as a whole, but in subsets on specific issues relevant to their departments. For a variety of reasons, partly related to Nixon's inability to provide policy direction, the idea was abandoned.

In his second term, however, Nixon promoted a somewhat similar idea: using **super-secretaries**, or combining secretaries with similar functions into committees and then placing them under the direction of one cabinet member who would direct policy in that area. Nixon abandoned the super-secretaries idea in 1973 because the idea had little support in Congress and Watergate now permeated the political agenda. The idea of creating a new organizational mechanism for the cabinet did not end with Nixon's presidency, however.

Super-secretaries: Secretaries who performed similar functions and were combined into committees and then placed under the direction of one cabinet member who directed policy in that area.

12-6e Ford and Carter and Their Use of the Cabinet

The Ford presidency saw a return to cabinet government. Following Nixon's resignation, many pundits argued that the Watergate scandal could be attributed to the president's misuse of his White House staff. Too much power had flowed to the chief of staff and a small cadre of other White House staffers. The president was kept isolated from his cabinet and therefore from constructive advice.

When Ford became president in August 1974, he promised a return to cabinet government. Gone was a strong chief of staff. In its place, the cabinet was promised increased access to the president. Coming to the White House as he did, unexpectedly following Nixon's resignation, Ford struggled to put together a coherent policy agenda. In the end, he failed in this task. Policy making was largely run out of the departments, but the White House staff did not provide sufficient coordination of departmental initiatives. As a result, the Ford administration drifted policy-wise, never finding its voice (see Warshaw 1996: Chapter 4).

In his 1976 campaign for president, Jimmy Carter likewise promised to restore cabinet government and to reduce the influence of the White House staff. Once elected, he proceeded to do so, choosing cabinet secretaries on the basis of their policy expertise, promising them access to the president, allowing departments to set the policy agenda, allowing secretaries to select their own subordinates, and restricting the influence of the White House staff. In addition, Carter created cabinet clusters, based loosely on the operating concept of Nixon's Urban Affairs Council. Carter created the clusters "to bring groups of Cabinet officers together to work on specific policy issues" (Warshaw 1996: 108).

During his first year, Carter "held two-hour weekly meetings with the Cabinet." According to Attorney General Griffin Bell, "the discussions were disjointed, given the range of cabinet positions. . . . It was adult show-and-tell" (Hess 1988: 159). By Carter's second year, cabinet meetings were held twice a month, and proposals from cabinet secretaries had to be routed through either Stuart Eisenstat (domestic policy) or Zbigniew Brzezinski (foreign policy). Additional oversight was provided by Hamilton Jordan, who eventually became Carter's chief of staff. These meetings "created friction between the White House staff and the departments. By Carter's third year, he had finally named a chief of staff and fired five of his cabinet secretaries in an ineptly handled summer purge" (ibid., 160).[1] Thus, Carter's experiment with cabinet government ended in failure (see also Weko 1995: 72–73).

Again, as was the case with Nixon, Carter's secretaries advocated policies with which the president did not agree. The many policy initiatives emanating from the departments were not properly screened by White House personnel to ensure they were consistent with the president's political agenda. As a result, the White House embarrassingly criticized departmental initiatives after they were publicly aired. Disagreements were fought out in public, and a perception developed that Carter was not in control of his own administration. As a result, Carter eventually transferred considerable authority to his White House staff. In a politically damaging move, he also asked for the resignation of all of his cabinet members and then accepted several of them. By the summer of 1979, it appeared that the Carter administration was in complete disarray (see Warshaw 1996: Chapter 5). Carter never recovered from the perception that he was well meaning but inept. The cabinet government system that he had initially employed contributed greatly to his failure as president.

12-6f Ronald Reagan's Innovations

Ronald Reagan did not make the same mistakes as Ford or Carter. Rather, even during the transition period before he was inaugurated, Reagan developed a clear conceptualization of how he would govern. He essentially would use both the White House staff and the cabinet to govern in tandem.

Reagan's administration employed a number of individuals who had served in the Nixon administration and were thus familiar with and amenable to the idea of employing a variation on the super-cabinet structure. Of equal importance, Reagan learned from Gerald Ford's and Jimmy Carter's failures. Reagan also centralized all appointments through the White House staff, ensuring that they were loyal to the president and his political philosophy. Unlike the Ford and Carter presidencies, the Reagan administration worked hard to ensure that it spoke with a single voice.

Cabinet councils: Councils consisting of cabinet members who Reagan organized into subcabinets along the lines of Nixon's super-secretaries. There were six councils in Reagan's first term, each with distinct authority over a policy area.

Reagan also employed **cabinet councils.** As Hess (1988: 161–62) writes, "The main feature was five cabinet councils, later six, each composed of four to six department heads who met to review policy and develop options. The president chaired a fifth of the council meetings in the first year; the others were chaired by the official with primary responsibility for the issues. During the first year, there were more than 500 meetings, over half of them relating to economic affairs."

Warshaw (1996) refers to the system that Reagan employed as "powersharing" (see Figure 12-1). Rather than using a pure cabinet form of government or relying primarily on the White House staff, Reagan blended the two in a way that allowed both to share power. The president set the overall policy direction for his

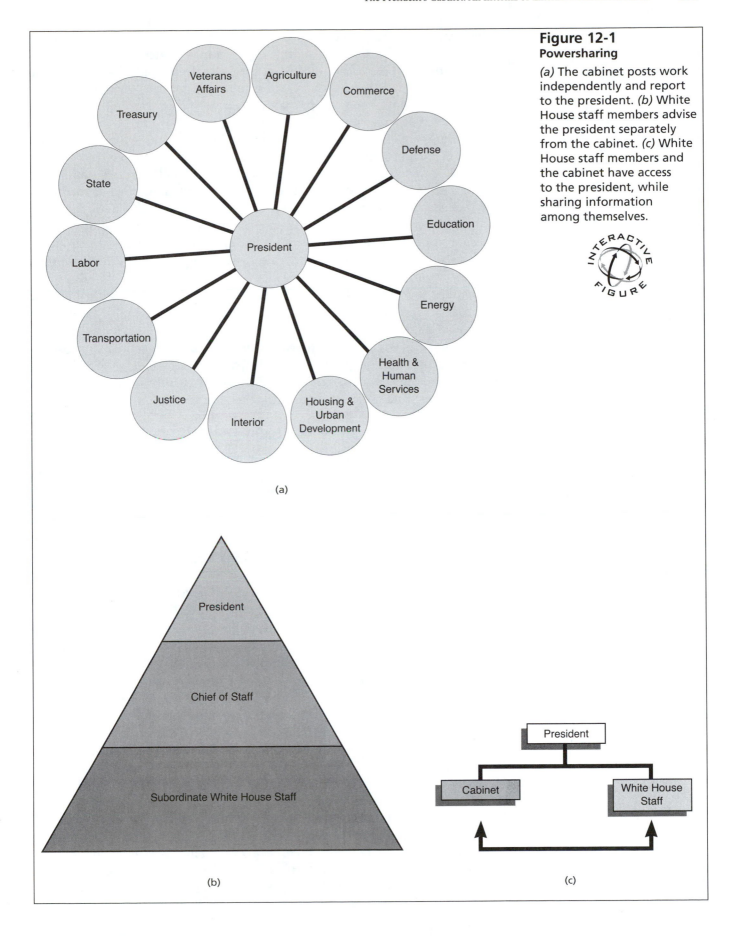

Figure 12-1
Powersharing

(a) The cabinet posts work independently and report to the president. *(b)* White House staff members advise the president separately from the cabinet. *(c)* White House staff members and the cabinet have access to the president, while sharing information among themselves.

INTERACTIVE FIGURE

(a)

(b)

(c)

government: tax cuts, balanced budgets, smaller government, less regulation, cuts in domestic programs, increases in defense programs, a greater reliance on state and local control, and less reliance on federal programs. Departments were allowed to develop specific policy proposals so long as they were consistent with the administration's overall philosophical approach. To ensure that they were, White House staff reviewed departmental policies. Cabinet secretaries worked side by side with White House staffers, each sharing the same political philosophy, on cabinet councils that met in the Roosevelt Room next to the Oval Office. They also met on a regular basis, providing continuing contact between cabinet secretaries and White House staff. Cabinet secretaries were encouraged to attend cabinet council meetings themselves and were discouraged from sending subordinates in their place. In addition, the president met regularly with cabinet secretaries, providing opportunities for him to make sure that everyone understood his general policy proposals. Reagan also met often (about 14 percent of the meetings during the first year of his administration) with the cabinet councils. In all these ways, then, the administration worked to make sure that the cabinet and White House staff worked together for a common purpose: to promote the president's conservative policy agenda (see Warshaw: Chapter 6).

While the powersharing arrangement deteriorated, to some extent, during Reagan's second term (as exemplified by the Iran-Contra scandal), the administration provided a new model of cabinet-White House staff interaction. It was a model Reagan's immediate successors used with much less success.

12-6g Bush, Clinton, and Bush and Their Use of the Cabinet

George H. W. Bush employed a system similar in many respects to that employed by Ronald Reagan. The difference was that Bush did not articulate a political philosophy that his subordinates could follow. Likewise, he showed little interest in domestic policy formulation. As a result, domestic policy initiatives drifted back to the departments. The White House staff provided little organizational or ideological guidance to the departments. Consequently, the resulting system bore little resemblance to the well-oiled machine Reagan's team had crafted (for more, see Warshaw, Chapter 7).

Bill Clinton had more interest in developing domestic policy than did his predecessor, but he did not move quickly to employ the Reagan model of powersharing. Rather, he created a system in which policy was coordinated and eventually controlled out of the White House, with cabinet secretaries encouraged to work in teams (in essence, variations of the cabinet councils, though there were many more of them and they received less oversight direction from the White House). The teams fit Clinton's personality. They allowed him to become engaged in wideranging policy debates, which he thoroughly enjoyed. They provided useful policy advice, but they also encouraged a cacophony of voices to emerge from the White House, creating the perception, as was the case during Carter's administration, that no one was firmly in charge of the White House. Like Carter then, Clinton eventually centralized greater control over policy development in the White House. By the time he did so, however, considerable political damage had been done. While Clinton survived—he was re-elected, whereas Carter was not—and while the policies adopted during this period contributed to the favorable economic conditions that characterized his presidency, there were considerable short-term political costs. Clinton was widely perceived as not being in control of his own administration, which contributed to the Republican party takeover of Congress in 1994.

Figure 12-2
Speaking with One Voice
(a) When the president is the one strong voice in government, his voice commands total attention, and he appears to be in control. *(b)* When members of an administration have public disagreements, opinion is split, and the administration suffers because it looks unstable and out of the president's control.

The lesson here is that administrations should speak with one voice (see Figure 12-2). Following the terrorist attacks of September 11, 2001, the administration of George W. Bush spoke clearly with one voice. By the spring of 2002, however, with the problems in the Middle East now the focus of attention, reports surfaced of disagreements between cabinet secretaries (particularly Secretary of State Colin Powell and Secretary of Defense Donald Rumsfeld) and between the cabinet and the White House staff. These disagreements intensified as the administration argued, often in the press, about an attack on the government of Iraq designed to unseat its leader, Saddam Hussein. These public policy disagreements threatened George W. Bush's reputation as a strong leader.

Chapter Summary

The lesson from the most recent presidencies is that presidents need to devise organizational mechanisms where policy disagreements can be worked out in house, that is, not in public view. Also, organizational mechanisms need to be constructed so that the White House staff and the cabinet can work in tandem, rather than at cross purposes. The evidence to date is that few presidents have succeeded with either of these tasks.

As presidents seek new organizational resources, they have not ignored their cabinet, but the age of pure cabinet government appears to be at an end. The cabinet continues to exist, but as the experiences of the Nixon, Ford, Carter, and Clinton presidencies demonstrate, presidents are likely to make greater use of their institutional presidential resources over time. In other words, as we will see in the next chapter, they consistently have developed new internal resources because the cabinet does not serve their needs. This is in part due to the cabinet's unique nature as a part external and part internal resource. It clearly has attributes of both types of political resources. As presidents desire greater control over their resources—that is, as they move to the development and use of new political resources—the influence of the cabinet likely will continue to decline.

Review Questions

1. Which of the following was the first cabinet position created by Congress?
   a. Secretary of War
   b. Secretary of the Treasury
   c. Attorney General
   d. Secretary of State

2. Which of the following is a member of the inner cabinet?
   a. Attorney General
   b. Housing and Urban Development
   c. Health and Welfare
   d. Education

3. Which of the following departments no longer exists?
   a. Housing and Urban Development
   b. Interior
   c. War
   d. Defense

4. The Constitution
   a. provides for a cabinet.
   b. says that the president must meet with cabinet officers.
   c. says that the president can meet with cabinet officers if he wishes.
   d. does not mention a cabinet.

5. The Senate
   a. often rejects cabinet nominees.
   b. often forces presidents to use their recess appointment power.
   c. seldom rejects cabinet nominees.
   d. seldom rejects recess appointments.

6. Which of the following presidents went so far as to decline to submit questions to his cabinet for a vote?
   a. George Washington
   b. Thomas Jefferson
   c. Andrew Jackson
   d. Abraham Lincoln

7. Which of the following presidents created the kitchen cabinet?
   a. George Washington
   b. Thomas Jefferson
   c. Andrew Jackson
   d. Abraham Lincoln

8. After allowing his cabinet members to choose their own subordinates, which of the following presidents later came to believe that the president should select cabinet secretaries and even subcabinet appointees who agreed with the president's policy positions?
   a. Lyndon Johnson
   b. Richard Nixon
   c. Jimmy Carter
   d. Bill Clinton

9. Which of the following presidents used cabinet government?
   a. Dwight Eisenhower
   b. Gerald Ford
   c. George H. W. Bush
   d. all of the above

10. Which of the following presidents was interested in creating teams so that the cabinet and White House staff could work together?
    a. Richard Nixon
    b. Gerald Ford
    d. Jimmy Carter
    d. Bill Clinton

Discussion Questions

1. Why are presidents reluctant to use their cabinets?

2. Should presidents make greater use of their cabinets?

Note

1. Carter was not the first to purge his cabinet. Andrew Jackson famously dissolved his cabinet in 1830. Likewise, after Nixon was re-elected in 1972, he asked for the resignations of all members of his administration (see Fallows 1988). In each case, however, these actions proved controversial and raised questions about presidential competence.

Chapter

The Search for New Political Resources

Key Terms

Brownlow Committee
cabinet secretariat
chief of staff
Special Assistant to the
  President for National
  Security Affairs
spokes of the wheel

13-1 The Search for New Political Resources

One can argue that presidents today face an untenable situation. Much of their constitutional authority is ambiguous. They also benefit less from elections than they once did (e.g., a declining coattail effect, electoral coalitions are less useful at the governing phase). In addition, the American public has excessive and unrealistic expectations of presidential performance (see Wayne 1982). At the same time, as the political environment becomes more hostile, presidents are finding it harder to work with a variety of external political actors. In short, there are too many demands on the presidency and the result is overload.

For these reasons, scholars have warned that the presidency is "under siege" (Rose 1997); e.g., three recent incumbents were defeated for re-election, another was forced to resign, while another was impeached. This argument is convincing as far as it goes, but it does not tell us the whole story of the presidency. Rather, thus far, we have focused on only four types of political resources—personal, legal, electoral, and external—or what I call the president's traditional political resources. When we focus solely on these resources, the prognosis appears to be bleak. Yet, what happens when we add two new resources to the analysis? An examination of the president's internal and informational resources is the subject of this chapter.

13-2 Centralization during the Transitional Presidential Era

According to Moe (1985b: 238),

> [B]asic features have structured the incentives of all modern presidents along the same basic lines. The president has increasingly been held responsible for designing, proposing, legislating, administering, and modifying public policy, that is, for governing. Whatever his particular policy objectives, whatever his personality and style, the modern president is driven by these formidable expectations to seek control over structures and processes of the government.

How, then, have presidents responded to these "formidable expectations"? Moe explains that presidents have a rational incentive to create new institutional mechanisms within the White House that allow them to (1) deal with myriad and expanding public expectations and (2) identify individuals who primarily are *responsive* to the president and his or her political needs. In other words, presidents have the incentive to create what scholars have long called "institutional resources" and what I call internal resources, or those resources over which the president has direct hierarchical control. Since many of these resources provide presidents with increased information about the political system, I also refer to the president's informational resources.

If we examine the changing political ecosystem—see Chapter 11, "The Presidency and the Political Ecosystem"—then what Moe suggests is part of an evolutionary development in the history of the presidency. In the traditional era of the presidency (see Figure 11-1), relatively little was expected of presidents in both domestic and foreign policy, and the political parties and the legislative branch largely isolated presidents from the external political world. Presidents did not need to respond directly to the public, the media, interest groups, state and local governments, or other external political actors. The bureaucracy was still diminutive, and the courts had yet to be politicized. Likewise, the State Department was capable of handling most foreign policy issues, and the Treasury Department actively worked with Congress on domestic policy. Consequently, there was little need for the presidency to create new institutional mechanisms inside the White House. As Neustadt (1982: 1) notes, the institutionalization of the White House was "more or less unknown before" the twentieth century.

13-2a Innovations in the Transitional Era

As the president's relationship within the political ecosystem changed, new demands on the presidency created the need for new organizational mechanisms. For example, when Grover Cleveland decided to cultivate positive media coverage, he appointed a prototype for the modern press secretary, an innovation his successors followed and developed (Nelson 1998).

Likewise, when William Howard Taft employed his secretary, Charles Norton, as a political operative, other presidents followed the practice: Wilson, Harding, and Coolidge then continued the practice. Under Herbert Hoover, there was a further expansion of the secretary's staff: It now included a former member of Congress and a couple of journalists (ibid., 229–30).

In the transitional period, presidents also began to establish the rudiments of what later would be called "congressional liaison." Woodrow Wilson "relied on legislative leaders in Congress to link the branches, but he also depended on Postmaster General Albert Burkson to carry out the duties of congressional liaison" (Fisher 1981: 40).

There also were more formal moves toward institutionalization. As Theodore Roosevelt became more active as an initiator of domestic policy, he used commissions to investigate "certain factual situations" and to report "their findings to the President" (Corwin 1984: 86), thus providing him with an independent source of information. For instance, in 1905 Roosevelt established the Keep Commission, which "generated a mass of recommendations for administrative improvements. . . ." As Arnold (1993: 227–28) notes, it was remarkable because "it was initiated by the president and responsible to him. . . ." Following Roosevelt's example, William Howard Taft then appointed the President's Committee on Economy and Efficiency, also known as the Cleveland Committee after its head, Frederick A. Cleveland. The committee's principal recommendation was to establish a federal budget to bring order to the budgetary process.[1] Cleveland's "diagnosis" was that the presidency "was enfeebled by its lack of resources and its position in the American regime" (ibid., 222). Again, while the Cleveland Committee's recommendations had little impact, the committee provided a precedent for Franklin Roosevelt's **Brownlow Committee** report two decades later.

Undoubtedly, the most important of the institutional innovations of the transitional era was the creation of the Bureau of the Budget (BOB). Sundquist (1981: 39) notes, "The modern presidency, judged in terms of institutional responsibilities, began on June 10, 1921, the day that President Harding signed the Budget and Accounting Act." Although the BOB initially was located in the Treasury Department, its first director, General Charles Dawes, "arranged for President Harding to inaugurate semiannual meetings of the president and the budget director with what was named the Business Organization of the Government—an assembly of officials from department and agency heads to unit chiefs and chief clerks that soon numbered two thousand. . . ." (ibid., 45). He also developed the central clearance technique discussed in section 10-5, "The Tools of Presidential Control of the Bureaucracy" (see Fisher 1981: 40).

Consequently, before Franklin Roosevelt was elected and before the modern presidency was established, the institutional presidency had begun to emerge. As presidents became more active in dealing with the press, Congress, domestic policy,

Brownlow Committee: Franklin Roosevelt's Committee on Administrative Management, also known as the Brownlow Committee, which recommended in 1937 that the "president needs help." Their recommendation became the foundation for the establishment of the Executive Office of the President in 1939.

and the budget, political advisers were designated, committees were formed, and some institutions (BOB) were established.

Still, a question remained for those individuals who advocated a stronger presidency: Could the presidency be transformed without a fundamental change in our constitutional system? Some Progressive era reformers thought it could not and therefore advocated the creation of a parliamentary system with the president as prime minister. Eventually, however, "progressive-era public administration envisioned a more modest and ingenious means to the same end. The solution was to strengthen the presidency by endowing it with tools for the direction of government—managerial solutions" (Arnold 1993: 222). Frederick Cleveland best expressed the idea (quoted in Arnold 1993: 223):

> What the country needs is not a change in the form of Government, but constructive leadership by a real Executive . . . leadership which will be used to keep the Executive informed about what is going on; leadership which is based on a knowledge of existing conditions. . . . There has never been developed in the . . . United States a regular organization for doing these things. . . .

Then, as if to emphasize how limited the resources available to the presidency currently were, he added, "The organization of the office of the Chief Executive . . . is about the same as would be established to conduct the correspondence and manage the household of a society belle in the city of New York" (ibid.). Cleveland's message was clear: The presidency needed additional resources before real executive leadership could emerge.

Hence, as Arnold (1993: 236–37) writes, "The institutionalized presidency is a twentieth-century response to the weakness of the presidency within the constitutional design of the American regime. The Constitution's design of the presidency left presidents unequally matched with Congress and without the resources for new expectations of it." The development of new organizational structures provided a means for presidents to redress this power imbalance. According to Leonard White, the transformation in presidential/congressional powers began with the Keep and Cleveland Commissions, which were "the visible symbols not only of a transfer of initiative for administrative reform from legislative to the executive branch, but also of the tipping of the constitutional balance from Congress to the President of the United States" (quoted in Arnold 1993: 228). In short, the movement toward the development of internal political resources not only began prior to the establishment of the modern presidency, but also reflected the later shift in the constitutional balance of power from Congress to the president. This process continued and achieved greater legitimacy under Franklin Roosevelt.

13-3 Centralization in the Modern Presidential Era

Arnold (1993: 230) writes, "Political scientists and historians see institutionalization as a characteristic of the modern presidency and claim Franklin D. Roosevelt (FDR) as the first modern president. Yet, FDR entered a presidency in which three key elements of institutionalization were already in place: executive budgeting, organizational activity, and expanding staff resources." Still, when Roosevelt entered the White House, he discovered his resources were inadequate for dealing with the problems created by the Great Depression. Roosevelt therefore acted quickly to develop the president's organizational resources, establishing the Emergency Council in November 1933 to coordinate the work of the various New Deal field agencies. He also created the National Resources Board and the National

Resources Committee. Thus, from "the very outset he had a keen interest in reorganizing the government, and over time that concern developed from a desire to cut costs, which had been the traditional rationale, to a determination to strengthen the president's managerial capacity" (Leuchtenburg 1988: 32).

Other organizational changes soon were forthcoming. Partly because he was confined to a wheelchair, Roosevelt sent personal representatives to work with members of Congress on presidential proposals (Mezey 1989: 95)—another evolutionary factor in the development of specialized congressional liaison staff. Roosevelt also created new agencies and staffed them with university-trained experts instead of using existing departments to deal with newly established tasks (Leuchtenburg 1988: 28, 30). The result was a management system that encouraged duplication and competition fostered between advisers. To everyone but Roosevelt, administrative chaos apparently prevailed.[2] This resulted in an "administrative monstrosity, proliferating the number of executives who had the right and obligation to report directly to the president" (Hess 1976: 36). By the beginning of Roosevelt's second term, then, it was generally recognized that something had to be done to reform the White House organization. The result was the creation of the president's Committee on Administrative Management, better known as the Brownlow Committee.

13-4 The Executive Office of the President and the Chief of Staff

The Brownlow Committee offered a wide range of recommendations to strengthen presidential influence over the administrative state. In words reminiscent of the Cleveland Committee, the members of the Brownlow Committee wrote "managerial direction and control of all departments and agencies of the Executive Branch . . . should be centered in the President; that while he now has popular responsibility for this direction . . . he is not equipped with adequate legal authority or administrative machinery to enable him to exercise it. . . ." (Arnold 1986: 103). The Brownlow Committee then recommended the creation of the Executive Office of the President, with the Bureau of the Budget at its fulcrum, to provide the president with the staff and resources for effective management of the bureaucracy. The report also recommended the abolition of the Civil Service Commission and the creation of a new agency headed by a single administrator answerable directly to the president. Finally, the report called for the creation of Departments of Conservation, Social Welfare, and Public Works (Arnold 1986: 103–07).

13-4a The Executive Office of the President

The timing of the Brownlow Committee's report and the president's subsequent request for congressional legislation to enact its provisions could not have come at a less propitious political time. FDR asked for reorganization authority in 1937; at the same time, he attempted to change the composition of the Supreme Court (see section 11-4a, "FDR and Court Packing"). Rather than judging the president's request for new staff resources on its own merits, members of Congress (of both political parties) perceived it as additional evidence of Roosevelt's dictatorial ambitions. The bill therefore died and no congressional action was taken until 1939. The Reorganization Act of 1939 followed the spirit of the Brownlow report, but did not give Roosevelt everything he had asked for—in particular, the abolition of the Civil Service Commission and the creation of additional departments.[3] Congress, like the Brownlow Committee, however, did recognize that "the president needs help."

Armed with new authority, in 1939 Roosevelt sent five reorganization plans to Congress. These plans embodied the recommendations of the Brownlow Committee, while they omitted some aspects that FDR's advisers considered too controversial—e.g., civil service reform. Congress did not legislatively veto any of the five plans. Thus, the Executive Office of the President (EOP) was created. It consisted of five divisions: the White House Office, containing six new administrative assistants; the Bureau of the Budget, transferred from the Treasury Department; the National Security Resources Board, established from the National Resources Committee; the Office of Government Reports; and the Liaison Office for Personnel Management, which is all that remained of the Brownlow Committee's more ambitious plan for civil service reform (Sundquist 1981: 54).

According to Sundquist (1981: 57–58), "After 1939 the central organizational apparatus for the president as general manager was fixed in place." The EOP was "endowed with presidential staff agencies for budgeting, planning, personnel, reorganization studies, and legislative clearance." Within a year, Roosevelt added to it an office of Emergency Management, designed to provide the president with the ability to deal with mounting wartime leadership burdens (Arnold 1993: 232). In fact, while the EOP consisted of six agencies in 1940, by 1972, it consisted of sixteen units and by then forty-five different units had resided in the EOP. Congress created 44 percent of these units, with only about 40 percent established by the president via executive order (ibid., 233).

One can argue that Roosevelt accustomed "the nation to expect that the president would be aided by a battery of policy advisers and implementers" (Greenstein 1988b: 300). His successor, Harry Truman, then brought the modern presidential organization into sharper focus. He dramatically increased the size of the presidential staff, from 51 during Roosevelt's third term to 256 by Truman's second term (King and Ragsdale 1988: 205). He also provided greater differentiation of staff functions, moving policy advocacy to the White House, building staff support around chief presidential assistants, adding (through congressional legislation) the National Security Council (NSC) and the Council of Economic Advisers (CEA), and most importantly, building "majority acceptance of the President as the locus of federal responsibility" (Hess 1976: 57). Eisenhower then took the next step, creating a variety of new positions and institutional units within the White House, providing greater formal structure (Henderson 1988).

Consequently, over time and across presidencies, Democratic and Republican, "the EOP institutionalized and legitimized the ideas of presidential central staff and planning. Its existence made it more likely that future presidential staff and planning mechanisms could be developed without having to battle Congress anew over each innovation. In effect, the existence of the EOP was itself the justification for such activities" (Arnold 1993: 233).

13-4b The EOP Evolves through the Involvement of Each President

Evidence that the EOP could evolve without congressional approval is provided by the fact that a variety of presidential commissions over time recommended further expansions of the White House staff apparatus: The Hoover Commission (1949), the President's Advisory Committee on Government Organization (1953), the Commission of Intergovernmental Relations (1955), the President's Task Force on Government Organization (1967), and the Advisory Council on Executive Organization in 1970 or the Ash Council (Hess 1976: 2). The latter council also recommended reformulating the Bureau of the Budget as a new Office of

Management and Budget, as well as a restructuring of the National Security Council (Hoff-Wilson 1988: 172).

Table 13-1 delineates the various units of the Executive Office of the President from 1939–1994. As is evident, numerous divisions have performed myriad functions over time. It also is apparent that a number of these units were later discontinued. An examination of the various EOP offices allows us to see the priorities of various presidents over time, by examining the offices they created and the ones they dissolved. It is important to note that the size, role, and very existence of these units depend on the inclinations of individual presidents (see Wyszomirski 1985: 133; Weko 1995: 108). One president, for example, may be more or less interested in promoting science and technology policy and therefore may establish or terminate a unit dealing with these policy areas. Indeed, by examining the range of specific policies (environment, trade, drugs, etc.) that are included among the functions of the EOP offices, we have a rough idea of which issues are important for particular presidents, as well as an indication of how issues move onto and off the policy agenda over time.

While the composition of the EOP has changed over time, its basic structure provides all presidents with continuity. As King and Ragsdale (1988: 486) note, "Although members of the White House staff change with some frequency, the broader institution of the presidency is hardly recreated each time a new administration enters office." Such key institutions as the National Security Council and the Bureau of the Budget, now the Office of Management and Budget, provide resources and invaluable institutional memory for presidents (see Heclo 1975).

In addition to creating new offices, the expansion of the EOP increased the number of staff working at the behest of the president. Figure 13-1 delineates the number of White House and EOP staff at five-year intervals from 1945 through 1995.[4] These numbers indicate an increase in White House staffing from 1945 to 1950, with the numbers fluctuating somewhat since then, increasing to more than 500 in the Ford administration. Likewise, there have been changes in the number of White House staff and EOP employees, from 820 in 1945, to almost 5,000 during Nixon's first term, with a decline in staff since then. Since, however, we do not have a reliable measure of the number of detailees or officials working for departments and agencies who are assigned to the White House and therefore not listed as members of the White House staff, these reductions may be nothing more than cosmetic. Presidents may merely be using staff from the line agencies or the military instead of White House staff. Regardless of whether the White House and EOP staff has declined over time, presidents clearly have numerous individuals working directly

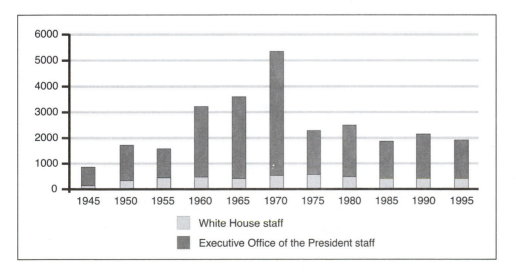

Figure 13-1
Number of White House Staff to Total EOP Employees at Five-Year Intervals, 1945–1995
Source: Stanley and Niemi (2000: 250–51).

T A B L E **13-1** **The Divisions of the Executive Office of the President, 1939–1994**

Division	Established	Status
White House Office	1939	Still in operation
Bureau of the Budget	1939	Replaced by Office of Management and Budget in 1970
National Resources Planning Board	1939	Terminated in 1943
Office of Government Reports	1939	Terminated in 1948
Liaison Office for Personnel Management	1939	Terminated in 1953
Office of Emergency Management	1940	Terminated in 1953
Office of War Mobilization	1943	Terminated in 1944
Office of War Mobilization and Reconversion	1944	Terminated in 1946
Council of Economic Advisers	1946	Still in operation
National Security Council	1949	Still in operation
National Security Resources Board	1949	Terminated in 1953
Office of Defense Mobilization	1950	Terminated in 1958
Office of the Director of Mutual Security	1951	Terminated in 1953
Telecommunications Adviser to the President	1951	Terminated in 1953
President's Advisory Committee on Government Organization	1953	Terminated in 1961
National Aeronautics and Space Administration	1958	Removed from EOP 1973
Office of Defense and Civilian Mobilization	1958	Renamed one month later as the Office of Civil and Defense Mobilization (terminated in 1961)
Office of Science and Technology	1962	Terminated in 1973
Office of Special Representative for Trade Negotiations	1963	Reorganized in 1975
Office of Economic Opportunity	1964	Terminated in 1975
National Council on Marine Resources and Engineering	1966	Terminated in 1971
Office of Emergency Preparedness	1968	Terminated in 1973
Council for Urban Affairs	1969	Terminated in 1970
President's Foreign Intelligence Advisory Board	1969	Terminated in 1977
Council on Environmental Quality	1969	Still in operation
Office of Telecommunications Policy	1970	Terminated in 1978
Office of Management and Budget	1970	Still in operation
Domestic Council	1970	Terminated in 1977
Council on International Economic Policy	1971	Terminated in 1977
Office of Consumer Affairs	1971	Terminated in 1973
Special Action Office for Drug Abuse Prevention	1971	Terminated in 1975
Federal Property Council	1973	Terminated in 1977
Energy Policy Office	1973	Terminated in 1974
Council on Wage and Price Stability	1974	Terminated in 1981
Presidential Clemency Board	1974	Terminated in 1975
Office of the Special Representative for Trade Negotiations	1975	Renamed the Office of the U.S. Trade Representative (1979)
Office of Drug Abuse Policy	1976	Terminated in 1978
Office of Science and Technology Policy	1976	Still in operation
Domestic Policy Staff	1977	Renamed the Office of Policy Development (1981; replaced by Domestic Policy Council in 1993)
Office of Administration	1977	Still in operation
National Critical Materials Council	1984	Terminated in 1993
National Space Council	1988	Terminated in 1993
Office of National Drug Control Policy	1988	Still in operation
National Economic Council	1993	Still in operation
Domestic Policy Council	1993	Still in operation

Source: Hart (1995: 242–44)

for them. Hart (1995) refers to the office as a "presidential branch." In many ways, this new branch of government has become highly controversial.

While they are responsive and loyal to the president, the White House staff are not *accountable* to other constitutional actors (e.g., the Congress), few are confirmed by the Senate (and thus are not required to testify before Congress), and none are subject to impeachment. Only the president decides to appoint and remove them from office. Hence, the staff can introduce blind ambition rather than policy neutrality or political expertise to the White House, thus violating one of the basic qualifications identified by the Brownlow Committee for competent White House staffers: They should have a "passion for anonymity." In practice, many have had only a passion for political power.

13-4c Problems with the White House Staff

There have been many problems over time with the White House staff. Eisenhower created the positions of **chief of staff,** the **Special Assistant to the President for National Security Affairs,** and the **cabinet secretariat.** While Kennedy eliminated the latter position (though it did periodically re-emerge under later presidents), the other two positions became vital organizational components of the modern presidency. Both are among the most powerful positions in the United States government today. Over time, both were related to serious presidential scandals.

The history of the chief of staff has been decidedly checkered. Eisenhower named former New Hampshire Governor Sherman Adams to be his chief of staff. Because Eisenhower preferred to delegate functions to his subordinates, Adams's new position immediately became prominent. In this position, loosely based on the idea of a military chief of staff, Adams not only oversaw the various components of the White House staff, but he also brought organizational order to the entire White House apparatus. The chief of staff became the person to see if one wanted an appointment with the president or simply wanted to pass along information to him. As the gatekeeper to the president, Adams, not surprisingly, developed a considerable power base in a relatively short period of time. Yet, he also made enemies, and his fall from political grace was sudden.

In Adams's amazing rise and fall, ironically, the basic parameters of the chief of staff position were established: Chiefs of staff would have extraordinary influence that could, in turn, engender a powerful political backlash against them. As a result, chiefs of staff would survive only if they had the president's complete support. Consequently, they, along with other top White House staffers, have an inherent reason to be loyal to the president: political survival. A personalized White House bureaucracy, centered on the presidency, was therefore created, one that could greatly serve the president's needs, but one that also could isolate the president from contrary political opinions. Over time, each of these scenarios has occurred.

In the short term, however, Kennedy decided to abandon many of Eisenhower's rigid organizational structures, such as the chief of staff, and develop a more loosely organized White House. Since Kennedy preferred to be the center of political debate, rather than routinely delegating issues to his subordinates, he organized the White House along a collegial spokes of the wheel governance model, as illustrated in Figure 13-2 (Campbell 1986; Buchanan 1987).[5]

Even during Kennedy's presidency, however, the size and functions of the presidency expanded, and this organizational framework actually placed increased demands on the president. While he formerly abolished the position of chief of staff, Kennedy depended on a chief of staff surrogate, Kenneth O'Donnell, to perform these myriad functions. As Press Secretary Pierre Salinger noted, "O'Donnell

Chief of staff: The chief of the White House staff. The position was created by Eisenhower as a policy and political coordinator, but the chief of staff has become (in many administrations) one of the most powerful officials in the U.S. government.

Special Assistant to the President for National Security Affairs: The National Security Adviser or the head of the National Security Council. The position was established by Eisenhower as a policy coordinator in foreign affairs but has become a political operative in some administrations. As with the chief of staff, this is one of the most powerful positions in the U.S. government.

Cabinet secretariat: A position created by Eisenhower to organize the agenda and materials for cabinet meetings. While the position was abandoned by Kennedy, other presidents have resurrected the cabinet secretariat.

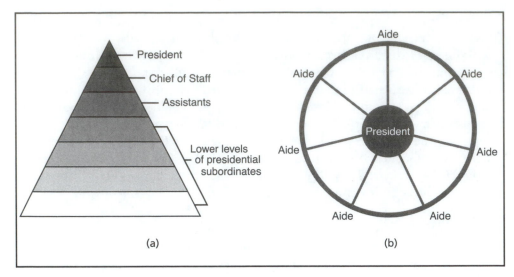

Figure 13-2

Spokes of the Wheel Model vs. Pyramid Model

(a) While Eisenhower based his administrative structure loosely on a military hierarchy (the pyramid), *(b)* Kennedy preferred to be in the center of debate and used a spokes of the wheel approach.

had the greatest influence in shaping the President's most important decisions" (quoted in Walcott and Hult 1995: 231). He was chief of staff in all but title.

When Lyndon Johnson became president, "his appointment secretary and office manager, Walter Jenkins, was generally regarded as the nearest thing to a chief of staff in the Johnson White House" (ibid., 232). After Jenkins was forced to resign following a sex scandal, the task went first to Jack Valenti and Bill Moyers, then to Marvin Watson. While Watson developed considerable influence, he never took on the formal task of chief of staff (ibid., 232–33). Over time, Joseph Califano became a de facto chief of staff, with more real power than Sherman Adams ever had (Hess 1976: 11). Still, LBJ chose not to formally assign anyone as chief of staff, thus creating organizational problems and some confusion throughout his presidency.

13-4d Nixon's Staff and Its Legacy

Not until Richard Nixon assumed the presidency was the chief of staff model again employed. Nixon's chief of staff, Robert (H. R.) Haldeman, became one of the most powerful men in the United States government, as did Nixon's National Security Adviser, Henry Kissinger. With power, however, came controversy. Kissinger was involved in allegations that the administration wiretapped journalists and even other officials in the Nixon administration, including some of his subordinates. While Kissinger's term as National Security Adviser was controversial, he was awarded the Nobel Peace Prize and rose to the position of Secretary of State. Haldeman's tenure as chief of staff was far less successful; he ultimately ended up in a jail cell.

Nixon's White House staff became infamous for a variety of reasons. It was charged with isolating the president of the United States from his top advisers, shielding the president even from contact with his own cabinet and vice president (see Haldeman 1994: 52; Warshaw 1996). From Nixon's point of view, this so-called White House "palace guard" protected him so that he could concentrate more of his time and attention on the important tasks of presidential leadership—in particular, foreign policy. As Nixon's own White House tapes demonstrate, however, he also had plenty of time to conspire with Haldeman, John Ehrlichman, Charles Colson, and other top White House staffers about petty political grudges. Often, he discussed retribution against his political opponents in agonizing detail. In this process, Haldeman and other staffers appeared to feed Nixon's mounting paranoia, thus undermining his entire presidency (see Reeves 2001; Kutler 1997).

In the end, Haldeman was convicted of obstruction of justice and sentenced to prison, along with Ehrlichman, Colson, Nixon's legal adviser John Dean, and a number of other top White House staffers. Cabinet and campaign officials also were implicated, indicted, convicted, and sentenced, but it was the White House staff's reputation that was most severely undermined. Immediately, scholars began to question the accountability and utility of the White House staff (see Hess 1976). Did the White House staff have too much power? Should staffers be accountable to more than just the president? Shouldn't presidents rely on the cabinet instead of the White House staff? The experiences of the Carter presidency provided some answers to these questions.

After the experiences of the Nixon presidency, Carter refused to name a chief of staff. He also decided to make regular use of his cabinet and to decrease the size and role of his White House staff. From the beginning of his administration, there were serious problems with these organizational choices. His use of a **spokes of the wheel** model of decision-making meant that there were too many access points to the president: Too many people had unrestricted access to Carter, thus inundating him in administrative and policy details rather than allowing him to step back and see the big picture. Carter himself seemed to relish this role, going so far as to dedicate precious presidential time to making out the schedule for the White House tennis court. With internal conflict ever inherent in White House staff operations, however, and no one in charge of it, chaos eventually prevailed.

As noted in section 12-6e, "Ford and Carter and Their Use of the Cabinet," the cabinet proved to be an ineffective organization for decision-making. As Carter's organization floundered, his presidency also was wounded fatally by the perception that he was not a competent manager of his own staff. Carter's subsequent achievements (Camp David, energy policy legislation, the Panama Canal treaty, civil service reform) could not undo the image of incompetence created during the first two years of his presidency (see Waterman, Wright, and St. Clair 1999). By the time Carter decided to name Hamilton Jordan as his first chief of staff, the damage essentially was done. While there is evidence that management of the White House improved substantially during Carter's last two years in office, under Jordan and then Jack Watson, and the president himself became more focused over time, politically speaking, Carter's presidency appeared beyond repair. Among the

Spokes of the wheel: A model of White House decision-making in which the president allows access from a variety of White House staffers but remains at the center of the decision-making process—the president is the fulcrum with the advisers representing each of the spokes in the wheel. The problem with this approach is that it allows too many access points, meaning too many people have unrestricted access to the president, thus inundating him in administrative and policy details rather than allowing him to step back and see the big picture.

Despite his achievements in office, Carter was seen as weak and disorganized, and his term is remembered mostly for the Iran hostage crisis (depicted here) and the oil embargo.

AP Photo

primary reasons for the failure of his presidency: bad organizational choices. Ronald Reagan would not make the same mistakes.

While Reagan introduced a new organizational structure, a triumvirate, or "troika," consisting of Edwin Meese, James Baker, and Michael Deaver, it was Baker who assumed clear responsibility as chief of staff.[6] He played a prominent role in the key legislative victories of 1981 and was given considerable credit for the administration's first-term successes. Baker demonstrated how critical a chief of staff could be to the success of a president. For instance, he convinced the president to focus on three major policy objectives in 1981 (tax cuts, spending cuts, and increased funds for the military) rather than promoting a broader-based agenda, as Carter initially had done. By setting clear legislative priorities, Reagan was able to achieve his key goals, which helped him develop a reputation as an effective leader.

While Baker helped develop the president's agenda and reputation, his successor, Donald Regan, was far less successful. The problems with Donald Regan's tenure as chief of staff derived from the very process by which he was selected for the post. After serving as chief of staff during Reagan's first term, Baker became bored and began to look to a cabinet position for the second term. At a lunch meeting with Secretary of the Treasury Donald Regan, Baker expressed his interest in a cabinet post and growing dissatisfaction with his job as chief of staff. Regan was bored as Treasury Secretary but was eager to work as chief of staff. The two men therefore approached the president with the idea of switching jobs. Without questioning its merits, Reagan agreed and Baker became his new Treasury Secretary, while Donald Regan became his new chief of staff.

Regan's tenure was much different than that of Baker. While Baker had heeded the recommendation of the Brownlow Committee and remained as much in the background as is possible for a chief of staff today, Regan longed for the limelight. For a while, the relationship seemed to work well: Regan's hands-on approach complemented the president's propensity to delegate.

Clearly, for presidents who delegate, a strong chief of staff is required, but presidents must still perform continual oversight, even if they delegate. Otherwise, they risk losing control of their staff. This is what appears to have happened in the second Reagan term. Not only did Regan take on a more aggressive role as chief of staff, but the president's various advisers for national security affairs turned the National Security Council from an agency that coordinates information into an operational decision-making body. With the president providing leadership only in the broadest of terms, the staff was free to interpret his policy pronouncements however they so desired, with little supervision. The result was a constitutional crisis: the Iran-Contra affair.

13-4e Iran-Contra

Iran-Contra raised such fundamental constitutional issues as, Who is in charge of foreign policy, the president or the Congress? The two institutions had battled over Nicaraguan policy for several years, with Congress increasingly tying the president's hands. As Reagan became more frustrated about the fate of the contra rebels in Nicaragua, and simultaneously lamented the fate of American hostages held in captivity in Iran, National Security staff struggled to develop policy options. In the end, NSC staff decided on a scheme that raised serious constitutional questions. U.S. arms were sold to so-called moderates inside Iran, an incentive for the release of American hostages. The profits from these legally dubious sales, which should have been the property of the U.S. government, were then transferred illegally to the contras in Nicaragua. This "neat idea," as NSC staffer Oliver North later called it, came close to destroying the Reagan presidency.

The Tower Commission, appointed by the president, later found that the NSC had moved beyond its formal mandate and thus inappropriately had become a policy player—a role legitimately handled by the State and Defense Departments, among others. The report also concluded that Chief of Staff Donald Regan had not provided appropriate oversight of the policy process. Regan angrily denounced the Tower Commission report (see Regan 1990), but following a subsequent confrontation with the First Lady (he apparently ended a telephone conversation by summarily hanging up on her), he was dismissed.

With the presidency again on the precipice, insiders turned to Howard Baker, a distinguished former Senate Majority Leader, to assume the post of chief of staff. Baker was tentative about accepting the job. He wanted to know whether the president was still mentally in charge. After meeting with the president, his concerns assuaged, Baker assumed control of the White House staff and, like James Baker before him, restored order to the Reagan White House. Baker's tenure was short-lived, however; he had returned to government service with a promise that he would leave within about a year. Hence, during the last year of the Reagan presidency, Ken Duberstein became chief of staff. Duberstein, like Baker, did much to restore confidence in the Reagan presidency.

A chief of staff has the potential for extraordinary power at any time, but particularly when the president's leadership style involves delegating broad authority to subordinates. The Reagan years, then, demonstrated both the best and worst aspects of the chief of staff position. James Baker helped Reagan achieve his greatest policy successes, and Howard Baker and Ken Duberstein restored order and prestige to the White House. Donald Regan's tenure, however, combined with an NSC staff that was out of control, raised fundamental questions about the legitimacy of the White House staff. If, within slightly more than a decade, the White House staff could contribute to the resignation of one president and involve a second president in a serious scandal, wasn't it time for presidents to make greater use of their cabinet and less use of their White House staff?

Additional questions were raised by the experiences of George H. W. Bush. His chief of staff, John Sununu, was widely recognized as a brilliant man. Yet, he also was acerbic and had a propensity to make political enemies, while cultivating few political friends. When a controversy arose whether Sununu inappropriately used government transportation to attend private events, the chief of staff had few political friends left to defend him. Faced with mounting controversy just as he was preparing to run for re-election, Bush removed Sununu from office. As happened with the first chief of staff, Sherman Adams, a relatively trivial event led to Sununu's downfall. In the process, however, the president was politically damaged. Not only was he forced to appoint a new untried chief of staff just as he was heading into a campaign for re-election, but the removal of a top White House official also raised questions about the president's competence. Sununu's case provided further evidence to support the argument that presidents should not employ a high-profile chief of staff.

Bill Clinton heeded that lesson, and like Jimmy Carter, he quickly came to regret it. Clinton did name a chief of staff, Thomas McClarty, but he gave McClarty relatively little authority, preferring instead to leave access to the president relatively open. The result is that Clinton's first chief of staff was resoundingly criticized for being "Mack the Nice."

Clinton, like Carter, learned the hard way that he needed a strong chief of staff to structure his contacts and to provide a policy focus for his administration. His choice of Leon Panetta, a former congressman who had once been a Republican, proved more successful. Panetta restored order to the White House and though there were many scandals associated with the Clinton White House, it is indeed a key reflection on Panetta's character and abilities that he was implicated in none of them. Instead, he is given considerable credit for redirecting the Clinton White House and putting the president on a path to re-election. George W. Bush then named Andrew Card as his chief of staff and employed an active chief of staff model.

13-4f Lessons Learned from Staffing History

The experiences of presidents since Eisenhower present us with a conundrum. With the increased size and complexity of the presidential staff, presidents must name a strong chief of staff. Yet, when they do so, they often risk the possibility that their staff will run out of control, severely damaging the president's reputation and political standing.

While a good case can be made that the organization of the White House can create serious problems for the presidency (in particular, see Hess 1976/1988), there seems to be no turning back (see Warshaw 1996; Waterman 1993). It is not likely that presidents will make greater use of the cabinet than the White House staff. As we saw in sections 12-6d through 12-6g, most modern presidents who have used the cabinet have not been satisfied with the results. Hence, the movement toward the development of internal and informational political resources appears to be inevitable. As Patterson (1988: 6) writes,[7]

> A divided nation at home and a bare-knuckled world abroad translate into the need for an American president who can synchronize all the resources the Constitution and the laws afford him for leadership and governance. Many of those resources are in his Cabinet, but it is the White House Staff who are his synchronizers; neither he nor they should apologize that they are energetic in this role. There should be less fighting, therefore, about the size of the staff, and more attention to the unique core functions that it performs and how the whole is managed and controlled.

Still, while the move toward greater staff use appears inevitable,[8] no one organizational formula guarantees success (Jones 1994: 101), though not taking advantage of a strong chief of staff may indeed open the door for policy confusion and political failure. Furthermore, it is clear that since the function of the White House staff is not merely governance but also politics (Podhoretz 1993: 79), White House staffers increasingly will be on the front lines of the policy battles in Washington. The opposition knows that if they can take down or embarrass a prominent White House staff member (such as Sherman Adams or John Sununu), they also can damage the leadership reputation of the president in the process. The White House staff represents other dangers: An expanded White House staff also can pull new functions into the White House (Weko 1995: 103), thus providing the president with little space to run if things go wrong. Attracting new functions to the White House also can exacerbate the overload problem identified in section 11-2a, "How Does Overload Occur?"—the problem the White House staff ostensibly is there to handle. For all of these reasons, the relationship between the president and his staff represents a presidential conundrum (Waterman 1988). In many respects, it is a veritable "*damned if you do and damned if you don't*" situation, one that calls for a new dimension of presidential leadership: managerial skill. Since the institutional presidency is so fraught with potential hazard, we need to more clearly determine why presidents adopt and employ these new political resources.

13-5 Internal Resources and the Changing Political Ecosystem

As we learned in section 11-7, "Why Do Political Ecosystems Change?" the modern presidency is inundated with a number of new demands, expectations, functions, and responsibilities. When we consider these various demands, the fact that presidents must respond to Congress, the public, the media, special interests (representing widely different political perspectives), the bureaucracy, as well as state and local governments, foreign countries, international organizations, and sundry other political actors, we can see why it is so difficult for presidents to govern without institutional help. When we add to the calculus the fact that issues move on and off the political agenda both rapidly and often unpredictably and the president plays an integral role in both setting and responding to the policy agenda (see Kingdon 1983), we further can understand why presidential scholars are concerned that the presidency is too big a job for any individual (Buchanan 1978). The demands and expectations placed on the presidency are excessive. Furthermore, the cabinet is of limited utility in providing presidents with the kind of help that the Brownlow Committee suggested the president needs. To deal with overload then, presidents (following the Brownlow Committee and Franklin Roosevelt) have turned their attention to a variety of institutions created directly inside the White House and thus primarily responsive to the president of the United States.

These internal resources often have been created to respond to changing demands and expectations as the president's place in the American political ecosystem has evolved. As Weko (1995: 154) notes, the trend toward greater centralization is related to the "vastly increased importance of television news, and the disintegration of 'policy networks' in response to the multiplying of interest groups and the dispersion of authority within the U.S. Congress. Taken together, these changes swiftly increased the costs—and diminished the rewards—of permitting departments to operate as 'semi-independent fiefdoms.'" As a result, "presidents responded by sharply accelerating the personnel staff's size and reach."

To better understand how changes in the political ecosystem translate into the need for centralization, let's turn our attention back to the various actors in Figure 11-2, which delineates some of the institutions presidents deal with on a regular basis. We see that demands on the presidency from various segments of the political ecosystem have increased. Now let's look separately at some of these actors and see how the institutional presidency deals with them.

13-5a The New Constituencies: The Media and the Public

The media are among the new constituencies of the presidency. Whereas presidents were largely shielded from the media in the nineteenth century, today they must respond to the various news outlets (including 24/7 TV news networks; radio; national newspapers such as the *New York Times,* the *Washington Post,* and the *Los Angeles Times;* the local press; weekly news magazines such as *Time, Newsweek,* and *U.S. News and World Report;* Internet news services; and even the foreign press). In addition, the size of the media expanded greatly—from about 350 at the time that Herbert Hoover took office to about 1,260 by the time Lyndon Johnson left office (Walcott and Hult 1995: 60). Press coverage of the president also has vastly increased, and presidents not only respond to these various news sources, but they also try to shape the news, manipulating it so that they can get the best possible coverage.[9] Obviously, no president alone could interact with all of these different types of media personnel, never mind develop strategies for controlling the message the media reports. To do these things, presidents need help. They need qualified staff capable of carrying out these functions. This is what presidents in the modern era have created.

At first, the innovations in press relations came slowly. Under Roosevelt and Truman, the press secretary had but two assistants who "interacted informally with the president and his intimates in the White House" (Walcott and Hult 1995: 53). Eisenhower, with his military background, however, had a penchant for management and organization. He therefore created organizational structures that performed specific functions, thus allowing the president to dedicate his time to bigger questions and issues. His press secretary, James Hagerty, "was an organizational innovator, as well." Hagerty expanded the tasks the office performed and paid closer attention to press operations in other executive departments, thus bringing greater coordination to the media operation (ibid., 57).

To perform these tasks, Eisenhower and his successors established a series of different offices in the Executive Office of the President. Grossman and Kumar (1981: 7) write,

> [T]he Press Office and the Media Liaison operation were designed in part to assist news organizations in covering the agenda of activities the President and his advisers wished to set before the public; the Office of Public Liaison was created to promote the President and his programs; and other offices assumed the function of planning and coordinating direct press operations, White House promotion, and other political communication. White House officials learned that when they combined the resources of these offices with more traditional avenues of public exposure such as presidential speeches, press conferences, and the regular activities of the press secretary, they had tools that enabled them to deal more effectively with news organizations and thus get the President's message to the appropriate audience.

The press office expanded from fewer than ten employees in 1953 to more than thirty in the 1960s and 1970s (ibid., 23). New offices also were created to improve presidential-media relations. During the Nixon administration, a number of media functions were combined when the Office of Communications was established. The Nixon administration misused this new resource. According to the Watergate investigation, the office "was shown to be a major organ of the Nixon administration's efforts to discredit and circumvent the Washington press corps" (ibid., 25). Still, the office has continued to operate under Nixon's successors. Successive presidents realized that they needed the organizational expertise that the Communications Office offered.

In short, the "White House is a vast political communications center that sends messages to Congress, foreign governments, interest groups, bureaucrats, and the American public" (ibid., 81). To perform these myriad public relations tasks, as well as to manage the day-to-day news operations, presidents need organizational resources that can assist them in their daily tasks. Reaching out to the press is thus of vital presidential interest. Organizationally, media relations reflect that priority.

13-5b Reaching Out to the Public

Presidents use the various communications/media relations units to reach out to the public and to shape their message and image. For this reason, they also are concerned with public opinion. Initially, presidential responses to public opinion were "idiosyncratic and did not involve the White House staff until LBJ brought the first public-opinion analyst into the White House; the aide was incorporated into the overall staff hierarchy without significant additional governance structuring" (Walcott and Hult 1995: 61). Jimmy Carter then became the first president to have his own pollster in the White House. Carter's successors have expanded the public opinion role. Now the White House conducts regular polling of the public to determine its mood.

Besides measuring public opinion, other efforts have been made to coordinate administration efforts at public relations. During the New Deal, the National Emergency Council brought various heads of recovery programs together to discuss and plot strategies for using promotional campaigns and the media to build public support for New Deal programs (ibid., 63). After the Executive Office of the President was established in 1939, the Office of Government Reports was created to provide a "central public information office that would serve as a clearinghouse for the distribution of information about the activities of government agencies and as a tool for keeping the Roosevelt administration abreast of public opinion on government activities" (ibid., 63).

Again reflecting his interest in organizations, Eisenhower established the Executive Branch Liaison Office, a "specialized public-relations unit." It had three tasks: "issuing weekly 'fact papers' to be used in speeches by agency and department officials," providing liaison with the Republican National Committee (RNC), and "coordinating executive branch speakers" (ibid., 65–66). Kennedy generally and derisively rejected the formalized structures created by Eisenhower, and public relations were no exception. A formal counterpart to the Eisenhower system was not established until Nixon created the Office of Communications, which included among its many functions those previously performed by Eisenhower's Executive Branch Liaison Office. Hence, since Nixon's presidency, a formal mechanism for coordinating administration responses to the public has been in place, even if its specific contours have varied somewhat from president to president.

13-5c Specific Areas of Presidential Interest

Presidents also have established different organizational units in the White House to reach out to specific constituencies of interest to them. These offices vary considerably from president to president as their policy and political interests differ. What does not differ, however, is the need for public outreach. Again, this practice largely began with Franklin Roosevelt, who used White House staff to reach out and "help monitor relations with farmers, labor, nationality groups, and Jewish organizations, all considered electorally important" (Pika 1993: 151). Truman used aides to work with business and labor, Catholics, and veterans (ibid., 152).

Pika (1993: 152) writes, "Eisenhower's situation was quite different. His electoral support rested less heavily on a coalition of distinctive voting blocs and he saw less importance in maintaining White House liaison." Still, as Pika (ibid., 152) writes, "despite this reluctance to appoint group contacts, several resident staff assignments emerged over time." A Jewish staff member worked closely with the Jewish community, while a congregational minister worked closely with other church groups. In addition, both farm and veteran's organizations had designated specialists, and although he did not officially name a representative for minority liaison, Eisenhower was the first president to name an African American to a professional White House staff position (ibid.). In addition to these efforts, "Eisenhower was the first president to use group liaison as a part of a coordinated effort to advance the administration's legislative program" (ibid.). In numerous ways, then, Eisenhower contributed to the institutionalization of the presidency in the field of public liaison.

While Kennedy and Johnson "restored the need to maintain ties with key Democratic voting blocs including blacks, Catholics, organized labor . . . , Jewish groups, and Protestants" (ibid.), it was not until the Nixon administration that

Presidents rely on public liaison to maintain ties with many groups, including civil rights organizations, women's groups, and ethnically and religiously affiliated groups. Here, Lyndon Johnson meets with civil rights leader Martin Luther King, Jr.

"public liaison assumed a more coherent organizational form within the White House staff" when the Office of Public Liaison (OPL) was created (ibid., 153). The "Nixon White House had aides looking after the interests of civil rights organizations, Jewish groups, Catholics, consumers, women, youth, and Hispanics in units other than" the OPL (ibid., 153–54). Carter also used his public liaison office to build up grass-roots support (Light 1983: 95).

13-5d Recent Liaison Presidents

Reagan was also active in public liaison. His administration "established a zealous band of lobbyists and skilled persuaders inside his Office of Public Liaison, the unit that served as the White House's eyes and ears with the American public" (Kolb 1994: 5). Reagan and George H. W. Bush, however, took "group liaison in a somewhat different direction. Since the 1970s, liaison has increasingly involved the distribution of factsheets and newsletters to specialized audiences" (ibid., 154–55). In this process, "the array of interests receiving White House attention has grown even larger, though not all enjoy a 'resident' contact. Business, labor, Jews, consumers, blacks, women, Hispanics, conservatives, the elderly have received major attention."[10] During Clinton's presidency, a unit for outreach to gays and lesbians was established.

Beyond specific interest groups, presidents also have added offices that provide outreach to state and local governments, as well as representing constituency interest on specific issues. Hence, various presidents created offices to deal with the environment, drugs, crime, AIDS, telecommunications, economic development, and many other issues, providing both substantive policy advice for presidents, as well as symbolic cues to interested publics that the White House cares about a particular issue. When a president disbands an office, as when the administration of George W. Bush eliminated the AIDS office, that too can send a policy signal. Consequently, as the constituencies that presidents interact with expand, the public liaison function takes on a larger role.

In sum, as media and public demands have increased, as public expectations have expanded, presidents have created new organizational mechanisms to help them deal with these new political constituencies. They have not used these institutional mechanisms in the same way, however. Presidents mold these institutions to their own needs. Therefore, the institutional presidency is really semi-institutional—constantly adjusting to the needs of different presidents and different political times.

13-5e Chief Legislator: Congressional Liaison

As noted in section 9-8a, "New Expectations for Presidential-Congressional Relations," the president's relationship with Congress also has changed considerably since the beginning of the twentieth century. Congress delegated greater authority to the presidency over specific functions, such as the budget and economic policy. In addition, the president's role as chief legislator is now accepted as a central function of the president's job (see Rossiter 1960). Presidents now initiate legislation, giving meaning to the rhyme: "the president proposes, Congress disposes."

As presidents have adopted a more active role in congressional relations, they have likewise expanded their internal and informational resources in this area. Like media and public relations, congressional liaison is a central task of the institutional presidency. As Walcott and Hult (1995: 27) write, "Presidential skill in dealing with Congress—one of the most important targets of presidential outreach—is a sine qua non of a successful presidency. During the early modern era, White House structures emerged to abet presidential efforts at legislative leadership."

13-5f Origins of the Current Congressional Liaison

As noted in section 13-3, Franklin Roosevelt began the practice of sending a personal envoy to Capitol Hill. It is not surprising, then, that the first White House mechanism for congressional liaison was established in the Executive Office of the President in 1939. The EOP White House Office was partially composed of secretaries whose mission was to "facilitate and maintain quick and easy communication with the Congress, the individual members of the Congress, the heads of executive departments and agencies, the press, the radio, and the general public" (Fisher 1981: 43). FDR did not fully take advantage of these new organizational resources because he preferred to retain and use his own personal contacts with the leaders of Congress.

Truman went further than Franklin Roosevelt by assigning specific staff the congressional liaison function (Hess 1976: 5). Once again, however, it was "Eisenhower who elevated the legislative affairs function to top rank in the White House, and appointed his deputy chief of staff, retired Major Wilton B. Persons, to take charge of it" (Patterson 1988: 152). In 1953, Eisenhower assigned a staff of senior assistants the responsibility of legislative liaison. The staff began with just three people, but increased to eight by 1961, when Eisenhower left the White House (Fisher 1981: 45).

According to Seligman and Covington (1988: 87), the Office of Congressional Relations (OCR) "is an institutional adaptation to the president's need to build congressional coalitions. Presidents needed help to fulfill increasingly insistent public and congressional expectations for legislative leadership." Consequently, it is not surprising that every president has adopted Eisenhower's innovation, though in somewhat different organizational forms (Patterson 1988: 152.). These coalitions help presidents to get a sense of the mood on Capitol Hill, apprise them of the needs and voting propensities of individual members of Congress, and provide a means for presidents to communicate with members, as well as for members to express their concerns about presidents and their programs.

13-6 Declining Political Party Influence and New Structures for Presidential Transitions

Presidents have created functions in the White House to deal not only with increasing demands for action, but also because of the declining influence of other institutions. As the political parties' influence declined, for example, presidents took on a more prominent role in the appointment process—see section 15-4d, "Party Decline and a New Appointment Process." Many roles and functions once performed by the parties (including public and congressional liaison) now are the purview of what Hart (1995) calls the presidential branch: As the party organizations declined, presidential organizations took their place. One example is the presidential transition function.

13-6a Declining Role of the Political Parties and Emergence of Transition Teams

Historically, the political parties provided the basic institutional structure for presidential transitions. When a new president was elected, the political parties played an integral role in identifying nominees for governmental positions, including top posts in the president's cabinet. As noted in section 6-8a, "The Presidential Primaries of 1952," beginning with the Eisenhower presidency, presidents developed their own campaign organizations, separate and distinct from the political parties. By the time Nixon ran for re-election in 1972, the Republican Party apparatus was largely irrelevant. As the parties were relegated to the backseat in elections, their influence in the transition process also declined. Hence, presidents created new transition organizations to fill the void left by the declining influence of the political parties.

During his transition, John Kennedy had two individuals—Clark Clifford and Richard Neustadt—writing transition reports, with each working independent of the other and without the other's knowledge. In addition to the Clifford and Neustadt operations, Kennedy also used several task forces to help with his transition. He designated seven after his nomination, nineteen more after his election, and three more in January 1961. By inauguration day, twenty-four of twenty-nine had reported to him. Out of these reports, Kennedy developed his ideas for legislative initiatives. The reports provided briefing material for the president and enlarged his circle of advisers (ibid., 11). Kennedy relied on these transition task forces to such an extent that, as president, he recommended government funding for transition costs. In response, Congress enacted the Presidential Transition Act of 1963. The act provided that "to promote the orderly transfer of a President and the inauguration of a new President," the Administrator of the General Services Administration (GSA) would provide office space whenever the president-elect wanted, as well as staff, travel, communication, and printing expenses. The act authorized $900,000 to be spent on transitions (ibid., 9). The Presidential Transition Act thus institutionalized the change from one presidential administration to another.[11]

Nixon was the first president entering office to use the act's provisions: Johnson became president when Kennedy was assassinated and thus was already in office when he used the act in 1964. Nixon appointed some twenty task forces under the supervision of Paul McCracken. The task forces developed various policy approaches, and many of their members became part of the administration (Pfiffner 1988: 13).

The first systematic preparation during a presidential campaign occurred with Jimmy Carter, a Democrat, who entered office after eight years of Republican rule. Yet, the transition planning caused serious problems. "The transition planning group was intentionally segregated from the campaign organization in order to keep day-to-day brush fires from driving out long-range planning, but therein lay the seeds of discord that were to damage the transition planning effort after the Carter election victory. Friction began to develop between the transitions planning group in Atlanta and the campaign organization." The election organization saw the transition team as "usurpers trying to steal from them the fruits of victory while they worked on getting the candidate elected" (ibid., 14). In other words, many campaign staff believed that they were being systematically eliminated from consideration for administration positions by the transition staff, even as they were working to get Carter elected. The bitter rivalries thus created continued into the Carter presidency, undermining unity from the very beginning.

Reagan's transition was more elaborate and benefited from the experience of Carter's failures. In April 1980, Reagan asked a group of supporters to begin planning for his first 100 days in office. As a result, Richard Allen, later Reagan's first National Security Adviser, "headed a group of 132 people in 23 issue-area groups led by Martin Anderson. No pre-election central transition planning office was set up as Carter had done, but Edwin Meese oversaw several low-visibility planning operations including a personnel operation headed by Pendleton James" (ibid., 16). After his election, Reagan's transition team was seated in Washington; to emphasize his independence from Washington politics, Carter's had been run out of Atlanta, Georgia. About 100 transition teams were spread throughout the government. The teams were given office space in various agencies and departments, where they had full access to budgetary and program information. In this way, the Reagan team was able to plan the transition, not only of the president's team, but also throughout the bureaucracy, ensuring that Reagan staffed his administration with individuals who shared the president's personal political philosophy (ibid., 17). In this sense, Reagan's transition team, like the new president himself, was more ideological than his predecessors (Moe 1985b: 260).

Consequently, by the time of the Kennedy presidency, institutionalization of the presidential transition function had begun, and by the Carter and Reagan presidencies, fully developed institutional procedures had been established. The different experiences of the Carter and Reagan presidencies demonstrate that how these resources are employed goes a long way toward determining a president's success. Management skill is required even before a president assumes office.

13-7 The Development of Institutional Mechanisms after September 11, 2001

As I noted in Chapter 11, shocks to the political ecosystem also create the need for new institutional mechanisms. In section 11-7c, I provided several examples of shocks to the ecosystem: the Great Depression and the New Deal, World War II, the Cold War, the Vietnam War, and the various Watergate-related scandals. The terrorist attack on the World Trade Center in New York City and the concomitant attack on the Pentagon in Washington suddenly altered the policy environment. In September and October 2001, George W. Bush was scheduled to discuss his education reforms. Instead, the September 11 terrorist attacks dramatically altered the president's political agenda. Overnight, domestic security and the fight against terrorism became the dominant themes of Bush's administration. Organizational changes soon reflected this change in the policy agenda.

13-7a The Creation of New Offices

In the aftermath of the September 11, 2001, terrorist attacks, the Office of Homeland Security was quickly announced as a new organization for coordinating internal security needs. A new Homeland Security Council also was created, to consist of Tom Ridge, the new director of Homeland Security; the Attorney General; the Secretaries of Defense, Treasury, Health and Human Services, and Agriculture; as well as the directors of the Federal Bureau of Investigation, and the director of the Federal Emergency Management Agency (NYT 9-28-01: B5). In addition, a new office of Cyber Security was announced.

The creation of these new offices demonstrated anew why presidents increase the size and functions of their White House staff. It also demonstrated the difficulties of establishing such instant agencies. While Ridge had a mission, he had no real organizational unit or staff support to assist him in his task. He had no clearly delineated role, initially making it difficult for him to get others to defer to his new office.

Created on the run to fill a newly created need, the office was soon attacked as inadequate. Senator Joseph Lieberman recommended creating a cabinet-level department of Homeland Security, while the Bush administration initially resisted creating either a department or further expanding the office's size and functions. A similar debate surrounded whether airport security should be federalized or privatized. As the functions of the new offices were debated, some newspapers criticized Ridge for not acting quickly enough to bring order to the homeland security issues, especially as a new threat, anthrax, invaded the postal system (see Figure 13-3). In fact, it would take time to establish a new office, clearly define its role, and convince existing organizations to defer to it. Eventually, the president conceded that a new Department of Homeland Security would be required. In short, simply establishing a new agency to deal with an emerging problem is not enough, though it often is a necessary starting point.

Figure 13-3
The Homeland Security Advisory System

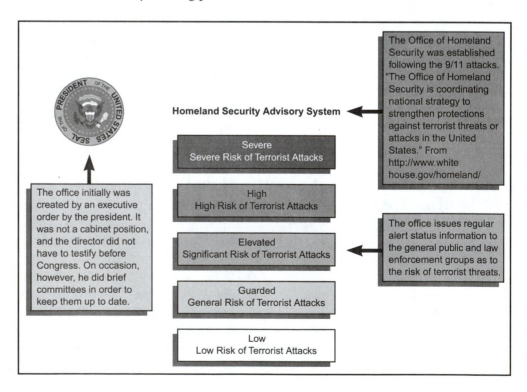

The Office of Homeland Security was established following the 9/11 attacks. "The Office of Homeland Security is coordinating national strategy to strengthen protections against terrorist threats or attacks in the United States." From http://www.white house.gov/homeland/

Homeland Security Advisory System

Severe
Severe Risk of Terrorist Attacks

High
High Risk of Terrorist Attacks

Elevated
Significant Risk of Terrorist Attacks

Guarded
General Risk of Terrorist Attacks

Low
Low Risk of Terrorist Attacks

The office initially was created by an executive order by the president. It was not a cabinet position, and the director did not have to testify before Congress. On occasion, however, he did brief committees in order to keep them up to date.

The office issues regular alert status information to the general public and law enforcement groups as to the risk of terrorist threats.

13-8 Domestic Policy and Informational Resources

Thus far, I have examined various components of the president's internal White House resources. Mostly, I have examined three factors that internal resources bring to the presidency:

1. outreach to the broader political community such as through the various liaison offices presidents have created,
2. coordination such as the chief of staff provides, and
3. expertise, both policy and political, as provided by various White House units, the chief of staff, and the new vice presidency.

Internal political resources also provide mechanisms for decision-making. As Kessel (1975: vii) notes, "The president himself makes the most important decisions, but scores of other persons gather the information he needs to make many vital decisions themselves." Hence, particularly in the realm of decision-making, the president's internal resources also involve informational resources such as political knowledge (provided by the Legislative Liaison Office regarding the voting propensities of members of Congress), budgetary information (provided by the Office of Management and Budget for the various departments and agencies throughout the executive branch), and national security data, including various military options (provided by the National Security Council, the Central Intelligence Agency, the Joint Chiefs of Staff, and other organizations). Without access to this information, presidents are at a distinct disadvantage in the policy-making process.

In the past, presidents did not have direct access to information about the political process. Even as skilled a political operator as Franklin Roosevelt was forced to use a network of outside political advisers, his brain trust, to provide information on domestic policy. In the realm of foreign policy, especially prior to World War II, Roosevelt was forced to rely on a number of informal contacts and networks to provide him with vital information on Japan's and Germany's military intentions (see Persico 2001). As the demands of the modern presidency expanded, however, it was clear that presidents not only needed more staff, but they also needed more and better information in order to govern effectively. While this is most clearly understood with regard to foreign policy, information also plays a vital role in the development of domestic policy.

For example, institutionally, the president's greatest asset in the budgetary process is the Office of Management and Budget (OMB), formerly the Bureau of the Budget (BOB). The OMB provides an organizational means for presidents to gain greater control over the budget. By requiring all departments and agencies to submit their proposed budgets to the OMB, the Nixon and Reagan administrations gained greater influence over the budgetary process. In the case of the Reagan administration, the OMB went so far as to inform various agencies of the exact amount of funding they would receive and how much they had to cut out of their proposed budgets. The OMB also included detailed plans regarding the number of layoffs and proposals for the reorganization of functional units (for various departments).

By providing a point of central clearance for all executive branch budgetary requests, the OMB likewise reduced the ability of individual agencies to make an end run around the president and request more money from Congress. Increasing the president's information advantages therefore concomitantly increased the president's influence over the budgetary process.[12]

13-8a The Council of Economic Advisers

Congress provided presidents with numerous organizational resources to provide them with greater information and coordination of domestic policy. One of these, the Council of Economic Advisers (CEA), was established via the Employment Act of 1946. The original idea was to limit presidential influence by forcing presidents to listen to the expertise of supposedly nonpartisan economists when formulating economic policy. Truman was therefore initially skeptical of the CEA. What Congress did not fully understand, though, is that once internal resources are established, presidents can use them pretty much as they wish. Over time, as he realized its utility, Truman made greater use of the CEA.

Eisenhower then reorganized the CEA in June 1953, granting the chairman of the CEA greater authority over the council's operations. Hess (1976: 75–76) writes, "The CEA survived the first crucial transition in administrations because of the increased stake of the President in the behavior of the economy, because the council members and their staff were congenial to the President, and because they provided the President with information that he considered immediately useful." With new central leadership, it was easier for Eisenhower's successors to exert control over the council, ensuring that it would not be an impediment to administration policy, but rather would provide useful economic information to presidents of both parties. Thus, Eisenhower's reorganization opened the door for more active use of the CEA by Kennedy and Johnson (see Hart 1987: 50–53).

Under the Kennedy administration, the CEA came to play its most prominent role. Kennedy's CEA chairman, Walter Heller, was as influential as the Secretary of the Treasury, Douglas Dillon (Hess 1976: 89). The CEA, however, played a lesser role under Presidents Nixon and Ford.

13-8b The Economic Policy Board, the Economic Policy Group, and the National Economic Council

In September 1974, Gerald Ford established a new mechanism for economic policy formulation—the Economic Policy Board (EPB).[13] Chaired by Treasury Secretary William Simon, the EPB provided a broad base of advice to the president on domestic and international economic policy. In fact, the "EPB became *the* formal vehicle for conveying policy advice to the president" (Porter 1988: 224; see also Porter 1980). Ford himself considered it to be the "most important institutional innovation of my administration" (quoted in Hess 1988: 135).

Still, once Ford was defeated, the new president, Jimmy Carter, disbanded the EPB and replaced it with his own organization, the Economic Policy Group (EPG). Staffed largely by Treasury Department personnel, the EPG had no direct access to the Oval Office; consequently, its utility was greatly constrained from the very beginning. The failure of the EPG led Reagan to abandon it, employing instead a cabinet Council of Economic Advisers, not to be confused with the CEA. The Council was particularly active during the first two years of the Reagan presidency (Hart 1987: 58–62). The model for the new council system was, in fact, Ford's Economic Policy Board—bringing both cabinet and White House staff together to deal with economic policy (Pfiffner 1988: 54).

While George H. W. Bush used many of the same organizational mechanisms as Reagan, Clinton made greater use of the National Economic Council. Since his interest was in international economic policy, as well as domestic economics, Clinton believed the National Economic Council provided him with a broader base of advice than did the Council of Economic Advisers, the Office of Management and Budget, or the Treasury Department. Since international trade agreements, Latin American debt problems, and the collapse of the Asian market became central concerns of the Clinton presidency, his reliance on advisers with expertise in these areas, including his second Treasury Secretary, Robert Rubin, proved highly useful.

What these various institutions used by recent presidents indicate, then, is that the president's internal and informational political resources are highly fluid, often changing from administration to administration, to meet the changing needs of new presidents. Each president prefers a particular organizational structure. In addition, presidents emphasize different policies. Consequently, the institutional presidency changes to satisfy these changing needs. This can be seen not only in the economic institutions presidents have used, but also in the domestic policy organizations.

13-9 Domestic Policy Organizations

Presidents Kennedy and Johnson "firmly recognized that prevailing arrangements could not be counted upon to generate or even support innovative domestic programs." As a result, they "centralized the policy process more fully in the White House, with the pivotal role played by a domestic policy staff." Policy proposals now took one of two tracks: Routine matters went to the departments and bureaus, while important ones were sent to the White House (Moe 1985b: 252–53). Nixon then expanded the Kennedy and Johnson innovation when he established the Domestic Policy Council in 1970. The council's task was to propose, formulate, and advocate policy options. It played a key if often-controversial role in policy development because it centralized functions once performed by the cabinet departments directly inside the White House. While Nixon was criticized for this move, his successors generally followed suit. This did not mean, however, that the domestic policy office always exerted the same level of influence. For example, under Ford, the Domestic Council, headed by Vice President Nelson Rockefeller, had minimal influence over policy making (Wyszomirski 1985). All administrations, however, had some form of a domestic policy unit or even multiple units.

For instance, Carter used his reorganization authority to replace the Domestic Council with the Domestic Policy Staff (DPS). It was no longer a deliberative council, but rather an advisory and coordinating staff. With a staff of between forty and fifty, its director, Stuart Eisenstat, put together a more experienced and talented unit than was characterized by other aspects of the Carter White House staff (which tended to be anti-Washington, relishing its outsider role). The staff, organized around about a dozen associate directors, provided the president with expertise on a variety of policy issues. It was, by most accounts, one of the most competent units in the Carter administration, an administration not generally known for its organizational prowess (Wyszomirski 1985: 138–40).

Despite its relative success under Carter's administration, the Domestic Council system played a much less influential role. The Office of Policy Development (OPD), chaired by Martin Anderson, and developed along the lines of Eisenstat's office in the Carter administration, was designed to "build a process that kept the cabinet officers directly involved in policy development, both to ensure their support for the policies and to ensure that policies were in line with broad administration goals" (Warshaw 1997: 125). While OPD was successful in this regard, the cabinet councils eclipsed its influence. Over time, Martin Anderson, the head of OPD, "became a messenger for [OMB Director David] Stockman's economic policy and essentially abdicated a policy-making role for the Office of Policy Development. Domestic policy was so closely tied to economic policy that it was difficult to separate the two" (ibid., 129).

During George H. W. Bush's administration, domestic policy "fell under the umbrella of 'all aspects of White House operations' and was rapidly pulled within" the jurisdiction of Chief of Staff John Sununu. Domestic policy was divided under two broad umbrellas: White House policy development was placed under the direction of the Assistant to the President for Economic and Domestic Policy, while cabinet-initiated policy development was assigned to a cabinet secretary (ibid., 160). The basic structure used by the Assistant to the President for Economic and Domestic Policy, Roger Porter, was again the Office of Policy Development, carried over from the Reagan administration. "Although Porter had carefully structured his office to be the dominant player in policy development, few major initiatives arose from either the Office of Policy Development (OPD) or the Office of Policy Planning (OPP) during the course of the administration" (ibid., 166). Then again, domestic policy formulation was never a priority of the first Bush presidency.

On the other hand, Bill Clinton had a clear interest in domestic affairs from the very beginning of his administration. The Office of Policy Development proved to be the primary mechanism through which the Clinton administration devised policy. Within the OPD, there were three subdivisions: one for the Domestic Policy Council, the second for the National Economic Council, and the third for the Environment Policy Council (ibid., 190). Clinton established the Domestic Policy Council. Clinton's council consisted of both cabinet members and White House staff (ibid., 194). Hence, another characteristic of White House organizations, over time, is the way in which they combine White House staff and cabinet secretaries and their staff into viable working groups. In such a manner, presidents combine their various resources in an attempt to gain greater utility from their cabinet members, while reducing some of the hostility that naturally exists between the cabinet and the White House staff. Thus, in both economic and domestic policy, the institutions have been fluid over time. Is the same true, however, of foreign affairs?

13-10 Foreign Policy and Informational Resources

Kellerman and Barilleaux (1991: 41) write, "The fact that a strong foreign affairs presidency has evolved over time is no accident. The main reasons for this development are: the president's pre-eminent position in the political system; the powers that have accrued in this [the twentieth] century to the executive office; the president's political, informational, and bureaucratic resources; and the nature of the American foreign policy system in the late twentieth century." Of particular interest to us here is "the president's political, informational, and bureaucratic resources." While the internal resources of the presidency in domestic affairs often have proven controversial, the same also can be said for the president's internal foreign policy resources. Like the internal domestic resources we examined in section 13-5, however, presidents have come to rely on these resources. In fact, they have become a vital component of the presidency and a major contributor to the accretion of presidential power.

As I noted in sections 2-6 through 2-6g, throughout much of our nation's history, America had virtually no standing army. Philosophically, our military was characterized by a fear of standing armies and an ardent belief in isolationism. By the end of World War II, isolationism fell by the wayside, and though there was a brief movement toward disarmament, by the end of the 1940s, policy makers on both sides of the political aisle recognized the need for a continuing military presence. They also recognized another need: the need for new institutional resources.

Naively, however, Congress envisioned a new institution, the National Security Council (NSC), as a means of limiting presidential power. The idea, as was the case when Congress established the Council of Economic Advisers, was to constrain presidential prerogative by forcing presidents to consult with experts. Consequently, when Congress insisted on creating the NSC as part of the reorganization and creation of the new Defense Department, Truman was not enthusiastic. Realizing that it was a condition of the agreement, however, he acquiesced and then ignored the NSC, as he had the CEA (Hess 1976: 56). Truman did not want someone to lecture him on what he should or should not do. Ironically, then, Congress forced the NSC, one of the most powerful arms of the institutional presidency, on a reluctant president. It did not take Truman long, however, to learn that Congress had given him an extraordinary gift of presidential power.

In 1950, Truman restructured the NSC. "The staff and consultants were replaced by a senior staff and staff assistants who, while still located in the agencies, were now under the direction of the NSC's executive secretary." In making these changes, Truman "set institutional precedents that would shape future uses of the council and its staff" (Mulcahy and Crabb 1991: 253). With a reorganized staff, as the Korean War continued, Truman found that the NSC provided him "with information that was immediately and politically useful" (Hess 1976: 56). In fact, the NSC's statutory role was to coordinate information to the president (Henderson 1988: 71–72). This was a valuable function, for presidents received information from a variety of sources, some more dubious than others. Presidents needed someone who could make sense of this information flow and then provide recommendations for action. The NSC thus commenced as a coordinating agency, not an operational one—that is, not as a decision-making body, but one that helps to facilitate decision-making.

Eisenhower made great use of the NSC in this capacity. Eisenhower listened to the various information presented to him and then reached a tentative decision. A "Record of Action" statement was then drafted; it expressed the president's policy views and became the basis for administration policy. These records were then presented to all members of the NSC (ibid., 85). To further implement his decisions, Eisenhower, via executive order, created the Operations Coordinating Board (OCB). As part of this process, the OCB would report to the president on the progress departments and agencies were making in implementing the president's decision. Chief of Staff Sherman Adams said, the OCB's purpose was to prevent the execution of administration policy from "falling between the stairs. It was meticulous hard work, the follow-up that ensued after decisions had been made" (quoted in Henderson 1988: 86).

13-10a Eisenhower's Innovations

As he had in domestic affairs, Eisenhower established a highly centralized decision-making process. It worked well for him. "In its first two years, the Eisenhower administration recorded actions on 656 of the items considered at NSC meetings. Comparatively speaking, this was a huge workload; the Truman administration, for instance, recorded action on only 699 matters in the entire five-year period of the Council's existence" (ibid., 84). What is also remarkable is that Eisenhower regularly attended NSC meetings (ibid., 80). Part of the reason for the success of the council was another innovation Eisenhower initiated: He was the "first president to appoint a Special Assistant for National Security Affairs with the responsibility for long-term planning" (Hess 1976: 71–72). The main functions of this new position were determining (subject to the President's approval) the Council agenda, briefing the President in advance of Council meetings, presenting matters for discussion at Council meetings, and supervising the overall operations of the NSC staff and Council (Henderson 1988: 74).

By creating a position, providing as its key function the reporting of sensitive national security information, and placing that position in proximity to the Oval Office, Eisenhower, whether inadvertently or not, had created a position of potentially enormous power. Over the years, it would develop into one of the most powerful offices in the United States government. Eisenhower also expanded the NSC's professional staff, and along with the OCB created the Planning Board. Through these mechanisms, Eisenhower institutionalized the NSC and gave it "clear lines of responsibility and authority" (ibid., 74). The basic contours of the NSC system were now available to future presidents who were wise enough to use it.

Initially, Kennedy was not. As noted, he was suspicious of all of Eisenhower's institutional innovations, and his election "marked the beginning of the end of the highly organized and institutionalized National Security Council apparatus that had flourished under Eisenhower" (ibid., 123). Kennedy's reasoning was based, in part, on the recommendations of Democratic Senator Henry "Scoop" Jackson's committee, which found the NSC apparatus had "not formulated a broad enough strategy and committed sufficient resources to winning the Cold War" (ibid., 124). One foreign policy expert, Douglas Kinnard, argued that the Jackson report misinformed a decade of scholars (Kinnard 1977: 133).

Because of the committee's recommendations, Eisenhower briefed the president-elect on the virtues of his administrative system, but Kennedy instead chose an informal organizational style, based on FDR's experiences (Henderson 1988: 127–30). What Kennedy did not realize was that politics and the world had changed since FDR's time, and the organizational systems that FDR had employed were outdated by 1961. The amounts of information presidents receive had expanded vastly. There now was a need for an organization that could make sense of this information.

Kennedy quickly learned this lesson. His new scaled-back administrative system contributed to his first foreign policy failure: the Bay of Pigs. Still Kennedy did not reorganize his NSC. His successor, Lyndon Johnson, likewise preferred an informal NSC system (ibid., 132). Because Eisenhower's two successors did not trust his penchant for organization, they did not reap the full benefits of the NSC system. This fact led 1968 Republican presidential hopeful Nelson Rockefeller to state,

> There exists no regular staff for arriving at decisions; instead, ad hoc groups are formed as the need arises. No staff agency to monitor the carrying out of decisions is available. There is no focal point for long-range planning on an interagency basis. Without a central administrative focus, foreign policy turns into a series of unrelated decisions—crisis-oriented, ad hoc, and after-the-fact in nature. We become the prisoners of events. (Quoted in Henderson 1988: 135)

13-10b Nixon's Innovations

Richard Nixon, Eisenhower's vice president, was elected in the fall of 1968. Following upon Rockefeller's criticism, one of Nixon's first presidential acts was to overhaul the NSC system. In so doing, he "reestablished the policy making supremacy of the NSC" (Mulcahy and Crabb 1991: 257). Like Rockefeller, Nixon too had vowed to reform the NSC in a campaign speech he delivered on October 24, 1968. Nixon charged that "most of our serious reverses abroad" were attributable to "the inability of Eisenhower's successors to make use of his important Council" (quoted in Henderson 1988: 134). Consequently, after he was elected, Nixon instructed Henry Kissinger, designated as his Special Assistant for National Security Affairs, "to begin work on revitalizing the Council as the primary channel for shaping national security policy" (ibid.).

Nixon, however, did more than restore the authority of the NSC; he began its transformation to a decision-making rather than a coordinating body—a potentially dangerous step that went beyond the NSC's original purpose. During Nixon's presidency, the traditional role of the Secretary of State, under William Rogers, was circumscribed. "Rogers was virtually displaced by Kissinger, who would eventually combine both positions in an unprecedented consolidation of policy-making powers." While Kissinger would be lauded for his successes, even receiving the Nobel Peace Prize, his "very success, as he later acknowledged, tempted his successors and serves as a warning about the dangers inherent in having so all-powerful a presidential agent" (Mulcahy and Crabb 1991: 257). In fact, even during the Nixon administration, there were problems with the new NSC structure. There was increased conflict with the State Department, with the Secretary of State often unaware of major policy developments (such as Kissinger's secret trip to China) until they already were operational.

Furthermore, over time, Nixon's "NSC system became more informal than had originally been envisioned. Crucial issues were maneuvered to committees chaired by Kissinger. The frequency of full NSC meetings diminished from thirty-seven in 1969 to twenty-one in 1970, and to a mere ten meetings in the first nine months of 1971." In time, the "NSC committee system commanded by Kissinger grew to be more important than the NSC itself" (Henderson 1988: 137).

13-10c Restoring Harmony?

Befitting his role as a president whose main task was to heal the nation's wounds following Watergate, Gerald Ford restored harmony between the State Department and the NSC (ibid., 138). For his NSC adviser, Ford chose Brent Scowcroft, who later would serve in the same capacity for George H. W. Bush. "Scowcroft's highly professional demeanor and low-profile approach to coordination revived the spirit of teamwork that had characterized the Eisenhower years" (ibid.). But this spirit would not long prevail.

Ironically, given his aversion to Nixon's organizational systems, it was Jimmy Carter who named a high-profile NSC adviser, Zbigniew Brzezinski, and gave him a dual role of policy protagonist and coordinator (ibid.). These roles, however, were contradictory: Coordination required the NSC to be neutral—that is, not to take sides in a policy debate—while the role of policy protagonist meant that Brzezinski would indeed take sides. An element of policy schizophrenia was therefore introduced into the NSC adviser's position, as well as the Council itself. A precedent was established that would soon have disastrous consequences.

The NSC's role appeared innocent enough in the first years of the Reagan presidency. The first NSC adviser, Richard Allen, "was one of those rare presidential assistants who actually had 'a passion for anonymity'" (Mulcahy and Crabb 1991: 260). The role of the NSC also was constrained, with an apparently strong Secretary of State, Alexander Haig, in charge of foreign policy. Haig's tenure in the administration proved to be stormy, however, and though George Shultz, another strong Secretary of State, replaced him, the NSC's role was allowed to change over time. When Allen departed, his successor, William Clark, had daily access to the president and direct contact with cabinet officials (Henderson 1988: 151). The position of

NSC adviser then shifted to Robert McFarlane. While he worked well with Shultz, the NSC entered a period of "insurgency and disarray" under his successor Admiral John Poindexter. This process ultimately "threatened the president's political survival" (Mulcahy and Crabb 1991: 261).

During the Reagan years, the NSC went from a policy coordinator to a policy initiator. It was this shift to an operational status that eventually created problems. In the case of the invasion of Grenada and the administration's response to the Achille Lauro incident, the NSC's operational role served the president's interests quite well. Yet, in the case of the sale of arms to Iran and the subsequent illegal transfer of funds derived from these sales to the Nicaraguan contras, the liabilities of using the NSC as an operational entity became apparent. Because the NSC took sides in this case, there was "no agency in (the) government to objectively scrutinize, challenge and evaluate plans and activities" (U.S. Congress 1987: 17). In other words, there was no check on the administration's policies, no one to present the president with other options.

The Iran-Contra affair threatened to destroy the Reagan presidency. Only after it was determined that Ronald Reagan did not approve of or know of the transfer of funds to the contras was his presidency saved. But Poindexter's declaration that the buck stopped with him was widely ridiculed. Harry Truman had put the reminder "the buck stops here" on his Oval Office desk. Now, a presidential subordinate was declaring that he, not the duly elected president of the United States, was the ultimate source of foreign policy responsibility. It was too much for many policy makers. Proposals were discussed which would have made the NSC adviser subject to Senate confirmation and radically altered the legislative NSC's mandate. Indeed, reorganization did occur, but not through congressional fiat. Rather, the Reagan administration itself initiated a series of reforms. Still, the damage already had been done. While Reagan survived in office and in time his approval ratings increased, his historical reputation had been damaged. Once praised for his keen prowess as a delegator, by the end of his second term of office, his managerial style was widely derided. Whatever history's final judgment on Reagan, the Iran-Contra scandal and the NSC's role in it left an indelible stain on the Reagan presidency.

Chapter Summary

The president's internal foreign policy resources, like his domestic ones, provide us with a further insight into the yin and yang of institutional resources. On the one hand, they appear to provide a necessary organizational basis that can increase presidential power. On the other hand, they appear to undermine that power and can utterly destroy a president's reputation. Besides the NSC, other internal resources can be either highly useful or offer considerable risks, often simultaneously. As we move into an age in which international terrorism is of predominant concern, there will be a continuing need for a capable NSC, as well as the National Security Agency, the Central Intelligence Agency, and other executive branch information-gathering and processing institutions. Yet, all of these institutions raise questions, whether it is about their representativeness (since they often are accused of representing only the president's interests) or their accountability.

They also raise anew the specter of abuses of presidential power. In our own age, we can wonder, Are these agencies providing the administration of George W. Bush with vital information in the war against terrorism, or are they a threat to our fundamental rights to free speech and a free press? Where do we draw the line, and how much power and authority should the institutional presidency have? These are important practical and philosophical questions.

While we can debate these questions endlessly, one point is clear. The internal and informational resources of the presidency are here to stay. Presidents need them, even if they provide a risk of promoting presidential failure and raise fundamental questions about the role of powerful institutions in a democratic government. Given their prominence and their potential peril, what is amazing is how little these institutional resources are discussed in the popular press or debated in presidential elections. Clearly, for many people, the institutional presidency operates under the radar screen of American politics. We are aware of it only when we see the ubiquitous presidential spokesperson on CNN or in times of scandal. Otherwise, the institutional presidency goes about its work, beyond the klieg lights, but not quite in the realm of anonymity that the Brownlow Committee long ago recommended.

What the Brownlow Committee overlooked or ignored is that proximity to the presidency provides power; therefore, people of ambition, as well as those who truly have the president's best interests at heart, are likely to be drawn to employment in the institutional presidency. One measure of presidential leadership today, then, is the ability to tell these people apart—certainly not an easy task but a vital one. For a president to succeed today, being a skilled chief manager is of critical importance. In short, one of the key tasks of presidential scholars should be to discuss and identify the skills required for the managerial presidency (for example, see Pfiffner 1991).

Review Questions

1. After which of the following presidents employed his secretary, Charles Norton, as a political operative, did other presidents follow the practice?
   a. Theodore Roosevelt
   b. William Howard Taft
   c. Woodrow Wilson
   d. Warren Harding

2. Under which of the following presidents was the Executive Office of the President (EOP) created?
   a. Theodore Roosevelt
   b. Franklin Roosevelt
   c. Lyndon Johnson
   d. Richard Nixon

3. The greatest accomplishment of which of the following presidents was to accustom "the nation to expect that the president would be aided by a battery of policy advisers and implementers"?
   a. Theodore Roosevelt
   b. Franklin Roosevelt
   c. Lyndon Johnson
   d. Richard Nixon

4. Who of the following was the first chief of staff?
   a. Herbert Brownlow
   b. Frederick Cleveland
   c. Sherman Adams
   d. Richard Cheney

5. Which of the following presidents turned the positions of chief of staff and Assistant to the President for National Security Affairs into two of the most powerful positions in the U.S. government?
   a Dwight Eisenhower
   b. Lyndon Johnson
   c. Richard Nixon
   d. Jimmy Carter

6. Which of the following presidents used a new organizational structure—the troika— for his White House?
   a. Ronald Reagan
   b. George H. W. Bush
   c. Bill Clinton
   d. George W. Bush

7. Which of the following presidents learned the hard way that he needed a strong chief of staff and subsequently named Leon Panetta to the position?
   a. Ronald Reagan
   b. George H. W. Bush
   c. Bill Clinton
   d. George W. Bush

8. Which of the following presidents was the first to specifically identify a staff member for the congressional liaison function?
   a. Franklin Roosevelt
   b. Harry Truman
   c. Dwight Eisenhower
   d. Richard Nixon

9. Which of the following presidents established the Office of Homeland Security?
   a. Ronald Reagan
   b. George H. W. Bush
   c. Bill Clinton
   d. George W. Bush

Discussion Questions

1. Why do presidents use the White House staff instead of the cabinet?
2. Is the White House staff constitutionally accountable? Should it be?
3. What are the political risks of presidential use of the White House staff? What are the benefits? Do the benefits exceed the risks?
4. Which presidents have made better use of their White House staff? Which ones have not used their staff well?

Notes

1. Polk was the only nineteenth century president to create an executive budget. Taft was then the first twentieth century president to submit a budget to Congress in 1913 just before he left office. Congress ignored it.

2. To many scholars, such as Buchanan (1987b), this system seemed inefficient, though Leuchtenburg (1988: 28) notes that it served Roosevelt's needs by alerting him "to policy conflicts and permitting him to resolve them when they were ripe." Dickinson (1997) argues that it was a sound and effective management style.

3. The new Civil Service Administration was to be established in the new EOP. This recommendation offered the possibility of greatly increasing presidential control over the bureaucracy. Many members of Congress, however, feared that the reforms would recreate the spoils system of party patronage. Largely as a result of these concerns, the proposal made little headway in Congress. It would take until the Carter presidency before Civil Service reform became a reality (Fisher 1981: 126).

4. Securing a reliable count of the White House staff is notoriously difficult because many members of the staff are not on the White House payroll; they serve as detailees from the departments, the military, and other institutions. The numbers in Figure 13-1 thus must be interpreted with some caution.

5. A number of chiefs of staff who served under presidents who utilized the collegial model have been highly critical of the approach. Donald Rumsfeld and Richard Cheney, former Ford chiefs of staff, and Jack Watson, former Carter chief of staff, have criticized the approach as reducing presidential control over management of the White House by increasing the likelihood that presidents will not be fully informed when making decisions, that dissent is discouraged, and that the president becomes overinvolved in policy making (Kernell and Popkins, 1986). Thus, the argument against the spokes of the wheel model is that as the presidency becomes more complex, there is a greater need for hierarchy, standard operating procedures, and a strong chief of staff (Buchanan 1987b: 14).

6. Buchanan (1987b: 26) argues that the troika of Meese, Baker, and Deaver was short-lived. Each clearly adopted different functions, and though they continued to meet on a regular basis, each remained primarily responsible for issues under his special purview (e.g., Deaver and public relations).

7. Also see Patterson (2000) for a detailed analysis of the functions and roles of the White House staff.

8. Walcott and Hult (1987: 1995) argue that the growth of new "governance structures" in the White House is related to changes in the political environment. This is consistent with the argument I advance in section 13-5 as I discuss how changes in the nation's political ecosystem have encouraged the development of new institutional resources. Pfiffner (1988) also argues that it may be impossible for presidents to function without a chief of staff.

9. See Kurtz (1998) for an interesting look at how the Clinton presidency used spin control and the impacts—positive and negative—it had on the press.

10. G. H. W. Bush also further altered the public liaison role by "placing his speechwriting and Public Liaison operations under the centralized control of David Demarest . . . [but he] had no idea whatsoever about how to make the linkage between presidential rhetoric and actually moving the American public to support a presidential initiative" (Kolb 1994: 5).

11. Schlesinger (1986: 323–34) found the Presidential Transition Act to be a disaster, creating a temporary bureaucracy to establish a new administration. Consequently, he recommended repealing the act.

12. Much has been made of the politicization of the OMB. While Nixon clearly played a major role in this development, Heclo (1975: 95) argues that Eisenhower, Kennedy, and Johnson used the OMB's forerunner, the Bureau of the Budget (BOB), for policy purposes. Likewise, Tomkins's (1998) analysis of the OMB shows that there are variations in the level of politicization from one administration to another, with some presidents (e.g., Nixon and Reagan) more likely to politicize it. Still, as Berman (1979) argues, the OMB has been more political than was the BOB (see also Tomkins 1985).

13. The EPB was not in the Executive Office of the President.

Chapter

14

A New Role
for the Vice President

14-1 A New Role for the Vice President

The administration of George W. Bush added another innovation to the development of the presidency by elevating the vice presidency to a position of considerable organizational and political influence. While I do not argue that the vice presidency is part of the institutional presidency, it can be argued that the vice president has become a new internal political resource for presidents over the past three decades. How did this come about?

14-2 The Original Role of the Vice President

The vice presidential role has been evolving for some time. Although the vice president is elected with the president,[1] the vice president was traditionally described as a member of the legislative branch. In their memoirs, both Truman (1955) and Eisenhower (1963) argued that the vice president was not an officer of the executive branch and thus not subject to presidential direction. The vice president's office was located in the Capitol building, and his main constitutional function was to serve as President of the Senate—a role vice presidents employ when we see them seated behind the president during the state of the union address and other speeches before a joint session of Congress. Hence, when William Howard Taft asked his vice president, James S. Sherman, to serve as the administration's liaison with the House of Representatives, Sherman said no, proclaiming, "Acting as messenger boy is not part of the duties of a Vice President" (quoted in Schlesinger 1986: 346).

Scholar Woodrow Wilson (1981: 162) noted the confusing nature of the vice president's constitutional heritage as well as the limited stature of the office:

> It would, doubtless, be considered quite improper to omit from an essay on the Senate all mention of the Senate's President; and yet, there is very little to be said about the Vice-President of the United States. His position is one of anomalous insignificance and curious uncertainty. Apparently he is not, strictly speaking, a part of the legislature—he is clearly not a member—yet, neither is he an officer of the executive. It is one of the remarkable things about him, that it is hard to find in sketching the government any proper place to discuss him . . . his importance consists in the fact that he may cease to be Vice-President. His chief dignity, next to presiding over the Senate, lies in the circumstance that he is awaiting the death or disability of the President. And the chief embarrassment in discussing his office is, that in explaining how little there is to be said about it one has evidently said all there is to say.

The vice presidency was a strange amalgam: a largely inconsequential office, yet at the same time, one breath away from power.

From the very beginning, the vice president had little of substance to do. Vice President John Adams attended cabinet meetings, but he was the last to do so until Woodrow Wilson became president (Pika 1988: 469). Wilson's vice president, Thomas Marshall, presided at cabinet meetings while Wilson was at Versailles negotiating the treaty ending World War I. Since, however, Marshall considered himself to be "a member of the legislative branch," he told the cabinet that he was doing so only "in obedience to a request" and therefore "in an unofficial and informal way" (quoted in Schlesinger 1986: 347; see also Hargrove and Nelson 1984: 30). It was not until Warren G. Harding that a president actually made his vice president a regular member of the cabinet. Coolidge attempted to continue the process, but his vice president, Charles Dawes, refused, arguing it was a "wrong principle" (Schlesinger 1986: 347–48).

14-3 The Under-Used Vice President

Other than serving as President of the Senate, the vice president's only other function was to succeed the president upon his death or disability. But even here, the Constitution was not clear. John Tyler was the first vice president to ascend to the presidency, upon the death of William Henry Harrison (see Table 14-1). Until this time, it was not clear whether the vice president would become president upon the death or disability of the president or merely serve in an acting presidential capacity until another president was elected. In a sense, Tyler "staged a constitutional coup" (Schlesinger 1986: 344) when he insisted that he was president. Former president John Quincy Adams characterized Tyler's action as in "direct violation both of the grammar and context of the Constitution" (quoted in ibid.). Some members of Harrison's cabinet registered protests and "there were unavailing protests from senators who thought a man could gain the Presidency only by election. But Tyler won his point, though the point did not gain explicit constitutional sanction until 125 years later in the Twenty-fifth Amendment" (ibid.).

John Tyler, Millard Fillmore, Andrew Johnson, and Chester A. Arthur in the nineteenth century and Theodore Roosevelt, Calvin Coolidge, Harry Truman, and Lyndon Johnson in the twentieth century rose to the presidency after the death of a president. Gerald Ford became president after Nixon's resignation. Of the nation's forty-three presidencies (forty-two presidents if we do not count Grover Cleveland twice), nine succeeded the presidency. Four others—John Adams, Thomas Jefferson, Martin Van Buren, and George H. W. Bush—were elected to the presidency after serving as vice president. Consequently, thirteen individuals out of forty-two, or 31 percent, found their way directly to the presidential office from the vice presidency. Considered in this manner, serving in the vice presidency, despite its lack of constitutional authority, is a solid stepping-stone to the presidency.[2]

14-4 Presidential–Vice Presidential Relations

The ascensions described in section 14-2 demonstrate the potential of the vice presidency as a road to the White House. Other than presidential succession, though, the office offered little influence for most of our nation's history. Presidents and their vice presidents often were not even particularly close. Prior to 1940, it was common for a vice president to disagree with a president over substantive policy concerns. Charles Dawes supported farm legislation that Coolidge later vetoed (Schlesinger 1986: 347–48). John Nance Garner, FDR's first vice president, openly opposed Roosevelt's decision to expand the Supreme Court in 1937 and then opposed Roosevelt's decision to run for a third term in 1940. This disagreement between presidents and their vice presidents led Roosevelt in 1940 to demand the right to name his own running mate. Until this time, party bosses had traditionally picked the vice president, and they often chose individuals who represented different wings of the party, almost ensuring that the president and vice president would have little in common, politically speaking (Pika 1988: 470; Schlesinger 1986: 346). After 1940, however, presidents, though slowly at first, gained the right to name their own running mate.[3] In this manner, vice presidents are now more likely to become trusted presidential advisers than they once were (Pika 1988: 470).

Presidential control of vice presidential selection allowed presidents to delegate more authority to the vice presidency. Even the vice president's ceremonial role, the butt of many jokes today (e.g., the propensity of vice presidents to attend funerals), was not established until recent times. John Nance Garner was the first vice president to travel abroad in an official administrative capacity and his successor, Henry Wallace, also traveled on several wartime missions (Pika 1988: 469). Even with regard

TABLE **14-1** Vice Presidents

Vice President	President Served	Became President?
John Adams (1735–1826)	George Washington	Yes
Thomas Jefferson (1743–1826)	John Adams	Yes
Aaron Burr (1756–1836)	Thomas Jefferson	No
George Clinton (1739–1812)	Thomas Jefferson	No
Elbridge Gerry (1744–1814)	James Madison	No
Daniel D. Tompkins (1744–1825)	James Monroe	No
John C. Calhoun (1782–1850)	John Quincy Adams and Andrew Jackson	No
Martin Van Buren (1782–1862)	Andrew Jackson	Yes
Richard M. Johnson (1780–1850)	Martin Van Buren	No
John Tyler (1790–1862)	William H. Harrison	Yes
George M. Dallas (1792–1864)	James Polk	No
Millard Fillmore (1800–1874)	Zachary Taylor	Yes
William R. D. King (1786–1853)	Franklin Pierce	No
John C. Breckinridge (1821–1875)	James Buchanan	No
Hannibal Hamlin (1809–1891)	Abraham Lincoln	No
Andrew Johnson (1808–1875)	Abraham Lincoln	Yes
Schuyler Colfax (1823–1885)	Ulysses S. Grant	No
Henry Wilson (1812–1875)	Ulysses S. Grant	No
William A. Wheeler (1819–1887)	Rutherford Hayes	No
Chester A. Arthur (1829–1886)	James A. Garfield	Yes
Thomas A. Hendricks (1819–1885)	Grover Cleveland	No
Levi P. Morton (1824–1920)	Benjamin Harrison	No
Adlai E. Stevenson (1835–1914)	Grover Cleveland	No
Garret A. Hobart (1844–1899)	William McKinley	No
Theodore Roosevelt (1858–1919)	William McKinley	Yes
Charles W. Fairbanks (1852–1918)	Theodore Roosevelt	No
James S. Sherman (1855–1912)	William H. Taft	No
Thomas R. Marshall (1854–1925)	Woodrow Wilson	No
Calvin Coolidge (1872–1933)	Warren G. Harding	Yes
Charles G. Dawes (1865–1951)	Calvin Coolidge	No
Charles Curtis (1860–1936)	Herbert C. Hoover	No
John N. Garner (1868–1967)	Franklin D. Roosevelt	No
Henry A. Wallace (1888–1965)	Franklin D. Roosevelt	No
Harry S. Truman (1884–1972)	Franklin D. Roosevelt	Yes
Alben W. Barkley (1877–1956)	Harry S. Truman	No
Richard M. Nixon (1913–1995)	Dwight D. Eisenhower	Yes
Lyndon B. Johnson (1908–1973)	John F. Kennedy	Yes
Hubert H. Humphrey (1911–1978)	Lyndon B. Johnson	No
Spiro T. Agnew (1918–1995)	Richard Nixon	No
Gerald R. Ford (1913–)	Richard Nixon	Yes
Nelson A. Rockefeller (1908–1979)	Gerald Ford	No
Walter F. Mondale (1928–)	Jimmy Carter	No
George H. W. Bush (1924–)	Ronald Reagan	Yes
J. Danforth Quayle (1947–)	George H. W. Bush	No
Albert A. Gore, Jr. (1948–)	William Clinton	No
Richard B. Cheney (1941–)	George W. Bush	

to ceremonial matters, Thomas Marshall, Wilson's vice president, was heavily involved in the World War I Liberty Loan campaign, but not as an administration spokesperson. Alben Barkley, Harry Truman's vice president, expanded these cere-monial activities, which are now regularly performed by vice presidents (ibid., 469).

14-5 Vice Presidents Gain Real Power

Substantive policy involvement in administration activities, like the vice president's ceremonial role, also is a recent development (see Figure 14-1). Franklin Roosevelt was the first president to give his vice president a real position of authority when, ten days after the attack on Pearl Harbor, he named Henry Wallace as the chairman of the new Board of Economic Warfare. This experience proved to be a failure. When Wallace and other top administration officials, though particularly Jesse Jones, disagreed over policy, FDR removed Wallace from his post (Schlesinger 1986: 348; Hess 1976: 41). With the Wallace experiment deemed a failure, presidents had little incentive to give their vice presidents a more active role. In fact, until 1961, the vice president's office was housed on Capitol Hill. Kennedy was the first president to provide his vice president, Lyndon Johnson, with space in the Old Executive Office building adjoining the White House. Even in this case administration officials did not "consider the constitutional implications of moving the Vice Presidency from the Capitol to the Executive Office Building—that is, from the legislative to the executive." Rather, this move was merely "a reasonable act of courtesy and convenience" (Schlesinger 1986: 350). Other than being included, via legislation, as a member of the National Security Council in the early 1950s, the vice president had few statutory responsibilities. It was therefore easy for presidents to treat the vice president as a constitutional irrelevancy.

14-6 Changing Perceptions of the Vice Presidency

The perception of the vice presidency began to change when Harry Truman became president after Franklin Roosevelt died suddenly of a cerebral hemorrhage in April 1945. Truman, who had been vice president for less than three months, was not an insider in the Roosevelt White House. Only after FDR died was he told about the Manhattan Project and the existence of the atomic bomb. He also was not sufficiently briefed on wartime or post-wartime policy. In short, the vice president was not ready to assume command. Truman's experience demonstrated that in the modern presidential era, the vice president should be more involved in presidential business. Though Truman treated his vice president, Alben Barkley, little better than Roosevelt had treated him, given the realities of the modern world, Eisenhower decided that the vice president would have to be better informed and

Figure 14-1
Relationships between Presidents and Their Vice Presidents

Franklin D. Roosevelt	John F. Kennedy	Jimmy Carter	Ronald Reagan	George W. Bush
Roosevelt named his vice president, Henry Wallace, chairman of the Board of Economic Warfare, but the position was short-lived; he was removed after internal disagreements over policy.	Kennedy gave his vice president, Lyndon Johnson, office space in the White House, signifying a closer relationship, but in reality, Johnson's role was minimal.	Relying on Walter Mondale's experience and delegating broader authority to him, Carter raised the value of the vice president as an advisor to the president.	Like Carter, Reagan chose for his vice president a Washington insider, George H.W. Bush. Bush brought experience in a variety of political arenas and received unprecedented status as a vice president, including a staff of seventy and a budget of $2 million.	The younger Bush has relied on his vice president, Dick Cheney, and delegated so much work to him that Cheney enjoys the most powerful vice presidency in history, causing some to dub him the "Co-President."

prepared should he need to assume office suddenly (Hargrove 1984: 30–31). When Eisenhower suffered a heart attack, Nixon did indeed step into the breach. Still, while Eisenhower elevated the vice president's role, he mainly saw Nixon as a political surrogate. He therefore dispensed him to the campaign trail, where Nixon gave partisan speeches in the midterm elections of 1954 and 1958 (Hess 1976: 66).

14-7 The Vice Presidency since the 1960s

Other than the modest changes described in section 14-6, the vice presidency continued to languish for the next three decades after Truman became president. Kennedy delegated little authority to Lyndon Johnson. In fact, many Kennedy staffers had utter contempt for Johnson, including Attorney General Robert Kennedy, the president's brother, thus creating unwelcome tensions when LBJ became president in November 1963. Richard Nixon, despite his perceived humiliation as vice president under Eisenhower, treated his vice president little better. He had little respect for his vice president, Spiro Agnew. The White House tapes reveal that he joked that Agnew was his insurance policy. No one would want to kill Nixon with Agnew in line to be president!

Agnew resigned from office before Nixon's own fall, and thus Nixon named Gerald Ford as his second vice president. Ford assumed office under the Twenty-fifth Amendment, thus becoming the first un-elected vice president in our nation's history. Ford saw the vice presidency as a "constitutional hybrid . . . with one foot in the legislative branch and the other in the executive. . . ." The office, therefore, "belongs to both the President and the Congress" (quoted in Bonafede 1988: 3257). When Ford became president upon Nixon's resignation, he also became the first un-elected president. Ford then named Nelson Rockefeller as his vice president with a promise to make him an active policy maker in his administration.

Before Rockefeller accepted the vice presidency, he "sought an explicit mandate from Ford to direct the Domestic [Policy] Council, an important center of White House decision making in domestic policy since its inception in the Nixon White House. From this vantage point, Rockefeller expected to direct the nation's domestic policy agenda much as Henry Kissinger had dominated foreign policy from his position as head of the National Security Council" (Pika 1988: 464; Porter 1988: 220–21). Rockefeller was soon to be disappointed. While he did have some successes (particularly in developing innovative ideas for energy policy and establishing a White House office of Science and Technology Policy), overall he received only a shadow of the influence he had been promised (Pika 1988: 465; Porter 1988: 222–23). As for the Domestic Council, its influence was negligible. The council was given little chance to develop as an important presidential advisory institution, and its influence waned. Rockefeller then announced that he would not run for re-election in 1976 and resigned from the Domestic Council (Wyszomirski 1985: 136–38).

Like Ford, Jimmy Carter promised his vice president, Walter Mondale, a more active role in administration politics. Whereas Ford had twenty-five years of experience in Washington as a member of Congress (before serving as vice president), Carter came to Washington as a true outsider. His experience as governor of Georgia did not prepare him for the rough inside-the-beltway politics of Washington political life. He therefore needed to rely on Mondale more than Ford had needed Rockefeller. One media representative told scholar Paul Light (1983: 180) that Mondale "was virtually the only member of the top staff to have extensive federal experience, and it affected his stock in the White House. As Carter began to suffer, Mondale began to rise. He knew how to move the pieces."

Carter thus delegated broader authority to Mondale. While Mondale's influence grew, it had existed even during the transition process. Mondale says, "I was invited to every meeting, I saw every piece of paper that went to Carter" (quoted in Bonafede 1988: 3256). Mondale played a crucial role in the selection of several cabinet secretaries, and two of his aides were named to top administration posts. The vice president's staff was even allowed to attend various White House meetings, a perk that was not even offered to George H. W. Bush when he served as Reagan's vice president (ibid., 3255). As vice president, Mondale received a West Wing office, a clear symbol of his influence in the Carter administration. In addition, "Carter instructed that Mondale be fully informed of U.S. military capabilities and be kept up to date on the use of secret codes to alert the armed forces in the event of a nuclear conflict, steps that were unprecedented in scope" (ibid., 3256).

In fact, Mondale had a more active role than did his successor, George H. W. Bush (Hess 1988: 163). Still, both Presidents Carter and Reagan increased the visibility and role of the vice presidency. Reagan, like Carter, a Washington outsider, chose a Washington insider for his vice president. He named George Herbert Walker Bush as his vice president after briefly toying with the idea of naming former President Gerald Ford to the post. Bush's experience included being director of the Central Intelligence Agency, ambassador to the United Nations, special envoy to China (essentially the equivalent of an ambassador), head of the Republican Party, and a two-term member of Congress. Reagan, as the former governor of California, benefited from Bush's knowledge of Washington politics, as Carter had relied on Mondale. Bush therefore inherited Mondale's West Wing office and was given access and briefings on national security matters. By 1984, the Office of the Vice President even had a $2 million budget and a staff of seventy, making it the fifth largest unit in the EOP (Schlesinger 1986: 359).

Writing about the vice presidential office, Bush notes (in Bush and Gold 1987: 7),

> The prestige, if not the power, of the office has grown since the end of World War Two. When Harry Truman succeeded FDR, he didn't know about the A-bomb and needed a crash course to deal with the major decisions facing him in the final days of World War Two. That experience led later Presidents to keep their Vice Presidents informed about the White House decision-making process. Given the right President, it's possible for the right Vice President to have an impact on administration policy.

Other factors also drew more power to the vice presidency than merely the right president and the right vice president. As Washington outsiders increasingly were elected to the presidency (e.g., presidents without a great deal of Washington experience—such as Carter, Reagan, Clinton, and G. W. Bush), an insider vice president became more necessary (e.g., Walter Mondale, G. H. W. Bush, Al Gore, and Dick Cheney). These insiders could provide the outsider presidents with beneficial and largely anonymous advice on the nature of Washington politics. Second, precedent was making it harder for presidents to go back to the days in which their vice presidents were largely constitutional irrelevancies (Pika 1988: 465–66). Vice presidents knew that the office had been transformed and would demand a significant role in the administration when elected. The institutionalization of various vice presidential roles (e.g., on the National Security Council) and the informal institutionalization of vice presidential functions (e.g., vice presidential debates have been held since Mondale debated Senator Robert Dole, Ford's 1976 vice presidential nominee) made it more difficult for presidents to put the vice presidency back into the political closet.

14-8 The Media and the Vice President

The decline of the political parties and the rise of the media, two factors related to the changing American political ecosystem, also contributed to a larger vice presidential role (see section 11-7, "Why Do Political Ecosystems Change?"). The rise of the media contributed to greater exposure for the vice president as well as the president. As Schlesinger (1986: 358) comments, "The Vice Presidency is the only place except the Presidency itself that ensures its occupant automatic and comprehensive national exposure. The Vice President is forever on television, even if mostly shaking the hands of foreign dignitaries or attending their funeral." With the decline of the political parties, the vice president became a "national political luminary." Once "the Vice Presidency achieved star billing, the iron law of status escalation decrees that the Vice President must have the staff, the budget, the residence, the airplane and all the other perquisites appropriate to a star." Schlesinger concludes, "In short, institutionalization did not take place because new duties required new vice presidential machinery. Rather, the contrary: new machinery produced the vice presidential search for new duties" (ibid.).

14-9 The Vice President as Incumbent

With the decline of the political parties, vice presidents today also are more likely to win their party's nomination (Thomas, Pika, and Watson 1993: 52), thus making the vice presidency a more attractive office for individuals who seek the presidency. From 1836, when Vice President Martin Van Buren was elected, to 1960, when Richard Nixon sought the presidency, the vice presidency was not a viable stepping-stone to the White House outside of direct presidential succession upon the death of the president. Today, vice presidents do not have to step over the president's corpse to secure the presidency. A number of former vice presidents (Nixon, Johnson, Humphrey, Ford, Mondale, G. H. W. Bush, Gore) and even failed vice presidential candidates, such as Bob Dole and Joseph Lieberman (who is interested in the 2004 Democratic nomination), have sought the presidency in their own right since 1960, thus making the vice presidency a more attractive political office for those with presidential ambitions.

14-10 The Vice President as Primary Advisor

All of the factors described in sections 14-2 through 14-9 were in place, then, when George W. Bush further elevated the vice president's role in 2001. Richard "Dick" Cheney became the most powerful vice president in history. Not only did he play an integral role in the transition period, but he also chaired a number of policy-related committees. While he was less interested in the political limelight than his immediate vice presidential predecessors and it has been suggested that he has no interest in the presidency itself, in some respects, his power and influence made him almost a co-president; Bush even joked about the nation having two presidents.

George W. Bush seems content with this relationship, relying on Cheney for advice on a wide range of issues, while allowing the vice president unprecedented access and authority. It is not clear whether or how this co-presidency model of the vice presidency will translate into an institutionalized expectation of vice presidential influence.

Chapter Summary

The vice president's influence likely will continue to wax and wane, depending on the president's skill, level of Washington experience, and temperament (Bush is not threatened by an active vice president, while others with less self-confidence might be). While the vice presidency may have reached its zenith under Cheney, however, it is doubtful that future presidents will ignore the office, as was long the vice presidency's lot. From the present vantage point, it appears that the vice presidential office, like the chief of staff, has become an institutional necessity and a valuable presidential resource.

Review Questions

1. For much of the nation's history, the vice presidency was considered to be part of which of the following branches of government?
   a. the legislative branch
   b. the executive branch
   c. the judicial branch
   d. the military industrial complex

2. Under the Constitution, the vice president serves as
   a. President Pro Tempore.
   b. President-elect.
   c. President of the Senate.
   d. President of the House.

3. Which of the following presidents was the first to give his vice president a real position of authority?
   a. George Washington
   b. Abraham Lincoln
   c. Theodore Roosevelt
   d. Franklin Roosevelt

4. Which of the following vice presidents resigned?
   a. John Adams
   b. John Nance Garner
   c. Spiro Agnew
   d. Albert Gore

5. Which of the following vice presidents received a West Wing White House office, signifying the increasing influence of the vice president?
   a. Lyndon Johnson
   b. Hubert Humphrey
   c. Gerald Ford
   d. Walter Mondale

Discussion Questions

1. Why has the vice presidency largely been an inconsequential office? Why is it more powerful today?

2. Should presidents name the vice president to a cabinet position such as Secretary of State or Defense? What are the pros and cons of such a choice?

Notes

1. "Most academics . . . regard the Twelfth Amendment as having reduced 'the vice presidency to an insignificant office, sought only by insignificant men,' an outcome that was correctly predicted by some members of Congress at the time of its passage" (Wilson 1887/1981: 162).

2. In addition, Richard Nixon in 1960, Hubert Humphrey in 1968, and Albert Gore in 2000 came exceedingly close to winning the presidency after having served as vice president. Both Nixon and Humphrey narrowly lost the popular vote, and Gore actually won more votes than his opponent. Eventually, Nixon was elected president in 1968, beating Humphrey, and again in 1972.

3. In 1944, FDR showed much less interest in his choice of vice president. The choice of Truman then reflected the will of the party as well as Roosevelt's acquiescence, but not his insistence, as had been the case with his 1940 vice presidential choice of Henry Wallace. Wallace was never popular with many wings of the Democratic Party and party leaders. It is interesting, then, that Roosevelt delegated much more authority to Wallace than he did to Truman.

How Internal and Informational Resources Can Increase Presidential Influence: The Case of Presidential Appointments

15-1 How Internal and Informational Resources Can Increase Presidential Influence: The Case of Presidential Appointments[1]

In this chapter, I provide an example to demonstrate why presidents internalize their political resources. I examine the centralization of the president's appointment resources in the White House and how this step provides presidents with an opportunity to make greater use of this constitutional power.

The Constitution's appointment provision is one of the most clearly articulated grants of presidential authority. When we compare it to such other provisions as the executive vesting clause, the take care (that the laws be faithfully executed) clause, or even the commander-in-chief clause, three constitutional provisions that have been the subject of much controversy in recent decades (see section 4-4, "The Vesting Clause," section 4-5, "The Take Care Clause," and section 5-6, "Commander-in-Chief"), the appointment provision stands out as a far less ambiguous delegation of presidential power. Hence, one could assume that the appointment power historically has been one of the presidency's most effective political resources. While it has provided presidents with some influence, it has only been in recent years that presidents have consistently employed it to nominate individuals who are responsive to their programmatic needs. Given the relative clarity of the appointment power, the obvious question is: Why haven't presidents traditionally made better use of this authority?

The primary reason was best expressed by then newly elected President John F. Kennedy when he commented, "I thought I knew everybody and it turned out I only knew a few politicians . . . I must make appointments now; a year hence I will know who I really want to appoint" (quoted in Pfiffner 1988: 70). Kennedy's problem was that he lacked the capacity to identify a large number of qualified potential officeholders. This is a problem that all presidents face. For the modern presidents, however, it is an even greater concern, since as the number of executive branch agencies has expanded, the number of appointive positions likewise has grown. Without an adequate mechanism for identifying, recruiting, and evaluating potential officeholders, presidents traditionally have found themselves at the mercy of a few close advisers, the defeated factions of their party, pressure groups with clearly vested interests, senators with their own political concerns, and anyone with the ability to forward a resume to the White House. The result is that presidents often appointed individuals who did not represent their personal political objectives, and presidents did not take full advantage of their appointment authority. A brief glance at history underscores this point.

15-1a Washington's Criteria for Appointments

George Washington was responsible for only a relatively few appointments, yet he had considerable difficulty identifying individuals to serve in his administration—this despite the fact that he had established clearly articulated appointment criteria. Washington announced that he wanted the best man for the job and would base his appointments on specific criteria. For example, Washington employed a "rule of fitness" for office by which he included more than technical competence. "The standard of expertise, of pure technical competence, individual training and individual ability—the 'merit system' as seen by the civil service reformers of a later day—still fell a good deal short of what Washington required of his appointees" (Elkins and McKitrick 1993: 53). More important than "technical competence for any specific office" was "a moral character whereby some men assume an authority over others so natural that it cannot be politely contested" (Koritansky 1989:

296). While Washington never clearly defined what he meant by "fitness of character" or "the first characters of the union," he did examine the "personal experience and reputation" of potential nominees. Indeed, some factors excluded a candidate from consideration, such as indolence and drink, while having sound family relationships was certainly a positive factor (ibid., 296–97).

Character was Washington's primary criterion for appointment (see Figure 15-1). Second was an evaluation of comparative assertions of competence based on a person's "former merits and sufferings in service," and third was an equality of distribution among the states (Goldsmith 1980: 160–61). "The balance of Massachusetts, New York, and Virginia in the cabinet gave general satisfaction, as did that of six states on the Supreme Court, whose first chief justice was John Jay of New York." Yet, while merit and geographical distribution were important, "the fundamental standard was that of 'first charactership'" (Elkins and McKitrick 1993: 54).

In addition to having criteria for the kinds of individuals he wanted in his administration, Washington also was decidedly thorough in his personal evaluation of each potential candidate for office. As Vice President John Adams wrote, [Washington] "seeks information from all quarters and judges more independently than any man I ever knew" (quoted in Flexner 1970: 223).

Yet, despite his thoroughness and the relative clarity of appointment criteria, Washington ran into immediate, and as his successors would soon learn, familiar problems. Although few would dare to suggest that Thomas Jefferson and Alexander Hamilton were not among the most qualified men of their time, their appointments did not fully serve Washington's stated political objectives. Rather than building the harmonious spirit of cooperation that Washington desired, Jefferson's and Hamilton's policy disagreements opened the door for the establishment of faction and the nation's first political parties. It is interesting to note, then, that neither man represented Washington's first choice for the cabinet.

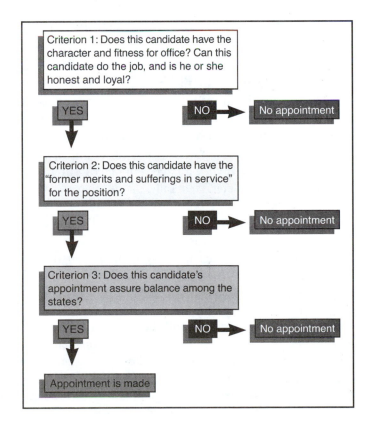

Figure 15-1
Washington's Criteria for Appointments

How closely do modern leaders follow Washington's criteria? Is character still the first consideration for an appointment? What about equal distribution of appointments between states?

15-1b Difficulties in Appointments in Washington's Presidency

Washington, like most of our presidents, had no formal mechanism to assist him in making his appointments. Rather, he relied on the advice of his most trusted personal advisers. Of his four cabinet appointments, two provided him with no problems. In selecting the Secretary of War, Washington decided to retain the services of Henry Knox, who had held the same post under the government of the Articles of Confederation. For attorney general, Washington set a precedent that would be followed by many of his successors. He selected a personal friend and confidant, Edmond Randolph. The two other cabinet posts, however, would not be filled as easily. For the position of Secretary of State, Washington preferred the services of John Jay, but Jay wanted to be Chief Justice of the Supreme Court. Washington eventually relented, thus leaving him without a suitable candidate for the new State Department. Since he did not have a ready choice at hand, Washington turned to his circle of personal advisers to identify possible candidates. On the advice of his close personal confidant, James Madison, the president nominated Thomas Jefferson as the nation's first Secretary of State. Though Washington was able to nominate a man of impeccable character and qualifications, he was not able to secure his first choice for that office (Flexner 1970: 235).

Likewise, both of the men Washington preferred for the position of Secretary of the Treasury were unavailable. Washington's first choice was Robert Morris. Because Morris was a senator, he was constitutionally prohibited from serving in the executive branch. Gouvenor Morris (Robert's brother) was Washington's second choice. Unfortunately, he was abroad and therefore unavailable. While unwilling to accept the Treasury post, the Morris brothers did offer Washington advice. They recommended Alexander Hamilton, who shared their opinions on economic matters. Washington was already quite familiar with Hamilton, and with his former subordinate's political ambition. Despite this reservation, however, Washington nominated Hamilton to serve as the nation's first Treasury Secretary (ibid.).

15-1c Washington's Precedent for Identifying Candidates

In naming his cabinet, Washington employed an informal network of friends and political confidants to identify potential candidates for office. Washington's experiences were not unique. Rather, it became a common practice for each new president to seek advice from a variety of personal advisers and for many preferred candidates to turn aside the president's solemn request for governmental service. Over time, as the number of executive branch positions increased, and particularly following Andrew Jackson's establishment of the "spoils system," presidents found themselves inundated with a large number of potential job seekers and sponsors for particular candidates. Generally, the number of office seekers far outnumbered the number of available positions. As a result, each president came to view his appointment authority as an unpleasant burden, rather than a clear opportunity to advance his own power. It is interesting to note that the opposition Whig Party at first soundly criticized the spoils system, but when the Whigs secured the White House in 1840 and a "mob of some 30,000 to 40,000 office-seekers showed up for the inauguration, the Whigs decided that it was prudent to throw the Jacksonian rascals out and replace them with their own" (McDonald 1994: 319). Consequently, the president and the political parties had a vastly increased number of appointments to fill at the beginning of each new administration. This dispensation of patronage would overwhelm many presidents. Lincoln, among many, complained vociferously about the difficulties it created. Yet, as president, Lincoln affected "the most thorough change of all" to his time in administrative personnel, with "1,457 removals and 1,639 'places within his gift'" (McDonald 1994: 320; see also Paludan 1994: 35).

Yet, the only organizational mechanisms in place to help presidents such as Lincoln were the political parties and Congress. The parties promised jobs for those who worked to get their candidates elected. Patronage thus became a characteristic of nineteenth-century appointments. Congress also recommended individuals for particular posts. Senators, who play a vital role in the confirmation process, also influenced presidents through the process of senatorial courtesy, whereby a senator has influence over appointments that fall within his or her state's jurisdiction. Senators could recommend and even block presidential appointees that they did not like. Hence, both patronage and senatorial courtesy provided the presidents with appointees, but not with individuals who necessarily were loyal to the president and his policies. These mechanisms also had the tendency of constraining presidential power, particularly after the Civil War, when the Senate boldly tried to nominate its own candidates for the executive branch, including cabinet posts. Rutherford B. Hayes restored balance in the appointment process by submitting his own nominees and once again relegating the Senate to its constitutional role in the confirmation process (King and Riddlesperger 1987: 4).

The Pendleton Act, also sometimes colloquially referred to as the Civil Service Act of 1883, was enacted after James Garfield's assassination by a disgruntled job seeker. It constrained the political parties' role in the appointment process (Lowi 1985: 66).[2] As presidents increased the number of positions subject to the Pendleton Act, the influence of the parties further declined (Milkis and Nelson 1994: 217).

15-2 BOGSAT!

While the Pendleton Act constrained the party's influence, presidents still lacked an organizational basis for identifying, recruiting, and evaluating potential appointees. Instead, most presidents relied on what Dan Fenn, John Kennedy's head of personnel, later characterized as the BOGSAT approach—"a bunch of guys sitting around a table saying, 'whom do you know'" (quoted in Pfiffner 1988: 71). While this approach may have been sufficient when the number of governmental posts was small, it did not provide presidents with the names of individuals who would best serve their policy interests; that is, loyalty to the president could not be guaranteed.

Despite the limitations of the BOGSAT approach, most of Washington's successors employed some variation of it. Beyond the parties and the Senate, presidents relied on informal advisers. James K. Polk, for example, relied on the advice of former president Andrew Jackson and a few other close political allies in developing the names of potential candidates for his cabinet. The appointment strategy they devised was designed to assuage regional interests (Begeron 1974: 24), a strategy many of Polk's successors adopted. James Buchanan also relied on the advice of his intimate political advisers in fashioning his cabinet. Because Buchanan's advisers were more sympathetic to the plight of the South, however, Buchanan's cabinet expressed a clear Southern bias. The advice Buchanan received later would contribute to one of his greatest political blunders: his decision to support congressional approval of the LeCompton Constitution for Kansas's statehood (Stampp 1990).

15-2a Lack of Advice

Some presidents lacked even the limited advice provided by the BOGSAT approach. Ulysses S. Grant's selection of his Secretary of State, considered the prize cabinet appointment, was apparently made on the basis of serendipity, rather than calculated political advice. According to Grant's biographer, William S. McFeeley (1981: 289–95), Grant nominated Elihu Washburne as Secretary of State on the basis of a casual promise made at a dinner party. Later realizing his mistake in promising such an important post to a clearly unqualified individual, Grant then offered Washburne the position of ambassador to France, a clearly subordinate position, if he would resign as Secretary of State shortly after his confirmation. Grant's nomination of Washburne and his subsequent resignation presented the new president in a most unfavorable light. Without a political mechanism to identify qualified potential officeholders or advisers who could protect him, Grant's worst political instincts were allowed to surface uncontrolled. Partly as a result, the Senate ultimately adopted a more active role in identifying candidates for office, at times essentially selecting the president's cabinet.

15-2b Wilson's Problems with the BOGSAT Approach

Grant's appointment problems can be greatly attributed to his lack of political skill. Yet, other men with greater political acuity also had problems locating qualified individuals for their cabinets. Although Woodrow Wilson is now considered to have been an able statesman and one of the nation's best presidents (see section 3-3, "Presidential Greatness"), his appointment strategy initially raised serious questions about his competence. One of Wilson's closest advisers, Colonel House, wrote shortly after the election: "The thing that impresses me most is the casual way in which the President-elect is making up his Cabinet. I can see no end of trouble for him in the future unless he proceeds with more care" (Seymour 1926: 111).

Colonel House was particularly upset because Wilson, who was not a Washington insider, was considering the possibility of appointing several individuals who had voted for William Howard Taft (his Republican opponent) in the 1912 election. To avert disaster, House confided to Mrs. Wilson that "in twenty years . . . no one would know how the different departments of Government had been run and that the President's fame would rest entirely upon the big constructive measures he was able to get through Congress, and in order to get them through he had to be on more or less good terms with that body" (ibid., 103). This meant that Wilson would have to appoint traditional, mainstream members of the Democratic Party to his cabinet. To this end, and on the advice of Colonel House and others, Wilson appointed William Jennings Bryan, the quintessential Democrat, as his Secretary of State. Bryan had three times, each in a losing cause, carried the party's banner in presidential elections. Although this appointment served Wilson's short-term political goal of party unity, Bryan later left the administration in a highly publicized policy dispute with the president.

Wilson made other appointments on the advice of Colonel House, Joseph Tumulty, and other personal advisers. An example of how poorly this BOGSAT approach served Wilson is provided by the excruciatingly elongated search for a nominee for the post of Secretary of War. Several people were initially considered for the position. Wilson's preference was A. Mitchell Palmer, who became the first man to receive an invitation from Wilson to serve as War Secretary. He would not, however, be the last. Because Wilson lacked a mechanism for collecting information on the qualifications of prospective candidates, he was unaware that Palmer was a Quaker and thus might have serious theological objections to serving as Secretary of War. In fact, after making the offer, Wilson was unable to convince Palmer to accept the position. As a result, Wilson and his advisers were forced to identify another candidate. Again, several individuals were considered for the post, with Wilson finally deciding on Franklin Lane. Lane already had been tentatively assigned to Wilson's cabinet as the new Interior Secretary. His appointment to the War Department was now based on the assumption that Walter Page would take over at Interior. Page, however, was a Southerner, and several members of Congress registered their displeasure with his possible nomination to the Interior post, which traditionally had gone to a Westerner. Again, lacking a formal mechanism for collecting information on prospective candidates, Wilson was unaware of this potential source of congressional opposition. As a result, Wilson again was forced to reconsider. He decided to leave Lane at Interior and identify someone else for the War post. On the advice of Colonel House, Wilson next offered the post to H. C. Wallace, who promptly turned it down, though he later accepted the post of ambassador to France.

Time was now running out before inauguration day, and Wilson and his advisers were frantic to identify someone for the post. As a result, as House commented, "The ultimate decision was made on the spur of the moment" (ibid., 100–11). Joseph Tumulty advised the president-elect to select someone from his own home state of New Jersey. Tumulty selected a candidate by scanning through the *Lawyer's Directory* until he came across the name of Lindley Garrison, who at the time was the vice chancellor of the highest court in New Jersey. Both Tumulty and Wilson were familiar with Garrison's impeccable reputation, and on this basis, his nomination was quickly secured (Daniels 1944: 117–18). Unfortunately, little was known of Garrison's qualifications for office or of his policy views. Lacking this information, Wilson again made an appointment that ultimately did not serve his policy needs. The new Secretary of War was a strict constitutional constructionist and disagreed with many of Wilson's progressive domestic and military policies. In time, this disagreement led to Garrison's resignation (ibid., 115).

Thus, the unstructured BOGSAT approach that promoted the Bryan and Garrison appointments did not serve the new president's policy needs. Rather than identifying qualified individuals who would support the president's political agenda, the BOGSAT approach produced two policy rivals to the president in Bryan and Garrison. Furthermore, Garrison lacked even the rudimentary qualifications to serve as Secretary of War.

15-2c Limitations of the BOGSAT Approach

The examples described in sections 15-2a and 15-2b illustrate the limitations of the BOGSAT approach. Without an effective and systematic mechanism for identifying, recruiting, and evaluating potential nominees, and a means of identifying which executive branch positions need to be filled (or likely would become vacant in the near future), most presidents were forced to rely on randomly collected information from a shifting coterie of personal advisers. Whereas history reveals that many excellent appointments were made over the years while presidents employed the BOGSAT approach, the utility of the appointment power was greatly constrained, especially during the modern presidential era.

15-3 Appointments in the Modern Presidency

As the modern presidency dawned, and as the size of the government continued to expand, presidents found themselves with an even larger number of appointive positions to fill. Congress, by law, augmented presidential appointment power as the government expanded. For example, presidents were delegated new authority to nominate judges to the Federal District and Appellate Courts as well as the members of the independent regulatory commissions. These increases in the number of presidential appointed positions over the years were extensive. By the time

Jimmy Carter assumed the office of president in 1977, the president was responsible for nominating individuals to more than 1,500 governmental positions (Mackenzie 1981: 5). With less than three months from election to inauguration, presidents had difficulty rendering considered judgments in the selection of even some top administration positions. As a result, most presidents limited their active participation to no more than 500 or 600 positions, while cabinet secretaries, the White House staff, or agency chairmen generally filled other positions, including assistant secretaries. Still, using the BOGSAT approach, presidents found it virtually impossible to identify even 500 to 600 qualified and loyal individuals to serve in a variety of governmental posts.

In addition, as public expectations continued to proliferate, while the utility of many of the presidency's traditional political resources declined, presidents also discovered that they needed greater responsiveness from their political appointees. To achieve this goal, a more reliable mechanism than the BOGSAT approach had to be established.

Finally, the adoption of the Twentieth Amendment to the Constitution in 1933 limited the time between election and inauguration day, reducing the transition period from four months to about ten and a half weeks. As a result, presidents-elect had less time to get their new team in place (McDonald 1994: 460). Consequently, with more appointments to make, less time to make them, and a perceived greater need for loyalty, a better system for identifying and evaluating appointments was needed. Such a system would evolve slowly along with the institutional development of the modern presidency.

15-4 Internalizing the Appointment Process

According to Bonafede (1987: 30), "A common denominator among modern presidents is their incessant search for a fail-safe formula for finding and appointing dedicated, qualified people to represent the administration with energy, imagination, and distinction. Upon entering office, indeed if not before, they learn that they cannot govern without the assistance of others." Likewise, as Nathan (1983: 90) writes, "Making the right appointments at the outset of a new government is one of the keys for a president in getting a grip on the office." For many presidents, making "the right appointments" means identifying and nominating individuals who are personally loyal to the president and his political agenda (see section 10-6, "Appointment Power"). In an age of escalating public expectations, presidents came to view loyalty and responsiveness as critically important attributes (Moe 1985b).

While the modern presidents are greatly concerned with loyalty, they were not the first to recognize its importance. For example, following the policy disagreements between Jefferson and Hamilton, George Washington wrote, "I shall not, while I have the honor to administer the government, bring a man into an office of consequence knowingly, whose political tenets are adverse to the measures which the general government are pursuing; for this, in my opinion, would be a sort of political suicide" (Goldsmith 1980: 159). Washington's Secretary of State, Thomas Jefferson, expressed similar sentiments shortly before he assumed the presidential office. According to McDonald (1976: 34; 36–37), Jefferson wanted to surround himself with a "loyal crew for steering the ship of state on a republican track." Likewise, Andrew Jackson considered loyalty to be a primary attribute for his political appointees. In a message to Congress on December 8, 1829, Jackson wrote, "In a country where offices are created solely for the benefit of the people no one man has any more intrinsic right to official station than another. . . . No individual wrong is, therefore, done by removal, since neither appointment to nor continuance in office is a matter of right" (Goldsmith 1980: 176).

Thus, a presidential concern with loyalty did not commence with the modern presidents: It long has been a presidential concern. As such, the modern presidency's preoccupation with loyalty and responsiveness cannot alone explain why the BOGSAT approach was superseded by newly evolving institutional mechanisms. Instead, the essential reason for these developments is that the modern presidents realized that as the size of the government expanded, and thus their need to appoint individuals to a greater number of federal positions expanded, presidents needed the loyal support of their appointed subordinates to satisfy ever-growing public expectations for presidential action in a wide variety of policy areas. In satisfying these expectations, the BOGSAT approach simply was not adequate (see Figure 15-2).

In addition, a change in the political ecosystem encouraged a move away from the BOGSAT approach. Slowly, over time, as the power of the political parties waned, presidents realized they needed to develop more formal mechanisms for identifying qualified candidates for office. Consequently, over a period of some sixty years, the appointment power, a legal political resource, was increasingly centralized within the White House (an internal resource) for the purpose of procuring additional information (i.e., an informational resource) about the availability of prospective officeholders. This new internal appointment mechanism was not developed overnight, however. Rather, as Bonafede (1987: 34) writes, "[It] grew piecemeal, with successive administrations adding and changing pieces of its structure and operational procedures. . . . Mainly, the ebb and flow of its fortunes coincided with the fluctuating needs and interest of the incumbent White House occupant and the prevailing national political climate."

15-4a The Evolution of the Appointment Process, Beginning with Roosevelt

A major period in the evolution of the appointment process occurred during Franklin Roosevelt's presidency, when Congress passed the Reorganization Act of 1939 (see section 13-4a, "The Executive Office of the President"), establishing six formal new administrative assistants to the president. Roosevelt assigned one of

Figure 15-2
Common Problems with the BOGSAT Approach

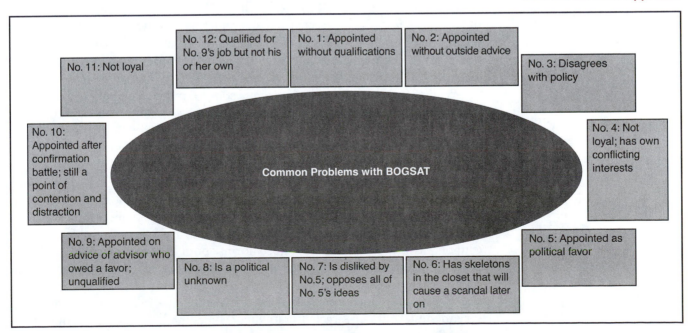

them as his liaison officer for personnel management, an impressive title with little real responsibility. Roosevelt's personnel adviser was responsible only for coordinating activities between the White House and the Civil Service Commission, while the president and his top advisers retained the important job of identifying prospective political appointees (ibid., 34). Thus, while Roosevelt assigned an official to be responsible for personnel matters, his actual appointment strategy remained the BOGSAT approach.

Roosevelt's first step was but a modest one. Much more significant were the actions of his successors. Harry Truman was the first president to establish a personnel office within the White House that was separate from the Democratic Party's political organization (see Weko 1995). By 1950, Truman was having trouble attracting qualified candidates for executive branch appointments. Truman named Donald Dawson, who formulated the "Committee on Executive Personnel" in March 1950. The Committee attempted to devise a mechanism for identifying the names of qualified personnel who could serve in various posts in the Truman administration. As Weko (1995: 19) writes, "the committee was careful to keep its proposals confidential, 'because of the controversy that its recommendations might have aroused' among party officials." In fact, Dawson's operation did engender controversy. "Dawson never presented . . . the committee's final report to the cabinet. As the committee completed its study, party officials weighed in with their views, making it clear that they saw the committee's plan for a fortified presidential staff as a threat. . . ." (ibid., 20). The committee's report therefore was buried. While a "talent bank" was established, it proved to be a mere shadow of the proposals Dawson initially had discussed. As Weko (1995: 20) comments, "This was a truly insignificant accretion to the president's staff, no more than a clerical tidying-up of the status quo. It did nothing to fortify the president's capabilities as a participant in staffing his administration, but it did have one virtue: it kept the president and his staff from violating the expectations of those whose support was essential, leaders of the Democratic party."

15-4b Truman's and Eisenhower's Use of BOGSAT

After the situation involving the Committee on Executive Personnel described in section 15-4a, BOGSAT was again employed by the Truman administration. For Dawson and his successor, Martin Friedman, who prepared files on prospective candidates, but did not take an active role in evaluating or recruiting candidates, much of their time was, in fact, "devoted to placing candidates proffered by Democratic politicians, campaign contributors, and clientele groups, an activity that Dawson and his boss deemed to be particularly valuable" (ibid., 17, 35).

While BOGSAT thus prevailed, the need for a more integrated personnel system was still apparent. During Truman's presidency, there were roughly "twenty-two thousand presidentially appointed posts" (Weko 1995: 15–16). According to Weko (ibid.), Truman was able to fill these posts because "virtually all of these appointments were 'presidential' in name only." Most "decisions about staffing the executive branch were still made outside the White House. During the Truman administration, as in past administrations, most political appointments were the product of negotiations among cabinet secretaries, congressmen from the president's party (particularly senators), party officials, and clientele groups, and bargaining was structured by well-defined norms about 'who gets what' and backed by powerful sanctions." In contrast, only "a thin layer of subcabinet appointments, roughly 100 posts at mid century, linked the president to the Washington bureaucracy." As Weko (ibid.) notes, even here, however, "the role of the president was very modest, confined largely to ratifying choices made by politicians outside the White House."

Yet, this situation reflected the dynamics of a political ecosystem that swiftly was changing. As noted in section 8-5, "Franklin Roosevelt and the Decline of the Parties," the Democratic political party's influence declined throughout the first half of the twentieth century and particularly during Franklin Roosevelt's presidency. While it still exerted influence over appointments during Truman's administration, its influence was about to be further undercut.

As noted in section 6-8a, "The Presidential Primaries of 1952," Eisenhower became the first president to use the primary elections to secure his party's nomination. The rationale for party influence over the presidency (control of the nomination) was evaporating. Still, the Republican Party played an important role during the Eisenhower presidency. Weko (1995: 15) writes, "Eisenhower's appointment staffer recalled, 'Every day, invariably, I would walk across the street to the Republican National Committee headquarters . . . and sit down with [RNC Chairman] Len Hall and his staff.' Each day the president's aide would solicit recommendations from Hall, clear candidates with him, and elicit political intelligence about prospective appointees."

Still, while Eisenhower showed deference to the Republican Party, from the very outset of his presidency, he recognized the need for an organization capable of coordinating information on prospective political appointees. In his memoirs, Eisenhower (1963: 117) wrote, "There had to be a place to direct applications for governmental appointments. This section also had the responsibility for keeping lists of qualified individuals from among whom I would later select men and women for particular tasks as they should arise." Eisenhower thus established the Office of the Special Assistant to the President for Personnel Management and then institutionalized it within the White House. Charles Willis was selected to handle personnel matters, under the direction of Eisenhower's chief of staff, Sherman Adams. The new special assistant served as a liaison to the executive departments, providing the administration with information such as when vacancies would occur, when terms would expire, as well as descriptions of the duties of vacant and soon-to-be-vacated positions. Through the Republican National Committee, members of Congress, the cabinet, and other political officials, the office also collected lists of potential nominees (Bonafede 1987: 35–36). Thus, by the time Eisenhower left office, an effective appointment mechanism was in place within the White House. It would, however, take another decade before Eisenhower's successors fully exploited its political potential. The evolution of this new internal political resource therefore also involved a certain amount of presidential learning. To replace the BOGSAT approach, not only was it necessary to create a mechanism inside the White House, but it was also necessary for presidents to learn how to use it.

15-4c Changes to the Appointments Process under Kennedy and Johnson

Initially, John Kennedy was hesitant to adopt Eisenhower's formal, organizational structure. Unlike his predecessor, Kennedy was less amenable to formal organizations, preferring instead to run things personally and directly from the Oval Office. Consequently, under Kennedy, there was an initial return to the BOGSAT approach. This regression, however, did not last long. As one Kennedy administration official, Ralph Dungan, states, "Generally, when a job was open we'd offer the president a single nominee, although sometimes we'd put in some others. He would assume we had worked it out. Of course, we made a heck of a lot of mistakes and occasionally he might say, 'Why'd you get that lame-brain?'" (quoted in Bonafede 1987: 37).

It soon became apparent to Kennedy and his advisers that he needed a more effective process for identifying qualified individuals than BOGSAT. As a result, midway through Kennedy's first year in office, Dungan brought in Dan Fenn to run the personnel office. In June 1961, Fenn concluded, "We were going to be in the recruitment business and not in the screening business. We are not going to be just going through the junk that was coming in over the transom" (quoted in Pfiffner 1988: 71).

The Kennedy administration's move toward an active, internalized recruitment process was yet another indication that presidents could no longer solely rely on informal mechanisms to locate qualified candidates for office. It also was part of the presidential learning process. Kennedy and his successors realized that they required an organization capable of providing them with information on a large number of potential nominees. While Kennedy's basic innovation would be adopted by each of his successors (Mackenzie 1981: 11, 79), it did not mean that each president would use it in the same manner or that the BOGSAT approach was yet obsolete.

While Lyndon Johnson inherited Kennedy's appointment process, he employed it in a different manner. Johnson's first major change, which he instituted shortly after his election in 1964, was to assign John Macy as the new director of the personnel office. According to Macy, the personnel office under Johnson was highly institutionalized:

> By 1968, we had accumulated thirty thousand names in our files. When reviewing a candidate, we'd consult with the agencies and commissions and winnow the list down to three to six candidates. Then a brief summary of the candidate's qualifications would be sent to the president; usually I'd select a favorite. At the bottom of the memorandum was a ballot allowing the president to indicate his preference or, if none was satisfactory, we were to look further. If a candidate was approved, we'd order an FBI check. (Quoted in Bonafede 1987: 38–39)

Johnson retained and further developed Kennedy's appointment organization: He was the first president to install a computer in the White House for processing information on potential candidates (ibid., 29). He also established a concurrent informal appointment system. In many cases, this informal system was more influential than Macy's operation. As Schott and Hamilton (1983: 9) note, it was "more fluid, more personal, and . . . left fewer traces in the written record." This informal network consisted of "the constant (often verbal) flow of advice and impressions of individuals given the president by his White House aides, by his cabinet secretaries, by his old friends, and by his personal confidants outside of the government." Hence, even as a new organizational mechanism was evolving, Johnson continued to rely on advisers, an approach similar in many respects to the BOGSAT approach. The difference was that the formal organization provided an alternative to BOGSAT.

15-4d Party Decline and a New Appointment Process

Weko (1995: 22) asks, "Why were Kennedy and Johnson able to expand the size and reach of their White House staff in ways that Truman's aides could only furtively contemplate?" His answer "lies in the sharply reduced leverage of the party figures. Between 1950 and the mid-1960s, the role that parties played during elections and between them diminished appreciably. The weakening hold of party organizations over presidential nominations was due, in part, to the expanding role of primary elections in the selection of convention delegates" (ibid., 23). Consequently, as the parties lost control of the nomination process and the critical selection of delegates, presidential candidates were less dependent on them and therefore had more freedom to ignore the parties and name their own appointees. With these changes to the political ecosystem already underway, Richard Nixon entered the White House at a most propitious time to further expand the White House personnel function.

15-4e Loyalty to the President: Nixon and BOGSAT

Whereas Johnson was intimately involved in the details of personnel matters, Richard Nixon initially distanced himself from the appointment process (Weko 1995: 109–10). On taking office, Nixon was determined to locate men of independent mind for his cabinet. He then allowed his cabinet secretaries to select their own subordinates, including such important posts as the under and deputy secretaries for each department. In so doing, Nixon was simply following a traditional presidential practice. Previous presidents simply did not have the time or the institutional capability to identify candidates for these many sub-cabinet positions. Traditionally, this task was left to department and agency heads, with the result that the sub-cabinet appointees often reflected the policy views of their immediate super-ordinates, rather than the president.[3]

During his first two years in office, however, Nixon's view of the appointment process changed. First, he decided that his top appointments should be made on the basis of loyalty to the president. Second, Nixon decided that he also would have to assume the responsibility for appointing sub-cabinet positions, that is, if he were to ensure loyalty to the president throughout the executive branch. Nixon (1978: 768) reflected on this changed appointment philosophy in his memoirs:

> I regretted that during the first term we had done a very poor job in the most basic business of every new administration of either party: we had failed to fill all the key posts in the departments and agencies with people who were loyal to the President and his programs. Without this kind of leadership in appointive positions, there is no way for a president to make any major impact on the bureaucracy.

Nixon's failure to appoint loyalists to his administration was related to his idea that cabinet secretaries should be individuals of independent mind. It also, however, resulted from the administration's initially chaotic appointment process. Prior to Nixon's election, Harry S. Flemming had solicited the names of potential appointees by making a list of individuals from the publication *Who's Who in America*. His subsequent contacts with these individuals resulted in an avalanche of dubious referrals. After Nixon's election, Peter Flanigan assumed the personnel function, assisted at first by fifteen employees. Over time, Flanigan's staff ballooned to some sixty employees (Pfiffner 1988: 72). With this new personnel operation in place, Nixon finally possessed a mechanism for implementing a more aggressive appointment strategy. What Nixon now required was an articulation of such an appointment strategy. The details of the new approach were provided in a forty-five-page report written for Chief of Staff H. R. Haldeman by Deputy Under Secretary of Health, Education, and Welfare Frederick Malek. In the report titled "Management of Non-Career Personnel: Recommendations For Improvement," Malek called on the president to appoint qualified and loyal individuals, to promote them, and to remove from office those who were not loyal.

Malek's recommendations so impressed Haldeman that he soon named Malek as head of the White House Personnel Office (WHPO). Under Malek's control, the WHPO adopted a variety of new techniques for increasing White House control over the appointment process. First, he broadened the search for new, loyal political appointees. Second, he kept lines open to departments and agencies regarding lower-level positions. Third, Malek instituted a process for evaluating incumbent personnel to guarantee that they were living up to the new standards of loyalty and competence that had been set by the Nixon administration.

As noted, an important innovation of Malek's approach was to gain control over lower-level appointments. Rather than following the age-old tradition of allowing department or agency heads to appoint their own subordinates, Nixon himself (or his top advisers) selected sub-cabinet officials. Now an appointee's primary commitment was to the president, particularly if he or she was interested in advancement within the administration. The strategy was designed to prevent department and agency heads from establishing their own autonomous bureaucratic fiefdoms and to ensure that bureaucratic policy was truly consistent with presidential intent.

Of course, the strategy of making the president personally responsible for such a staggering number of new appointments would not have been feasible without the new internal resources that had been developed by Nixon's predecessors. Now, more than ever, the president needed an effective mechanism for identifying and evaluating prospective officeholders. A system established in its most nascent form by Roosevelt and Truman, institutionalized by Eisenhower, expanded by Kennedy and Johnson, now was further transformed to serve Nixon's organizational needs.

15-4f Nixon's Appointment Arsenal

The Nixon administration's development of a clear appointment strategy was indeed impressive, but it had negative ramifications as well (see Figure 15-3). The new appointment strategy provided Nixon with greater control over his subordinates, but by internalizing the recruitment function and the process for evaluating the conduct of incumbent appointees, Nixon created a powerful tool, one might even say a weapon, for enforcing conformity with his political viewpoints. In turn, the new appointment process provoked political opposition, since it created a political environment that was ripe with opportunities for abuse. Nixon's appointment strategy, particularly with regard to his second-term decision to establish a super-cabinet of super loyalists, was stridently criticized by members of Congress and the press as a usurpation of the legitimate, statutory authority of the various executive departments and agencies. In addition, there were specific charges of impropriety, such as the administration's attempts to remove career civil servants from the bureaucracy and the revelation that Malek had been asked to delineate a list of all Jewish officeholders serving in the Nixon administration. Thus, the strategy as implemented, while it promised increased presidential control of the executive branch, concomitantly raised serious political, legal, and moral claims that eventually reduced Nixon's influence, particularly as one Nixon appointee after another was indicted, convicted, and sentenced to prison for his role in the Watergate-related crimes.

The case of the Nixon presidency demonstrates that the internalization of political resources can, when abused, threaten a president's very legitimacy (see Hess 1976/1988). Even such a comparatively unambiguous constitutional delegation of authority as the president's appointment power can become the subject of intense political scrutiny. Yet, at the same time, the internalization of the appointment power established a potentially powerful new political resource. If presidents could avoid the abuses of the Nixon years, they could employ this new internal and informational resource in a manner that would help them to identify and evaluate a wider number of potential nominees for a variety of diverse executive branch positions. In fact, after Carter decided to decentralize the appointment process,

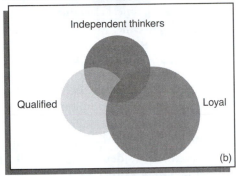

Nixon's initial plan for appointments: Nixon originally sought out independent thinkers and allowed Cabinet members to appoint their own subordinates. Loyalty, independence of thought, and qualification for the position were regarded equally.

(a)

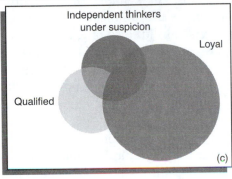

Nixon became increasingly concerned with loyalty and insisted that it be the primary standard by which candidates be evaluated. He also removed the power of his Cabinet members to appoint their own subordinates, doing so himself. The balance of criteria for appointment became unstable.

(b)

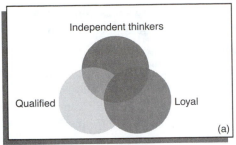

Using White House Personnel Office head Frederick Malek's recommendations, certain groups and individuals were removed from the lists of potential appointees. Nixon now required that his appointees be loyal (this elusive trait was evaluated by Malek's department). Independent thinkers were under suspicion. Loyalty to the president was valued above all, creating a grotesque abuse of the appointment process.

(c)

Figure 15-3
Nixon's Control over Appointments and Abuses Therein

with disastrous policy consequences (see section 13-4d, "Nixon's Staff and Its Legacy"), Ronald Reagan exploited these new internal and informational political resources to their fullest potential to date.

15-4g Reagan and Carter's TIP

With the election of Ronald Reagan in 1980, the stage was set for an aggressive employment of the president's appointment power. The primary qualifications for service in the new Reagan administration were, from the very outset, loyalty to the president and conformity with the president's conservative political agenda. During the election, Reagan's advisers borrowed an innovation Jimmy Carter established for the transition process in 1976. Carter created the Talent Inventory Process (TIP) prior to his 1976 election victory so that he could identify qualified candidates before he was elected. Unfortunately, intense infighting between Carter aides Jack Watson and Hamilton Jordan, and their respective campaign and transition teams, greatly reduced the utility of the TIP process (Pfiffner 1988).

Despite TIP's failure, in 1980 Reagan and his top aides employed a similar system to identify talent for a prospective Reagan administration. Free from the internecine warfare that had characterized Carter's transition, however, Reagan successfully employed a variation of TIP. Under the direction of E. Pendleton James, Reagan commenced an unprecedented search to identify individuals who could pass the strictest of ideological litmus tests, as well as demonstrate personal loyalty to the new president. One key feature of his new appointment strategy was its complete control by the White House. As Pfiffner (1988: 75) writes,

> The Reagan administration resolved that it would not make the mistakes of earlier presidencies and lose control of its personnel appointments, but that close control of all appointments at all levels would come from the White House. In order to do this they set up an elaborate clearance procedure to be followed in appointing personnel. Each nomination had to run a formidable gauntlet running from the cabinet secretary and the personnel office to Lyn Nofziger (political clearance), to White House counsel Fred Fielding (conflict of interest), to either Martin Anderson (domestic) or Richard Allen (national security), to the triad James Baker, Michael Deaver, and Edwin Meese . . . and finally to the president himself.

Never in the history of the presidency had such a rigorous process been established for recruiting, screening, and evaluating potential appointees. The new centralized mechanisms worked to Reagan's political advantage. His legislative achievements during his first year in office owed much to an administration united by clear ideological principles. Like the Nixon presidency, however, Reagan's appointment strategy encountered problems. For example, the appointment of Anne Gorsuch Burford as Administrator of the Environmental Protection Agency resulted in considerable political controversy, as did some of Reagan's other regulatory appointments (such as the EEOC; see Wood 1990) and two of his Supreme Court nominees. For the most part, the Reagan appointment strategy was successful. As Wood and Waterman (1991; 1993; 1994) empirically demonstrate, Reagan's appointees were able to alter the enforcement behavior of a variety of different executive branch agencies.[4]

Thus, an examination of the Reagan presidency demonstrates that by taking a constitutionally enumerated power, that is, a legal political resource, and internalizing it within the White House, a president gained additional political influence by increasing the probability that his appointees would actively support his political agenda. As the Iran-Contra scandal shows, however, there are limits to this approach, as well. Once again, the presidential appointees faced the specter of congressional investigation, indictment, trial, and sentencing.

Given the experiences of Watergate and Iran-Contra, why have presidents continued to employ the new appointment strategy? One clear answer is that Reagan achieved many policy successes as a result of his control over the appointment process. Despite the risks, then, it is not surprising that his successors have followed his example. George H. W. Bush made loyalty a key criterion in his appointment approach. Podhoretz (1993: 89) writes, "To clear the personnel hurdle, Republicans had to demonstrate their personal loyalty to Bush with hard evidence. The forms that job seekers had to fill out asked candidates to specify their 'Bush experience'— not their general Republican experience."

15-4h George H. W. Bush's Criteria

While George H. W. Bush, like Reagan, stressed loyalty, his selection process was more deliberate than Reagan's: His selection of important positions, particularly at the sub-cabinet level, was delayed far beyond the president's inauguration. This slower pace partly was due to the fact that the Bush transition was a friendly takeover, that is, a Republican president replacing another Republican president. Yet, Bush also told his personnel director, Chase Untermeyer, not to set up a computer search for prospective candidates until after the election (as noted, the Reagan team had begun to search much earlier in 1980, when it was apparent that Reagan had secured the

Republican nomination). There were other differences, as well. Whereas Reagan had set up an elaborate process for testing the loyalty of his appointments, the Bush system merely called for Untermeyer and the appropriate cabinet secretary (or secretary designate) to agree on a list, which was then forwarded to Chief of Staff John Sununu and then on to Bush (Solomon 1989: 142–43).

Bush may have adopted this less rigorous system because he had a different conceptualization of loyalty than his predecessor. While Ronald Reagan based loyalty on the acceptance of a corps of conservative philosophical principles, Bush saw it in a more personal way. He preferred to surround himself with people he knew or who had a background similar to his own (see Michaels 1997; Solomon 1989). In fact, Bush's governing philosophy was less clearly enumerated than was Reagan's.[5] This, in turn, created problems as administration officials found it more difficult to follow the president's lead.

Consequently, the first Bush presidency shows that the centralization strategy works best if the president has a clear sense of the kinds of people he wants to attract to his new administration and a consistent policy vision. When such commendable goals as Carter's desire to name a greater percentage of women or minorities to administration posts (see Fishel 1985: 35) predominate, loyalty to the president and his program may take on a lesser priority. Furthermore, when presidents have less clearly articulated policy goals or do not express a clear political philosophy, it is more difficult to recruit and evaluate individuals who share the president's policy goals. Reagan therefore had a distinct advantage that many presidents do not have: He knew what he wanted before he became president. Many presidents are less clear about their policy objectives, or their goals change as their presidency unfolds. In these cases, the centralized appointment strategy is of less utility than it was for Reagan.

A second problem experienced by the first Bush presidency was that as presidents centralize and take more control over the appointment process, they run the risk of elongating the time required to get their governing team in place. The Bush and Clinton presidencies experienced a significant elongation in the time period needed to appoint individuals to key administration posts, with some positions remaining vacant for over a year (see Waterman, Stewart, and Morris 1995). If presidents cannot get their appointees confirmed expeditiously, and key positions are left vacant, this will do little to increase presidential influence. With the Senate confirmation process also more divisive than in the past (see Carter 1994), questions arise about the utility of the centralized appointment strategy. Yet, while there are questions, there appears to be little alternative other than to return to the BOGSAT approach. With the political parties far weaker today than they once were, they clearly are not in a position to dominate the appointment process, as they once did. With greater conflict between the president and Congress, and with the increasing likelihood of divided government (see section 9-8b, "Divided Government"), presidents also are not likely to ask Congress to play a larger role in the appointment process. Hence, while it certainly has limitations, the centralized appointment strategy likely will remain the most viable option.

15-4i The Bureaucracy of Appointments under Clinton

The Clinton presidency provides a test of the idea that the centralized appointment strategy is the most viable option: Bill Clinton's aides "constructed a personnel staff that resembled Ronald Reagan's in its size, procedures and influence" (Weko 1995: 124). It also developed another innovation: "in yet another bow to the demands of sharply ideological and media-centered politics, Clinton's personnel organization broke new ground by creating a 'vetting staff.'" The staff consisted of "upward of

30 lawyers and researchers" who performed the tasks of searching for negative information on their own prospective appointees (ibid., 101). As the Washington political environment has become more hostile, it has become necessary for presidents to discover negative information about their own appointees before the opposition does. Thus, the personnel staff had yet another task to perform in addition to recruitment. Evaluation now meant doing the opposition party's job first so that the opposition would not have a chance to later embarrass the administration with salacious details about an appointee's financial or personal life.

Yet, at the same time that Clinton expanded his staff's functions, he also reduced the size of his White House staff, following through on a promise he had made during the campaign to reduce it by one-third. The Presidential Personnel Office (PPO) was therefore reduced from 105 in March 1993 to 55 by late August. Clinton's PPO aides "privately warned, 'we're losing control.'" They noted that "we lose the ability to set direction, we become hostage to what the agencies want to do.'" By October 1, the staff was further reduced to 35 and by late November 1993 to just 25, "smaller than any since Carter's PPO of 1978–1979." In this diminished capacity, "the Clinton PPO was sharply circumscribed in its capacity to exercise influence over the staffing of the government as well" (ibid., 125).

Clinton's payoff for following through on a campaign promise to cut the size of the White House staff was modest, if in fact there was any political benefit to it at all. In contrast, by cutting his PPO staff, he ensured that it would take even longer for his appointees to get into their jobs than had been the case with George H. W. Bush. There were serious political repercussions for the new administration. The "slowness with which posts were filled generated anger inside the Clinton White House, criticism from Capitol Hill, and a torrent of critical news stories and commentary from Washington journalists" (ibid., 102).

Inadvertently, Clinton had demonstrated what would happen if a president dispensed with the centralized White House personnel staff operation. The result was political and organizational chaos. In fact, it proved to be a serious governing hindrance to the Clinton administration throughout its first term. The lesson from the Clinton presidency was clear: A centralized White House staff is needed, and presidents who do not take full advantage of it raise questions about their very competence.

15-4j Bush the Younger Looks Back for Advice and Appointments

It is not surprising that George W. Bush did not make the same mistake as Clinton. His appointment process was not only centralized, but he relied heavily on the vast experience of his vice president, Richard Cheney, to identify and evaluate prospective nominees. He also used a pool of Republican officials established over the years, nominating a large number of former Nixon and Ford officials to key positions in his administration. Even though he had less time to put his team in place, due to the inconclusive nature of the 2000 presidential election and the thirty-six days its result lay in the balance, he was able to surround himself with a large number of experienced individuals who also expressed personal loyalty to the new president. Consequently, the presidency of George W. Bush provides no evidence of a further retreat from a hierarchical White House–dominated personnel-staffing system. Presidents now can look to the experience of the first Clinton administration if they want to know what would happen if they do not use their centralized White House Personnel Office to its fullest potential.

Chapter Summary

The internalization of the presidential appointment power offers presidents a clear benefit: It increases the likelihood that presidents will be able to identify and evaluate individuals who will be loyal to them and their policies. Yet, it also incurs risks. The Iran-Contra case in the Reagan presidency, no less than Watergate in the Nixon presidency, shows that loyal individuals, especially if they are not properly supervised by a vigilant president, may do more damage than good to a president's reputation.

Hence, the case of the presidential appointment strategy demonstrates the two contradictory features of the internalization of presidential resources. On the one hand, it offers the presidency the possibility of palpable influence, which presidents need, particularly as changes in the political ecosystem place greater demands on them and as the relationship between the presidency and its various external political actors becomes more hostile. Yet, internal resources also can decrease presidential power, can delay the time necessary to get the president's team on board the ship of state, and in extreme cases, can even leave a presidency in political ruins. It is therefore important to remember the risks as well as the potential benefits of the centralization strategy.

Weko (1995: 149–51) identifies three problems that the centralization of the appointment process creates. "First, the aggrandizement of the president's White House appointments staff has produced a tremendous surge in demands and expectations aimed at the White House." Second, there has been an "intensification of conflict within the White House office." Third, "conflict between the appointments staff and executive departments" has increased.

Consequently, the choice to adopt internal resources involves potential benefits and costs. So far, presidents have been willing to accept the inherent risks, but for those who believe that this move is too dangerous, it appears the genie already is out of the bottle. As Clinton's reduction of his personnel staff inadvertently shows us, it is too late for presidents to go back to the days before internal resources dominated the presidency. Presidents need these various organizational mechanisms to help them identify prospective appointments, as well as to perform a variety of other tasks associated with outreach, coordination, and decision-making to bring expertise to the White House. The presidential conundrum, then, continues to be how to balance the potential benefits and risks of these new internal and informational political resources.

Review Questions

1. George Washington made appointments on the basis of which of the following?
   a. fitness for office
   b. competence
   c. an equal distribution of appointments across the states
   d. all of the above

2. Which of the following was the only organizational mechanism in place to help presidents such as Abraham Lincoln make appointments?
   a. the White House Personnel Office
   b. the congressional personnel office
   c. the political parties
   d. all of the above

3. Which of the following constrained the role of the parties in the political process?
   a. the Civil War
   b. the Pendleton Act
   c. the Einstein Act
   d. World War I

4. Which of the following presidents' casual promise at a dinner party led to the appointment of Elihu Washburne as Secretary of State?
   a. George Washington
   b. Abraham Lincoln
   c. Ulysses Grant
   d. Grover Cleveland

5. By the time Jimmy Carter became president, the president was responsible for how many appointments?
    a. 100
    b. 1,000
    c. 1,500
    d. 10,000

6. Which of the following presidents established the Office of the Special Assistant to the President for Personnel Management and then institutionalized it within the White House?
    a. Franklin Roosevelt
    b. Harry Truman
    c. Dwight Eisenhower
    d. John Kennedy

7. Which of the following presidents established the Talent Inventory Process (TIP) prior to his election victory so that he could begin the process of identifying qualified candidates before he was elected?
    a. Richard Nixon
    b. Jimmy Carter
    c. Ronald Reagan
    d. Bill Clinton

8. Which of the following presidents promised to cut the size of his White House staff and then cut personnel staff, creating problems recruiting qualified candidates in a timely fashion?
    a. Richard Nixon
    b. Jimmy Carter
    c. Ronald Reagan
    d. Bill Clinton

Discussion Questions

1. What does BOGSAT stand for? What were the limitations of the BOGSAT approach?

2. Why do presidents need a White House Personnel Office?

Notes

1. An earlier version of this chapter appeared as "Combining Political Resources: The Internalization of the President's Appointment Power" in Richard W. Waterman (ed.) *The Presidency Reconsidered.* Itasca, IL: F. E. Peacock Publishers (1993: 195–214).

2. Garfield struggled with the Senate, and particularly Senator Conklin of New York, over the issue of senatorial courtesy. In the short time before his assassination, Garfield was able to reclaim additional presidential appointment authority from the Senate (see Milkis and Nelson 1994: 186–87).

3. For example, Mann and Jamison (1965) find that Truman, Eisenhower, and Kennedy left the appointment of departmental assistant secretaries to the department secretaries.

4. These agencies included the Food and Drug Administration, the Federal Trade Commission, the Nuclear Regulatory Commission, the Interstate Commerce Commission, and for a time, the Equal Employment Opportunity Commission.

5. So was Carter's. He was unable to send a clear signal to his appointees about his governing philosophy that, in turn, did little to prevent disagreements within the bureaucracy over the intent of administration policy (see Landy, Roberts, and Thomas 1994: 67).

Chapter 16

Of the Presidency:
Past, Present, and Future

Key Term

impact presidents

16-1 Of the Presidency: Past, Present, and Future

In this book, I have argued that while the constitutional basis of the presidency is essentially the same as it was in 1787, the office itself has been transformed. The changing American presidency is the result of altered contextual factors (from rural to urban, from agricultural to industrial, from isolationist to interventionist, as well as the development of a national media, radio, television, improved transportation systems, and new weapons systems). These contextual factors, in turn, have an impact on public and elite expectations, primarily by placing new demands for political action on the federal government or specific policy actors. This process has had a particularly important impact on the power of the presidency over time. Changing expectations increased the tendency to look toward Washington and the White House for leadership. By the 1960s and 1970s, however, greater distrust in government (another form of public expectations) fostered a more hostile political environment and, along with escalating expectations, helped create scholarly concerns that the presidency is threatened by an expectations gap. Meanwhile, various shocks to the political ecosystem, such as the Great Depression, World War II, the Cold War, Vietnam, Watergate, and September 11, 2001, either undercut the rationalization for laissez-faire economics or provided a rationale for a more active foreign policy role. Both rationalizations provided an impetus for increased presidential power.

As a result of all of these factors, plus ongoing incremental changes over time, the nation's political ecosystem has been significantly altered with the influence of some policy actors declining over time (e.g., the political parties) and others ascending (the presidency). Likewise, new institutions developed (the bureaucracy), and others found new constituencies (the public and the media shifting from the parties to the presidency). As new demands were placed on the presidency, a variety of new White House organizations were created, further altering how the presidency works by transferring influence from the cabinet to the White House staff.

In sum, five main factors examined throughout this book contributed to the accretion of presidential power and its ascension to a position of considerable prominence in our political ecosystem: (1) changes in contextual factors encouraged a move toward an executive-centered governmental system; (2) these contextual changes also stimulated new public and elite expectations of political actors, but particularly of the presidency; (3) incremental shifts in the balance of power between different institutions in the political ecosystem led to a decline in the power of the parties and an increased role for the media, as well as a more direct connection between the public and the presidency; (4) various shocks to the political ecosystem resulted in altered public and elite expectations of presidential performance, usually in ways that led to the accretion of presidential power; and (5) presidents created an institutionalized presidency which further centralized demands for domestic and foreign policy responses from the executive branch.

In this chapter, I use two frameworks to summarize and further develop these various stimuli for presidential power. The first is a presentation of what I call the twelve impact presidents: the presidents who I believe promoted (both in positive and negative ways) changes in the office of the presidency. Then I will re-examine the framework I introduced in section 1-3, "Political Resources," and employed throughout this book, by analyzing the six political resources of the presidency.

16-2 The Twelve Impact Presidents

While to some extent almost all of our presidents have contributed to the evolution of the presidential office, twelve have had the most significant impact. I call them the **impact presidents,** comparing them in sports terminology to impact players

Impact presidents: The presidents who have played the most important role in changing the presidency, but they are not necessarily the great presidents.

who are vital to a team's success. They are the presidents who played the most important role in changing the presidency: George Washington, Thomas Jefferson, Andrew Jackson, Abraham Lincoln, William McKinley, Theodore Roosevelt, Woodrow Wilson, Franklin Roosevelt, Harry Truman, Dwight Eisenhower, Lyndon Johnson, and Richard Nixon. This is not a list of the great presidents; hence, worthy presidents such as John Adams and James Polk are not listed here, though they clearly had important policy successes. As presidential innovators, they also had some impact (e.g., Adams eventually replaced Washington's cabinet with his own, thus setting an important precedent; Polk was the first president to use a budget and was an active commander-in-chief), but they did not leave behind them fundamental changes in the office, as I believe the other twelve presidents did.

Five presidents from the nineteenth century can be characterized as impact presidents: George Washington, Thomas Jefferson, Andrew Jackson, Abraham Lincoln, and William McKinley. Washington played an obvious and important role in setting precedents for all of his successors. He developed the basic parameters for the presidential office. Jefferson demonstrated that the presidency could play an active political role, working with Congress and the Democratic/Republican party to set the policy agenda. He provided the basis for the growth of presidential power by providing a powerful rationale for presidential leadership and a means of accomplishing it. Part of Jefferson's rationale was an expanded concept of democracy. Like Jefferson, Andrew Jackson expanded the connection between the president and the public, even providing a clear rationale for combining presidential power with popular support. In this process, Jackson transformed the electoral order—promoting an era in which party government prevailed. Jackson also provided a model for a more active presidency, making greater use of the presidential veto power, removing recalcitrant officials from office, establishing the spoils system, taking an active role as a policy initiator, and establishing the power of the presidency as separate and distinct from that of Congress.

Abraham Lincoln also set a number of precedents for presidential power. Governing in the unique times of the Civil War, Lincoln expanded presidential power in both domestic and foreign affairs and played an active role as commander-in-chief, even more active than James Polk, whom he had once criticized for initiating war with Mexico. Finally, William McKinley was the first president to sense the changing nature of the political ecosystem. He began the process of reaching out to the public and the media. He also witnessed the beginnings of a permanent transformation in the president's role as commander-in-chief—even if, ironically, Congress pressured him to declare war on Spain. McKinley's election in 1896 coincided with a fundamental realignment in the political electorate, which led to the establishment of the third electoral order: when the presidency began to emerge from the party's shadows. While McKinley was not an active participant in fomenting some of these changes, his presidency nonetheless reflects a fundamental dividing point between the politics of the past and those of the future.

16-2a Twentieth Century Impact Presidents

In some respects, the fact that McKinley's presidency symbolizes the dividing point in presidential politics relates more to factors beyond his control, such as the aggressive and innovative leadership approach employed by his successor in the White House, Theodore Roosevelt. Roosevelt was the first of seven twentieth-century presidents who had a significant impact on the presidency. He helped to create the rhetorical presidency. He reached out to the public and the media, thus helping the presidency to develop a new constituency and a new intermediary to it, as well as shifting public expectations toward the White House. He expanded the president's role as chief legislator, vastly expanded the president's role in foreign affairs, and provided a new interpretation of the Constitution that opened the door for a more active presidency.

Woodrow Wilson also came to office with a clearly articulated view of presidential power and then further refashioned the presidency. He further elevated the president's rhetorical role by delivering his state of the union address in person before Congress and attempting to go public over the heads of legislators to sell the Treaty of Versailles and the League of Nations. He also became an active chief legislator and later commander-in-chief. While his presidency ultimately demonstrated the limitations of these approaches, Wilson provided the foundation for many of Franklin Roosevelt's later political innovations.

Franklin Roosevelt often is credited with creating the modern presidency. While the innovations necessary for the establishment of the modern presidency were well underway prior to FDR's arrival at 1600 Pennsylvania Avenue, he clearly accelerated and contributed to these changes in myriad ways. From his presidency onward, there was no doubt that the president was expected to provide primary leadership in establishing the policy agenda. Roosevelt expanded both public expectations and the scope of presidential activities. He used radio to directly reach out to the public and public opinion polls to gauge public sentiment. In so doing, he fundamentally changed the way people interact with the president and the federal government. In sum, his presidency marks a true symbiosis between the public and the presidency. In addition, he also increased presidential outreach to the media and expanded the size and functions of the White House itself (including the development of the Executive Office of the President). As commander-in-chief in World War II, he also provided a model for a new foreign policy presidency.

Harry Truman then institutionalized that model. Governing at the beginning of the Cold War, he played a major role in promoting interventionist policies and driving isolationism to the backbench of American politics. He also oversaw important developments in the institutionalization of the foreign policy presidency, including the creation of the Defense Department, the National Security Council, and the Central Intelligence Agency.[1] The U.S.'s foreign policy role also further expanded, as it became an active member of the United Nations, the North Atlantic Treaty Organization, and other international organizations. Treaty obligations not only solidified an internationalist foreign policy, but they also provided additional legal rationales for presidential action. Hence, when Truman went to war in Korea, he did not ask for a congressional declaration, but rather justified it under treaty obligations and the UN Charter. A fundamentally new age of presidential war making without congressional acquiescence had begun.

Dwight Eisenhower also played a critical role in altering the presidency. His electoral innovations, including creating his own campaign organization, successfully using the primaries to unseat the party favorite, and using television advertisements in his fall campaign, transformed electoral politics, marking the way for the fourth and present electoral order. As president, Eisenhower also further expanded the institutional presidency, creating a number of institutional units that, in somewhat different forms, have been used by his successors. He also established the positions of chief of staff and the President's Special Assistant for National Security Affairs, as well as the cabinet secretariat (which reappeared in several administrations). Today, the first two of these positions are among the most powerful in the U.S. government.

16-2b Negative Impacts

Lyndon Johnson and Richard Nixon changed the political climate in a fundamentally important way that has impacted all presidents since their time. Vietnam and Watergate provided fundamental shocks to the political system, resulting in vastly increased levels of public distrust with government. The hostility that pervades Washington politics had its roots in these presidencies and, according to many scholars cited throughout this book, undermined the ability of Presidents Ford, Carter, Reagan, G. H. W. Bush, Clinton, and G. W. Bush to govern. In addition, from Nixon's presidency onward, divided government became the norm in American politics. Open conflict developed between the presidency and the media. Congressional investigations of the presidency became commonplace: One president was impeached, one resigned rather than face impeachment, and another survived a major foreign policy scandal. With the rise of divisive single-issue interest groups, the further decline of the political parties, and an environment of unrealistic and excessive public expectations, scholars wondered if the presidency itself was too powerful (Schlesinger 1973) or doomed to failure (Lowi 1985). Johnson and Nixon, for all of their policy successes, have to take much of the blame for the cannibalistic political environment they helped to create (see Figure 16-1).

16-2c Four Other Candidates

The twelve presidents described in sections 16-2 through 16-2b, then, had the greatest impact, good and bad, on the development of the presidency. Others clearly contributed, as well. Ronald Reagan provided a new model for presidential bureaucratic relations, expanding ideas initially developed by Nixon. Reagan also expanded the public relations and image focus of the presidency, which again Nixon had done much to create (see Waterman, Wright, and St. Clair 1999). Kennedy also played a major role in developing the public presidency, including expanded use of public ceremonies and a greater reliance on television skills. Likewise, Taft played a major role in developing the rationale for the present budgetary system, and Polk added to concerns about the propriety of presidential power when he sent troops into disputed territory in Mexico. Consequently, Reagan, Kennedy, Taft, and Polk also made impacts on the presidency, but I believe lesser ones than the twelve impact presidents I identified.

16-2d The Impact Presidents and the Great Presidents

It is interesting to note that the names of the same twelve presidents that I identified as the impact presidents appear with regularity on lists of the great presidents. In fact, nine of the twelve presidents I identified (see names in bold print in poll that follows) are ranked in the top ten of the 1982 *Chicago Tribune* poll, presented

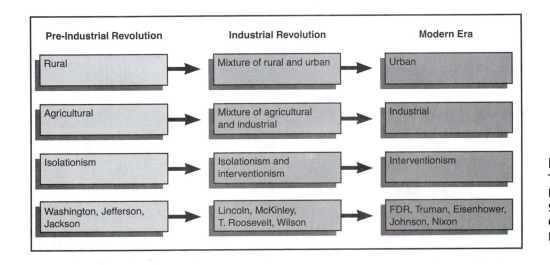

Figure 16-1
The Gradually Shifting Landscape of American Society, Showing Contextual Factors in Domestic and Foreign Policy

below (and in section 3-3a, "Other Poll Results"), while McKinley is listed as number 11, and Lyndon Johnson, 12. Only Polk, who I believe had a somewhat lesser impact on the presidency, is in the top ten list. Nixon ranked next to last in the *Chicago Tribune* poll, reflecting no doubt the ill effects of the Watergate scandal. The poll results suggest that historians appreciate the contributions that these impact presidents have made to the evolution of the modern presidency.

1982 Chicago Tribune Poll

1. **Lincoln**
2. **Washington**
3. **F. Roosevelt**
4. **T. Roosevelt**
5. **Jefferson**
6. **Wilson**
7. **Jackson**
8. **Truman**
9. **Eisenhower**
10. Polk
11. **McKinley**
12. **L. Johnson**

To further illustrate how these presidents impacted the presidency, I next return to an examination of the six political resources, originally presented in Chapter 1, "Public Expectations and the Political Resources of the Presidency," and then used as the organizational basis for the chapters in this book. By examining these political resources, we can determine how each impact president contributed to the development of presidential power.

16-3 The Six Political Resources

In this book, we have examined each of the political resources presently available to the modern presidents (see Figure 16-2). In sections 16-4 through 16-8, I provide a summation and elaboration of each political resource. I begin with an examination of the president's personal resources.

Figure 16-2
An Overview of the Six Political Resources

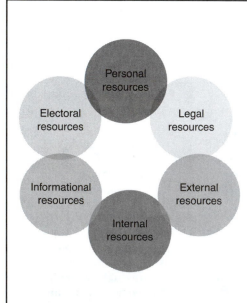

Personal resources: These factors relate to the personal beliefs and qualifications that individual presidents bring to the White House when they assume the presidential office, including personality and rhetorical skills.

Legal resources: Legal resources come from the enumerated powers of the Constitution, precedent, executive orders and presidential proclamations, treaties, defense pacts, and foreign agreements.

Electoral resources: Elections generally provide presidents with legitimacy. Presidents can argue that they are carrying out the will of the people as expressed in the outcome of the last election.

External resources: These resources include the U.S. Congress, the courts, political parties, the bureaucracy, the public, interest groups, and the media, as well as the federal bureaucracy.

Internal resources: These resources involve the development of institutional frameworks within the White House or the EOP. They may be either formal organizations or an informal collection of individuals motivated by a common purpose.

Informational resources: Informational resources involve gathering, maintaining, manipulating, and dispensing a variety of different types of intelligence, involving such diverse functions as monitoring bureaucratic policy proposals through the use of central clearance procedures, collecting information on potential nominees for federal office through a systematized personnel unit, collecting data on the budget, or counting votes on Capitol Hill.

16-4 Personal Resources

What constitutes personal political resources? They are factors that relate to the personal beliefs and qualifications that individual presidents bring to the White House when they assume the presidential office. Each individual comes to office with different skills, ideologies, belief systems, and ideas about how the presidency operates. One of the most detailed analyses of the president's personal resources is provided by Richard Neustadt's (1960) classic study of presidential power. Neustadt identifies several personal resources that presidents employ to promote their policy objectives. For example, Dwight Eisenhower brought an impeccable "reputation" as a military leader and expert on foreign affairs to the White House. This reputation proved to be of considerable value to him throughout his eight years in the White House. Policy-wise, it was useful in his dealings with other nations during foreign policy crises. Domestically, it provided a statesmanlike public image and the "prestige" that goes with that image. This translated into consistently high public approval ratings and an image of effective leadership. This image was useful in compensating for his shortcomings (his poor speaking style). It also improved his bargaining position with other politicians.

Beyond reputation and prestige, Neustadt also identifies several legislative skills. In particular, he discusses the presidential ability to persuade and bargain. These personal skills clearly differentiate Lyndon Johnson's presidency from that of Jimmy Carter. Whereas Carter had great difficulty understanding how to deal with Congress, particularly during his first two years in office, Lyndon Johnson was a master at legislative maneuvering. One cannot fully understand the legislative dealings of either presidency without first examining the personal bargaining skills each man possessed.

16-4a Rhetorical Skills

As with previous presidents' bargaining skills, one cannot understand the presidencies of John Kennedy, Ronald Reagan, or Bill Clinton without examining another personal skill: the art of political rhetoric. These president's exhibited extraordinary ability to communicate with the media and the public, a skill now required by all modern presidents. In an age when media influence is pervasive, communications skills are one of the president's most important political resources. As Kernell (1997) argues, presidents who face an uncooperative Congress can go over the heads of the legislature directly to the public. This "going public" strategy requires first and foremost an ability to skillfully communicate with the public.

As these examples demonstrate, personal skills (such as communication and bargaining ability) are important attributes that can advance presidential power. They also can be a detriment, however. For example, Richard Nixon's lack of people skills and his deep suspicion of his political rivals (real or perceived) undermined his presidency. Likewise, Reedy (1970) argues that Lyndon Johnson's personality contributed to the failure of his presidency. Like Nixon, he was obsessed with his political opponents. Johnson also lacked a basic ability to communicate to mass audiences, though he was unusually skilled at dealing with small groups and individuals.

16-4b Presidential Personality

Lyndon Johnson and Richard Nixon show us that with the rise of media technologies, presidential personality—both the good and bad aspects of it—has taken on greater importance. Unlike the presidents of the eighteenth and nineteenth century, presidents now can reach out directly to the American voter. They do so through such technologies as radio, television, mass mailings, faxes, and the Internet, and through personal appearances facilitated by advances in transportation technology (e.g., Air Force One). Presidents with well-developed personal communication skills, such as Franklin Roosevelt, John Kennedy, Ronald Reagan, and Bill Clinton, had a distinct strategic political advantage over other modern presidents who lacked these same skills (Eisenhower, Johnson, Nixon, Ford, Carter, and George H. W. Bush). Other personal attributes also can be used to advance a president's political influence. For example, while they lacked communications skills, Gerald Ford and Jimmy Carter portrayed themselves as decent, common men. George Herbert Walker Bush presented himself as a man who understood and even relished the details of government. George W. Bush, lacking his father's knowledge base, portrays an image of congeniality and toughness. During the 2000 presidential campaign, one focus group found that of the two major candidates (Bush and Gore), more people preferred to go to a barbecue with George W. Bush, which was evidence of his perceived likability. On the other hand, after September 11, 2001, Bush showed considerable toughness in his rhetoric and his actions in dealing with the terrorist threat. Richard Nixon, on the other hand, lacking a congenial nature, tried to portray himself as a statesman and as tough on crime, while Lyndon Johnson cultivated an image as a master politician. Both tried to emphasize personal attributes that the public liked or that they thought portrayed the president in the most positive light possible. These same men functioned best when they avoided settings that exacerbated concerns about their personal weaknesses.

16-4c Developing Personal Resources

Often, constructing a favorable personal image or taking full advantage of other personal political resources requires the development of an institutional innovation (an internal political resource). The greatest such innovations in recent years have involved the development and expansion of public relations, press offices, and legislative liaison functions directly within the White House. Presidents with greater frequency also have turned to political consultants, image-makers, and speechwriters as a way of crafting a desirable governing image. For example, Ronald Reagan developed an extensive public relations network that was designed to popularize his image as an affable but tough-minded leader. White House aides spent considerable time and effort identifying precisely the right activities, functions, and settings to develop a favorable image. Speeches were focus-group tested. Locations for events were chosen to determine how they (and the president) would appear on television. Even issues were screened to determine if they would promote a desirable presidential image (see Waterman, Wright, and St. Clair 1999). Similar efforts also were made to limit occasions where the president was less personally skilled, such as news conferences. These combined efforts paid off handsomely. Reagan's personal image proved to be one of his greatest political resources. It translated into consistently high public approval ratings (especially after his first two years in office) and re-election in 1984 by a comfortable margin. When the details of the Iran-Contra affair exploded onto the front pages in November 1986, his personal image helped to sustain him through some difficult political times. While a new image began to emerge, a perception that Reagan was not up to the job, his image of congeniality continued to work in his favor.

16-5 Legal Resources

Legal mechanisms are a second political resource available to presidents. Legal resources derive from a variety of sources such as the enumerated powers of the Constitution, precedent, extra-constitutional actions such as executive orders and presidential proclamations, congressional delegations of authority to the executive branch, treaties, defense pacts, and foreign agreements. Legal resources provide presidential power with considerable legitimacy: through a citation of the enumerated powers of the Constitution, a particular court decision (e.g., the Supreme Court's decision in *Bush v. Gore* [2000]), a precedent, a treaty, or a legal statute, the application of presidential authority becomes much more defensible. For example, the entire legitimacy of George W. Bush's presidency initially rested on a Supreme Court decision, even though a full count of the votes did not occur in Florida until after the election, and some of those counts found that Bush's opponent, Democrat Al Gore, actually won the state (while other counts confirmed a Bush victory). Likewise, George Herbert Walker Bush was granted authority by Congress—in January 1991— to "use all necessary force" in the Persian Gulf. This provided legitimacy for the war against Iraq, despite the fact that the public was about evenly divided on the question of whether our nation should go to war. So long, then, as presidents can cite their legal authority to act in a particular situation, their subsequent actions gain greater legitimacy. Even if the action is not popular, it is still protected by a veil of legal legitimacy.

The action can still, however, be challenged on political grounds. The problem in citing legal authority is that often the president's constitutional authority is limited or otherwise poorly defined (see Corwin 1984). As a result of this constitutional ambiguity, Tulis (1988) argues that presidents are forced to seek out new political resources to advance their influence. Likewise, legal precedent also is permeated by uncertainty. Schlesinger (1973) and Berger (1974) demonstrate how presidents employ remarkable creativity in citing precedent, particularly when it relates to issues of war and national security. Some of the precedents clearly contradict the Founders' intent.

A further problem is raised by the judicial branch's extreme reluctance to adjudicate what it considers to be essentially political matters involving conflicts between the legislative and executive branches of government. As a result, so-called political matters are most often left to the political arena for adjudication where they are more likely to attract greater controversy.

16-5a Changing Perceptions of Legal Resources

Perceptions of the president's legal resources are in constant flux. As we saw in section 3-2, "Different Perceptions of the Presidency," due to a variety of factors (e.g., the growth of the U.S. military, America's prominent role on the world political stage, the presence of nuclear weapons, the Cold War), perceptions of the president's role as commander-in-chief radically changed over time. As a result, a legal resource that originally was quite limited in terms of actual power has become one of the president's most potent political resources.

Also contributing to the change in the president's legal resources, since 1921 and the enactment of the Budget and Accounting Act (see section 9-6c, "Presidential Influence Further Expands"), Congress has delegated considerable legal authority to the presidency (see Sundquist 1981). Even when Congress attempted to limit presidential power—for instance, with the 1973 War Powers Resolution—it often inadvertently granted the president additional power. In this case, prior to passage of the resolution, the president did not have the legal authority to commit troops without a declaration of war.

16-5b Foreign Affairs

In the area of foreign affairs, the modern presidents also gained authority from treaties, trade and defense pacts, and from both formal and informal international agreements. These documents often refer to the president as commander-in-chief, thus accentuating the prestige and power of that constitutional role. While these powers provide presidents with considerable authority and legitimacy in international affairs, they are less influential when it comes to the formulation and implementation of domestic policy.

16-5c Impeachment

The Constitution also provides constraints on presidential power. For instance, the impeachment power, a legal resource, was designed to promote presidential accountability. Two presidents have been impeached: Andrew Johnson and Bill Clinton. Neither impeachment by the House of Representatives (similar to an indictment in a court of law) led to an actual conviction by the Senate. Therefore, neither Johnson nor Clinton was removed from office, though history will label both as impeached presidents. Impeachment therefore is a constraint, but thus far, it has not proved to be a particularly effective one. While the threat of impeachment undoubtedly convinced Richard Nixon to resign from office, critics argue that the process is driven by political motivations and therefore is not really used to ensure accountability.

For example, while a good case can be made that Clinton lied to the American public, to members of his own administration, and to the Office of the Independent Counsel, a good case also can be made that the impeachment investigation was driven by political considerations. As we move into a period of increased hostility between the president and Congress, the possibility increases that impeachment can be used as a political weapon. While this would constrain presidential power, it means that impeachment would be used more as a "no confidence vote" in a parliamentary system than as a means of protecting the nation from presidential "high crimes and misdemeanors."

16-5d Other Political Resources Are Needed

In domestic affairs, in particular, the president's legal resources are often ambiguous. Commonly, they are subject to intense, even incendiary political debate. While presidents can cite their legal resources to legitimize their actions, as Neustadt (1980) notes, presidents do not have the power to command. These political resources, therefore, do not provide presidents with all of the authority they need to exert real influence in domestic or foreign affairs. As a result, presidents are forced to employ other types of political resources in an attempt to supplement their limited and sometimes confusing legal authority.

16-6 Electoral Resources

One resource that presidents can use derives from the electoral process. Like legal resources, elections generally provide presidents with legitimacy because, along with the vice president, the president is the only governmental official elected by a national constituency. Presidents, therefore, can and often do argue that they are carrying out the will of the people as expressed in the outcome of the last election. As Polsby (1978) argues, however, legitimacy can be interpreted in different ways. We can conceptualize it in discrete terms as having derived from a particular election, or we can interpret it as a continuous process. According to the latter method, declining public approval ratings or a lame duck status can quickly rob a president of influence and an important source of political legitimacy.

There are times, however, when elections raise questions about legitimacy. The elections of 1824 (John Quincy Adams), 1876 (Rutherford B. Hayes), 1888 (Benjamin Harrison), and 2000 (George W. Bush) raised questions about the legitimacy of the winners. Ironically, three of the four winners in these disputed elections were directly related to a former president (John Quincy Adams was the son of John Adams, Benjamin Harrison was the grandson of William Henry Harrison, and George W. Bush is the son of George Herbert Walker Bush).

In 1824, no one candidate received a majority of the electoral votes. Despite the fact that John Quincy Adams finished second in the popular vote, the House of Representatives chose him as the nation's sixth president. Adams's legitimacy was further undercut by the fact that Henry Clay of Kentucky (who had finished fourth in the presidential contest) became his Secretary of State. Despite the fact that Adams was not even on the ballot in Kentucky and thus received no votes in the state, the Kentucky House delegation awarded him the state's electoral votes. The candidate who received the most popular votes, Andrew Jackson, then accused Adams and Clay of a "corrupt bargain," thus directly challenging the legitimacy of Adams's selection. Just four years later Jackson defeated Adams in an electoral rematch.

Furthermore, when Rutherford B. Hayes was elected in 1876, an election in which several state delegations (including Florida) were in dispute, many felt that Samuel Tilden was the real winner. As a result, Hayes lacked legitimacy, facing taunts throughout his one term in office, such as being called "His Fraudulency" and "Rutherfraud B. Hayes."

Just twelve years later, Benjamin Harrison won a majority of the Electoral College vote, but lost the popular vote to the incumbent, Grover Cleveland. Four years later, Cleveland defeated Harrison in a rematch.

Most recently, George W. Bush's election raised questions about his legitimacy. Bush also lost the popular vote to Al Gore by about half a million votes, and the controversial decision in the Supreme Court case of *Bush v. Gore* left many Americans dissatisfied. Even before Bush's inauguration, protestors greeted the new president with taunts of "Hail to the Thief." Again, legitimacy was the issue.

16-6a Other Controversial Elections

Presidential legitimacy has been raised in other elections and contexts, as well. The 1800 election resulted in an Electoral College vote tie between Thomas Jefferson and Aaron Burr. As a result, the Constitution was amended so that the president and vice president would run together as a team. In 1841, upon the death of President William Henry Harrison, many people questioned the right of his vice president, John Tyler, to assume the presidential office. Even though Tyler was elected with Harrison in 1840, some politicians argued that a new election should

"Now boy, I gave it to you. Don't blow it!"

rayberry.com / toons ©

Controversy over the 2000 presidential election cast George W. Bush's legitimacy into doubt.

rayberry.com/toons ©

be held to choose a permanent successor for Harrison, with Tyler serving only as acting president until that time. Finally, the presidency of Gerald Ford provided an interesting test of legitimacy. Ford was appointed to the vice presidency by Richard Nixon after Vice President Spiro Agnew resigned. Ford then became president when Nixon resigned. Hence, for the first and only time (to date) in American history, the nation had as president a man who had not faced the electorate and thus had received no votes for president or vice president (outside of the Congress, which confirmed him).

In all of these cases, presidents had to deal with the question of legitimacy. In only one of these cases, that of Thomas Jefferson, was the president successful, either as a governing president or in winning a second term in office; though the case of George W. Bush is yet to be decided by the voters in 2004. All of these other presidents served one term, and several (Adams, Harrison, Ford) were defeated in their re-election bids. None, other than Jefferson, is ranked among the great presidents of history. As we look to the election of 2004, the legitimacy of the George W. Bush presidency will be on the minds of some voters. One poll (prior to September 11, 2001) showed that 90 percent of African Americans did not consider him to be the nation's legitimate president. Until the terrorist attacks of September 2001, polls also showed that large percentages of Democrats shared the same opinion. Given the changed political climate since then, it is unclear whether legitimacy will be a major obstacle for George W. Bush, but it is likely the issue will be raised, if only to encourage increased fund-raising by opposing political forces.

16-6b Electoral Benefits Can Be Transitory

While elections can provide legitimacy and even influence, the latter benefit is often transitory. For example, the so-called *honeymoon*—consisting of the weeks and/or months immediately following the president's inauguration—is the period in which presidents possess their greatest political influence. Yet, this period is generally quite brief. It generally lasts for four or five months, but our forty-second president, Bill Clinton, had no honeymoon. His decision to promote a new policy toward gays in the military, which he announced prior to inauguration day, ignited a firestorm of political opposition that essentially robbed him of a true honeymoon with the American electorate, the media, and the political opposition. The forty-third president, George W. Bush, had a different problem. His honeymoon initially was eclipsed by the scandals surrounding the outgoing Clinton administration. While Bush hoped to bask in the political limelight, he watched helplessly as Republican members of Congress and the press examined whether the Clintons illegally removed furniture from the White House, whether Clinton's aides damaged White House equipment, and whether the former president had accepted contributions for his presidential library in return for granting pardons to fugitives and other unsavory individuals. While the press treated Bush with deference, as is the common practice during the honeymoon period, the new president received relatively little press attention, even when he introduced key components of his political agenda.

Even so, the honeymoon is an electoral resource that offers scant benefits—that is, unless a president is ready to "hit the ground running," as Pfiffner (1988) recommends. Ronald Reagan and Lyndon Johnson were able to use their honeymoons effectively to promote congressional adoption of key aspects of their agenda. For presidents who are not ready to hit the ground running on inauguration day, however, the honeymoon provides only a limited window of opportunity for advancing their political influence. As Light (1983) argues, it comes at a time when presidents are still learning their job. As a result, most are not yet fully prepared to take advantage of this time-limited opportunity.

16-6c Presidential Mandates

Another type of electoral resource is the political *mandate*. Mandates (when they exist), like honeymoons, generally are short-lived. According to Conley (2001: 1), "No concept invokes the connection between the public and a president more than the electoral mandate, for it implies that the president shall work to make the will of the people into law." Mandates generally are claimed by presidents when there is a policy explanation for a president's election (e.g., the president touted a particular policy as a central theme in the campaign) and when the president believes he or she can mobilize members of Congress and the public behind that policy (ibid., 2). Conley contends that presidents have claimed mandates in about half of the elections since 1828 (ibid., 54).

For example, Ronald Reagan claimed a mandate based on his 1980 election victory over an incumbent, Jimmy Carter, and on the basis of the fact that the Republican Party gained seats in the House of Representatives and actually took back control of the Senate. As a result, in 1981, Southern House Democrats provided Reagan with his margin of victory for his tax cut, spending cuts, military defense spending increases, and other legislative initiatives. This political influence was only temporary, however. By 1982, with Reagan's approval ratings in a free fall, with the unemployment rate at more than 10 percent, and with the midterm elections on the horizon, Democrats abandoned Reagan's self-styled "Reagan Revolution."

While mandates do exist, they do not occur after each election. There was no mandate for George H. W. Bush in 1988 (despite the fact that he was the first vice president to win the White House since Martin Van Buren in 1836). True mandate elections (as opposed to when presidents claim they have a mandate), then, tend to be an exception in American politics rather than the rule.

The explanation for why most elections provide no mandate is that real mandates most often occur when the public is dissatisfied with the status quo and therefore anticipate significant political change following the election of a new president (e.g., Franklin Roosevelt in 1932 and Ronald Reagan in 1980; though an exception is Lyndon Johnson in 1964). Dwight Eisenhower (1952) had a mandate to slow federal governmental activity, following sixteen years of activist Democratic government. Re-election campaigns and elections based on promises to continue the status quo (e.g., George H. W. Bush's 1988 campaign) or largely issue-less campaigns (more common generally in recent decades) therefore seldom produce a tangible mandate.

16-6d Presidential Coattails and Midterm Elections

When they exist, mandates and honeymoons provide presidents with a temporary source of political influence. On the other hand, the presidential coattail effect and electoral coalitions once provided presidents with palpable long-term electoral resources. The coattail effect refers to the ability of a popular presidential candidate to transfer electoral support to congressional candidates of the president's political party. Through this process, the president helps to elect some congressional partisans who otherwise would have been defeated. During the period following the Civil War, and even during the first three decades of the twentieth century, the coattail effect provided presidents with considerable influence over the course of a presidential term. A president could count on loyalty from congressional members whose political careers depended on the president's electoral success.

Since the 1930s, however, there is empirical evidence that the presidential coattail effect has declined (see Ferejohn and Calvert 1983; 1984; Waterman, Oppenheimer, and Stimson 1991; though for a different perspective, see Campbell

1986). As a result, with a few exceptions, such as Reagan's election in 1980, presidents no longer derive this benefit from their electoral victories; that is, they can no longer count on the same level of congressional loyalty that existed in the period in which members owed their very election to the president. Instead, today, presidents most often secure a lower percentage of the vote in House districts than do the members of Congress who ultimately win those same districts. In this sense, then, the coattail effect may have been reversed. Members of Congress now feel that they are helping the president to win the election, not the other way around. As a result of the decline of the coattail effect, members of Congress, even those from the president's own party, are more likely to defy the president on votes on key issues (see Edwards 1989).

Alternatively, the midterm election effect, in which the party of the president generally loses seats in congressional elections, is still important. Three times since the 1930s, the party of the president actually has picked up seats: during the presidency of Franklin Roosevelt in 1934, during Bill Clinton's second term in 1998, and in 2002 during the presidency of George W. Bush. Erikson (1989) refers to the result in congressional midterm elections as the "presidential penalty effect." Voters displeased with the president's performance go to the polls to punish the president. Since the president is not on the ticket, they punish members of the president's party in Congress. Hence, presidents do not help many members of Congress to secure election through the coattail effect, but (like Clinton in the disastrous—for Democrats—1994 congressional midterm elections) they do place their partisans in a position of considerable electoral peril at midterm. It is no doubt, then, why so many members of the president's own party try to distance themselves from the president at election time and may therefore be less likely to support critical components of the president's agenda. This situation may be changing, however. Since the last two midterm elections resulted in House seat gains for the party of the president, it may be that the presidential penalty effect is no longer relevant. Both Clinton and Bush had approval ratings in the 60 percent range, and individual circumstances, impeachment, and terrorism also may account for these election results.

16-6e Electoral Coalitions

Another electoral resource that once provided long-term political benefits is the electoral coalition. In putting together an electoral coalition, presidents traditionally constructed the framework for an effective governing coalition (e.g., Franklin Roosevelt's New Deal Coalition, which survived well into the 1960s). As Seligman and Covington (1989) convincingly argue, this is no longer the case. Now presidents must put together separate electoral and governing coalitions, the latter usually on the basis of each issue. This can be a daunting task.

16-6f A Temporary Source of Legitimacy and Influence

While elections generally provide presidents with legitimacy and influence, this effect is largely transitory. At present, political influence is generally limited to a few months at the beginning of a president's first term (there generally is little benefit at the beginning of a second or lame duck term, as the media immediately begin to speculate on who will replace the president in four years). As a president's term in office continues, the focus quickly changes from a concentration on the last campaign to a concern with the next one. Thus, the president's electoral resources provide mainly short-term benefits. With regard to long-term political influence, the benefits once provided by the presidential coattail effect and the construction of an effective electoral/governing coalition have declined considerably.

16-7 External Resources

After a president is elected, a number of institutions and other political entities share power with the president. They include the U.S. Congress, the courts, political parties, the bureaucracy, the public, interest groups, and the media. I refer to these institutions or groups as external resources because they are external to the White House; that is, they are not under the direct hierarchy of the White House itself. This is true of even the federal bureaucracy. Although located within the executive branch, it retains considerable legal autonomy from the White House (see Waterman 1989).

Of all the external resources available to the presidency, Congress is without question the most important. Contrary to some modern misconceptions of the relationship between the presidency and Congress, the Founding Fathers purposely devised a system in which the president and Congress share power (see Neustadt 1980; Fisher 1981; Jones 1994, 1995). This fact greatly complicates the reality of presidential-legislative relations in an era in which different political parties most often control the executive and legislative branches (i.e., divided government). Presidents can exert influence with Congress, but as Neustadt (1980) suggests, it is influence that has to be developed over time through a process of bargaining, compromise, and coalition building. Still, as other scholars (e.g., Edwards 1989; Seligman and Covington 1989; Kernell 1997) argue, building coalitions with members of Congress is an exceedingly difficult process.

In fact, many political scientists have noted that presidential influence over Congress appears to have diminished considerably in recent years (e.g., Mezey 1989). Seligman and Covington (1989), in particular, argue that presidents have fewer political resources today to influence Congress. For example, they cite declining coattails, the greater propensity toward divided government, the election of a new class of independent-minded legislators, declining party discipline, the collapse of the seniority system, and an escalation in the number and importance of subcommittees as reasons why presidents now find it more difficult to work with Congress.

Despite these political obstacles, presidents still need the support of Congress to achieve their domestic policy objectives and their foreign policy goals. Presidents cannot simply ignore Congress, nor can they ignore the developments that have made Congress a less willing and able political partner. As a result, important issues have become more difficult issues for presidents to address.

16-7a Other External Actors

Congress is not the only external resource that has become less amenable to direct presidential influence. Scholars long have argued that the influence of political parties is declining (see Broder 1971; Crotty and Jacobson 1980; Sorauf 1980; Sundquist 1983). Lowi (1985) and Seligman and Covington (1989) further argue that without the discipline and the organizational abilities of the political parties, there is no available mechanism for promoting a president's program in Congress. Rather, the decline of the parties has left a political void that robs the presidency of the ability to influence Congress and other external political actors.

This trend of the declining utility of external resources does not end with Congress and the political parties. Interest groups have become less predictable, particularly with their greater propensity to form single-issue groups. The media have become more combative and prone to report the sordid details of political scandals (real or imagined) with or without reliance on multiple sources and other objective journalistic standards.

Thus, the utility of external resources has decreased over time. As I argued in section 16-6, so have many of the president's electoral resources. Furthermore, neither a president's legal nor personal resources are sufficient to ensure political success. Thus, the paradox for the modern presidency is that as its political resource base has diminished, public expectations of presidential performance have proliferated. Given this trend, how can presidents satisfy increasing public demands for action? Many presidential scholars have answered this question with forecasts of a doomed presidency—that is, a series of failed presidencies and continual deadlock between the presidency and Congress (see especially Lowi 1985).

16-7b Traditional Versus New Political Resources

I argue that because the utility of the president's traditional political resource base has declined in recent decades, presidents have had an incentive to develop new political resources. Modern presidents since the days of Franklin Roosevelt have, whenever possible, internalized their political resources directly within the White House or within the Executive Office of the President (EOP). They also have increased their access to information that can provide them with distinct political advantages in their dealings with other external political actors. Through these two developments presidents have attempted, but not always succeeded, to increase their influence and to close the expectations gap. While this internalization of presidential resources may be criticized on normative grounds (it shifts too much power to individuals who are unaccountable to constitutional actors such as Congress), this trend is a logical presidential strategy given two concomitant developments: expanding expectations and declining traditional political resources.

16-8 Internal and Informational Resources

Since the days of Franklin Roosevelt, presidents have developed and employed two types of political resources—internal and informational—to increase their political influence. Internal resources involve the development of institutional frameworks within the White House or the EOP. They may be either formal organizations or an informal collection of individuals motivated by a common purpose (e.g., to develop an agenda for the president or to plan political strategy). Because the needs of each president are different, the internal political resources employed by each will also be different. It is expected that presidents will establish new organizational mechanisms or use existing ones in fundamentally different ways. They may also dispense with (or simply ignore) other existing White House units. This variability in the use of the president's internal resources is both a function of the president's policy needs and the president's own distinct personality.

Informational resources involve gathering, maintaining, manipulating, and dispensing a variety of different types of intelligence. They can involve such diverse functions as monitoring bureaucratic policy proposals through the use of central clearance procedures, collecting information on potential nominees for federal office through a systematized personnel unit, collecting data on the budget, or counting votes on Capitol Hill. Presidents often use their internal resources as a mechanism for collecting, managing, and even disseminating information.

The primary political advantage of internal and informational political resources is that they provide presidents with a greater degree of political responsiveness (see Moe 1985b). Since the president's overall political environment has become more uncertain in recent decades, presidents have developed new political resources that are specifically attentive and responsive to their own needs (Walcott and Hult 1987). Thus, whereas presidents may not be able to count on a responsive Congress, they can count on responsiveness from their own White House bureaucracy—or what Hart (1993) calls "The Presidential Branch."

16-8a Executive Orders

Since the Reagan presidency, there has been a greater presidential propensity to make policy by nonlegislative means, such as altering or removing bureaucratic rules and regulations via executive orders.[2] Mayer (2001: 4) argues that presidents today are making greater use of executive orders—"presidential directives that require or authorize some action within the executive branch"—because presidents can issue them unilaterally. On the other hand, an executive order simply can be countermanded by the next president.

Still, despite this limitation, as the president's relationship with Congress has become more conflict ridden over time, and the likelihood of enacting new legislation declines, presidents have found that they can make significant policy changes (in areas such as abortion, for example) via executive order. Although executive orders are a legal resource, the increased use of such orders is consistent with the internalization strategy—that is, running policy unilaterally from the White House. If the prevalence of divided government continues, we should expect presidents to issue even more policy-substantive executive orders.

16-8b The Administrative Presidency

Another form of presidential unilateralism was Nixon's formulation of the administrative presidency strategy (see Nathan 1983; Waterman 1989). This strategy used the president's appointment, removal, budgetary, and reorganization authority to alter bureaucratic behavior. As a result, presidents could make policy change through the bureaucracy, again without the need for new legislation. While Nixon developed the strategy, it was Reagan who took full advantage of it. Again, as with the case of executive orders, presidents are more likely to act unilaterally to develop policy.

16-8c Examples of Internal and Informational Resources

One example of both an internal and informational political resource is the Office of Management and Budget (OMB). It provides an organizational apparatus that is responsive to the president's policy objectives. It also provides a mechanism for collecting and managing information on the state of the economy (for long-term planning and action on the immediate budget), on budgetary allocations, and on the cost and possible impact of proposed bureaucratic regulations through its central clearance function. Therefore, OMB is an important political resource that counterbalances what presidents perceive as the recalcitrant tendencies of both the bureaucracy and Congress.

Another example is the Legislative Liaison Office (which has existed under various names during different presidential administrations). As Congress has become less amenable to direct presidential influence, presidents have been forced to make greater use of their legislative liaison capabilities. This function provides presidents with information on each member of Congress, which can be useful (as the utility of electoral coalitions and coattails decline) as presidents attempt to bargain with 535 individuals on a variety of different legislative proposals. It also provides an institutional framework that facilitates contacts between the legislative and executive branches of government.

Along with the legislative liaison function, presidents also established White House mechanisms to facilitate political outreach with the media, interest groups, state and local governments, and various segments of the public. They have

Figure 16-3
New Resources
Used by Presidents

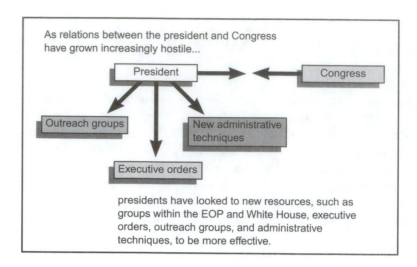

As relations between the president and Congress have grown increasingly hostile...

President → ← Congress

President → Outreach groups

President → Executive orders

President → New administrative techniques

presidents have looked to new resources, such as groups within the EOP and White House, executive orders, outreach groups, and administrative techniques, to be more effective.

established mechanisms to deal with such specific policy areas as civil rights, science and technology, defense and national security, telecommunications, urban affairs, emergency preparedness, consumer affairs, the environment, drug abuse, energy policy, AIDS, and the economy (see Figure 16-3). These organizational mechanisms provide presidents with the ability to simultaneously deal with a wide variety of different constituencies and issues. Thus, as public expectations proliferate, regarding a variety of different issues, and as the president's policy responsibilities expand, the number of formal and informal organizational mechanisms within the White House and the EOP likewise increase. This internalization of the president's resources is both a logical and, from the president's point of view, a necessary development in an era of growing political uncertainty.

16-8d The Risks of Internalization

Still, while the expansion of the presidency's internal and informational political resources is designed to advance presidential power and influence, not all of these innovations have had that effect. In fact, some scholars argue that the greater centralization and institutionalization of the presidency have diminished presidential influence (see Hess 1988). Internal political resources can have this effect when they are abused. *No organizational mechanism or information-gathering technique automatically provides presidents with increased influence; if that were the case, all presidents who employed the same internal and informational political resources would be equally successful.* What, then, accounts for the fact that some internal and informational political resources have failed to promote presidential influence?

While the development of these resources can provide presidents with additional influence, they also can threaten a president's legitimacy if they are perceived as lacking accountability. Internal and informational political resources have received their greatest criticism when presidents attempt to centralize the political process to such an extent that they exclude other legitimate political actors from the policy process, as occurred during both Watergate and Iran-Contra. For example, when cabinet secretaries are unable to get past the unelected and nonappointed guardians of the Oval Office (as often was the case during the Nixon presidency), legitimacy is challenged. When the media refer to the chief of staff, who is accountable only to the president, as the second most powerful person in the American government, this, too, raises questions of legitimacy. When nonappointed officials place the presidency in harm's way by reckless and illegal actions, legitimacy is threatened. Consequently, as various scholars argue,[3] centralization can indeed rob presidents of legitimacy and ultimately of political influence.

16-8e Why Then Do Presidents Use These Resources?

Even with the dangers described in section 16-8d, given the uncertainty of the existing political environment (that is, expanding expectations and a decline in the utility of electoral and external political resources), it is likely that presidents will continue to internalize their resources (see Warshaw 1996). This is a logical (if somewhat dangerous) development in an era of rising public expectations and decreasing traditional political resources. How, then, can presidents internalize their resources without losing legitimacy? This is an extraordinarily difficult but important question. I argue that by combining internal and informational resources with existing traditional political resources (e.g., legal, electoral, and external), presidents can retain legitimacy while increasing their influence. In this way, they can achieve greater responsiveness without sacrificing legitimacy. How can presidents accomplish this task?

Largely due to the way I have presented the typology of political resources, it is tempting to conceptualize them as mutually exclusive categories. That is not the case. In fact, presidents often gain their greatest political advantage when they use one type of resource in combination with another. See section 15-4, "Internalizing the Appointment Process," where I examined how presidents combined a legal resource, their appointment power, with an internal resource, personnel offices in the White House. This combination of political resources enabled presidents to recruit and evaluate prospective candidates for office.

Additionally, as I showed in section 13-2, "Centralization during the Transitional Presidential Era," various administrations have employed institutional innovations within the White House (internal and informational resources) to reach out to members of Congress, interest groups, and the public (external resources). Presidents have used advanced methods of personnel management (internal and informational resources) to identify individuals who represent their political views at the bureaucratic level (an external resource). Presidents also have created sophisticated communications operations (internal resources) to take advantage of the president's communications skills or lack thereof (a personal resource).

On the other hand, not all combinations of resources have proven beneficial for presidents. The creation of their own campaign committees (an internal resource) further divorced the presidency from the political parties. Likewise, the fact that presidents run on their own makes it harder for them to use elections to build coalitions with members of Congress that can later help them at the governing stage.

Hence, one task for future research is to examine how the six political resources I have identified here interact in ways that are beneficial to the presidency; that is, how do they increase presidential influence? Which add to the legitimacy of the presidency, and which detract from it? Understanding how these resources interact may provide us with an even better means of understanding the changing nature of presidential power.

Chapter Summary

In addition to the six political resources of the presidency, this book also introduced the concept of political ecosystems—see Chapter 11, "The Presidency and the Political Ecosystem." The idea is that we need to focus on the institutions of government and how they change over time. As the analysis in this chapter shows, the president's political resources are in a constant state of transition. This transition is related to changes in the political ecosystem that I have described throughout this book. For example, as the presidency gains influence in the political system, the political parties lose influence, public opinion becomes more important, the media gain prominence by becoming the new intermediary between the public and the president, the nascent bureaucracy expands rapidly, becoming a dominant aspect of American life, and Congress goes from being the initiator of legislation to the disposer of it. All of these factors change the president's relationship with his or her external political resources.

In sum, I argue that we simply cannot understand American history and the president's role in it unless we examine the changing nature of its institutions over time. This work has examined the presidency, but other institutions, particularly the courts, likewise have been entirely transformed over time. Understanding how and why this change occurs can be an invaluable asset to our understanding of how our governmental system operates today.

I have identified a series of reasons why the presidency has changed. I also demonstrated how the utility of six different political resources has changed over time. I also endeavored to show how these resources are interrelated—how changes in one resource can lead to changes in others.

Despite the changing contextual factors, demands, and expectations documented in this book, the presidency that we have today was far from an inevitable outcome. Congress did not have to delegate greater authority to the presidency, such as the Budget and Accounting Act of 1921. It could have established a position in Congress, such as the Speaker of the House, the Senate Majority Leader, or even the President Pro Tempore as the equivalent of a prime minister. The president, then, could have developed as more of a symbolic office or as primarily a foreign policy leader. In other words, the presidency as it exists today was not in any sense predestined or even a direct outgrowth of the Founders' intent.

This means that the presidency and other governmental institutions will continue to evolve and change over time. As a result, the study of changing political ecosystems is always a work in progress. Like an evolving organism, the political ecosystem will continue to evolve and so will the president's place in it and its relationship with its six political resources. In short, the presidency is much changed, and we should expect it to continue to change in the future.

Review Questions

1. Who of the following is *not* an impact president from the nineteenth century?
   a. Andrew Jackson
   b. Abraham Lincoln
   c. William McKinley
   d. Theodore Roosevelt

2. Which of the following impact presidents and scholars came to office with a clearly articulated view of presidential power?
   a. Woodrow Wilson
   b. Jimmy Carter
   c. Franklin Roosevelt
   d. Bill Clinton

3. Which of the following impact presidents had a negative impact on the presidency?
   a. George Washington
   b. Thomas Jefferson
   c. Richard Nixon
   d. Ronald Reagan

4. Many people felt that which of the following presidents actually won the election of 1876?
   a. Albert Gore
   b. Rutherford B. Hayes
   c. Samuel Tilden
   d. Grover Cleveland

Discussion Questions

1. Of the twelve impact presidents, who do you think had the greatest impact on the development of the presidency?
2. Of the twelve impact presidents, who do you think had the least impact on the development of the presidency?
3. Is there another president who you think should be on this list of impact presidents? If so, who and why?
4. Why has the utility of the president's traditional resources declined over time? Do you agree that they have?

Notes

1. Though Congress forced the National Security Council on a recalcitrant Truman, this innovation was adopted during his presidency. Furthermore, while he at first was reluctant to use it, he later made considerable use of it during the Korean War, thus setting a precedent for an active NSC.
2. As with so many other innovations related to the presidency, Theodore Roosevelt was the first president to make "extensive use" of executive orders (Mayer 2001: 10).
3. See, for example, Reedy (1970), Hess (1988), Bonafede (1977), and Campbell (1986).

The Gallery of Presidents

The information presented for each president contains a link to that president's page at the POTUS website and the White House site, where you can find biographical information and suggested readings. Short biographies of the twelve impact presidents (see section 16-2) also are presented.

1. **George Washington**
   b. 1732 d. 1799
   Served as president 1789–1797
   Federalist party; home state: Virginia
   http://www.potus.com/gwashington.html
   http://www.whitehouse.gov/history/presidents/gw1.html

Washington played an obvious and important role in setting precedents for all of his successors. The first president, Washington established the use of the Cabinet and set standards for presidential conduct in terms of dealings with Congress and in domestic and foreign affairs.

2. **John Adams**
   b. 1735 d. 1826
   Served as president 1797–1801
   Federalist party; home state: Massachusetts
   http://www.potus.com/jadams.html
   http://www.whitehouse.gov/history/presidents/ja2.html

3. **Thomas Jefferson**
   b. 1743 d. 1826
   Served as president 1801–1809
   Democratic–Republican party; home state: Virginia
   http://www.potus.com/tjefferson.html
   http://www.whitehouse.gov/history/presidents/tj3.html

Jefferson demonstrated that the presidency could play an active role, working with Congress, to set the policy agenda. He therefore provided the basis for the growth of presidential power by providing a powerful rationale for presidential leadership and a means of accomplishing it. Part of Jefferson's rationale was an expanded concept of democracy, one that more prominently included the American public.

4. **James Madison**
   b. 1751 d. 1836
   Served as president 1809–1817
   Democratic–Republican party; home state: Virginia
   http://www.potus.com/jmadison.html
   http://www.whitehouse.gov/history/presidents/jm4.html

George Washington

Thomas Jefferson

5. **James Monroe**
   b. 1758 d. 1831
   Served as president 1817–1825
   Democratic–Republican party; home state: Virginia
   http://www.potus.com/jmonroe.html
   http://www.whitehouse.gov/history/presidents/jm5.html

6. **John Quincy Adams**
   b. 1767 d. 1848
   Served as president 1825–1829
   Democratic–Republican party; home state: Massachusetts
   http://www.potus.com/jqadams.html
   http://www.whitehouse.gov/history/presidents/ja6.html

7. **Andrew Jackson**
   b. 1767 d. 1845
   Served as president 1829–1837
   Democrat party; home state: South Carolina
   http://www.potus.com/ajackson.html
   http://www.whitehouse.gov/history/presidents/aj7.html

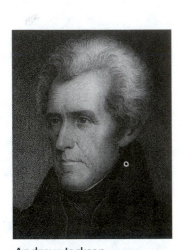

Andrew Jackson

Andrew Jackson expanded the connection between the president and the public, even providing a clear rationale for combining presidential power with popular support. In this process, Jackson transformed the electoral order—promoting an era in which party government prevailed. Jackson also provided a model for a more active presidency, making greater use of the presidential veto power, removing officials he considered to be recalcitrant from office, establishing the spoils system, taking a more active role as a policy initiator, and establishing the power of the presidency as separate and distinct from that of Congress.

8. **Martin Van Buren**
   b. 1782 d. 1862
   Served as president 1837–1841
   Democrat party; home state: New York
   http://www.potus.com/mvanburen.html
   http://www.whitehouse.gov/history/presidents/mb8.html

9. **William Henry Harrison**
   b. 1773 d. 1841
   Served as president 1841
   Whig party; home state: Virginia
   Died in office
   http://www.potus.com/whharrison.html
   http://www.whitehouse.gov/history/presidents/wh9.html

10. **John Tyler**
    b. 1790 d. 1862
    Served as president 1841–1845
    Whig party; home state: Virginia
    http://www.potus.com/jtyler.html
    http://www.whitehouse.gov/history/presidents/jt10.html

11. **James Polk**
    b. 1795 d. 1849
    Served as president 1845–1849
    Democrat party; home state: North Carolina
    http://www.potus.com/jkpolk.html
    http://www.whitehouse.gov/history/presidents/jp11.html

12. **Zachary Taylor**
    b. 1784 d. 1850
    Served as president 1849–1850
    Whig party; home state: Virginia
    Died in office
    http://www.potus.com/ztaylor.html
    http://www.whitehouse.gov/history/presidents/zt12.html

13. **Millard Fillmore**
    b. 1800 d. 1874
    Served as president 1850–1853
    Whig party; home state: New York
    http://www.potus.com/mfillmore.html
    http://www.whitehouse.gov/history/presidents/mf13.html

14. **Franklin Pierce**
    b. 1804 d. 1869
    Served as president 1853–1857
    Democrat party; home state: New Hampshire
    http://www.potus.com/fpierce.html
    http://www.whitehouse.gov/history/presidents/fp14.html

15. **James Buchanan**
    b. 1791 d. 1868
    Served as president 1857–1861
    Democrat party; home state: Pennsylvania
    http://www.potus.com/jbuchanan.html
    http://www.whitehouse.gov/history/presidents/jb15.html

16. **Abraham Lincoln**
    b. 1809 d. 1865
    Served as president 1861–1865
    Republican/Union party; home state: Kentucky
    Assassinated in office
    http://www.potus.com/alincoln.html
    http://www.whitehouse.gov/history/presidents/al16.html

Abraham Lincoln

Abraham Lincoln also set a number of precedents for presidential power. Governing in the unique times of the Civil War, Lincoln expanded presidential power in both domestic and foreign affairs and played an active role as commander-in-chief, even more active than James Polk, whom he had once criticized for initiating war with Mexico.

17. **Andrew Johnson**
    b. 1808 d. 1875
    Served as president 1865–1869
    Union party; home state: North Carolina
    http://www.potus.com/ajohnson.html
    http://www.whitehouse.gov/history/presidents/aj17.html

18. **Ulysses S. Grant**
    b. 1822 d. 1885
    Served as president 1869–1877
    Republican party; home state: Ohio
    http://www.potus.com/usgrant.html
    http://www.whitehouse.gov/history/presidents/ug18.html

19. **Rutherford B. Hayes**
    b. 1822 d. 1893
    Served as president 1877–1881
    Republican party; home state: Ohio
    http://www.potus.com/rbhayes.html
    http://www.whitehouse.gov/history/presidents/rh19.html

20. **James A. Garfield**
    b. 1831 d. 1881
    Served as president 1881
    Republican party; home state: Ohio
    Assassinated in office
    http://www.potus.com/jagarfield.html
    http://www.whitehouse.gov/history/presidents/jg20.html

21. **Chester A. Arthur**
    b. 1830 d. 1886
    Served as president 1881–1885
    Republican party; home state: Vermont
    http://www.potus.com/caarthur.html
    http://www.whitehouse.gov/history/presidents/ca21.html

22. **Grover Cleveland**
    b. 1837 d. 1908
    Served as president 1885–1889, 1893–1897
    Democrat party; home state: New Jersey
    http://www.potus.com/gcleveland.html
    http://www.whitehouse.gov/history/presidents/gc2224.html

23. **Benjamin Harrison**
    b. 1833 d. 1901
    Served as president 1889–1893
    Republican party; home state: Ohio
    http://www.potus.com/bharrison.html
    http://www.whitehouse.gov/history/presidents/bh23.html

24. **Grover Cleveland**
    b. 1837 d. 1908
    Served as president 1885–1889, 1893–1897
    Democrat party; home state: New Jersey
    http://www.potus.com/gcleveland.html
    http://www.whitehouse.gov/history/presidents/gc2224.html

25. **William McKinley**
    b. 1843 d. 1901
    Served as president 1897–1901
    Republican party; home state: Ohio
    Assassinated in office
    http://www.potus.com/wmckinley.html
    http://www.whitehouse.gov/history/presidents/wm25.html

William McKinley

William McKinley was the first president to sense the changing nature of the political ecosystem. He began the process of reaching out to the public and the media. He also witnessed the beginnings of a permanent transformation in the president's role as commander-in-chief, even if ironically Congress pressured him to declare war on Spain. His election in 1896 coincided with a fundamental realignment in the political electorate, which led to the establishment of the third electoral order: where the presidency began to emerge from the party's shadows. While McKinley was not an active participant in fomenting some of the changes that occurred during his time, his presidency nonetheless reflects a fundamental division point between the politics of the past and those of the future.

26. Theodore Roosevelt
b. 1858 d. 1919
Served as president 1901–1909
Republican party; home state: New York
http://www.potus.com/troosevelt.html
http://www.whitehouse.gov/history/presidents/tr26.html

Theodore Roosevelt began the transformation of the rhetorical presidency. He reached out to the public and the media, thus helping the presidency to develop a new constituency and a new intermediary to it. He expanded the president's role as chief legislator, vastly expanded the president's role in foreign affairs, and provided a new interpretation of the Constitution that opened the door for a more active presidency.

27. William Howard Taft
b. 1857 d. 1930
Served as president 1909–1913
Republican party; home state: Ohio
http://www.potus.com/whtaft.html
http://www.whitehouse.gov/history/presidents/wt27.html

28. Woodrow Wilson
b. 1856 d. 1924
Served as president 1913–1921
Democrat party; home state: Virginia
http://www.potus.com/wwilson.html
http://www.whitehouse.gov/history/presidents/ww28.html

Woodrow Wilson came to office with a clearly articulated view of presidential power and then further refashioned the presidency. He elevated the president's rhetorical role significantly by delivering the State of the Union address in person before Congress. He also became an active chief legislator and later commander-in-chief. While his presidency ultimately demonstrated the limitations of these approaches, Wilson provided the foundation for many of Franklin Roosevelt's later political innovations.

29. Warren G. Harding
b. 1865 d. 1923
Served as president 1921–1923
Republican party; home state: Ohio
Died in office
http://www.potus.com/wgharding.html
http://www.whitehouse.gov/history/presidents/wh29.html

30. Calvin Coolidge
b. 1872 d. 1933
Served as president 1923–1929
Republican party; home state: Vermont
http://www.potus.com/ccoolidge.html
http://www.whitehouse.gov/history/presidents/cc30.html

31. Herbert Hoover
b. 1874 d. 1964
Served as president 1929–1933
Republican party; home state: Iowa
http://www.potus.com/hchoover.html
http://www.whitehouse.gov/history/presidents/hh31.html

Theodore Roosevelt

Woodrow Wilson

Franklin D. Roosevelt

Harry S. Truman

Dwight D. Eisenhower

32. Franklin D. Roosevelt

b. 1882 d. 1945
Served as president 1933–1945
Democrat party; home state: New York
Died in office
http://www.potus.com/fdroosevelt.html
http://www.whitehouse.gov/history/presidents/fr32.html

Franklin Roosevelt often is credited with creating the modern presidency. From his presidency onward, there was no doubt that the president was expected to provide primary leadership in establishing the policy agenda. Roosevelt expanded both public expectations and the scope of presidential activities. He changed the way people interacted with the president and the government. His presidency marks a true symbiosis between the public and the presidency. He also further expanded presidential outreach to the media and greatly expanded the size and functions of the White House itself (including the development of the Executive Office of the President). As commander-in-chief in World War II, he also provided a model for a new foreign policy presidency.

33. Harry S. Truman

b. 1884 d. 1972
Served as president 1945–1953
Democrat party; home state: Missouri
http://www.potus.com/hstruman.html
http://www.whitehouse.gov/history/presidents/ht33.html

Harry Truman institutionalized Roosevelt's model. Governing at the beginning of the Cold War, he played a major role in promoting interventionist policies and driving isolationism to the backbench of American politics. He also oversaw important developments in the institutionalization of the foreign policy presidency, including the creation of the Defense Department, the National Security Council, and the Central Intelligence Agency. The U.S.'s foreign policy role also further expanded, as it became an active member of the United Nations, the North Atlantic Treaty Organization, and other international organizations. Treaty obligations not only solidified an internationalist foreign policy, they also provided clear legal rationales for presidential action. Hence, when Truman went to war in Korea, he did not ask for a congressional declaration, but rather justified it under treaty obligations and the UN Charter. A fundamentally new age of presidential war-making without congressional acquiescence had begun.

34. Dwight D. Eisenhower

b. 1890 d. 1969
Served as president 1953–1961
Republican party; home state: Texas
http://www.potus.com/ddeisenhower.html
http://www.whitehouse.gov/history/presidents/de34.html

Dwight Eisenhower played a critical role in altering the presidency. His electoral innovations, including creating his own campaign organization, using the primaries to unseat the party favorite, and utilizing television advertisements in his fall campaign, transformed electoral politics, making way for the fourth and present electoral order. As president, Eisenhower also played a major role in expanding the institutional presidency. His administration created a number of institutional units that, in somewhat different forms, were used by his successors. He also established the positions of Chief of Staff and the President's Advisor for National Security Affairs, as well as the Cabinet Secretariat (which reappeared in several administrations). Today, the first two of these are among the most powerful positions in the U.S. government.

35. John F. Kennedy

b. 1917 d. 1963
Served as president 1961–1963
Democrat party; home state: Massachusetts
Assassinated in office
http://www.potus.com/jfkennedy.html
http://www.whitehouse.gov/history/presidents/jk35.html

36. Lyndon B. Johnson

b. 1908 d. 1973
Served as president 1963–1969
Democrat party; home state: Texas
http://www.potus.com/lbjohnson.html
http://www.whitehouse.gov/history/presidents/lj36.html

Lyndon Johnson and Richard Nixon then changed the political climate in a fundamentally important way that has affected all presidents since their time. Vietnam and Watergate provided fundamental shocks to the political system, resulting in vastly increased levels of public distrust with government. The hostility that pervades Washington politics had its roots in these presidencies and, according to many scholars cited throughout this book, undermined the ability of Presidents Ford, Carter, Reagan, G. H. W. Bush, and Clinton to govern.

Lyndon B. Johnson

37. Richard M. Nixon

b. 1913 d. 1994
Served as president 1969–1974
Republican party; home state: California
Resigned the presidency
http://www.potus.com/rmnixon.html
http://www.whitehouse.gov/history/presidents/rn37.html

From Nixon's presidency onward, divided government became the norm in American politics. Open conflict developed between the presidency and the media. Congressional investigations of the presidency became commonplace: One president was impeached, one resigned rather than face impeachment, and another survived a major foreign policy scandal. With the rise of divisive single-issue interest groups, the further decline of the political parties, and an environment of unrealistic and excessive public expectations, scholars wondered if the presidency itself was doomed to failure (Lowi 1985). Johnson and Nixon, for all of their policy successes, have to take much of the blame for the often cannibalistic political environment they left behind in their wake.

Richard M. Nixon

38. Gerald Ford

b. 1913
Served as president 1974–1977
Republican party; home state: Nebraska
http://www.potus.com/grford.html
http://www.whitehouse.gov/history/presidents/gf38.html

39. Jimmy Carter

b. 1924
Served as president 1977–1981
Democrat party; home state: Georgia
http://www.potus.com/jecarter.html
http://www.whitehouse.gov/history/presidents/jc39.html

40. Ronald Reagan

b. 1911
Served as president 1981–1989
Republican party; home state: California
http://www.potus.com/rwreagan.html
http://www.whitehouse.gov/history/presidents/rr40.html

41. George H. W. Bush

b. 1924
Served as president 1989–1993
Republican party; home state: Texas
http://www.potus.com/ghwbush.html
http://www.whitehouse.gov/history/presidents/gb41.html

42. **William J. Clinton**
    b. 1946
    Served as president 1994–2000
    Democrat party; home state: Arkansas
    http://www.potus.com/wjclinton.html
    http://www.whitehouse.gov/history/presidents/bc42.html

43. **George W. Bush**
    b. 1946
    Served as president 2001–
    Republican party; home state: Texas
    http://www.potus.com/gwbush.html
    http://www.whitehouse.gov/president/gwbbio.html

Glossary

A

Activist presidency: A presidency motivated by the goal of accomplishing domestic and/or foreign policies while increasing the power of the office. The alternatives are the idea that presidents should be managers or magistrates rather than activist initiators of policy or that they should be purely passive, leaving responsibility for policy making to the legislative branch.

Adjourn: When Congress ends a session. Presidents have this constitutional authority when there is a disagreement between the House of Representatives and the Senate regarding the time of adjournment. As with the power to convene Congress, this provision is little used.

B

Borked: A term that refers to a political appointee's fate being deleteriously determined by political considerations.

Brownlow Committee: Franklin Roosevelt's Committee on Administrative Management, also known as the Brownlow Committee, which recommended in 1937 that the "president needs help." Their recommendation became the foundation for the establishment of the Executive Office of the President in 1939.

C

Cabinet councils: Councils consisting of cabinet members who Reagan organized into subcabinets along the lines of Nixon's super-secretaries. There were six councils in Reagan's first term, each with distinct authority over a policy area.

Cabinet secretariat: A position created by Eisenhower to organize the agenda and materials for cabinet meetings. While the position was abandoned by Kennedy, other presidents have resurrected the cabinet secretariat.

Capture theory: A theory describing the relationships of regulatory agencies, regulated interest groups, and congressional committees. The idea is that regulated agencies are captured by the groups they are supposed to regulate. Therefore, the public interest is not protected. Also called iron triangle theory.

Chief diplomat: One of the "hats" or tasks of the presidency, as identified by historian Clinton Rossiter. It involves the president's diplomatic functions, including those functions covered by the Constitution involving treaty making and receiving foreign dignitaries.

Chief of staff: The chief of the White House staff. The position was created by Eisenhower as a policy and political coordinator, but the chief of staff has become (in many administrations) one of the most powerful officials in the U.S. government.

Commander-in-chief: A constitutional role of the presidency. As commander and chief, the president, as a nonmilitary official, is the head of the military. This was part of the Founders' intent to limit the power of the military by placing it under civilian control.

Congressional hegemony: A system in which the Congress dominates the political system.

Convene: To bring Congress back into session after it has adjourned. Presidents have the constitutional authority to use this provision, which has become less influential over time, as Congress now meets throughout most of its two-year session.

D

Dark horse candidate: A candidate who has come out of nowhere to secure a party's nomination. This person is often a little-known candidate who gets the nomination because of political compromises.

Divided government: When different political parties control the presidency and at least one branch of Congress.

E

Electoral resources: Resources that derive from elections and include such elements as how presidents are nominated (King Caucus, party conventions, presidential primaries), how presidents campaign, the technologies (radio and television) and political organizations (parties, independent committees) they use to present themselves to the public, whether the president is a lame duck or faces competition in his or her re-election campaign, the scope of the president's margin of victory, the accompanying "mandate," the so-called "honeymoon" period, the presidential coattail effect, and the midterm penalty effect.

Executive hegemony: A system in which the president dominates the political system.

Executive privilege: The idea that presidents can keep certain information secret or privileged even from Congress.

Expectations: A central concept in the presidential literature. The idea is that how we perceive the presidential office, what we demand from it, and where we look for leadership have a direct impact on the extent of presidential power. In short, the greater our expectations of the presidency, the greater is the potential for increased presidential power. Since expectations can change more quickly than constitutional provisions, laws, or the president's legal authority, it is also a central concept explaining change in the American presidency over time.

Expectations gap: The difference between what the public expects presidents to do and what presidents are actually capable of doing.

External resources: Resources that relate to the exogenous political environment and consist of such diverse entities as public opinion, the media, Congress, political parties, interest groups, the courts, state and local governments, foreign governments, international organizations, and the bureaucracy. These are various actors and institutions that presidents must interact with on a regular basis, but they are actors or institutions over which the president does not have direct hierarchical authority.

Extra-constitutional powers: The roles, identified by Rossiter, as Party Chief and Voice of the People, which are not identified in the Constitution but are important roles that presidents now play nonetheless.

F

Favorite son: A candidate who runs for president essentially because he or she represents a particular state or sometimes region of the country.

Fireside chats: Franklin Roosevelt's radio communications with the public. He talked to the American public via radio as individuals in their homes and built a personal bond with them.

H

Honeymoon: The period after the presidential inauguration, usually the first four or five months of a new president's term, when the new president receives generally positive press and muted criticism from the political opposition.

I

Impact presidents: The presidents who have played the most important role in changing the presidency, but they are not necessarily the great presidents.

Informational resources: Resources that consist of intelligence the president alone can acquire. Many agencies are involved in collecting information for the presidency (from the Central Intelligence Agency, or CIA, to the National Security Council, or NSC). Presidents also use White House organizations (an internal resource) to acquire information (e.g., the Legislative Liaison Office provides the president with information on vote counts in Congress). These sources of information place presidents in a more advantageous bargaining position with other external political actors, both in domestic and foreign affairs.

Internal resources: Formal and informal mechanisms that have been developed directly within the White House itself. They include the creation of organizations and staff within the White House that are directly under the president's hierarchical control.

Iron triangle theory: A theory describing the relationships of regulatory agencies, regulated interest groups, and congressional committees. The idea is that regulated agencies are captured by the groups they are supposed to regulate. Therefore, the public interest is not protected. Also called capture theory.

Isolationism: The idea that America was isolated from Europe by a great ocean and, hence, was largely invulnerable to foreign attack. As a result, America could (and should) try to stay out of European politics (that is, to isolate itself from Europe). Interestingly, although the Pacific Ocean also separated the nation from Asia, isolationism would be used more often as an argument for staying out of European affairs than Asian politics. Isolationism was the framework of American foreign policy throughout most of the nineteenth century and even well into the twentieth century. Indeed, a consensus did not exist to replace isolationism with internationalism until after World War II.

K

Kitchen cabinet: Advisers outside the administration that some presidents use instead of or in addition to the cabinet for advice.

L

Laissez-faire: A central concept of economic theory. It is the idea that the government should take a hands-off approach to economic policy.

Legal resources: Resources that derive directly from the Constitution (e.g., the president's enumerated power) or indirectly from it (inherent powers). They also derive from Supreme Court (and other court) decisions and legal precedent that define the parameters of presidential power, from congressional delegation of authority, treaties, defense pacts, and other agreements with other nations and international organizations.

Linkage mechanisms: The various policy actors that link constitutional political actors to the American public. The media and political parties, plus interest groups, perform these functions in the American political system.

M

Militia system: An alternative to a standing army. The militia system created by the Constitution gave primary control for creating a militia (similar to today's National Guard) to Congress. Congress also had the authority to provide regulations for the new militia. The militias would then be under the control of the state governors except in times of war or when war was imminent. Then the president as commander-in-chief could ask the governors to call forth the militias of the several states in defense of the nation. The militias, in theory, were meant to be the "bulwark of democracy." In reality, while some states had "well regulated militias," most state militias were not efficient or competent. During the War of 1812, governors of several states refused President James Madison's request to call up the militias. Hence, over time, the nation turned from the militia as the primary method of defense to a professional, standing army.

Modern presidency: A concept used to describe the period in which the presidency has assumed dominance in our governmental system. Most scholars begin the modern presidency with Franklin Roosevelt, although others have argued that the roots of the modern presidency were laid by presidents such as Theodore Roosevelt and Woodrow Wilson.

N

National party chairman: The head of the Democratic or the Republican national committee, which is the national (as opposed to state or local) organization for each party.

National security: This is actually a term of fairly recent usage. Although security was an issue that the Founders were concerned with (note that the first several *Federalist Papers* deal primarily with security issues), they did not refer to a concept of national security until after World War II. Since then, the national security state (including the Department of Defense, the National Security Council, the Central Intelligence Agency, etc.) has been established, and the president's authority as commander-in-chief has greatly expanded. In this book, I refer to a national security presidency, which combines the president's role as commander-in-chief with the national security machinery and the goal of national security.

New political resources: Resources that consist of the president's internal and informational resources.

O

Overload: A situation in which too many demands and expectations are aimed at the presidential office. As the presidency is overloaded, it is more difficult for presidents to respond to growing demands for action.

P

Patronage system: A system whereby jobs in bureaucratic agencies were made generally on the basis of whether a job candidate worked for and supported a particular political candidate and/or political party.

Personal resources: The resources (speaking ability, personal likeability, intelligence, ability to compromise, experience, etc.) presidents bring with them when they enter the presidential office.

Photo opportunities (photo-ops): Events at which the president is photographed in a setting that emphasizes a particular policy or pre-selected image—president as leader, president as concerned American, president as patriot.

Pocket veto: A president's ability to veto a bill without sending it back to Congress for reconsideration if Congress has adjourned.

Political ecosystem/political ecology: The political system as a whole, rather than its individual components (president, Congress, courts, public, interest groups, etc.). The focus is on where the public and other political actors look for leadership (or aim their demands for leadership) in the governmental system. The idea is that the political ecosystem is constantly changing or evolving over time, as individual institutions gain or lose influence, as public expectations of these institutions change, and as demands for action are aimed at different political actors.

Post-modern presidency: Richard Rose's idea that the United States is no longer capable of leading the world on its own, but now is but one of the world leaders. The idea is that the presidency, in this age, is constrained by various resource limitations.

Press conference: A meeting of the president and various members of the press. The basic purpose is for presidents to communicate a desired message to the media so that the press can report it to the public.

R

Rally round the flag effect: During a crisis, the effect seen when the public supports the president as the symbol of the nation. The president's popularity often increases suddenly as a result, though the effect is generally limited over time.

Realignment: The idea that there are certain elections in American history in which the electorate (or important segments of it) change or realign from one party to another. Most scholars argue that there were realigning elections in 1828, 1860, 1896, and 1932. Some have argued that 1964 and 1980 were also realigning elections, though there is lesser consensus regarding the long-term electoral implications of these latter two elections.

S

Session: The two-year time period in which Congress meets. Every two years, a new House of Representatives is elected, as well as one-third of the Senate. The newly elected Congress then governs within a two-year session.

Shays's Rebellion: A farmers' rebellion that was led by Revolutionary War veteran Daniel Shays in rural western Massachusetts to oppose higher taxes. The rebellion forced several courts to close, thus preventing them from conducting foreclosure proceedings against farmers. An attack on the federal arsenal at Springfield also occurred. Although unsuccessful, the rebellion sent a shockwave through the new nation and was an important factor leading to the replacement of the Articles of Confederation with a new Constitution.

Special Assistant to the President for National Security Affairs: The National Security Adviser or the head of the National Security Council. The position was established by Eisenhower as a policy coordinator in foreign affairs but has become a political operative in some administrations. As with the chief of staff, this is one of the most powerful positions in the U.S. government.

Spin control: The effort made by presidential officials and other political actors to create (for the media) a positive spin or interpretation on a presidential speech or decision.

Spokes of the wheel: A model of White House decision-making in which the president allows access from a variety of White House staffers but remains at the center of the decision-making process—the president is the fulcrum with the advisers representing each of the spokes in the wheel. The problem with this approach is that it allows too many access points, meaning too many people have unrestricted access to the president, thus inundating him in administrative and policy details rather than allowing him to step back and see the big picture.

Super-secretaries: Secretaries who performed similar functions and were combined into committees and then placed under the direction of one cabinet member who directed policy in that area.

T

Traditional political resources: Resources that consist of the president's personal, legal, electoral, and external political resources.

W

Watergate: A political scandal precipitated when officials of the Nixon administration broke into the Democratic Party headquarters in the Watergate building in Washington, D.C. The Watergate scandals represented a wide assortment of abuses of government by the Nixon administration.

White Fleet: A fleet (painted white and therefore called the White Fleet) that Theodore Roosevelt sent around the world in the early 1900s as a symbol of America's growing military prominence. Roosevelt considered his decision to send the White Fleet around the world as the most significant of his administration.

References

A

Aberback, Joel D. 1990. *Keeping a Watchful Eye: The Politics of Congressional Oversight.* Washington, D.C.: Brookings Institution.

Abramowitz, Alan I., Dan J. Lanoue, and Susan Remesh. 1988. "Economic Conditions, Causal Attributions, and Political Evaluations in the 1984 Presidential Election." *Journal of Politics.* 50: 849–63.

Acheson, Dean. 1987 edition/1969. *Present at the Creation: My Years in the State Department.* New York: Norton.

Adams, Henry. 1986. *History of the United States of America During the Administrations of James Madison.* New York: Library of America.

Adler, David Gray. 1989. "The President's War-Making Power." In Thomas E. Cronin (ed.) *Inventing the Presidency.* Lawrence, KS: University Press of Kansas. 119–53.

Allen, W. B. 1988. *George Washington: A Collection.* Indianapolis: Liberty Classics.

Allenby, Braden R. 1999. *Industrial Ecology: Policy Framework and Implementation.* Upper Saddle River, NJ: Prentice-Hall.

Altschuler, Bruce E. 1991. "Lyndon Johnson: Campaign Innovator." *PS: Political Science and Politics.* XXIV (March): 42–44.

Anderson, Patrick. 1968. *The President's Men: White House Assistants of Franklin D. Roosevelt, Harry S. Truman, Dwight D. Eisenhower, John F. Kennedy, and Lyndon B. Johnson.* Garden City, NY: Doubleday.

Arnold, Peri E. 1986. *Making the Managerial Presidency: Comprehensive Reorganization Planning 1905–1980.* Princeton: Princeton University Press.

———. 1993. "The Institutionalized Presidency and the American Regime." In Richard W. Waterman (ed.) *The Presidency Reconsidered.* Itasca, IL: Peacock. 215–45.

Arnold, R. Douglas. 1979. *Congress and the Bureaucracy: A Theory of Influence.* New Haven: Yale University Press.

B

Bailyn, Bernard. 1992. *The Ideological Origins of the American Revolution.* Cambridge, MA: Belknap Press.

Barber, James David. 1992. *The Presidential Character: Predicting Performance in the White House.* Englewood Cliffs, NJ: Prentice-Hall.

Barnet, Richard J. 1990. *The Rocket's Red Glare: When America Goes To War: The Presidents and the People.* New York: Simon and Schuster.

Barone, Michael. 1990. *The Shaping of America from Roosevelt to Reagan.* New York: Free Press.

Basler, Roy P. (ed.) 1953. *The Collected Works of Abraham Lincoln.* Volume 1. New Brunswick, NJ: Rutgers University Press.

Beck, Nathaniel. 1982. "Presidential Influence on the Federal Reserve in the 1970s." *American Journal of Political Science.* 3: 415–45.

Begeron, Paul H. 1974. *The Presidency of James K. Polk.* Lawrence, KS: University Press of Kansas.

Benze, Maes G. Jr. 1985. "Presidential Reorganization as a Tactical Weapon: Putting Politics Back into Administration." *Presidential Studies Quarterly.* 15: 145–56.

Berger, Raoul. 1974. *Executive Privilege: A Constitutional Myth.* Cambridge, MA: Harvard University Press.

Berman, Larry. 1979. *The Office of Management and Budget and the Presidency, 1921–1979.* Princeton: Princeton University Press.

———. 2001. *No Peace, No Honor: Nixon, Kissinger, and Betrayal in Vietnam.* New York: Free Press.

Bessette, Joseph M. and Jeffrey K. Tulis. 1981. *The Presidency in The Constitutional Order.* Baton Rouge: Louisiana State University Press.

Best, Gary Dean. 1993. *The Critical Press and the New Deal: The Press versus Presidential Power, 1933–1938.* Westport, CT: Praeger Press.

Bibby, John F. and Roger H. Davidson. 1972. *On Capitol Hill.* Hinsdale, IL: Dryden Press.

Binkley, Wilfred E. 1956. "The President as Chief Legislator." *The Office of the American Presidency.* Philadelphia: The Academy of Political and Social Science.

Black, Charles L. 1976. "Some Thoughts on the Veto." *Law and Contemporary Problems.* 40: 87.

Bonafede, Dom. 1977. "White House Staffing: The Nixon-Ford Era." In Thomas E. Cronin and Rexford G. Tugwell (eds.) *The Presidency Reappraised.* New York: Praeger Press.

———. 1987. "The White House Personnel Office from Roosevelt to Reagan." In Calvin Mackenzie (ed.) *The In-and-Outers: Presidential Appointees and Transient Government in Washington.* Baltimore: John Hopkins University Press.

———. 1988. "Quayle's Quandry." *National Journal.* (December 31): 3254–57.

Bond, Jon and Richard Fleisher. 1990. *The President in the Legislative Arena.* Chicago: University of Chicago Press.

Bowen, Catherine Drinker. 1966. *Miracle at Philadelphia.* Boston: Little, Brown and Co.

Brace, Paul and Barbara Hinckley. 1992. *Follow the Leader: Opinion Polls and the Modern Presidents.* New York: Basic Books.

Brauer, Carl. 1987. "Tenure, Turnover, and Postgovernment Trends of Presidential Appointees." In G. Calvin Mackenzie (ed.) *The In-and-Outers: Presidential Appointees and Transient Government in Washington.* Baltimore: John Hopkins University Press. 174–94.

Brigman, William E. 1981. "The Executive Branch and the Independent Regulatory Agencies." *Presidential Studies Quarterly.* 11: 244–61.

Broder, David S. 1972. *The Party's Over: The Failure of Politics in America.* New York: Harper Torchbooks.

Brody, Richard A. 1991. *Assessing the President: The Media, Elite Opinion, and Public Support.* Stanford: Stanford University Press.

Boughton, D. H. 1907. "Evolution of the National Guard." In Robert Marion La Follette (ed.) *The Making of America.* Chicago: De Bower-Chapline Co. 128–40.

Brownlow, Louis. 1969. "What We Expect the President to Do." In Aaron Wildavsky (ed.) *The Presidency.* Boston: Little, Brown and Co.

Bryce, James Lord. 1888/1908. *The American Commonwealth.* London: Macmillan.

Bryner, Gary C. 1987. *Bureaucratic Discretion: Law and Policy in Federal Regulatory Agencies.* New York: Pergamon Press.

Buchanan, Bruce. 1978. *The Presidential Experience: What the Office Does to the Man.* Englewood Cliffs, NJ: Prentice-Hall.

———. 1987a. *The Citizen's Presidency.* Washington, D.C.: Congressional Quarterly Press.

———. 1987b. "Constrained Diversity: The Organization Theory of the Presidency." Presented at the annual meeting of the American Political Science Association. Chicago, IL.

Burnham, Walter Dean. 1970. *Critical Elections and the Mainsprings of American Politics.* New York: W. W. Norton.

Burns, James MacGregor. 1965. *Presidential Government: The Crucible of Leadership.* Boston: Houghton Miflin.

———. 1984. *Roosevelt: The Lion and the Fox.* New York: Harcourt Brace Jovanovich Publishers.

———. 1989. *The Crosswinds of Freedom.* New York: Alfred A. Knopf.

Bush, George H. W. and Victor Gold. 1987. *Looking Forward: An Autobiography.* New York: Doubleday.

C

Calvert, Randall L. and John A. Ferejohn. 1983. "Coattail Voting in Recent Presidential Elections." *American Political Science Review.* 77: 407–19.

Cameron, Charles M. 2000. *Veto Bargaining: Presidents and the Politics of Negative Power.* New York: Cambridge University Press.

Campbell, Angus. 1960. "Surge and Decline: A Study of Electoral Change." *Public Opinion Quarterly.* 24: 397–418.

Campbell, Colin. 1986. *Managing the Presidency: Carter, Reagan, and the Search for Executive Harmony.* Pittsburgh: University of Pittsburgh Press.

Campbell, James E. 1986. "Predicting Seat Gains from Presidential Coattails." *American Journal of Political Science.* 30: 165–83.

Carp, Robert and C. K. Rowland. 1983. *Policymaking and Politics in the Federal District Courts.* Knoxville, TN: University of Tennessee Press.

Carter, Stephen L. 1994. *The Confirmation Mess: Cleaning Up the Federal Appointment Process.* New York: Basic Books.

Cater, Douglass. 1964. *Power in Washington: A Critical Look at Today's Struggle to Govern in the Nation's Capitol.* New York: Random House.

Catton, Bruce. 1953. *A Stillness at Appomattox.* New York: Doubleday.

Chandler, Alfred D. 1977. *The Visible Hand: The Managerial Revolution in American Business.* Cambridge, MA: Harvard University Press.

Chubb, John and Paul Peterson. 1985. *Can the Government Govern?* Washington, D.C.: Brookings Institution.

Citrin, Jack and Donald Philip Green. 1986. "Presidential Leadership and the Resurgence of Trust in Government." *British Journal of Political Science.* 5: 1–31.

Clausen, Aage R. 1973. *How Congressmen Decide: A Policy Focus.* New York: St. Martin's Press.

Cohen, Jeffrey E. 1982. "A Historical Reassessment of Wildavksy's Two Presidencies' Thesis." *Social Science Quarterly.* 63: 549–55.

———. 1985. "Presidential Control of Independent Regulatory Commissions Through Appointment: The Case of the ICC." *Administration and Society.* 17: 61–71.

———. 1986. "On the Tenure of Appointive Political Executives: The American Cabinet, 1952–1984." *American Journal of Political Science.* 30: 507–16.

———. 1988. *The Politics of the U.S. Cabinet: Representation in the Executive Branch, 1789–1984.* Pittsburgh: University of Pittsburgh Press.

Conley, Patricia H. 2001. *Presidential Mandates: How Elections Shape the National Agenda.* Chicago: University of Chicago Press.

Cooke, Jacob E. 1961. *The Federalist.* New York: Meridian Books.

Corbett, Michael. 2001. *Research Methods in Political Science: An Introduction Using Microcase.* Belmont, CA: Wadsworth Thomas Learning.

Cornwell, Elmer E. 1965. *Presidential Leadership of Public Opinion.* Bloomington, IN: Indiana University Press.

Corwin, Edward S. 1984. *The President: Office and Powers, 1787–1984.* Randall W. Bland, Theodore T. Hindson, and Jack W. Peltason (eds.) New York: New York University Press.

Crabb, Cecil V. Jr. and Pat M. Holt. 1989. *Invitation to Struggle: Congress, the President, and Foreign Policy.* Washington, D.C.: Congressional Quarterly Press.

Cronin, Thomas E. 1974. "The Textbook Presidency and Political Science." In Stanley Bach and George T. Sulzner (eds.) *Perspectives on the Presidency.* Lexington, MA: D. C. Heath and Co. 54–74.

———. 1980. *The State of the Presidency.* Boston: Little, Brown and Co.

Crotty, William J. and Gary C. Jacobson. 1980. *American Parties in Decline.* Boston: Little, Brown and Co.

D

Daniels, Josephus. 1924. *The Life of Woodrow Wilson.* New York: United Publishers.

———. 1944. *The Wilson Era: Years of Peace—1910–1917.* Chapel Hill, NC: University of North Carolina Press.

Davis, James W. 1967. *Presidential Primaries: Road to the White House.* New York: Thomas Y. Crowell Company.

Davis, Kenneth S. 1986. *FDR: The New Deal Years 1933–1937.* New York: Random House.

———. 1993. *FDR: Into the Storm 1937–1940.* New York: Random House.

Davis, Lance E. and Douglass C. North. 1971. *Institutional Change and American Economic Growth.* New York: Cambridge University Press.

DeClerico, Robert E. 1993. "The Role of the Media in Heightened Expectations and Diminished Leadership Capacity." In Richard W. Waterman (ed.) *The Presidency Reconsidered.* Itasca, IL: F. E. Peacock. 115–43.

———. 1979. *The American President.* Englewood Cliffs, NJ: Prentice-Hall.

Deering, Christopher. 1987. "Damned If You Do and Damned If You Don't: The Senate's Role in the Appointment Process." In G. Calvin Mackenzie (ed.) *The In-and-Outers: Presidential Appointees and Transient Government in Washington.* Baltimore: John Hopkins Press. 100–19.

Destler, I. M. 1981. "National Security II. The Rise of the Assistant (1961–1981)." In Hugh Heclo and Lester M. Salmon (eds.) *The Illusion of Presidential Government.* Boulder, CO: Westview Press. 263–85.

Dickinson, Matthew J. 1997. *Bitter Harvest: FDR, Presidential Power and the Growth of the Executive Branch.* New York: Cambridge University Press.

Divine, Robert A., T. H. Breen, George M. Fredrickson, and R. Hal Williams. 1984. *America Past and Present.* Glenview, IL: Scot, Foresman and Co.

Dodd, Lawrence C. and Richard L. Schott. 1979. *Congress and the Administrative State.* New York: John Wiley and Sons.

E

Edwards, George C. III. 1980. *Presidential Influence in Congress.* San Francisco: W. H. Freeman and Company.

———. 1983. *The Public Presidency: The Pursuit of Popular Support.* New York: St. Martin's Press.

———. 1989. *At the Margins: Presidential Leadership of Congress.* New Haven: Yale University Press.

Edwards, George C. III. and Alec M. Gallup. 1990. *Presidential Approval: A Sourcebook.* Baltimore: John Hopkins University Press.

Eisenhower, Dwight D. 1963. *Mandate for Change, 1953–1956.* Garden City, NY: Doubleday and Co.

Elkins, Stanley and Eric McKitrick. 1993. *The Age of Federalism: The Early American Republic, 1788-1800.* New York: Oxford University Press.

Epstein, David and Sharyn O'Halloran. 1999. *Delegating Powers: A Transaction Cost Politics Approach to Policy Making under Separate Powers.* New York: Cambridge University Press.

Erikson, Robert S. 1988. "The Puzzle of Midterm Loss." *Journal of Politics.* 25: 1011–29.

———. 1989. "Economic Conditions and the Presidential Vote." *American Political Science Review.* 83: 567–73.

Erikson, Robert S. and Kent L. Tedin. 1981. "The 1928–1936 Partisan Realignment: The Case for the Conversion Hypothesis." *American Political Science Review.* 75: 951–62.

F

Fallows, James. 1988. "The Presidency and the Press." In Michael Nelson (ed.) *The Presidency and the Political System.* Washington, D.C.: Congressional Quarterly Press. 293–310.

Farrand, Max. 1913. *The Framing of the Constitution of the United States.* New Haven: Yale University Press.

Farrand, Max (ed.) 1966. *The Records of the Federal Convention of 1787.* Four volumes. New Haven: Yale University Press.

Fausold, Martin L. 1985. *The Presidency of Herbert C. Hoover.* Lawrence, KS: University Press of Kansas.

Fels, Rendigs. 1951. "American Business Cycles, 1867–79." *American Economic Review.* June: 349.

Fenno, Richard F. Jr. 1959. *The President's Cabinet.* New York: Vintage Books.

———. 1973. *Congressmen in Committees.* Boston: Little, Brown and Co.

Ferejohn, John A. and Randall L. Calvert. 1984. "Presidential Coattails in Historical Perspective." *American Journal of Political Science.* 28: 127–46.

Finer, Herman. 1960. *The Presidency: Crisis and Regeneration.* Chicago: University of Chicago Press.

Fishel, Jeff. 1985. *Presidents & Promises.* Washington, D.C.: Congressional Quarterly Press.

Fisher, Linda. 1986. "Appointments and Presidential Control: The Importance of Role." Paper presented at the annual meeting of the American Political Science Association. Washington, D.C.

Fisher, Louis. 1975. *Presidential Spending Power.* Princeton, NJ: Princeton University Press.

———. 1978. *The Constitution Between Friends: Congress, the President, and the Law.* New York: St. Martin's Press.

———. 1981/1987. *The Politics of Shared Power.* Washington, D.C.: Congressional Quarterly Press.

———. 1986. "The Administrative State: What's Next after Chadha and Bowsher." Delivered at the annual meeting of the American Political Science Association. Washington, D.C.

———. 1989. "Micromanagement by Congress: Reality and Mythology." In L. Gordon Crovitz and Jeremy A. Rabkin (eds.) *The Fettered Presidency: Legal Constraints on the Executive Branch.* Washington, D.C.: American Enterprise Institute: 139–57.

———. 1995. *Presidential War Power.* Lawrence, KS: University Press of Kansas.

Fisher, Louis and Ronald C. Moe. 1981. "Presidential Reorganization: Is It Worth the Cost? *Political Science Quarterly.* 96: 301–18.

Fite, Gilbert C. 1972. "Election of 1896." In Arthur Schlesinger, Jr. (ed.) *The Coming To Power: Critical Presidential Elections in American History.* New York: McGraw-Hill. 225–63.

Fitzpatrick, John C. 1932. *The Writings of George Washington.* Washington, D.C.: Government Printing Office. Volume 26.

Flexner, James Thomas. 1968. *George Washington in the American Revolution (1775–1783).* Boston: Little, Brown and Co.

———. 1970. *George Washington and the New Nation (1783–1793).* Boston: Little, Brown and Co.

Foner, Eric. 1970. *Free Soil, Free Labor, Free Men: The Ideology of the Republican Party before the Civil War.* New York: Oxford University Press.

Foner, Philip S. (ed.) 1944. *Basic Writings of Thomas Jefferson.* Garden City, NY: Halcyon House.

Foote, Shelby. 1958. *The Civil War: A Narrative Fort Sumter to Perryville.* New York: Vintage Books.

Ford, Gerald R. 1979. *A Time to Heal: The Autobiography of Gerald R. Ford.* New York: Harper and Row.

Freeman, J. Leiper. 1965. *The Political Process: Executive Bureau-Legislative Committee Relations.* New York: Random House.

Fuchs, Edward Paul. 1988. *Presidents, Management, and Regulation.* Englewood Cliffs, NJ: Prentice-Hall.

G

Gaddie, Ronald Keith and Charles S. Bullock, III. 2000. *Election to Open Seats in the U.S. House: Where the Action Is.* New York: Rowman and Littlefield.

Gamm, Gerald and Renee M. Smith. 1998. "Presidents, Parties and the Public: Evolving Patterns of Interaction, 1877–1929." In Richard J. Ellis (ed.) *Speaking to the People: The Rhetorical Presidency in Historical Perspective.* Amherst, MA: University of Massachusetts Press. 87–111.

Gant, Michael M. and Dwight F. Davis. 1984. "Negative Voter Support in Presidential Elections." *Western Political Quarterly.* 37: 272–90.

Gant, Michael M. and Lee Sigelman. 1985. "Anti-Candidate Voting in Presidential Elections." *Polity.* 18: 329–39.

Gant, Michael M. and Lilliard E. Richardson, Jr., 1993. "Presidential Performance, the Expectations Gap and Negative Voter Support." In Richard W. Waterman (ed.) *The Presidency Reconsidered.* Itasca, IL: P. E. Peacock Publishers. 47–74.

Gant, Michael M., Lilliard Richardson, and Richard W. Waterman. 1992. "Negative Voting in Presidential Elections: An Explanation of the Decline of the Coattail Effect." Paper presented at the annual meeting of the Midwest Political Science Association. Chicago, IL.

Gelderman, Carol. 1997. *All the President's Words: The Bully Pulpit and the Creation of the Virtual Presidency.* New York: Walker and Company.

Genovese, Michael A. 1995. *The Presidential Dilemma: Leadership in the American System.* New York: Harper Collins.

George, Alexander L. 1980. *Presidential Decisionmaking in Foreign Policy: The Effective Use of Information and Advice.* Boulder, CO: Westview Press.

Gergen, David. 2000. *Eyewitness to Power: The Essence of Leadership Nixon to Clinton.* New York: Simon and Schuster.

Gerhardt, Michael J. 2000. *The Federal Appointment Process: A Constitutional and Historical Analysis.* Durham, NC: Duke University Press.

Gilmour, Robert. 1976. "Policy Formulation in the Executive Branch: Central Legislative Clearance." In James Anderson (ed.) *Case Studies in Public Policy Making.* New York: Holt, Rinehard, and Winston. 80–96.

Ginsberg, Benjamin, Walter R. Mebane, Jr., and Martin Shefter. 1995. "The Presidency and Interest Groups: Why Presidents Cannot Govern." In Michael Nelson (ed.) *The Presidency and the Political System.* Washington, D.C.: Congressional Quarterly Press. 331–47.

Goldsmith, William M. (ed.) 1980. *The Growth of Presidential Power: A Documented History.* New York: Confucian Press.

Goodnow, Frank J. 1900. *Politics and Administration: A Study of Government.* New York: Russell and Russell.

Greenberg, Stanley B. 1995. *Middle Class Dreams: The Politics and Power of the New American Majority.* New York: Times Books/Random House.

Greenstein, Fred I. 1982. *The Hidden Hand Presidency: Eisenhower as Leader.* New York: Basic Books.

———. 1988a. "Toward a Modern Presidency." In Fred I. Greenstein (ed.) *Leadership in the Modern Presidency.* Cambridge, MA: Harvard University Press. 1–6.

———. 1988b. "In Search of a Modern Presidency." In Fred I. Greenstein (ed.) *Leadership in the Modern Presidency.* Cambridge, MA: Harvard University Press: 296–352.

Grossman, Michael Baruch and Martha Joynt Kumar. 1981. *Portraying the President: The White House and the News Media.* Baltimore: John Hopkins University Press.

H

Halberstam, David. 1993. *The Fifties*. New York: Villard Books.

Haldeman, H. R. 1994. *The Haldeman Diaries: Inside the Nixon White House*. New York: G. P. Putnam's Sons.

Hamby, Alonzo L. 1988. "Harry S. Truman: Insecurity and Responsibility." In Fred I. Greenstein (ed.) *Leadership in the Modern Presidency*. Cambridge, MA: Harvard University Press: 41–75.

Hardin, Charles M. 1974. *Presidential Power and Accountability toward a New Institution*. Chicago: University of Chicago Press.

Hargrove, Erwin and Michael Nelson. 1984. *Presidents, Politics, and Policy*. New York: Alfred Knopf.

Hart, John. 1987/1995. *The Presidential Branch*. New York: Pergamon Press.

Hart, Roderick P. 1987. *The Sound of Leadership: Presidential Communication in the Modern Age*. Chicago: University of Chicago Press.

Haskin, Frederic J. 1923. *The American Government*. Washington, D.C.: Fred Haskin.

Heclo, Hugh. 1975. "OMB and the Presidency—The Problems of Neutral Competence." *The Public Interest*. 38: 80–98.

———. 1978. "Issue Networks and the Executive Establishment." In Anthony A. King (ed.) *The New American Political System*. Washington, D.C.: American Enterprise Institute.

Heclo, Hugh and Lester M. Salamon (eds.) 1981. *The Illusion of Presidential Government*. Boulder, CO: Westview.

Henderson, Phillip G. 1988. *Managing the Presidency: The Eisenhower Legacy—from Kennedy to Reagan*. Boulder, CO: Westview.

Hertsgaard, Mark. 1988. *On Bended Knee: The Press and the Reagan Presidency*. New York: Farrar, Straus and Giroux.

Hess, Stephen. 1976/1988. *Organizing the Presidency*. Washington, D.C.: Brookings Institution.

Hetherington, Marc J. 1999. "The Effect of Political Trust on the Presidential Vote, 1968–96." *American Political Science Review*. 93: 311–26.

Hickey, Donald R. 1989. *The War of 1812: The Forgotten Conflict*. Chicago: University of Illinois Press.

Higginbotham, Don. 1983. *The War of American Independence: Military Attitudes, Policies, and Practice 1763–1789*. Boston: Northeastern University Press.

Hinckley, Barbara. 1985. *Problems of the Presidency: A Text with Readings*. Glenview, IL: Scott, Foresman, and Co.

Hoar, George F. 1903. *Autobiography of Seventy Years*. New York: Scribners.

Hoff-Wilson, Joan. 1988. "Richard M. Nixon: The Corporate Presidency." In Fred I. Greenstein (ed.). *Leadership in the Modern Presidency*. Cambridge, MA: Harvard University Press: 164–98.

Hofstadter, Richard. 1955. *The Age of Reform*. New York: Vintage Books.

———. 1948/1973. *The American Political Tradition & The Men Who Made It*. New York: Vintage Books.

Hunt, John Gabriel. 1995. *The Inaugural Addresses of the Presidents*. New York: Gramercy Books.

Hunter, Susan and Richard W. Waterman. 1996. *Enforcing the Law: The Case of the Clean Water Acts*. Armonk, NY: M. E. Sharpe.

Huntington, Samuel P. 1952. "The Marasmus of the ICC: The Commission, the Railroads, and the Public Interest. *Yale Law Journal*. 61: 467–509.

———. 1956. "Civilian Control and the Constitution." *American Political Science Review*. 50: 676–99.

J

Jacobson, Gary C. 1990. *The Electoral Origins of Divided Government: Competition in U.S. House Elections, 1946–1988*. Boulder, CO: Westview Press.

Jacobson, Gary C. and Samuel Kernell. 1981. *Strategy and Choice in Congressional Elections*. New Haven, CT: Yale University Press.

Jamieson, Kathleen Hall and David S. Birdsell. 1988. *Presidential Debates: The Challenge of Creating an Informed Electorate*. New York: Oxford University Press.

Jeffers, H. Paul. 2001. *An Honest President: The Life and Presidencies of Grover Cleveland*. New York: Harper Perennial.

Johnson, Charles and Danette Brickman. 2001. *Independent Counsel: The Law and the Investigations*. Washington, D.C.: Congressional Quarterly Press.

Johnson, Haynes. 1980. *In the Absence of Power: Governing in America*. New York: Viking Press.

Jones, Charles O. 1994. *The Presidency in a Separated System*. Washington, D.C.: The Brookings Institution.

———. 1995. *Separate But Equal Branches: Congress and the President*. Chatham, NJ: Chatham House Publishers.

K

Katzman, Robert A. 1980a. "The Federal Trade Commission." In James Q. Wilson (ed.) *The Politics of Regulation*. New York: Basic Books.

———. 1980b. *Regulatory Bureaucracy: The Federal Trade Commission and Antitrust Policy*. Cambridge, MA: MIT Press.

Kellerman, Barbara and Ryan J. Barilleaux. 1991. *The President as World Leader*. New York: St. Martin's Press.

Kennedy, David M. 2000. *Freedom from Fear: The American People in the Depression and War, 1929–1945*. New York: Oxford University Press.

Kernell, Samuel. 1986/1997. *Going Public: New Strategies of Presidential Leadership*. Washington, D.C.: Congressional Quarterly Press.

Kernell, Samuel and Samuel L. Popkin. 1986. *Chief of Staff: Twenty-Five Years of Managing the Presidency*. Berkeley, CA: University of California Press.

Kessel, John H. 1975. *The Domestic Presidency: Decision-Making in the White House*. North Scituate, MA: Duxbury Press.

Kessler, Frank. 1982. *The Dilemmas of Presidential Leadership: of Caretakers and Kings*. Englewood Cliffs, NJ: Prentice-Hall.

Ketcham, Ralph (ed.) 1986. *The Anti-Federalist Papers and the Constitutional Debates*. New York: New American Library.

Ketchum, Richard M. 1973. *The Winter Soldiers*. Garden City, NY: Doubleday and Co.

Kinder, Donald R. and D. Roderick Kiewiet. 1979. "Economic Discontent and Political Behavior: The Role of Personal Grievances and Collective Economic Judgments in Congressional Voting." *American Journal of Political Science*. 23: 495–527.

———. 1981. "Sociotropic Politics: The American Case." *British Journal of Political Science*. 11: 126–61.

Kinder, Donald R., Gordon S. Adams, and Paul W. Gronke. 1989. "Economics and Politics in the 1984 American Presidential Election." *American Journal of Political Science*. 33: 491–515.

King, Gary and Lyn Ragsdale. 1988. *The Elusive Executive: Discovering Statistical Patterns in the Presidency*. Washington, D.C.: Congressional Quarterly Press.

King, James D. and James W. Riddlesperger, Jr. 1987. "Senate Confirmation of Appointments to the Cabinet and Executive Office of the President." Presented at the annual meeting of the American Political Science Association. Chicago, IL.

Kingdon, John W. 1973. *Congressmen's Voting Decisions*. New York: Harper and Row.

———. 1983. *Agendas, Alternatives, and Public Policies*. Boston: Little, Brown and Co.

Kinnard, Douglas. 1977. *President Eisenhower and Strategy Management: A Study in Defense Policy*. Lexington: University of Kentucky Press.

Koenig, Louis W. 1975. *The Chief Executive*. New York: Harcourt Brace, and Jovanovich Publishers.

Kolb, Charles. 1994. *White House Daze: The Unmaking of Domestic Policy in the Bush Years*. New York: Free Press.

Kolko, Gabriel. 1963. *The Triumph of Conservatism: A Reinterpretation of American History, 1900–1916*. New York: Macmillan.

Kolko, Gabriel. 1965. *Railroads and Regulation, 1877–1916*. Princeton: Princeton University Press.

Koritansky, John C. 1989. "Alexander Hamilton and the Presidency." In Thomas Cronin (ed.) *Inventing the American Presidency*. Lawrence, KS: University Press of Kansas. 282–303.

Kramer, Gerald. 1971. "Short-Term Fluctuations in U.S. Voting Behavior." *American Political Science Review*. 65: 131–43.

Krich, Arthur A. Jr. 1966. *Idea, Ideals, and American Diplomacy: A History of Their Growth and Interaction*. New York: Appleton-Century-Crofts.

Kurtz, Howard. 1998. *Spin Control: How the White House and the Media Manipulate the News*. New York: Touchstone Book/Simon and Schuster.

Kutler, Stanley I. (ed.) 1997. *Abuse of Power: The New Nixon Tapes*. New York: Free Press.

L

Lammers, William W. and Michael A. Genovese. 2000. *The President and Domestic Policy: Comparing Leadership Styles, FDR to Clinton*. Washington, D.C.: Congressional Quarterly Press.

Landy, Mark and Sidney M. Milkis. 2000. *Presidential Greatness*. Lawrence, KS: University Press of Kansas.

Landy, Mark K., Marc J. Roberts, and Stephen R. Thomas. 1994. *The Environmental Protection Agency: Asking the Wrong Questions from Nixon to Clinton*. New York: Oxford University Press.

Ledeen , Michael and William Lewis. 1981. *Debacle: American Failure in Iran*. New York: Knopf.

Leffler, Melvyn P. 1992. *A Preponderance of Power: National Security, the Truman Administration, and the Cold War*. Stanford, CA: Stanford University Press.

LeLoup, Lance T. 1980. *Budgetary Politics*. Brunswick, OH: King's Court.

LeLoup, Lance T. and Steven A. Shull. 1979. "Congress versus the Executive: The Two Presidencies' Reconsidered." *Social Science Quarterly*. 59: 704–19.

———. 1999. *The President and Congress: Collaboration and Combat in National Policymaking*. Needham Heights, MA: Allyn and Bacon.

Leuchtenburg, William E. 1963. *Franklin D. Roosevelt and the New Deal*. New York: Harper and Row Publishers.

———. 1988. "Franklin D. Roosevelt: The First Modern President." In Fred I. Greenstein (ed.) *Leadership in the Modern Presidency*. Cambridge, MA: Harvard University Press. 7–40.

Lewis, William Draper. 1919. *The Life of Theodore Roosevelt*. New York: United Publishers.

Lewis-Beck, Michael S. and Tom W. Rice. 1992. *Forecasting Elections*. Washington, D.C.: Congressional Quarterly Press.

Light, Paul C. 1983. *The President's Agenda: Domestic Policy Choice from Kennedy to Carter*. Baltimore: John Hopkins University Press.

———. 1987. "When Worlds Collide: The Political-Career Nexus." In G. Calvin Mackenzie (ed.) *The In-and-Outers: Presidential Appointees and Transient Government in Washington*. Baltimore: John Hopkins University Press: 156–73.

Lloyd, Mark. 1988. *History of the United States ARMY*. London: Chevprime Limited.

Lowi, Theodore J. 1964. "American Business, Public Policy, Case Studies, and Political Theory." *World Politics*. 16: 667–715.

———. 1985. *The Personal Presidency: Power Invested Promise Unfulfilled*. Ithaca, NY: Cornell University Press.

Lynn, Laurence E. Jr. 1984. "The Reagan Administration and the Renitent Bureaucracy." In Lester M. Salamon and Michael S. Lund (eds.) *The Reagan Presidency and the Governing of America*. Washington, D.C.: Urban Institute.

M

Mackenzie, G. Calvin. 1981. *The Politics of Presidential Appointments*. New York: Free Press.

———. 1987. "If You Want to Play, You've Got to Pay: Ethics Regulation and the Presidential Appointment System." In G. Calvin Mackenzie (ed.) *The In-and-Outers: Presidential Appointees and Transient Government in Washington*. Baltimore: John Hopkins University Press: 77–89.

MacKuen, Michael B., Robert S. Erikson, and James A. Stimson. 1992. "Peasants or Bankers? The American Electorate." *American Political Science Review*. 86: 597–611.

Mahan, John K. 1972. *The War of 1812*. Gainesville, FL: Da Capo Press.

Malone, Dumas. 1970. *Jefferson the President: First Term 1801–1805*. Boston: Little, Brown and Co.

Mann, Dean and Jamison Doig. 1965. *The Assistant Secretaries*. Washington, D.C.: Brookings Institution.

Markus, Gregory B. 1992. "The Impact of Personal and National Economic Conditions on Presidential Voting, 1956–1988." *American Journal of Political Science*. 36: 829–34.

———. 1988. "The Impact of Personal and National Economic Conditions on the Presidential Vote: A Pooled Cross–Sectional Analysis." *American Journal of Political Science*. 32:137–54.

Mayer, Kenneth R. 2001. *With the Stroke of a Pen: Executive Orders and Presidential Power*. Princeton: Princeton University Press.

Mayhew, David R. 1991. *Divided We Govern: Party Control, Lawmaking, and Investigations 1946–1990*. New Haven: Yale University Press.

McConnell, Grant. 1966. *Private Power and American Democracy*. New York: Vintage Press.

McCoy, Donald R. 1984. *The Presidency of Harry S. Truman*. Lawrence, KS: University Press of Kansas.

McCubbins, Mathew D. 1985. "The Legislative Design of Regulatory Structure." *American Journal of Political Science*. 29: 721–48.

McCubbins, Mathew D. and Thomas Schwartz. 1984. "Congressional Oversight Overlooked: Police Patrols Versus Fire Alarms." *American Journal of Political Science*. 28: 165–79.

McCullough, David. 1977. *The Path Between the Seas: The Creation of the Panama Canal 1870–1914*. New York: Simon and Schuster.

———. 2001. *John Adams*. New York: Simon and Schuster.

McDonald, Forrest. 1976. *The Presidency of Thomas Jefferson*. Lawrence, KS: University Press of Kansas.

———. 1994. *The American Presidency: An Intellectual History*. Lawrence, KS: University Press of Kansas.

McFeeley, William S. 1981. *Grant: A Biography*. New York: W. W. Norton.

McGinniss, Joe. 1970. *The Selling of the President, 1968*. New York: Trident Press.

Menefee-Libey, David. 2000. *The Triumph of Campaign-Centered Politics*. New York: Chatham House Publishers.

Menzel, Donald C. 1983. "Redirecting the Implementation of a Law: The Reagan Administration and Coal Surface Mining Regulation." *Public Administration Review*. 43: 411–20.

Mezey, Michael L. 1989. *Congress, the President, & Public Policy*. Boulder, CO: Westview Press.

Michaels, Judith E. 1997. *The President's Call: Executive Leadership from FDR to George Bush*. Pittsburgh, PA: University of Pittsburgh Press.

Milkis, Stanley M. 1988. "The Presidency and Political Parties." In Michael Nelson (ed.) *The Presidency and the Political System*. Washington, D.C.: Congressional Quarterly Press. 331–49.

———. 1993. *The President and the Parties: The Transformation of the American Party System Since the New Deal*. New York: Oxford University Press.

Milkis, Stanley M. and Michael Nelson. 1994/1998. *The American Presidency: Origins and Development*. Washington, D.C.: Congressional Quarterly Press.

Miller, Nathan. 1992. *Theodore Roosevelt: A Life*. New York: William Morrow and Co.

Millis, Walter. 1956. *Arms and Men: A Study of American Military History*. New York: Mentor Books.

Miroff, Bruce. 1988. "John Adams and the Presidency." In Thomas E. Cronin (ed.) *Inventing the American Presidency*. Lawrence, KS: University Press of Kansas.

Moe, Terry M. 1982. "Regulatory Performance and Presidential Administration." *American Journal of Political Science*. 26: 197–225.

———. 1985a. "Control and Feedback in Economic Regulations: The Case of the NLRB." *American Political Science Review*. 79: 1094–1116.

———. 1985b. "The Politicized Presidency." In John E. Chubb and Paul E. Peterson (eds.) *New Directions in American Politics*. Washington, D.C.: Brookings Institution. 235–71.

Mollenhoff, Clark R. 1980. *The President Who Failed: Carter Out of Control*. New York: Macmillan.

Morris, Edmund. 2001. *The Rise of Theodore Roosevelt.* New York: Modern Library.

Mosher, Frederick C. 1982. *Democracy and the Public Service.* New York: Oxford University Press.

Mueller, John. 1973. *War, Presidents and Public Opinion.* New York: John Wiley and Sons.

Mulcahy, Kevin and Cecil V. Crabb. 1991. "Presidential Management of National Security Policy Making, 1947–1987." In James P. Pfiffner (ed.) *The Managerial Presidency.* Pacific Grove, CA: Brookscole. 250–64.

Murray, Tim H. and Robert K. Blessing. 1994. *Greatness in The White House: Rating the Presidents from George Washington through Ronald Reagan.* University Park: Pennsylvania State University Press.

N

Nadeau, Richard, Richard G. Niemi, David P. Fan, and Timothy Amato. 1999. "Elite Economic Forecasts, Economic News, Mass Economic Judgments, and Presidential Approval." *Journal of Politics.* 61: 109–35.

Nathan, Richard P. 1983. *The Administrative Presidency.* New York: John Wiley and Sons.

Nelson, W. Dale. 1998. *Who Speaks for the President? The White House Press Secretary from Cleveland to Clinton.* Syracuse, NY: Syracuse University Press.

Neustadt, Richard E. 1954. "Presidency and Legislation: The Growth of Central Clearance." *American Political Science Review.* 48: 641–71.

———. 1960/1980. *Presidential Power: The Politics of Leadership from FDR to Carter.* New York: John Wiley and Sons.

———. 1982. "Presidential Leadership: The Clerk Against the Preacher." In J. S. Young (ed.). *Problems and Prospects of Presidential Leadership in the Nineteen-Eighties.* Volume 1. Washington, D.C.: University Press of America. 1–36.

Nevins, Allan. 1947. *The Ordeal of the Union: The Fruits of Manifest Destiny, 1847–1852.* New York: Charles Scribner's Sons.

———. 1959. *The War for the Union: The Organized War 1863–1864.* New York: Charles Scribner's Sons.

Newman, Bruce I. 1994. *The Marketing of the President: Political Marketing as Campaign Strategy.* Thousand Oaks, CA: Sage Publications.

Nixon, Richard M. 1978. *RN: The Memoirs of Richard Nixon.* New York: Grosset & Dunlap.

———. 1979. *Six Crises.* New York: Warner Books.

Noll, Roger G. 1971. *Reforming Regulation.* Washington, D.C.: Brookings Institution.

Noll, Roger G. and Bruce M. Owen. 1983. *The Political Economy of Deregulation: Interest Groups in the Regulatory Process.* Washington, D.C.: American Enterprise Institute.

North, Douglass C. 1981. *Structure and Change in Economic History.* New York: Norton.

O

Ogul, Morris. 1976. *Congress Oversees the Bureaucracy.* Pittsburgh: University of Pittsburgh Press.

———. 1981. "Congressional Oversight: Structures and Incentives." In Lawrence C. Dodd and Bruce I. Oppenheimer (ed.) *Congress Reconsidered.* Washington, D.C.: Congressional Quarterly Press.

Oppenheimer, Bruce I. 1993. "Declining Presidential Success with Congress." In Richard W. Waterman (ed.) *The Presidency Reconsidered.* Itasca, IL: F. E. Peacock Publishers: 75–92.

Oppenheimer, Bruce, James Stimson, and Richard W. Waterman. 1986. "Interpreting U.S. Congressional Elections: The Exposure Thesis." *Legislative Studies Quarterly.* XI (May): 227–47.

Ornstein, Norman and Thomas Mann. 2000. *The Permanent Campaign and Its Future.* Washington, D.C.: The American Enterprise Institute.

Ostrom, Charles W. Jr. and Dennis M. Simon. 1985. "Promise and Performance: A Dynamic Model of Presidential Popularity." *American Political Science Review.* 79: 334–58.

P

Palludan, Phillip. 1994. *The Presidency of Abraham Lincoln.* Lawrence, KS: University Press of Kansas.

Palmer, Dave R. 1994. *1794: America, Its Army, and the Birth of the Nation.* Novato, CA: Presidio Press.

Patterson, Bradley H. Jr. 1988. *The Ring of Power: The White House Staff and Its Expanding Role in Government.* New York: Basic Books.

———. 2000. *The White House Staff: Inside the West Wing and Beyond.* Washington, D.C.: Brookings Institution.

Patterson, Thomas. 1993. *Out of Control: How the decline of the political parties and the growing power of the news media undermine the American way of electing presidents.* New York: Knopf.

Persico, Joseph E. 2001. *Roosevelt's Secret War: FDR and World War II Espionage.* New York: Random House.

Peterson, Mark A. 1990. *Legislating Together: The White House and Capitol Hill from Eisenhower to Reagan.* Cambridge, MA: Harvard University Press.

Pfiffner, James P. 1987. "Strangers in a Strange Land: Orienting New Presidential Appointees." In G. Calvin Mackenzie (ed.) *The In-and-Outers: Presidential Appointees and Transient Government in Washington.* Baltimore: John Hopkins University Press: 141–55.

———. 1988. *The Strategic Presidency: Hitting the Ground Running.* Chicago: The Dorsey Press.

———. 2002. "Reevaluating the Electoral College." In James P. Pfiffner and Roger H. Davidson (eds.) *Understanding the Presidency.* New York: Longman.

Phelps, Glenn A. 1989. "George Washington: Precedent Setter." In Thomas E. Cronin (ed.) *Inventing the American Presidency.* Lawrence, KS: University Press of Kansas. 259–81.

Pika, Joseph A. 1988. "A New Vice Presidency?" In Michael Nelson (ed.) *The Presidency and the Political System.* Washington, D.C.: Congressional Quarterly Press. 463–82.

———. 1993. "Reaching Out to Organized Interests: Public Liaison in the Modern White House." In Richard W. Waterman (ed.) *The Presidency Reconsidered.* Itasca, IL: F. E. Peacock Publishers: 145–68.

Pious, Richard M. 1979. *The American Presidency.* New York: Basic Books.

———. 1996. *The Presidency.* Boston: Allyn and Bacon.

Podhoretz, John. 1993. *Hell of a Ride: Backstage at the White House Follies 1989–1993.* New York: Simon and Schuster.

Polsby, Nelson W. 1978. "Presidential Cabinet Making: Lessons for the Political System." *Political Science Quarterly.* 93: 15–25.

Porter, Roger B. 1980. *Presidential Decision Making: The Economic Policy Board.* Cambridge, MA: Cambridge University Press.

———. 1988. "A Healing Presidency." In Fred I. Greenstein (ed.) *Leadership in the Modern Presidency.* Cambridge, MA: Harvard University Press. 199–227.

Q

Quayle, Dan. 1994. *Standing Firm: A Vice-Presidential Memoir.* New York: Harper Collins.

R

Raichur, Arvind, and Richard W. Waterman. 1993. "The Presidency, the Public, and the Expectations Gap." In Richard W. Waterman (ed.) *The Presidency Reconsidered.* Itasca, IL: F. E. Peacock Publishers. 1–21.

Randall, J. G. and David Donald. 1969. *The Civil War and Reconstruction,* 2nd ed. Lexington, MA: D. C. Heath and Co.

Reddy, George. 1970. *The Twilight of the Presidency.* New York: New American Library.

Redford, Emmette S. 1969. *Democracy and the Administrative State.* New York: Oxford University Press.

Redford, Emmette S. and Marlan Blissett. 1981. *Organizing the Executive Branch: The Johnson Presidency.* Chicago: University of Chicago Press.

Reeves, Richard. 2001. *President Nixon: Alone in the White House.* New York: Simon and Schuster.

Regan, Donald. 1990. *For the Record: From Wall Street to Washington.* New York: Harcourt Brace Jovanovich Publishers.

Remini, Robert V. 1972. "Election of 1828." In Arthur Schlesinger, Jr. (ed.) *The Coming To Power: Critical Presidential Elections in American History.* New York: McGraw-Hill. 67–90.

Riccards, Michael P. 1995. *The Ferocious Engine of Democracy: A History of the American Presidency.* Volume 1. New York: Madison Books.

Rivers, Douglas and Nancy L. Rose. 1985. "Passing the President's Program: Public Opinion and Presidential Influence in Congress." *American Journal of Political Science.* 29: 183–96.

Robinson, Donald. 1987. *"To the Best of My Ability": The Presidency and the Constitution.* New York: W. W. Norton.

Romasco, Albert V. 1974. "Herbert Hoover's Policies for Dealing with the Great Depression: The End of the Old Order or the Beginning of the New?" In Martin L. Fausold and George T. Mazuzan (eds.) *The Hoover Presidency.* Albany: State University of New York Press.

Roosevelt, Theodore. 1913. *An Autobiography.* New York: Scribners.

Rose, Gary L. 1997. *The American Presidency Under Siege.* Albany: State University of New York Press.

Rose, Richard. 1988/1991. *The Post-Modern Presidency: The White House Meets the World.* Chatham, NJ: Chatham House Publishers.

Roseboom, Eugene H. and Alfred E. Eckes, Jr. 1979. *A History of Presidential Elections: From George Washington to Jimmy Carter.* New York: Collier Books.

Rossiter, Clinton. 1960. *The American Presidency.* New York: Harcourt Brace and World.

———. 1966. *1787 The Grand Convention: The Year That Made a Nation.* New York: Macmillan Co.

Rourke, Francis. 1969. *Bureaucracy, Politics and Public Policy.* Boston: Little, Brown and Co.

Russell, Francis. 1968. *The Shadow of Blooming Grove: Warren G. Harding in His Times.* New York: McGraw Hill.

Rutland, Robert Allen. 1990. *The Presidency of James Madison.* Lawrence, KS: University Press of Kansas.

S

Sabatier, Paul A. and Hank C. Jenkins-Smith. 1993. "The Advocacy Coalition Framework: Assessment, Revisions, and Implications for Scholars and Practitioners." In Paul A. Sabatier and Hank C. Jenkins-Smith (eds.) *Policy Change and Learning: An Advocacy Coalition Approach.* Boulder, CO: Westview.

Sabatier, Paul A. and Neil Pelkey. 1987. "Incorporating Multiple Actors and Guidance Instruments into Models of Regulatory Policy-making: An Advocacy Coalition Framework." *Administration and Society.* 19: 236–63.

Salamon, Lester M. 1981. "The Question of Goals." In Peter Szanton (ed.) *Federal Reorganization: What Have We Learned?* Chatham, NJ: Chatham House. 58–84.

Sanders, Elizabeth. 1988. "The Presidency and the Bureaucratic State." In Michael Nelson (ed.) *The Presidency and the Political System.* Washington, D.C.: Congressional Quarterly Press. 379–409.

Schick, Allen. 1981. "The Problem of Presidential Budgeting." In Hugh Heclo and Lester M. Salamon (eds.) *The Illusion of Presidential Government.* Boulder, CO: Westview Press. 85–111.

Schlereth, Thomas J. 1991. *Victorian America: Transformations in Everyday Life, 1876–1915.* New York: Harper Collins.

Schlesinger, Arthur Jr. 1945. *The Age of Jackson.* Boston: Little, Brown and Co.

———. 1957. *The Crisis of the Old Order: The Age of Roosevelt.* Boston: Houghton Mifflin.

———. 1958. *The Coming of the New Deal: The Age of Roosevelt.* Boston: Houghton Mifflin.

———. 1960. *The Politics of Upheaval: The Age of Roosevelt.* Boston: Houghton Mifflin.

———. 1973. *The Imperial Presidency.* Boston: Houghton Mifflin.

———. 1986. *The Cycles of American History.* Boston: Houghton Mifflin.

———. (ed.) 1994a. *Running for President: The Candidates and Their Images 1789–1896.* New York: Simon and Schuster.

———. (ed.) 1994b. *Running for President: The Candidates and Their Images 1900–1992.* New York: Simon and Schuster.

Schott, Richard L. and Richard L. Hamilton. 1983. *People, Positions, and Power: The Political Appointments of Lyndon Johnson.* Chicago: University of Chicago Press.

Schroedel, Jean Reith. 1994. *Congress, the President, and Policymaking: A Historical Analysis.* Armonk, NY: M. E. Sharpe.

Scigliano, Robert. 1988. "The Presidency and the Judiciary." In Michael Nelson (ed.) *The Presidency and the Political System.* Washington, D.C.: Congressional Quarterly Press. 435–61.

Scott, Ruth K. and Ronald J. Hrebenar. 1979. *Parties in Crisis: Party Politics in America.* New York: John Wiley and Sons.

Seidman, Harold. 1980. *Politics, Position, and Power: The Dynamics of Federal Organization.* Oxford: Oxford University Press.

Seligman, Lester G. and Cary R. Covington. 1989. *The Coalitional Presidency.* Chicago: The Dorsey Press.

Seligman, Lester G. and Michael A. Baer. 1969. "Expectations of Presidential Leadership and Decision-Making." In Aaron Wildavsky (ed.) *The Presidency.* Boston: Little, Brown and Co.

Seymour, Charles (ed.) 1926. *The Intimate Papers of Colonel House.* Boston: Houghton Mifflin.

Sharp, James Roger. 1993. *American Politics in The Early Republic: The New Nation in Crisis.* New Haven: Yale University Press.

Shogan, Robert. 1991. *The Riddle of Power: Presidential Leadership from Truman to Bush.* New York: Dutton.

Shull, Steven A. (ed.) 1991. *The Two Presidencies: A Quarter Century Assessment.* Chicago: Nelson-Hall.

Shuman, Howard E. 1992. *The Politics and the Budget: The Struggle Between the President and Congress.* Englewood Cliffs, NJ: Prentice-Hall.

Sigelman, Lee. 1979. "A Reassessment of the Two Presidencies' Thesis." *Journal of Politics.* 41: 1195–1205.

Sigelman, Lee and Michael M. Gant. 1989. "Anticandidate Voting in the 1984 Presidential Election." *Political Behavior.* 11: 81–92.

Sinclair, Barbara. 1983. *Majority Leadership in the U.S. House.* Baltimore: John Hopkins University Press.

Skelton, William B. 1992. *An American Profession of Arms: The Army Officer Corps, 1784–1861.* Lawrence, KS: University Press of Kansas.

Skowronek, Stephen. 1993. *The Politics Presidents Make: Leadership from John Adams to George Bush.* Cambridge, MA: Harvard University Press.

Smith, Goldwin. 1974. *A History of England.* New York: Scribners.

Smith, Hedrick. 1988. *The Power Game.* New York: Ballantine Books.

Smith, Steven S. and Christopher J. Deering. 1984. *Committees in Congress.* Washington, D.C.: Congressional Quarterly Press.

Soloman, Burt. 1989. "Bush Promised Fresh Faces . . . But He's Hiring Old Friends." *National Journal.* (1/21): 142–43.

Sorauf, Frank J. 1980. *Party Politics in America.* Boston: Little, Brown and Co.

Sorenson, Leonard R. 1989. "The Federalist Papers on the Constitutionality of Executive Prerogatives." *Presidential Studies Quarterly.* XIX: 267–83.

Spitzer, Robert J. 1993. *President & Congress: Executive Hegemony at the Crossroads of American Government.* New York: McGraw Hill.

Stampp, Kenneth M. 1990. *America in 1857: A Nation on the Brink.* New York: Oxford University Press.

Stanley, Harold W. and Richard G. Niemi. 2000. *Vital Statistics on American Politics 1999–2000.* Washington, D.C.: Congressional Quarterly Press.

Stein, Herbert. 1969. *The Fiscal Revolution in America*. Chicago: University of Chicago Press.

Stewart, Joseph Jr. and Jane S. Cromartie. 1982. "Partisan Presidential Change and Regulatory Policy: The Case of the FTC and Deceptive Practices Enforcement, 1938–1974." *Presidential Studies Quarterly*. 12: 568–73.

Still, Baryd. 1974. *Urban America: A History with Documents*. Boston: Little, Brown and Co.

Stimson, James A. 1976. "Public Support for American Presidents: A Cyclical Model." *Public Opinion Quarterly*. 40 (Spring): 1–21.

———. 1976/1977. "On Disillusionment with the Expectation/Disillusion Theory: A Rejoinder." *Public Opinion Quarterly*. 40 (Winter): 541–43.

Stockman, David A. 1986. *The Triumph of Politics: Why the Reagan Revolution Failed*. New York: Harper and Row.

Strober, Gerald S. and Deborah Hart Strober. 1994. *Nixon: An Oral History of His Presidency*. New York: Harper Collins.

Stuckey, Mary E. 1991. *The President as Interpreter-in-Chief*. Chatham, NJ: Chatham House.

Sundquist, James L. 1981. *The Decline and Resurgence of Congress*. Washington, DC: Brookings Institution.

———. 1983. *Dynamics of the Party System: Alignment and Realignment of Political Parties in the United States*. Washington, D.C.: Brookings Institution.

T

Tebbel, John and Sarah Miles Watts. 1985. *The Press and the Presidency: From George Washington to Ronald Reagan*. New York: Oxford University Press.

Thach, Charles C. Jr. 1969. *The Creation of the Presidency, 1775–1789: A Study in Constitutional Government*. Baltimore: John Hopkins University Press.

Thomas, Norman, Joseph Pika, and Thomas Watson. 1993. *The Politics of the Presidency*. Washington, D.C.: Congressional Quarterly Press.

Thurber, James A. 1991. *Divided Democracy: Cooperation and Conflict Between the President and Congress*. Washington, D.C.: Congressional Quarterly Press.

Tocqueville, Alexis de. 1945. *Democracy in America*. New York: Vintage Books.

Tomkin, Shelley Lynne. 1985. "Playing Politics in OMB: Civil Servants Join the Game." *Presidential Studies Quarterly*. XV: 158–70.

———. 1998. *Inside OMB: Politics and Process in the President's Budget Office*. Armonk, NY: M. E. Sharpe.

Trefousse, Hans L. 1989. *Andrew Johnson: A Biography*. New York: W. W. Norton.

Tribe, Lawrence H. 1972. "Policy Science: Analysis or Ideology?" *Philosophy and Public Affairs*. 2: 66–110.

Truman, Harry S. 1955. *Memoirs by Harry S. Truman: Year of Decisions*. Garden City, NY: Doubleday.

———. 1956. *Memoirs by Harry S. Truman: Years of Trial and Hope*. Garden City, NY: Doubleday.

Tufte, Edward R. 1975. "Determinants of Outcomes of Midterm Congressional Elections." *American Political Science Review*. 69: 812–26.

———. 1978. *Political Control of the Economy*. Princeton: University of Princeton Press.

Tulis, Jeffrey K. 1987. *The Rhetorical Presidency*. Princeton: Princeton University Press.

———. 1988. "The Two Constitutional Presidencies." In Michael Nelson (ed.) *The Presidency and the Political System*. Washington, D.C.: Congressional Quarterly Press. 85–113.

U

U.S. Government. 1937. President's Committee on Administrative Management. *Administrative Management in the Government of the United States, January 8, 1937*. Washington, D.C.: Government Printing Office.

———. 1977. *Report of the Congressional Committee Investigating the Iran-contra Affair with Supplemental, Minority and Additional Views*. Washington, D.C.: Government Printing Office.

V

Vanderbilt, Arthur T. 1989. *Fortune's Children: The Fall of the House of Vanderbilt*. New York: William Morrow and Co.

Vig, Norman J. 1984. "The President and the Environment: Revolution or Retreat." In Norman J. Vig and Michael E. Kraft (eds.) *Environmental Policy in the 1980s: Reagan's New Agenda*. Washington, D.C.: Congressional Quarterly Press: 77–95.

W

Walcott, Charles E. and Karen M. Hult. 1987. "Organizing the White House: Structure, Environment, and Organizational Governance." *American Journal of Political Science*. 31: 109–25.

———. 1995. *Governing the White House: From Hoover through LBJ*. Lawrence, KS: University Press of Kansas.

Walker, David B. 1981. *Toward a Functioning Federalism*. Boston, Little, Brown and Co.

Warshaw, Shirley Anne. 1996. *Powersharing: White House-Cabinet Relations in the Modern Presidency*. Albany: State University of New York.

———. 1997. *The Domestic Presidency: Policy Making in the White House*. Boston: Allyn and Bacon.

Waterman, Richard W. 1988. "The Presidential Conundrum: The Benefits and Risks of the New Strategies for Presidential Leadership." Paper presented at the annual meeting of the Midwest Political Science Association. Chicago, IL.

———. 1989. *Presidential Influence and the Administrative State*. Knoxville: University of Tennessee Press.

———. 1990. "Comparing Senate and House Electoral Outcomes: The Exposure Thesis." *Legislative Studies Quarterly*. XV (February): 99–114.

———. 1993. "Closing the Expectations Gap: The Presidential Search for New Political Resources." In Richard W. Waterman (ed.) *The Presidency Reconsidered*. Wood Dale, IL: Peacock Publishers. 23–46.

———. 1996. "Storm Clouds on the Political Horizon: George Bush at the Dawn of the 1992 Presidential Election." *Presidential Studies Quarterly*. XXVI (Spring): 337–49.

———. 1999. "Bureaucratic Views of the President." In Steven A. Shull (ed.) *Presidential Policymaking: An End-of-Century Assessment*. Armonk, NY: M. E. Sharpe.

Waterman, Richard W., Bruce Oppenheimer, and James Stimson. 1991. "Sequence and Equilibrium in Congressional Elections: An Integrated Approach." *Journal of Politics*. 53 (May): 372–93.

Waterman, Richard W., Joseph Stewart, and Melinda McCrocklin Morris. 1995. "The Appointment Paradox: Obstacles to Hitting the Ground Running." Paper presented at the annual meeting of the American Political Science Association. Chicago, IL.

Waterman, Richard W., Amelia A. Rouse, and Robert L. Wright. 1998. "The Venues of Influence: A New Theory of Political Control of the Bureaucracy." *Journal of Public Administration Research and Theory*. 8 (January): 13–38.

Waterman, Richard W., Hank C. Jenkins-Smith, and Carol L. Silva. 1999. "The Expectations Gap Thesis: Public Attitudes Toward an Incumbent President." *Journal of Politics*. 61 (November): 944–66.

Waterman, Richard W., Robert Wright, and Gilbert St. Clair. 1999. *The Image-Is-Everything Presidency: Dilemmas in American Politics*. Boulder, CO: Westview Press.

Wayne, Stephen J. 1978. *The Legislative Presidency*. New York: Harper and Row.

———. 1982. "Great Expectations: What People Want from Presidents." In Thomas E. Cronin (ed.) *Rethinking the Presidency*. Boston: Little, Brown and Co. 185–99.

Weingast, Barry R. 1984. "The Congressional-Bureaucratic System: A Principal-Agent Perspective (with Applications to the SEC). *Public Choice.* 44: 147–91.

Weingast, Barry R. and Mark J. Moran. 1983. "Bureaucratic Discretion or Congressional Control: Regulatory Policymaking by the Federal Trade Commission. *Journal of Political Economy.* 91: 756–800.

Weko, Thomas J. 1995. *The Politicizing Presidency: The White House Personnel Office, 1948–1994.* Lawrence, KS: University Press of Kansas.

Welborn, David M. 1977. *Governance of Federal Regulatory Agencies.* Knoxville, TN: University of Tennessee Press.

Wildavsky, Aaron. 1969. "The Two Presidencies." In Aaron Wildavsky (ed.) *The Presidency.* Boston: Little, Brown and Co. 230–43.

Wilson, Major L. 1984. *The Presidency of Martin Van Buren.* Lawrence, KS: University Press of Kansas.

Wilson, Woodrow. 1885/1981. *Congressional Government: A Study in American Politics.* Baltimore: John Hopkins Press.

———. 1887/1987. "The Study of Administration." In Jay M. Shafritz and Albert C. Hyde (eds.) *Classics in Public Administration.* New York: Dorsey Press.

———. 1908. *Constitutional Government in the United States.* New York: Columbia University Press.

Wood, B. Dan. 1988. "Principals, Bureaucrats, and Responsiveness in Clear Air Enforcements." *American Political Science Review.* 82: 213–34.

———. 1990. "Does Politics Make a Difference at the EEOC? *American Journal of Political Science.* 34: 503–30.

Wood, B. Dan and James Anderson. 1993. "The Politics of U.S. Antitrust Regulation." *American Journal of Political Science.* 37: 1–39.

Wood, B. Dan and Richard W. Waterman. 1994. *Bureaucratic Dynamics: The Role of Bureaucracy in a Democracy.* Boulder, CO: Westview.

———. 1993. "The Dynamics of Political-Bureaucratic Adaptation." *American Journal of Political Science.* 37 (May): 497–528.

———. 1991. "The Dynamics of Political Control of the Bureaucracy." *American Political Science Review.* 85 (September): 801–28.

Wood, Gordon S. 1969. *The Creation of the American Republic 1776–1787.* New York: Norton.

Woodward, Bob. 1999. *Shadow: Five Presidents and the Legacy of Watergate.* New York: Simon and Schuster.

Wyszomirski, Margaret Jane. 1985. "The Roles of a Presidential Office for Domestic Policy: Three Models and Four Cases." In George C. Edwards III, Steven A. Shull, and Norman C. Thomas (eds.) *The Presidency and Public Policy Making.* Pittsburgh: University of Pittsburgh Press.

Y

Yandle, Bruce. 1985. "FTC Activity and Presidential Effects." *Presidential Studies Quarterly.* 15: 128–35.

Young, James S. 1966. *The Washington Community.* New York: Columbia University Press.

Index

Note: Page numbers in *italics* indicate illustrative material; a *t* in italics indicates a table.